YEATS ANNUAL No. 20

W. B. Yeats and T. S. Eliot in the United States, December 1932.

ESSAYS IN HONOUR OF EAMONN CANTWELL

YEATS ANNUAL No. 20

A Special Number

Edited by Warwick Gould

OpenBook
Publishers

in association with the Institute of English Studies
School of Advanced Study, University of London

ISBN Paperback: 978-1-78374-177-9
ISBN Hardback: 978-1-78374-178-6
ISBN Digital (PDF): 978-1-78374-179-3
ISBN Digital ebook (epub): 978-1-78374-180-9
ISBN Digital ebook (mobi): 978-1-78374-181-6
Series ISSN: 0278-7687 (Print); 2054-3611 (Online)
DOI: 10.11647/OBP.0081

Cover image: The heraldic device is taken from Althea Gyles's top board design for the revised and enlarged edition of W. B. Yeats, *The Celtic Twilight* (London: A. H. Bullen, English edition only, 1902). Private collection, London.

All paper used by Open Book Publishers is SFI (Sustainable Forestry Initiative), PEFC (Programme for the Endorsement of Forest Certification Schemes) and Forest Stewardship Council(r)(FSC(r) certified.

Printed in the United Kingdom, United States and Australia
by Lightning Source for Open Book Publishers (Cambridge, UK).

For Eamonn and Anne Cantwell, benefactors of
University College, Cork, and who both care for
'what old books tell'.

Contents

ESSAYS IN HONOUR OF EAMONN CANTWELL

RESEARCH UPDATES AND OBITUARIES

'MASTERING WHAT IS MOST ABSTRACT':
A FORUM ON A VISION

List of Illustrations

Cover Images: The *Yeats Annual* fleuron on the spine is based upon Thomas Sturge Moore's rose design, as used in his illustrations for H. P. R. Finberg's translation of Count Villiers de L'Isle Adam's *Axel* with Yeats's preface (London: Jarrolds Publishers, Ltd., 1925), and elsewhere on cover designs for Yeats's books, most notably that for *Per Amica Silentia Lunae* (1918), courtesy of the late Riette Sturge Moore. The heraldic device is taken from Althea Gyles's top board design for the revised and enlarged *The Celtic Twilight* (London: A. H. Bullen, English edition only, 1902; *Wade* 35), her last cover design for Yeats.

Frontispiece: W. B. Yeats and T. S. Eliot in the United States, December 1932. © private collection, London, All rights reserved.

Plates

List of Illustrations

Abbreviations

Au	*Autobiographies* (London: Macmillan, 1955).
AVA	*A Vision: An Explanation of Life Founded upon the Writings of Giraldus and upon certain Doctrines attributed to Kusta Ben Luka* (London: privately printed for subscribers only by T. Werner Laurie, Ltd., 1925). See also *CVA*.
AVB	*A Vision* (London: Macmillan, 1962).
Berg	Books and Manuscripts, The Berg Collection, New York Public Library (Astor, Lenox and Tilden Foundations).
BIV1, 2	*A Book of Irish Verse* (London: Methuen, 1895; 1900).
BL Add. MS	Additional Manuscript, The British Library, London (followed by number).
BL Macmillan	Later papers from the Macmillan Archive, British Library, London.
Bodley	Bodleian Library, Oxford.
Bradford	Curtis B. Bradford, *Yeats at Work* (Carbondale and Edwardsville: Southern Illinois University Press, 1965).
Brotherton	Manuscript, The Brotherton Collection, Brotherton Library, University of Leeds.
CH	W. B. Yeats, *The Critical Heritage*, edited by A. Norman Jeffares (London: Henley; Boston: Routledge & Kegan Paul, 1977).
ChronY	*A W. B. Yeats Chronology* by John S. Kelly (Basingstoke: Palgrave Macmillan, 2003).
CL1, 2, 3, 4	*The Collected Letters of W. B. Yeats: Volume I, 1865–1895*, edited by John Kelly and Eric Domville; *Volume II, 1896–1900*, edited by Warwick Gould, John Kelly and Deirdre Toomey; *Volume III, 1901–1904*, and *Volume IV, 1905–1907*, edited by John Kelly and Ronald Schuchard (Oxford: Clarendon Press, 1986, 1997, 1994, 2005).

CL InteLex	*The Collected Letters of W. B. Yeats*, General editor John Kelly, Oxford University Press (InteLex Electronic Edition) 2002, http://www.nlx.com/collections/130. Letters cited by Accession number.
CM	*W. B. Yeats: A Census of the Manuscripts*, by Conrad A. Balliet, with the assistance of Christine Mawhinney (New York and London: Garland Publishing, 1990).
CVA	*A Critical Edition of Yeats's A Vision (1925)*, edited by George Mills Harper and Walter Kelly Hood (London: Macmillan, 1978).
CW1	*The Poems: Second Edition* (New York: Scribner, 1997), edited by Richard J. Finneran and replacing *The Poems: Revised* (New York: Macmillan, 1989; London: Macmillan, 1989), *PR*, which replaced *The Poems: A New Edition* (New York: Macmillan, 1983; London: Macmillan, 1984), *PNE*, as the first volume of *The Collected Works of W. B. Yeats* (formerly *The Collected Edition of the Works of W. B. Yeat*s).
CW2	*The Plays*, edited by David R. Clark and Rosalind E. Clark (New York: Scribner, 2001), volume II of *The Collected Works of W. B. Yeats* (formerly *The Collected Edition of the Works of W. B. Yeats*).
CW3	*Autobiographies*, edited by William H. O'Donnell and Douglas N. Archibald, assisted by J. Fraser Cocks III and Gretchen Schwenker (New York: Scribner, 1999), volume III of *The Collected Works of W. B. Yeats* (formerly *The Collected Edition of the Works of W. B. Yeats*).
CW5	*Later Essays*, edited by William H. O'Donnell, with assistance from Elizabeth Bergmann Loizeaux (New York: Charles Scribner's Sons, 1994), volume V of *The Collected Works of W. B. Yeats* (formerly *The Collected Edition of the Works of W. B. Yeats*).
CW6	*Prefaces and Introductions: Uncollected Prefaces and Introductions by Yeats to Works by other Authors and to Anthologies edited by Yeats*, edited by William H. O'Donnell (London: Macmillan, 1988), volume VI of *The Collected Works of W. B. Yeats* (formerly *The Collected Edition of the Works of W. B. Yeats*).
CW7	*Letters to the New Island*, edited by George Bornstein and Hugh Witemeyer (London: Macmillan, 1989), volume VII of *The Collected Works of W. B. Yeats* (formerly *The Collected Edition of the Works of W. B. Yeats*).
CW8	*The Irish Dramatic Movement*, edited by Mary FitzGerald and Richard J. Finneran (New York: Scribner, 2003), volume VIII of *The Collected Works of W. B. Yeats* (formerly *The Collected Edition of the Works of W. B. Yeats*).

CW9   *Early Articles and Reviews: Uncollected Articles and Reviews Written between 1886 and 1900*, edited by John P. Frayne and Madeleine Marchaterre (New York: Scribner, 2004), volume IX of *The Collected Works of W. B. Yeats* (formerly *The Collected Edition of the Works of W. B. Yeats*).

CW10   *Later Articles and Reviews: Uncollected Articles, Reviews, and Radio Broadcasts Written after 1900*, edited by Colton Johnson (New York: Scribner, 2000), volume X of *The Collected Works of W. B. Yeats* (formerly *The Collected Edition of the Works of W. B. Yeats*).

CW12   *John Sherman and Dhoya*, edited by Richard J. Finneran (New York: Macmillan, 1991), volume XII of *The Collected Works of W. B. Yeats* (formerly *The Collected Edition of the Works of W. B. Yeats*).

CW13   *A Vision: The Original 1925 Version*, edited by Catherine E. Paul and Margaret Mills Harper (New York: Scribner 2008), Vol. XIII of *The Collected Works of W. B. Yeats* (formerly *The Collected Edition of the Works of W. B. Yeats*).

CWVP1–8   *The Collected Works in Verse and Prose of William Butler Yeats* (Stratford-on-Avon: The Shakespeare Head Press, 1908), 8 vols.

DC   *Druid Craft: The Writing of The Shadowy Waters, Manuscripts of W. B. Yeats*, transcribed, edited and with a commentary by Michael J. Sidnell, George P. Mayhew and David R. Clark (Amherst: The University of Massachusetts Press, 1971).

Diaries   *Lady Gregory's Diaries 1892–1902*, edited by James Pethica (Gerrards Cross: Colin Smythe, 1996).

E&I   *Essays and Introductions* (London and New York: Macmillan, 1961).

Emory   Books and Manuscripts in the Robert W. Woodruff Library, Emory University.

Ex   *Explorations*, sel. Mrs W. B. Yeats (London: Macmillan, 1962; New York: Macmillan, 1963).

FFTIP   *Fairy and Folk Tales of the Irish Peasantry*. Edited and selected by W. B. Yeats (London: Walter Scott, Ltd., 1888).

G-YL   *The Gonne-Yeats Letters 1893–1938: Always Your Friend*, edited by Anna MacBride White and A. Norman Jeffares (London: Hutchinson, 1992).

Harvard   Manuscript, Houghton Library, Harvard University.

HRHRC   Books and Manuscripts, Harry Ransom Humanities Research Center, University of Texas at Austin.

I&R   *W. B. Yeats: Interviews and Recollections*, edited by E. H. Mikhail (London: Macmillan, 1977), 2 vols.

IFT   *Irish Fairy Tales*, edited with an introduction by W. B. Yeats (London: T. Fisher Unwin, 1892).

J   *W. B. Yeats: A Classified Bibliography of Criticism*, 2nd ed., revised and enlarged by K. P. S. Jochum (Urbana and Chicago: University of Illinois Press, 1990). Item nos. or page no. preceded by 'p.'

JBYL   *Letters to his Son W. B. Yeats and Others 1869–1922 by J.B. Yeats*, edited with a Memoir by Joseph Hone and a Preface by Oliver Elton (London: Faber & Faber, 1944).

Kansas Manuscripts in the Kenneth Spencer Research Library, University of Kansas, Lawrence.

L   *The Letters of W. B. Yeats*, edited by Allan Wade (London: Rupert Hart-Davis, 1954; New York: Macmillan, 1955).

LBP   *Letters from Bedford Park: A Selection from the Correspondence (1890–1901) of John Butler Yeats*, edited with an introduction and notes by William M. Murphy (Dublin: The Cuala Press, 1972).

LDW   *Letters on Poetry from W. B. Yeats to Dorothy Wellesley*, intro. Kathleen Raine (London and New York: Oxford University Press, 1964).

Life 1   *W. B. Yeats: A Life, I: The Apprentice Mage*, by R. F. Foster (Oxford and New York: Oxford University Press, 1997).

Life 2   *W. B. Yeats: A Life, II: The Arch-Poet*, by R. F. Foster (Oxford and New York: Oxford University Press, 2003).

Lilly   Manuscript in the Lilly Library, Indiana University, Bloomington.

LJQ   *The Letters of John Quinn to W. B. Yeats*, edited by Alan B. Himber, with the assistance of George Mills Harper (Ann Arbor: UMI Research Press, 1983).

LMR   'Ah, Sweet Dancer': W. B. Yeats and Margot Ruddock, A Correspondence, edited by Roger McHugh (London and New York: Macmillan, 1970).

LNI   *Letters to the New Island*, by William Butler Yeats, edited and with an introduction by Horace Reynolds (Cambridge, Mass.: Harvard University Press, 1934).

LRB   *The Correspondence of Robert Bridges and W. B. Yeats*, edited by Richard J. Finneran (London: Macmillan, 1977; Toronto: Macmillan of Canada, 1978).

LTWBY1, 2 *Letters to W. B. Yeats*, edited by Richard J. Finneran, George Mills Harper and William M. Murphy, with the assistance of Alan B. Himber (London: Macmillan; New York: Columbia University Press, 1977), 2 vols.

MBY   Manuscript in the collection of Michael Butler Yeats.

McGarry   *Places Names in the Writings of W. B. Yeats*, by James P. McGarry, edited with additional material by Edward Malins and a Preface by Kathleen Raine (Gerrards Cross: Colin Smythe, Ltd., 1976).

Mem   *Memoirs: Autobiography—First Draft: Journal*, transcribed and edited by Denis Donoghue (London: Macmillan, 1972; New York: Macmillan, 1973).

Myth   *Mythologies* (London and New York: Macmillan, 1959).

Myth 2005 *Mythologies*, edited by Warwick Gould and Deirdre Toomey (Houndmills, Basingstoke: Palgrave Macmillan, 2005).

MYV1, 2   *The Making of Yeats's 'A Vision': A Study of the Automatic Script*, by George Mills Harper (London: Macmillan; Carbondale and Edwardsville: Southern Illinois University Press, 1987), 2 vols.

NLI   Manuscripts in the National Library of Ireland, Dublin.

NLS   Manuscripts in the National Library of Scotland, Edinburgh.

NYPL   Manuscripts in the New York Public Library.

Norwood   Manuscripts, Norwood Historical Society, Day House, Norwood, Mass.

OBMV   *The Oxford Book of Modern Verse 1895–1935*, chosen by W. B. Yeats (Oxford: Clarendon Press, 1936).

Princeton   Manuscript in the Scribner Archive, Firestone Library, Princeton University.

Quinn Cat. Complete Catalogue of the Library of John Quinn sold by auction in five parts [with printed prices] (New York: The Anderson Galleries, 1924), 2 vols.

SB   *The Speckled Bird by William Butler Yeats: An Autobiographical Novel with Variant Versions: New Edition, Incorporating Recently Discovered Manuscripts*, edited and annotated by William H. O'Donnell (Basingstoke: Palgrave Macmillan, 2003).

SQ   *A Servant of the Queen: Reminiscences*, by Maud Gonne MacBride, edited by A. Norman Jeffares and Anna MacBride White (Gerrards Cross: Colin Smythe, 1994).

SS   *The Senate Speeches of W. B. Yeats*, edited by Donald R. Pearce (Bloomington: Indiana University Press, 1960; London: Faber & Faber, 1961).

TB   *Theatre Business: The Correspondence of the First Abbey Theatre Directors: William Butler Yeats, Lady Gregory and J. M. Synge*, edited by Ann Saddlemyer (Gerrards Cross: Colin Smythe; University Park: Pennsylvania State University Press, 1982).

TSMC	*W. B. Yeats and T. Sturge Moore: Their Correspondence, 1901–1937*, edited by Ursula Bridge (London: Routledge & Kegan Paul; New York: Oxford University Press, 1953).
UP1	*Uncollected Prose by W. B. Yeats, Vol. I*, edited by John P. Frayne (London: Macmillan; New York: Columbia University Press, 1970).
UP2	*Uncollected Prose by W. B. Yeats, Vol. 2*, edited by John P. Frayne and Colton Johnson (London: Macmillan, 1975; New York: Columbia University Press, 1976).
VBWI	*Visions and Beliefs in the West of Ireland*, collected and arranged by Lady Gregory: with two Essays and Notes by W. B. Yeats with a foreword by Elizabeth Coxhead (Gerrards Cross: Colin Smythe, Ltd.; New York: Oxford University Press, 1970).
VP	*The Variorum Edition of the Poems of W. B. Yeats*, edited by Peter Allt and Russell K. Alspach (New York: The Macmillan Company, 1957). Cited from the corrected third printing of 1966.
VPl	*The Variorum Edition of the Plays of W. B. Yeats*, edited by Russell K. Alspach, assisted by Catherine C. Alspach (London and New York: Macmillan, 1966). Cited from the corrected second printing of 1966.
VSR	*The Secret Rose, Stories by W. B. Yeats: A Variorum Edition*, edited by Warwick Gould, Phillip L. Marcus and Michael J. Sidnell (London: Macmillan, 1992). 2nd ed., revised and enlarged.
Wade	Allan Wade, *A Bibliography of the Writings of W. B. Yeats*, 3rd ed., revised by Russell K. Alspach (London: Rupert Hart-Davis, 1968). Cited by item no. and/or page no. preceded by 'p'..
WWB1, 2, 3	*The Works of William Blake Poetic, Symbolic, and Critical, edited with lithographs of the illustrated 'Prophetic Books'*, and a memoir and interpretation by Edwin John Ellis and William Butler Yeats (London: Bernard Quaritch, 1893), 3 vols.
YA1, 2, etc.	*Yeats Annual* (London: Macmillan, 1–17, 1982–2007; Cambridge: Open Book Publishers nos. 18-), http://www.openbookpublishers.com/section/39/1. Cited by no.
YAACTS	*Yeats: An Annual of Critical and Textual Studies*, edited by Richard J. Finneran (publishers vary, 1983–99). Cited by no.
YGYL	*W. B. Yeats and George Yeats: The Letters*, edited by Ann Saddlemyer (Oxford: Oxford University Press, 2011).

YL   Edward O'Shea, *A Descriptive Catalogue of W. B. Yeats's Library* (New York and London: Garland Publishing, 1985).

YO   *Yeats and the Occult*, edited by George Mills Harper (Toronto: Macmillan of Canada; Niagara Falls, New York: Maclean-Hunter Press, 1975).

YP   *Yeats's Poems*, edited and annotated by A. Norman Jeffares, with an Appendix by Warwick Gould (London: Macmillan, 1989). Cited from the second, revised edition of 1991.

YT   *Yeats and the Theatre*, edited by Robert O'Driscoll and Lorna Reynolds (Toronto: Macmillan of Canada; Niagara Falls, New York: Maclean-Hunter Press, 1975).

YVP1, 2, 3, 4   *Yeats's Vision* Papers (London: Macmillan, 1992; Palgrave 2001), George Mills Harper (General Editor) assisted by Mary Jane Harper, *Vol.1: The Automatic Script: 5 November 1917–18 June 1918*, edited by Steve L. Adams, Barbara J. Frieling and Sandra L. Sprayberry; *Vol. 2: The Automatic Script: 25 June 1918–29 March 1920*, edited by Steve L. Adams, Barbara J. Frieling and Sandra L. Sprayberry; *Vol. 3: Sleep and Dream Notebooks, Vision Notebooks 1 and 2, Card File*, edited by Robert Anthony Martinich and Margaret Mills Harper; Vol. 4: *'The Discoveries of Michael Robartes' Version B ['The Great Wheel' and 'The Twenty-Eight Embodiments']*, edited by George Mills Harper and Margaret Mills Harper assisted by Richard W. Stoops, Jr.

Editorial Board

Notes on Contributors

Jad Adams is an historian working as an author and an independent television producer. He specializes on radical characters from the nineteenth and twentieth centuries and the Decadence of the 1890s. His books include biographies of Tony Benn, Gandhi, Emmeline Pankhurst and of the Nehru dynasty. His literary work includes a biography of Kipling, *Madder Music, Stronger Wine: The Life of Ernest Dowson* (2000) and *Hideous Absinthe: History of the Devil in a Bottle* (2004). His television work includes biographies of Kitchener, Bill and Hillary Clinton and of characters from London's East End. He is an Associate Research Fellow of the Institute of English Studies, University of London.

Nicolas Barker OBE, FBA succeeded John Hayward as Editor of *The Book Collector* (founded in 1952 by Ian Fleming) in 1965, and edited it until 2016. He has been a publisher with Rupert Hart-Davis and Macmillan, a Keeper at the National Portrait Gallery and the British Library, a Sandars Reader in Bibliography at Cambridge, a Panizzi Lecturer at the British Library, and is a Senior Research Fellow of the Institute of English Studies, University of London. Notable among his prolific stream of studies and editions in all fields of Bibliography is his application of the methods of John Carter and Pollard in investigating the forgeries of Thomas J. Wise (a study which he edited and to which he co-wrote a sequel) to the forgeries by Frederic Prokosh: see his *The Butterfly Books: An Enquiry into the Nature of Certain Twentieth Century Pamphlets* (1987).

Richard Allen Cave is Emeritus Professor of Drama and Theatre Arts at Royal Holloway, University of London. He has published extensively on Irish theatre, and edited the manuscripts of *The King of the Great Clock Tower* and *A Full Moon in March* (2007). His *Collaborations: Ninette de Valois and W. B. Yeats* appeared in 2008.

Michael Edwards is Professor of Classics and Head of the Department of Humanities at the University of Roehampton, London. He was formerly in the School of English and Drama at Queen Mary, University of London, Director of the Institute of Classical Studies, and Head of Classics at the University of Wales Trinity Saint David. He is the President of the International Society for the History of Rhetoric. He has published widely on classical Greek oratory, including commentaries on speeches of Antiphon, Andocides, and Lysias, and a translation of the speeches of Isaeus. Professor Edwards was recently a co-editor of a three-volume edition of the Latin poet Statius (Newcastle upon Tyne: Cambridge Scholars Publishing, 2007) and he is currently working on an Oxford Classical Text of Isaeus and a commentary on Aeschines, *Against Ctesiphon*.

R. F. Foster FBA, FRSL, FRHS, MRHA retires this year from the Carroll Chair of Irish History at Hertford College, in the University of Oxford, a post founded for him in 1991. His books include *Charles Stewart Parnell: The Man and His Family* (1976), *Lord Randolph Churchill: A Political Life* (1981), *Modern Ireland 1600–1972* (1988), *The Oxford Illustrated History of Ireland* (1989), *The Sub Prefect Should Have Held His Tongue: Selected Essays of Hubert Butler* (1990), *Paddy and Mr Punch: Connections in Irish and English History* (1993), *The Irish Story: Telling Tales and Making It Up in Ireland* (2001), *W. B. Yeats, A Life. I: The Apprentice Mage 1865–1914* (1997) and *II: The Arch-Poet, 1915–1939* (2003); *Conquering England: The Irish in the Victorian Metropolis* (2005), co-written with Fintan Cullen, *Luck and the Irish: a brief history of change 1970–2000* (2006), *Words Alone: Yeats and his inheritances* (2011), derived from his Clark Lectures at the University of Cambridge; and *Vivid Faces: The Revolutionary Generation in Ireland* (2014), based on the Ford Lectures which he delivered at Oxford in 2012. He is also a well-known critic, reviewer and broadcaster. Email: Roy.Foster@hertford.ox.ac.uk

Warwick Gould FRSL, FRSA, FEA is Emeritus Professor of English Literature in the University of London (at Royal Holloway), and Senior Research Fellow of the Institute of English Studies (in the School of Advanced Study), of which he was Founder-Director 1999–2013. He is co-author of *Joachim of Fiore and the Myth of the Eternal Evangel in the Nineteenth and Twentieth Centuries* (1988, revised 2001), and co-editor of *The Secret Rose, Stories by W. B. Yeats: A Variorum Edition* (1981, revised 1992), *The Collected Letters of W. B. Yeats, Volume II, 1896–1900* (1997), and *Mythologies* (2005). He has edited *Yeats Annual* for thirty years. Email: Warwick.Gould@sas.ac.uk

John Kelly is an Emeritus Research Fellow at St John's College, Oxford, and the Donald Keough Professor in Irish Studies at the University of Notre Dame. He taught English and Irish Literature at the University of Oxford from 1976 to 2009, and has written extensively on nineteenth- and twentieth-century literature. He is General Editor of *The Collected Letters of W. B. Yeats*, Volume 4 (2005) of which was awarded the Cohen Prize by the Modern Languages Association, and has also edited and introduced a 12-volume series of Irish fiction, poetry and essays of the nineteenth century, under the title *Hibernia: State and Nation*. His *W. B. Yeats Chronology* appeared in 2003.

Geert Lernout is an Emeritus Professor of Comparative Literature at the University of Antwerp. His books in English include *The French Joyce* (Ann Arbor: University of Michigan Press, 1990), *The Poet as Thinker: Hölderlin in France* (1994) and *Help My Unbelief: James Joyce and Religion* (2010). With Vincent Deane and Daniel Ferrer he edited twelve of Joyce's Buffalo Notebooks for *Finnegans Wake* and with Wim Van Mierlo two volumes on the European reception of Joyce's work. His scholarly articles are mostly in the fields of comparative literature and editorial theory. He is a member of the Academia Europaea and President of the International James Joyce Foundation. Email: geert.lernout@uantwerpen.be

Colin McDowell retired several years ago after what he describes as 'a long and undistinguished career in the Australian Public Service', during which he has been the mainstay of this journal's commitment to 'Mastering what is most abstract' in *A Vision*, with numerous closely-observed elucidations of its system and its textual puzzles. He continues to read widely, review questioningly, and to write essays on Yeats. Email: colin.richard.mcdowell@gmail.com

Paul Muldoon FRSL, Poet and Howard G. B. Clark '21 Chair of the Humanities, Princeton University, is also an editor, critic and translator. His collections of poetry include *New Weather* (1973), *Mules* (1977), *Why Brownlee Left* (1980), *Quoof* (1983), *Meeting the British* (1987), *Madoc: A Mystery* (1990), *The Annals of Chile* (1994), *Hay* (1998), *Moy Sand and Gravel* (2002), *Horse Latitudes* (2006), *Maggot* (2010), and *One Thousand Things Worth Knowing* (2015). He was Professor of Poetry at Oxford University 1990–2004, and has been poetry editor of *The New Yorker* since 2007. A Fellow of the American Academy of Arts and Sciences and the American Academy of Arts and Letters and a Pulitzer Prize winner, he has also won the American Academy of Arts and Letters award in literature, the T. S. Eliot Prize (1994), the *Irish Times* Poetry Prize (1997), the Griffin International Prize for Excellence in Poetry (2003), the American Ireland Fund Literary Award (2004), the Shakespeare Prize (2004), the Aspen Prize for Poetry (2005), and the European Prize for Poetry (2006).

Bernard O'Donoghue FRSL is a noted Irish poet and Emeritus Fellow of Wadham College, Oxford. His books include his translation of *Sir Gawain and the Green Knight*, his collection, *The Courtly Love Tradition* (1982), *Seamus Heaney and the Language of Poetry* (1995), and his edited *Oxford Irish Quotations* (1999). His poetry collections include *Poaching Rights* (1987), *The Absent Signifier* (1990), *The Weakness* (1991), *Gunpowder* (1995, which won the Whitbread Prize for Poetry), *Here Nor There* (1999), *Poaching Rights* (1999), *Outliving* (2003), *Selected Poems* (2008) and *Farmers Cross* (2011). He is an editor of the distinguished Oxford Poets imprint of Carcanet Press, and the senior member of the Oxford University Poetry Society.

Crónán Ó Doibhlin is Head of Research Collections and Communications in the Boole Library, *Coláiste na hOllscoile Corcaigh* (University College, Cork, now known as a constituent University of the National University of Ireland system). Email: bernard. odonoghue@wadh.ox.ac.uk

Günther Schmigalle, now retired, was a librarian at the Badische Landesbibliothek, Karlsruhe, Germany. He was also for some years (1988–94) a professor of literature and library science at the Universidad Centroamericana, Managua, Nicaragua. He has written about the literature of the Spanish Civil War (Malraux, Hemingway, Arthur Koestler) and has published critical editions of the prose works of Rubén Darío. Email: schmigalle2000@yahoo.de

Colin Smythe is presently working on a new bibliography of W. B. Yeats, correcting, enlarging and updating that by Alan Wade (3rd ed., 1968). He is General Editor of his publishing company's Irish Literary Studies Series (53 titles), and (with the late T. R. Henn) the *Coole Edition of Lady Gregory's Works* (15 volumes so far published, and with *Early Irish Writings 1883–1893*, edited by James Pethica, due shortly as the 16th: that volume will include 'An Emigrant's Note Book', the Angus Grey' stories, and 'A Phantom's Pilgrimage'.) With Henry Summerfield, Dr Smythe is co-General Editor the *Collected Works of G.W. Russell (AE)*, of which four volumes are now published. He is also the late Sir Terry Pratchett's literary agent (and first publisher). He received a Hon. LLD from Dublin University for services to Irish Literature in 1998. Email: cpsmythe@aol.com

Deirdre Toomey is editor of *Yeats and Women: Yeats Annual No. 9* (1991), revised and augmented as *Yeats and Women* (1997). She is co-editor of *The Collected Letters of W. B. Yeats, Volume II, 1896–1900* (1997) and *Mythologies* (2005). She is working with Warwick Gould on a complete revision of A. Norman Jeffares's *A New Commentary on the Poems of Yeats* and is Research Editor of *Yeats Annual*. Email: yeatsresearch@sas.ac.uk

Helen Vendler is A. Kingsley Porter University Professor at Harvard University. Among her many books are *Yeats's Vision and the Later Plays* (1963), *Poets Thinking, Coming of Age as a Poet, The Art of Shakespeare's Sonnets*, and *Our Secret Discipline: Yeats and Lyric Form* (2007). Her latest book is *The Ocean, the Bird and the Scholar: Essays on Poets and Poetry* (2015). Email: vendler@fas.harvard.edu

http://dx.doi.org/10.11647/OBP.0081.01

Introduction

This *Yeats Annual* collects for the first time all of lectures given under the aegis of the University College Cork/ESB International Annual W. B. Yeats Lecture Series. These lectures were delivered between 2003 and 2008. *Coláiste na hOllscoile Corcaigh* (UCC) hosted the series in its Boole Library with funding from the Electricity Supply Board International. UCC is now known as a constituent *university* of the National University of Ireland system.

The key figure in realizing this endowment was the UCC alumnus, Eamonn Cantwell, who took his degree in 1960 in Electrical Engineering, and joined the ESB, and developed the overseas consultancy business, ESB International. Inspired by the late Gus Martin of University College Dublin and a regular attender at the Yeats International Summer School, Eamonn Cantwell became a fastidious international collector of Yeats first editions. On his retirement from ESB International in 1997 he undertook the MPhil in Anglo-Irish Literature. He was awarded a Doctorate of the University of Dublin for his thesis on Yeats's reception in Ireland— '"To Write for My Own Race": The Irish Response to Yeats in his Lifetime', completed in 2003 after working with Professor Terence Brown of Trinity College, Dublin.

The same year, Eamonn Cantwell's magnificent collection of books by Yeats was given to UCC. A Catalogue, *W. B. Yeats: A Collector's Gift* was compiled for the inaugural exhibition (24 June-30 July 2003) by Olivia Fitzpatrick and Carol Quinn, with help from Julia Walton and Michael Holland. 'The Cantwell Collection' compiled for this volume by Crónán Ó Doibhlin, provides in essence an update (and occasional correction) of 'A Collector's Gift', augmented both in terms of bibliographical description and in terms of items bought by the Librarians since 2003.

This volume takes great pride in offering the first publication of Professor John Kelly's 'Eliot and Yeats' which, delivered on 30 April 2008 as 'A "Mutual Illumination"? W. B. Yeats and T. S. Eliot' was the sixth and final UCC W. B. Yeats Lecture. It will subsequently be issued in pamphlet form to conclude the Boole library's now much sought-after series. Illustrations used in the lectures were delivered by PowerPoint or handout. As many of these as possible have been collected in this volume.

Readers familiar with the traditional format of *Yeats Annual* will observe that the section formerly devoted to Shorter Notes now includes what we have termed 'Research Updates'. The reasons are to be found in the content of that which is on offer and which recognizes that since the great period of editorial scholarship on Yeats began in the early 1970s, much more has been rediscovered than has been incorporated into the standard editions, especially the earlier volumes in the *Collected Works* Series with their highly restricted parameters of annotation. It has been possible, therefore, for John Kelly to recover some of Yeats's ghost-writing for Sarah Allgood omitted from the *Collected Works*, and for Warwick Gould, Geert Lernout and Günther Schmigalle to begin to repair some inadequacies in the annotation of *The Poems* and *Autobiographies*. Deirdre Toomey collects and edits some new letters not recovered before the publication of the second volume of *The Collected Letters* (1997).

Colin Smythe, Yeats's bibliographer, has this year added to his occasional series of focused studies of particular examples of Yeats's publications, addressing a new phase in his descriptive bibliography. Census-taking of surviving copies of Yeats's rarest books allows us to map more closely the history of Yeats's dealings with his publishers, agents, patrons and that inner circle of admirers of his work who were happy to bankroll his publications and to regard that duty as a privileged path to collecting early, rare, or embellished states of his books. It also allows us to trace the histories of their price and value and to think about what it is that creates such value, be it the esteem placed on an author's first published 'book', the desires of 'completist' collectors, the intrinsic literary value of a text, its embellishment as a book, or its history of ownership and thus its accrued associations.

This time, Smythe tackles *Mosada* (1886) which, though the first of Yeats's separate publications, is not the rarest either in terms of the original numbers printed nor in terms of its survival. Nevertheless, it is a book which, published at 1/- in 1886, commanded in 2016 at the London Olympia Book Fair the seemingly plausible price of £98,000 for a copy held in the same family for 100 years.

This volume also records the deaths of the Yeats scholars, Katharine Worth (1922–2015) of the University of London, Daniel Albright (1945–2015) of Harvard, Phillip L. Marcus (1941–2015) of the Florida International University and Yves Bonnefoy (1923–2016) the French poet, critic, and essayist, David Bradshaw (1955–2016) Worcester College, Oxford, and Jon Stallworthy (1935–2014) of Wolfson College, Oxford. In this volume, we publish obituaries of Katharine Worth (an indefatigable colleague, first in English and then founding the Department of Drama and Theatre Studies at Royal Holloway College, University of London) and Jon Stallworthy (whom I first met as a student in early 1970 when he was working at the old Ely House office of Oxford University Press in Dover St., in London's West End).

It seemed appropriate, however, to add a personal word here about Daniel Albright, David Bradshaw, Phillip Marcus and Yves Bonnefoy. Yeats remained a pivotal point for the massively curious and restless Albright from his early *The Myth against Myth: A Study of Yeats's Imagination in Old Age* (Oxford, 1972). He had contributed, at Ron Schuchard's request, 'The Fool by the Pool' for *Yeats Annual No. 7: Essays in Memory of Richard Ellmann* and later published his much-admired edition of Yeats's *The Poems* (J. M. Dent, 1990 and later), by far the best annotated American edition of Yeats's poetry, amid a huge range of studies of lyric poetry and music.[1]

---

[1] See Annie E. Schugart, 'Albright Remembered as Whimsical English and Music Teacher', *Harvard Crimson*, 10 January 2015, http://www.thecrimson.com/article/2015/1/10/daniel-albright-obituary

Professor David Bradshaw (d. 13 September 2016) taught at Queen Mary College, University of London before taking the Hawthorden Fellowship at Worcester College, Oxford, where he subsequently also got his Chair. A scholar of Woolf, Huxley, and Evelyn Waugh, and the co-editor (with Rachel Potter) of and major contributor to *Prudes on the Prowl: Fiction and Obscenity in England, 1850 to the Present Day* (Oxford, 2013) he will best be known to readers of this journal as the author of two extended, uncompromising essays. 'The Eugenics Movement and the Emergence of *On the Boiler*' in *Yeats and Women: YA9* (1992, 189–215) foredoomed by the depth of its scholarship— Bradshaw even joined the then Eugenics Society[2] to deepen that understanding and access the references to Yeats in its papers—what it certainly pre-dated, unsatisfactory (because anachronistic) writing on Eugenics and the writers of the period. His more recent piece, 'Oxford Poets: Yeats, T. S. Eliot and William Force Stead' brought all his scholarship to bear on Oxford poets known to Yeats. In this endeavour he used his own College archives; Stead, the priest who baptized T. S. Eliot, having been Chaplain of Worcester until his own conversion to Roman Catholicism (*Yeats's Mask: YA19*, 2013, 77–102). I had known him from his London days, but came to know him best when his cancer was already far-developed. He was unflinchingly brave, and, towards the end, 'absolute for death'.

I first met Phillip Marcus in the mid-1970s when we were co-editing with Michael Sidnell the first edition of *The Secret Rose, Stories by W. B. Yeats: A Variorum Edition* (Ithaca, 1981). He and his family came to Oxford and swapped houses, cars, school places and rooms with Stephen Gill, the Wordsworth scholar at Lincoln College, who took his family to Ithaca while working on the Cornell Wordsworth. It was a time when Cornell University Press was also

---

[2] Founded in 1907 as the Eugenics Education Society, with the aim of promoting the research and understanding of eugenics, the Eugenics Society from 1926 published *The Eugenics Review* (1909–68). It tactfully changed its name to the Galton Institute in 1989, and it is a learned society which aims 'to promote the public understanding of human heredity and to facilitate informed debate about the ethical issues raised by advances in reproductive technology'. See https://en.wikipedia.org/wiki/Galton_Institute.

mounting the Cornell Yeats Manuscripts Series (of which Marcus was co-general editor, and of which he edited the inaugural volume, *The Death of Cuchulain* (Ithaca, 1982). As a student I had read his brilliant early and pioneering study *Yeats and the Beginning of the Irish Renaissance* (Ithaca, 1970), and I saw much more of him in Ithaca in the autumn of 1988, when we worked on the 1992 *Variorum* edition of *The Secret Rose*. He met me at the little airfield waving a copy of the first edition of that book, just in case I did not recognize him after his hair transplant. Jacques Derrida was lecturing on 'The Politics of Friendship' in that department as Cornell's 'Professor at Large', and the politics of hair may have been an issue. The politics of Theory were also at the time pretty vivid in the department, for on several of its doors, including Marcus's, were displayed signs reading 'Just say "No" to Theory'. To retreat to Marcus's own house, amid his splendid Yeats library, to 'swim' around his living-room under his fibre-glass facsimiles of his big-game fishing catches strikingly displayed with his pre-Raphaelite pictures (including one masterpiece by Arthur Hughes) was to deal at once with a wonderfully easy and flexible collaborator and a very private man, intensely difficult to know, one later to seem far more at ease with himself after he moved to a new life at Florida International University.

Yves Bonnefoy (1923–2016) translated Leopardi, Donne, Keats, Yeats and Shakespeare into French, and was the first poet since Paul Valéry to be elected to the Collège de France, where he held the Chaire d'études comparées de la fonction poétique. I recall with some trepidation asking him, after Kathleen Raine had enthusiastically endorsed the idea, to offer a translation of an extended lyric to *YA6*. After an extended silence, a reply came with a typescript translation of the *grand poème* 'Mille neuf cent dix-neuf'. Later he rang and asked me what I thought of it. I thought there was a slight problem with one line and after we had discussed it for a while he was inclined to agree, but concluded that he had better leave it as it stood, for he could for the moment not recompose it. His 'poetic project' was, as John Naughton has written, 'profoundly spiritual', he sought to 'almost identify, poetry and hope' and he 'never ceased insisting that happiness and fulfilment were not to be sought in some other world, but rather in the here and now of our earthly condition and in the simple realities that all people share'.[3]

Colin McDowell contributes an extensive and learned review essay on the new edition of *A Vision* (1937), while among the book reviews, Jad Adams looks at the late Winifred Dawson's new biography of Amy Audrey Locke (1881–1916), platonically beloved by Yeats's friend W. T. Horton, and thus celebrated by Yeats in 'All Soul's Night' as Horton's 'slight companionable ghost | Wild with divinity' (*VP* 471–72).

Dawson's book is a creditable sample of a new trend towards necessary (and necessitous) self-publishing of books otherwise unpublishable in a noisy marketplace. In anticipation or celebration of Yeats's sesquicentenary within Ireland's decade of centenaries, there has been an upsurge in self- and crowd-funded publication of fiction about him, and some few titles are listed in the 'Publications Received' list at the end of this volume.

There seems little point in getting too heavy-handed with the trend, except to say that it exists in a realm of fancy permissible only through willed ignorance of the world of past facts, as found in archives, and re-established through biographical scholarship and critical thinking, a world foisted on the unsuspecting now that W. B. Yeats has emerged from copyright and self-publishing has unleashed authors from the usual gatekeepers. These self-published books have sought to cash in on 'Yeats 150'.

One of these, *Secret Rose* ('© 2015 Orna Ross, & 1897 WB [*sic*] Yeats'), was sent to us for notice. It was printed by Clays plc, St Ives in 2015, and published by Font Publications, London, marking a sad decline in book-making since Richard Clay & Sons printed Yeats's 1897 book, if it possible to judge by the proof copy sent out to *Yeats Annual*. The first volume of Ross's 'biographical' novel about Yeats and Maud Gonne, *Her Secret Rose*, narrated by one Rosie Cross, is ostensibly a 352 pages curtain-raiser to 'pave the way, John The Baptist-like', for her idiosyncratic presentation of *The Secret Rose*

---

[3] 'Yves Bonnefoy: French poet, critic and essayist who believed in the sacred nature of the here and now', *The Guardian*, 3 August 2016, 13.

(1897) including *The Tables of the Law*. *The Adoration of the Magi* (1897), but omitting 'The Rose of Shadow' and 'The Binding of the Hair'. The Yeats texts make up an odd 180 pages assemblage which ignores Yeats's changing intentions for that book as recorded in the scholarly texts from the variorum edition, the various volumes of Yeats's *Collected Letters*, and the 2005 *Mythologies* (for which I register my shared responsibilities) in favour of textual unreliability.

Just one sample will suffice: in the 1897 text of 'Rosa Alchemica', Eros is a 'faint solitary figure with a veiled face' (p. 258, 1897 ed.) while Ross's text offers 'a faint solitary figure with a Rosa veiled face' (p. 522). *Her Secret Rose* forewarns us that it is the first volume of a trilogy, *Between The Words*, about 'the relationship between WB Yeats and the Gonnes, mother and daughter, Maud and Iseult… bringing WB and Maud Gonne face-to-face with the terrible beauty they've created' (p. 353), showing rather rakingly how Yeats's own language can be rattled in readers' faces as the loose change of clichéd 'biographese'.

The cover design, too, has been simply appropriated from Althea Gyles's original cover design for the 1897 edition.[4] Photoshopped so as to eliminate W. B. Yeats's name from its integral place at the foot of the design, and with its integrated title, *The Secret Rose*, simply changed in the design to *Secret Rose*, Gyles's work is then 'bloated' for a book way beyond Bullen's, using a cloth very different in hue and finish from either Yeats's ribbed or smooth cloth versions, and much more open-pored in texture, and so already holding the gold very poorly. Yeats's and Gyles's proportions are simply distorted, and Ross's title and Yeats's are imposed on the lower board, depressing Gyles's lower board design from more or less its centralized position.

How one longs for a faithful facsimile edition of this, and of others of Gyles's books for Yeats. *Secret Rose* is a 'sick rose', its 'invisible worm' seemingly a parasitic envy of Yeats. The preface insists that

---

[4]   The interpretation of the symbolism of the cover, and of its sources, is over-egged and under-researched. Gyles was emphatically not a member of the Golden Dawn: Contrast *VSR* 272–77 especially 273 n. 3, with the account offered to the *Bookseller*, 20 August, 2015 at http://www.thebookseller.com/futurebook/orna-ross-digital-secrets-two-roses-309722.

'WB [*sic*] Yeats was an Indie Author' (as Ross terms herself), an absurd claim given the facts of Yeats's writing life and of the lives of his texts, as found in the long histories of his dealings with numerous publishers. The very thought of what is, in essence, a retro-hijack had given Ross, she tells us, 'a real *frisson*' (p. xi). 'My book and Yeats's book together, between two covers. The audacity! But hey, it's 2015'.

On the very brightest side of the sesquicentenary celebrations, however, are the new programmes about Yeats to have come from RTE, Ireland's national television and radio broadcaster, and other media. One of the best is 'Yeats and the Beastly Coinage', directed by Laura McNicholas and Ann Marie Hourihane (who also did the writing and some of the voice-overs) for 925 Productions (email: 925productions@gmail.com).

Acknowledgements and Editorial Information

Our chief debt of gratitude is to the Yeats Estate over many years for granting permission (through A. P. Watt, Ltd., now part of United Agents Partnership, Ltd.) to use published and unpublished materials by W. B. Yeats. Many of our contributors are further indebted to the Yeats family and Estate for making unpublished materials available for study and for many other kindnesses, as is the Editor. Linda Shaughnessy of United Agents has recently retired after a long and distinguished career, and stewardship of the Yeats Estate is now in the hands of Amy Mitchell (amitchell@unitedagents.co.uk) also formerly of A. P. Watt and her Assistant, Kat Aitken (kaitken@unitedagents. co.uk) at +44 (0)2032140931, who also handle, in addition to their estate work, foreign rights in a large number of countries.

Declan Kiely of the Pierpont Morgan Library, New York, Dr Cathy Henderson and Dr Richard Oram at the Harry Ransom Humanities Research Center, Austin, Catherine Fahy at the National Library of Ireland continue to provide us with research materials and research assistance. At the British Museum, Mr Iain Calderwood and at the British Library, the Curator of the Macmillan Archive, Dr Elizabeth James, rendered invaluable assistance to the Editor, while the research librarians at the Robert W. Woodruff Library at Emory University are equally generous and prompt in recovering specialist materials. Dr Karen Attar in Special Collections at the Senate House Library, University of London has been unfailingly helpful, especially in respect of the Thomas Sturge Moore Collection. Riette Sturge Moore (who died in 1995) allowed us to use in the livery of the *Yeats Annuals* the rose symbol adapted from Thomas Sturge Moore's designs for the H. P. R. Finberg translation of *Axel* (1925).

Martin Enright, President of the Yeats Society, Sligo, alerted us to the existence of Constance Gore-Booth's drawing of Yeats in the Sligo County Museum and Library, and the County Librarian, Dónal Tinney, kindly provided it. Professors Roy Foster, F.B.A. and John Kelly on behalf of Oxford University Press, are generous with permissions. Individuals, institutions private collectors and estates which gave permission for the reproductions of images are profoundly to be thanked for helping us to take advantage of the digital publishing. Every effort has been made to trace copyright holders, and while some images are by unknown photographers, the editor would be grateful to acknowledge any omissions in the next issue.

At Open Book Publishers, William St. Clair FBA, Dr Rupert Gatti, Dr Alessandra Tosi and Bianca Gualandi provided patient assistance and invaluable advice to facilitate our transfer to Open Access publishing. Members of the Advisory Board continue to read a large number of submissions and we are grateful to them, and also to Mr R. A. Gilbert and other specialist readers who offered valuable assistance.

Deirdre Toomey as Research Editor of this journal continues to take up the challenges which routinely defeat contributors, finding innumerable ways to make good articles better by means of her restless curiosity and indefatigable reading. All of us associated with the volume (as well as its readers) continue to be grateful for her persistence with intractabilities.

Contributions for *Yeats Annual No. 21* should reach me, preferably by email as soon as possible after publication of this volume at:

The Institute of English Studies,
University of London,
Senate House, Malet Street,
London WC1E 7HU
United Kingdom
Email: warwick.gould@sas.ac.uk

A style sheet, instructions for the submission of articles to the Editorial Board and consequent editorial procedures are available on our website at http://www.ies.sas.ac.uk/publications/yeats-annual where it is also possible to find full information about, and to purchase, in-print numbers from the *Yeats Annual* backlist. The website is being further developed to complement the online and print availability of the current issues through Open Book Publishers (http://www.openbookpublishers.com).

Professor John Kelly of St John's College, Oxford is General Editor of *The Collected Letters of W. B. Yeats*. Later years of the letters are available in the InteLex electronic edition, which is now online at http://www.nlx.com/collections/130. This resource presently includes only the first three fully annotated volumes as well as the 'B' text of all subsequent letters which have come to light. Priority in the publication of newly discovered letters remains, however, with the print-based volumes, the fifth of which is shortly to be published by the Clarendon Press.

Colin Smythe (PO Box 6, Gerrards Cross, Bucks, SL9 8XA, UK, cpsmythe@aol.com) is completing his revision of the Wade-Alspach *Bibliography* for Colin Smythe, Ltd., while an authorised edition of *Yeats's Occult Diaries, 1898–1901* is being prepared by Deirdre Toomey and myself. We continue to revise A. Norman Jeffares' *New Commentary on the Poems of W. B. Yeats*. All the above would be very grateful to hear of new letters, and to receive new information from readers.

We are grateful to receive offprints and review copies and other bibliographical information (acknowledged at the end of each volume).

Warwick Gould, 1 September 2016

ESSAYS
IN HONOUR OF
EAMONN CANTWELL

from
THE UNIVERSITY COLLEGE
CORK/ESB INTERNATIONAL
ANNUAL YEATS LECTURE SERIES,
2003–08

http://dx.doi.org/10.11647/OBP.0081.02

Yeats and his Books[1]

Warwick Gould

EAMONN CANTWELL—Yeats scholar, booklover, genial philanthropist —has honoured his *alma mater* with a great and timely gift, and I count it a privilege and a distinction to have been asked by University College Cork to inaugurate a series of lectures which will annually celebrate that gift. It is no easy thing to assemble a major Yeats collection. A number of the books in the Cantwell benefaction are over a hundred years old and all of them have been prized collectors' items for generations. The heroic prices Yeats's books now command put such items beyond the reach of scholars, who need them now as never before. Yeats, of course, is the greatest poet in the English language since Shakespeare (more certainly since Milton), and it is already very late in his reception to be buying books of such beauty and distinction. Nobody in Ireland is buying Yeats with Eamonn Cantwell's care, shrewdness, and determination to seek the best surviving copies.

---

[1] This first lecture in the Cork Series was delivered on 24 June 2003. Further information may have been gathered since this article was prepared for publication. If you would like to find out if any further information has been discovered that may help your own research, why not write to the author at Warwick.Gould@sas. ac.uk? Quite apart from anything else, feedback is always welcomed.

There is, however, a further reason for urgency beyond a limited (and depleted) book stock. Scholarly attention has recently turned to what would seem to be a comparatively new subject, the History of the Book. It proves, of course, to be a new way of thinking about a number of older subjects, including, of course, Historical Bibliography. National histories of the book have been essayed in numerous countries around the world.[2] Against this background, we seek to understand what Robert Darnton has called the communications circuit between author, publisher, printer, binder, bookseller, reader, and back to author again, through a process of feedback into new writing from the reception of books.[3] Far too little is known about the last, mysterious phase whereby reading contributes to new writing, and much can only be gleaned from the patient study of the material forms of the text itself, even down to the histories that surviving copies of books have to tell about their own readership. The study of books themselves, as objects, has taken on a new urgency: even as the books themselves become scarcer, acidify, decay, or are cropped and rebound.

This is why Eamonn Cantwell's patient fastidiousness and bibliographical curiosity in respect of Yeats are so important. His doctorate from the University of Dublin concerns itself with the reception of Yeats in Ireland, and of course we receive literary texts in a number of forms other than in books—on the stage, or in other oral communities, in newspapers and periodicals or even by manuscript circulation. Yeats himself claimed in 'Speaking to the Psaltery' (1902) that he naturally dislike[d] print and paper, but now at last [he understood] why

I have just heard a poem spoken with so delicate a sense of its rhythm, with so perfect a respect for its meaning, that if I were a wise man and could persuade a few people to learn the art I would never open a book of verses again.

---

[2] Oxford University Press is publishing a five volume *History of the Irish Book* under the general editorship of the late Professor Robert Welch and Professor Brian Walker. See Clare Hutton and Patrick Walsh (eds.), *The Oxford History of the Irish Book, Vol. V: The Twentieth Century* (Oxford: Clarendon, 2011).

[3] See Robert Darnton, 'What is the History of Books?', in his *The Kiss of Lamourette: Reflections in Cultural History* (London: Faber & Faber, 1990).

This was the origin of his project for the performance of verse by chanting.

Since I was a boy I have always longed to hear poems spoken to a harp, as I imagined Homer to have spoken his, for it is not natural to enjoy an art only when one is by oneself. Whenever one finds a fine verse one wants to read it to somebody, and it would be much less trouble and much pleasanter if we could all listen, friend by friend, lover by beloved (*E&I* 13–14; *CW4* 13).

But Homeric memory had been replaced by the book. The performative, oral culture that Yeats sought to encourage had to be based, as he acknowledged, on the pre-existing literate culture.

It has long been asserted by critics who had the privilege of knowing Mrs George Yeats that Yeats thought in terms of books as much as he did in terms of the individual poem, that the unity of his work and many keys to its patterns of meanings, are to be found in the locations and collocations of his poems. Hugh Kenner in 1955 had published an essay entitled 'The Sacred Book of the Arts' taking his title from Yeats himself and arguing that the order of the poems in *The Tower* is an aspect of their meaning. Yeats, he wrote, 'was an architect, not a decorator; he didn't accumulate poems, he wrote books'.[4] He then extrapolated his argument to the life-arrangement of *Poems* (149), long known as the 'Definitive Edition', which begins with *The Wanderings of Oisin* of 1889 and ends with Yeats's epitaph.[5] Kenner discerned an authorial structure of 'progressive revelation', but when George Yeats complimented him on the essay she also told him that it was not Yeats who was responsible for the order of the *Last Poems* in that posthumous volume.[6]

---

[4] 'The Sacred Book of the Arts', *Irish Writing* (W. B. Yeats: A Special Number), 31 (Summer 1955), 24–35; also *Sewanee Review* 64:4 (October-December 1956), 574–90. Also reprinted in Kenner's *Gnomon: Essays on Contemporary Literature* (New York, 1958), 9–29 and elsewhere.

[5] The arrangement of this edition accords with Yeats's own preference, though whether he would have sanctioned the order chosen by his editor and his wife for the last poems in that collection is not knowable. It differs radically from that which Yeats himself judged appropriate for what was published after his death as *Last Poems and Two Plays* (Dublin: Cuala, 1939). See Warwick Gould, 'W. B. Yeats and the Resurrection of the Author', *The Library* 16: 2 (June 1994), 101–34. Both *The Tower* (1928) and *Poems* (1949) are in the Cantwell Collection.

[6] See Warwick Gould, 'W. B. Yeats and the Resurrection of the Author', 108.

This was crucial, and consistent with her rigorous respect for Yeats's own poem order and volume arrangement. Donald R. Pearce, who worked with the Yeats manuscripts in 1949, recalls Mrs Yeats's telling him:

The poems in any one collection are carefully arranged by W. B. to give an effect, you see, of poetic unity to the volume—a little like successive paragraphs in a story. And so when you open one of his volumes, if you're already familiar with the poems in it, you have an experience somewhat like entering a room full of mirrors; you touch one poem and immediately see reflections of it... there, and there, and there... at different places in the same volume. It was a very serious business with W. B. He worked very hard to get the arrangement exactly right. But, of course, it made things very difficult for the printer; because so often he'd stop the press with, 'The volume needs a little more color just there!' And everything had to come to a halt till he found or made the color he wanted. Then things could start up again![7]

One could go much further, and say that Yeats thought in terms of books as he wrote. He wrote out fair copies of poems in blank vellum-bound volumes of heavy, hand-made paper and gave them as gifts to Maud Gonne. When Katharine Tynan interviewed him in 1893 she found '[p]rominent in the disorder' of his room a manuscript book, first used on 29 August of that year and already the chief repository for poems eventually published in *The Wind Among the Reeds*. It was

a book bound like a mediæval missal in cherry-coloured brocade and tarnished gold... 'What may that fine thing be?' I ask. He answers with a slight blush, 'That is my MS. book. A friend [Maud Gonne] brought me the cover from Paris, and I had the book made to fit it'. I inspect the book. It is such thick paper as one finds in *éditions de luxe*, and, one imagines, must be rather uncomfortable to write upon.[8]

---

[7]   'Hours with the Domestic Sibyl: Remembering George Yeats', *The Southern Review* 28:3 (July 1992), 485–501, at p. 500. The memoir is made up of such fully quoted conversations remembered from 1949 and it lacks documentation. Nevertheless, Dr Anthony Roche of University College Dublin, a former student of the late Professor Pearce, tells me that Pearce kept prodigious contemporary written records of such encounters. Their present whereabouts is unknown.

[8]   *The Sketch*, 29 November 1893, 256. Maud Gonne's cover and the notebook itself are described by Carolyn Holdsworth in W. B. Yeats, The Wind Among

Composition was for Yeats a chaotic process, and composing poems in such books meant violating or disturbing the order which their sequence of pages implied. After all, a book is a machine which allows for both sequential and hypertextual reading (the latter some of us still refer to as skipping), but beyond the security which its binding conveys to working sheets, it is a machine which works best with settled forms of the text. It is not easy to erase ink from paper. Yet the ruling idea of Yeats's poems was so frequently the book with its settled arrangement and order that he first divulged the title of *The Wind Among the Reeds* (1899) to Tynan in this interview, some six years before he completed it, and then had to put up with others plagiarizing it in the interim.

He also *reconceived* poems in terms of the books and the markets for which they were designed. Thus, early on, he had a strong sense that the American market was financially important, but that he did not wish to remain the hostage of an Irish-American sentimentality unacceptable here in Ireland, or in England. His 'Dedication to a Book of Stories from the Irish Novelists' had been consciously aimed at the Irish-American audience for whom his *Representative Irish Tales* was assembled. He chose to rewrite it for all audiences in 1924–25, the pressures of public life in the new Free State being such as to leave him feeling 'battered, badgered and destroyed' (*VP* 129–30).

He had made a special arrangement of his work for the Macmillan Company of New York specifically to outwit that American piracy of his work which threatened after he had first lectured there in 1903–04 and had created a huge potential audience.[9] These two volumes the publishers entitled *The Poetical Works of William B. Yeats*, and when you look at the Cantwell copies you will see how the 'name, initial, name' reformulates Yeats into a plausibly American poet. The presence on the title page of Macmillan & Co., London is a bit of international swaggering of the Macmillan Company of New York.

---

the Reeds: *Manuscript Materials* (Ithaca and London: Cornell University Press, 1993), 215ff. So heavy is the paper of several of Yeats's manuscript books that the uneven surface adds to the difficulty of reading his always obscure script.

[9] See Warwick Gould, 'Yeats in the States: Piracy, Copyright and the Shaping of the Canon', *Publishing History*, 51: 2002, 61–82.

Copyright deposit copies of these volumes, evidently never issued in Britain, are not to be found in the British Library. Preparing the first of these volumes (1906), Yeats saw too that his own explanatory notes had to be modified for the American audience. Yet, in spite of such pressures in Yeats's dealings with the major audiences who paid for his books—primarily English, increasingly American—he was insistent about one thing, his Irish identity. In 1896 he threw this imperative to Henry-D. Davray, his French translator.

I want you to understand that I am an Irish poet, looking to my own people for my ultimate best audience & trying to express the things that interest them & which will make them care for the land in which they live (*CL2* 15, 19 Mar. [1896]).

He was given to steering (though not controlling) his reception in such ways, but this issue could sound simple only when packaged for export. He was at odds with the journalistic and literary establishment here in Ireland. His textual self begins obviously enough with his early collections—*The Wanderings of Oisin: and Other Poems* (1889), *The Countess Kathleen and Various Legends and Lyrics* (1892) and *The Celtic Twilight* (1893), but it is multivalent and, famously, shape-changing. Moreover, it has a mysterious companion in his perceived image in the press. Yeats's struggles with that *doppelgänger* are intriguing, and result in his creation of different textual identities for different Irish markets. The several Yeatses include the Protestant IRB man, the *'declassé* Protestant Magician' (Roy Foster's phrase[10]), the Mariolatrous mystic, the Connacht man, the Sligo folklorist, the Clare/Galway border man, the eighteenth-century throwback, the national dramaturge, the Free State politician, the Londoner, the Nobel prizewinner. His Irish audience had multiple identities, and the Irish press through which he reached them was at least as fissiparous.

---

[10] See 'Protestant Magic: W. B. Yeats and the Spell of Irish History', in R. F. Foster, *Paddy and Mr Punch: Connections in Irish History* (London: Allen Lane, 1993), 212–32.

Plate 1. W. T. Horton's caricature of Yeats among his books and William Blake's alchemical equipment and astrological *grimoires*, from *The Academy*, 59, no. 1418 (8 July 1899), 28. Private collection, London.

When his publisher A. H. Bullen, himself from Clonakilty, tried to sell his books in Dublin in late 1900, it wasn't easy. Yeats complained that Bullen 'was amazed to find the hostility to me of the booksellers'.[11] Gill, he declared,

seemed to hardly like to speak my name. I am looked upon as hetredox it seems. 'The Secret Rose' was strange to say particularly disapproved of, but they spoke with hostility of even 'The Shadowy Waters'. Russell told me before I saw Bullen that clerical influence was he beleived working against me because of my mysticism.[12] He accuses Father Finlay & his jesuits of working behind [D. P.] Moran. Memory of 'The Countess Cathleen' dispute accounts for a good deal. Bullen found the protestant booksellers little better & asked me if TCD disliked me. Magee, the College publisher,

[11] Censorship by the Dublin firm of Eason & Son (including of their library) was 'taken for granted, and, far from attracting hostile criticism, was considered one of the proofs that the firm was discharging its moral responsibilities seriously'. See L. M. Cullen, *Eason and Son: A History* (Dublin: Eason & Son, Ltd., 1989), 246.

[12] W. T. Horton's caricature of WBY (Plate 1) as 'the Irish poet and mystic' in the *Academy* on 8 July 1899 showed Yeats standing on and surrounded by various *grimoires*, together with copies of his *Poems*, *The Secret Rose*, his Blake edition, 'Rosa Alchemica', and a wand and halo. The accompanying letterpress pointed out that Horton 'as joint author with Mr. Yeats of *A Book of Images*, should know his subject well. He has made his picture both a portrait and criticism. Mr. Yeats's experiments in necromancy are suggested by the retort and the volume on which he stands, his poetry and mysticism by other books; and there is, in fact, nothing in the drawing that has not special significance'. One thing, however, the artist has not quite realised—Mr. Yeats's height. The poet is long and willowy (28).

said 'What is he doing here Why doesnt he go away & leave us in peace'. He seems to have suspected me of some deep revolutionary design.... must not go near the Constitutional Club, where I have no desire to go.[13] This because of my letter about the late queen. Between my politics & my mysticism I shall hardly have my head turned with popularity.[14]

At this point, Yeats took a literary agent, A. P. Watt, Mr. 10% himself. For many years thereafter, Yeats pointedly instructed his publishers not to send any of his books for review in Ireland.

Such interactions with the market—real or imagined—are particularly noteworthy, and this issue of an author's sense of his audience is a mysterious but a formative matter. In Yeats's case, the feedback loop from readers to writer is of profound importance because he was not only a writer but a rewriter, and a rewriter whose rewriting helped him to find new sources of inspiration. Lafcadio Hearn protested in 1901 about revisions to 'The Host of the Air':

You have mangled it, maimed it, deformed it, extenuated it—destroyed it totally. ...you have really sinned a great sin! *Do* try to be sorry for it!— reprint the original version,—tell critics to go to perdition, if they don't like it,—and, above all things, *n'y touchez plus!*

Even as Yeats assured Hearn that he would restore parts of the poem, he confided, in the immediately following letter that:—

even when one certainly improves ones work, as when one disengages a half hidden meaning or gets rid of a needless inversion, no body who liked the old will like the new. One changes for the sake of new readers, not for the sake of old ones (*CL3* 101–02).

For the moment, however, I want to stress how the young writer sought to find and to shape his audience, even as he struggled to get published, and I shall do so with reference to a recent discovery. Another private collector here in Ireland once showed me a scruffy treasure, the *Minute Book of the Literary Sub-Committee of the Irish Literary Society of London, 1893–1896*. Yeats was a member, and the committee had the responsibility of 'superintend[ing] the Literary

---

[13] George Pollexfen's club in Sligo, Protestant and Unionist.
[14] To Lady Gregory [21 May 1901], *CL3* 70–73, cf. *Au* 447–48.

Work' of the Society. Who was involved? How did they go to work, and why? The committee consisted of interested amateurs of Irish Literature, prominent members of the London Irish community such as Francis Fahy of Kinvarra (author of 'The Ould Plaid Shawl'), journalists such as R. Barry O'Brien, author of lives of Wolfe Tone and Parnell, the bibliographer of Irish poetry, D. J. O'Donoghue, Edward Garnett from the British Museum, the Irish publisher Edmund Downey, the Irish folklorist Eleanor Hull. The rest were Irish writers: Lionel Johnson, Yeats, Stopford Brooke, John Todhunter, T. W. Rolleston, Emily Hickey and Alfred Percival Graves.[15]

Their ultimate concern was the creation of the taste by which they wanted to be enjoyed. They attempted to build markets for Irish books, which the publishers would then supply at discounted prices, and to that end, the writers sat down with the publishers and journalists. They devised plans for the creation of reading groups, to read Irish writing. It all sounds fashionably recent, but it is not. Nor is there anything new about our preoccupation with the idea that we read too little. Here is Stephen Gwynn, later an Irish Nationalist MP at Westminster and a founder of Maunsel & Co. the Dublin publisher, recalling the Dublin of the 1880s and early 1890s.

The New Irish Library... like every other literary venture in Ireland... had to contend with the reluctance of the Irish people to spend money on print. Newspapers in Ireland are bought, but they are carefully handed from one reader to another, and it is rare to see a man leave one in a tram or train: in this respect, our people are admirably frugal. So far as concerns the purchase of books, we are a nation of asbstainers with a few drunkards: but the bookworm in Ireland is almost invariably an amasser of old books. There was never a harder country for a literary man to make his money out of.... Later, I was to some degree concerned in starting the firm of Maunsel and Company in Ireland and did my utmost to develop the sale of books in Ireland itself. But in my wanderings I reached the town of Ballaghaderreen and in the big shop over which Mr. Dillon still at least nominally presides, I was authorized to interview the manager about setting up a sale of Irish

---

A vivid sense of the self-help culture of the London Irish Literary Society can be found in 'Francis Fahy's "Ireland in London—Reminiscences" (1921)' edited by Clare Hutton in Wayne K. Chapman and Warwick Gould (eds.), *Yeats's Collaborations: YA15* 233–80.

books. One work in particular seemed particularly hopeful, but it cost two shillings. Two shillings! No one would give the like of that for a book in Ballaghaderreen.

Gwynn noticed, however, that a case of expensive pipes in the same shop were selling well at 7/6 each. These were an 'intelligible expenditure. But that any body should pay two shillings—let alone seven and sixpence—for a book was apparently unthinkable in County Mayo'.[16] All this changed (as he conceded in 1926): by then there were 'more bookshops... in Irish towns, but the good bookshops have gone down in the world'.

One thing is clear. The output of writing in Ireland has increased immensely, and the standard of it has improved out of all comparison: it has gained a rank of its own in the world of letters...

To Gwynn, the 'men to whom this change is mainly attributable... stood deliberately and consciously apart' from Parnell's movement but capitalized on the 'loneliness and expectancy' after the 'ebb of the land war'. The 'two moving forces were, of course, W. B. Yeats and Douglas Hyde'.[17]

Moreover, the London manoeuvres had their predictable politics. The reading groups were to be affiliated to the National Home Reading Union. For 2/- per year, one could sign up to a reading circle, receive lists of what to read, and get on with it. The poets, the publishers, the journalists drew up impressive lists of what to read in Irish literature, logrolled for each other, advertised their ideas and tried to co-ordinate a programme of lectures and original nights to accompany the scheme. It was, perhaps inevitably, not a great success. Dissension followed, including a split with the Dublin-based National Literary Society, and Yeats's famous quarrel with Gavan Duffy who used the occasion to force a Davisite diet onto Irish audiences against all Yeats's instincts: Roy Foster is excellent on this episode (*Life 1*, 112–34).

[16] Stephen Gwynn, *Experiences of a Literary Man* (London: Thornton Butterworth, 1926), 60–61.
[17] *Ibid.*, 62.

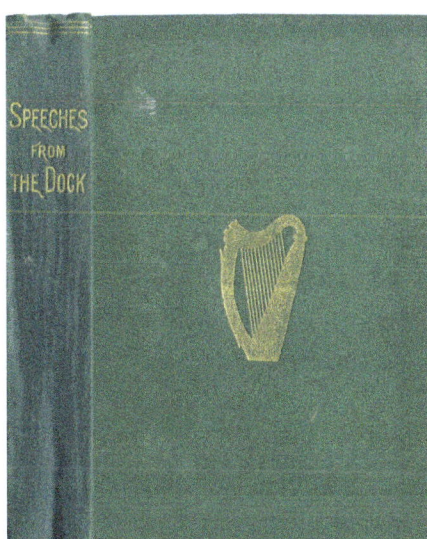

Plates 2a & b. Top boards of *Speeches from the Dock*, 48th edition and alternative cover emblem, showing Shamrocks, Harp, Shield with Red Hand of Ulster, and Spear, from the 53rd edition. Private collection, London.

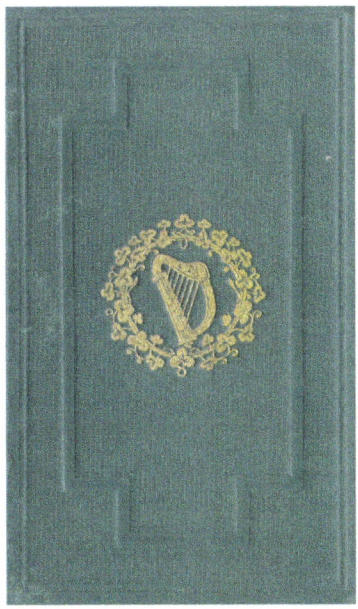

Plate 3. *Spirit of the Nation*, 50th edition of 1876. Private collection, London.

My point is that for Yeats to succeed was to succeed in London, to create an English or an Irish expatriate reading community to buy books, in order to begin to build the reputation at home which might reinvigorate Dublin culture. In London Yeats had to learn to roll literary logs, to lecture, and, in the Irish Literary Society, to create his own audience.[18] Until a decent publishing house was established in Dublin, 'a city which has long published little but school-books and prayer-books',[19] he would have to publish in London and be a literary presence there. He hated the look of Irish books, the livery of *The Spirit of the Nation*, *Speeches from the Dock*, or *National Ballads, Songs and Poems* of Thomas Davis, anything produced by James Duffy, or M. H. Gill, or Sealey, Bryers and Walker (Plates 2a & b, 3). Thus, in 'The Union of the Gael', his Presidential speech to a banquet on 13 April, 1898, Yeats deplored the era when 'No Irish books were read except books of rhetorical or melodramatic journalism, bound in staring green, and covered with shamrocks'.[20] The association of such covers with the rhetoric of the 'harp and pepperpot' school of Irish literary endeavour was, for Yeats, insufferable, largely because of its freight of Young Ireland images and metaphors.[21]

---

[18] Its first meeting was at 3 Blenheim Rd., 28 December, 1891: see *CL1* xv. Yeats glimpsed its possibilities from within the Celtic majority of the Rhymers' Club, which he and Ernest Rhys had founded in January 1890. See *CW7* 57; also Karl Beckson, 'Yeats and the Rhymers' Club', *Yeats Studies: An International Journal* 1 (Bealtaine, 1971), 20–41 at pp. 22, 25. A journal, the *Irish Home Reading Magazine* was founded in 1894; see *CL1* 344 and n., 355.

[19] So Yeats complained in 'Dublin Mystics' (*The Bookman* May 1895), perennially hoping that a Dublin publisher had been found to advance the 'imaginative awakening of our time'. See *CW9* 259–60; *UP1* 357. While the periodical press in Dublin was vibrant, Yeats, who been involved in *The Irish Home Reading Magazine* with Sealy, Bryers and Walker in Dublin, was well versed in the costs and returns of such ventures.

[20] See Yeats's speech 'The Union of the Gael', in *'98 Centennial Association of Great Britain and France: Report of Speeches etc* [Dublin: Bernard Doyle, 1898], 8–9.

[21] *Au* 203, 219. T. D., A. M., and D. B. Sullivan, *Speeches from the Dock, or Protests of Irish Patriotism, containing, with introductory sketches and biographical notices, Speeches delivered in the Dock* (Dublin, T. D. Sullivan, 1887) was in its 39th edition. Yeats knew the work well, and even troped on some of the more renowned speeches, e.g. that of Emmet, which is alluded to in 'September 1913', a poem which overall responds to Thomas Davis's 'The Green above the Red'. The similarly adorned *The Spirit of the Nation*, was in its fiftieth edition: see WBY's comments in *Mem* 65.

Irish literature had fallen into contempt; no educated man ever bought an Irish book; in Dublin Professor Dowden, the one man of letters with an international influence, was accustomed to say that he knew an Irish book by its smell, because he had once seen some books whose binding had been fastened together by rotten glue (*Au* 200).

On 18 May, 1903, John Quinn wrote to George P. Brett of the Macmillan Company to record Yeats's view that 'I prefer my books to be bound in any other colour than green because if one binds an Irish book in green one is thought to have done so on patriotic grounds' (*CL3* 361). Yeats continued for many years to hate having green covers on his books, and even after the establishment of the Free State transfigured other emblems of nationalism, the shamrock remained a symbol to be despised.[22]

In all this London literary work, Yeats was not the dreamy poet with the floppy bow tie, but a working writer interacting with the means by which his work would be produced, marketed, and read. He had been so from the outset, and his books would seem to show that he was always prepared to operate within the fields of two contrary forces. On the one hand he knew how individual was his vision, and how important it was to stamp his own personality, image, livery or symbolic force onto his books as objects as well as onto his texts.

From his own debut, it was Yeats's own personality and image which were thrust on our attention. *Mosada. A Dramatic Poem* (1886), reprinted by Sealy, Bryers, and Walker from the *Dublin University Review* had a 'Frontispiece Portrait of the Author by J. B. Yeats' announced on the front cover (Plate 4). While not all young poets have a portrait painter for a father, not all would presume to embellish their first publication with a self-image.[23]

---

[22] See below, n. 135.

[23] When Elkin Mathews asked Will Rothenstein to provide a portrait drawing of Lionel Johnson for the latter's *Poems* (1895), Johnson replied on 24 October 1894 'Too great an honour! or shall I say, premature? I should be charmed to sit to you at any time, when you want an excellent model for nothing: but a portrait in my book would be too great a vanity, even for me. Wait till the Laureateship is mine, or—don't be insulted—the P.R.A. is yours. I am explaining to Mathews that the very portrait itself would blush: which is undesirable for a lithograph by

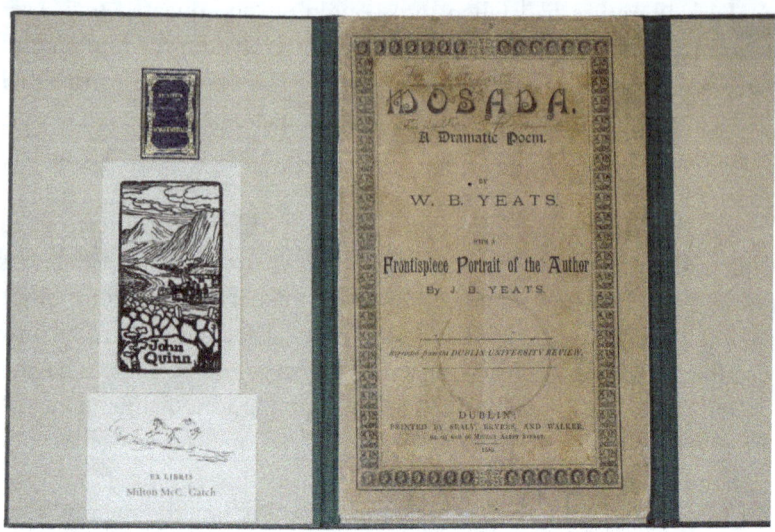

Plate 4. Review copy of *Mosada: A Dramatic Poem* (1886) with bookplates, including those of John Quinn (centre, by Jack B. Yeats), Major William van R. Whitall (top), and Milton McC. Gatch (bottom). Courtesy of Maggs Bros., London.

Gerard Manley Hopkins, reporting on the Dublin poets to Coventry Patmore, commented upon a certain 'young Mr. Yeats' whose 'striking verses' were in the Trinity College journal, and who had been 'perhaps unduly pushed by Ferguson'.[24] Hopkins, who was not predisposed to think well of it, recalled a visit to John Butler Yeats's studio where, 'with some emphasis of manner', JBY had presented him with a copy of the book, no doubt drawing attention to the portrait. Hopkins was

> you. Only Academicians' portraits ought to blush. Seriously, in a first volume of verse, it would be a little absurd: greatly as I should appreciate the honour of immortality from your hands. You must give it to me later'. See *Men and Memories: Recollections of William Rothenstein 1872–1900* (London: Faber & Faber, 1931), 157. 'Enoch Soames' was more insistent, and Max Beerbohm has Rothenstein fleeing to the country to avoid the commission for a portrait drawing as frontispiece to that 'dim' figure's poems. See *Seven Men* (London: William Heinemann, Ltd., 1919), 10.

24   These poets included Katharine Tynan—'a simple brightlooking Biddy with glossy very pretty red hair, a farmer's daughter in the County Dublin'. See Claude Colleer Abbott (ed.), *Further Letters of Gerard Manley Hopkins including his correspondence with Coventry Patmore* (London: Oxford University Press, 2nd ed., 1956), 373–74.

impressed, 'the young man having finely cut intellectual features and his father being a fine draughtsman' but

[f]or a young man's pamphlet this was something too much; but you will understand a father's feeling. Now this *Mosada* I cannot think highly of, but I was happily not required to praise what presumably I had not then read…'.[25]

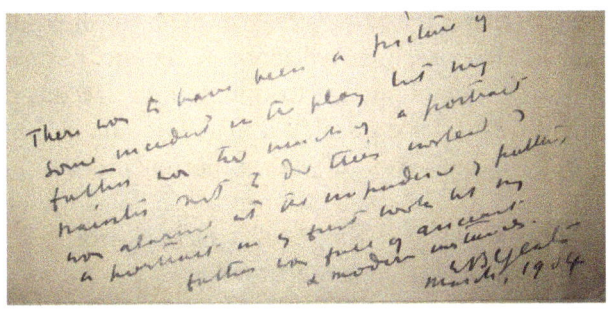

Plate 5. A detail of Yeats's inscription on the frontispiece page of Quinn's copy of *Mosada*. Courtesy of Maggs Bros., London.

Yeats had planned 'a picture of some incident in the play' but his 'father was too much of a portrait painter' and prevailed. Though Yeats was 'alarmed at the impudence of putting a portrait in my first book' his father was 'full of ancient and modern instances', as Yeats recorded in 1904 on John Quinn's copy (Plate 5).[26] Since JBY had, in a moment characteristic only in its financial misjudgment, actually paid (or promised to pay) for the printing, Yeats was in no position

[25] *Ibid.*, 374. He had recently found Yeats's 'The Two Titans: A Political Poem', a 'strained and unworkable allegory about a young man and a sphinx on a rock in the sea (how did they get there? what did they eat? and so on: people think such criticisms very prosaic; but commonsense is never out of place anywhere…) but still containing fine lines and vivid imagery' (*ibid.*). William M. Murphy's account of this episode misquotes Hopkins and conflates 'The Two Titans' with *Mosada*: see *Prodigal Father: The Life of John Butler Yeats (1839–1922)* (Ithaca and London: Cornell University Press, 1978), 146–47.

[26] *Wade* 1, frontispiece, and pp. 19–20. Quinn's copy, inscribed March 1904, was most recently sold by Maggs Bros., London, from the collection of Milton McC. Gatch: see Gatch and Ed Maggs, *A Little Dust: The Gatch Collection of Yeats* (London: Maggs Bros., 2012), and *Yeats: The McC. Gatch Collection* (London: Maggs Catalogue 1492, 2015). See also below, p. 242 (Smythe).

to protest—not even about the shamrocks in the cover's border design.[27] The portrait is of a somewhat callow-looking and bearded Yeats looking a good deal older than his twenty-one years.[28] It was duly noticed by Katharine Tynan who prophesied 'great things... we to whom he belongs by blood and birth, will watch his career with especial trust and pride' (Plate 6).[29] The image helped to turn the book into a very preliminary auto-icon, perhaps all the more necessary given that it is a Moorish tale of the Spanish Inquisition.

Mosada like all books, was a collaborative venture. Early on, then, Yeats learned that an author has to compromise. He was prepared to compromise or to strike a deal, if it might get him closer to what he wanted. It became a habit of JBY's to portray his son in his own poems. When John McGrath commented on John Butler Yeats's portrait of Yeats as the mad 'King Goll' which, vigorously rethought as it was engraved to accompany that poem in *The Leisure Hour* in September 1887 (Plates 7a & b),[30] Yeats conceded that it had been 'done from me & is probably like though it was not intend[ed] as a portrait. Be sure I would never have had myself painted as the mad

---

[27] There are twenty-one shamrock medallions in each vertical border, with seven male heads facing seven female heads across a scroll in the top and bottom borders. See above Plate 4 and below pp. 253, 255, Plates 37 and 38 (Smythe).

[28] Yeats inscribed another copy on 10 November 1923 'The play... had of course no success of any kind. It was my father who insisted on the portrait, as he refused to consider anybody's diffidence where a portrait is concerned, it was also his insistence that kept me bearded'. (HRHRC).

[29] The 'new singer in Erin' would 'take high place among the world's future singers' (*Irish Monthly* XV: 165 [March 1887], 166–8). See also John Kelly, 'Books and Numberless Dreams: Yeats's Relations with his Early Publishers', in A. Norman Jeffares (ed.), *Yeats, Sligo and Ireland: Essays to mark the 21st Yeats International Summer School* (Gerrards Cross: Colin Smythe, 1980), 233 (hereafter Kelly, 'Books'). When Tynan first saw Yeats he had 'the saddest, most poetical, face I ever saw.... I am the only poet I have ever met whose face does not show something of the divine art. O dear, I wish I was in the least degree poetical-looking'. (Letter to Mrs Pritchard, 30 June 1885, in *Apex One, Katherine [sic] Tynan Letters 1884–1885* ([London?], 1973), 23). Most of the 100 copies of the pamphlet were given away. Allen R. Grossman traces the origin of Yeats's 'self-image as the overthrown artist, the reed bowed by the wind' to JBY's early portraits 'where the son is exhibited either as a youth too effeminate to be in any sense threatening or as a giant destroyed by his own self-destructive power'. See *Poetic Knowledge in the Early Yeats: A Study of* The Wind Among the Reeds (Charlottesville: The University Press of Virginia, 1969), 47–48.

[30] *The Leisure Hour*, 36, September 1887, 637.

"King Goll" of my own poem had I thought it was going to turn out the portrait it has. I was merely the cheapest & handiest model to be found'.[31]

Plate 6. J. B. Yeats's frontispiece drawing of W. B. Yeats, from *Mosada* (1886). Courtesy Colin Smythe.

Plate 7a. J. B. Yeats's pastel portrait of W. B. Yeats as King Goll. Private collection, Ireland. Courtesy Colin Smythe.

Plate 7b. J. B. Yeats's portrait of W. B. Yeats as King Goll, *The Leisure Hour*, September 1887. Private collection, London.

[31] *CL4* 939; *CL InteLex*, 14 [19 January 1892].

Nevertheless, Yeats kept the portrait and on 26 May, 1924 told Olivia Shakespear that it had been painted at the age of twenty when his father had 'painted me as "King Goll", quite insane, tearing the strings out [of] a harp, being insane with youth, but looking very desirable—alas no woman noticed it at the time—with dreamy eyes & a great mass of black hair. It hangs in our drawing room now a pathetic memory of a really dreadful time'.[32] Nine years later, JBY was still at it, offering an image of Yeats as a Firbolg with an Irish wolf hound, in an illustration for a reprint of 'The Lake Isle of Innisfree' in the same journal.[33] By then Yeats had established himself enough to have a marketable image.

This was not yet the case when he assembled his first collection in 1889, *The Wanderings of Oisin: and Other Poems*, Eamonn Cantwell's copy of which is the cornerstone of the collection we celebrate today. Despite Yeats's London connexions, that volume was immensely difficult to realize.[34] It was in effect a vanity publication, but such was a common and honourable mode of publication in the period, and it was probably Katharine Tynan who suggested Charles Kegan Paul as publisher, and for his Irish sympathies.[35] In 1885 Paul had taken her first book at her father's expense—£ 20 as she tells us—found he could sell it, reprinted it, and took her second book, *Shamrocks*, at his own (dubiously rewarded) risk.[36] He took Yeats's book on 'the good old-fashioned method of publishing on half profits',[37] whereby the

[32] *CL InteLex* 4556; *L* 705. See also *YA4* Plate 16; *YA8* 194. The portrait remains in the Yeats family collection. I am indebted to Colin Smythe and Colin Smythe, Ltd. For this image.
[33] *The Leisure Hour* (1896), 638–39.
[34] London: Kegan Paul, Trench & Co., January 1889; Wade 2.
[35] On Charles Kegan Paul see Leslie Howsam, *Kegan Paul: A Victorian Imprint: Publishers, Books and Cultural History* (London: Kegan Paul International; Toronto: University of Toronto Press, 1998).
[36] *CL1* 24 n., 517. See also Tynan's *Twenty-Five Years: Reminiscences* (London: Smith, Elder, 1913), 140. The volume was *Louise de la Vallière and Other Poems* (1885). Paul also published John Todhunter, the Yeatses' neighbour in Bedford Park, and a friend of Dr George Coffey, see also John Kelly, 'Books', 233.
[37] 'Publishers of Today. Messrs. Kegan Paul, Trench Trübner & Co., Limited', *The Publishers' Circular and General Record of British and Foreign Literature*, 1319 (10 October 1891), 424–26 at p. 426. Redway was opposing the views of the Society of Authors.

publisher bears the cost of production (itself a debatable or inflatable entity) and the author makes no money until costs are recovered, at which point profits are shared by author and publisher. In Yeats's case, Kegan Paul demanded guarantees from subscribers before being prepared even to consider the matter.

The business of publishing by subscription was one which Yeats, O'Leary and others including Tynan knew well from *Poems and Ballads of Young Ireland*. John O'Leary had found 'almost all the subscribers' for *The Wanderings of Oisin: and Other Poems*, but Yeats too was involved.[38] Beyond the drumming up of the initial subscribers, which Yeats began in autumn 1887, there was the difficulty of matching their numbers, commitments and expectations to Charles Kegan Paul's extremely close appreciation of the likely costs and the likely market. In January 1888 Yeats had sought to impress the Irishness of his work upon the Irish journalist Stephen Gwynn (who was putting his name down for four copies): the title poem was not merely 'an irish poem' it was also 'about my best' and was to dominate the collection—'irish a good many of them'—which Yeats even then felt he might 'modify... indefinately' (*CL1* 44). Kegan Paul—in whom Yeats professed to discover a 'compound of the superciliousness of the man of letters with the oiliness of the tradesman'—thought of lowering the price from the proposed 5/- to 3/6d without bothering too much about the labour this would involve for those organizing the subscription list (*CL1* 54). When John Todhunter enterprisingly suggesting offering each subscriber two copies of a more cheaply produced book at 2/6d, Yeats saw at once that the arrangement would use up 400 of the 500 to be printed and be 'a somewhat unceremonious as well as a losing arrangement exausting my whole edition but 100'.[39]

Yeats's business acumen was sharp, but he was green enough in every sense to imagine that the unsubscribed copies of his first book were going to sell widely on the open market. He was faced with a dilemma: should he exhaust himself and his supporters' patience by

---

[38] 'I Became an Author', *The Listener* (4 August 1938), *UP2* 509. See also Kelly, 'Books', 233–39.

[39] *CL1* 58–59. See also Kelly, 'Books', 235–37.

endeavouring to increase the number of subscribers, or should he cut his losses and the book? 'Friction with the market' (in the shape of Kegan Paul, that champion of its values) made Yeats confront artistic priorities.[40]

perhap[s] I will reduce the size of the book. At any rate 3/6 is likely to be the price. A 5/- book should be over 200 pages. I will decide this week after seeing Keegan Paul. Whatever may be decided on I will submit to O'Leary for his opinion he having got so many names for me. If it comes to lightening the ship I will hardly know what to throw overboard... the Irish poems must all be kept, making the personality of the book—or as few thrown over as may be.[41]

Yeats as yet was too near to his poems to be a ruthless excluder—but the principle that his books would have their own Irish personality was established.[42] There were other, practical difficulties to be addressed. A book of 156 numbered and six preliminary pages, *The Wanderings of Oisin: and Other Poems* was estimated to cost £30.7.6 to produce. Kegan Paul's final costs were almost twice that, at £59.15. 2, including 'fee, advertisements, postage and booksellers' discount'. 500 quires of the octavo were printed by 12 December 1888, and 300 bound, to be sold at 5/-. There were 208 pledged subscribers, some of whom Yeats had signed up to pay only 3/6d.[43] There was yet endless work in dunning those who did not pay their subscriptions (only 146 obliged at once). The subscribers got their copies in January, and the book was actually published in the first fortnight of February 1889.[44]

---

[40] Such a situation was exactly that commented upon by Henry James, when he alerted Hendrik Anderson to 'that benefit of *friction with the market* which is so *true* a one for solitary artists too much steeped in their mere personal dreams' (unpublished letter, 25 November 1906, University of Virginia, quoted in Michael Anesko, *Friction with the Market* (New York: Oxford University Press, 1986), 6.

[41] *CL1* 59, and Kelly, 'Books', 238.

[42] This was a key expression of the problem considered by Ian Jack in 'A Choice of Orders: The Arrangement of "The Poetical Works"', in Jerome J. McGann (ed.), *Textual Criticism and Literary Interpretation* (Chicago and London: University of Chicago Press, 1985), 127–43, at 138ff.

[43] *CL1* 123. See also Kelly, 'Books', 238–39.

[44] *Publishers' Circular* 52:1234 (15 February 1889), 178, cf. *Wade* 2, p. 21, which offers 'January 1889'.

While 50 extra quires were bound on 1 February and a similar number on 15 July, only 174 of the 270 copies disposed of had actually been sold by June. Further, only 35 of the 204 copies sold in the first year had been 'bought on the open market'. In 1890 and 1891 about thirty copies per year were sold (including nineteen in the first year to subscribers) and an increasing number went to purchasers on the open market. The total sold to such buyers, however, did not exceed 75 copies.[45]

The subscribers Yeats found were Irish sympathizers, and few casual buyers who knew his work through *The Dublin University Review*, *The Irish Monthly*, *The Irish Fireside*, *United Ireland* or *The Gael* had not been tapped. Kegan Paul was relying on an ordinary English paying public consisting of those who could lay out about one sixth of a clerk's weekly wage for a book of poems by an Irishman known in England only through the pages of *The Leisure Hour*, *The Vegetarian* and *Lucifer*. There was no American contract for this book, so readers of *The Boston Pilot* or *The Providence Sunday Journal* were left out of account. No doubt Yeats would have liked an American issue, but the decision to publish solely in London meant that he was appealing largely to an English public—to which even the poems of Ferguson were not well known. These poetry buyers would have found Yeats's subject matter and treatment in 'The Wanderings of Oisin' as strange as they would have found his hero's name unpronounceable.

Yet the book was widely reviewed as friends and logrollers got to work. Rather than temporize about promise, Oscar Wilde openly defied the anticipated charge of logrolling by reviewing it twice and

<hr/>

[45] More difficulties followed. Yeats took 35 copies 'although some of these went to subscribers whose contributions he had diverted to his own chronically empty pocket' says Kelly. Fifty-one review copies were sent out, and the remaining six copies went to five copyright libraries and to a friend (Kelly, 'Books', 239, see also *CL1* 230). The figures upon which Kelly's excellent summary is based can be found in *British Publishers' Archive on Microfilm: The Archives of Kegan Paul, Trench, Trübner & Henry S. King 1858–1912* (Bishops Stortford: Chadwyck-Healey, 1974), Reel 3 'Publication Books', A6, 337; Reel 10 'Commission Book', 215–16; Reel 17 'Print and Paper Books', D4, 161; Reel 19 'Sheet Stock and Binding Book', E1, 371, Reel 23 'Royalty and Commission Accounts' G3, 429.

talking about it.[46] He boldly identified for *The Pall Mall Gazette*'s readership the central achievement of the book, Yeats's Irish 'largeness of vision'.

Books of poetry by young writers are usually promissory notes that are never met. Now and then, however, one comes across a volume that is so far above the average that one can hardly resist the fascinating temptation of prophesying a fine future for its author. Such a volume Mr. Yeats's 'Wanderings of Oisin' certainly is…. If he has not the grand simplicity of epic treatment, he has at least something of that largeness of vision that belongs to the epical temper. He does not rob of their stature the great heroes of Celtic mythology. He is very naïve, and very primitive, and speaks of his giants with the awe of a child.[47]

Yeats had been prepared to declare that Irish 'personality' from the outset of this book, not entirely without vacillation.[48] By 1893 he had no such doubts. Acknowledging to Katharine Tynan the influence

[46] *CL1* 126. Talk was 'worth more than any review', Yeats recalled (*Autobiographies* 134). An excellent and subtle log-roller himself, Yeats may even have manufactured a charge against himself of log-rolling in order to do so more effectively: see *CL3* 589 n. 1; 592–93.

[47] Unsigned review, 'Three New Poets: Yeats, FitzGerald, Le Gallienne', *The Pall Mall Gazette* XLIX: 7587 (12 July 1889), 3; reprinted in Richard Ellmann (ed.), *The Artist as Critic: Critical Writings of Oscar Wilde* (London: W. H. Allen, 1970), 150–51). Yeats's response was acute. Wilde found 'populace' in 'And a small and a feeble populace stooping with mattock and spade' (see *VP* 58) to be 'infelicitous' (151). Yeats substituted 'race' in *Poems* (1895) but restored the infinitely stronger, contemptuous 'populace' in 1912. Wilde's second review was 'Some Literary Notes', *Women's World* 2:17 (March 1889), 277–80.

[48] A half-hearted argument privileging Yeats's 'English origins' and claiming that his 'long poems are [to be] understood as a kind of adjunct to the fundamentally lyric achievement' has been advanced by Richard J. Finneran in 'Text and Interpretation in the Poems of W. B. Yeats', in George Bornstein (ed.), *Representing Modernist Texts: Editing as Interpretation* (Ann Arbor: University of Michigan Press, 1991), 17–48. It bolsters Finneran's choice of the overall arrangement of *Collected Poems* (1933) for his *The Poems: A New Edition* (London: Macmillan, 1984). He wonders if Yeats's lists of 'Irish Poems' and 'Arcadian Poems' (together with his added comment '46 pages of poems on non-Irish subjects') were made 'with pride or with anguish?' (29). The lists are to be found in a copy of *The Wanderings of Oisin: and Other Poems* lost from Yeats's working library and discovered in a bookshop in the Charing Cross Road, London, by George Yeats who gave it to Thomas Mark in March, 1949, as he was preparing the two-volumes of *The Poems* for publication in November. That copy is now in The Morgan Library, New York (Plates 8a and 8b).

of Shelley on his first (abandoned) dramatic poem and his schoolboy reading of Scott and Macaulay, he declared 'I am going back to Dublin this week… and intend to stay there. I want my work to be as Irish as possible, and I find that here my impressions get blunted'.[49]

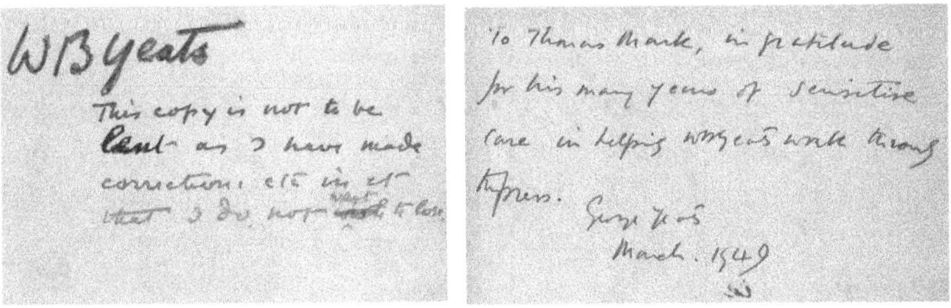

Plates 8a & b. Inscriptions by W. B. Yeats [n.d.] and George Yeats (March, 1949) in Yeats's working copy of *The Wanderings of Oisin and Other Poems* (1889). Images © and courtesy of The Morgan Library, New York. All rights reserved.

In his chosen arrangement, 'The Wanderings of Oisin', hitherto unpublished and unknown, dominates the title and the volume. It is placed first in spite of the fact that many of the lyrics rather loosely aggregated in the volume had been written and published before it. It occupies exactly one third of the printed pages. An assertion of boldness and character, the placement of an epic with the defiant penultimate line 'I will go to the house of the Fenians, be they in flames or at feast', was an explicit political statement (*VP* 63v.). He had joined the Irish Republican Brotherhood in 1886, as O'Leary's protégé.[50]

Although Yeats put 'The Wanderings of Oisin' last in *Poems* (1899), where it stayed during the life of that popular edition, by 1925 he had returned it to pride of place in his *Early Poems and Stories*, and had no doubt that it was the poem in which 'my subject-matter became Irish'.[51] This was not how he felt about all the poems

---

[49] *The Sketch*, 29 November 1893, 526.

[50] This is well before his more active commitment to 'dangerous hope' took him into Mark Ryan's Irish National Alliance (*Mem* 82 and n.).

[51] *VP* 841. Seeing his own work in bound form gave him the confidence in its own geography to invoke *A Midsummer Night's Dream* V:1. 17: 'All poetry should have a local habitation when at all possible', declared Yeats in a letter to Katharine

in the book, and he inscribed the title page of Quinn's copy with a rueful echo of Shakespeare's epitaph: 'My first book of poems & full of mixed influences "Cursed be he who moves" the worst of these verses to reprint them W B Yeats March 1904'.[52] And yet, the proud emphasis with which Yeats uses the word 'book' here is not to be lost: this was a book, not (as had been *Mosada*), an off-print, and as such, his first collection.

Kegan Paul still had 98 unbound copies of *The Wanderings of Oisin: and Other Poems*, plus a further 19 on which subscriptions had not been paid.[53] £2.3.10 was outstanding from subscribers, and he began to 'threaten [Yeats] with lawyers'. Yeats wrote to O'Leary for help

I want to take the remaining [i.e. unbound] 100 copies out of their hand & get Fisher Unwin to sell them which he will do with ease—There is as it is, some slight sale & a steadily increasing one. The new book [i.e. *The Countess Kathleen and Various Legends and Lyrics*] will sell the rest of the copies. I want you to lend me £2.10.0 so that I can make the transfer at once.[54]

Tynan of 21 March 1889 (*CL1* 157). Like 'Endymion', though with an Irish habitation, the poem was 'a region into which one should wander from the cares of life'. The idea had been derived from 'a small thicket… at Howth (*CL1* 135). 'Endymion' was to Keats a 'trial of my… invention' but his answer to Leigh Hunt's question 'why endeavour after a long Poem' was that 'the Lovers of Poetry like to have a little *Region to wander in* [emphasis added] where they may pick and choose, and in which the images are so numerous that many are forgotten and found new in a second Reading; which may be food for a Week's stroll in the Summer'. See Keats's letter to Benjamin Bailey, 8 October 1817 in Robert Gittings (ed.), *Letters of John Keats: a Selection*, 27. Yeats had 'constantly tested' his 'own ambition with Keats's praise of him who left "great verse unto a little clan"' (*Autobiographies*, 120) in his 'Fragments of an Ode to Maia' (1818). See also *CL3* 389.

52 See Plate 8c. Yeats reused the curse from Shakespeare's epitaph in *The Collected Works in Verse and Prose* of 1908: see *VP* 779. The volume is now Copy 4 of *The Wanderings of Oisin* in the Berg Collection, New York Public Library.

53 See Kelly, 'Books' 245–46.

54 *CL1* 280 [*c*.15 January 1892]. Unwin had seventy-three unbound quires bound from the original sheets, and made a second issue in May 1892 *Wade* 3, p. 23. Yeats also received twenty-five bound copies. For full details see *CL1* 283 n.

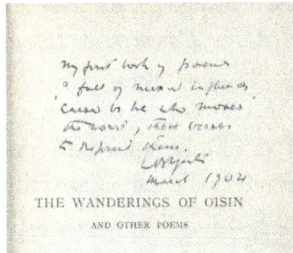

Plate 8c. W. B. Yeats's inscription of March 1904 in John Quinn's copy of *The Wanderings of Oisin and Other Poems* (1889), now Copy 4 in the Berg Collection, New York Public Library. © and courtesy of the Henry W. and Albert A. Berg Collection, and the Astor, Lenox and Tilden Foundations, New York Public Library. All rights reserved.

O'Leary came to the rescue and Unwin duly took over, bound and issued the remainder in late May on a commission contract which put their interest at 10%. The idea had been proposed in late January, a contract issued on 8 February but it was not signed until 25 May. Kegan Paul, sensing that Unwin's sales drive on the remainder could do him some good too, bound for his own sale 25 of the 98 he was holding and probably procrastinated over the transfer.[55] '[A]ll expenses connected with the deletion of the previous publisher's imprint, such as printing & insertion of fresh s, reblocking, or, if necessary, rebinding the bound copies' were to be borne by Yeats who was to 'offer no hindrance to such deletion, printing, blocking, or binding'.[56] The rebinding alone of the 73 remaining copies cost Yeats £1. 7. 8, but he got a new title, *The Wanderings of Oisin. Dramatic Sketches, Ballads & Lyrics*. This new array of generic sub-classifications showed Yeats for the first time taking stock of the generic shift from compositional texts (e.g. plays, stories) into new (and effectively discrete) republished contexts. The 'various legends and lyrics' of the next volume were already on his mind. Unwin published seventy three copies in May in a gray-green cloth, with T. Fisher Unwin's device on the upper board, gold lettering spiraled diagonally up the parchment spine, top edge gilt, others were trimmed (*Wade* 3, p. 23). This 'handsomer' binding was in fact the Cameo Series format, designed or approved by Edward Garnett and the Gresham Press,

---

[55] This led to binding variants (Wade, item 2, p. 23); see also Kelly, 'Books' 245.
[56] NLI 30654, *CL2* 637–38.

Unwin Brothers, and quite skillfully adapted to Kegan Paul's sheets (*CL1* 287). It exactly matches the binding of *The Countess Kathleen and Various Legends and Lyrics* in the Cantwell Collection.

Working from a copy of the first edition containing corrections Yeats had dictated, Edwin J. Ellis designed and lithographed a sepia frontispiece of Niam in a panel portrait, dominating the colloquy of the aged St Patrick (with mitre and crozier) and Oisin.[57] Tipped in with the cancel title, it imposed a symbolic personality on the relaunched book. Yeats cautiously found it 'charming' (*CL1* 28: see Plate 9).

Plate 9. Edwin J. Ellis's Frontispiece of Niam [*sic*], St Patrick and Oisin, in The *Wanderings of Oisin. Dramatic Sketches. Ballads* & *Lyrics* (1892). Image © private collection, London. All rights reserved.

It was a mark of the success of *John Sherman AND Dhoya* that T. Fisher Unwin had taken the opportunity to help Yeats out of his

---

[57] The corrected copy is now in the University of Reading, has the lower edge untrimmed. Copies of the 1892 edition may be found in Reading, the DeLury Collection, Thomas Fisher Rare Book Library, University of Toronto and in the British Library (11661.de 72). See also Michael J. Sidnell, 'J. B. Yeats's Marginalia in *The Wanderings of Oisin: and Other Poems*' YA13 265–91.

financial difficulty with Kegan Paul. Collaborations with other artists followed. John Nettleship supplied the frontispiece for *The Countess Kathleen and Various Legends and Lyrics* (also in the Cantwell Collection), and Beardsley, whose cover design for *The Land of Heart's Desire* also functioned as the poster to advertise the book.

In these early books, two forces are endlessly at play, Yeats's desire for an individual personality for his books and the limitations of the market. As early as 1895 he wanted a collected works, and a uniform edition of all of his books which none of his publishers could afford. *Poems* (1895) represents his first attempt at uniform size, shape and typography. A fine copy of this elusive book has been secured by Eamonn Cantwell. *Poems* (1895) is Yeats's first attempt to deploy work previously published in single volume form into discrete sections of what is envisaged not just as a collection, but as a book-of-books. Its internal subdivisions are accomplished by rendering the titles of individual works, and previous volume-units as sections, bibliographically and typographically indistinguishable from units such as CROSSWAYS and THE ROSE, especially made up for this book. All such units have their own half-titles, with dedications, and epigraphs on the versos, as do the 'sections' such as THE COUNTESS CATHLEEN. CROSSWAYS and THE ROSE were to be as enduring as if Yeats had actually published collections with those titles. Their contents were not invariable, but the method remained a fixed one through which Yeats remade collections of poems as units in subsequent textual selves.

The arrangement of *Poems* (1895) was ultimately determined by the desire to put major work first in chronological array.[58] Lyrics were accorded third place after the epic and the dramatic poems. The epic and the lyric collections are dedicated to men, the plays to women. The later lyrics are privileged over earlier ones, with two from the collection which is stylized into THE ROSE pushed back to form part of CROSSWAYS presumably because Yeats felt they belonged in

---

[58] For an earlier attempt at a different arrangement which grouped 'The Wanderings of Oisin' in a section called 'Under the Moon' with *The Land of Heart's Desire*, *The Countess Kathleen* and the undifferentiated lyrics later grouped as THE ROSE, see *CL1* 411–13. In this arrangement, earlier lyrics (mostly from *The Wanderings of Oisin: and Other Poems*) were relegated to a section called *Crossways*.

subject and style to an earlier period.[59] In that section, some of the poems are dated and the first two, 'The Song of the Happy Shepherd' and 'The Sad Shepherd' (which Yeats had thought to place in the penultimate and antepenultimate positions respectively) are given the earliest of the affixed dates (1885). The overall order of the section is not however chronological either in terms of composition or of publication: these facts of life yield before the imposition of a created personality.

This emergence from drama into lyric is congruent with the fact that the first seven or eight poems in CROSSWAYS are unwoven from abandoned dramas, collections, or series. 'The Wanderings of Oisin' remained in first place as the true Irish beginning of his whole poetic endeavour. Consigning his origins quite literally to Irish by-ways, Yeats named CROSSWAYS for the 'many pathways' he had tried in its poems.[60] The trunk road was signposted in THE ROSE, 'the only pathway whereon he can hope to see with his own eyes the Eternal Rose of Beauty and of Peace' (*VP* 845–46).

Yeats insisted on approving the paper, and samples of printing, on choosing the page size (crown octavo), on 'title page & cover design—not a frontispiece', 'no headlines, the number of the page to be at the bottom & single commas for quotation marks', 'rough edges' (*CL1* 434, 436, 439). This was an act of self-definition. *TO SOME I HAVE TALKED WITH BY THE FIRE* stands in italic to signify the dedication of the whole volume. Other framing poems such as 'To the Rose upon the Rood of Time' and 'To Ireland in the Coming Times' continue to be printed in italic, while elsewhere italic is used for sung sections of poems or song-lyrics in plays, or for prayers or inwardly spoken thoughts, offering an implicitly linked second level of discourse.[61]

---

[59] 'The Ballad of Father O'Hart' and 'The Ballad of the Foxhunter'. This was not the only occasion upon which Yeats would shuffle the chronologies of composition or publication in order to achieve consistencies of theme or genre.

[60] The Christian pun sometimes claimed is an anachronism: cf. the *pensée* of 1907 'the nobleness of the arts is in the mingling of contraries... its red rose opens at the meeting of the two beams of the cross... [n]o new man has ever plucked that rose' (*E&I* 255).

[61] Yeats was to develop the habit in such highly articulated volume-sequences as *Responsibilities: Poems and a Play* (Churchtown, Dundrum: Cuala Press, 1914).

Though a decisive act of self-formation, *Poems* (1895) was not a 'total book' and it was not a wholly successful self-image. In explicitly ruling out a frontispiece as 'an external and extrinsic decoration which I would be very glad of, but only if I also had my decorative title page, which I look upon as making an essential part of the book more beautiful' (*CL1* 439) he was perhaps rebelling against a self-image proffered by his father. He had initially wanted the book decorated by Fernand Khnopff or Charles Hazlewood Shannon, but eventually chose H. Granville Fell whose work had been exhibited in the autumn of 1894.[62] As a former 'Art student myself', Yeats declared, he was 'opinionated and crotchety over this question of design'.[63]

Later in the nineties the 'facile meaninglessness' of Fell's cover-design began to irritate Yeats, although he had been enthusiastic about it at the start (*CL2* 357). An early copy had 'caused quite a flutter of aproval among [Unwin's] clerks... Fells design... is very admirable. I have chosen for the substance a curious dove-grey (*CL1* 471, 31 July 1895). However, Yeats did not get the 'dark colour' he had originally stipulated, but a buff cloth to match the full vellum of the 25 copy issue printed on Japan vellum.[64] Fell gave him a front-and-back design of an aureoled, winged and helmeted angel, presumably St Michael (who appears at the apotheosis of the Countess in 'The Countess Cathleen'),

---

[62] The exhibition was at the Royal Institute of Painters in Water Colours in September-October 1894 (*CL1* 462 n.). A puff for *Poems* (1895) says that Fell's 'water colour, "The Virgin Mary's Toumbler" attracted some attention at Mr. Dent's "black and white" exhibition last year' (*Bookman* VIII:47 [August 1895], 129). Fell's work appealed to the poet of 'The Cap and Bells'. See also Allen Grossman, *Poetic Knowledge in the Early Yeats: A Study of* The Wind Among the Reeds (Charlottesville: The University Press of Virginia, 1969), 48.

[63] *CL1* 462, 465. Fell responded to *The Countess Cathleen*.

[64] *CL1* 434. It has darkened in most surviving examples of the 750-copy cloth issue. With its 135 x 200 mm boards (cf. 128 x 198 mm cloth issue), the 25 copy full vellum issue is far more handsome, in all aspects except the spine which is a mere 22 mm across. The spinal design is, as a result, heavily pinched. (The Japan vellum upon which this issue is printed is a good deal less bulky than the ordinary paper of the cloth issue, while the ordinary issue is more fully rounded, measuring 40 mm across. It would seem that Fell designed the top and bottom panel designs with the more spacious dimensions of the vellum issue in mind, but drew the spinal design to a thickness copy of the ordinary paper issue. By September 1896 Yeats wrote that he 'much prefer[red] the ordinary 6/- edition' (*CL2* 53).

vanquishing a serpent, all enclosed within a celestial harp-shaped border of thorned roses (Plate 10).

Plate 10. Top board of wraparound covers by H. Granville Fell
for W. B. Yeats's *Poems* (1895). Private collection, London.

The angel 'more closely resembled St George and the Dragon', as the editors of Yeats's letters have suggested (*ibid.*, n. 4). On 27 January 1895, Yeats had given 'a firm command' to Unwin that the cover design for *Poems* (1895) 'be not green & have no shamrocks' (*CL1* 434). The livery of *Poems* (1895) is religiose, with its celestial dove, harp and roses. The resultant banal, debased Pre-Raphaelitism extends to the title page, which depicts rather poorly Paracelsus' mysterious epigraph (*'He who tastes a crust of bread tastes all the stars and all the heavens'*: placed on the verso[65]) by means of a knight receiving Communion. Yeats had made clear his preferences. He had wished to leave the artist free to choose his own expression of Yeats's themes. This was, no doubt, in line with advanced thinking of the day that 'the illustrations of a volume should sum up in themselves

[65] On the source, see Warwick Gould, 'Paracelsus in Excelcis', *YA11* 176–84.

the printed matter, they should be decorative in character'.[66] Yeats came, as he said, to 'hate that expressionless angel of his'. Worse, perhaps—though Yeats does not say so—Fell had smuggled some weedy shamrocks onto the spine. Before the next edition in 1899, Yeats had 'abolished' the cover (*CL2* 357).

If *oeuvre* was a destabilizing force, Yeats had also a turbulent time with publishers. He had too many because he did not earn enough for any of them, and none could envisage a *Collected Works in Verse and Prose* except A. H. Bullen, who eventually gave him the only satisfactory one he had in his life (there is a set in the Cantwell Collection). With such an ambition deferred, he sought other modes of uniformity for his books through some sort of immediately recognizable livery.

Enter a Cork woman, Althea Gyles, estranged from her family in Kilmurry, a family, according to Yeats, 'so haughty that their neighbours called them the Royal family'.[67] Yeats first met her in that Ely Place commune which she shared with George Russell and other Theosophists. Later she slept on a heap of rags in London, had an affair with Yeats's publisher, Leonard Smithers, and lived from hand to mouth, leaving her rare books with Yeats to prevent them being distrained when the bailiffs forced their way in. She was, however, the genius who invented a symbolic personality for Yeats. Here I want to talk about her first book for him, not yet in Eamonn Cantwell's collection, *The Secret Rose* (1897).[68]

This book shows everything about collaboration and compromise. For a start this collection of Irish stories about 'the war between spiritual and natural order' had an arrangement not only chronological but culminative, and the last two stories appeared too heterodox to the publishers, Lawrence and Bullen. A. H. Bullen was, as we have

---

[66] Albert Louis Cotton, 'The Kelmscott Press and the new Printing', *Contemporary Review* 64 (July-December 1898), 221–31 at p. 224.

[67] *Au* 237. Alithea Emma, daughter of the Hon. and Rev. Edward Grey, Bishop of Hereford, married the 'mad' George Gyles in 1862. On Althea (b. Margaret Alethea) Gyles, see the *Oxford Dictionary of National Biography*, 2004.

[68] The internal illustrations to the stories were by John Butler Yeats, and Lily Yeats was the model for a number involving female subjects. On the subsequently added copy of the book in the Cantwell Collection, see below, p. 235.

seen, proved right. At proof stage he cut those stories and privately printed them from the same plates in an edition of 110 copies as *The Tables of the Law. The Adoration of the Magi* (1897) just three months later (the Cantwell collection has a later reprint of these).

For the moment, let us look at Althea Gyles's cover design (Plate 11), and two of its likely sources. The first of these visual precursors is from the Sacramentary Fleury (Plate 12a) attributed to Nivardus of Milan and wrought for Robert the Pious, King of France (r. 996–1031), perhaps at the behest of the Bishop of Beauvais, who crowned him in 1017.[69] If the field of Gyles's visual sources is, as I suggest, international, then an image of the cover decoration of a Qu'ran (Plate 12b) held in the Library of the Escorial, Spain, was also available to Gyles in a lavishly illustrated reference work in the then British Museum Library.[70] Granted the contrast in styles between these two very different examples of mediaeval representations of knot work, the designer in Gyles seems to have focused upon what they have in common. After all, that international fascination with knot work runs from the Copts to the Celts. Icovellavna, or knot work, often showing interlacing and/or 'endless' ball patterns, some employing triskelia, are to be found on ancient Celtic Crosses.

---

[69] This manuscript had been in the collection of the Reverend Walter Sneyd (1809–88), sold at Sotheby's on 16 December 1903. It is not yet known if Gyles saw the manuscript or a facsimile of this leaf by Lord John Thynne (*c.*1882) in the Victoria and Albert Museum. The manuscript is now in the Getty Museum, California. See also *Masterpieces of the J. Paul Getty Museum: Illuminated Manuscripts*, texts prepared by Thomas Kren, Elizabeth C. Teviotdale, Adam S. Cohen, and Kurtis Barstow (London: Thames & Hudson, co-published with the J. Paul Getty Museum, 1997), 14–15; and Anton von Euw und Joachim M. Plotzek, *die Handschriften der Sammlung Ludwig* (Köln: Herausgegeben vom Schnütgen-Museum der Stadt Köln etc., 1979), Band 1, 219–22. See also Gould, 'Byzantine Materiality and Byzantine Vision etc.', esp. at p. 100 where various versions of this image are reproduced.

[70] *Museo Español de Antigüedades* bajo la direccion del doctor Don Juan de D. de la Rada y Delgado, etc. (Madrid, 1872–80, 3 [1874], pp. 408ff. See also the accompanying analysis by Florencio Janér, 'El-Koran: códice árabe llamado de Muley Cidan, rey de Marruecos, conservado en la Biblioteca del Escorial' 3 (1874): 409–32.

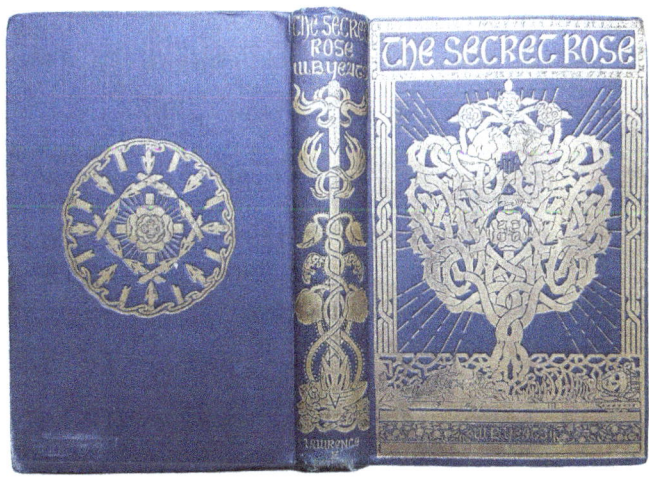

Plate 11. Althea Gyles's wraparound design for *The Secret Rose* (1897), first state, ribbed cloth. Private collection, London.

Plate 12a. Decorated initial letter from the Sacramentary Fleury, early eleventh century, attributed to Nivardus of Milan, MS. Ludwig v, 1, f. 9. Tempera colours, gold, silver and ink on parchment. Courtesy of the Getty Museum, California.

Plate 12b. Front board of Muley Zidan's *Qu'ran* (*El Koran, Códikce Árabe Llamado de Muley Cidan, Rey del Marruęcos*, Library of the Escorial, Spain). Private collection, London, from a copy of *Museo Español de Antigüedades* (Madrid, 1872–80, vol. 3 [1874]).

The sacramentary's early eleventh century decoration and its embellishment shows an initial letter 'D' in uncial script, as the *incipit* of the Mass for Easter Day, its framing columns each spirally bound by climbing vines which intermingle in an arch over a ball-like tangle of vine in a maze of knot work, and forming the uncial 'D' for 'Deus'. Given the subject, we may assume the vines are the triune God, the 'true vine', with its two climbing husbandmen intent on harvesting its grapes, or tending its new shoots, some of which are in triskeles. Perhaps its pillars also show the vine spiralling upwards. It grows from twin roots around a fourfold knot which may resemble a Cross. The Arabesque pattern of the Qu'ran codex cover, on the other hand, has its labyrinthine filigree woven around a stylized rose, with two roots seemingly growing not just from the bottom panel of its inner frame, but from each of the four planes which make up that roped-over frame. Taken together, these two designs offer immense potential for Gyles to impose Yeats's symbolist and occult programme upon the pattern they have in common.

Now, in the story entitled 'Rosa Alchemica', the unnamed narrator is being initiated into an occult Order out in Connemara. He sits down to read its rituals before the ceremony. He takes its ancient Ritual MS book from its bronze box. The wrap-around Gyles design for Yeats's cover may be compared to Yeats's description of the Order's Ritual Book found in the following passage from the page proofs of the 1897 edition, the italicized section having been cut by Yeats from the published book:

In the box was a book bound in vellum, and having *a rose-tree growing from an armed anatomy, and enclosing the faces of two lovers painted on the one side, to symbolize certainly the coming of beauty out of corruption, and probably much else*; and upon the other, the alchemical rose with many spears thrusting against it, but in vain, as was shown by the shattered points of those nearest. The book was written upon vellum...[71]

---

[71] Italics added. See *VSR* 274. Hereafter *VSR*. The passage has been discussed (but mis-transcribed) in a stimulating account of the 1896 page proofs for *The Secret Rose* (1897): see Curtis Bradford, *Yeats at Work* (Carbondale and Edwardsville: Southern Illinois University Press, 1965), 317–28, at p. 324.

This precise symbolism Gyles put onto the top and lower boards of Yeats's book. She was not a member of the Order of the Golden Dawn, but she turns the Ritual Book of the Order of the Alchemical Rose into Yeats's personal talisman, or *grimoire*. (There are, by the way, other fatal books in other stories in *The Secret Rose*, e.g., the *Grimoire of Pope Honorius* in 'The Book of the Great Dhoul and Hanrahan the Red' and a Hebrew manuscript in 'The Heart of Spring', and the splendidly adorned sole copy of the 'secret book' Yeats attributes to Joachim of Fiore, the *Liber Inducens in Evangelium Æternum*, in 'The Tables of the Law'.)

Althea Gyles's pillars employ Celtic knot-work, which is evident in both central ball-like interweavings of rose-bush. Nivardus's two figures have clambered above the central knot of their true vine. In Gyles's design, the tight interlacing imitates the paths of the Kabbalistic Tree of Life, encloses a rose cross, and has the two figures portrayed as lovers, kissing just beneath the crowning blossoms of the tree. There is a great deal more to be said of her symbolism, both esoteric and exoteric: I pause only to add that her Tree of Life growing from the body of the armed knight is also the Tree of Jesse, and that its lovers appear in such of Yeats's poems as 'The Two Trees', and that she may have been drawn to Nivardus's interpenetrating vines by the motif of the interwoven ash trees which grow from the graves of Tumaus Costello and Oona MacDermott on Insula Trinitatis in Lough Key, at the end of Yeats's story 'Of Costello the Proud, of Oona the Daughter of Dermott, and of the Bitter Tongue' in Yeats's book of stories (*VSR* 81).

The symbolism of the spine is also Celtic, and also drawn from 'Rosa Alchemica' ('the [...]. overflowing cauldron: Lu, [*sic*] with his spear dipped in poppy-juice, lest it rush forth hot for battle...').[72] The wreathed poppies cling to a spear plunged in a chalice rather than a cauldron, and such an association might have suggested affinities with the lance and chalice of the Grail legends, at least in the mind of the designer.

---

[72] *VSR* 139vv.

Gyles's design was stamped in gold upon the dark blue[73] cloth of the book, which was ribbed cloth in the first issues of the first binding state, although many copies of the first state have smooth cloth.[74] It is perhaps an indication of just how satisfied Yeats was with the design that he cut much of the passage just quoted.[75] At all events, it would have been otiose in such a resplendently bound volume. Cover designs of such 'total' books are part of the text which they enclose,[76] and their symbolism divides the readers into esoteric and exoteric groups (though neophytes can become initiates).

With this livery, Althea Gyles established the image or call-sign of Yeats for the next thirty years. You will have seen it on his next two books, *The Wind Among the Reeds* and *Poems* both issued in 1899

---

[73] Two copies survive in which the designs, or part of them, are stamped upon dark crimson or reddish brown cloth. One copy is in the D. B. Weldon Library, University of Western Ontario. It has been discussed by Steven Winnett and Beth Miller in 'Addenda to Wade. Item 21: *The Secret Rose*', in *The Canadian Association for Irish Studies Newsletter*, 5 (November 1974). It has 'Lawrence & Bullen' stamped on the spine, in common with copies of the first issue, but there is no design upon the lower board. I am grateful to Beth Miller for supplying further details in letters of 1975. This saturated crimson cloth is redolent of a late nineteenth century Masonic or Rosicrucian manual. See also Virginia Hyde, 'Variant Covers of *The Secret Rose*' *YA13* 292–95. The second copy is in the Harry Ransom Humanities Research Center, University of Texas, where it is copy PR 5904 53 1897 HRC No 5 (R Y 141). It lacks all plates and also has 'Lawrence & Bullen' stamped on the spine. Both copies seem most likely to have been publisher's trial bindings.

[74] Copies 1 and 4 of PR 5904 53 1897 HRC at the Humanities Research Center, University of Texas at Austin, are respectively the copies inscribed to Arthur Symons and Olivia Shakespear, the latter dated on the day of publication, 'April Ist, 1897'. Both are bound in ribbed cloth. Lionel Johnson's copy, also inscribed by Yeats in April, 1897, is now in the Berg Collection, New York Public Library, and also has the design stamped on ribbed cloth.

[75] Deirdre Toomey alerted me to this conjecture.

[76] See *VSR* 271–78. On this principle *VSR* (2nd ed., 1992) includes reproductions of cover-designs and illustrations from the two 'talismanic' editions of *The Secret Rose*: 1897 (with Gyles) and 1927 (with Norah McGuinness). In 1927 Yeats schooled the young Norah McGuinness in Byzantine wall-pictures. His placement of 'Sailing to Byzantium' before the text and his dedication of the poem to her extend the Byzantine iconography of certain stories first introduced in *Early Poems and Stories* (1925) by means of allusions to Byzantine artefacts (*VSR* 278–86). See also Warwick Gould, 'Byzantine Materiality and Byzantine Vision: "Hammered Gold and Gold Enamelling"', in Declan J. Foley (ed.), *Yeats 150* (Dublin: Lilliput, 2016), 94–137.

in time for the first stagings of the Irish Literary Theatre in Dublin, and both in the Cantwell Collection. In another copy of the former Yeats wrote that he had 'great trouble with the designer' who had 'demanded' it back 'because the publisher [Elkin Mathews] had not answered a letter of hers. "He is not worthy" she said. She was a strange attractive person who came to nothing through ill health or indolence or both'.[77] Despite such difficulties, Yeats was determined to spread his symbolical selves on '[t]he blue and the dim and the dark cloths', 'enwrought with golden... light' (*VP* 176). Alas, that the most personal of her symbolical selves for Yeats had to be omitted from *The Wind Among the Reeds* partly through Yeats's diffidence, but principally because Gyles just could never bring herself to finish it and let it go (Plate 13).[78]

Plate 13. Althea Gyles's abandoned frontispiece (*c*.1897) for *The Wind Among the Reeds*. Courtesy of the Trustees of the British Museum. All rights reserved.

[77] Vellum-bound copy, private collection, USA. The inscription is Yeats's, to Kazumi Yano, provided in 1927.
[78] See *CL2* 263, 271.

Plate 14. Althea Gyles's wraparound design for the vellum-bound 4th edition of *The Wind Among the Reeds* (London, 1903). Image © private collection, London. All rights reserved.

That determination can be seen in a letter which was written during one of Yeats's wrangles with Elkin Mathews, to whom he had promised *The Wind Among the Reeds*. Having finally got Gyles to submit her design to Mathews, Yeats took an instant dislike to a trial version of the binding, with an image in yellow on the reviled green cloth:

First the colour of the cloth wont do. It is a colour I particularly dislike. The colour should be the same dark blue as my 'Secret Rose'. Secondly the yellow lines wont do. This cover is simply ugly. The lines should be in gold or the cover should be perfectly plain. I thought it was understood that the design was to be in gold. Please get this design printed in gold or abolish it altogeather letting me know what the block has cost. Surely you must see yourself that it is absurd to print a book of verse of any kind of importance with the same kind of common stuff on the cover that you put on a novel.[79]

---

[79] Writing (or not writing) *The Speckled Bird*, Yeats had invested little pride in the novelist's trade.

What you have to consider is whether you can do the things in gold, increasing the price of the book to 5/- if you like, though I should think this unnecessary. If not print in a perfectly plain blue cover... In either case let me have another proof. I have the strongest objection to designs printed in yellow or any other colour or in anything except gold. The cover you sent me would do neither of us credit.... if you make it a really charming book to look at you will help the book greatly (*CL2* 279–80, 25 October 1898).

Mathews capitulated but penny-pinched, using some 'schlagmetal', 'Dutch gold', 'green gold' or some other copper alloy which briefly glistered but was not gold, and few if any copies survive in good condition. The decay was well and truly evident by 1902 when in any case, the old block was badly worn. Robert Gregory, Archibald G. B. Russell and other like-minded Oxford students and graduates raised enough promises from existing owners and others for a new block to be made, redrawn from Gyles's design, but in slightly variant proportions. About 25 new covers were made, some for copies of earlier editions to be rebound, others newly printed for the 1903 4th edition, and were bound in full vellum, with real gold.[80] I've taken my image from one of these rather than from the Cantwell copy which is gold on blue (Plate 14). At the centre of *The Wind Among the Reeds* is a complex projection of a hopeless love triangle, the lover, his beloved, and a pale woman whom passion has worn, or Yeats, Maud Gonne, and Olivia Shakespear. Bulked out to sixty-two pages of poems, it has a further forty-six pages of recondite, essay-like notes on the book's symbolism. Gyles's rather Japanese design cuts through its extraordinary complexity to get to its central narrative of failure and pain. Based on her reading of one poem, 'Breasal the Fisherman', is the elaborate woven net of reeds on the front cover, suggesting perhaps the planned entrapment of the beloved. It is reduced to chaos, tangle and escape on the back, as fire gives way to water. The fire of the front cover is replaced by water on the back, just as one of the central symbolic 'principles of the mind', Michael Robartes, is 'fire reflected in water'.[81] The process of reading from

---

[80] See *CL3* 227, 231–32.

[81] Yeats thought it 'probable that only students of the magical tradition' would 'understand' him (*VP* 803). One such student, Dorothea Hunter, Soror Deo Date, drafted an answer (which she did not send) to this conundrum for Richard

the front cover through to the back is thus figured in the boards themselves, while on the spine, a 'hyssop-heavy sponge' impaled on a reed from another poem dares us to compare the sufferings of sexual passion with those of Christ on the Cross. Gyles's frontispiece portrait of Yeats, never finished to her standards or his, was omitted, but its three-petalled Tudor rose and blown fourth petal found their way onto *The Shadowy Waters*, 1900, also in the Cantwell collection, in stamped gold on blue.

The rose also dominates the second (1899) edition of *Poems*[82] (Plate 15). Yeats had again to nudge a publisher to spend on a cover design, and to nurse Althea Gyles and Unwin through its production, liaising between the wretched and ill designer, the binder, and the publisher in order to get the finest design he had even seen on 'the best looking book I have ever had', a 'perfect' combination of cloth and gold (*CL2* 402). The rose petals swirl in clouds rather like incense from the rose on the cross at the centre, which acts as a thurible or censer. Henry Woodd Nevinson had praised the cover as (in John Masefield's words),

the most beautiful modern cover that [he] had seen... Soon, I was at a book-shop, looking at the... beautiful cover, dark blue, with a design, in gold, of a rose upon a cross spilling petals everywhere. Even now, after more than half a century, many copies still show those drifting golden rose-petals

Ellmann, 15 November 1946, to the effect that his 'cabbalistic emphasis on the action of the pairs of opposites in all life' was at the back of his thinking, and that 'fire reflected in water' would be represented by two triangles (one inverted) superimposed to form 'the seal of Solomon i.e. a sign of power'. See also Warwick Gould, '"The Music of Heaven": Dorothea Hunter', in Deirdre Toomey (ed.), *Yeats and Women* (Basingstoke: Macmillan Press, 1997), 73–134 at pp. 117–18 and nn. 175, 182. By refining the 'actual personages' of his *Secret Rose* stories to 'principles of the mind', Yeats seems to have found what amounts to an avatar to the later Mask theories: much later the Fool in Abbey productions of *The Hour-Glass* in wore a mask by Edward Gordon Craig that made him 'seem less a human being than a principle of the mind' (*VPl* 645).

[82] This time too, Yeats was happy to have a new portrait by his father for the new edition of his *Poems* in 1899. The pencil drawing was reproduced in subsequent editions of *Poems*. Signed and dated, 28 January 1899, 23 x 19.5 cm (coll. MBY). It would take several lectures to discuss textual change and rearrangement in this and the subsequent issues that kept this book in print until 1928.

in all their glory and beauty. Ah, when that gold was new, the cover alone seemed well worth the money...[83]

Plate 15. Althea Gyles's wraparound design for
Poems (1899). Private collection, London.

The lower board image recalls that of *The Secret Rose*, while the spine is like a new close-up view of the rose-tree on the top board of *The Secret Rose*, as the imploring hands of the lover reach for the beloved among the birds, branches and roses of the Tree. Yet it is also suggestive of a symbolical narrative which begins with the spine (plucked from a bookshelf) before the top board is revealed.[84] The head with half-opened mouth which hangs by a plume of hair is indeed, a severed head, a development of the iconography of the bard

[83] John Masefield, *So Long to Learn: Chapters of an Autobiography* (London: William Heinemann, 1952), 125–28. On the friendship between Nevinson and Masefield which Yeats fostered, see also Ronald Schuchard, "An Attendant Lord": H. W. Nevinson's Friendship with W. B. Yeats', *YA7* 90–130, at 94–95.

[84] Dora Sigerson, *Illustrated London News*, 22 July 1899 (in Yeats's Cuttings Book, NLI).

Aodh in 'The Binding of the Hair', the opening story of *The Secret Rose*.[85]

Poems (1899) became Yeats's most enduring bibliographical self almost by dint of a publisher's grudge.[86] Unwin refused to deal with literary agents, and after Yeats put his affairs into A. P. Watt's hands in 1900 he was forced to deal with Unwin by himself, and even secured a limited issue of the 4th (1904) edition on full parchment boards (Plate 16), available at 10/6d. Yeats sought new publishers for newer work, but left *Poems*, *The Land of Heart's Desire* and *The Countess Cathleen* in Unwin's hands because they made money (*Poems* at about £35 per year, accounted for nearly half Yeats's income). Thus it was that these books created a separate publishing category for what he came to call early work.[87]

These spinal designs and blue-and-gold liveries by Gyles established Yeats's image across five further titles (*The Celtic Twilight*, 1902, *Poems 1899–1905*, *Poems Second Series*, *The Poetical Works of William B. Yeats*, *The Unicorn from the Stars*, and across four publishers (Unwin, Bullen, Ernest Benn and the Macmillan Company, in two hemispheres. After 1913 gold was discontinued and the boards *Poems* were blind stamped. After 1926, *Poems* lost even the blind stamped boards. The spine alone remained recognizable, a small but prudent gesture, no doubt to aid sales.[88] Finally in 1929 *Poems* was reissued by Ernest Benn without even a vestige of the Gyles design, in plain blue-green cloth, lettered in gold on the spine, with top edges stained green and trimmed edges, but there was little enterprise in going

---

[85] Gyles subsequently planned but never finished a book plate for WBY for which she suggested a 'hanging head' motif (*Visions* Notebook, 25 November 1899, Private). On Yeats's continuing interest in severed heads (as in *The King of the Great Clock Tower* and *A Full Moon in March*), see Genevieve Brennan, "'The Binding of the Hair' and Yeats's Reading of Eugene O'Curry', *YA5* 214–23.

[86] In mid-1998 Maggs Bros. sold a copy of the 1899 text bound presumably to Unwin's specification in a rather overstretched 1895 case. I am grateful to Edward Maggs and to Colin Smythe for a sight of it.

[87] Yeats's habit of revising texts on actual copies of his books therefore led to several instances of bifurcated textual stemmae as revisions made in the Unwin copies were not always incorporated in Bullen's volumes. See e.g., *CL3* 58 no. 1.

[88] Gone also are the frontispiece and the rubric of title and half title. The title page imprint with its 'T. FISHER UNWIN LIMITED' underscored by '(*ERNEST BENN LIMITED*)' bears witness to new management.

naked, and within two years the publisher managed to cut the sales of Yeats's most popular book to one tenth of what they had been. Stripped of its talismanic livery with its increasingly nostalgic appeal, *Poems* was as effaced as a well-rubbed coin. Yeats was a victim of its success. Its image kept his early work in front of later work, and he increasingly sought a new image.

Plate 16. Althea Gyles's top board design on a parchment copy of *Poems* (1904). Courtesy the Rose Library, Emory University, Atlanta, Georgia.

NEW LIVERIES

The fading of Althea Gyles brought Yeats into numerous other relationships with book artists and designers, of which the most difficult was with his sisters in the production of the Dun Emer and Cuala editions. His long association with A. H. Bullen, who remained his mentor and publisher until 1916, was fruitful in all that it taught him about book making and remaking, typography and layout. When finally he went to Macmillan in 1916, he began to work closely with the London poet and artist Thomas Sturge Moore whom he had known since the 1890s, and whose book covers for

Yeats eventually become almost a visual encyclopaedia of Yeats's leading symbols.[89]

They began to work with William Rothenstein on the problem of putting Rabindranath Tagore's poems into English in 1912, making *Gitanjali* made it an extraordinary best-seller for Macmillan & Co., London.[90] In 1916, however, with Yeats at the top of his powers, Macmillan took over his books from the near-bankrupt A. H. Bullen. By 10 April of that year, Yeats was revising *Responsibilities* for Macmillan.[91] He was content to leave to Macmillan the date of publication, but wondered if the poems might not be published at the same time as *Reveries over Childhood and Youth*. Copies of both books are in the Cantwell collection.

The latter volume was already in production with the Macmillan Company in New York. Yeats thought Sturge Moore's American design for *Reveries* 'show[ed] signs of haste' and wanted it modified

---

[89] A number of images of Sturge Moore's original designs for Yeats's books, held in the Thomas Sturge Moore Papers in the Senate House Library of the University of London have been published in previous *Yeats Annuals*. See, e.g., *YA4* Plates 9–15 (illustrating the article by Pamela M. Baker and Helen M. Young, 'W. B. Yeats Material in the University of London'), 175–80; *YA18* Plates 11–12, 19–20; *YA19* Plate 25.

[90] See Warwick Gould, 'W. B. Yeats on the Road to St. Martin's Street', in Elizabeth James (ed.), *Macmillan: A Publishing Tradition* (Basingstoke: Palgrave Macmillan, 2002), 192–217. Macmillan had rejected Yeats in 1900, despite his being urged upon them by Stephen Gwynn, who had been retained them in 1898 to foster connexions with younger writers. The reasons lay in Yeats's anti-Boer War politics. One of the firm's readers who pronounced against him was John Morley, the former Chief Secretary for Ireland who had lost his Newcastle seat when Maud Gonne campaigned against him, citing his failure to honour pledges of amnesty for Irish prisoners in Portland Jail. See Warwick Gould, '"Playing at Treason with Miss Maud Gonne": Yeats and his Publishers in 1900', in Ian Willison, Warwick Gould and Warren Chernaik (eds.), *Modernist Writers and the Marketplace* (London: Macmillan, 1996), 36–80.

[91] *The Letters of W. B. Yeats*, ed. Allan Wade (London: Rupert Hart-Davis, 1954), 612. 'I send under a separate cover the contents of my new book of verse. It contains one book published by my sister "Responsibilities" <with a play> & part of the contents of another. Neither of the books has ever been sent for review. I have much more verse written since but am keeping this book to make a small book for my sister sometime next winter' (British Library Add. MS. 55003 f. 26). The letter was sent on by Watt to Sir Frederick Macmillan and is stamped F.M. dated Sunday, April 30 [1916].

for the English edition.[92] Sturge Moore's design for the American
edition is crowded with symbols: tower, baby, female figure,
mysterious sea and ship, and finger of God dominate, but it is
easy to be baffled by the proliferation of human grotesques—men,
women, babies—that throng the lower, predella-like, border panel.
These Sturge Moore eliminated for the revised design on the top
board and spine of the English edition. Simplified and stylized
even further—the sea loses its ship, its waves become a pattern of
scales—it loses the elaborateness of allegory whilst yet preserving the
symbols of tower, woman, and baby in swaddling clutching the finger
of God imposed above the tower from out of a halo. As with the
cover designs of Althea Gyles, Yeats here is again in charge of the
symbolic programme of a book cover which summarized in emblems
the currently ruling symbol of his art (Plates 17a & b).

 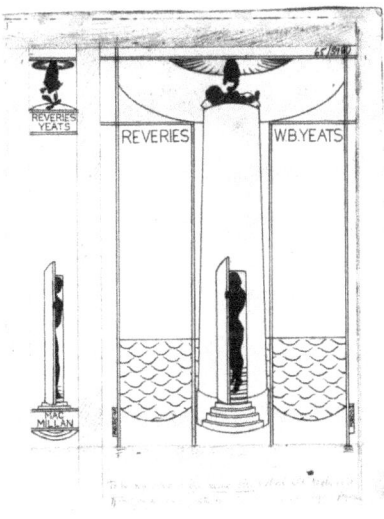

Plate 17a & b. T. Sturge Moore's designs for the Macmillan (New York) and
Macmillan (London) editions of *Reveries over Childhood and Youth* (1916),

---

[92] B.L. Add. MS. 55003 f. 26. Unlike their London counterparts, the American
editions of *Reveries* and *Responsibilities* are not bound in cloth, with gold
blocking. Instead, the Sturge Moore designs were printed in black on blue-grey
paper, glued to buff cloth in the case of *Reveries*, on blue-grey paper boards with
a buff linen spine in the case of *Responsibilities*.

Plate 18. The American *Reveries over Childhood and Youth* cover design by Thomas Sturge Moore as adapted and reused on the cloth issue of the Macmillan (New York) edition of *Selected Poems* (1921). Private collection, London.

Plate 19. Generic design for copies of Yeats's various American editions, including an alternative design for books with thicker spines by Thomas Sturge Moore, *c*.1917–18. © Senate House Library, University of London. All rights reserved.

Sturge Moore had been instructed by Yeats to provide a cover design which could be used by the Macmillan Company of New York on all of Yeats's American editions. He sought a design of 'great beauty… better suited for my American books in general than the design for "Reveries"'[93] Yeats wrote, hoping that Macmillan in London would also use it (though not for all of his books). He concluded that 'the block should be made in London & that the expense of this will not fall on me'.[94]

Yeats wanted something which would confer a more general symbolical autograph, even a new identity which would nevertheless provide continuity with the slowly fading icon of his youth provided by Althea Gyles's designs for *The Secret Rose*, *The Celtic Twilight* (1902), *Poems, 1899–1905* and *Poems: Second Series*, as well as that for the much-reprinted Unwin *Poems* in the UK market, and for *The Poetical Works of William B. Yeats* and *The Unicorn from the Stars and Other Plays* in the United States.[95] Sturge Moore provided a panelled design of a stylized rose and thorns which was to Yeats a 'fine grave design', first used upon both English and American editions of *Per Amica Silentia Lunae* (1918) and the American edition (but not the English edition) of *The Wild Swans at Coole* (1919) and upon the paper board issue of the American *Selected Poems* (1921).[96] Sturge Moore had even provided for spines of different thicknesses, offering one spinal design of a single thorned stem, and another of a pair of such stems, although the double-stemmed spine was not used in the end for the thicker volumes, such as the 1921 *Selected Poems* (*Wade* 121, Plate 19). The Rose emblem also offered Yeats a way of forestalling anonymous American book designers chosen by the Macmillan Company and whose work he much disliked. *The Green Helmet and Other Poems* (1912) must stand as the volume most reviled by its

---

[93] Nevertheless, Macmillan, New York did use the *Reveries* design on the cloth issue of *Selected Poems* (1921). See Plate 18.

[94] B.L. Add. MS. 55003 f. 26.

[95] Wade, *Bibliography*, items 65, 71, 73.

[96] Ibid., items 120–21, 130, 128. The cloth issue of *Selected Poems* uses the rejected Sturge Moore design made for the American edition of *Reveries*. Only the book title itself has been changed. Wade implies that the cloth issue came first, which might suggest that Yeats decided to restore the Rose design on the paper issue, but evidence is scanty.

author for its cover design. This had been Macmillan New York's first new collection of Yeats's poems since 1906, and it was issued in tan paper boards with a green ornamental design which enclosed its title within a helmet absurdly reminiscent of contemporary diving suits. No doubt the designer (who is unknown, but who, from similarities of style, was also responsible for the regrettable cover image on the American 1905 John Lane re-issue of *The Wind Among the Reeds*) thought he was paying a sincere tribute to the title play, and perhaps to Yeats's half-forgotten helmets and crowns of his *Poems* (1895) period. Yeats had so loathed this 'hateful American copy decorated in my despite' as he told Robert Bridges, that he inscribed Sturge Moore's copy 'The cover is the unaided work of the American publisher. He says it is he believes the kind of cover I like', branding other copies with similar sentiments (Plate 20).[97] By contrast, Sturge Moore's gold-blocked blue cloth covers on the English editions from *Reveries over Childhood and Youth*, *Responsibilities and Other Poems*, *Per Amica Silentia Lunae*, *The Cutting of an Agate* and *The Wild Swans at Coole* afforded some unity of livery, a tonal congruity with the Gyles covers, and some symbolic individuality for the various volumes. I choose but one example, the cover of *The Cutting of an Agate* (1919), an image noble in its restraint (Plate 21a).[98]

The design for *Responsibilities* (1916) offers the chance to watch Sturge Moore at work. Framing, panelling and boxing are a key feature of Sturge Moore's designs, one learned from the work of Charles Ricketts (Plate 21b).[99] A glance at the evolution of the design for *Responsibilities* is possible, because almost all the documents for that process are in the Sturge Moore Archive, Senate House Library, University of London. Its dominant symbols are the well, tree, and hawk from *At the Hawk's Well* (the hawk of course later becoming an important personal symbol for Yeats).[100]

---

[97] See, e.g., *L* 596. The presentation copy to Sturge Moore is inscribed 'December 1912' and is in the Sterling Library, University of London. Similar inscriptions showing how Yeats amusedly reviled the design can be found in other presentation copies, e.g., Allan Wade's, John Masefield's, and Lady Gregory's. See *CM* 20–21.

[98] The design may be found in *YA19* Plate 25, p. 375.

[99] The design for the top board and of the later *Four Plays for Dancers* (1921) offers a more severe example.

[100] See Ronald Schuchard, 'Hawk and Butterfly: The Double Vision of *The Wild Swans at Coole*' *YA10* 111–34. See also *LTSM* 132 for Yeats's letter of 6 July

Plate 20. Design for the top board of *The Green Helmet and Other Poems* (New York, 1912) by unknown artist. © private collection, London. All rights reserved.

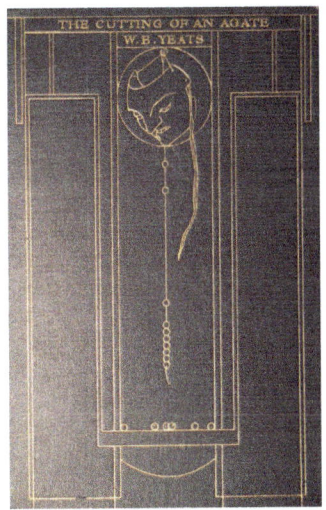

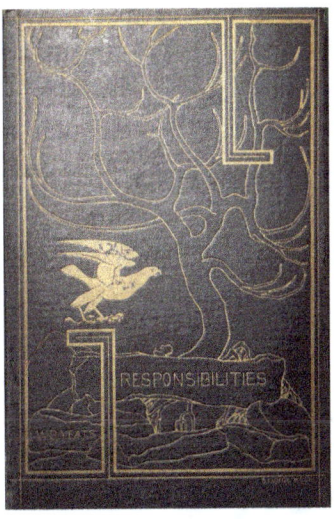

Plate 21a. Top board of *The Cutting of an Agate* (London, 1919), designed by Thomas Sturge Moore. Private collection, London.

Plate 21b. Top board, *Responsibilities* (London, 1916) by Thomas Sturge Moore. Private collection, London.

[1925] commissioning a book label design for use when signing books with what had become his signature motto, 'For wisdom is a butterfly | And not a gloomy bird of prey' (*VP* 337–38 and 827) where Yeats speaks of his ring, with its hawk and butterfly, in the Notes to 'Meditations in Time of Civil War', very much on his mind when writing to Sturge Moore about *The Tower*.

Responsibilities (1916) shows ingenious use of the top board's double outer gold frame. It breaks the illusion, obtruding into the image it supposedly encloses, in the lower left and upper right hand corners, and providing a perch for the hawk depicted above the '[d]ry stones in a well' and 'withered tree' of 'The Well and the Tree', a lyric uniquely included as such in this volume, and later published by Yeats only within the play, where it forms the closing lyric, 'The Man that I Praise' (*VP* 780; *VPl* 413–14) for the folding of the cloth at the end of the play. *Responsibilities*, however, was published on 2 October 1916, when the play was yet unpublished. As the hawk is not mentioned in the song lyric, I suggest that Sturge Moore must have been present in the audience in Lady Cunard's drawing-room, when *At the Hawk's Well* was first played on 2 April, 1916 (*VPl* 1315). Or he may have subsequently had sight of the manuscript. Sturge Moore was at the same time designing a table centre for the Yeats family, using the lion of St Mark and similar angular devices (Plate 22a). Both tablecloth and book cover have a common source in a tracing or copy Sturge Moore did in the Bibliothèque Nationale of the eighth-century boards of the Latin Gospels of St Willebrord (d. 739), an important analogue of the Lindisfarne Gospels, as Sturge Moore notes in the illegible pencilled note on the side of the drawing (Plate 22b).

Plate 22a. Table centre design for the Yeats Family by Thomas Sturge Moore, featuring the Lion of St Mark. © Senate House Library, University of London.

Plate 22b. A Tracing after f. 75 of the *Evangéliaire de saint Willibrord* (Bibliothèque Nationale, Paris, B. N. Latin 9389) by Thomas Sturge Moore, with the title RESPONSIBILITIES blocked in on bottom r.h.s. The almost illegible pencilled note reads as far as can be made out 'From the Latin Gospels at Paris attested to have belonged to St Willibrord who died 739 the oldest of which [?] resemble [?] gospels of Lindisfarne'. The lettering in the original also reads 'IMAGO LEONII'. © Senate House Library, University of London. All rights reserved.

This is certainly insular work, but Sturge Moore went further, declaring in the note 'Irish work'. Pencilled in to the bottom right hand of the drawing is the title, 'RESPONSIBILITIES'. The further development can be traced in the finished design (Plate 21b, above). The finest of course, is the tower reflected in the stream at Ballylee, the most famous image perhaps in all of Yeats's work (Plate 23a), done from a tiny sepia and white snapshot sent by Yeats and still among Sturge Moore's papers in the Senate House Library, University of London (Plate 23b). The snapshot offers the tower at Ballylee and the stream beside it, but Sturge Moore's reconception moves quite a long way from a realistic depiction, particularly in that he gives us so complete a reflection of the tower in the water. I have often wondered whether Sturge Moore, in formulating this idea, and in using such masses of gold not have in mind Yeats's early passion for the symbolism of 'fire reflected in water', which Yeats figures under the persona of Michael Robartes as 'the pride of the imagination brooding on the greatness of its possessions, or the adoration of the Magi'.[101] The volume, of course, opens with the Byzantine 'sages standing in God's holy fire | As in the gold mosaic of a wall' (*VP* 408), and if my suggestion has any merit,

---

[101] From the Notes to *The Wind Among the Reeds*: see *VP* 803.

Sturge Moore is reading 'Sailing to Byzantium' by the light of Yeats's older symbolic system. In 'Blood and the Moon' (published in *The Exile*, Spring 1928) Yeats was to 'declare this tower my symbol', but arguably Sturge Moore had already done so, with the publication of *The Tower* on St Valentine's Day of that year.

One could of course follow through nearly every Sturge Moore design on copies in the Cantwell Collection. The sequence of designs for what became the cover design of *The Winding Stair* is recoverable, and the track of Sturge Moore's attempts is a record of both his and Yeats's changing intentions for the volume. This is collaboration in the deepest sense: Sturge Moore's dissatisfaction with 'Sailing to Byzantium' having provided the seed for the growth of 'Byzantium' out of the earlier poem and Yeats, having been told by Lady Gregory that *The Winding Stair* was a title already used on some other book, wrote to his wife on 27 September [1930] to ask if he should change his planned title to *Byzantium*, in which case he would 'send Sturge Moore the new Byzantium poem 'which will give him a mass of symbols. "Byzantium" would follow up my old "Sailing to Byzantium" which people liked'.[102] By 4 October, he wrote to Sturge Moore,

I have decided to call the book 'Byzantium'. I enclose the poem from which the name is taken, hoping that it may suggest symbolism for the cover. The poem originates from a criticism of yours. You objected to the last verse of 'Sailing to Byzantium' because a bird made by a goldsmith was just as natural as anything else. That showed me that the idea needed exposition. Gongs were used in the Byzantine churches.[103]

Sturge Moore's preliminary sketch is a harvest of symbols from the Byzantium poems, the bird in the tree, the bird in flames, the boy on a dolphin (which seems to have large ears, rather than fins), the moon, the gyre, the dome of Hagia Sophia (Plate 24a). But there was excessive delay it the publication of the book, economic conditions worsened, its name was changed back to *The Winding Stair* after all, and the publisher's drive for economy forced the cover design (here best seen in that of the printed dustjacket) to be issued in blind stamping, except for its checker-board spine (Plate 24b).

[102] *CL InteLex* 5389.
[103] *Ibid.* 5390.

Plate 23a. *The Tower* (1928), top board design by Thomas Sturge Moore. © private collection, London. All rights reserved.

Plate 23b. Photograph sent by Yeats to Sturge Moore of Thoor Ballylee, to be used as the basis for the design in Plate 23a. The back is inscribed 'The cottage at back is my kitchen. The front you will see is over parapet of the old bridge. The other [parapet] was blown up during our civil war. WBY'. © Senate House Library, London. All rights reserved.

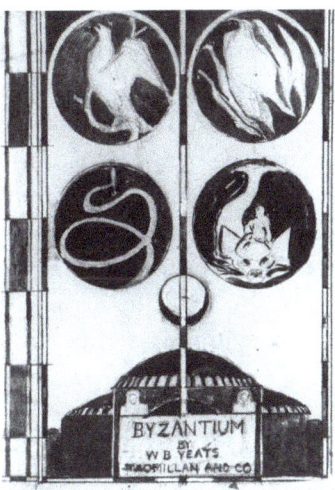

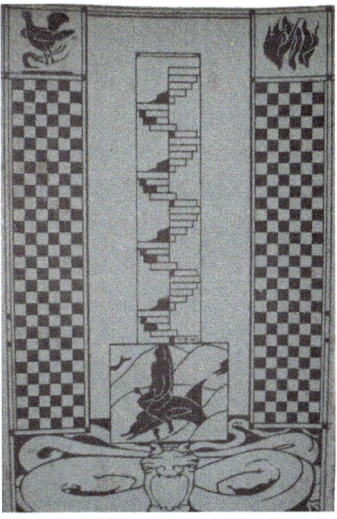

Plate 24a. Thomas Sturge Moore's preliminary sketch for the top board of *Byzantium* (later *The Winding Stair and Other Poems*). © Senate House Library, London. All rights reserved.

Plate 24b. Thomas Sturge Moore's dust jacket for *The Winding Stair and Other Poems* (1933). © private collection, London. All rights reserved.

TRIBUTORY BOOKS

Sturge Moore's most elaborate tribute to Yeats's symbols came in his decoration to H. P. R. Finberg's translation of Villiers de L'Isle Adam's *Axel* (1925), for which Yeats provided a preface. Sturge Moore was a close associate of Finberg's father, A. J. Finberg the Turner scholar, and Finberg himself was a former Oxford student who had met Yeats while he was living in Oxford. *Axel* was one of the sacred books of Yeats's youth, and Sturge Moore designed a new total book as a tribute to Yeats's love for this play (which he had first seen in Paris in 1894 with Maud Gonne). The result is that *Axel* comes adorned throughout with Yeats's leading symbols—Solomon's seal and lamp, Christ on the cross, with spear or sponge on a reed, the Janus-headed Magi, the lion and the sphinx. Many of these, the rose and thorns, also allude to Sturge Moore's own previous work for Yeats. If one compares the tower struck by lightning and unicorn bookplate for Mrs Yeats of 1918, which Yeats thought 'magnificent', and 'a masterpiece'[104] with the spine of *Axel* one can see the justifiable pride in these private associations (Plates 25a & b).

Another kind of tribute is effected by the Janus-headed Magi and Sphinx, repeated from the top board in the frontispiece (Plates 26 and 27). These take their source in a pair of attendant gods (*c.*810–800 BC) from the Temple of Nabu, god of wisdom and writing or learning, at Nimrûd, found in the lower Assyrian Transept of the British Museum, where both Yeats and Sturge Moore had regularly seen them. Sturge Moore's design for the Janus-headed statues which symbolize the 'immortality' of 'Magi, such as Axel's tutor', develop the back-and-front, hair-and-beard balance evident in the profile of this little god of wisdom and writing from the temple of Nabu (Plate 28a).[105] Sturge Moore's Janus, appropriate after 2700

---

[104] Ursula Bridge (ed.), *W. B. Yeats and T. Sturge Moore, Their Correspondence 1901–1937* (London: Routledge & Kegan Paul, 1953), 31–35, 54, 91.

[105] One of the pair of limestone statues of attendant gods dedicated to Nabu by Adad-Nirari III and Sammuramat (BM.118888–89). Nabu was the god of learning, in the temple of Ezida at Calah. Sammuramat was probably the original of the legendary Semiramis. They came to the Museum in 1856. In Yeats's time and Sturge Moore's, both little gods stood at the lower end of the Assyrian transept

years of writing, has a double-aspect and is 'four-eyed, two unbaffled by the veiling past, two unduped by the seductive future'.[106] The Sphinx is just as evidently based on the colossal winged lions, also found at Nimrûd (Plate 28b). These huge portal deities, ten ton sphinxes also with 'crowns' or horned helmets which signify sacred character or supernatural stature in ancient Assyrian art, had been unearthed in the North-West Palace of Ashurnasirpal II in Nimrûd 1845–51 by Sir Austen Henry Layard (1817–94), husband of Lady Gregory's close friend Enid Layard, with whom she and Yeats stayed in Venice in 1907. Sturge Moore had no textual authority for these Assyrian sphinxes in *Axel* itself.[107] But in bringing them into his designs, he gestures openly at Yeats's iconographical source for the 'brazen winged beast' of the play *Where there is Nothing*, '[a]fterwards described in my poem "The Second Coming"', as Yeats indicates in his note to *The Resurrection*.[108]

---

on the way to the old readers' tea room, adjacent to the monolithic wingèd lion temple doorway guardians. Their collation perhaps suggested to Sturge Moore their combination into his Janus figure.

[106] *Axel*, 12–13.

[107] British Museum curators comment that a pair of guardian figures that flanked one of the entrances into the throne room of Ashurnasirpal II (883–859 BC). Lamassu, or stone mythological guardians 'sculpted in relief or in the round, were often placed at gateways to ancient Mesopotamian palaces, to protect them from demonic forces. This winged lion has five legs so that when viewed from the front it is standing firm, and when viewed from the side it appears to be striding forward against any evil. It wears ropes like other protective spirits. Between the legs is inscribed the 'Standard Inscription' of Ashurnasirpal which is repeated over many of his reliefs. It records the king's titles, ancestry and achievements…. [Layard] suggested that these composite creatures embodied the strength of the lion, the swiftness of birds indicated by the wings, and the intelligence of the human head'. (http://www.britishmuseum.org/visiting/galleries/middle_east/room_6_assyrian_sculpture.aspx). The arrival of the monoliths in 1850–52 caused immense public interest among classes not accustomed to visit the British Museum. Layard's discoveries fired the minds of those who built the Nineveh Court in the Crystal Palace. Less remarked, however, is the impact on poets and designers. 'The Burden of Nineveh', for instance, finds Dante Gabriel Rossetti leaving the Grecian galleries and seeing a 'wingèd beast from Nineveh' being hoisted into the building. See the illustration in the *Illustrated London News*, 28 February, 1852 (184).

[108] See *The Variorum Edition of the Plays of W. B. Yeats*, edited by Russell K. Alspach, assisted by Catharine C. Alspach (London: Macmillan & Co., 1966), 932, 1102, 1099; *VP* 402.

Plate 25a. Proof of design for Book Plate for Mrs Yeats, by Thomas Sturge Moore. © Senate House Library, London. All rights reserved.

Plate 25b. Design for top board and spine of Villiers de L'Isle Adam's *Axel* by Thomas Sturge Moore. © Senate House Library, London. All rights reserved.

Plate 26. Top board and spine of published *Axel*. Image © private collection, London. All rights reserved.

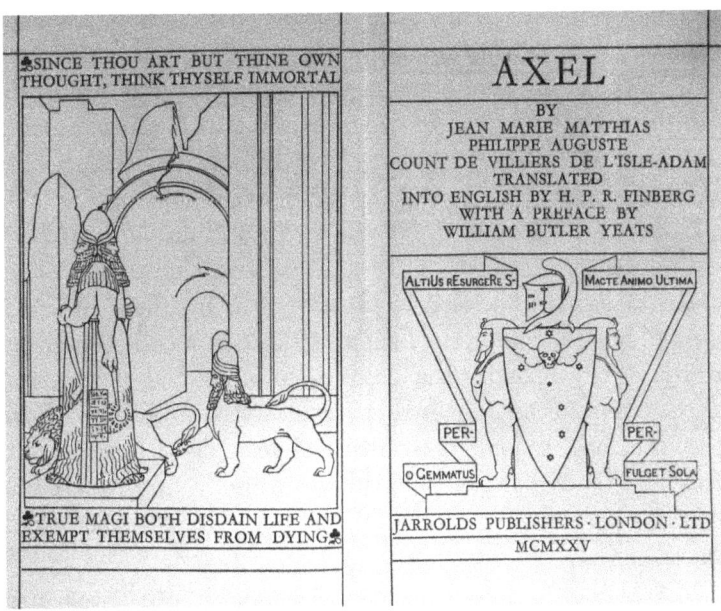

I shall end with a different kind of tributary book, one occasioned as a tribute to an artist in whom Yeats had placed enormous faith in his project of bringing Byzantine imagery back into contemporary Irish art. In turn, the artist and designer, Norah McGuinness, produced an artist's book decorated wholly as a tribute to Yeats. *Stories of Red Hanrahan and the Secret Rose* (1927), a fine copy of which is in the Cantwell Collection.[109] The illustrator and decorator is Norah McGuinness (1904–80), painter, illustrator, costume-designer, born in Derry, and married to Geoffrey Phibbs. She went to the Metropolitan School of Art, Dublin, 1921, and was long connected with the Abbey Theatre. She designed costumes and masks for *The Only Jealousy of Emer*, directed by Lennox Robinson under Yeats's supervision and presented by the Dublin Drama League at the Abbey on 9 and 10 May, 1926 (in which production McGuinness danced the part of the Woman of the Sidhe).[110] In 1969 she designed *Waiting for Godot* for the Abbey.

On 4 January, 1925, Yeats wrote a letter of introduction to Sir Frederick Macmillan for Norah McGuinness, 'one of the most promising Irish artists of the younger generation'.[111] Sir Frederick replied seeking a Yeats title for her to illustrate, having summoned her and inspected samples of her work on 22 January.[112] Yeats parried, replying 'I don't want any of my own work done for I have always refused illustrators and would give offence if I made an exception', but went on to suggest that Macmillan let her illustrate Sheridan Le Fanu's *In a Glass Darkly*, as he thought it

Le Fanu's most famous book… and I have often tried to get a copy. It has long been out of print and so I may exagerrate [*sic*] its merits. I am confident

---

[109] My account of it is drawn from my Appendix on 'The Illustrations and Cover Designs', in *The Secret Rose: Stories by W. B. Yeats: A Variorum Edition*, 278ff.

[110] Liam Miller, *The Noble Drama of W. B. Yeats* (Dublin: The Dolmen Press, 1977), 246–47. Norah McGuinness's own memories of the occasion, on which a droll remark by Yeats about her gold body paint led to her poor performance, are vividly retold in her 'Young Painter and Elderly Genius' in *W. B. Yeats, 1865–1965: A Centenary Tribute*, Supplement to the *Irish Times*, 10 June, 1965, vi. See also Miller, *op. cit.*, 247–48 and Plate xxiii.

[111] B.L. Add. MS. 55003 f. 85.

[112] B.L. Add. MSS. 55613 f. 600; 55614 ff. 258–59.

however that it would suit the talent of that particular artist and there has been a revival of interest in Le Fanu of late.[113]

Gradually the real reason was drawn from Yeats: he had

> always objected to having my work illustrated... because I was in dread of having my tales emptied into some very British nursery.... I suggested to Miss McGuinness the other night that she might, if you cared for the idea, illustrate some stories of mine in the style of Byzantine wall-pictures—we spent the evening looking through photographs of Sicilian mosaics and the like, and she went away full of the idea.[114] The reason why I want Byzantium is that there was great Byzantine influence upon Ireland.[115]

Yeats then cited wooden crucifixes in the Byzantine style in Irish private collections, and gestured to what he called a North Connaught

---

[113] B.L. Add. MS. 55003 f. 87; see also f. 130.

[114] The books included O[rmonde] M[addock] Dalton's *Byzantine Art and Archaeology* (Oxford: Clarendon, 1911), a copy of which is preserved in Yeats's Library. A paper slip marks the opening of 210–11, which is illustrated by carved ivory book-covers, heavily compartmentalized; while a further slip marks the opening of 404–05, which includes a photograph of mosaics in the Martorana, Palermo. Many of Dalton's photographs of Byzantine mosaic decorations include architectural details such as the arch, usually of the apse or narthex of ecclesiastical buildings. McGuinness's illustrations are characterized by the employment of a curvilinear device — typically an arch or a hill—whereby this architectural feature seems absorbed into her drawing. In Josef Strygowski's *Origin of Christian Church Art* (Oxford: Clarendon, 1923), Yeats and McGuinness would have found a whole chapter on 'Hiberno-Saxon Art in the Time of Bede' stressing the 'individuality' of Celtic ecclesiastical art as well as its dependence on Byzantine tradition (233). Other books available for consultation in Yeats's collection of Byzantine and Celtic Art studies included W. G. Holmes, *The Age of Justinian and Theodora: A History of the Sixth Century* (London: G. Bell, 1912), which is not illustrated with reproductions of mosaics; Margaret Stokes *Handbook and Guide to Irish Antiquities Collection. Early Christian Art in Ireland. National Museum of Science and Art, Dublin* (Dublin: HMSO, 1911). See Edward O'Shea, *A Descriptive Catalog of W. B. Yeats's Library* (New York and London: Garland Publishing, Inc., 1985), items 461, 903, and 2009.

[115] On 8 September, 1931, in 'An Irish Programme', a BBC broadcast from Belfast, Yeats commented further on 'Sailing to Byzantium': 'When Irishmen were illuminating the Book of Kells [in the eighth century] and making the jewelled croziers in the National Museum, Byzantium was the centre of European civilization and the source of its spiritual philosophy, so I symbolise the search for the spiritual life by a journey to that city. The passage is quoted in A. Norman Jeffares (ed.), *Yeats's Poems* (London: Macmillan, 1989), 576.

tradition of such art down to 'about 80 years ago' before suggesting that 'a little book containing RED HANRAHAN and THE SECRET ROSE stories' might 'suit admirably for a first experiment'.[116] Sir Frederick's response to Yeats's suggestion was to consult Norah McGuinness, before offering Yeats one shilling per copy in royalties. The published price was 10/6d net. Norah McGuinness's fee was a handsome £100, and she retained ownership of the original drawings.[117] No formal agreement through A. P. Watt was made, nor did Yeats stipulate that he must see proof, nor did he express any interest in revising the text of the stories.

Stories of Red Hanrahan and The Secret Rose is thus a second attempt at the 'total' or 'talismanic' book, in the same tradition as Yeats's work with the Cork artist Althea Gyles, and it grows directly out of the writing of 'Sailing to Byzantium', which was, as we shall see, to be fittingly dedicated to Norah McGuinness.[118] Yeats preferred to keep himself in the background, and did not directly communicate with Sir Frederick about the volume until 23 August, 1927, when he sent a manuscript of 'Sailing to Byzantium' to be used as a 'prelude' to this Byzantine experiment in integrated book design.

---

[116] B.L. Add. MS. 55003 ff. 95–96. He also suggested as alternatives either *The Celtic Twilight* ('better known but not so suitable for illustration') or a book made up from that volume, together with the next two sections of *Early Poems and Stories*, 'The Secret Rose' (1897) and 'Stories of Red Hanrahan'. Yeats does not seem to have entertained the idea that the section headed 'Rosa Alchemica' and including 'The Tables of the Law' and 'The Adoration of the Magi' should be included in this 'first experiment'. The implication is that after so much rearrangement of his text, he had come to see each of these sections as discrete entities, and had ceased to view the three last-named stories as a part of an entity called *The Secret Rose*. However, the 'experimental' nature of the project should also be emphasized.

[117] B.L. Add. MSS. 55645 f. 482; 20 December, 1926; 55646 ff. 28, 222, 30 December, 1926 and 6 January, 1927. Many of the drawings remained in her collection until the end of her life. They are now in a private collection in Dublin. I remain grateful to the late Norah McGuinness who, in 1975, wrote to me about her work with Yeats, and provided through Anne Yeats copies of some of her original drawings for *Stories of Red Hanrahan and The Secret Rose*.

[118] The two typescripts of the poem are dated 26 September, 1926, and it was published first in August 1927, when the Cuala Press *October Blast* (finished in the first week of June, 1927), was finally published. Yeats submitted copy to Macmillan for *Stories of Red Hanrahan and The Secret Rose* on 23 August, 1927 (B.L. Add. MS. 55003 f. 99).

He has 'thought first of doing a preface to explain why I put it there' but then thought that 'the dedication to the maker of the pictures' was 'a better explanation'.[119]

Norah McGuinness was, from the outset, anxious about the 'total' effect of the book. She tirelessly but unsuccessfully sought a paper of weight and finish rather better than the 'machine' finish paper which the printers insisted was necessary to bear the 'solid' blacks and fine lines of her designs.[120] It was McGuinness who insisted on the basic 'arrangement of the text and the illustrations' so that each story was furnished with half-title, two vignettes on the next opening, with initial design on the verso facing the first full recto of text, and a closing design on the final recto of each of the book's two sections.[121] Again, she was careful to the point of obsession about getting her work exactly as she wanted it, and Sir Frederick was patient and accommodating of changes, even when designs had been proofed.[122] She also consulted Yeats over such matters as the colour plates and cover designs. As early as 4 May 1927, McGuinness had asked Sir Frederick about the possibility of using gold in the coloured plates, and had been assured that, provided she limited herself to two coloured plates, gold could indeed be used.[123] The implication perhaps is that at first she entertained an ambitious plan for the effect of the 'gold mosaic of a wall' (*VP* 408). The two coloured designs do not in fact employ gold.[124]

McGuinness had requested flat colours, doubtless in search of the finish of frescoes or of dulled, ancient mosaic. This had necessitated reproduction *not* (as Yeats apparently thought) by the 'ordinary three colour process' (which would have resulted in a 'spotty' finish),

---

[119] B.L. Add. MS. 55003 f. 99. Norah McGuinness's letters to Macmillan have been preserved in the firm's archive, and were presented to the British Library at the end of 2004. They are at present unavailable.

[120] B.L. Add. MSS. 55646 ff. 437, 643, 13, 20 January 1927; 55647 f. 86, 24 January 1927; 55653 f. 428, 1 June 1927; 55654 f. 528, 27 June 1927.

[121] B.L. Add. MSS. 55653 f. 614, 8 June 1927; also 55654 ff. 132, 204; 13, 15 June 1927.

[122] B.L. Add. MSS. 55653 ff. 428, 614, 1, 8 June 1927 55656 f. 355, 28 July 1927.

[123] B.L. Add. MS. 55652 f. 83.

[124] They were submitted on 24 June 1927 (B.L. Add. MS. 55654 f. 528, 27 June 1927).

but by 'separate super-imposed blocks'. Toning down the colours necessitated the return of the originals, but Sir Frederick was quite willing for his printers to continue experimenting.[125] At about this time, Yeats, in Dublin, saw the proofs of the coloured plates. He feared that the 'method' of colour-reproduction had 'destroy[ed]' McGuinness's 'excellent' work.

The effect of your colour designs depends upon the variety of tint in the colour masses. Had you worked for this three colour process you would have had to break up the flat colour with patterns, or in some similar way—I have seen Dulac spend days on a pattern made by the scales of a fish—but your method is different. You work by suggestion not only in your colour but your design. Your hand & finger convention, for instance, would not go with pattern which by its very nature is the opposite of suggestion. A tudor rose, in decoration, for instance, must be completely realized in its convention like a letter of the alphabet.

Yeats went on to suggest that she insist on only the one coloured plate, of the design which became at his suggestion, made also in this letter, the frontispiece. He was more ready to compromise with expense than was necessary, given Sir Frederick's accommodating attitude to Norah McGuinness. The frontispiece design (with Hanrahan and the hounds, Cathleen the Daughter of Hoolihan and the four women with the four sacred objects, cauldron, whetstone, sword and spear,) 'need[ed] colour greatly'[126] (Plate 29).

  On the matter of a suitable cover design, both the publisher and the designer took endless pains, and were not always in agreement. The initial suggestion from Sir Frederick, made on receipt of the front cover design, was for a design in gold on blue boards, the eventual choice.[127] By 21 June, four specimen cover colours were sent to the artist with a dummy copy (which McGuinness needed before knowing the dimensions within which she had to work for the spine design); Sir Frederick still preferred the 'dark purply blue' cloth.[128]

[125] B.L. Add. MS. 55656 f. 292, 27 July 1927.
[126] Sligo County Library [n.d.].
[127] B.L. Add. MS. 55653 f. 428, 1 June 1927. After the first issue, some copies were bound in red cloth, with the design in blue on the front cover, and the design and lettering in blue on the spine. See *Wade*, item 157, pp. 159–61.
[128] B.L. Add MS. 55654 f. 385.

Yeats was consulted by Norah McGuinness and on 25 June, Yeats wrote from Thoor Ballylee, about the cover design. He had seen the trial bindings, and wrote to praise McGuinness's 'fine design' which would do 'a great deal for the success of my book'. He and George Yeats preferred (and got) a binding of 'the darkest blue… a fine colour in itself' and one which 'shows up the gold' (Plate 30).[129] Macmillan tried to economize, with a further weakly expressed try, with

three more pulls of the cover—one in green with gilt side, and one each in green and purple with the side design in blind instead of gilt. We have the idea that the blind is less staring than the gilt one; but we will leave you to decide, as we have no strong feeling either way.[130]

Plate 29. Frontispiece and title page by Norah McGuinness for *Stories of Red Hanrahan and the Secret Rose* (1927). Image © private collection, London. All rights reserved.

---

[129] Sligo County Library, June 25 1927.
[130] B.L. Add. MS. 55658 ff. 98–99, 7 September 1927.

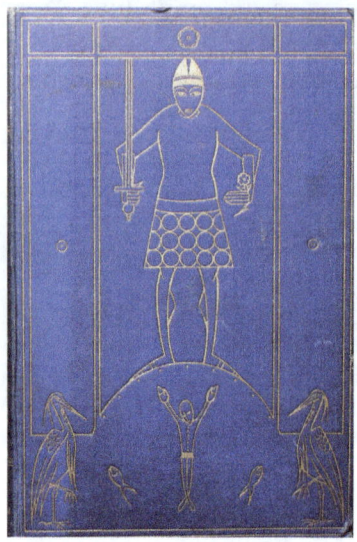

Plate 30. Top board design by Norah McGuinness for *Stories of Red Hanrahan and the Secret Rose* (1927). Image © private collection, London. All rights reserved.

On 13 March 1928 Yeats wrote from Rapallo, ill and conscious of his own delay, but eager to thank her for the 'great pleasure' her designs gave him. They were 'exactly right [in]... their powerful simplicity', and he 'like[d] them all'. He 'especially like[d]' the designs for 'The Death of Hanrahan and the vignettes for 'The Wisdom of the King', but found the 'best of all' to be the two opening vignettes for 'Proud Costello...', which 'made me think of some old carved stone on "Insula Trinitatis"'. These were the two vignettes of the lovers and the two mingled ash trees on Insula Trinitatis in Lough Key (Plate 31). Norah McGuinness had done him 'a great service', and the young Michael Yeats had said 'I like those pictures—they are not too like anything so I can tell myself stories about them'.[131]

George Russell writing in the *Irish Statesman*, considered the illustrations irrelevant, but what he had perhaps not seen was that the Byzantine decoration of *Stories of Red Hanrahan and The Secret Rose* was the imposition of an Irish visual concomitant to Yeats's new iconography, one announced in the textual changes which introduced

---

[131] Sligo County Library, March 13 [1928]. Yeats's last comment of course alludes to the ending of 'Proud Costello, MacDermot's Daughter, and the Bitter Tongue': see *VSR* 81, *Myth (2005)* 137.

Byzantium into 'Rosa Alchemica' in *Early Poems and Stories* (1925).[132] The composition of 'Sailing to Byzantium' completed, Yeats had come back, as it were, *from* Byzantium to Ireland, and, with Norah McGuinness, now undertook the revisionist task of bringing Byzantium itself back to Ireland. Through the medium of a young artist whose work in the theatre he had admired, he had come to feel that he might inspire a new generation of Irish art and design. Insisting upon that affinity between Byzantine and Celtic art, and sealing that insistence by the deployment of the poem and its dedication, Yeats was determined to demonstrate the living or recently deceased affinities between Byzantine and Celtic Art. It was an old enthusiasm, as 'Rosicrux' he had strongly endorsed such a connexion in 1899, in his review entitled 'High Crosses of Ireland'.[133] Moreover, it was to continue: as late as 1932, he added the opening Byzantine frame-tale to 'The Old Age of Queen Maeve' (1903) (*VP* 180).

Plate 31. Final vignette of the two woven ash trees over the graves on Insula Trinitatis, Lough Key, for 'Proud Costello, MacDermot's Daughter, and the Bitter Tongue' in *Stories of Red Hanrahan and the Secret Rose* (1927). © private collection, London. All rights reserved.

---

[132] See *VSR* 128 (lines 48–49).

[133] In the Dublin *Daily Express* (28 January, 1899), 3. See John P. Frayne and Colton Johnson (eds.), *Uncollected Prose by W. B. Yeats Volume II: Reviews, Articles and Other Miscellaneous Prose 1897–1939* (London: Macmillan Press, 1975), 142–45. ('Rosicrux' was a transparent pseudonym in the Dublin of the late nineties). His 'passion for the mystic rose... [had] saddened my friends' Yeats wrote, before proposing Behmenist and Blakean interpretations of the ground plan of a mediæval Irish monastery which he (and Margaret Stokes) read as a 'mystical symbol'. Praising her interpretation of Irish antiquities by means of Byzantine studies, he yet hoped that some future scholar 'as well as visionary... having mastered the mysticism of the middle ages' would 'tell us how much of it is reflected in the crosses and illuminated missals of this country' (*ibid.*, 144–45).

CONCLUSION

Publishing itself forced renewal onto Yeats. From 1903 he had an established publishing system or cycle—Dun Emer or Cuala edition, trade edition, revised collection and, endlessly deferred but always in prospect, a collected works. Such was the uniform Macmillan edition which began with *Later Poems* in 1922. 'You have perfect books at last' George Yeats said, when she saw the first volumes with their Charles Ricketts binding and unicorn end-paper motif. Yeats himself recalled that

at 17 there is an identity between an authors imagination & paper & book-cover one does not find in later life. I still do not quite seperate Shelley from the green cover, or Blake from the blue covers & brown reproductions of pictures, of the books in which I first read them. I do not separate Rossetti at all from his covers.[134]

As we can see in Eamonn Cantwell's copies, Ricketts had chosen green boards! After 1922, Yeats concluded that such symbols as the colour green and the harp (if not the shamrock) had 'ascended out of sentimentality', for obvious reasons.[135]

[134] B.L. Add. MS 58091 f. 190, cf. *L* 691. Lady Gregory recalled how the Gyles designs dominated her bookcase 'filled… with Yeats bounty from end to end'. The 'earlier volumes shine and glitter through the glass; golden designs, by a genius, of leaves and birds and the mystic rose'. (*Coole* by Lady Gregory, completed from the manuscript and edited by Colin Smythe with a foreword by Edward Malins [Dublin: Dolmen, 1971], 39).

[135] 'I walked along the south side of the Dublin quays a couple of years ago; looked at the funnels of certain Dublin steamers and found that something incredible had happened; I had not shuddered with disgust though they were painted green on patriotic grounds; that deep olive seemed beautiful. I hurried to the Parnell Monument and looked at the harp. Yes, that too was transfigured; it was a most beautiful symbol; it had ascended out of sentimentality, out of insincere rhetoric, out of mob emotion. When I reached home I took from the mantelpiece a bronze medal of myself and studied the little shamrock the American medallist [Theodore Spicer-Simson, 1922] had put after the date. But there had been no transformation; the disgust that will always keep me from printing that portrait in any book of mine, or forgiving its creator, had increased, as though the ascent of the other symbols left the shamrock the more alone with its associations of drink and jocularity ('Ireland, 1921–31', *The Spectator*, 30 January 1932; *UP2* 486–87). The medal is reproduced as frontispiece of Oliver St. John Gogarty's *William Butler Yeats: A Memoir* (Dublin: Dolmen Press, 1963).

Lecturing in America, Yeats was once asked what reading he would recommend, and told how Lionel Johnson said that a man should read all books until he was forty, and thereafter be satisfied with six. When asked what were his six, Yeats chose such authors as Balzac and Morris and *The Arabian Nights*, and when I thought I would offer just six books to introduce Eamonn Cantwell's library I did not foresee that the books I originally chose would lead into multitudinous pathways. I think with regret of so many other avenues: the books he wrote to keep Dun Emer and Cuala alive, which became not merely collectors' items nor even coterie publications for friends and critics, but a vital part of his publishing economy, a rolling dress rehearsal for his trade publishing; *A Vision* 'for my schoolmates only', most of all, perhaps, the great story of the *Collected Works in Verse and Prose* with its obsessive self-portraiture.

My inspiration has been Eamonn Cantwell's passion for collecting, and his taste. In mentioning some books which eluded him I am offering an unsubtle hint to the Boole Library. We cannot read Yeats in any depth today without study of these unique and precious objects, which bear continuing witness to what it was to read Yeats in his lifetime. No amount of literary theory or post-colonial discourse can help us do that. To examine these books tells us something new every time. Every one of them tells us a story of collaboration: author, agent, publisher, designer, plate manufacturer, publisher's reader, sub-editor, blurb writer, printer, binder, salesman.

Introducing a bibliography appended to *The Works of Max Beerbohm* John Lane remarked, 'It is impossible for one to compile a bibliography of a great man's works without making it in some sense a biography—and indeed in the minds of not a few people I have found a delusion that the one is identical with the other'.[136] Similarly, Yeats's books are not only central to the biography of the man of whom T. S. Eliot said that his history was the history

---

[136] London: John Lane, The Bodley Head; New York: Charles Scribner's Sons, 1896, 163.

of his 'own time',[137] they have a life, or lives, and a contingency of
their own. Yeats knew this. His textual field has about it all the
contingency that is implied in a remark to Florence Farr in 1914: 'I
have brought my memoirs down to my twentieth year. I will carry
them no further... partly because when one begins to write ones
books are a sufficient history'.[138]

[137] 'The Poetry of W. B. Yeats', the first annual Yeats Lecture, delivered to the
Friends of the Irish Academy at the Abbey Theatre, June 1940, and reprinted in
Purpose (xii:3–4, July-December 1940), 115–27 at 127.
[138] W. B. Yeats to Florence Emery, 4 October [1914] (private collection).

http://dx.doi.org/10.11647/OBP.0081.03

'Philosophy and Passion':
W. B. Yeats, Ireland and Europe

R. F. Foster

MY TITLE[1] comes from one of Yeats's volumes of autobiography—of which there are such beautiful editions in the Cantwell Collection of the Boole Library. In the passage I have chosen, he is recalling his early ambitions around 1890 for the revival of Irish culture—and, indeed, a distinctively Irish civilization.

I used to tell the few friends to whom I could speak these secret thoughts that I would make the attempt in Ireland but fail, for our civilization, its elements multiplying by division like certain low forms of life, was all-powerful; but in reality I had the wildest hopes. Today I add to that first conviction, to that first desire for unity, this other conviction, long a mere opinion vaguely or intermittently apprehended: Nations, races, and individual men are unified by an image, or bundle of related images, symbolical or evocative of the state of mind which is, of all states of mind not impossible, the most difficult to that man, race, or nation; because only the greatest obstacle that can be contemplated without despair rouses the will to full intensity.

---

[1] This was delivered as the second lecture in the series, on 3 June 2004. Further information may have been gathered since this article was prepared for publication. If you would like to find out if any further information has been discovered that may help your own research, why not write to the author at Roy.Foster@hertford.ox.ac.uk? Quite apart from anything else, feedback is always welcomed.

A powerful class by terror, rhetoric, and organized sentimentality may drive their people to war, but the day draws near when they cannot keep them there; and how shall they face the pure nations of the East when the day comes to do it with but equal arms? I had seen Ireland in my own time turn from the bragging rhetoric and gregarious humour of O'Connell's generation and school, and offer herself to the solitary and proud Parnell as to her anti-self, buskin followed hard on sock, and I had begun to hope, or to half hope, that we might be the first in Europe to seek unity as deliberately as it had been sought by theologian, poet, sculptor, architect from the eleventh to the thirteenth century. Doubtless we must seek it differently, no longer considering it convenient to epitomize all human knowledge, but find it we well might could we first find philosophy and a little passion.[2]

'Philosophy and passion' were the qualities he tried to bring both to creative and political endeavour, and I want to look at how he did this. But first I must point out that the passage above was written in the autumn of 1920. He had first revisited these years of his apprenticeship around 1890 in a draft written in 1917, too frank for publication; but the section called 'Four Years: 1887–1891', from which this passage is taken, was written in Oxford in 1920, as events in Ireland worsened. The Black and Tans were terrorizing the countryside around his Tower at Ballylee and the Anglo-Irish war was in full swing. He was writing his early life with this knowledge of contemporary dissolution, and was deliberately placing the thoughts and ambitions of his youth as a prelude to the Irish revolution which he wanted to be a revolution in consciousness too, towards 'unity of being'. In the late 1880s, 'philosophy and passion' were intended to provide the key to a political annunciation. But by the time he was writing in 1920, Ireland was in the throes of guerrilla war while Russia and Europe had been turned upside-down by war and revolution. Yeats wrote his recollections of these years with great excitement. But, he privately admitted, 'One thing I did not see, the growing murderousness of the world'.[3]

---

[2] This is the closing passage of 'Four Years: 1887–1891' (*Au* 194–95). In early versions (as in NLI 30, 536), 'Four Years' continues with what is now the opening passage of the next section, Ireland After Parnell': but Yeats clearly decided that the impact was greater if the section ended on the words 'philosophy and a little passion'.

[3] See *Life 2*, 180.

'The world', it should be noted: not just 'Ireland'. And these reflections of Yeats's on the roots of the Irish revolution were also inspired by the close attention he had been paying to European history, since the Russian revolutions of 1917, and the upheavals after the Great War ended a year later. Since then, too, Yeats had been assembling his own strange philosophy of history, published in 1925 as *A Vision*, which tried to interpret the phases of European history and civilization—constantly returning to the idea that around 1920 a new era was dawning. This would be a new era for Europe as well as for Ireland. I want here to try and show how his ideas about the two were connected, and how they relate to his doubts about the efficacy of democracy, and his belief in artistic freedom.

John Stuart Mill said long ago that Ireland was part of Europe, whereas England was isolated in some kind of tributary stream; recent developments in the history and politics of both countries may seem to bear this out. But when Mill wrote this, Ireland was part of a political Union with Britain; that was the historical and cultural reality which Yeats was born into, and in some ways he remained enmeshed in it all his life. Yet he has been enlisted as the voice of liberationist nationalism in the years when Ireland was moving towards independence in the early twentieth century, a process which he himself saw as Ireland assuming its rightful place in Europe. He begins his public and publishing life as a radical nationalist, a member of the revolutionary Fenian brotherhood, preaching the rejection of British domination in political as well as cultural terms; he moves to a stance of disillusionment with conventional nationalism, then emerges once more as the voice of national self-determination when politics radicalize after the 1916 Rising; he takes a leading part in the public life of the independent Irish State from 1922, but this too leads to disillusionment; and the work of his last ten years, in the 1930s, has been closely connected with an interest in fascist politics and the dark pseudo-science of eugenics. By then he had been indicted as the advocate of elite culture in Ireland— in effect, the culture of the colonizer—and this seems to trouble some critics more than his attitude towards reactionary politics in Europe.[4]

---

[4] See e.g. Seamus Deane, 'Heroic Styles: the tradition of an idea', in *Ireland's Field Day* (London: Hutchinson, 1995), 45–58; reprinted in Claire Connolly (ed.), *Theorizing Ireland* (Basingstoke: Palgrave, 2002), 14–26.

His early career did not prophesy this. Thanks partly to his influential book *The Celtic Twilight*, Yeats became the voice of the Celtic Revival in Britain during the 1890s, and it branded his image for many years after that.[5] If we are to explore the inheritances of Yeats, then this is one of the longest-established: the marketing of fashionable Irishness. And it is a theme uncomfortably familiar to us today. But it is also a European kind of identity. Celticism has its French dimension, and French literary fashion was vital to the young Yeats—not only the *Symbolistes* and Ernest Renan, but the lectures of Henri d'Arbois de Jubainville at the Sorbonne (which Maud Gonne translated for him) and occultist Jacobite groups in 1890s Paris. Yeats spent a lot of time in Paris as a young man, and had an uncanny instinct for seeking out the latest thing; he differs greatly from Joyce and Beckett in being a hopeless linguist, but like those other Irish writers, he found what he needed there. (One of the most marvellous passages in his autobiographies concerns his visit to Paul Verlaine, and it should be mandatory reading for anyone who denies that Yeats has a sense of humour.[6])

He was well aware of the European and avant-garde implications of Celticism—paralleled in our own day, in France as well as in America, though the concept looks more and more problematic to ethnologists as well as historians. (I refer you to a literary gathering in France in 1996 under the title 'L'imaginaire irlandais' where, according to one observer, 'Parisian intellectuals raved about *celtique* spirituality while Irish writers objected coarsely on the sidelines'.[7]) Yeats remained in touch with French literary developments, even after the shift of cultural energy back to Dublin in the early 1900s. This coincided with the period when he determined that Ireland take its part in the European avant-garde. His own work, especially his dramatic work, looked in this direction; and when considering his own London apprenticeship, he used a quintessential European

---

[5]   On the uses of literary Celticism, see Terence Brown (ed.), *Celticism* (Amsterdam: Rodopi, 1996) and Edna Longley, 'The Politics of Celt and Saxon', in *Poetry and Posterity* (Tarset: Bloodaxe, 2000), 52–89.

[6]   *Au* 341–42.

[7]   Longley, *op. cit.*, p. 59.

literary image, comparing himself to Lucien coming to Paris in Balzac's *Lost Illusions*. I think this receptiveness to European events, ideas and parallels conditions much of his political thought.

But I also want to look at the implications—political and aesthetic—of his apparent turn away from this role, and the significance of his return to Ireland when his country gained a kind of independence in 1922. This is a central theme of the second and final volume in my biography of the poet. Again, this involved a change of direction. Through the early 1900s, Yeats had in fact been moving away from conventional Irish nationalism. For one thing, Maud Gonne abandoned him; for another, the language of Irish nationalism began to express something alarmingly like a *Kulturkampf* between Catholic and Protestant (a European echo here too, perhaps); for another, the nationally-minded theatre which Yeats founded, was itself the object of attack from conventional nationalists, particularly when it put on the avant-garde plays of J. M. Synge. Yeats, like Synge, had a strong sense of Ireland's European identity, and direct experience of Parisian intellectual life. In the Abbey, he invoked Antoine's Theatre Libre, and Lugné-Poe's Theatre de l'Oeuvre, Wagner's Bayreuth, the stage designs of Edward Gordon Craig, and Stanislavsky and the Moscow Art Theatre; while Ibsen and Maeterlinck are deeply influential on the first Abbey generation. Norway, Russia and Germany could provide dramatic models, no less than Celtic myths. The inclination towards European models and the necessity to bring foreign masterpieces into the Irish orbit remained through Yeats's life.

It is true that by the time of the First World War, Yeats had retreated from his advanced nationalist posture; he supported constitutional Home Rule, but spent most of his time in England. Meanwhile the War was convulsing Irish politics, and radical nationalism was on the rise. He was by then nearly fifty, a member of the establishment, and indeed refused a knighthood in 1915. But I think his European sense helped him avoid what's called 'internalised colonisation' and enabled him to fly by the nets of exclusive national definitions. Certainly the Easter Rising of 1916, and the subsequent radicalisation of Irish political opinion, brought about Yeats's own repositioning in his relationship with Britain. In one of his first letters after the news of the Easter Rising, though, he reflected that it was time to go back and 'begin building again'.[8] I have traced how his poems, plays and public manifestoes in the period from 1916 to 1922 followed a cautious path between endorsing Irish revolution and calling for an accommodation with Britain.[9] Most significantly, he wrote his autobiography—with which I began. And he altered and re-shaped the pattern of his earlier life to fit with the story of his emerging country—changing perspective and even chronology to make the point. His public statements were equally careful. He tailored his speeches in the USA and elsewhere very cautiously; he withheld from publication poems and plays that seemed to take up the rebel cause; he stayed living (now in Oxford) with his new young English wife and their small children; he did not take part in political initiatives set up by friends, such as the Irish Convention of 1917.

It should also be noted that, though he was indeed writing poems and plays which carried a nationalist message, and circulating them in *samizdat* fashion at this time, he also wrote a strangely bitter poem about his old friend the revolutionary Constance Markiewicz, whom he had first known as a beautiful and aristocratic girl in her family's great country house, Lissadell. She was now imprisoned for her revolutionary activities, and (as a letter to her sister Eva of 1916 shows) Yeats was deeply struck by the contrast between her past and her present: 'Your sister & yourself, two beautiful figures

[8]   To John Quinn, 23 May 1916, *CL InteLex* 2960; *L* 614.
[9]   "Romantic Ireland's dead and gone" sounds old-fashioned now. It seemed true in 1913, but 1 did not foresee 1916. The late Dublin Rebellion, whatever one can say of its wisdom, will long be remembered for its heroism. 'They weighed so lightly what they gave', and gave too in some cases without hope of success. July 1916'. I am grateful to Eamonn Cantwell for pointing out this early salute to the 'heroism' of the 1916 Rising, which survived into the 1917 reprinting of that volume, and thereafter disappeared from Yeats's notes: see *VP* 820. He also pointed out that Ernest A. Boyd printed the first stanza of 'Easter, 1916', in *The Irish Commonwealth* (March 1919), a year before its first full printing in the *New Statesman*. Boyd's article was entitled 'The Drift of Irish Literature' (20–28), and the quotation came on p. 24. See also 'Yeats at War: Poetic Strategies and Political Reconstruction, 1916–1922', in my *The Irish Story: Telling Tales and Making It Up in Ireland* (London: Allen Lane, 2001), 58–79.

among the great trees of Lissadell, are among the dear memories of my youth.[10] That memory, as we'll see, persisted and was built into a great poem eleven years later when both sisters were dead. But the poem he wrote about Markiewicz at the time of her imprisonment in 1918 poem demonstrates an unequivocally contemptuous view of the company she kept. It also indicates the way that, at the end of World War I, he was already doubtful about the new democratic politics.

On a Political Prisoner

She that but little patience knew,
From childhood on, had now so much
A grey gull lost its fear and flew
Down to her cell and there alit,
And there endured her fingers' touch
And from her fingers ate its bit.

Did she in touching that lone wing
Recall the years before her mind
Became a bitter, an abstract thing.
Her thought some popular enmity:
Blind and leader of the blind
Drinking the foul ditch where they lie?

When long ago I saw her ride
Under Ben Bulben to the meet.
The beauty of her countryside
With all youth's lonely wildness stirred.
She seemed to have grown clean and sweet
Like any rock-bred, sea-borne bird:

Sea-borne, or balanced on the air
When first it sprang out of the nest
Upon some lofty rock to stare
Upon the cloudy canopy.
While under its storm-beaten breast
Cried out the hollows of the sea. (*VP* 397)

---

[10] Letter to Eva Gore-Booth, 23 July [1916], *CL InteLex* 3008.

This poem, written in January 1919, was not published until November 1920, though he read it on an American lecture tour earlier that year. A certain caution in releasing his political poems may be evident here (as, famously, with 'Easter 1916'). Ambiguity about endorsing extremist republicanism remained, along with his mounting anger at the government's actions against the insurgents and the Irish population at large. When he did 'come out' as a supporter of Sinn Fein, and condemned British policy in Ireland, he did it (after careful preparation) in an Oxford Union debate. And he expressed his horror at the doings of the British military mercenaries in Ireland by invoking Gladstone and Salisbury, and aligning himself with them and with the outmoded notions of honour that the nineteenth century represented. A contemporary witness has left a description.

In twelve minutes of bitter and blazing attack on the English in Ireland he ended pointing at the busts of the Union's Prime Ministers. "Gladstone! Salisbury! Asquith! They were Victorians. I am a Victorian. They knew the meaning of the words "truth" and "honour" and "justice". But you do not know the meaning of them. You do not know the language I speak, so I will sit down".

'No-one who heard that speech', added this witness, 'could question his sincerity as an Irish nationalist'.[11] We may also be struck in it by the anticipation of a bitter quatrain he would put into his great poem 'Nineteen Hundred and Nineteen':

> We who seven years ago
> Spoke of honour and of truth
> Shriek with pleasure if we show
> The weasel's twist, the weasel's tooth. (VP 431)

But he also claimed to be 'a Victorian'. This may seem a surprising identification for a figure seen as not only the poet of national liberation but as one of the founders of modernism; however, there is much about other aspects of Yeats's life that bears it out. (Long

---

[11] James O'Reilly, 'Memories of W. B. Yeats and Undergraduate Oxford', TS, HRHRC. See also *Life 2*, 188, 703 and 'Yeats at War', 75.

ago I interviewed Frederick Ashton, the great choreographer who had known Yeats in the 1930s; I described Yeats as 'avant-garde', and Ashton retorted, 'Avant-garde? My dear boy, he was *pure 'nineties'.*). The basic matter of his age might be kept in view.

Yeats was in his fifties when the European world was transformed by the Russian revolution and the upheaval of the old world order in the aftermath of World War I. His own world view often tended to the apocalyptic, and this was such a juncture. It is well known that 'Nineteen Hundred and Nineteen' began as 'Thoughts on the Present State of the World'; it seems to me, looking at its evolution, that it originated as a poem about the European crisis, and was only later turned into a commentary on Ireland. This might be borne out by other writings around this time, which show similar misgivings: notably an ominous essay called 'If I Were Four and Twenty'. Written in 1919, it responds directly to the Russian revolution. It should, I think, be directly related to apocalyptic poems like 'The Second Coming'. In this essay Yeats considers the motor of history, driven either by struggles of individual against individual, or family against family; he reviews the economics of egalitarianism *versus* traditional hierarchies, and stresses the family unit as the basis of civilization, and the need to privilege it.

Thus in 1919 he was already absorbed by the ideas which would emerge, ominously, in the 1930s. And he wrote at this time to a friend that he had decided 'the Marxian criterion of values in this age [is] the spear-head of materialism and leads to inevitable murder'.[12] He put some of his thoughts about political authority into 'If I Were Four and Twenty', where he discussed the primitive idea that 'ordinary men had no immortality, but obtained it through a magical bond with some priest or king' (an idea that would recur in his powerful poem about Irish politics, 'Parnell's Funeral').

---

[12] *CL InteLex* 3603, to George Russell [? 5 May 1919]: 'I consider the Markian criterion of value, as in this age the spear-head of materialism & leading to inevitable murder. From that criterion follows the well known phrase "can the bourgois be innocent?"'. See also *L* 655–56.

Perhaps it may be possible in a few years to apportion the values of idleness by a science that traces the connections of thought and by a religion that judges the result. With Christianity came the realization that a man must surrender his particular will to an implacable will, not his, though within his, and perhaps we are restless because we approach a realization that our general will must surrender itself to another will within it, interpreted by certain men, at once economists, patriots and inquisitors. As all realization is through opposites, men coming to believe the subjective opposite of what they do or think, we may be about to accept the most implacable authority the world has known. Do I desire it or dread it, loving as I do the gaming-table of Nature where many are ruined but none is judged, and where all is fortuitous, unforeseen? (*Ex* 279–80)

These are also the years when he was writing the first version of *A Vision*, eventually published in 1926. While scholars have struggled with its philosophical and historical schema, not many have noted the implicit political prophecy offered in its final section—written, as it happens, in Mussolini's Italy. Here, he prophesies the end of an era in 1927. 'It is as though myth and fact, united until the exhaustion of the Renaissance, have now fallen so far apart that man understands for the first time the rigidity of fact, and calls up, by that very recognition, myth—the *Mask*—which now but gropes its way out of the mind's dark but will shortly pursue and terrify' (*CV[A]* 212, *CW13* 175). (This is clearly the rough beast, slouching towards Bethlehem in 'The Second Coming'.) In another passage, later dropped, he questions the utility of democratic forms of government, faced with anarchic violence. A new era is coming, bringing its 'stream of irrational force'. All this is closely connected with his revulsion from the Soviet revolution, and his interest in the new Italian politics.

At the same time, from about 1920 Yeats had been repudiating the British dispensation, endorsing the Irish claim of independence, and planning to place his stamp on the cultural life of the new state. He was a firm supporter of the Treaty which established twenty-six counties of Ireland as an autonomous Dominion within the Commonwealth and felt no difficulty about the partition of Northern Ireland, telling Maud Gonne that if such unpleasant neighbours slammed the door in your face, it was better to turn the key in the lock. The Irish Free State would later negotiate its way to the status of a republic, but at the time of the Treaty there were those who believed that Dominion status and an oath of fidelity to the King as head of the Commonwealth was an unpardonable betrayal of the Revolution. A minority of irreconcilable republicans, led by Eamon de Valera, precipitated the brief and brutal Civil War of 1922–23. The forces of the Irish civil war seemed to fulfil many of Yeats's fears and prophecies. It also inspired one of his great poem-sequences, 'Meditations in Time of Civil War'. This deals with violence, aristocratic descent, and the creation of a new order. The ambivalent and retiring poet/observer comes up against the ruthless clarity of action, and the forces of hatred behind Irish—and world—history.

I have not time to explore it all, but one might look at the opening poem in the sequence, 'Ancestral Houses'. It begins as a country-house idyll, almost Arcadian in tone, but ends by raising the question of degeneration, and unworthy inheritors—which, again, would resurface in his very late work of the 1930s. The conclusion of 'Ancestral Houses' revolves around an uncomfortable question. Are violence, bitterness, and grandeur inseparable? Is the decline and destruction of inherited greatness and achievement not only inevitable, but somehow encoded within the qualities that founded an aristocratic culture in the first place? And if so, can it really be regretted?

> Some violent bitter man, some powerful man
> Called architect and artist in, that they
> Bitter and violent men, might rear in stone
> The sweetness that all longed for night and day.
> The gentleness none there had ever known;
> But when the master's buried mice can play.
> And maybe the great-grandson of that house
> For all its bronze and marble, 's but a mouse.
>
> O what if gardens where the peacock strays
> With delicate feet upon old terraces.
> Or else all Juno from an urn displays
> Before the indifferent garden deities;
> O what if levelled lawns and gravelled ways
> Where slippered Contemplation finds his ease
> And Childhood a delight for every sense.
> But take our greatness with our violence?

What if the glory of escutcheoned doors,
And buildings that a haughtier age designed.
The pacing to and fro on polished floors
Amid great chambers and long galleries, lined
With famous portraits of our ancestors;
What if those things the greatest of mankind
Consider most to magnify, or to bless.
But take our greatness with our bitterness? (*VP* 418)

Yet he opposed the anti-Treaty forces who sustained the violence and anarchy of revolution in Ireland. Yeats was in no doubt that the Treaty was the best deal possible; and while he felt that Irish cultural independence of English models was essential, he represented the Free State Government on several secret negotiations about the terms of the Oath of Allegiance. His political ambitions went further; he hoped to be made Minister for Arts in the new Government, which did not happen. But he became a Senator, speaking often and influentially; he was an organiser of cultural jamborees such as the Irish Race Congress, held in Paris just after independence, and the Tailteann Games (a sort of cultural Olympics). But he used occasions like his speech welcoming foreign visitors to Ireland for that occasion to declare gloomy expectations about the dawning post-democratic age, and to draw attention to Mussolini's Italian experiment, even quoting the Duce's call to 'trample upon the decomposing body of the Goddess of Liberty'.

Nonetheless, by the 1920s the poet of liberation has apparently become the father of his country: permitted—unlike, say, Adam Mickiewicz—to see the Promised Land which he has sung into being. But beware of answered prayers. The Free State rapidly became, in Yeats's view, prey to the wrong kind of pieties and restrictions, especially in the imposition of Catholic social law upon the constitution, outlawing divorce and contraception and imposing literary censorship in the interests of conservative Catholic standards of 'purity'. From the early 1920s Yeats took a deliberate and leading part in opposing such restrictions, mounting, for instance, a long-running campaign to have James Joyce recognized as the great Irish genius of his generation, as well as being a great European writer, as great as Tolstoy or Rabelais. If it is true, as Denis Donoghue has said, that Joyce made himself a European to get out from under Yeats's shadow, we see a nice irony here as Yeats tries to reclaim him for Ireland. He had already tried to interest the writers of the new state in French poets like Péguy and Claudel—whom he had discovered with Maud Gonne's daughter Iseult in France in 1916–17. We encounter once again that European preoccupation, with a right-wing twist.

For it should be pointed out that this did not make him a political radical. Alarmed by threatened unrest in the new Irish Army which produced a near-mutiny in 1924, he was also entering discussions with like-minded people about the need for a new conservative Irish Party—which was privately described as a 'Unionist' party. What Yeats meant by this is not entirely clear, but it seems that he was interested in the status which he thought Ireland enjoyed in the late eighteenth century, with its own parliament and autonomy, and with the English monarch king of Ireland too—rather than a federated association within the Commonwealth. He clearly did not realise the extent to which the late eighteenth-century arrangements reserved vital executive powers over Ireland to the British government of the day, but he was not alone in this. And it seems equally clear that this in turn was associated with his ideas about political authority, and where it should properly reside. It is incorrect to label these ideas as 'totalitarian', because Yeats was preoccupied with the free development of the creative individual—and, indeed, with the necessity of a leisured and cultured class. But his political ideas certainly tended towards the oligarchic, and increasingly—in the Irish context—to the idea of inherited authority as epitomised by the Ascendancy class of the pre-Union period, whom he idealised to an almost ludicrous level, revolving around his (highly partial) reading of Swift, Berkeley and Burke.

This is hardly new, but perhaps these inclinations have not been sufficiently mapped against his quarrels with the Catholic *demos* in the 1920s. (Nor have his subversive sexually frank 'Crazy Jane' lyrics been sufficiently related to the political and moral conflicts raging when he wrote them.) His ideas about aesthetic models for the new Irish state in the 1920s owe much to current European examples, such as the architecture of the Stockholm City Hall. His scheme for an Irish Academy of Letters, to recognize writers and bind them together into a body that would set standards and preserve intellectual independence, was much influenced by the French Academy. I believe that several of his most apparently visionary or cerebral poems of the late 1920s are firmly rooted in the socio-political arguments of the day—'Among School Children', for instance, is deeply infused with his readings in Italian educational treatises, the philosophy of Croce and Gentile, and his preoccupation with ensuring the free creative development of the individual in the increasingly repressive atmosphere of the Irish Free State. And 'In Memory of Eva Gore-Booth and Con Markiewicz' stands for far more than an elegy to lost youth: I read it as another instalment in the great fantasy of Ascendancy culture, which he had begun in poems like 'The Tower' and 'Blood and the Moon'. Moreover, I think that he is placing himself, with his ascendancy ancestors, against the levelling wind epitomised—now—by these two radical Anglo-Irishwomen.

Yeats wrote this marvellous poem in 1927, after hearing that Constance Markiewicz, his old friend and adversary, had died in the public ward of a poor Dublin hospital, worn out by years of frantic campaigning for republicanism and socialism; her sister Eva, also a committed radical, had died a year before. Like his earlier poem about Markiewicz, Yeats kept it unpublished for two years; but he eventually placed it first in his great 1933 collection, *The Winding Stair*, so it strikes the keynote for that collection. In fact, it is far more than an elegy for lost friends of his youth: it is an interrogation of the Irish propensity to hatred. It doesn't begin like that, but with a lovely evocation of a double portrait, like a painting by Sargent or Lavery.

> The light of evening, Lissadell,
> Great windows open to the south.
> Two girls in silk kimonos, both
> Beautiful, one a gazelle.
> But a raving autumn shears
> Blossom from the summer's wreath;
> The older is condemned to death.
> Pardoned, drags out lonely years
> Conspiring among the ignorant.

I know not what the younger dreams—
Some vague Utopia—and she seems.
When withered old and skeleton-gaunt.
An image of such politics.
Many a time I think to seek
One or the other out and speak
Of that old Georgian mansion, mix
Pictures of the mind, recall
That table and the talk of youth.
Two girls in silk kimonos, both
Beautiful, one a gazelle.

The beauty of the sisters is clearly sacrificed to their opinions as much as to the passing of years. And the second stanza takes this further, opening with a compassionate but despairing invocation to the ghosts of the dead girls, and ending with an enduringly mysterious image, which demands examination.

II

Dear shadows, now you know it all.
All the folly of a fight
With a common wrong or right.
The innocent and the beautiful
Have no enemy but time;
Arise and bid me strike a match
And strike another till time catch;
Should the conflagration climb.
Run till all the sages know.
We the great gazebo built.
They convicted us of guilt;
Bid me strike a match and blow.

October 1927 (VP 475–76)

If the poem simply expressed his wish to burn away the years and restore the girls to the innocence and beauty of their youth, it would be clear enough. But note the last couplet. It is possible to read the 'we' as uniting Yeats and the two sisters in the dreams of their youth, building a 'great gazebo' of hopes; while 'they' are faceless critics, modern Irish philistines, so-called sages. However, I think it means something different. A first draft, cancelled, reads 'I the great gazebo built | They brought home to me the guilt'.[13] The Georgian image of a 'great gazebo' suggests the fragile achievement of the eighteenth-century Irish ascendancy which Yeats now took as his own inheritance, and compared modern Ireland with, to the latter's detriment. So I think the 'we' in this couplet, the builders of the gazebo, are Yeats and his Ascendancy ancestors; while 'they' are the rebel girls themselves, who denounced the Anglo-Irish world whence they came. It is, therefore, another statement aligning himself with the forces of reaction against revolution. The abstract bitterness he had identified in his earlier poem, 'On a Political Prisoner', was now taken further. And I could quote, too, a letter he wrote to Olivia Shakespear at this time. 'In England you have never met the hatred that is a commonplace here. It lays hold upon our class, I think, more easily than upon the mass of the people—it finds a more complicated & determined conscience to prey upon'.[14] I think Constance Markiewicz was in his mind here: the nationalist and socialist hero whom he now placed among the phantoms of hatred, the innumerable harpies with their clanging wings, who haunt the last stanzas of 'Meditations in Time of Civil War'. If this is so, it is a distinctly uncomfortable thought, which would grow in his mind, and in his work—along with his preoccupation with the hatreds arising in contemporary Europe.

From 1930, his political ideas took a more aggressive direction. The long and polemical Introduction to his play *The Words Upon the Window Pane* is, I think, a barely-coded reply to a book by Daniel Corkery, *Synge and Anglo-Irish Literature*,[15] which had denied the claims of people from Yeats's background to represent any kind of Irish culture. Yeats responded further to what he privately called

---

[13]   W. B. Yeats, *The Winding Stair (1929) Manuscript Materials*, ed. David R. Clark (Ithaca and London: Cornell University Press, 1995), 7. See also my *Vivid Faces: The Revolutionary Generation in Ireland 1890–1923* (London: Allen Lane, Penguin Books, 2014), 314.

[14]   *CL InteLex* 5023, 7 September [1927], partly quoted in *L* 728.

[15]   Cork: Cork University Press, 1931.

'Corkery's troop' in a striking essay on 'Ireland 1921–1931', and his lecture on 'Modern Ireland' to American audiences in 1932. These pursue the same theme of glorifying the Irish Georgian Ascendancy. That eighteenth-century civilization, resting firmly on privilege and exclusion though it did, was linked in his mind to successive rises and falls of other civilizations through historical cycles; it also at its Swiftian best stood out against the naive and sentimental liberal democracy which Yeats now identified as the enemy (often under the name 'Whiggery'). He saw this as quintessentially English, and his ideas about Ireland's place in the European tradition now took a new turn. Ireland must, as ever, look to Europe, not to England. Georgian Dublin equalled Renaissance Urbino, in valuing style, intellect and aristocratic authority. This assertion makes no sense historically, and it aroused furious reactions in the Irish press, but it was one of Yeats's sustaining and inspirational inventions.

His idealization of Italy accompanied and influenced his idealization of Georgian Ireland. He had been wintering in Rapallo in the late 1920s, where his chief companion was Ezra Pound: the connection to fascism might seem easily made. But it is clear that Yeats neither shared Pound's political opinions nor took them very seriously. Nor, apparently, did he take much interest in what was happening in Italy around him, as poets like Montale found when they came on pilgrimages to him. There was a lack of communication not only because of the language difficulty, but also because of Yeats's ability to construct his own historical reality and determinedly inhabit it.

It was also wonderfully at odds with the ruling ideas of the new Irish Free State. And when Eamon de Valera, the republican irreconcilable, returned to constitutional politics and was elected to power in 1932, Yeats's political position became more embattled. De Valera was determined to complete Ireland's withdrawal from the Commonwealth; though Yeats was actually involved in some of the fruitless negotiations with the British government behind the scenes, there was much about de Valera's project that seemed to threaten all he held dear. From 1933 he was lending cautious support to the developing 'Blueshirt' party, which looked like becoming an Irish variant of fascism. The Blueshirt movement quickly mustered 30,000 followers; they took an aggressive and paramilitary stance, calling for the overthrow of elections and the 'assertion of the national will'; their rhetoric would eventually become both xenophobic and anti-Semitic. This happened at a point when Yeats had severed his connection with them. But his unpublished correspondence shows that he was closely in touch with early supporters of the movement like Desmond Fitzgerald, Ernest Blythe and Dermott MacManus. After writing some obscure and banal 'marching Songs' for them, he quickly dissociated himself. This was largely, I believe, because their kind of politics rapidly tended towards clericalism and Catholic *revanche*, as well as cultivated a support base of disgruntled famers, impoverished by de Valera's policy of economic war with England. Yeats rather approved of de Valera's ideas on this issue, and was personally impressed by de Valera himself.[16] On the other hand the Blueshirts and their leader, General O'Duffy, were now conjuring up the sort of demotic politics he had long ago set himself against.[17]

But in the first stages of their evolution, he had philosophical discussions with some of their political backers, and his unpublished letters and private notebooks show that he had a rather idiosyncratic view of the evolution of fascism as a right-wing descendant of Hegelianism (Communism being its left-wing cousin), which ensured the free development of the individual and the safeguarding of the cultured classes, unlike Communism, which stood for the elimination of those very social phenomena. He told Thomas MacGreevy that Mussolini 'represented the rise of the individual man as against what he considered the anti-human party machine', which seems to get it exactly the wrong way around. And at the height of his Blueshirt interest, he wrote in a notebook: 'What I think most important is to preserve the dynamic element of fascism, the clear picture of something to be worked for. We have to take

---

[16] See *Life 2*, 470–71.
[17] For a detailed treatment see my essay 'Our Chosen Colour is Blue', *Dublin Review* 11 (Summer 2003), 83–106.

everything we legitimately can from our opponents. Perhaps even more from communism than fascism has taken. Fascism is perhaps as much entangled with right-hand Hegelianism as communism is'. Significantly, these reflections were written at a time when he was rewriting *A Vision*, and contemplating the rise and fall of world systems through historical cycles. His personal encounters with General O'Duffy were hilariously unsuccessful; the General simply did not know what Yeats was talking about, and he never became the movement's D'Annunzio. Yeats recorded one meeting:

If the IRA attempt to seize power (& MacManus believes they will but I do not) or if the economic war brings chaos, then democratic politics will be discredited in this country & a substitute will have to be found. Talk was on the usual lines: the organized party directed from above, each district dominated by its ablest men, my own principle That every government is a tyranny but by the government of the educated classes & that the state must be hierarchical throughout'. De Valera has described himself to somebody as the autocrat expressing the feeling of the masses. If we must have an autocrat let him express what Swift called 'the bent & current of a people', not a momentary majority. I urged the getting of a recent 3-volume description of the Italian system (FitzGerald talks of it) & putting some Italian scholars to make a condensation of it. I urged also that unless a revolutionary crisis rose they must make no intervention. They should prepare themselves by study to act without hesitation should the crisis arise. Then, & then only, their full programme. I talked the 'historical dialectic', spoke of it as moving itself by events as the curvature of space was proved (after mathematics had it worked out) by observation during an eclipse (NLI, MS 30,280).

This probably confused O'Duffy sufficiently, but it is clarified by further notes made by Yeats, which emphasise his belief that in a new European order 'the family and the individual' must be given priority above governments, that creative individuals and their families deserve privilege in order to create culture and educate their children properly, and that 'structure and tradition' must be preserved. This is not much different from the oligarchic and aristocratic ideals he had been drawn to all his life, and discovered in his idea of courtly Italian culture when he first visited the country in 1907. It has very little to do with what Mussolini stood for by 1933. As MacManus later said, 'Yeats was not a fascist, but he was an authoritarian'.[18]

Why then did he write 'Marching Songs' for the movement, starting in November 1933, when it was already clear that the organisation was far from his own political principles? There is one extremely utilitarian reason: since Augusta Gregory's death in May 1932 he had written hardly any poetry, and was determined to galvanize his inspiration by any form of excitement possible. One of the very few poems he wrote was, significantly, the first part of 'Parnell's Funeral'.

He was also under some pressure from Ernest Blythe, in whose papers some drafts of the 'Marching Songs' have surfaced.[19] Yeats's efforts are a response, in fact, to a campaign to find a new 'National Song', which the Blueshirts tried to commandeer. They are set to the Irish tune. 'O'Donnell Abu', a lilting rhythm which is very hard to fit, and they are at once strident, obscure and bathetic.

> *Those fanatics all that we do would undo;*
> *Down the fanatic, down the clown;*
> *Down, down, hammer them down,*
> *Down to the tune of O'Donnell Abu. (VP 544)*

Yeats knew as much, rewriting them over and over again, and progressively disclaiming the apparent political intention behind them. Lines such as 'What's equality?—Muck in the yard', for instance, rapidly become 'Troy looked on Helen, it died and adored' (*VP* 547vv.). When he printed them, it was with a long explanatory note 'offer[ing]... these trivial songs and what remains of life' to any 'government or party' which would meet his conditions whilst being sure that 'no such government or party [exists] today', and so effectively withdrawing from the contemporary political upheavals.[20] Eventually he accompanied the 'Three Songs to the Same Tune'

[18]   Dermott MacManus, 'Notes for the Radio', W. R. Rogers Collection, HRHRC. See also *Life 2*, 475 and 744, n. 26.

[19]   First published in *The Spectator*, 23 February 1934 as 'Three Songs to the Same Tune' and first collected in *The King of the Great Clock Tower, Commentaries and Poems* (Dublin: Cuala, 1934), 30–38: see *VP* 543–49.

[20]   *Ibid.*, 37–38.

with an ironic squib, first called 'A Vain Hope', and then 'Church and State'.[21]

> Here is fresh matter, poet,
> Matter for old age meet;
> Might of the Church and the State,
> Their mobs put under their feet.
> O but heart's wine shall run pure,
> Mind's bread grow sweet.
>
> That were a cowardly song,
> Wander in dreams no more;
> What if the Church and the State
> Are the mob that howls at the door!
> Wine shall run thick to the end,
> Bread taste sour.

August 1934 (VP 553–54)

By then he had also added a coda, 'Forty Years Later', to his great political poem, 'Parnell's Funeral', which (first published in 1932) brought together many of the classical myths and themes which had dominated his imagination since Parnell's death in 1891. It also crystallized his disillusionment with Irish politics.

> The rest I pass, one sentence I unsay.
> Had de Valera eaten Parnell's heart
> No loose-lipped demagogue had won the day,
> No civil rancour torn the land apart.
>
> Had Cosgrave eaten Parnell's heart, the land's
> Imagination had been satisfied.
> Or lacking that, government in such hands,
> O'Higgins its sole statesman had not died.
>
> Had even O'Duffy—but I name no more—
> Their school a crowd, his master solitude;
> Through Jonathan Swift's dark grove he passed, and there
> Plucked bitter wisdom that enriched his blood. (*VP* 542–43)

---

[21] *Ibid.*, 34–38; see *VP* 553–54; 835–37.

This 'Coda' shows that, seen in the light of Parnell's aristocratic star, de Valera was a demagogue, and other politicians earthbound and uninspiring. True leadership inhabited the world illuminated by Fraser's *Golden Bough* and Dante's *Inferno*. Swift's brilliance of intellect was what should rule a nation, but never would. It might still be said that Yeats's disillusionment with the Blueshirts arose not from the fact that they became fascist, but that their commitment to fascism as he understood it did not go far enough. But one must then add at once that his understanding of fascism was not like anybody else's.[22] We are back with the convulsions he had expected in the early 1890s, when 1891 ushered in a new 'phase'.

But his fascination with European politics remained, and many of his late poems—such as 'Lapis Lazuli', with its references to fleeing refugees and the collapse of elite civilizations, and 'The Statues', where the Irish appear as Europeans playing their part in a predestined drama of cultural history—reflect it

> When Pearse summoned Cuchulain to his side,
> What stalked through the Post Office? What intellect,
> What calculation, number, measurement replied?
> We Irish, born into that ancient sect
> But thrown upon the filthy modern tide
> And by its formless spawning fury wrecked,
> Climb to our proper dark, that we may trace
> The lineaments of a plummet-measured face. (*VP* 611)

He is certainly looking towards the aesthetic idioms of classical European civilization as traditions which the new Irish may claim; but 'The Statues' also disturbingly evokes violence, totalitarianism and eugenics, while the anti-British politics of 'The Ghost of Roger Casement' indicate some pleasure in Germany's re-arming challenge to British military power in the late 1930s. How ominous is this?

Yeats's private writings and letters indicate his interest in the political aspects of fascism petered out—and he cannot be convicted

---

[22] For a more detailed treatment of Yeats and right-wing politics at this time see my essay 'Fascism', in David Holdeman and Ben Levitas (eds.), *W. B. Yeats in Context* (Cambridge: Cambridge University Press, 2010), 213–26.

either of support for the Third Reich, nor of anti-Semitism. His acceptance of the *Goethe-Plakette* from the Municipal Council of Frankfurt, when it had come under National Socialist domination, has been shown to have had no conscious political motivation; it was specifically for a performance of his ancient play *The Countess Cathleen*, and in any case the Nazi state subsequently banned Yeats's work as 'depressive art'.[23] But Yeats's late writing, reading and correspondence shows that he was—like many intellectuals of both Right and Left— increasingly preoccupied by eugenics, and what he conceived as the decline of the cultured classes through the unrestricted breeding of the proletariat. In fact, he used his belief in eugenic control to argue against some of the social policies of Fascist Italy and Nazi Germany. His very last political manifesto, published as *On the Boiler*, makes this stark—so do some of his most challenging late poems, such as 'The Statues', 'A Bronze Head' and 'Under Ben Bulben'. His play *Purgatory* suggests, perhaps, that independent Ireland itself is the result of a mésalliance and a misbegotten birth, and that old patterns of hatred will be eternally repeated until social and political authority returns to its proper possessors. The 'great gazebo' starts to look like a very exclusive enclosure indeed.

And yet Yeats in his latter days, even as a 'smiling public man', should be remembered as the defender of important liberties in independent Ireland, as a consistent advocate of artistic and intellectual freedom, and as a sometimes unconscious voice raised in defence of tolerance and inclusivity. On some artistic levels, he had liberated himself just as his country ostensibly underwent the same process. His poems from the mid-thirties interrogate old age, the roots of inspiration, the artistic process, and the gnawing dissatisfactions of sex. Perhaps the greatest of them—'Long-legged Fly', 'The Circus Animals' Desertion'—concern themselves with the individual impulse of creativity, rather than any collective theorizing. In its first draft the last stanza of 'The Circus Animals' Desertion' was a bombastic declaration about war, asserting that cannon

---

[23] On this incident see K. P. S. Jochum, 'Yeats and the *Goethe-Plakette*: An Unpublished Letter and Its Context', in *YA15 Yeats's Collaborations*, 281–87.

and thunder were the gods of mankind. If it had been left like that, it would be seen to reflect his thoughts on the contemporary Spanish Civil War, the Italian adventure in Abyssinia, and German rearmament. But Yeats rejected it, and wrote, very late in his life, the substitute ending which we know, bringing artistic inspiration and creativity back to the troubled self:

> Those masterful images because complete
> Grew in pure mind but out of what began?
> A mound of refuse or the sweepings of a street,
> Old kettles, old bottles, and a broken can,
> Old iron, old bones, that raving slut
> Who keeps the till. Now that my ladder's gone,
> I must lie down where all the ladders start,
> In the foul rag and bone shop of the heart. (*VP* 630)

Literally on his deathbed, he wrote a play and a series of poems which return to his very earliest inspirations of Gaelic legend as retold by Standish O'Grady. This had been the seedbed of his early nationalism, but now he plays it against the inadequacies of the new Irish order. His very last poem, was 'The Black Tower'. It can be traced back to a story and play by Standish O'Grady which Yeats had first encountered in the early 1890s; it portrays a band of disaffected warriors hiding out in a ruined fortress, awaiting the return of a deliverer.[24] Yeats's wife, very pertinently, described it as a political poem.

Yet that is not the full story either. Biographers always find a salient piece of evidence just after their book has gone to press, and I am no exception. A short while ago I went to Cambridge to look at some papers in Churchill College and found there the diary of Yeats's friend Edith Lyttelton, kept while she was visiting newly-independent Ireland in 1922. She was struck by the intensity of antagonism there, and wrote in a private notebook:

I have often thought of a thing W. B. Yeats said to me many years ago. I was asking how it was that he no longer went in for Revolution, nor drove about

[24] See Patrick Diskin, 'O'Grady's *Finn and his Companions*: A Source for Yeats's "The Black Tower"', *Notes & Queries* (March 1961), 107–08; *NC* 409.

in crepe when any big moment came to England, as he did in the streets of Dublin at Queen Victoria's Jubilee. (This last was a silent question.) He said 'I have learned to know that nothing great comes out of hatred and bitterness'.[25]

Thus he contradicted the message of 'Ancestral Houses', which I quoted earlier. The tension of this contradiction is sustained through Yeats's life and work, and gives it much of its power; and it is a tension which reflects his own social and political position, balanced between two worlds, the old and the new: the Ireland he had known under the Union, and the Ireland that had the potential to be a new European country. It is also true that this could take on a disturbingly reactionary colour. But I would like to suggest that Yeats's troubled and troubling reaction to the modern Irish world should be more closely historicized; and that it represents a pattern of response as well as challenge. Yeats, as his wife once remarked, had an extraordinary sense of how things would look to people afterwards; he spent much of his life constructing exactly how posterity should see things. Even the originally conceived contents of his last book of poems, beginning, not ending, with 'Under Ben Bulben', were to convey the sense that he was speaking from beyond the grave. And he was highly conscious, in his last decade, that the 'ceremony of innocence' was being well and truly drowned, and would be carried away in an apocalyptic flood of violence—which he dreaded.

One reason for Yeats's continuing resonance, celebrated in this series of lectures, is that he wrote at the intersection of literature and politics—which in Ireland can mean, as Conor Cruise O'Brien has said, a 'bloody crossroads'. Yeats made the territory all the more sensitive by thinking aloud on all the forbidden subjects: sex, religion, class, politics. After spending seventeen years writing his biography I remain astonished at his enduring relevance, his refusal to be taken for granted, and his superb disinclination to provide comfortable reassurance. Early in his career he had remarked that the old Irish 'did not weigh and measure their hatred' but focused hatred into a pure idea; 'and from this idealism', he added, 'comes, as I think, a

[25] Chandos Papers, Churchill College, CHAN 1 6/4.

certain power of saying and forgetting things, especially a power of saying and forgetting things in politics, which others do not say or forget'.[26] It is easy to be discomfited by a great deal of what Yeats says; and almost impossible to forget it.

[26] *E&I* 181; the reflection comes from 'The Celtic Element in Literature', first published in 1897.

http://dx.doi.org/10.11647/OBP.0081.04

Yeats the Love Poet

Bernard O'Donoghue

I COULD NOT IMAGINE a greater honour than to be standing here today[1] in this capacity, in University College Cork's great Boole library, for a multitude of reasons. The small-time prophet is being honoured in his own kingdom; I come from North Cork, from the edge of Sliabh Luachra, the territory of the great poets in Irish. But Cork city, with UCC where my sisters studied English and Irish at its cultural heart, was the height of our aspirations. Secondly, there is the Yeats connexion: I don't have to look far in the audience here to see several people who know a lot more about Yeats than I do, so I am setting out with some trepidation. Thirdly, it is wonderful to be here under the aegis of Eamonn Cantwell's great collection of Yeats in the library here. Nothing of course could be more appropriate to Yeats, with his yearning for patronage on the scale of Renaissance Tuscany, than that magnificent bequest. We are, all of us here, privileged to be linked with it in any way.

My topic is further self-indulgence. I first read Yeats when I was at Presentation College on the Western Road in 1962, learning English

---

[1] This third lecture in the series was delivered on 18 March 2005. Further information may have been gathered since this article was prepared for publication. If you would like to find out if any further information has been discovered that may help your own research, why not write to the author at bernard.odonoghue@ wadh.ox.ac.uk? Quite apart from anything else, feedback is always welcomed.

and Irish from the incomparable Dan Donovan. In fact, I had come
to Pres to do the new Maths—as we called Calculus then—from the
equally incomparable Freddie Holland (later of course poached by
UCC), but I was won away, permanently as it turned out, by Dan's
wonderful readings of English and Irish poetry and plays. And Yeats
was at the centre of all that, particularly as we listened on the new LP
record-player in Miss Cahill's flat in Donovan's Road (now of course
a department of UCC) to Cyril Cusack's wonderfully heart-breaking
reading of the love poems (There is grey in your hair!) on that ancient
Caedmon record. So here I am today, forty years on.

Yeats said himself that the occult was the great concern of his life
and work, only sharing centrality on some occasions with Ireland.
Certainly both of those things had immense significance in Yeats's
poetry; they are the things that have had the principal emphasis in
the two volumes of Roy Foster's majestic biography of the poet, the
first especially prominent in the title of the first of those volumes *The
Apprentice Mage*. But the surprising absentee from this statement of
priorities is love: Yeats, in particular as the lover of Maud Gonne,
documented the great unrequited poetic obsession of the century—
maybe the most intense in English since the Renaissance. We might
be tempted to think that that somehow goes without saying: that love
is a classic subject of poetry, like birds and religion. But what I hope to
show here is that Yeats is a very particular kind of love-poet—almost
unique in the language, and certainly unique in his time. Maybe it is
significant that most of the best recent discussions of Yeats and love
(pre-eminently Elizabeth Butler Cullingford's *Gender and History in
Yeats's Love-Poetry*[2]) have been concerned with something other than
love, or at least something as well as love, as in Butler Cullingford's
title. This mixedness in treating love is typical of the characterization
of Yeats, and it is very surprising when you think about it. A very
attractive selection of the love poetry was edited by A. N. Jeffares in
1990, *W. B. Yeats: the Love Poems*; but that book too has all kinds of
material in it, from 'A Prayer for my Daughter' to 'Coole and Ballylee

---

[2] Elizabeth Butler Cullingford, *Gender and History in Yeats's Love Poetry*
(Cambridge: Cambridge University Press, 1993). Hereafter 'Cullingford'.

1931', in praise of Lady Gregory. I think this is surprising because it does not make clear how concentrated on the role of lover, and its object, Yeats was. He is consciously setting himself up as a medieval courtly—love poet—that is the model of behaviour and sentiment he is following. In addition, he brings something quite different to that tradition by particularizing the object of that love. Maud Gonne is Yeats's *donna*, his *innamorata*; but she is also Maud Gonne—a woman who is big and beautiful but with unbeautiful small hands. I will touch more than once on the perfect poem that celebrates this imperfection, 'Broken Dreams'.

There is another way in which love has become oddly marginalized in the discussion of Yeats. A great deal of attention, and admiration, has been given to Yeats's harsh, late quatrain 'The Spur', addressed to Dorothy Wellesley:

> You think it horrible that lust and rage
> Should dance attendance upon my old age.
> They were not such a plague when I was young.
> What else have I to spur me into song? (*VP* 355)

There is indeed a grandeur about this survival of lasciviousness into old age. And ours is an age that has a lot of time and energy for lust, which maybe explains why this wild old wicked man' (to call him nothing worse) has tended to usurp the amorous area in Yeats. For most of his life, that was not his specialism.

So what exactly is love as Yeats specializes in it? Well, everyone knows about Yeats and Maud Gonne: that his unrequited love for her was the inspiration for many of his best-loved poems, and indeed for many of his best poems. In this respect he is the classic modern version of a long-established persona: the unrequited lover has had a long innings in literary popularity. From the troubadours to the present day this lovelorn and ineffectual figure has been a dominant presence in all literatures: not only in poetry, prominent as he is there (it is 'he' almost by definition, at least until the reversal of the myth by writers like Fay Weldon late in the twentieth century); there are also central texts of fiction like Flaubert's *Sentimental Education* and, with a questioning feminine nuance, *Madame Bovary*, and the heart-wrung novels of Turgenev. So Yeats's infatuation with what Thomas Hardy called *The Well-Beloved* is part of a long tradition.

It is indeed such a familiar phenomenon that it is often felt to need no explaining at all, or even remarking. Everybody falls in love. And there is a tendency for them to fall in love with the unattainable. Yet, over the past century or so, love has increasingly been felt to need scrutiny and explanation. It is a very unsatisfactory state of affairs after all. The arranged marriage works a lot better; the wife brings in her dowry to help finance the business, or the returning emigrant funds the woman's farm, in a successful economic organization. So why set out to find an object of love that is neither attainable nor, often, economically viable? I will deal later on with the view that this offering of a psychologically fulfilling alternative to more viable social arrangements was precisely what 'courtly love', so called, is: it is individual 'passion', or in more modern terms 'desire', which works against the socio-economic structures of a good political order.

It is particularly strange, given that this sounds like a matter of what we call common sense, that this familiar, unsatisfactory order of things has generally been believed to have a clear name and a definable point of origin. It is 'Courtly Love'; and, as C. S. Lewis said in 1936, 'everybody knows that it appeared quite suddenly in the eleventh century in Provence'.[3] Up to then, it is suggested, people selected sexual partners on more practical grounds, or at least they stuck with the partners that their society deemed appropriate for them. But the Provençal troubadours of the twelfth century were not sensible about this, and we are told they made the absence of sense the literary fashion in love for all subsequent eras and places in the western world.

Whether or not the pain of love (and it is always recognized that, as a subject if not as an experience, *liebesleid* has more power than *liebesfreud*) was an invention of twelfth-century Provence, there is no doubt that Yeats was a major exponent, or sufferer from it. He was so in a quite explicit and conscious way. He asks in 'The Tower' 'Does the imagination dwell the most | Upon a woman won or woman lost?' The answer is so obvious that the addressee, 'impatient to be gone',

---

[3]   C. S. Lewis, *The Allegory of Love* (London: Oxford University Press 1936), 2.

doesn't deign to state it (*VP* 413). Everyone knows that love lost is the more compelling. Yeats says it over and over again: the child dancing in the wind is a figure of innocence because she has not yet known love lost as soon as won' or 'the fool's triumph' (*VP* 312). According to the traditional account, Maud Gonne herself recognized that unrequited love was good material for the poet: better than requited love with the woman won. Thus (still according to the traditional account) she responded to his proposal in 1902—thirteen years after the 'troubling of [his] life began' in meeting her—by saying

'You make beautiful poetry out of what you call your unhappiness and you are happy in that. Marriage would be such a dull affair. Poets should never marry' (*SQ* 326–30).

The same view was expressed more coarsely by John Berryman:

If Miss Gonne had called Willie's bluff and gone to bed with him, she wouldn't have filled his days with misery. No misery, no poems. You can bet your life that what Yeats was after was *poems*.[4]

(As a matter of fact we now know that this might not have been literally true; it seems she did sleep with him, but this did not stop him from carefully nurturing the 'misery' as poetic inspiration.)

In any case, fairly recently this traditional interpretation of Yeats and Gonne—at least as far as his wish for love with her to be sexually consummated goes—has been persuasively contested (or refined on) by Deirdre Toomey in her 1992 essay 'Labyrinths'.[5] Toomey argues that Yeats's requirement that Maud Gonne should remain unrequiting and an unattainable dream was quite literally enforced by him, and whenever she showed any inclination to marry him (in 1898 she practically proposed to him, according to Toomey), it was Yeats who backed off and reinstalled her as the unattainable. This is what Gonne was acknowledging in her observation in 1902: that he was happy in making his beautiful poetry out of their spiritual union.

---

[4]   John Berryman quoted in Eileen Simpson, *Poets in their Youth* (London: Faber & Faber, 1982), 156.
[5]   Reprinted in Deirdre Toomey, *Yeats and Women* (Basingstoke: Macmillan, 1990), 1–40.

And as far as courtly love and the unattainable goes as inspiration, it doesn't make any difference who initiates the unattainability; the whole point is that it should be poetically productive. Indeed, part of what I will argue later on is that the Toomey view makes the Yeats-Gonne relations all the more classically courtly—*courtois*—according to the medieval definition of love. Petrarch hardly knew Laura; Dante was, it seems, relatively happily married to Gemma Donati; his transcendentalizing love Beatrice was married to a Venetian burgher until she died young, thereby making herself ready to encounter Dante when he visited Paradise. The role that the courtly love *donna* or *innamorata* or lady was required to fulfil was not sexual compliance but quite the opposite. I don't imagine Beatrice or Laura ever set out to tempt their great poets sexually, in the way Toomey suggests that Maud Gonne, at least once, did. But it is beyond question that they would have been stepping out of line if they had. Yeats had to respond decisively to ensure that Maud Gonne remained the cold inaccessible muse rather than the initiator of sexual love which was not at all the role of the 'lady' in courtly love. C. S. Lewis said with great severity that one of its prerequisites was 'adultery' (though this is not exactly true either).[6]

However, the situation described by Toomey is not only a well-attested one (she links it to Gonne's 'strangeness':[7] that is a word which might repay further scrutiny), but the apparently inconvenient circumstances she describes are precisely what were demanded in the case of the medieval faithful lover. One of the most famous (and now controversial) accounts of courtly love was a book written in French in 1939 by Denis de Rougemont called *L'Amour et L'Occident*: literally 'Love and the West', but translated the following year into English as *Passion and Society*.[8] What de Rougemont argues—and it is historically well-based—is that love-poetry of the kind that swept through Europe in the high Middle Ages was a Middle Eastern convention, written in Arabic and taken through Spain by Arabic

---

[6] Lewis, *ibid.*
[7] Toomey's argument here is based upon Yeats's 'Against Unworthy Praise': 'The labyrinth of her days | That her own strangeness perplexed' (*VP* 259–60): see Toomey, 18–19.
[8] London: Faber & Faber, 1940, translated by Montgomery Belgion.

scholars in the eleventh and twelfth centuries. This was the route by which the 'Love' of his title reached the West' of his title. His most interesting contention was that it was a view of love which did not suit the West and led to a permanent conflict at the core of western culture. The title of the English translation was designed to make this conflict between passion and society more explicit: Middle-Eastern love was informed by a passion which was inimical to the good operation of society. Society is made up of 'little boxes', as Pete Seeger put it, and the most indispensable arrangement of these is the nuclear family: mother, father and children who will go on to repeat the structure for ever, constructing a perfect history for the species.[9] Unfortunately, people are built with a genetic flaw, recognized and institutionalised by Courtly Love. The courtly lover, like Dante, Petrarch and the rest, was a happily married individual with children; but there was something in his nature—passion, desire or whatever we call it—that he also felt the need to respond to. It is precisely the fact that the good order of society requires that this illicit, extramarital impulse must not be entertained and hence requires rules forbidding the fulfilment of that impulse that causes a frustration which is expressed in poetry. John Donne, early in the seventeenth century says:-

> I am two fooles, I know,
> For loving, and for saying so
> In whining Poëtry.

The two things—love and poetry—go together. But Donne also says, in the same poem

> Grief brought to numbers cannot be so fierce,
> For he tames it that fetters it in verse.[10]

---

9 'Little Boxes' (1962) was composed by Malvina Reynolds. A political satire on suburbia, it became a hit for Pete Seeger in 1963.
10 'The Triple Foole', in John Donne, *Complete Poetry and Selected Prose*, ed. John Hayward (London: The Nonesuch Press, 1929, *YL* 530), 10. The last two quoted lines may be a source for Yeats's phrase in 'Shepherd and Goatherd', 'For rhyme may beat a measure out of trouble | And make the daylight sweet once more… (*VP* 339).

Expressing misery in poetic numbers somehow 'tames' it, making it
less painful.

What the followers of the troubadours progressively established
was that such illicit love, which was at once a natural instinct of
passion and doomed by social edict, was a fine thing, requiring
disinterestedness. There was no worldly reward for this passion; so
it became more and more high-minded and refined. The term used
was *fin amor*, as is often pointed out, the *fin* element is not related to
the word 'fine' but to 'faithful', *fidus*; this love required great fidelity
because it offered no rewards. In Joyce's *Portrait*, that most Dante-
like of modern young men, Stephen Dedalus calls it 'the spiritual-
heroic refrigerating apparatus, invented and patented in all countries
by Dante Alighieri'.[11] Dante didn't invent it, but he did patent it,
making it a central plank of European literature.

The second major consequence of this curious state of mind which
I will argue is important for Yeats follows logically enough from its
disinterestedness. Lack of interest in worldly reward is generally
accounted a Christian virtue. So courtly love becomes a kind of
heresy, another lack of interest in the practical, offering competition
as an alternative challenge to the orthodox moral arrangements which
were set up to serve society's interests and exalted monogamous
marriage. The lover makes a virtue out of his frustrations; by nursing
them, without physical outlet, he becomes more and more refined.
The object of his love, with whom he must not have sexual relations
on grounds of social utility, becomes in turn a fine and unattainable
ideal, a *Beatrice*, the blessing-conferrer. As expounded by Dante
and his friends, love of woman in this mode, because of its lack of
physical fulfilment and its attachment to the absent, transmutes into
love of God.

It might be objected that, if the literature of the courtly world
was so important for Yeats, we might expect to find it more fully
expounded by him. Yet his references to the figures of courtliness,

---

[11] James Joyce, *A Portrait of the Artist as a Young Man* (Harmondsworth: Penguin,
1960), 252.

and of medieval romance, are relatively few. The most obvious place to look is the beginning of section 5 of 'Dove or Swan', Book 5 of *A Vision*, dealing with A.D. 1050 onwards. Of course in a very evident way, the whole theme of 'Dove or Swan', Christian peace *versus* the harshness of artistic beauty, mirrors exactly the opposition between quiet-life orthodoxy and transgressive passion which courtly love centres on. It is striking, too, that the second edition of *A Vision* was being worked on, in the late 1930s, at the same time that De Rougemont was writing *Passion and Society* and a few years after Lewis wrote *The Allegory of Love*. Medievalism was in the air, especially the matter of courtly love. We might bear this in mind in reading this passage about *Parsifal*, the great thirteenth-century German epic of love and religion by Wolfram von Eschenbach. Yeats reminds us that

Throughout the German *Parsifal* there is no ceremony of the Church, neither Marriage nor Mass nor Baptism, but instead we discover that strangest creation of romance or of life, 'the love trance'.

Parsifal in such a trance, seeing nothing before his eyes but the image of his absent love, overcame knight after knight, and awakening at last looked amazed upon his dinted sword and shield; and it was to his lady and not to God or the Virgin that Parsifal prayed upon the day of battle, and it was his lady's soul, separated from her entranced or sleeping body, that went beside him and gave him victory (*AVB* 286–87).

A few paragraphs later Yeats is crediting Dante with writing 'the first sentence of modern autobiography' in the *Convito* (*AVB*, 289). But the Parsifal passage is highly revealing. Yeats's famous description of the first vision of Maud Gonne as 'the troubling of his life' is closely reminiscent of these moments of vision—the love-trance or love-potion—at the first encounter with the beloved. Dante called it his *Vita Nuova*, his 'new life'; Chaucer's Criseyde, intoxicated by her first sight of Troilus, exclaims 'who gave me drink?'

> Cryseyda gan al his chere aspien,
> And leet it so softe in hir herte sinke,
> That to hireself she seyde, `Who yaf me drinke?'

> For of hir owene thought she wex al reed,
> Remembrying hire right thus, `Lo, this is he
> Which that myn uncle swerith he moot be deed,
>
> But I on him have mercy and pitee';[12]

Who has given her a love-potion which acts with the irresistible potency that compels her to love, against all her economic interests and better instincts?—just as in the most famous love-story of all, Tristan and his Irish bride Iseult fatally drink the potion intended to tie Iseult and her husband King Mark together forever. The lives of Tristan and Iseult (like those of their literary relations Diarmuid and Grainne) are as a consequence both wrecked and exalted: the troubling of their lives indeed! It is one of the great literary conundrums: was it a blessing or a curse for Tristan and Iseult to have drunk the love-potion? Certainly it led to a grand Wagnerian passion and to a transcendent fidelity; but it led to their deaths at the end of a desperate career of subterfuge and flight from the social repercussions of their fated illicit love. We meet the dilemma again of course in the figures of Francesca da Rimini and Paolo in the fifth canto of Dante's *Inferno*. As punishment for their illicit love, the lovers are condemned to be never out of each other's sight for all eternity. But is this punishment or glory?

Yeats's other references and allusions to the major figures of courtly love are made with the passingness of what is casually well-known: thus one of his few references to Tristram (maybe the central figures) is thrown off in 1907 in the essay 'Poetry and Tradition': 'it is only before such things, before a love like that of Tristan and Iseult, before noble or ennobled death, that the free mind permits itself aught but brief sorrow' (*E&I* 252). Here we might note the early occurrence of the notion of tragic joy/tragic gaiety associated with the era of 'Lapis Lazuli' and the later poetry. This is important because, even though it is in the early poetry such as 'The Wanderings of Oisin' that the Medieval-Renaissance world of 'the old high way of love' (*VP* 206) is

---

[12] *Troilus and Criseyde* Book 2, 649–55, in F. N. Robinson (ed.), *The Works of Geoffrey Chaucer* (London: Oxford University Press, 2nd ed., 1957), 408.

explicitly evoked, many of the ideas mentioned there are embedded into Yeats's central concerns and are influential in the whole of his working life. The principal case I am arguing is that a framework of the grandeur and personal improvement effected by being in love is an assumption that underlies all Yeats's poetry, even where it is not spelled out. Moreover, it is not significant only in the poems of love; Yeats's whole conception of the poet is founded on the courtly social outlaw that emerged in the poetry schools of southern Europe in the Middle Ages and Renaissance. To summarise the relevant qualities: the poet-lover was in breach of official social edicts which were constructed for the good operation of society; he was a heretic, operating by an ethic which not only contradicted the Christian norms but was in competition with them for virtue; and above all he was a figure of refinement of sensibility. He was made more virtuous by love, as Chaucer says Troilus was. Yeats wanted to make all these three claims for himself as poet-lover.

I will conclude by arguing that the first of these—the political outcast—gradually extended into all Yeats's politics and forced him into positions of increasingly perverse individuality. Maud Gonne was the founding inspiration and troubler of his life; but the logic of his courtly love persona extended far beyond her: not only into other instances of the beautiful woman (notably Constance Gore-Booth/ Markiewicz) but into political realms which were not to do with love at all. Exactly the same thing happened with the medieval poets, where the love-troubadours who wrote their *cansos* of love extended their writing outwards into *sirventes*, poems of public comment.

Next though to return to where 'courtly love' and its world may be found explicitly in Yeats's writing: this is—as they say—a surprisingly neglected topic. There is only one book-length discussion of it, by Gloria C. Kline in 1983.[13] Kline begins by identifying Yeats's 'role-playing' as a 'poet in love'. In the best courtly tradition, Yeats fell in love, not with Maud Gonne 'whom he scarcely knew, but with his own projected *anima*, the "woman within himself"' (11). Kline develops

---

[13] Gloria C. Kline, *The Last Courtly Lover: Yeats and the Idea of Woman* (Ann Arbor: University of Michigan Press, 1983). Hereafter 'Kline'.

this Jungian view of Yeats—and it should be said that she does it
very well if you like that sort of thing. But her book is incidentally
useful for its enumeration of the courtly affinities in Yeats. As early as
'The Rose of Peace' in 1892, the archangel Michael looks down from
Heaven to acknowledge the glory of Yeats's beloved (Maud Gonne,
according to AE) and to 'weave a chaplet for her head'. Although it
is not exactly the same, we might recall that the end of the process
of refinement of the beloved in the courtly love process, according
to Dante and his friends, was 'Angelicization'. The idea was that the
Platonic, idealising lover was refined by the process of being in love;
his love transmutes and advances from love of woman to love of God.
The problem, from the twelfth century onwards, was what became of
the supplanted woman, the original object of the love and its material
cause. The solution, as I have said, was to exalt her dignity in parallel
with the increase in spiritual worth of the love she inspired. As the
love, and the lover, became more refined, the beloved became so
too, to the point where she was converted from a physical, sexual
entity into an angel: literally, according to medieval metaphysics.
(Incidentally, the controversial reputation of Maud Gonne might
also be linked to this: it is linked too perhaps to what Toomey calls
her 'strangeness'. The world at large has not been so ready to see her
as a Beatrice-figure as Yeats was, seeing indeed a marked disparity
between some of her views and actions, and the kind of claims Yeats
made for her. But that is a different topic.)

Nevertheless, the bearing of the general situation of the courtly
lover *vis-a-vis* the beloved on the relations and attitudes prevailing
between Yeats and Maud Gonne hardly needs elaboration. The most
obvious occurrence is in 'The Lover' poems of *The Wind Among
The Reeds* (1899). As is often remarked, this lover in earlier versions
had several personifications, as Aedh, Mongan and others. The
concentration into the generic term 'The Lover' or sometimes 'He',
referring back to 'the lover' as the antecedent in the title of previous
poems in the series, makes it clear that this is a classic love-sequence.
The best-loved of all these poems, 'He wishes for the Cloths of
Heaven', features an appeal to the beloved which could hardly be
more unphysical and idealising. He would like to offer the lady the
fabrics of which the night sky is composed, 'Enwrought with golden

and silver light', but being poor he hasn't anything as material even as the night sky. He has only his dreams to spread under her feet:

> Tread softly because you tread on my dreams. (*VP* 176)

The refining, idealising and unconsummating service (service is the word most commonly used) demanded of the courtly lover is certainly consistent with Toomey's revising view that, when Gonne made tentative attempts to reach out to Yeats sexually (such as taking the initiative in kissing him), she was not behaving according to the poetic stereotype that Yeats required her to follow. Of course we do not have to argue that this characterization of the inaccessible, ethereal beloved came straight from the Middle Ages to Yeats; there is a good deal of intervening poetry (the Elizabethan sonneteers, the metaphysical love-poets, and the nineteenth-century Romantics, not to mention Yeats's more immediate pre-Raphaelite and Beardsleyesque predecessors) that comes in between. Examples could be taken from almost anywhere; the whole point of the argument of books such as Lewis's *The Allegory of Love* is that the motif that we find so central in all love poetry—the pain of unrequited love— which we take to be a norm not only of writing but of experience, was in fact a creation of medieval poetics which became totally dominant: Lewis says with a characteristic sweeping gesture 'Compared with this revolution the Renaissance is a mere ripple on the surface of literature'.[14] We can link Bob Dylan's

> 'And only if my own true love were waiting'

to the theme of *amor de lonh*, love from afar, in the troubadours. Dylan's ending

> And only if she were lying by me
> And I in my bed once again,[15]

---

[14] Lewis, 4.
[15] "Tomorrow Is a Long Time", written by Bob Dylan in 1962 and first recorded by him in 1963, first appeared on the album *Bob Dylan's Greatest Hits Vol. II* (Columbia Records, 1971).

is almost identical to the end of the fervent sixteenth-century
'Westron Wynd':

> Christ! If my love were in my arms
> And I in my bed again.[16]

There is a perfect, brief example of the qualities and circumstances in
a poem from early in Yeats's writing life, in Housman's *A Shropshire
Lad* (1896):

> Oh, when I was in love with you,
> Then I was clean and brave,
> And miles around the wonder grew
> How well did I behave.
>
> And now the fancy passes by,
> And nothing will remain,
> And miles around they'll say that I
> Am quite myself again.[17]

(For the full effect you need to hear the beautiful song-version by
Ralph Vaughan Williams.[18]) Despite its apparent artlessness, this
captures the whole story of the refining power of love. The observing
world is astonished by the behaviour of the poet in love; but once he
falls back out of love (something of course you mustn't do in courtly
love), he is 'quite [him]self again'—the same old grouch he always
was.

Despite the universality of these instances, what I want to do for
the rest of the time today is to look at Yeats's love-poetry in the light
of medieval (and the derived Renaissance) precepts about love, and
to suggest that—for whatever psychological reason—Yeats observed
them, in the poems in particular but in prose and plays too, with far

---

[16] Frequently anthologized, but available in a modernized spelling version in e.g.,
Arthur Quiller-Couch's *The Oxford Book of English Verse* (Oxford: Clarendon,
1900 and later editions). There are two printings in *YL*, nos. 1653 and 2954,
where the poem is on p. 42 under the title 'The Lover in Winter Plaineth for the
Spring'.

[17] See *The Collected Poems of A. E. Housman* (London: Jonathan Cape, 1939, 1967),
24, 'A Shropshire Lad' n. 18.

[18] See https://www.youtube.com/watch?v=pwjUN0jfnIE

greater fidelity and explicitness, inspired perhaps by the ideas of the Pre-Raphaelite painters and poets of his father's milieu, than had been the case in European poetry since the Renaissance. There is a set of terms which was already developed as a technical vocabulary in the twelfth century that Yeats constantly returns to: words such as 'passion' and its derivatives (as famously noted by Conor Cruise O'Brien), 'trouble' and 'joy', and part of what I will do is to trace the way a few of these terms run through Yeats's love-poetry side-by-side with a terminology of his own. For a start it is clear from 'Adam's Curse' that Yeats like many of his pre-Raphaelite contemporaries thought of love as 'fine' or 'high' in this way:

> I said: 'It's certain there is no fine thing
> Since Adam's fall but needs much labouring.
> There have been lovers who thought love should be
> So much compounded of high courtesy
> That they would sigh and quote with learned looks
> Precedents out of beautiful old books;
> Yet now it seems an idle trade enough'. (*VP* 205)

What are learned looks'? And, a more obvious question, what are these 'beautiful old books? It is striking how closely the 'high courtesy' and the theorists of love follow on from the question of the 'fine thing'. Crucially too, what exactly does Yeats mean by the lightly thrown out last line? What exactly now seems 'an idle trade enough? Surely the implication is that love nowadays is not taken seriously enough. The argument seems to be that the ideals of 'high courtesy' ought to be revived as a 'fine thing'. 'Joy' is another term of *courtoisie* which repays scrutiny:

> The body calls it death,
> The heart remorse.
> But if these be right,
> What is Joy? (*VP* 500)

What is Joy?' was originally the title of the opening section of this poem Vacillation' (of which this is the end). 'Joy' doesn't sound like a very technical word in Yeats's time (though whole books have been written about its significance for the troubadours), and Yeats uses

it a great deal; from *The Wanderings of Oisin* to 'Vacillation', there
are sixty-six usages.[19] But the opposing of it here to remorse—the
appropriate Christian moral response to sin—is highly significant; in
the magnificent end of' 'A Dialogue of Self and Soul', Yeats declares
'When such as I cast out remorse... Everything we look upon is blest'
(*VP* 479). In the fourth poem of the 'Vacillation' series, the wonderful
mystical experience in a crowded London shop' culminates with a
priest-like sensation of power:

> It seemed, so great my happiness,
> That I was blessèd and could bless. (*VP* 501)

This is part of the extended answer to the question 'What is Joy?' It
is, as it was for the troubadours, an exalted—even religious—state of
mind which is the opposite of penitential remorse.

Yeats is clearly—and, as he might have put it, self-delightingly—
in the heretical world of courtly love here, where the state of mind
which, according to the priests, ought to be followed by remorse
is treated not only as a happiness but as a beatific (a Beatrice-like)
virtue. And I don't think we fully understand these references
if we don't see them in the poetic tradition they belong to. It has
sometimes been said to be a deficiency in the criticism of Yeats and
his contemporaries that biographical glossing and identification have
been treated as, so to speak, critical *solutions* to the issues raised in
poems. We don't need to go on reminding ourselves that the 'I' of the
poem is not just the writer: that as Sharon Olds famously put it: '"I"
is not I'. But an awareness of the tradition it is written in can stop us
looking, in solely biographical terms, at a poem like the 'The Lover
Mourns for the Loss of Love' (1898), the very title of which might
be seen as a reminder to move the identification of the lover into the
third person.[20]

> She looked in my heart one day
> And saw your image was there;
> She has gone weeping away. (*VP* 152)

---

[19] See Stephen Maxfield Parrish (ed.), and James Allan Painter (programmer), *A
Concordance to the Poems of W. B. Yeats* (Ithaca: Cornell, 1963), 414–15.
[20] First published as one of the 'Three Songs' grouped as 'Aodh to Dectora' in *The
Dome* May, 1898, the poem was retitled for the 1899 edition: see *VP* 152.

Certainly it does seem that your image' is Maud Gonne—Yeats's courtly lover—and the pale-browed, 'beautiful friend' is Olivia Shakespear, and it is useful to be told that. But we must not forget that we are in the world of Dante's *Vita Nuova* where the beautiful woman, often in a dream (and there is a dream in this poem), often goes 'weeping away'. And of course we know, from 'Ego Dominus Tuus' (which takes its title from Dante) and elsewhere that Dante's hugely influential work, compounded of poems, apparent biography and commentary, was a work of the first importance for Yeats and his Italophile predecessors. That is to say, Yeats—as Toomey implies— is organizing the whole turbulent and complicated cast of his love-drama according to well-established lines. As Conor Cruise O'Brien said in 1963, Yeats is the director of the drama, motivated by cunning (which by now we would see at least partly as the virtue of artistic control, operating in collaboration with 'passion', rather than only the socio-political irresponsibility that O'Brien represents it as).[21]

O'Brien's terms—passion and cunning—are highly significant and well chosen, to describe among other things Yeats's recklessly indulging and exalting his own individualizing love-agenda, to impress Maud Gonne, at the cost of social responsibility, with the result that he contributed to the violence of the 1916 Rising. In political terms O'Brien's argument is an important one, and one which of course the ageing Yeats came to worry about: 'Did that play of mine send out | Certain men the English shot?' But in literary terms O'Brien is King Mark to Yeats's Tristan, or King Arthur to his Lancelot: the figure of socio-political responsibility rather than individual expression. And for most of his career, however reprehensible this was, that was how Yeats wanted it. Although I think the counter-arguments, or at least complications, of O'Brien's charge offered by Elizabeth Cullingford and Marjorie Howes[22] seem

---

[21] 'Passion and Cunning: An Essay on the Politics of W. B. Yeats', first in *In Excited Reverie A Centenary Tribute to William Butler Yeats 1865–1939*, edited by A. Norman Jeffares and K. G. W. Cross (London: Macmillan, 1965), 207–78, and much reprinted elsewhere.

[22] See both Elizabeth Butler Cullingford, *Yeats, Ireland and Fascism* London: Macmillan, 1981) and Marjorie Howes, *Yeats's Nations: Gender, Class and Irishness* (Cambridge: Cambridge University Press, 1996), *passim* for their engagements with O'Brien's essay.

weighty to me, I think part of the value of his argument has not
been sufficiently acknowledged. That is the way O'Brien moves the
idea of passion—which seems at first glance to belong to a different
world altogether—into the public realm. Yeats used 'passion' and
its derivatives as a positive term ('a poem cold and passionate as
the dawn', and so on); but O'Brien restores to it a sense which is
opposed to good social order—to 'Society' in De Rougemont's
terms. This view has been much expounded in modern French post-
Freudian, Lacanian criticism: what Leo Bersani calls 'desire' as the
reprehensible but individually universal impulse. And we might
recall, too, C. S. Lewis's outraged Christian response to the great
documents of courtly love, especially Chretien de Troyes's *Lancelot*
from the 1180s. Lancelot is a figure of extramarital passion/desire,
like Diarmuid and Tristan. He and King Arthur's queen Guinevere
are fatally tied by the bonds of love in ways that led to the destruction
of the whole great ethical society represented by the fellowship of
the Round Table. There could be no clearer representation of how
individual passion undermines society. Lewis sees this well enough;
but his concern is less with the destruction of the social order than
with what he astonishingly calls 'these revolting passages' in which
Chretien 'deliberately apes religious devotion'.[23] He cares more about
the heresy than the politics. O'Brien cares more about the politics,
but he shows very acutely how this world of passion is in conflict
with the general ethics of society.

Interestingly, in *The Last Courtly Lover* Gloria Kline too traces
a movement in Yeats from the individual lover to a literary instance
which has wider repercussions, very different though her terms are.
Yeats was 'the poet who fell in love with Maud Gonne and began
to create a myth of courtly love about her' (63). She argues that he
gradually moved away from this myth and constructed an alternative
'Unity of Being' myth of his own. Enlighteningly, but perhaps a bit
too neatly, she argues that Yeats progresses chronologically from the
Maud Gonne period of medieval courtly love to a Lady Gregory
period of Renaissance palaces and patronage, which is of course a

---

[23] Lewis, 29.

shift which also has political ramifications. Her view of courtly love (she was writing at a time when the whole idea of courtly love was regarded as an 'impediment to the understanding of medieval texts' as one commentator put it) was a mode 'that nineteenth-century scholars had inferred from the literature of the twelfth, thirteenth, and fourteenth centuries' (101). Yeats had inherited the system from his father:

> Over the years the father... inculcated in the son the two basic precepts of Courtly Love: that what a man derives intuitively from a woman's image is of more value to him than what he can gain from her intellect[,] and that love of that image brings out in the lover his highest spiritual qualities' (Kline 51).

It is true that the idea of courtly love was formulated in the late nineteenth century; the term *amour courtois* was invented by the French critic Gaston Paris in the 1880s, to describe the extraordinary love that prevailed between Lancelot and Guinevere in Chretien's Lancelot as I have said. According to this strange morality the lover could—and almost invariably did—become involved sexually with women other than the courtly beloved. Repeatedly indeed the very women who aid the lover in his pursuit of the ideal courtly beloved sleep with him—or are slept with as a kind of bizarre recognition. Kline says that this view of things was found very satisfactory by Victorian mores: by 'the nineteenth-century middle-class turn of mind that balked at sex unless it could be elevated and turned away from the body... the turn of mind that elevated and delighted in courtly love, wherein the physical became spiritually transforming' (53). Thus Yeats's mother, the poet tells us, 'taught the young boy to feel disgust at the English who openly kissed at railway stations' (*Au* 34). And in her *Autobiography* Lady Gregory attributes to Yeats the view that

> 'We never love the woman we like, or like the woman we love, for she whom we like gives us peace, and she whom we love gives us unrest'.[24]

---

[24] *Seventy Years: Being the Autobiography of Lady Gregory*, edited and with foreword by Colin Smythe (Gerrards Cross: Colin Smythe, Ltd., 1973), 350. This view

None of this is that unfamiliar; most people have suffered unrest
as a consequence of love, whether or not the inclination was an
invention of the Middle Ages. Anyway, the 'she whom we love' here
is very recognizable as Maud Gonne in Yeats's poetry. The same
poems tend to recur in evidence, although the condition is general.
Ironically maybe, the classic text is Yeats's loose 1891 translation of
Ronsard, a poet from the mid-sixteenth century when, according to
the development persuasively proposed by Kline, Yeats should have
been on to the patronage of the Big House:

> How many loved your moments of glad grace,
> And loved your beauty with love false or true,
> But one man loved the pilgrim soul in you,
> And loved the sorrows of your changing face; (*VP* 121)

The 'pilgrim soul', as what was appreciated by the real lover, is the
essential thing here and the most cited; but the most medieval and
courtly thing is the almost unnoticeable 'love false or true'. The idea
of the false lover—the bodily lover, by contrast with the exalted
spiritually-motivated true lover—was the subject of many medieval
treatises. Again, there is a full terminology, developed in the Middle
Ages in all the major European literary vernaculars. For example,
in Provencal there is an opposition between *amors*—true love, and
the derived coinage *amars*—false love. The essence of the difference
was that true love was not sexually directed, loving the 'pilgrim soul'
rather than the yellow hair', the body to which false love was sexually
drawn (*VP* 492). This is another instance of the courtly ethic setting
up an opposition which corresponds to an official Christian order:
the *amors/amars* pairing is like such things as perfect *versus* imperfect
contrition, motivated respectively by pure love of God or more
pragmatic considerations such as fear of pain in Hell.

I am labouring the correspondences. I would like to finish with
two points: the political application of Yeats's ideas derived from
the courtly order (his indomitable Irishry, the 'people of Burke and

---

may be compared to Yeats's view that he 'could not give [Olivia Shakespear] the
love that was her beauty's right... she was too near my soul, too salutary and
wholesome to my inmost being' (*Mem* 88).

Grattan | Who gave though free to refuse' are a kind of ideal order, noble heretics corresponding to the Albigensian *perfecti* repressed and persecuted by the medieval Church, the seeds of the Inquisition). The political influences are wider and more complex though; for example, in *The Dreaming of the Bones*, Diarmuid (the other Diarmuid, MacMurrough who brought the Normans to Ireland) and Devorgilla are tied together for all eternity in the same kind of courtly determinism as Dante's Paolo and Francesca. They encounter an escapee from the GPO in 1916, in a context that believes that their alliance was politically disastrous for Ireland. Secondly, the way the courtly system hovers in the background of Yeats's later poetry of love and allied matters is often enriching. It enriches, I think, a poem such as 'Broken Dreams' in 1917—which of course is not in need of any enrichment. The addressee is obviously the beloved, so the first line is a bombshell, an extraordinary intrusion of the real world into a context where it is not to be expected:

There is grey in your hair. (*VP* 355)

One thing I do want to argue too is that familiarity with the requirements of the courtly-love situation can give pause to the tendency in Yeats criticism to explain poems in entirely biographical terms. Certainly Yeats did put a lot of himself into the poems. He is often confessional; the 'sixty-year-old smiling public man' is one way of characterizing Yeats at the time of 'Among School Children' (*VP* 443), and a pretty accurate one; but the 'lover' who loved the 'pilgrim soul' is a representative figure of wider meaning than W. B. Yeats.

http://dx.doi.org/10.11647/OBP.0081.05

The Puzzle of Sequence: Two Political Poems[1]

Helen Vendler

ALTHOUGH YEATS'S multi-poem sequences are the complex end-point of his lyric experimentation, I want to consider them at this early point to establish the intellectual and emotional accumulation toward which his mature lyrics tend. These sequences, which approach a single phenomenon (civil war) or concept (vacillation) from various angles, replaced in Yeats's ambition the narrative poems of his earlier poetic career. The famous sequences in English before Yeats had linked together poems, such as sonnets, that were identical in shape; but the characteristic Yeatsian sequence—for _ which my examples here will be 'Nineteen Hundred and Nineteen' and 'Blood and the Moon'—consists of poems of different shapes linked under one title. The individual members of the sequence are 'poems' (as Yeats usually referred to them),[2] but although many of these poems

---

[1]   First delivered as n. 4 in the Cork Series, on 21 February, 2006 and, after pamphlet publication by UCC in that year, was revised as Chapter III, 'The Puzzle of Sequence: Two Political Poems', in Helen Vendler (ed.), *Our Secret Discipline: Yeats and Lyric Form* (Cambridge, Mass.: The Belknap Press of Harvard University Press, 2007), 62–89 and nn. The present text is taken from that book. Grateful acknowledgement is made to Harvard University Press.
      Helen Vendler's e-mail is vendler@fas.harvard.edu

[2]   See Yeats's note (*VP* 827) on 'Meditations in Time of Civil War': 'These *poems* were written at Thoor Ballylee... The sixth *poem* is called *The Stare's Nest by My Window*... In the second stanza of the seventh *poem* occur the words "'vengeance upon the murderers'" (italics mine).

119

can stand singly as aesthetic units, they take on weight from their presence and placement within the sequence.

What is the imaginative impulse that wants to create a sequence rather than a single poem? And what are the characteristic methods by which such an impulse embodies itself? These methods, as we shall see, may be 'magical' in derivation, or they may be motivated by a desire to exemplify a particular genre, rhythm, or stanza form. Sometimes they seem fantastic. The poet's imaginative impulse when constructing a sequence fulfils itself in its act of discovering appropriate form-and by 'form' I mean not only the inner and outer shapes of the individual members of the sequence, but also the chosen ordering of the poems from which we derive the implicit argument of the whole. If Yeats's multiple choices of individual form and sequential order are not random (as they certainly are not), can we find plausible ways to describe the phenomenology both of the individual poems and of the sequence as a whole, and can we suggest the aims governing the poet's choices? And can we see the advantage to a poem, especially a political poem, in turning away from the topical and adopting forms of abstraction? Ezra Pound, always one for the topical, was amused by Yeats's inveterate belief that it was the symbol, abstracted from the quotidian, that could hold the quintessence of reality: in *The Pisan Cantos* (n. 83, 22–26), Pound, in Paris with Yeats, comments on that belief:

> Le Paradis n'est pas artificiel
> and Uncle William dawdling around Notre Dame
> in search of whatever
>   paused to admire the symbol
> with Notre Dame standing inside it[.][3]

Yeats's symbols for the acts of violence in the two sequences discussed here, and his confidence in those imagined abstractions, needed the implementation of form. For each of my two cases, I will sketch the themes and name the forms of the entire sequence, with the aim of improving our sense of Yeats's formal resources and his imperious management of them.

[3]   Ezra Pound, *The Cantos of Ezra Pound* (London: Faber & Faber, 1987), 528.

'Nineteen Hundred and Nineteen' (published in 1928 in *The Tower*) is a long six-part sequence of 130 lines, a work too massive to be understood without study and reflection. It was in part occasioned by the guerrilla conflicts in Ireland during 1919 and 1920 between Republicans and the British police, aided by the Black and Tans (an irregular military group, so named from their uniform), composed mostly of men demobilized from the War. (These conflicts anticipated the outbreak of civil war between Republicans and Free Staters in 1922.) But it must be recalled, in order to understand Yeats's concern with violence in 'Nineteen Hundred and Nineteen', that the poem was written in the wake of World War I, with its catastrophic rupture of the European *status quo*.

The formal organization of 'Nineteen Hundred and Nineteen' (outlined more fully in the appendix to this essay) appears to be heterogeneous, mutating spontaneously from part to part. Its six poems, ranging in length from one stanza to six, employ five different rhyme schemes, four distinguishable rhythmic schemes, and three different line lengths; they also represent distinct thematic and prosodic genres. They are voiced differently, too: Yeats writes only once in the first person singular, more frequently in the first person plural, and sometimes in an impersonal voice, narrative or philosophical by turns. How can we explain not only this prosodic and syntactic variety but also the sequential ordering of the poems?

'Nineteen Hundred and Nineteen' was originally entitled 'Thoughts upon the Present State of the World' and dated 'May, 1921'. On April 9, 1921, Yeats commented on his undertaking to Olivia Shakespear, remarking that he had been reading many books, 'searching out signs of the whirling gyres of the historical cone as we see it'.[4] In a letter to Lady Gregory, he said, 'The first poem is rather in the mood of the Anne poem ['A Prayer for my Daughter] but the rest are wilder'.[5] As Daniel Albright remarks, 'The retitling and

---

[4]   *CL InteLex* 3899; *L* 668. J. Hillis Miller, in *The Linguistic Moment: From Wordsworth to Stevens* (Princeton: Princeton University Press, 1985), sees the whole sequence as a manifestation of the whirling of the gyres, as image succeeds image in rapid succession (see esp. pp. 320ff.). Whether all of the sections whirl deconstructively around 'an absent center' seems more debatable: Yeats's centre— atrocity through the ages—is all too present.

[5]   *Life 2*, 193 n. 83.

redating [of the sequence] may reflect Yeats's sense of the importance of 1919, the year in which... the rebel Irish Republican Army was opposed by the Black and Tans'.[6] Lady Gregory's journal entry of 5 November, 1920, records the atrocity that lies at the heart of Yeats's sequence: Eileen Quinn, a young mother of three, was 'shot dead... with her child in her arms' by Black and Tan soldiers shooting from a passing lorry.[7] We might at first think that the whole of 'Nineteen Hundred and Nineteen' was written to show how that actual event, mentioned in part I, burst in upon the illusions of the past:

> Now days are dragon-ridden, the nightmare
> Rides upon sleep: a drunken soldiery
> Can leave the mother, murdered at her door,
> To crawl in her own blood, and go scot-free. (*VP* 429)

In 'Meditations in Time of Civil War', another political sequence, the comparable topical moment arrives late, in the penultimate poem:

> Somewhere
> A man is killed, or a house burned...
> Some fourteen days of civil war;
> Last night they trundled down the road
> That dead young soldier in his blood. (*VP* 425)

Another poet might have made more, in each case, of the local bloodshed and the earlier causes of the present tragedy; Yeats neither begins nor ends with the local event, nor does he treat it in any historical detail.[8] Irish events, though they stimulated

---

[6]   W. B. *Yeats: The Poems*, ed. Daniel Albright (London: J. M. Dent, 1990), 651.

[7]   *Lady Gregory's Journals*, ed. Daniel Murphy, 2 vols. (Gerrards Cross: Colin Smythe, 1978), I, 197.

[8]   Compare the slightly more extended account of the Troubles around Kiltartan Cross in Yeats's address to the dead Robert Gregory in 'Reprisals':
>   Half-drunk or whole-mad soldiery
>   Are murdering your tenants there.
>   Men that revere your father yet
>   Are shot at on the open plain.
>   Where may new-married women sit
>   And suckle children now? Armed men
>   May murder them in passing by
>   Nor law nor parliament take heed. (*VP* 791)

'Nineteen Hundred and Nineteen', are not Yeats's principal focus within the sequence; it is the enigma of human violence that is his subject. Why—to leap to the last enigma of 'Nineteen Hundred and Nineteen'—would the fourteenth-century high-born Lady Alice Kyteler abase herself to an 'evil spirit' (Yeats's words in his note to the poem) such as Robert Artisson, and bring him, by way of erotic offerings, the 'red combs' sliced off the heads of her cocks?[9] Why—to return to the first enigma of the sequence—would anyone in ancient Greece become such an 'incendiary or bigot' that he would burn religious monuments or melt down artworks for their gold? It is not solely, or even chiefly, political violence that perplexes Yeats in 'Nineteen Hundred and Nineteen'; it is rather the recurrent multiform and age-old violence of human beings— even if only the violence of animal sacrifice—that he investigates in the sequence. It is misleading to consider 'Nineteen Hundred and Nineteen' only in the context of contemporary Irish conflicts: Yeats himself takes great pains to widen the historical context within the sequence, ranging as far back as ancient Greece (in the burning of the statue of Athena) and ancient Palestine (in the decapitation of John the Baptist after Salome's dance).[10] Although the carnage in Ireland occasioned this sequence, its individual poems are neither comprehended nor exhausted by the events that prompted them.

---

[9] Dame Alice Kyteler was accused, in 1324–25, 'of being at the head of a band of sorcerers in the city of Kilkenny, and of offering sacrifice to demons. Her incubus, to whom she had made the sacrifice of nine red cocks and nine peacocks' eyes, sometimes made his appearance as a cat or black dog, sometimes as a black man'. See *Myth 2005* 289 n. 7. Yeats's own note adds, 'My last symbol, Robert Artisson, was an evil spirit much run after in Kilkenny at the start of the fourteenth century' (*VP*433).

[10] Jeffares, following Henn (NC, 234), speculates that Yeats, in collectivizing Salome's dance into the dance of 'the daughters of Herodias', may have been prompted not only by the medieval naming of the Sidhe, who, as Yeats noted in *The Wind Among the Reeds*, 'journey in whirling winds that were called the dance of the daughters of Herodias in the Middle Ages' (*VP* 800), but also by Arthur Symons's poem 'The Dance of the Daughters of Herodias'. Warwick Gould suggests to me that Symons's poem 'may take its title from Yeats's preoccupation with this subject as in the note to *The Wind Among the Reeds* rather than the other way around'.

The originating enigma of 'Nineteen Hundred and Nineteen' is the human race's urge to obliterate the very civilizations it has constructed. We might, says Yeats, expect 'common things' to be 'pitched about' by sublunary change, but surely 'ingenious lovely things' (the aesthetic heritage of the West) would be protected by Fate from such violence. Yeats instances, among those lovely things, religious icons such as the olive-wood image of Athena on the Acropolis, and artworks such as the ivory sculptures of Phidias or the inspired Greek simulacra in gold of humble grasshoppers and bees. The sequence begins in the voice of one who values such icons and images:

> There stood
> Amid the ornamental bronze and stone
> An ancient image made of olive wood—
> And gone are Phidias' famous ivories
> And all the golden grasshoppers and bees. (*VP* 428)

Exactly halfway through its length, this opening poem turns its face away from archaic Greece to comment on present-day Ireland— 'Now days are dragon-ridden, the nightmare | Rides upon sleep'— but it ends with a return to ancient Greece and a restatement of its original enigma. The poem is, then, a circular one, ending in the same perplexity with which it began. The initial confidence in the permanence of 'ingenious lovely things' is seen as illusion, and at the close the speaker's language descends to reproducing, in the indirect discourse of its last three lines, the attitudes natural to the destroyers: contempt ('that stump'), mercenary motives ('traffic in'), and heedless violence ('break in bits'):

> That country round
> None dared admit, if such a thought were his,
> Incendiary or bigot could be found
> To burn that stump on the acropolis,
> Or break in bits the famous ivories
> Or traffic in the grasshoppers or bees. (*VP* 430)

Poems that end where they began—with their emotions unresolved and their condition as hopeless as it was at the beginning—are a known form (Yeats was acquainted with Donne's 'A Nocturnall on St Lucie's Day'). But why would Yeats cast his opening enigma into *ottava rima*?

Ottava rima first appears in Yeats's work in the 1928 *Tower*, he continued to resort to it for the next ten years, through the composition of 'The Circus Animals' Desertion' in 1938. Yeats had used eight-line stanzas earlier, but not the stately and equable *ottava rima*, which he was to explore with such versatility.[11] Although 'Sailing to Byzantium' was the last composed of the poems in *The Tower*, its stanza form takes on, by standing first in the volume, an exemplary function: *ottava rima* (throughout Yeats) stands for Renaissance courtly achievement, for culture, for civilization, for 'monuments of unageing intellect', for an achieved artifice (whether of eternity or of time). The first two stanzas of 'Sailing to Byzantium' exhibit the normative form of *ottava rima* when it is undisturbed: six lines of description or speculation (*ababab*), resolved with a resonant couplet (*cc*). Readers of *The Tower*, then, encountering the *ottava rima* opening of 'Nineteen Hundred and Nineteen', might reasonably expect another salute to the perpetuity of art, Hebraic or Hellenic; and the poem's initial praise of ingenious lovely things is a theme suitable to *ottava rima*. But readers find themselves abandoned, in the course of the sequence, to enigmas, questions, and outlandish folk legend. And although the first two *ottava rima* stanzas of the opening poem of 'Nineteen Hundred and Nineteen' preserve the normative integrity of their closing couplets, the last four stanzas, one way or another, break that stability. The cultural products of civilization are in view, yes, but this poem's topic is their tragic fate. 'He who can read the signs' knows

> no work can stand,
> Whether health, wealth or peace of mind were spent
> On master-work of intellect or hand,
> No honour leave its mighty monument[.] (*VP* 429)

---

[11] See my 'Yeats and *Ottava Rima*' (*YA11* 26–44) revised into Chapter X, 'The Renaissance Aura: *Ottava Rima* Poems' in *Our Secret Discipline*, 262–90.

The first part of 'Nineteen Hundred and Nineteen' vacillates between creativity and annihilation, free will and determinism. On the one hand, man seems to possess the power not only to create, but also to 'read the signs' and, if he is strong enough, to withstand the temptation to 'sink unmanned | Into the half-deceit of some intoxicant', even while the free will of the incendiary or the bigot is expending itself on destruction. At another moment, however, the poem will declare that men are but 'weasels fighting in a hole', devoid of human reason. And in a third formulation, the poet asserts that the objects of love are not in fact destroyed by violent outside forces, but simply, and intransitively, 'vanish' as we look on: 'Man is in love and loves what vanishes, | What more is there to say?' (*VP* 429–30). These changing speculations within part I of 'Nineteen Hundred and Nineteen' are not arranged in any logical or cumulative order: art does not win, reason does not win, animal viciousness does not win, philosophical insight does not win. In this tumult, civilization, in its formal analogue of *ottava rima*, cannot survive further within the sequence; this cultivated stanza form, with its Renaissance aura, never returns after part I.

Yeats's stanzas in this opening poem—all but one—repeat inflexibly a single structure: that of illusion (usually voiced somewhere in the first six lines) and that of illusion disabused (expressed most frequently in the couplet, but sometimes earlier, as in the third stanza, with its biblical warning about cannon unbeaten into ploughshares). (In a poem, such a repeated psychological pattern stands for a determinism irresistible by human will.) For a brief moment, one single stanza, the fifth, resists this fated collapse, announcing (prematurely, as we will discover) a form of comfort: the wise and realistic man is solaced by his 'ghostly solitude', which would be marred if he took his superior philosophical knowledge to be a form of triumph. His objectivity in the midst of disaster is disinterested—or so the stanza believes. But as soon as Yeats finds this comfort for his intellect, his emotions rebel, and he denies his pretence that there is 'one comfort left'.[12]

---

[12] Warwick Gould finds here an allusion to *Richard II* (2.1.72): 'What comfort, man? How is't with aged Gaunt?'

> But is there any comfort to be found?
> Man is in love and loves what vanishes,
> What more is there to say? (*VP* 429–30)

After this admission, there is no more talk of defeating disaster by 'ghostly solitude'; instead, the *ottava rima* falls back, in conclusion, into its subjected pattern of illusion disabused, as the Greek ivories are broken and the golden jewellery traded for money. Where can Yeats's sequence go after this apparent philosophic resignation to the depredations of violence? What is he to do with his apprehension that 'days are dragon-ridden', that a dragon has been loosed upon his country?

To our surprise, the sequence proceeds, in its single-stanza part II, into an apparently trivial description of an orientalised modern dance, which, by means of its many veils wielded by the batons of 'Chinese' (actually Japanese) dancers, creates 'a dragon of air'. But the poet takes this modern choreography as a symbol ratifying his sense of present 'dragon-ridden' history:

> When Loie Fuller's Chinese dancers enwound
> A shining web, a floating ribbon of cloth,
> It seemed that a dragon of air
> Had fallen among dancers, had whirled them round
> Or hurried them off on its own furious path;
> So the Platonic Year
> Whirls out new right and wrong,
> Whirls in the old instead;
> All men are dancers and their tread
> Goes to the barbarous clangour of a gong. (*VP* 430)

The motion of Loie Fuller's dancers has no sooner been described than it is immediately—within the same single stanza—analogized to the largest motion of the cosmos, the 36,000-year journey of the constellations through the entire zodiac. The scale of space expands to the astronomical, while the index of time flees back to the primitive origins of music, here represented by an Asian 'gong' that beats out the deterministic measure that all men are compelled to tread. Later, in 'Supernatural Songs', primitive music will be made on a 'magic drum'; each of these instruments is capable of only a single on/off sound, representing the most basic form of music. Determinism asserts its absolute rule, paradoxically through the apparently spontaneous motion of the whirling dragon-dancers (directed in reality by an unseen choreographic force). Tennyson's 'Ring out the old' stands behind Yeats's more sinister variety of change in which new right and wrong are merely exchanged for old right and wrong.

What is the stanza form containing this grim statement? And why does this part of 'Nineteen Hundred and Nineteen' consist of a single peculiar and very uneasy stanza? And why will Yeats immediately resort to this stanza again in the next poem, part III of the sequence?[13] Here are the features of this ten-line stanza:

In *rhyme*, the ten-line stanza divides itself *asymmetrically*, 6–4, with a sestet (*abcabc*) followed immediately (no break) by an embraced-rhyme quatrain (*deed*).

In *logic* and *punctuation*, however, the stanza divides itself *symmetrically* (5–5) into two *equal* parts of five lines each, separated by a semicolon: the first part is about the dance, the second about the Platonic Year.

In *rhythm*, the stanza exhibits yet a third pattern, also *asymmetrical*: the first five lines place a *single* trimeter *between* two pentameter couplets (5–5–3–5–5); the second five lines offer *four* trimeters followed by a single pentameter (3–3–3–3–5).[14]

---

[13] He turns to it again for part II ('My House') of 'Meditations in Time of Civil War'. There, it is composed in a vortex-structure, in which external features of Ballylee (bridge, farmhouse, acre of ground) lead (in stanza 2) to entering the tower, going up the winding stair, finding a chamber and its fireplace, and finally, at the narrowed point of the vortex, stopping at 'A candle and a written page'. This 'gyre-structure' is repeated, in reverse, to show Yeats's literary ancestry, beginning with the single figure of Milton's 'Platonist' toiling 'in some like chamber', and widening out to the 'benighted travellers' passing outside who see his 'lighted candle glimmering'. The third vortex in the poem is one of time, not space: it begins with the ancient founder of the tower among his score of men; descends to Yeats, the present occupant; and at its narrowest point looks forward to his 'bodily heirs'. The vortex may be seen as a version of the labyrinth and of the gyre.

[14] It might seem that line 9 of the Loie Fuller stanza has four beats, not three; but a glance at the other stanzas of this pattern reveals that Yeats always intends lines 6, 7, 8, and 9 to be trimeters. The correct scansion is probably 'All men are dancers and their tread'.

The stanza is therefore a triply unsettling one: its asymmetrical 6 + 4 *rhyme* division does not match its 5 + 5 *logical* division into two equal parts; and the two *logically* analogous equal halves (dancer and year) are *rhythmically* entirely disparate. Graphically, the stanza as a whole begins broadly in pentameters, narrows to a trimeter, broadens again, narrows to trimeters again, ends in a pentameter: broad, narrow, broad, narrow, broad—a double gyre.

Yeats 'defines' this strange stanza for us in the poem for which he invented it, the 1920 'All Souls' Night' (*VP* 470–74). After telling us first that he wishes to be 'wound in mind's pondering | As mummies in the mummy cloth are wound', he closes the poem by echoing and enlarging that statement:

> Such thought—such thought have I that hold it tight
> Till meditation master all its parts...
> Such thought, that in it bound
> I need no other thing,
> Wound in mind's wandering
> As mummies in the mummy-cloth are wound.[15]

This ten-line stanza created for 'All Souls' Night' and reused in 'Nineteen Hundred and Nineteen' and 'Meditations in Time of Civil War' is the largest single unit in Yeats's poetic repertoire. (When the mature Yeats writes a stanza that is longer than ten lines, such as the eighteen-line stanza that closes 'Nineteen Hundred and Nineteen', he creates it by gathering together smaller uniform rhyming units, in that case, three sixains.) Because of its several asymmetries, the ten-line stanza never falls into a 'comfortable' shape; its syntax strains against its rhymes, its rhymes against its rhythms. In 'Nineteen Hundred and Nineteen' (though not in its other occurrences) the ten lines of the stanza invariably compose a single sentence, a single complex proposal in which several sub-proposals are enwound. We recall Yeats's statement in 'A General Introduction to My Work' of his desire for 'a complete coincidence between period and stanza'

---

[15] *VP* 474. 'All Souls' Night' was written in November 1920; Yeats began the composition of 'Nineteen Hundred and Nineteen' on April 9, 1921. See *CL InteLex* 3899 and 3900.

(*E&I* 522–23). The winding of the syntax through the long sentence is the winding of Loie Fuller's dancers' veils, or the winding of the constellations through the circuit of the zodiac, or the winding of the mummy-cloth about the mummy. The pride of the poet in composing such an expert stanza lies in having created a texture so dense that it permits the enwinding of the large with the small, the general with the particular, the symmetrical with the asymmetrical, the expanding with the contracting. The first half of the stanza (two solidly rhyming pentameter couplets enclosing a trimeter) offers stateliness: the second half, with its four successive lines in lilting trimeter, offers a dance-rhythm stabilized by a final pentameter. By means of the internally contrastive parts of the stanza, the poet wishes to enclose in one moment tragedy and joy, discursive weight and lightness of motion.

What can Yeats's purpose be—after the single-stanza part II poem of Loie Fuller and the Platonic Year—in returning to the very same stanza form for the next poem of 'Nineteen Hundred and Nineteen', the part III excursus comparing the soul to a swan? Why the emblematic winding stanza if there are, here, no mummy-bands, no complex veils, and no large scale heavenly circuit? It is not until the middle of part III that we find the new function of this irregular stanza: it is to represent, this time, the windings of a labyrinth, Yeats's own maze of 'art and politics':

> A man in his own secret meditation
> Is lost amid the labyrinth that he has made
> In art or politics.[16]

Yeats's soul—engaged in 'art or politics' not only in this poem but during his entire life—seeks an adequate emblem of its own nature. The central part III of 'Nineteen Hundred and Nineteen'—flanked on the left by parts I and II (the dragon-ridden present and the dragon of air that is the Platonic Year) and on the right by the three

---

[16] *VP* 431. Recall three other Yeatsian uses of the word 'labyrinth': 'The labyrinth of her days' ('Against Unworthy Praise') and 'the labyrinth of another's being' and 'From a great labyrinth out of pride' ('The Tower', II, lines 112, 116): see *VP* 260 and 413.

parts yet to come (IV, V, and VI)—is, strikingly, the only one among the six poems of the sequence that is written in the first person singular. In it, the Yeatsian 'I' speaks out in *propria persona* at the centre of the labyrinth he has made of art or politics. The rest of the sequence may be thought of as a series of indices pointing to the 'I' hidden among the many impersonal propositions about art and politics that are constantly being proffered and withdrawn. These several propositions, as we see them unfold within the sequence, are irreconcilable on any plane. In these various poems, we are sometimes agents of free will, sometimes helpless creatures of Fate. We are makers of beautiful things; we are destroyers of beautiful things. We live on a human scale; we live on a cosmic scale. We are rememberers; we are forgetters. We are believers; we are mockers. We are creative minds; we are creatures of erotic abjection. We are debased animals; we are the creators of abstract notions of honour and truth. All of these assertions are held in tension within the sequence.

When Yeats decides ('I am satisfied with that') to accept (from the unnamed 'mythological poet') the solitary swan as an image for the solitary soul, he frames his central symbol of the labyrinth with two postures of the swan. In the first, the swan represents the joy of potential choice: poised for flight, he is able still to choose 'Whether to play, or to ride | Those winds that clamour of approaching night'. But in the second posture, the moment of choice has passed: in present-perfect diction, we are told that 'The swan has leaped into the desolate heaven'. The word 'solitary' in the originating 'solitary soul' has at this point metamorphosed, via the word 'solitude' in the middle stanza (both of them derivatives of *solus*, 'alone'), into Keatsian word 'desolate' (from *desolare*, 'to abandon', ultimately also *solus*). (Each of these words contains in its syllable *sol* a graphic pun on *soul*.) The solitary soul has leaped not into the 'sky' but into a desolate 'heaven', desolate because it is a heaven with no resident God, and because all utopian hopes have shown themselves—in the opening poem—to be illusory. The swan in the desolate heaven is an image vacating life's labyrinth of meaning, forcing Yeats to descend from his grand symbolic swan-sweep to a first person apocalyptic self-obliteration:

> That image can bring wildness, bring a rage
> To end all things, to end
> What my laborious life imagined, even
> The half-imagined, the half-written page. (*VP* 431)

Determining on a fierce self-immolation even in the actual moment
of this writing Yeats checks himself and diverges—in keeping with
the rhythmical habit of his asymmetrical stanza—into a trimeter lilt,
this time embodying a Shakespearean song recalling *King Lear*:

> O but we dreamed to mend
> Whatever mischief seemed
> To afflict mankind, but now
> That winds of winter blow
> Learned that we were crack-pated when we dreamed. (*Ibid.*)

The frustrating search for an ethical centre to the labyrinth of art
and politics has been forsaken in favour of the tragicomic song of a
Shakespearean fool.

Parts II and III—four labyrinthine stanzas, each a single
labyrinthine sentence—are followed by another single-sentence
poem. But in violent contrast to the intricacy of its predecessors, part
IV is a biting trochaic epigram of collective self-mockery, repellently
thrusting the high abstractions 'honour' and 'truth' up against 'the
weasel's twist, the weasel's tooth':

> We, who seven years ago
> Talked of honour and of truth,
> Shriek with pleasure if we show
> The weasel's twist, the weasel's tooth. (*Ibid.*)

In part I, the speaker had said of himself and his contemporaries
'[We] are but weasels fighting in a hole'; this recapitulation in
part IV is merely the most visible of many in the poem, repetitions
that intensively link the members of the sequence to one another,
making the whole a sequence rather than a haphazard gathering
of independent poems.[17] The appearance of the coarse-imaged

---

[17] These include *bronze/bronzed; old wrong/new right and wrong/the old; habits/habit;
thought, thought, thought/thoughts/thought; triumph/triumph; solitude/solitary/*

epigram of the weasels suggests that the conditions of 1919–21 (Yeats began the poem on 9 April, 1921)—hitherto expressed in the aristocratic form of the *ottava rima* and the 'masterful' form of the labyrinthine stanza—have not yet been formulated comprehensively, or even correctly. The self-irony in part I was chiefly intellectual: 'O what fine thought we had because we thought | That the worst rogues and rascals had died out'; 'We pieced our thoughts into philosophy | And planned to bring the world under a rule'—with 'philosophy' pronounced as if in quotation marks. Although part I had momentarily lapsed into a bestial self-image ('weasels fighting in a hole'), it departed instantly from that insight into a lofty self-comfort of believing that the reflective man could read the signs and could refuse to sink into the deception of an intoxicant. Now, reverting to the image of the weasel, the poem reifies it into physical twist and vicious tooth, trochaically **shriek**ing in **plea**sure and sonically matching '**We** who' with '**wea**sel's' and '**wea**sel's'. The aural effects of part IV are so unpleasant that they put in question all the loftier effects of parts I, II, and III. Part IV's weasels bring the poem to a tone of mordant self-abasement, as their bestiality—uncountered in part IV by any other image—is savagely reiterated. Of all genres, the epigram is the one that most pretends to encapsulate the (debased) essence of its subject.[18] Now that Yeats seems to have repudiated, by this self-hating epigram, the discursive ground of philosophical

---

solitude/solitude; break/break; vanishes/vanish/vanish; dragon-ridden/dragon; traffic/ traffic; work/master-work/works; show/show; shriek/shrieked; winds/winds/wind/ wind/wind/wind/wind/wind; labyrinth/labyrinth; image/image/imagined/images; eyes/eyes; sun's/sun. This list does not mention all the internal repetitions within single poems, which are numerous; it gives only repetitions *across* from one poem in the sequence to another.

[18] See Ben Jonson's verse-preface to his *Epigrams*, 'To My Book':

> It will be looked for, booke, when some but see
> Thy title, *Epigrammes*, and nam'd of me,
> Thou should'st be bold, licentious, full of gall,
> Wormewood and sulphure, sharp and tooth'd withal,
> Become a petulant thing, hurle ink, and wit
> As mad-men stones: not caring whom they hit.

See *Poems*, ed. George Burke Johnston (Cambridge, Mass.: Harvard University Press, 1960), 7.

abstraction, aesthetic mastery, and labyrinthine thought on which he has so far stood during parts I-III, how can he continue his sequence?

He does so, in part V, with a peculiar genre—a first-person-plural exhortation to mockery. This poem is at first consistent with the baseness of weasel-pleasure, as its speaker sardonically recommends, as a form of collective enjoyment, that he and his companions turn to mocking the great, the wise, and the good. But in the fourth stanza the speaker turns on his own practice, mocking his own mockery, denouncing himself and his companions for refusing to bar the door against the ongoing political storm, and using—in the bitter phrase 'we | Traffic in mockery'—the low verb 'traffic' that was so unthinkable to him in the opening poem, when he could not imagine that anyone could be so mercenary as to 'traffic in the grasshoppers or bees':

> Mock mockers after that
> That would not lift a hand maybe
> To help good, wise or great
> To bar that foul storm out, for we
> Traffic in mockery. (*VP* 432)

Yeats's shamed self-abasement, carried over from part IV's weasels, provides a partial reason for the existence of this poem in the sequence. The true subject of part V is yet again evanescence, but this time what vanishes is not ivories and golden bees but rather striving human beings—the great who toiled to leave some monument behind, the wise who struggled with aching eyes to understand the documents of the past, the good who attempted to make virtue gay. T. R. Henn and Harold Bloom cite the devastating passage in Shelley (*Prometheus Unbound*, I, 625–628) from which Yeats borrows his categories of great, wise, and good:

> The good want power, but to weep barren tears.
> The powerful goodness want: worse need for them.
> The wise want love; and those who love want wisdom;
> And all best things are thus confused to ill.[19]

---

[19] The categories appear as well in lines 81–83 of Shelley's 'Mont Blanc', in which the mountain's voice is 'Not understood | By all, but which the wise, and great, and good | Interpret'.

In each of the first three stanzas of Yeats's part V, the seasonal turn to a 'foul storm' with its 'levelling wind' (which 'shrieks' like the weasels) has undone the work by which the great, the wise, and the good hoped to bar out the storm. 'Where are they?' Yeats cries of the vanished strivers, echoing the *ubi sunt* of earlier poets. What does the form of part V tell us? It is a very peculiar form. It looks like some form of ballad, as we see its rhymes beginning *abab*— but then it adds an extra *b* line. In each of the first three stanzas, the 'extra' fifth line serves as commentary, undoing what the first four lines have established: the great toiled, but they never 'thought of the levelling wind'; the wise studied, but now merely 'gape at the sun'; the good attempted a collective joy in virtue, but 'Wind shrieked—and where are they?' The effect is that of climbing up for three or four lines and then rapidly losing, in a single slide, all the ground gained. This might be a plausible stanza form, as I have so far described it, but it is rendered indigestible by its rhythms. Whereas a ballad stanza would be structured 4–3–4–3, following tetrameters with trimeters, this stanza up-ends the process, following trimeters with tetrameters, 3–4–3–4, and then closing with a trimeter, 3. This is a virtually unspeakable rhythm; I cannot think of another such example of 'doing the ballad backwards', as one might call it. Yeats may be casting a spell of undoing on the ballad stanza, and complicating it by a fifth-line coda. In any case, there is no ease in the form.[20]

The absolutely undanceable rhythm ironizes the initial convention of the 'come-all-ye' and contradicts the repeated folk-derived 'Come let us' of each stanza. Yeats's moral position in part V, even in the equivocal reversal of 'Mock mockers after that', is laden with self-contempt. The indubitable sympathy for the toils of the great, wise, and good is undone by the recurrence of their defeat. The first-person-plural part V, full of 'we's' like its epigrammatic predecessor

---

[20] Derek Attridge, perhaps unaware of this venture of Yeats into a backwards-ballad stanza (with an added line), invents (for his catalogue of rhythms) a 3–4–3–4 stanza, and comments, 'It's an invented example, since such stanzas don't occur normally in the tradition... The movement of the stanza is ungainly.... If we rearrange the lines [so as to give a 4–3–4–3 stanza], they take on the familiar lilt which tells us immediately that we're reading a deeply-ingrained rhythmic structure'. See his *Poetic Rhythm: An Introduction* (Cambridge: Cambridge University Press, 1995), 61.

(IV), refuses high discursive language and (for all the oddity of its invented stanza) similarly refuses, by its 'low' ballad-like appearance, Yeats's earlier aristocratic self-presentation, which he conveyed through *ottava rima* or its labyrinthine sequel, forms that imply the lofty complexity of their speaker's thought. If Yeats's earlier choice of 'high' forms belied the brutality of his savage subject, human violence, it is also true that neither the whiplash of his 'low' epigram nor the spell-casting of his ironic mock-ballad is equal to the theme of the sequence-murderous local and European bloodshed, with not a comfort to be had. The enigmas of violence and evanescence, free will and the agency of fate, still pose themselves, as does the implicit quarrel within the sequence between 'civilized' high form and 'debased' low form. If neither loftiness nor satire can finally illuminate the origins of human destructiveness, what form can Yeats invent to reveal more accurately the cause of the enigmas he has evoked?

The last of Yeats's attempts at understanding human violence is the three-scene visual fantasy of part VI. In the first of these scenes, a set of horses (most of them riderless and unadorned, but a few still garlanded and with 'handsome riders') run past, and, vanquished by the weariness of their repetitive courses, they break and vanish. Yeats's note explains them as apparitions seen by country people: 'I have assumed that these horsemen, now that the times worsen, give way to worse' (*VP* 433). In the second scene, the blind daughters of Herodias, personifying the levelling and labyrinthine wind, whirl in a clamorous 'thunder of feet, tumult of images' in which they become objects of desire to bystanders—but should someone dare to touch one of them, their response will be unpredictable: 'All turn with amorous cries, or angry cries, I According to the wind'. Amorous or angry, depending on the whim of the wind, these dancers incarnate Eros or Thanatos in turn; they are a violent version of Keats's gnats, 'Borne aloft I Or sinking, as the light wind lives or dies', and they represent the mystifying effects of a Fate-wind as blind as its subjects. Both the first and second scenes of Yeats's fantasy—unrestrained horses and clamorous dancers—are merely symbols of a hidden turbulence that invisibly and unaccountably generates them.

Behind these screen-images of supernatural incursions into the natural world, Yeats at last reveals the origin of human violence: the sexual satisfaction attending on it, a powerful satisfaction that is always irrational.[21] He borrows his final symbol for that demonic sexual undoing of culture from the chronicles of witchcraft, invoking the tale of the empty-eyed 'insolent fiend Robert Artisson', insusceptible in his 'insolence' to all the conventions of romance, who has exercised his sexual power over 'the love-lorn Lady Kyteler':

> But now wind drops, dust settles; thereupon
> There lurches past, his great eyes without thought
> Under the shadow of stupid straw-pale locks,
> That insolent fiend Robert Artisson
> To whom the love-lorn Lady Kyteler brought
> Bronzed peacock feathers, red combs of her cocks. (*VP* 433)

Already Robert Artisson has conquered; already the aristocratic woman described with irony as the 'love-lorn Lady Kyteler' has brought to him, as a token of her abjection, not only 'bronzed peacock feathers', themselves already torn from their original site, but also bloody body-parts, 'red combs of her cocks'. The outrageous obeisance of high-born lady to low incubus is a symbol, for Yeats, of the drivenness of human desire: it will abase itself before its object, it will commit violence for its object. Robert Artisson 'lurches' past, just as the rough beast 'slouches' toward Bethlehem; their gait is a mimic version of the monstrous formlessness of their dark-of-the-

---

[21] Warwick Gould argues that Yeats would ascribe the human practice of violence not to sexual desire but to 'belief in the supernatural', citing the passage in *Autobiographies* in which Yeats recalls accompanying Lady Gregory 'from cottage to cottage collecting folk-lore... My object was to find actual experience of the supernatural, for I did not believe, nor do I now, that it is possible to discover in the text-books of the schools, in the manuals sold by religious booksellers, even in the subtle reverie of saints, the most violent force in history' (*Au* 399–400; CW3 298–99). Yeats's scenes in part VI of 'Nineteen Hundred and Nineteen' are indeed expressed with the 'supernatural' symbols of the Sidhe, the Daughters of Herodias, and Robert Artisson; but the hand attempting to touch one of the daughters, and Alice Kyteler in her subjection to her incubus, are human beings motivated by sexual desire.

moon supernatural being. By coupling with the human, they have the power to bring about an unforeseeable new order of things.

What form did Yeats find for his concluding triple vision, which unrolls unbroken from the violent rout of beautiful if wearied horses and riders through the dust and wind, thunder and tumult, of the irrationally angry or amorous daughters of Herodias, to the single malign figure of Robert Artisson corrupting Alice Kyteler? Five lines for the horses, seven lines for the daughters of Herodias, six lines for the repellent liaison; the asymmetry of the lengths is belied by the symmetry of the rhymes (which I separate for clarity): *abcabc defdef ghighi*—or, more accurately, (*abcabc*) x 3. The three sixains succeed each other with no intervening blank space: one vision, three scenes, in a single tripartite pentameter stanza eighteen lines long. The rhymed pentameter sixains are 'aristocratic' in genre (because of their Petrarchan ancestry); in this they are kin to the *ottava rima* of part I and the long labyrinthine 'metaphysical' stanzas of parts II and III. However, these sixains are presented not as individual 'stanzas' of a lyric but as a single, impersonally voiced, ongoing flow. With their supernatural beings riding or whirling or lurching past, these sixains belong in content to the Romance tradition, and stand for the realm of fairy and folk tale, of suggestive but irrational narratives of symbolic people and actions. The horsemen and the daughters of the wind are Romance equivalents of the pagan gods called in Ireland the Sidhe; Lady Kyteler and Robert Artisson arise from narratives of witchcraft. The whole breathes Apocalypse.

What would impel Yeats to end his sequence, which presented at its beginning the 'ingenious lovely things' of civilization, with a witch's cauldron of these *dramatis personae*? We are reminded no longer of *Lear* but rather of *Macbeth*, of an uprising of dark impulse: as Yeats says, 'Evil gathers head'. In giving up, through this final fantasy, the possibility of any rational explanation of human violence and cultural destruction, Yeats rejects any solution that might be thought to lie within the modes so far explored—not only the 'civilized' modes of octave and labyrinth, but also the 'low' modes of epigram and bespelled ballad. Fantastic images of the supernatural thrown up from the unconscious seem to Yeats to offer a better insight into the enigma of violence than do other poetic modes. It is a daring way to end.[22]

Would 'Nineteen Hundred and Nineteen' be a different poem if the order of its component parts were rearranged? One feels immediately that an ending voiced in *ottava rima* discursiveness, or in a reductive folk-form, would carry a very different import from a visionary conclusion in Romance sixains—and one could say the same for any other conjectural order. In short, the order of the sequence contains an implicit argument about its speaker's successive responses to violence. It says that almost any intellectual person, when responding to a tragic contemporary event, begins by resorting to the intellectual tools (seen in part I) of historical analogy and philosophical speculation—or by espousing a resigned determinism such as that evoked by the Platonic Year (seen in part II). Despair at the apparently inevitable 'vanishing' of loved things governs part III, with its desire for self-destruction and the destruction of the page under the poet's pen. Sooner or later, however, one's own complicity in the socio-political order is bound to suggest itself, and intellectualizing is put aside (in parts IV and V) in favour of collective self-accusation and an attempt to deny the

---

22 It is also the mode with which Yeats decides to end 'Meditations in Time of Civil War'. There, too, he has a tripartite vision, as his subtitle tells us: 'I See Phantoms of Hatred and of the Heart's Fullness and of the Coming Emptiness'. The Phantoms of Hatred are medieval Templars crying for vengeance on the murderers of their Grand Master, Jacques Molay; the Phantoms of the Heart's Fullness are female figures riding upon unicorns, who represent the moment (Phase 14) when 'all thought becomes an image' ('The Phases of the Moon'); the Phantoms of the Coming Emptiness are brazen hawks whose wings have put out the moon; these hawks are symbols, according to Yeats, of 'the straight road of logic, and so of mechanism' (*VP* 827). But after this tripartite vision, Yeats adds— as he does not in 'Nineteen Hundred and Nineteen'—a personal postscript. He turns away from the local soldiers representing the life of action, and recommits himself to his poetic vocation: 'The abstract joy, | The half-read wisdom of demonic images, | Suffice the ageing man as once the growing boy'. Since this closing statement does not adopt a new form, but is included within the hexameter octaves of Yeats's tripartite vision, it does not undo the visionary Romance-mode that ends the sequence. The resemblance of the close of 'Meditations' to the ending of the later 'Nineteen Hundred and Nineteen' is striking, although by closing 'Nineteen Hundred and Nineteen' with 'Romance' pentameter sixains, Yeats distinguishes it from 'Meditations', with its 'Renaissance' hexameter octaves (*ababcdcd*).

efficacy, in human affairs, of intellectual and moral will. The only defence against complicity is an admission that, like everyone else, one is driven by implacable irrational impulses, sexual and violent, that are ultimately inexplicable—and such a realization produces part VI. The psychological order determining the succession of parts in 'Nineteen Hundred and Nineteen' determines as well the individual forms into which Yeats casts these poems—aristocratic, labyrinthine (collective and personal), epigrammatic, ballad-like, and Romance-derived.

But there is another force determining the forms of the individual parts of the sequence, and that is a 'magical' one. Yeats at times liked to guide his poems in 'magical' ways; the most evident instance to me is his implication of the date of the Easter Rising—the 24th day of the 4th month of the year 1916—in the forms of his poem on the event. In 'Nineteen Hundred and Nineteen' a comparable 'magical' intent is visible. Part I (which was, in its first printing in *The Dial*, an unnumbered prelude to the rest) is *sui generis*. Part II has two halves, the dance and its analogue in the Platonic year. Part III has three stanzas. Part IV has four lines of four beats each (4 X 4, a perfect square). Part V has stanzas of five lines; and Part VI is written in six-line rhyme-groups. It does not matter, perhaps, whether the reader notices any of these correspondences, but their existence is undeniable, and clearly not random. From its beginnings, Yeats's art had had room for such micro-techniques (as we see in his early work), and their appeal—not really distinct from the jigsaw-puzzle aspects of all prosody—ever quite faded. Constructing the grand architectonics of 'Nineteen Hundred and Nineteen' (and other sequences of comparable virtuosity) requires, of course, an intellectual concentration of a different order of magnitude, but for Yeats all orders, great and small, existed to cooperate in the final forming of the poem.

What do we learn from understanding 'Nineteen Hundred and Nineteen' in its formal proceedings as well as in its paraphrasable content? We learn its implicit argument: that, faced with complex historical phenomena, we must guard against resting in our premature intellectualizing impulses (whether 'aristocratic' or 'labyrinthine') but must also guard against a subsequent resorting to self-debasing judgments or reductive self-categorizations. At the same time, we must admit the likelihood in our responses of such intellectualizing or self-reproachful or over-simplifying reactions. We are brought forcibly face to face with our desire to 'make sense' of human behaviour, while being confronted with Yeats's final scepticism about such sense-making. We understand, too, that form for Yeats has ideological resonance: that some forms say 'stability and order' or 'aristocracy' or 'Romance', while others say 'complexity of thought' or 'folk-material' or 'essence of something'. We learn that the suppression of stanza breaks (and therefore of stanza-essence) denotes the refusal to grant successive scenes discrete reality, implying, by this flowing of one cursive and disturbing 'vision' of disorder into another, that they are all versions of one thing, fully revealed only in the last scene. We learn that stable forms (such as *ottava rima*) can be destabilized to significant effect; that forms possessing several competing inner structures (such as the ten-line 'labyrinthine' stanza) change shape as they are considered under different categories— rhythmically, or logically, or by rhyme-pattern; that reversed forms (as in the upside-down ballad) are disturbing; that tragedy and joy (as in the 'labyrinthine' stanza) can coexist in a stanza's asymmetrical and contrastive rhythms. We of course also see—as we do in all of Yeats's work—the usefulness of the other resources of poetry: symbol, analogy, irony, narrative suspense, distinct imaginative planes, and varied *dramatis personae*. We come to appreciate, above all, a powerful attempt by the poet to ingest his country's tragic contemporary moment whole, to analogize it to comparable moments of the human past, and to project his exploration of the abstract enigma of violence into a set of chosen symbolic forms, prosodic as well as thematic. An understanding of Yeats's decisions concerning form and arrangement keeps us from acquiescing in a merely biographical and historical interpretation of 'Nineteen Hundred and Nineteen', and invites us instead to consider the sequence as the product of a versatile formal imagination seeking 'befitting emblems of adversity' ('Meditations in Time of Civil War'). If they did not have befitting form, they would not be befitting emblems.

Does Yeats, we wonder, return to the poetic methods that we have seen here when he is constructing his other sequences? The short answer (as we would expect) is that he finds a new set of methods for each sequence. It might seem that 'Meditations in Time of Civil War' (1922) is imitating 'Nineteen Hundred and Nineteen' (1921): after all, both sequences open with an *ottava rima* poem, and 'Meditations' contains a three-stanza poem ('My House') in the ten-line 'labyrinthine' stanza used in parts II and III of 'Nineteen Hundred and Nineteen'; 'Meditations' exhibits ballad measures in parts V and VI, and ends, like 'Nineteen Hundred and Nineteen' with a tripartite visionary scheme.[23] Nonetheless, the total impression left by 'Meditations' is not at all like the one left by the earlier sequence. 'Nineteen Hundred and Nineteen' has, for instance, no subtitles prefacing its 'stations'. Who would have imagined, reading the running subtitles of 'Meditations'—'Ancestral Houses', 'My House', 'My Table', 'My Descendants', 'The Road at My Door', 'The Stare's Nest at My Window' and 'I See Phantoms, etc.'—that such topics could direct a poem on civil war? Where is the war? And even though part VI of 'Meditations' returns to the mode of tripartite vision seen in the close of 'Nineteen Hundred and Nineteen', it does so in an entirely different prosodic form—five eight-line double-quatrain stanzas (*ababcdcd*) composed in vague 'wavering' hexameters as 'Monstrous familiar images swim to the mind's eye'. In short, the two sequences remain imaginatively and prosodically distinct (and 'Meditations' has none of the numerical play of 'Nineteen Hundred and Nineteen'. By concentrating in 'Meditations' on the domestic place and objects around which the civil war rages, Yeats finds a new focus for a political poem, different from the cosmic range of 'Nineteen Hundred and Nineteen'.

---

[23] 'My Table', part III of 'Meditations', written in the same strange measure as 'Demon and Beast' (4–4–3–3, *aabb*), breaks the pattern of resemblance to 'Nineteen Hundred and Nineteen'. The 32 lines of part III appear as one unbroken block (while the 50-line 'Demon and Beast' is divided into stanzas of unequal length). Because 'Demon and Beast' adds a two-line 4–4 coda, it exhibits a more stable close than 'My Table'.

We can see Yeats turning to entirely different methods in his later sequences. Here I will offer evidence of his invention of structures in 'Blood and the Moon' (*VP* 480–82), a four-part sequence in the second of Yeats's volumes named from his tower, *The Winding Stair*.[24] 'Blood and the Moon' was occasioned by the 1927 assassination of Kevin O'Higgins, vice-president of the Free State government and a man whom Yeats considered a friend. 'I am now at a new Tower series, partially driven to it by this murder', Yeats wrote to Olivia Shakespear.[25] Foster remarks that Higgins was killed not so much for his policies in 1927 as by his having 'ordered seventy-seven executions of his ex-comrades during the civil war', when he was in the Free State cabinet (*Life 2*, 343). As earlier executions brought about later assassination, an unstoppable circuit of blood-shedding seemed to have become an established fact in Ireland.

Yeats's sequence opposes the terrene stain of blood to the moon's unstainable celestial light—but its way to that opposition is a winding one. Foster considers the sequence 'an uneven performance, obscure and declamatory by turns', though he adds that it is 'replete with wonderful phrases' (*Life 2*, 346). I believe there is more to be said for 'Blood and the Moon' if one comes to understand its strange and at first inexplicable structure, which consists of the following parts:

I. a slender twelve-line block of three trimeter *abba* quatrains without stanza breaks;
II. an eighteen-line segment consisting of six irregularly long-lined *aaa* tercet stanzas;
III. a square douzain (twelve-line verse-block) consisting of three *abba* pentameter quatrains; and
IV. a second douzain identical in form with III.

Why the tall trimeter-block as an opening? Why the straggling uneven tercets in the middle, separated by stanza breaks (the only stanza breaks of the poem)? Why two identical pentameter blocks at

24 First published in *The Exile*, Spring 1928 and first collected in *The Winding Stair* (New York: The Fountain Press, 1929).
25 *CL InteLex* 5013; *L*, 727.

the end? And why do the two closing pentameter douzains have the same *abba* rhyme-pattern as the trimeter part I?

I confess to being long baffled by this structure. And yet (as it turns out, and as I was slow to see), Yeats himself has explained it as he goes. The tall part I is '*this* tower'; part II's six-tercet climb through history is '*this* winding gyring, spiring treadmill of a stair,... my ancestral stair'; and the prosodically identical parts III and IV (identically square in appearance on the page) represent two ways of looking at 'the dusty, glittering windows' of the tower. One can see the windows as transparently 'glittering' as they permit the light of the moon to fall on the tower floor (III); or one can focus on their 'dusty' inside surface on which doomed butterflies, unable to fly out, 'cling' (IV).[26] Yeats chooses, in 'Blood and the Moon' (as in no other sequence), a graphic, pictorial method of arrangement. In the first 'station' of the sequence he will show us, from the outside, the tall shape of the tower he has restored; then, in the second station (part II) he will laboriously climb its stair, stopping from time to time; and finally, in the third and fourth stations in the upper chamber of the tower (parts III and IV), he will contemplate its windows. (He is tempted to rise to the upper ruined battlement, but he breaks off before he does so, and the battlement does not generate any pictorial equivalent of itself.) The underlying symbolic unit of the poem is clearly three-ness: *three* quatrains in I, six (that is, two times *three*) stanzas of *three* lines each in II, *three* quatrains in III, *three* quatrains in IV. These threes stand, I believe, for the three architectural features of Yeats's location depicted in the sequence: tower, stair, and windows. (In school, Yeats found geometry easy.)

The laborious actual 'rise' of the tower in stone is long past, as is the 'rise' of the race that built it; therefore, Yeats's symbolic tower-of-words lifts rapidly before us in a tall, slender verse. With the vertical effort of its medieval construction now over, the tower has taken on its secondary, intellectual function as an emblem: this 'decided-upon' status is denoted by the 'forethought' of the *abba* non-linear choice

---

[26] These two ways of looking through or at a surface in 'Sailing to Byzantium', as the poet confronts the sage-mosaic, are discussed in *Our Secret Discipline*, pp. 32–33.

of rhyme-form (repeated in III and IV). The tower's former defensive use prompts Yeats's choice in first station of the martial trimeter over his original tetrameter (which be too wide and would make the image of the tower on the page too squat),[27] but the tower is a ruin, 'half dead at the top', and so the poet's additive song ('rhyme upon rhyme') becomes a 'mockery', as he makes a 'mock' word-tower arise on a virtual, not a real, plane. The whole poem—tower, stair, and windows—is the powerful 'emblem' the poet has set up: it 'mocks' (is the image of) the physical tower, stair, and windows, and 'mocks' (repudiates) the nation-state which is, like the tower, already 'half dead at the top'.

Although part I began in the first draft as a verbless noun-list of the features of the tower and its surroundings, Yeats converted the passage to an authoritative, performative speech-act, 'Blessed be this place':

> Blessed be this place,
> More blessed still this tower;
> A bloody, arrogant power
> Rose out of the race
> Uttering, mastering it,
> Rose like these walls from these
> Storm beaten cottages—
> In mockery I have set
> A powerful emblem up,
> And sing it rhyme upon rhyme
> In mockery of a time
> Half dead at the top. (*VP* 480)

Although this opening part introduces two of the central nouns of the sequence—'blood' and 'power'—the relative 'weightlessness' of this trimeter tower denotes its purely virtual existence, its construction

---

[27] The drafts of 'Blood and the Moon' show that part I was originally in tetrameter, and part III in hexameter. Yeats quickly decided on the non-linear *abba* rhyme scheme for part I, but the pentameter for part III was longer in arriving. Part II always had its 'spiring' staircase-shape in ungainly tercets. See *The Winding Stair* (1929): Manuscript Materials by W. B. Yeats, ed. David R. Clark (Ithaca: Cornell University Press, 1995), 61–99. Hereafter *WS*.

out of rhymes, not stones. It is the only 'song' of the sequence: Yeats 'sing[s]' it.

A real effort, however, is necessary as the poet subsequently climbs the winding stair within the tower to arrive at a high vantage-point. The six distinct and unwieldy tercets (two threes, of course) exert a gravitational drag, stair-portion by stair-portion, as the elderly Yeats mounts one step at a time, line by line, pausing after each three steps, finding the climb physically tiring. (The tercet-lines are based loosely on the hexameter, the measure used to mimic stilt-walking in 'High Talk'.) As Yeats enters upon the gyre-stair of history, he recalls past towers (two real ones in Alexandria and Babylon, and other emblematical ones, Shelley's 'thought's crowned powers' in *Prometheus Unbound*). Still ascending, he pauses to declare (in another performative utterance) the symbolic status of this stair, what he has ordained that it should represent:

I declare this tower is my symbol; I declare
This winding, gyring, spiring treadmill of a stair is my ancestral stair;
That Goldsmith and the Dean, Berkeley and Burke have travelled there.[28]

The strain of climbing the stair generates more outrageously lengthy lines as the poet summons to mind his predecessors Swift, Goldsmith, Burke, and Berkeley, describing the last of these, Berkeley, in a stanza the like of which Yeats had never before written, and which is inexplicable except as an equivalent to physical exertion: step, step, step, as in 'this pragmatical, preposterous pig' and 'so solid seem':

And God-appointed Berkeley that proved all things a dream,
That this pragmatical, preposterous pig of a world, its farrow that so solid
    seem,
Must vanish on the instant if the mind but change its theme. (*Ibid.*)

In the next, and last, tercet, the poet reaches the top of his tower-stair. He pauses at that point to summarize, in a newly 'high' diction, the views and principles bequeathed to him by his mental 'ancestors',

---

[28] *VP* 480–81. Warwick Gould recalls that in Yeats's tale *Rosa Alchemica*, Swift and his ilk were to be found 'joking and railing' on the staircase of the narrator's house in Dublin. See *Myth* 179; *Myth 2005* 179 and n. 20.

citing their achievements in the order in which he had mentioned them earlier, Swift and Goldsmith in the first line of the tercet, then, each with his own line, Burke and Berkeley:

Saeva Indignatio and the labourer's hire,
The strength that gives our blood and state magnanimity of its own desire;
Everything that is not God consumed with intellectual fire. (*Ibid.*)

Now that the stair has been climbed, and the poet has arrived at the last inhabited (therefore windowed) room, what does he see? That 'seven centuries' of the bloody slaughter of innocents on this terrain have left no stain on the unearthly moon, that it remains wholly untouched by human affairs. For all the efforts of executioners to cast blood upon it, it has maintained its purity. And yet it is blood that saturates this first douzain, as though the poet, having absorbed the 'Odour of blood on the ancestral stair' cannot forget that he, like Swift, owns a human 'blood-sodden breast'. As he contemplates the 'arrowy shaft' of light aimed by the unclouded moon at the tower floor, he rages with anger at the thought that the moon remains perpetually and serenely uncontaminated. (Although the *abba* quatrain rhyme ensures the greatest possible distance between the 'moon' that ends line 1 and the 'stain' that ends line 4, the fact that they rhyme, even if inexactly, suggests that they are here conceptually inextricable, as are purity and contamination. By contrast, when Yeats rhymes the two words again in part IV, as the inner rhymes of the last quatrain of the poem, he reverses the order in which they rhyme: 'stain: moon', just as he had reversed 'come: Byzantium' to 'Byzantium: come' at the end of 'Sailing to Byzantium'. Such reversals represent, I believe, the doing and undoing of a poetic 'spell'.)

The poet refers to the blood-stained floor on which he stands by the distal deictic 'there', as though denying his own connection with it. He will not group himself with the past assassins by saying 'here'. The first ten lines of the douzain are themselves blood-saturated:

> The purity of the unclouded moon
> Has flung its arrowy shaft upon the floor.
> Seven centuries have passed and it is pure,
> The blood of innocence has left no stain.

> There, on blood-saturated ground, have stood
> Soldier, assassin, executioner,
> Whether for daily pittance or in blind fear
> Or out of abstract hatred, and shed blood,
> But could not cast a single jet thereon.
> Odour of blood on the ancestral stair! (*VP* 482)

Four 'blood's' in ten lines: the pure moon is still steadily shining, no matter how many 'blood's' the poet casts up at it like gouts of gore, no matter how many varieties of shedders of blood ('soldier, assassin, executioner') he enumerates, no matter how many motives for blood-shedding ('daily pittance... blind fear... abstract hatred') he can summon, no matter how many centuries have passed—seven—in which innocent blood has been shed. The douzain is extraordinary in its mimicry of hurled blots of blood, all of them ineffectual.

Even if we have shed no blood ourselves, the 'blood-saturated' ground of the earth repels us from its very surface, and (resisting the fact that we cannot leave the earth), we submit ourselves to 'some intoxicant' to make ourselves drunkenly think that we can choose a purer destiny than our mortal one. The tenth line of the douzain leads to a fantasy that one can join the moon in its purity:

> Odour of blood on the ancestral stair!
> And we that have shed none must gather there
> And clamour in drunken frenzy for the moon.[29]

Yeats's part III douzain, as he gazes at the moon, expresses two sorts of disgust—a disgust for ancestral violence (the bloody stair, like the bloody floor, is 'there', not 'here'), and a disgust for man's 'drunken' desire to evade his own condition. These revulsions drive the poem to its final rage against the corrupt, even 'lunatic' human frenzy of longing for the ideal realm of the moon.

So far, nothing in 'Blood and the Moon' has suggested, against the horrors of blood-slaughter mocked by an unattainable moon-

---

[29] *VP* 482. The pictorial quality of this statement may recall Blake's engraving of a long ladder reaching from earth toward the moon, with the caption referring to the cry of the child at the foot of the ladder yearning for the moon: 'I want! I want!'

purity, an alternate way of viewing the human condition. Wrenched by admitting that even his own ancestral stair reeks of blood, the poet looks a second time at a window—one of those through which he had seen, and clamoured for, the moon. (This second look explains why parts III and IV are prosodically identical: the window-frames are the same size, or the poems represent two different ways of looking at the same window.) This time, the poet does not look *through* the window to the inaccessible and uncontaminated moon; he looks instead *at* the window, stopping his gaze at the inside of the glass pane.[30] All the windows in the tower, glittering on the outside with lunar light, are, he sees, covered on the dusty inside with multicoloured butterflies, butterflies with wings like tortoise-shell, wings like peacock-feathers, butterflies who, unable to escape, cling dying to the pane:

> Upon the dusty, glittering windows cling,
> And seem to cling upon the moonlit skies,
> Tortoiseshell butterflies, peacock butterflies,
> A couple of night-moths are on the wing.
> Is every modern nation like the tower,
> Half dead at the top? (*VP* 482)

The poet's change in vision-focus, from the lunar absolute to the trapped butterflies, brings into view the pathos of life, rather than its violence. With pathos comes pity; with pity comes fellow-feeling, with fellow-feeling comes resignation to the ineluctable difference between the mortal and the incorruptible. The moon, remote and pure and dead, is as it is; human beings are as they are, ever subject to the greed for power that leads to the shedding of blood. Earth-

---

30 It may not be too fanciful to think that Yeats is here reversing George Herbert's famous window-looks in 'The Elixir', which Yeats had imitated in his look at and through the mosaic in 'Sailing to Byzantium':

> A man may look on glass,
> And on it stay his eye,
> Or if he pleaseth, through it pass,
> And then the heaven espy.

In 'Blood and the Moon', Yeats, dissatisfied with espying the heaven and its moon, chooses to 'stay his eye' on the surface; he replaces Herbert's stained glass with the multicoloured butterflies. (In one of his more creative spellings in the drafts, Yeats refers to 'tortashel' butterflies, proving how much the sound, rather than the derivation, of words mattered to him.)

creatures cannot aspire to moon-purity, moon-wisdom. Yeats closes in deep acknowledgment of that true 'vision of reality', using for his final conclusions Aristotelian abstractions carefully worded so as to distinguish definite from indefinite article: 'the property... a something... everything... a property':

> No matter what I said,
> For wisdom is the property of the dead,
> A something incompatible with life; and power,
> Like everything that has the stain of blood,
> A property of the living; but no stain
> Can come upon the visage of the moon
> When it has looked in glory from a cloud.[31]

By the final quatrain, as we pass from 'blood' to 'stain' to 'moon', we see that Yeats is ready to bless, and not to clamour for, the moon. He is remembering Shelley's 'Ode to a Skylark', as it compares the song of the lark to the exalted moment when 'from one lonely cloud | The moon rains out her beams, and heaven is overflowed'. Yeats's moon looks in glory from a cloud, and the poet, having acquired at last the gift of pity in lieu of the torment of rage, is no longer futilely compelled to cast blood at it.

'Blood and the Moon' has become an 'abstract' political poem (one might say) because it has abstracted the topical events of O'Higgins's executions and his consequent assassination into a confrontation between the stained and the pure, blood and the moon. The sequence would not have made its philosophical abstractions ('wisdom', 'power', 'a property') and its historical abstractions ('soldier, assassin, executioner') so humanly credible if it had not been grounded in its solid graphic representations: Yeats's lithe virtual

---

[31] *VP* 482. Yeats was originally unwilling to give unequivocal glory to the lunar light. In the drafts, we read two antitheses: 'Wisdom has no stain, | Whether a crescent or a waning moon, | Whether unclouded, or in clouds beset' (*WS*, 95). If the moon is 'waning', or 'beset' by clouds, it might seem diminished in power, even in its own celestial realm. In 'Blood and the Moon', Yeats finally decides that there can be no commerce between ideal power and political power: the moon remains full and unstained, the tower is irremediably tainted by blood.

tower, its exhausting real stair, its two windows. These locate the poet firmly in space as he contends with the opposition of blood and moon; and by miming the swift rise of the tower, the difficult, intermittently pausing ascent up the winding stair, and the flanking views of the windows, Yeats gradually gives us the whole tower and himself moving within it. The poet's last question–'Is every modern nation like the tower, | Half dead at the top?' takes us up beyond the windowed room to the ruined battlement, and makes us wonder if that region, like the tower, the stair, and the windows, will also shape itself into an emblematic lesson. But instead of looking for an answer, Yeats dismisses his question: 'No matter what I said'. He dismisses it because the poem is dissolving into resignation to the human and admiration for the celestial. The moon does not (as, say, in Whitman) 'look down' on the human scene; it remains within its own region, as it looks in glory from a cloud.

'Nineteen Hundred and Nineteen' and 'Blood and the Moon' attest to Yeats's extraordinary capacity to confront a contemporary event, generalize it into abstraction, and deploy his reflections on it through a number of poems and symbolic forms into a meaningful sequential order. Each of the great sequences, similarly scrutinized, would reveal other Yeatsian strategies for investigating multiple aspects of complex events or concepts. I have merely wanted to claim here that Yeats's formal choices in his sequences are not made at random, but are motivated; that we can explain Yeats's choices and deduce his presumed intentions as he decided to cast his material into these forms and not others. With a sense of Yeats's care in inventing adequate emblematic forms for individual poems, paired poems,[32] and the sequences described here, we can go on to a more systematic study of Yeatsian forms.

---

[32] Individual poems are considered in Chapter I, and paired poems (such as the Byzantium and Oracle poems) in Chapter II of my *Our Secret Discipline*, pp. 1–26 and 27–61.

APPENDIX: SCHEMATIC SUMMARY OF
'NINETEEN HUNDRED AND NINETEEN'

I: 'Many ingenious lovely things are gone'

Rhyme form:	*ababab cc*	
Feet in line:	5 throughout (pentameter)	(*ottava rima*)
Rhythm:	iambic	
Stanza-length:	8 lines	
Length of poem:	6 stanzas	
Voice(s):	'We'	

II: 'When Loie Fuller's Chinese dancers enwound'

Rhyme form:	*abcabcdeed*
Feet in line:	5535533335
Rhythm:	iambic
Stanza-length:	10 lines
Length of poem:	1 stanza
Voice(s):	impersonal

III: 'Some moralist or mythological poet' (same stanza form as in II)

Rhyme form:	*abcabcdeed*
Feet in line:	5535533335
Rhythm:	iambic
Stanza-length:	10 lines
Length of poem:	3 stanzas
Voice(s):	'I', impersonal, 'We'

IV: 'We, who seven years ago': (4 X 4, a perfect square)

Rhyme form:	*abab*
Feet in line:	4 throughout (tetrameter)
Rhythm:	trochaic
Stanza-length:	4 lines
Length of poem:	1 quatrain-stanza
Voice(s):	'We'

V: 'Come let us mock at the great'

Rhyme form:	*ababb*
Feet in line:	343434
Rhythm:	iambic (with trochaic substitution)
Stanza-length:	5 lines
Length of poem:	4 stanzas
Voices:	'We'

VI: 'Violence upon the roads: violence of horses'

Rhyme form:	*abcabc* (x 3)
Feet in line:	5
Rhythm:	iambic (with dactylic and trochaic substitution)
Stanza-length:	18 lines
Length of poem:	1 stanza
Voices:	Impersonal

'NINETEEN HUNDRED AND NINETEEN': SUMMARY

Number of poems:	6
Number of rhyme forms:	5 (II and III have the same rhyme form)
Number of rhythms:	4 (iambic, iambic/trochaic, iambic/dactylic/trochaic, trochaic)
Number of line lengths:	3 (trimeter, tetrameter, pentameter)
Number of stanzas:	1 (II, IV; and VI)
	3 (III)
	4 (V)
	6 (1)
Stanza-lengths	4 lines (IV)
	5 lines (V)
	8 lines (1)
	10 lines (II, III)
	18 lines [3 x 6] (VI)

http://dx.doi.org/10.11647/OBP.0081.06

Moving on Silence: Yeats and the Refrain as Symbol[1]

Paul Muldoon

I

IN HIS STUDY of *The Poetry of W.B. Yeats*, published in 1941, Louis MacNeice addresses the subject of Yeats and the refrain with admirable chutzpah (perhaps even a hint of hauteur) and a sense of the historical moment out of which Yeats arose:

It is worth considering the principle of refrain at some length because refrain in the twentieth century was in many circles for a long time under taboo. We suspected it, firstly, as an easy form of conventional decoration (we could point to Morris and Rossetti) and, secondly, as a well known prop for sentimentality (we could point to Alfred Noyes) or for any poetry where it is risky to examine the content critically (we could point to the patriotic poems of Kipling and Newbolt). Housman had used it effectively, but even his effects we found suspiciously pat. The twentieth century suspected most poetic repetition-devices on the ground that repetition saves thinking or excuses the lack of thought, that by sheer hypnotic force it can persuade the reader to buy his twopence coloured when he would certainly reject the penny plain. If we are honest, however, we must admit that all poetry involves this danger of hypnosis. (We must remember too that hypnosis can be illuminating.)[2]

---

[1] Delivered on 16 January 2007.
[2] Louis MacNeice, *The Poetry of W.B Yeats* (Oxford: Oxford University Press, 1941), 164. Hereafter 'MacNeice'.

I'd like to take MacNeice's idea of 'this danger of hypnosis' and try to extend it to the fact that the hypnotized 'has usually no remembrance of what he has said or done during the hypnotic state'.[3] He is, in other words, in a state of ecstatic trance in which the concept of duration has no meaning. I want to try today to discuss what one might call the triumph over time, ecstasy in stasis, which is implicit in all writing and reading, with a particular focus on the peculiar power of the refrain to represent at once fixity and fracture, regularity and rupture, constancy and change. I'll be suggesting that, far from being patriotic or pat, the refrain is integral to Yeats's symbolic system, a physical manifestation of the winding stair and the perning gyre, a perfect crossing of the butterfly with the hawk. I'll be mulling over, and musing upon, some Yeatsian symbols that spring to mind less frequently—the moorfowl, the mouse, the mayfly and the refrain itself, this last a reification of eternal intervention. While I'll be concentrating on a small number of poems by Yeats himself, notably 'Easter, 1916' and 'Long-legged Fly', I'll also be skipping sideways to take in Anonymous, a Browning or two, Donne, Poe, Wyatt and Wordsworth. I'll be appealing to informants as diverse as Arthur Schopenhauer and Stephen Sondheim on the subjects of clarity and contamination, allusiveness and elusiveness. Here's Sondheim, for example, speaking in New York in 1973 on the subject of 'Lyrics and Lyricists':

First, lyrics exist in time—as opposed to poetry, for example. You can read a poem at your own speed. I find most poetry very difficult, and there are a few poets I like very much. Wallace Stevens is one, but it takes me a good 20 minutes to get through a medium-length Wallace Stevens poem, and even then I don't understand a lot of it, yet I enjoy it and can read it at my own speed. That's the point. On the stage, the lyrics come at you and you hear them once. If there's a reprise you hear them twice, if there are two reprises you hear them three times, but that's all.[4]

This negotiation between exigency and excess is rather neatly summed up by the repetitive device used by John Donne in his three-stanza poem, 'A Hymn to God the Father':

---

[3]   *OED.*
[4]   George Martin (ed.), *Making Music* (London: Muller, 1983), 74.

> When thou hast done, thou hast not done,
> For, I have more.

These two lines are repeated at the end of the second stanza and then, at the end of the third stanza, are transmogrified into:

> And having done that, Thou hast done,
> I feare no more.[5]

One would be hard put to say if this represents merely a triple repetition of the kind that is at the heart of every form of art, or a refrain *per se* in Sondheim's 'two reprises' sense, in the way it's being used by Thomas Wyatt, say, in his majestic 'In Eternum I was Ons Determed'. Something of the tension between being finished (Donne playing there on his own name) and unfinished (there being 'more' with its play on the name of Donne's wife, Ann More), contributes to an effect of stasis which might properly be seen as one aspect of the refrain. This device of sheer repetition is sometimes known as 'incremental repetition', particularly when it doesn't repeat 'verbatim' the 'line, lines, or part of a line' that is usually associated with the refrain.[6] This is the kind of proto-refrain of which Yeats often avails himself. Stanzas 1 and 2 of 'Easter, 1916', for example, end with the lines 'All changed, changed utterly: | A terrible beauty is born' and 'He, too, has been changed in his turn, | Transformed utterly: A terrible beauty is born' while the fourth and final stanza ends:

> I write it out in a verse—
> MacDonagh and MacBride
> And Connolly and Pearse
> Now and in time to be,
> Wherever green is worn,
> Are changed, changed utterly:
> A terrible beauty is born. (*VP* 394)

---

[5] Text from John Hayward (ed.), John Donne, *The Complete Poems and Selected Prose* (London: Nonesuch, 1929), 321–22, of which Yeats had a copy (*YL* 530). See also John Carey (ed.), *John Donne: The Major Works* (Oxford: Oxford University Press, 1990), 333.

[6] Alex Preminger and T. V. F. Brogan (eds.), *The New Princeton Encyclopaedia of Poetry and Poetics* (Princeton: Princeton University Press, 1993), 1018.

One cannot but be amused by the fact that a device used to suggest that nothing has changed should assert that things have 'changed, changed utterly'. Perhaps they've not changed utterly? Perhaps they've changed *slightly*? The tension between form and content is an indicator of Yeats's own predicament, the sense of frustration expressed in his famous letter to Lady Gregory of May 11 1916:

I had no idea that any public event could so deeply move me—and I am very despondent about the future. At the moment I feel that all the work of years has been overturned, all the bringing together of classes, all the freeing of Irish literature and criticism from politics.[7]

This letter was written on the very day Yeats began to compose 'Easter, 1916'[8] and one cannot help but think that the subject of the poem is in some sense stasis, just as stasis is the subject of the couplet—the free standing refrain, one might say—'Parnell':

> Parnell came down the road, he said to a cheering man;
> 'Ireland shall get her freedom and you still break stone'. (*VP* 353)

The 'break' in 'break stone' is not irrelevant here, since the OED definition of the word refrain points us to its root in the Latin word *refrangere*, meaning 'to break again'. Some notion of breaking is central to the idea of a refrain as 'a phrase or verse occurring at intervals, esp. at the end of each stanza of a poem or song; a burden, chorus'. The 'still' in 'still break stone' will resonate for readers of 'Easter, 1916' both in the sense of 'now as before' and 'motionless':

> A shadow of cloud on the stream
> Changes minute by minute;
> A horse-hoof slides on the brim,
> And a horse plashes within it;
> The long-legged moor-hens dive,
> And hens to moor-cocks call;
> Minute by minute they live:
> The stone's in the midst of all. (*VP* 393)

---

[7] *CL InteLex* 2950 [11 May, 1916], *L* 612–13.

[8] 'I am trying to write a poem on the men executed; "terrible beauty has been born again"' (*ibid.*).

The 'stone' that's *still* 'in the midst of all' is of course the stone rolled away by the angel of the Lord to reveal the risen Christ on Easter morning. That stone is central to Christian iconography. One might say it's the icon of the moment that gives Christianity momentum. In the context of the Irish Easter 'rising', though, stone is again connected in less than ameliorative ways to notions of insensitivity and intransigence:

> Too long a sacrifice
> Can make a *stone* of the heart.
> O when may it suffice? (*VP* 394, emphasis added)

Again, Yeats allows the form of his poem to comment on its content, since the conclusion of stanza 3 of 'Easter, 1916' is not the ringing of some small change on 'All changed, changed utterly: | A terrible beauty is born' but what is *ipso facto* an utter transformation in the structure of the poem, the stone itself breaking the established order:

> Minute by minute they live:
> The stone's in the midst of all. (*VP* 393)

Perhaps one interpretation of this poem, which would be of a piece with the frustration that Yeats expresses to Lady Gregory and in keeping, too, with the fact of his withholding of the poem until it was published in *The New Statesman* 23 October and *The Dial*, November 1920,[9] is that things have changed not even slightly but have changed *not at all*. R. F. Foster, in his biography of Yeats, asserts that 'in 1916 it would have been read principally as a passionate endorsement of the rebels' cause, and WBY was extremely cautious about releasing it'.[10] I incline much more to the view, alluded to by Foster, that Irish readers would be much more like Maud Gonne

---

[9]   As distinct from private circulation in—and stemming from—Clement Shorter's pamphlet *Easter, 1916* (*Wade* 117), which Tom Paulin rather oddly calls 'a sort of underground pamphlet': see Tom Paulin (ed.), *The Faber Book of Political Verse* (London: Faber & Faber, 1986), 20. WBY subsequently tested the water, as it were, by printing the first stanza in *The Irish Commonwealth* (March 1919): see above n. 8, and Roy Foster's essay above, 'Philosophy and Passion': W. B. Yeats, Ireland and Europe', n. 9.

[10] *Life 2*, 64.

MacBride, whom Foster describes as having 'unerringly spotted the poem's central ambivalence, missed by those who concentrate on the images of terrible beauty and rebirth through sacrifice',[11] and disliked the poem at least as much as she did, which was rather a lot. I write 'poem', but that's not what Yeats writes, in these lines that summon and sum up Maud Gonne's husband:

> This other man I had dreamed
> A drunken, vainglorious lout.
> He had done most bitter wrong
> To some who are near my heart,
> Yet I number him in the *song*.
>   (*VP* 393, emphasis added)

In other words, 'Easter, 1916' is quite seen by Yeats as a song, a song that alludes quite specifically, in the phrase 'wherever green is worn' to 'The Wearing of the Green', the political ballad associated with the 1798 rebellion which Yeats had anthologized in 1895:

> I met with Napper Tandy, and he took me by the hand,
> And he said, 'How's poor old Ireland, and how does she stand?'
> She's the most distressful country that ever yet was seen,
> They are hanging men and women there for the wearing of the green'.
>   (*BIV* 236)

Again, Yeats has introduced a less than ameliorative aspect to the past participle of 'wearing' to 'Easter, 1916' since the word 'worn' may mean 'impaired by wear or use, or by exposure; showing the results of use or attrition' or, even more relevantly, 'hackneyed by use or *repetition*'[12] like the 'polite meaningless words' in line 6 of 'Easter, 1916' followed by the 'polite meaningless words' in line 8. Again, there is a commentary on both content and form implicit in that word 'worn' which brings us back to the effect of 'the living stream' on the stone that's 'in the midst of all', its very smoothness leading to the insensitivity and intransigence to which I referred earlier, to the stone-heart being untroubled in troubling ways:

---

[11] *Ibid.*, 63.
[12] *OED.*

> Hearts with one purpose alone
> Through summer and winter seem
> Enchanted to a stone
> To trouble the living stream. (*VP* 393)

The paradox is extraordinary. It might be said that inaction rather than action, including political action, may trouble the living stream, including the living stream of Irish history and the Irish *Troubles*, just as a work of art that seems inert may trouble in the sense of 'disturb, agitate, ruffle':[13]

> Michael Angelo left a proof
> On the Sistine Chapel roof,
> Where but half-awakened Adam
> Can *disturb* globe-trotting Madam
> Till her bowels are in heat,
> Proof that there's a purpose set
> Before the secret working mind:
> Profane perfection of mankind.
> (*VP* 638–39, emphasis added)

This image of Michael Angelo working on the Sistine Chapel comes from 'Under Ben Bulben', a poem written on September 4, 1938 which is in dialogue with 'Easter, 1916' in several significant ways. The stone that's in the midst of 'Under Ben Bulben' is of course the marker of Yeats's own grave:

> On lime*stone* quarried near the spot
> By his command these words are cut:
>
> *Cast a cold eye*
> *On life, on death.*
> *Horseman, pass by!* (*VP* 640, emphasis added)

This horseman is one of the 'hard-riding country gentlemen' who appears earlier in 'Under Ben Bulben', but it's the hoof of his horse, surely, that 'slides on the brim' of the stream in 'Easter, 1916', his horse that 'plashes within it'. That 'plashes' will send many readers back to the most famous use of the word in English literature:

[13] *Ibid.*

> The hare is running races in her mirth;
> And with her feet she from the *plashy* earth
> Raises a mist; that, glittering in the sun,
> Runs with her all the way, wherever she doth run.

Wordsworth's description of the hare comes from 'Resolution and Independence' his great hymn of praise to the old leech-gatherer whom he meets 'beside a pool bare to the eye of heaven' and who lies 'As a huge *stone* is sometimes seen to lie | Couched on the bald top of an eminence' and who roams 'from moor to moor'. The 'moor' in Wordsworth's poem seeps into 'Easter, 1916':

> The long-legged moor-hens dive,
> And hens to moor-cocks call.

As Daniel Albright hints, in a note on this poem in his great edition of *Yeats: The Poems*, among those that might recognize this call—perhaps even respond to it—are the moorfowl in 'The Indian upon God':[14]

> I passed along the water's edge below the humid trees,
> My spirit rocked in evening light, the rushes round my knees,
> My spirit rocked in sleep and sighs; and saw the *moorfowl* pace
> All dripping on a grassy slope, and saw them cease to chase
> Each other round in circles, and heard the eldest speak:
> *Who holds the world between His bill and made us strong or weak*
> *Is an undying moorfowl, and He lives beyond the sky.*
> *The rains are from His dripping wing, the moonbeams from His eye.*
> (*VP* 76 emphasis added in third quoted line)

'The Indian Upon God' was written in 1886, exactly 30 years before 'Easter, 1916', yet the two poems are cut from the same, part-Connemara, part-embroidered, cloth. The structure of 'The Indian Upon God' not only relies on the formal device of incremental repetition, a sequence of italicized utterances from, in turn, a moorfowl, a lotus, a roebuck and a peacock, but its very subject matter is repetition, the burden of each utterance being the tendency

---

[14] See Daniel Albright (ed.), *W. B. Yeats: The Poems* (London: J. M. Dent, 1990), 418.

of the speaker to perceive its godhead as a replica of itself, in the case of the peacock '*He is a monstrous peacock*', a version, one might say, of 'a terrible beauty'. The lines

> My spirit rocked in sleep and sighs; and saw the moorfowl pace
> All dripping on a grassy slope, and saw them cease to chase
> Each other round in circles...

are just as much under the spell of Wordsworth as that section of 'Easter, 1916', the hare 'running races in her mirth' from 'Resolution and Independence' replayed in the moorfowl that 'cease to chase | each other round in circles'.

II

Now, I'm going to take my cue from the moorfowl and chase around in circles for a little while, in hopes of returning to the subject of replication and replay. For the moment, I'll try to get to get under the surface of that most surface-engaged of Yeats's poems, 'Long-legged Fly'. Written between November 1937 and April 1938, just a year before Yeats's death, Long-legged Fly' is a poem of contemplation, partly self-contemplation, as this self-alluding final stanza makes clear:

> That girls at puberty may find
> The first Adam in their thought,
> Shut the door of the Pope's chapel,
> Keep those children out.
> There on that scaffolding reclines
> Michael Angelo.
> With no more sound than the mice make
> His hand moves to and fro.
> *Like a long-legged fly upon the stream*
> *His mind moves upon silence.* (*VP* 617–18)

This stanza of 'Long-legged Fly', collected as the ninth poem in *Last Poems and Two Plays*,[15] has an antiphonal relationship to the first poem in that book, 'Under Ben Bulben', if only in the figure of

---

[15] Dublin: Cuala, 1939, 19–20.

Michael Angelo causing a shudder in the loins despite, as I remarked on earlier, the inertness of the paint. It's as if art, in the making as in the taking, combines mechanical movement ('his hand moves to and fro') with tranquillity (Michael Angelo being the embodiment of the cliché 'as quiet as a mouse'). Those mice in 'Long-legged Fly' are town cousins of the country mice who have walk on parts in two poems written fifty years earlier and collected, along with 'The Indian Upon God', in *Crossways* (1889). The poems are 'The Falling of the Leaves' and 'The Stolen Child':

> Autumn is over the long leaves that love us,
> And over the *mice* in the barley sheaves;
> Yellow the leaves of the rowan above us,
> And yellow the wet wild-strawberry leaves.
> (*VP* 79, emphasis added)

How stealthily, by his repetition of the word 'leaves' three times in four lines, does Yeats introduce his subject, the subject of *leaving*:

> The hour of the waning of love has beset us,
> And weary and worn are our sad souls now;
> Let us part, ere the season of passion forget us,
> With a kiss and a tear on thy drooping brow. (*VP* 79)

That 'mice' are associated in Yeats's mind with the end of a season, with some sense of the waning of a cycle ('Hickory, Dickory, Dock'), with what is 'weary and worn' in the secondary sense of 'wherever green is *worn*, is substantiated by their appearance in 'The Stolen Child':

> Away with us he's going,
> The solemn-eyed:
> He'll hear no more the lowing
> Of the calves on the warm hillside
> Or the kettle on the hob
> Sing peace into his breast,
> Or see the brown *mice* bob
> Round and round the oatmeal-chest.
> (*VP* 88, emphasis added)

That phrase 'the brown mice bob' has always struck me as being such a strange touch that I can only think that Yeats is unconsciously connecting a story about a stolen child and a rodent to that most famous of poems about stolen children and rodents, 'The Pied Piper of Hamelin'.[16] The rats have already scurried into the poem:

> Where dips the rocky highland
> Of Sleuth Wood in the lake,
> There lies a leafy island
> Where flapping herons wake
> The drowsy water-rats,
> There we've our faery vats
> Full of berries
> And of reddest stolen cherries. (*VP* 87)

If I were, like Yeats, a whodunit-loving sleuth, going into *Sleuth* Wood, as Slish Wood (as it is locally known) is here named, I might well discern a near version of Robert Browning's name appearing there in '*brown* mice *bob*'. As the OED reminds us, the word 'bob' more often denotes 'to move up and down like a buoyant body in water, or an elastic body on land; *hence*, to dance; to move to and fro with a similar motion, esp. said of hanging things rebounding from objects lightly struck by them'.[17] That 'to and fro' motion is precisely that of Michael Angelo's hand, and it might well describe a 'long-legged fly' moving 'up and down like a buoyant body in water'. Now, what type of fly moves on water? A clue may lie in a poem that falls right between 'The Falling of the Leaves' and 'The Stolen Child' in *Crossways*, yet another poem about a Browningesque parting:

> 'Your eyes that once were never weary of mine
> Are bowed in sorrow under pendulous lids,
> Because our love is waning'. (*VP* 79)

---

[16] Yeats probably first encountered this fairy story from the Brothers Grimm in Robert Browning's poem, 'The Pied Piper of Hamelin', with which 'The Stolen Child' has certain formal affinities. He retained two volumes of his father's set of Browning's *Poetical Works* (YL 296–97), but this poem is found in Vol. 1: *Lyrics, Romances, Men, and Women*, 234–46.

[17] OED.

This is one of the two lovers who take the stage to say their say in 'Ephemera', a poem Yeats wrote in 1884, the ephemera of the title referring to 'an insect that (in its imago or winged form) lives only for a day. In mod[ern] Entomology the name of a genus of pseudo-neuropterous insects belonging to the group *Ephemeridae* (Day-flies, May-flies.)'[18] Indeed, Robert Browning had written in his 1875 poem, *Aristophanes' Apology*, with an unconscious pun on the first word:

> 'May I, the *ephemeral*, ne'er scrutinize
> Who made the heaven and earth and all things there!'[19]

The fact that 'Easter, 1916' begins with the line 'I have met them *at close of day*' might be seen to establish immediately the theme of the poem as the tension between the ephemeral and the eternal, the evanescent and the everlasting, and to point immediately to the identity of the long-legged fly. The legs of the male mayfly are indeed particularly long so as to facilitate finding and grasping females for brief, mid-flight couplings on their day of days. 'I am still of opinion', wrote Yeats, in oft-quoted mode, 'that only two topics can be of the least interest to a serious & studious mind—sex & the dead'.[20] The mayfly is the perfect emblem for that double major of sex and the dead, its positioning of itself on the surface of the water the perfect emblem for self-reflection. The 'studious mood' in which Yeats poses himself is one of meditation, one of a Browningesque scrutiny, that he shares with the main characters of 'Long-legged Fly', including Julius Caesar:

> That civilization may not sink,
> Its great battle lost,
> Quiet the dog, tether the pony
> To a distant post.
> Our master Caesar is in the tent
> Where the maps are spread,

---

[18] *Ibid.*
[19] *The Poetical Works of Robert Browning* (London: Smith, Elder & Co., 1889), XIII, 90.
[20] *CL InteLex* 5034, to Olivia Shakespear, 2 October [1927]; *L* 730.

> His eyes fixed upon nothing,
> A hand under his head.
> *Like a long-legged fly upon the stream*
> *His mind moves upon silence.* (*VP* 617)

'Long-legged Fly' was written between November 1937 and April 1938, a period in which the map of Europe was being redrawn with a particular vengeance. Though *Kaiser* Wilhelm II had been forced out of Germany after World War I, Adolph Hitler was continuing to strengthen his position as a Caesar in the making. In this he was comforted by the ideas of the redoubtable Arthur Schopenhauer:

The highest civilization and culture, apart from the ancient Hindus and Egyptians, are found exclusively among the white races.[21]

It turns out that when, at a secret conference on 5 November 1937, Hitler had revealed his plan for extending the *Lebensraum*, or 'living space', for the Aryan nation, he pointed to Ireland's fight for independence from Britain as an indicator that Britain could no longer expect to rule its Empire. On 13 March 1938, Hitler annexed Austria, giving the master race a little more room for their great hatred. This November-March period of European political expansionism coincides precisely with the writing of 'Long-legged fly', giving a chilling aspect to the words 'our' and 'master' in 'Our master Caesar'. The use of the word 'our' also raises the question of who speaks 'Long-legged Fly', or at least this section of it. Harold Bloom, in his *Yeats*, asserts:

I hear only one speaker in Yeats's poem, the poet himself, who intercedes magically as a keeper of solitude for Caesar, Helen, Michael Angelo.[22]

I think Harold Bloom is perhaps overly influenced by the received view, not immediately evident from the poem itself, that Helen of Troy is not so much Helen of Troy as Maud Gonne:

---

[21] Arthur Schopenhauer, *Parerga and Paralipomena: Short Philosophical Essays*, tr. E. F. J. Payne (Oxford: Clarendon Press, 1974), Vol. 2, Section 92, 158.
[22] Harold Bloom, *Yeats* (New York: Oxford University Press, 1970), 450.

> She thinks, part woman, three parts a child,
> That nobody looks; her feet
> Practise a tinker shuffle
> Picked up on the street.
> *Like a long-legged fly upon the stream*
> *Her mind moves upon silence.* (*VP* 617)

This is a stroke of brilliance on the part of Yeats, since the propinquity of the dancer's 'feet' to the 'long-legged fly' has us envision Helen as a mayfly on the surface of the stream. The 'tinker' is just one letter shy of a 'thinker' and indeed the word 'thinks' is introduced to prepare for, and perpetuate, that slippage. The dance in which Helen is engaged may be construed as the technical term for the swarming of male mayflies to attract a mate, the 'dance' of the ephemera, a far cry from the dance of *Michael Robartes and the Dancer*. Yeats is engaged in a rather complex little shuffle himself, perhaps under the influence of Laurel and Hardy's *Way Out West*, a film released in this same year of 1937 and featuring, of all things, a soft-shoe shuffle. One might, with Bloom, wish the speaker who exhorts us to 'Move most gently if move you must | In this lonely place' to be a version of Yeats himself. The repetition of 'move' in '*Move* most gently if *move* you must' in the body of the verse, reminiscent as it is of the repetition of 'leaves' in 'The Falling of the Leaves', should weaken the impact of the refrain, or burden, of '*Like a long-legged fly upon a stream* | *Her mind* moves *upon silence*'. Instead, the impact is even greater. Part of Yeats's genius here is to make the burden have to do with an image of a burden being borne, the form of the poem yet again commenting on its subject matter in a mimetic way. In 'Three Songs to the One Burden', the poem which immediately follows 'Under Ben Bulben' in *Last Poems*, the first of three speakers, or singers, introduces himself as a 'tinker', and goes on to propose a theory of eugenics, a topic with which Yeats himself was much taken:

> The Roaring Tinker if you like,
> But Mannion is my name,
> And I beat up the common sort
> And think it is no shame.
> The common breeds the common,

A lout begets a lout,
So when I take on half a score
I knock their heads about.
From mountain to mountain ride the fierce horsemen. (*VP* 605)

Though Yeats's hope that this particular burden be multipurpose, perhaps even 'one-size-fits-all', is unfounded, giving substance to MacNeice's complaint that some refrains 'save thinking or excuse the lack of thought', the poem is not without its revelations, at least one of which Yeats may not have taken into account.[23] That is that the name 'Mannion' is one letter different from the name of one of Yeats's later lovers, Ethel *Mannin*, herself a firm believer in eugenics, in the desirability of rooting out 'base-born products of base beds' (*VP* 639). As Daniel Albright points out, it's in a letter to Ethel Mannin, written in 1936, that Yeats identifies himself as 'a forerunner of that horde that will some day come down the mountains'. He is himself one of these 'fierce horsemen', himself another contender for having 'trouble [d] the living stream' in 'Easter, 1916'. Here, the sense of 'trouble' is the sense beloved of eugenicists and other advocates of the pure drop, that's to say 'to mar' or 'to stir up (water) so as to make it thick or muddy; to make (wine) thick by stirring up the lees; to make turbid, dim, or cloudy',[24] as in 'the blood-*dimmed* tide' from 'The Second Coming', written in January 1919 and the seventh poem after 'Easter, 1916' in *Michael Robartes and the Dancer*. The 'lout' who 'begets louts' has already sent us back to the 'drunken vainglorious *lout* in 'Easter, 1916'.

'On a Political Prisoner', the third poem after 'Easter, 1916' in *Michael Robartes and the Dancer*, was also written in January 1919.

When long ago I saw her ride
Under Ben Bulben to the meet,
The beauty of her country-side
With all youth's lonely wildness stirred[25]

---

[23] MacNeice, 164–65.
[24] *OED*.
[25] *VP* 397. Yeats stayed with the Gore-Booth sisters from 20 November 1894 for a few days, during which Constance Gore-Booth drew him (dated 11 '94). See Plate 32.

Plate 32. Constance Gore-Booth's drawing of W. B. Yeats, Image, © Sligo County Library, Ireland and courtesy of the County Librarian, Dónal Tinney.

At this moment, Constance Markiewicz is indivisible from a sexualized Irish landscape (if I may speak of the 'side' as a flank, and 'country' matters as just those) in which she is the embodiment of the living stream troubled by a stone. The 'stirred' suggests agitation both the sense of 'to excite or provoke passion' and 'to rise in revolt or insurrection'. Yeats wrote to Lady Gregory on 29 January:

'I wrote a good poem on Madam Markeivitch at Lucan to escape the necessity of writing one on Maud Gonne who is now sane & amicable again & I think anxious to make up'.[26]

It now seems that the only 'stirring' of which Markiewicz (as a proxy for Gonne) is capable, either in herself or others, is to 'practice a tinker shuffle I picked up on the street'. Like those other long-legged flies, Caesar and Michael Angelo, Gonne/Markiewicz seems to have had her day.

---

[26] *CL InteLex* 3562. For a recent claim that the poem is about Gonne, see Anne Margaret Daniel, 'Moura is in Holloway: A famous "prophylactic love poem" by W. B. Yeats', *TLS*, 29 January, 2016, 14–15. For a definitive refutation, see Roy Foster, 'W. B. Yeats and Maud Gonne', *TLS* 12 February 2016, 6.

III

As I myself shuffle and slouch towards some conclusion, I want to consider for a moment that strange description of Maud Gonne as 'part woman, three parts a child'. The conventional phrase, as it were, would be something like 'one part woman, three parts child'. Such infelicitous phrasing as 'part woman, three parts a child' is more often than not an indicator of a little disturbance below the surface of the living stream of the poem. In this case it's an unconscious allusion to the ballad tradition, the tradition which (like the 'tinker shuffle'), is 'picked up on the street'. This is the tradition so categorically codified by James Francis Child in the original 10 volume edition of *The English and Scottish Popular Ballads* (1882–98) that the words 'Child' and 'ballad' are virtually indistinguishable. We've already seen the word child 'stolen' in the title of a poem in which 'peace' is sung 'into the breast' of 'The Stolen Child'. The poem was written in 1886, two years after the publication of Volume 2 of *The English and Scottish Popular Ballads*, the first ballad which, No. 54, has to do with another stolen child.[27]

> When Joseph was an old man, an old man was he,
> He married Virgin Mary, the queen of Galilee.
> He married Virgin Mary, the queen of Galilee.
> Joseph and Mary walked through an orchard green,
> There were berries and cherries as thick as might be seen.
> There were berries and cherries as thick as might be seen.[28]

---

[27] Francis James Child (ed.), *The English and Scottish Popular Ballad* (Boston and New York: Houghton, Mifflin & Co.; London: H. Stevens, Son & Stiles, [1882–98]), II, 2.

[28] In this and the two succeeding quotations, I use not Child's ballad versions, but 'The Cherry-Tree Carol', the refrained version known from sung carols with musical settings, in which the lines of each quatrain double up into dimeters, with the second line repeated as a refrain, added for sung versions. The earliest published version of this carol (which he may have encountered as a Christmas carol in his Protestant childhood), is that of Cecil Sharp (1909), who took the carol-tune down from in Gloucestershire on 13 January and 6 April 1909, using dimeters with a repeated second line, as well as the ballad in quatrains which he evidently checked in the *Oxford Book of Carols*. The carol was also available from numerous nineteenth-century sources, several before Child. Certainly Yeats knew the ballad in unrefrained quatrains from the Irish and English versions taken down by Douglas Hyde in and published in *The Religious Songs of Connacht*

These 'berries and cherries' find their way into 'The Stolen Child' with its faery vats, 'full of *berries*' and of reddest stolen *cherries*', the word 'stolen' related both to 'cherries' as it was to the 'child' because of the connection between 'a *baby*, with no crying' and the '*cherry* that has no stone', the ballad of that title that's also known as Child #46.[29] The attraction of the ballad tradition to Yeats is manifold. That riddling quality in 'The Cherry That Has No Stone' connects to the worlds of magic and religion. Its antiphonal aspect connects further to the world of public prayer just as the mantra is a feature of private prayer or meditation. The relationship been chanting and enchantment is firmly established in 'Easter, 1916' in 'the hearts with one purpose alone' that are '*enchanted* to a stone'. This is a version of the hypnotic trance, to which the refrain may be a contributing device, in which the three main characters in 'Long-legged Fly' find themselves caught up, the 'sheer hypnotic force' which MacNeice diagnosed as an intrinsic danger of the refrain.[30] It is the hypnosis associated with repetitive action—including the labour of the stonebreakers in 'Parnell' (*VP* 590)—which may be one of the sources of dance. It is also the hypnosis associated with such work song forms as the villanelle and the blues, which is barely a breath away from the ballad:

> And Mary spoke to Joseph, so meek and so mild,
> 'Joseph, gather me some cherries, for I am with child.
> Joseph, gather me some cherries, for I am with child'.
> And Joseph flew in anger, in anger flew he,
> 'Let the father of the baby gather cherries for thee.
> Let the father of the baby gather cherries for thee'.

Yet again, the 'to and fro' of the ballad tradition takes Yeats in the direction of a more conventional drama, with speaker handing off to speaker:

(1906), 1, 279–85, and the unrefrained quatrains in Jack Yeats's illustrated Cuala Broadside of 1909. The version I quote is that found in modern renditions by Joan Baez or Peter, Paul and Mary, found in a number of American folk versions.

29 I.e., 'Captain Wedderburn's Courtship', Child, 1, 414ff.

30 MacNeice, 164.

> Then up spoke the baby Jesus from in Mary's womb,
> 'Bend down the tallest tree that my mother might have some.
> Bend down the tallest tree that my mother might have some'.
> And bent down the tallest branch, till it touched Mary's hand.
> Cried she, 'Oh look thou Joseph, I have cherries by command'.
> Cried she, 'Oh look thou Joseph, I have cherries by command'.

The exchange of direct speech by Jesus, Mary, and Joseph is a feature of the ballad which is carried over to many of Yeats's poems including, as it happens, 'Ephemera' and 'The Indian Upon God', with the moorhen whose god is a replica of itself. In addition to being at the root of drama, it gave rise, yet again, to verse forms associated with dance. I'm thinking of the rondeau, for example, which is 'derived from dance-rounds (*rondes* or rondels) with singing accompaniment: the refrain was sung by the chorus—the general body of dancers— and the variable section by the leader'.[31]

Now, I promised earlier to get back to the idea of replication and replay, to what goes by rote, and that time has come around. Again, I want to suggest that the refrain is itself a symbol in Yeats. Let me return for a moment to the 'bob' of the mice in 'The Stolen Child'. One sense of the word 'bob' I've not raised until now is the sense given in the OED as '*the refrain or burden of a song*', a sense related perhaps to its connotations with dance. Coincidentally, Yeats's use of the refrain connects almost literally with a strand of symbolism I mentioned earlier. The 'bob' of the refrain is related, at least in sound, to the 'bobbin', a corruption of the Gaelic word *babán*,[32] a tuft, a tassel', meaning a spool or reel 'used to receive thread or yarn'. It is, in other words, one of 'the still expanding and ascending gyres' we might remember from Mrs Bob Browning's *Aurora Leigh*, her long poem of 1857, the gyres we've long since known to be central to Yeats's work. The wider context of that phrase in Elizabeth Barrett Browning is well worth remembering:

---

[31] *The New Princeton Encyclopaedia of Poetry and Poetics* (Princeton: Princeton University Press, 1993), 1097.

[32] Patrick S. Dineen, *An Irish-English Dictionary* (Dublin: Irish Texts Society, 1927), 66.

> I answered, smiling gently. 'Let it be.
> You scarcely found the poet of Vaucluse
> As drowsy as the shepherds. What is art
> But life upon the larger scale, the higher,
> When, graduating up in a spiral line
> Of still expanding and ascending gyres,
> It pushes toward the intense significance
> Of all things, hungry for the Infinite?
> Art's life,—and where we live, we suffer and toil'.[33]

The wider context, therefore, is a discussion of the meaning of art, a discussion which is obviously very much akin to that in 'Long-legged Fly', less obviously akin to 'Easter, 1916'. The kinship may have to do with the figure of 'the poet of Vaucluse', i.e. Francesco Petrarch (1304–74), who's rather glancingly mentioned there in Aurora Leigh. Petrarch is known for the play on his own name in, for example, Sonnet 51, where he associates himself with *petra*, or 'stone', a self-identification that was taken up by that stonebreaker of stonebreakers, Michelangelo Buonarroti (1475–1564), in his own sonnets. For Yeats may think of Michael Angelo as much sonneteer as stonebreaker, though he does of course tend to position him under the 'Sistine roof', as he describes it in 'Michael Robartes and the Dancer', the first poem in the 1921 volume of that same name in which 'Easter, 1916' follows four poems later:

> While Michael Angelo's Sistine roof,
> His 'Morning' and his 'Night' disclose
> How sinew that has been pulled tight,
> Or it may be loosened in repose,
> Can rule by supernatural right
> Yet be but sinew. (*VP* 386)

The centrality of what is 'loosened in repose' is carried over from *Aurora Leigh* through 'Michael Robartes and the Dancer' to 'Easter, 1916' and the system of the 'stone' that has it in it 'to trouble the living stream'. That art might have as its end toil, with its deep sense

---

[33] Elizabeth Barrett Browning, *Aurora Leigh*, With an Introductory Note by E. Wingate Rinder (London: Walter Scott, [n.d.]), Bk IV, ll. 1149–54, p. 151; *Aurora Leigh* (London: The Women's Press, 1978), Bk iv, l. 1154, p. 192.

of 'to stir up, make a stir or agitation' (*OED*) rather than tranquillity, of rupture rather than 'repose', stands in direct contradiction to Walter Pater's view, restated by Yeats in 'To a Wealthy Man who promised a Second Subscription to the Dublin Municipal Gallery if it were proved the People wanted Pictures', where he writes of Michelozzo's San Marco Library, 'Whence turbulent Italy should draw | Delight in Art whose end is peace' (*VP* 288). What Michael Angelo's mind is moving on in 'Long-legged Fly' is not merely a post-Schopenhauerean 'silence' by Buddhism out of Pessimism, nor even a post-Schopenhauerean 'silence' by Boredom out of Brevity of Life, but the paradoxical nature of the intersection of the eternal with the ephemeral that is *the refrain itself*. The eternal is made flesh in the refrain just as Helen or Christ are made flesh. The refrain itself is the point at which the crooked road of intuition intersects with the straight road of logic, symbolized for Yeats by the butterfly and the hawk (*VP* 338, 827). The refrain is itself the point at which the fluttering 'to and fro' of the butterfly intersects with the 'fixed' path of the hawk, the butterfly's 'limbs that had run wild' intersects with the hawk's heart 'with one purpose alone'. We can easily appreciate that sense of the word gyre as meaning 'a vortex' if we visualize what happens when 'the stone's in the midst of all' and the living stream is 'troubled'. There is a mini-gyre in the 'vortex' sense, as given by the *OED*, just as there's a mini-gyre (in a slightly different, if related, sense) when the minds of Caesar, Helen and Michael Angelo 'move upon silence' (*VP* 617). Caesar's eyes are 'fixed' alright, but 'fixed upon nothing' because he is in a gyre in the very specific sense of 'a trance', presumably one brought on by whirling. This is a usage which, though obsolete and, as the *OED* tells us, probably based on 'a mistake', is very much of a piece with the description of the hypnotic state MacNeice divined as being a danger to the refrainer. In a poem like 'Long-legged Fly', the refrain is itself conducive to this hypnotic state, and may not be entirely distinguishable from it, even when it functions in much the way so famously outlined by Edgar Allan Poe in his essay on 'The Philosophy of Composition':

As commonly used, the *refrain*, or burden, not only is limited to lyric verse, but depends for its impression upon the force of monotone—both in sound and thought. The pleasure is deduced solely from the sense of identity—of repetition. I resolved to diversify, and heighten the effect, adhering in general to the monotone of sound, while I continually varied that of thought: that is to say, I determined to produce continuously novel effects, by the variation *of the application* of the refrain—the refrain itself remaining for the most part unvaried.[34]

It's as if Poe's refrain in 'The Raven'—the tolling 'Nevermore'—were an ironic commentary on Wyatt's 'In Eternum':

> In eternum I was ons determed
> For to have lovid and my minde affirmed,
> That with my herte it shuld be confermed
> In eternum.[35]

The two tags 'in eternum' (evermore) and 'Nevermore' may themselves be read as one-size-fits-all refrains, since every refrain manages to fall between the two, between some sense of the endlessly ongoing stream that runs under and behind the poem and the fact that it surfaces only at intervals and, like its own long-legged fly, only ephemerally. A particular variation of that word springs to mind just now, like a cog caught in mid-cogitation. I'm thinking of the word 'Ephemeris', a term with which Yeats was almost certainly familiar, and one relevant to his system of gyres, referring as it does to 'a table showing the predicted (rarely the observed) positions of a heavenly body for every day during a given period' (*OED*). Yet again, it's the shuffling from the predictable to the unforeseen and back again to the predictable that, as MacNeice describes it, gives the Yeatsian refrain its particular power:

A refrain again, when it means anything, tends to be simpler in meaning than the rest of the poem; it gives the reader or hearer relief. Yeats's use of it, therefore, is often in two respects unusual. First the music of his refrain

---

[34] Edgar Allan Poe, *Poems and Essays*, edited with a new memoir, by John H. Ingram (Leipzig: Bernhard Tauchnitz, 1884), 276. On Yeats's reading of early Poe see *Myth 2005*, 308, 371, 396, 416, 418.

[35] See Sir Thomas Wyatt, *Collected Poems*, ed. Kenneth Muir (London: Routledge and Kegan Paul, 1949), 54.

is often less obvious or smooth than that of the verses themselves, being sometimes flat, sometimes halting, sometimes strongly counterpointed.

Secondly, his refrains tend to have either an intellectual meaning which is subtle and concentrated, or a symbolist or nonsense meaning which hits the reader below the belt.[36]

What's striking about the refrain in 'Long-legged Fly', and perhaps even the refrain in 'Easter, 1916', is that they have a nonce quality, as if to suggest that the speech that comes after long silence might be confused and confusing. It was, of course, this rivulet of the oddly dissociative quality of a nursery rhyme that MacNeice so brilliantly diverted from Yeats into his own stream. In this way, 'There's not a pilot on the perch | Knows I have lived so long', from 'Three Songs To the One Burden' (*VP* 607), takes off and lands in a cage in the form of 'Budgie', a poem in MacNeice's final book, *The Burning Perch*.[37] The mechanical birds of 'Byzantium', like the 'birds made to sing, and be silent alternately by flowing water' by the great inventor Hero of Alexandria,[38] transcend their moment and, through poetic influence and poetic allusion, achieve in reality a synthesis of constancy and change that Yeats achieves rhetorically at the end of 'Ephemera':

> 'Ah, do not mourn', he said,
> 'That we are tired, for other loves await us;
> Hate on and love through unrepining hours.
> Before us lies eternity; our souls
> Are love, and a continual farewell'. (*VP* 80–81)

This continual farewell is represented, yet again, by the refrain itself which, in the midst of all that momentum and surfeit must, for a moment, suffice.

[36] MacNeice, 167.
[37] Louis MacNeice, *The Burning Perch* (London: Faber & Faber, 1963), 37
[38] See *The Pneumatics of Hero of Alexandria*, tr. for (by J. G. Leonard) and ed. Bennet Woodcroft (London: Charles Whittingham, 1851), Section 15, 31–32.

http://dx.doi.org/10.11647/OBP.0081.07

Eliot and Yeats

John Kelly

YEATS AND ELIOT are generally supposed to have had little in common, either in their thinking or in the manner and style of their work.[1] Indeed, it is generally assumed that they were at best chary of each other and at worst antagonistic. This view has been powerfully put by a poet who knew them both as close friends: in a letter of 21 November 1957 Ezra Pound wrote to George Yeats, W. B. Yeats's widow:

My benevolent speculation | not retrospective but as insemination was as to whether TSE and Uncle Wm | didn't tend to bring out the worst of each other, or at least neglected to develop a mutual illumination.[2]

Since Yeats, 'Uncle Wm' had by this time been dead almost twenty years it might be thought that Pound's speculation could not help but be retrospective, but his description of it as 'insemination' seems to suggest more fertile possibilities, even that he considers the relationship

---

[1]   This sixth annual UCC W. B. Yeats Lecture was delivered on 30 April, 2008 as 'A "Mutual Illumination"? W. B. Yeats and T. S. Eliot'. When delivered, it began with a tribute to 'that renaissance man Eamonn Cantwell [who] spent the first part of his life bringing physical light to Ireland in the ESB and the second part intellectual light in his work on Yeats and his generous bequest to the National University, Cork, of his superb Yeats library'.

[2]   Ezra Pound to George Yeats, 21 Nov 1957 (Private).

between two of the greatest poets writing in the twentieth century is still pregnant with possibilities. Later critics have almost uniformly agreed with Pound's estimation that the two writers were suspicious or hostile towards each other's work—although it is conceded that after Yeats was safely dead Eliot's attitude towards him softened, and that he made amends with a noble commemorative lecture in Dublin in 1940, and with the inclusion of Yeats as a significant element in the 'compound' ghost in his last great poem *Little Gidding*.

Reading the newly available letters between both poets, as well as hitherto uncollected articles and prose, suggests that the relationship between Yeats and Eliot was more complex and less antipathetic than has been hitherto thought, and I want to argue that under an apparent indifference, or lack of 'mutual illumination', the two men were not only far more conscious of each other than is generally recognised, but that, ironically, they were more alike in their thinking, or at least in sharing common concerns in their thinking, than they were like Pound—although he impinged more obviously, and boisterously, on both their careers. And there is this implication in Pound's very words. His regret is not that there was no 'mutual illumination' between Yeats and Eliot but that such a potential illumination regrettably lacked sufficient wattage, so that it did not refract and reflect as brightly as he thought it could and should have done. In this sense it is worth exploring just what was 'mutual' in the two poets' 'illumination', and in what ways they might be said to have 'neglected to develop' it. And we might remark that, as in the case of matches and flint, illumination may be generated from friction as much as from recognition and assent.

The attitudes of both Yeats and Eliot to their age and their art was deeply inflected both in theme and practice by philosophical, religious and social anxieties that had incubated in the nineteenth century, and these anxieties pre-occupied them more agonizingly than they did Pound, Joyce or Wyndham Lewis, writers usually numbered with them as the major Modernists. If, as is now fashionable, we see the Modernist Movement as a reaction to Modernity, as a realisation that the secular ethics and clear thinking of the Enlightenment had not only failed to deliver the earthly paradise but had in fact begotten a world of fragmentation and entropy, then Yeats and Eliot can be said to have addressed this condition from the outset of their careers. In both cases, the perception led them to seek meaning in what Eliot was to call 'the immense panorama of futility and anarchy which is contemporary history' and Yeats, more succinctly, 'the preposterous pig of the world'.[3] In seeking to find meaning both were drawn, if from different directions and with different conclusions, towards what was for them a central mystery: a comprehension of the implications of Logos, which Eliot eventually understood as the Christian Incarnation and Yeats as a less orthodox process of sometimes violent incarnations—supernatural irruptions into the processes of human history.

Yeats was already an established poet of forty-nine in 1914, when Eliot arrived in England for what turned out to be a permanent residence. His radical change in style and theme, increasingly evident after he had 'got down off his stilts' at the turn of the century, was unmistakably registered in his book *Responsibilities* of that year, a fact that Pound understood but Eliot did not. Indeed, Pound, if not the catalytic influence some critics have claimed, certainly encouraged Yeats to be bolder in his poetic experiments. He also exerted an important influence on Eliot—but again, as in his dealings with Yeats, this was less in converting him to new forms and styles than in encouraging him to persevere and develop the poetry he was already writing. Pound at once understood the precocity and individuality of the twenty-six-year-old Eliot, recalling later that he was so poetically gifted as to have evolved his own modernist style apparently by himself. This very self-fashioning kept Eliot aloof from Yeats. Whereas Pound had arrived in London, five years before him, eager to become a disciple (Dorothy Shakespear recalled in her journal that in February 1909 he 'talked of Yeats, as one of the Twenty of the world who have added to the World's poetic matter' and 'read a short piece of Yeats, in a voice dropping with emotion, in a voice like Yeats's own'[4]), Eliot needed no such addition to his poetic matter.

[3] Eliot 'Ulysses, Order, and Myth', the *Dial*, LXXV, 1923, 480-83; Yeats, 'Blood and the Moon' (*VP* 481).
[4] *Ezra Pound and Dorothy Shakespear; their letters 1910–1914*, ed. Omar Pound and A. Walton Litz (London: Faber & Faber, 1985), v.

Although, as he acknowledged in a lecture delivered shortly after Yeats's death, 'Yeats was already a considerable figure in the world of poetry' when he began to write, he could not 'remember that his poetry at this stage made any deep impression on me', because, as he went on to explain, the poetry he needed to quicken his consciousness only existed in France; for this reason 'the poetry of the young Yeats hardly existed for me until after my enthusiasm had been won by the poetry of the older Yeats; and by that time—I mean from 1919 on my own course of evolution was already determined'.[5]

If not influenced by Yeats, Eliot was, from early in his English career, keenly aware of him and within a few months of his arrival in Oxford engineered a meeting. In February 1915 he intimated to Pound that he hoped to make Yeats's acquaintance, and Pound, who had recently acted as Yeats's secretary, took the hint and brought him to one of Yeats's famous 'Monday Evening' gatherings, probably on 8 March. Thus by 4 April 1915 Eliot could report that he had 'had the pleasure of meeting Yeats': 'he is now in Ireland', he went on, but 'I am hoping for him to return—he is a very agreeable talker'.[6] It is probable that the two bumped into each other reasonably often over the next few years, particularly given their shared friendship with Pound; there is evidence, for instance, that Eliot attended one of the exclusive performances of Yeats's first Noh play, *At the Hawk's Well*, in London in April 1916. On 2 March 1917 he was constrained to curtail the pleasure of Yeats's 'agreeable' talk by the intervention of a popular novelist when, as he reported in a letter to Eleanor Hinkley, he found himself at 'a gathering of a curious zoo of people known as the Omega Club, and was sitting on a mat (as is the custom in such circles) discussing psychical research with William Butler Yeats (the only thing he ever talks about, except Dublin gossip) when a red-faced, sprucely dressed man with an air of impertinent prosperity and the aspect of a successful wholesale grocer came up

---

[5] 'The First Annual Yeats Lecture', delivered to the Friends of the Irish Academy at the Abbey Theatre, Dublin, 30 June 1940, in *On Poetry and Poets* (London: Faber & Faber, 1957), 252.

[6] *The Letters of T. S. Eliot, Volume I: 1898–1922*, eds. Valerie Eliot and Hugh Haughton (London: Faber & Faber, 2009), 103. Hereafter TSE, *Letters* I.

and interrupted us with a most disagreeable Cockney accent.... I was so irritated by the man that I left for another part of the room almost at once—later I found out it was Arnold Bennett'.[7] Despite his striking, if uncarbuncular, resemblance to a small house agent's clerk, Bennett was later to go out of his way to try to help Eliot, and, since he sometimes attended séances with Yeats, was probably genuinely engaged by the conversation on this occasion. It is also quite possible that Eliot was genuinely interested in it. In an interview after Yeats's death he told Richard Ellmann about these discussions, and Ellmann assumed that he had been bored by them,[8] although in the light of his warm response to Yeats in 1915, and the fact that he began a review of *Per Amica Silentia Luna* in 1917 with the observation that it was 'always a pleasure to have Mr. Yeats talking', it is far from certain that this was the case. But, if not wearied by Yeats's fascination with psychical research, he was on philosophical grounds suspicious of it, and also of his recourse to folklore and myth in addressing metaphysical and theological questions.

Part of his disquiet was prompted by the perception that they were both troubled by the same questions. In his very first published essay, an article on the poetry of the Irish writer, Sir Samuel Ferguson, which appeared in October 1886, Yeats had extolled Ferguson's heroic style, as offering an alternative to what he describes as 'that leprosy of the modern—tepid emotions and many aims' (*UP1* 104). Yeats from the very first opposed in his art and criticism what he saw as the psychological and social torpor induced by modernity and the consequent undermining of traditional social and religious beliefs. It is significant that shortly after moving to London in 1887 he articulated his increasing sense of alienation with the very allusion that Eliot was later to employ in *The Waste Land*. Writing to his Dublin correspondent, the poet Katharine Tynan, he complained that many of those he met reminded him of the lost souls in Dante's *Inferno*, consigned there not because they had committed any great

---

[7] TSE, *Letters* I, 185–86.
[8] Richard Ellmann, *Eminent Domain* (New York: Oxford University Press, 1967), 90. It is significant that the chapter on Yeats and Eliot is by far the shortest in this excellent study of Yeats's encounters with five major contemporaries.

sin, but because they had made the *gran refuso*—they had failed
to do anything virtuous (*CL1* 91). Thirty-five years later Eliot
was to identify these souls as the quotidian denizens of his Waste
Land—the crowd flowing over London bridge 'so many, I had not
thought death had undone so many, I Sighs short and infrequent,
were exhaled I And each man fixed his eyes before his feet'.[9] The
allusions, as Eliot reminds us in his notes, are to the First Circle
of the *Inferno*, and it is these crowds which set the moral tone of
his poem: not great sinners (for great sins, as he argues in his essay
on Baudelaire, require energy and audacity) but the trivial and the
venial, represented elsewhere in his work by Prufrock and Gerontion
and the Hollow Men. Yeats prescribed as the antidote to 'the leprosy
of the modern' an heroic form of poetry based on myth and legend,
and in the nineties he was fond of citing not (as Eliot misrepresented
him) Matthew Arnold's assertion that poetry was 'a criticism of life',
but William Blake's more robust and positive insistence that Art
was a 'celebration' of life, and that all arts strove to bring about the
Golden Age again (*E&I* 137, 167).

And here we strike on a fundamental difference between Yeats
and Eliot: both were haunted by the prospect that the world may be
'Absurd', in so far as it has no purpose; that history is merely a process
of endless repetition. But whereas Yeats defiantly sought to redeem
the world through the Imagination, Eliot took it as the inevitable
consequence of the human condition, a state which, following his
conversion to Christianity, he would associate with original sin. In
a thoughtful essay on Yeats and Eliot, George Fraser argues that
the crucial difference between the two is that 'Eliot is a Christian.
Yeats was not'.[10] There is much truth in this, but we need to remind
ourselves that Eliot was not always a Christian and that his form
of theology was based on attitudes and perplexities that preceded
his conversion. These perplexities overlapped with those of Yeats,
who was certainly not indifferent to Christianity, so that, while their

---

[9] T. S. Eliot, *Collected Poems and Plays* (London: Faber & Faber, 1969), 62.
     Hereafter TSE, *Collected Poems and Plays*.
[10] George S. Fraser, 'W. B. Yeats and T. S. Eliot', in Neville Braybrooke (ed.), *T. S.
     Eliot: A Symposium* (London: Hart-Davis, 1958), 196–216.

search for answers that would satisfy them differed markedly, the origins and motives of their quest were markedly similar.

Yeats's concern to counter the leprosy of the modern and its many aims was grounded before 1900 in his attempts to find what he called Unity of Being through Unity of Culture. In a poignant passage in *Autobiographies*, one to which, significantly, Eliot returned on a number of occasions, Yeats laments that, unlike others of his generation, he was deeply religious but, 'deprived... of the simple-minded religion of my childhood' by the post-Darwinians, he made a new religion out of poetic tradition, and that this tradition was steeped in the supernatural (*Au* 115–16). If Yeats's predicament was not as untypical as he alleges of one born in the mid-nineteenth century, and thus inescapably the heir of Darwin and German Higher Criticism, his reaction to it was less usual. Eliot would later charge him with trying to promulgate what was essentially an individual and idiosyncratic religion, but this was far from the case. On the contrary, no matter how unorthodox the directions it may have taken, Yeats's search for faith always included a search for authentication: in the Tibetan authorities Madame Blavatsky claimed for her form of theosophy, in the supposed Rosicrucian or Hermetic origins of the Golden Dawn, in medieval mysticism and Gnosticism, and, in later life, in the study of the *Upanishads*. Moreover, in his interest in theosophy and the religions of India, Yeats was anticipating, in a less rigorous and less scholarly fashion, Eliot's purpose in taking academic courses on Eastern religions at Harvard. Like many of their generations both sought enlightenment from the East, and Eliot was propelled to take these courses because he was seeking what Yeats was seeking. Both in their youth found themselves cut off from the faith of their childhood. In Yeats's case this was the orthodox Protestantism of the Church of Ireland; for Eliot it was the Unitarianism of his family, a creed which denied the Trinity, questioned the divinity of Christ, and tended to convert issues of good and evil into conflicts in rational ethics.

So, if Yeats was, as he supposed, unlike others in his generation in being very religious, he was not unlike at least one person in the next generation, that is to say Eliot. Both were deeply unsettled by the inroads science had made into religious belief in the nineteenth century. The Higher Criticism of the Bible had challenged the orthodox account of creation and the divinity of Christ, while natural selection seemed, at its most reductive, to deny life any purpose beyond mere survival. Yet, for all his denunciation of Huxley and Tyndall ('whom I detested' [*Au* 115]), Darwinism was not the major factor in this process for Yeats, who readily rejected social and political evolution for a historiography based on sudden revolutionary, or counter-revolutionary, change. Nor was it for Eliot, who was to dismiss post-Darwinian meliorism as 'a partial fallacy Encouraged by superficial notions of evolution' and override it with a view of History as 'a pattern of timeless moments'.[11] Rather, both men were anguished by the loss of the numinous, the reduction of life to drab secularism, by those scientific and intellectual movements that contributed to what is now often described as the 'decentring' of man from his hitherto sovereign position in the scheme of things: a decentring which involved psychology, social change and politics as well as religion. In psychology the destabilization was a product of the growing perception that the self is a plural, unstable entity, and yet the troublesome realization that this plural and unstable entity has become crucial in the authentication of certain kinds of essential knowledge.

In confronting these problems their philosophic goals were not dissimilar: to find and articulate significance, to bring individuals and society to a richer and larger view of themselves and their destiny. The relationship between Yeats's quest for Unity of Being and Eliot's nostalgia for an undissociated sensibility would repay a more detailed study than I have time for here, as indeed would the question of why and how both saw Puritanism as a key factor in undermining this condition. Both saw the necessity for authority—in both cases discipline without regimentation—and both argued that any authentic community must ultimately appeal to a religious sense. Both were aware that in the modernist age psychological intuition must be an important constituent of belief but both were worried by the danger of

---

[11] *Collected Poems and Plays*, 186, 197.

mere eccentricity and solipsism that this threatened. Their concerns are therefore similar, but their temperaments different. Deprived of the simple faith of his childhood Yeats plunged into Theosophy and the Golden Dawn. The problem for him, as for the Romantics (and, indeed, for Eliot), was to authenticate private moments of seeming insight by relating them to universal truths. Yeats, a self-styled 'last Romantic', placed his hopes in the passionately engaged Imagination, sanctioned and corroborated by those movements and ideas—Theosophy, the Golden Dawn, Spiritualism—which seemed to offer a sort of inside track to illumination. There was in all this, as Eliot noted, something willed. Yeats, as an avid reader of Blake and Shelley, believed in the value of passion and energy as paths to Understanding, and, like Blake, never doubted that the road of excess lead to the palace of wisdom. But Yeats was not, as he himself ruefully confessed, a natural visionary or mystic. His unpublished 'Visions Notebooks' (the first started, significantly, at the very time when Freud was embarking on his research for *The Interpretation of Dreams*) bear witness to his elaborate attempts not only to analyse but also direct his dreaming states. Yeats wanted to believe that individual consciousness is part of a universal power (which he variously designates as 'anima mundi', 'primum mobile', or 'God'—concepts which in his theology derive from Platonic rather than Christian sources), and which he desperately wants to access. His poems of the 1890s, of 'The Rose' and *The Wind Among the Reeds*, are full of the desire for some revelation, a revelation that he seems perpetually on the brink of attaining: 'The Everlasting Voices' that cry of a remembered but unattained paradisiacal, Edenic State, 'The Secret Rose' which will bring with it the passionate ecstasy of spiritual Illumination, but which though urgently and eloquently invoked leaves the poet still waiting at the end of the poem, still wondering 'When will my hour come round at last…'

Eliot's approach was apparently much cooler. He, too, was haunted by revelation: but his revelations were not willed, or even at first desired. To the very end they remained 'unattended moments', and he was fastidiously cautious about questioning their origin or interpreting their meaning. And yet one might argue that there was

far more of the genuine mystic in Eliot than in Yeats. In this respect
he was (as he himself understood) closer to Tennyson but, unlike
Tennyson, he subjected such experiences to rigorous intellectual
monitoring and retained an abiding suspicion of what he calls 'the
inner voice', unmediated by divine grace. His early poems, those
now published in *Inventions of the March Hare*, are haunted by
such bleak epiphanies—'Silence', 'Oh Little Voices' and 'The First
Debate Between Body and Soul'—and by the gulf between quotidian
triviality and ultimate meaning as in 'Afternoon':

> The ladies who are interested in Assyrian art
> Gather in the hall of the British Museum.
> The faint perfume of last year's tailor suits
> And the steam from drying rubber overshoes
> And the green and purple feathers in their hats
> Vanish in the sombre Sunday afternoon
>
> As they fade beyond the Roman statuary
> Like amateur comedians across a lawn
> Towards the unconscious, the ineffable, the absolute.[12]

The details (even to the modish expression 'tailor suits') are exact
and economical, and the tone Laforgian. But the final line owes
less to Laforgue than to Francis Herbert Bradley, whose philosophy
was the subject of Eliot's doctoral dissertation. It is the apparently
absolute gulf between the Absolute and the mundane that haunts
and anguishes Eliot—and in his early poetry for all the apparent
flippancy of the ironical or even clownish mode which he borrowed
from Laforgue, for all his philosophic scepticism, there is a real
torment—something far more disturbing, far more profound than
Laforgue ever registered. The young Yeats had faced similar problems
in attempting to articulate the ineffable, and found recourse in the
iconography of the Rose and a symbolism based on Gaelic myth and
esoteric and folkloric sources. But he does not share Eliot's apparent
resignation. In 'Afternoon' the juxtaposition of the banal and the

---

[12] T. S. Eliot, *Inventions of the March Hare: Poems 1909–1917*, ed. Christopher
Ricks (London: Faber & Faber, 1996), 53.

sublime are an intentional and carefully worked effect: in the trite normality of the afternoon awesome cultural and religious artefacts of ancient civilizations are reduced to objects—mere objects—of disinterested contemplation rather than, as Yeats would have wanted them, recognized as the repositories of a still potential ancient wisdom. As in so many of Eliot's early poems, neither thought nor language can bridge the gulf between appearance and reality.

Eliot bought F. H. Bradley's *Appearance and Reality* in June 1913, and found that the philosopher, too, was concerned with the gulf between hints of the Absolute and everyday experience. Bradley debated in urbane prose the question that Eliot had agonised over in his recent poem 'Oh little voices' but, as Lyndall Gordon eloquently puts it, 'admitted bafflement without Eliot's sense of defeat'.[13] Bradley's attraction for Eliot was not intellectual daring but graceful intellectual poise with which he accepted failure to know final truth. It was, characteristically, just this detachment which appalled Yeats: in a footnote to *A Vision* he commented disapprovingly that Bradley 'found it difficult to reconcile personal immortality with his form of Absolute idealism, and besides he hated the common heart; an arrogant, sapless man' (*AVB* 219). This view, shorn of Yeats's aggressive rhetoric, was not so very far from Eliot's later estimation of Bradley. While he would never have thought of Bradley as 'arrogant', and although he continued to admire his 'scrupulous respect' for words and meanings, Eliot was from the beginning disturbed by Bradley's insistence that the individual soul was lost in the undifferentiated entity of the Absolute and he came to regard Bradley's Absolute as the Void, a state of Nothingness which horrified—and terrified—him. Thus his thesis strives beyond the bounds of enquiry Bradley thought appropriate, countering the assertion that 'my experience is not the whole world' by insisting that it is only in finite experiences that reality is to be apprehended, 'experiences so mad and strange that they will be boiled away before you boil them down to one homogeneous mass'. In this sense he can claim that '[a]ll significant

---

[13] Lyndall Gordon, *Eliot's Early Years* (Oxford: Oxford University Press, 1977), 50.

truths are private truths'.[14] But the problem remained of how those private truths related to more objective 'significant' truths and much of Eliot's dissertation, *Knowledge and Experience in the Philosophy of F. H. Bradley*, is concerned with exploring the extent to which distinctions between subjective and objective, mental and physical, external and internal, are tenuous, relative, and ambiguous.

As many commentators have pointed out, *Knowledge and Experience* is a painful and troubled work, in which Eliot turns Bradley's sceptical procedures on Bradley himself and upon his own immediate experience and fragmentary mental visions. He was hesitantly but rigorously to explore the relationship between private insight and larger revelation through his readings of Dante, George Herbert and the Christian mystics, readings which enabled him to associate private vision to the concept of the Logos and a Christian Incarnation. The process was a slow one, and is charted in a number of his belief in the reviews for the *International Journal of Ethics* and the *Monist* from 1916 onwards—for instance in his review of *Mens Creatia* by William Temple, later Archbishop of Canterbury and a personal friend, and *Religion and Philosophy* by R. G. Collingwood[15]— and, more obliquely, in the poems he published from 1917 to 1922: in 'Mr Eliot's Sunday Morning Service', 'Gerontion', and, masked in the mythological method, in 'The Waste Land'.

During this period of anguished intellectual questioning Yeats lurked perplexingly, even irritatingly, within Eliot's ken, and he attempted in two reviews to pluck the heart of his mystery: in the summer of 1918 he wrote a short notice of *Per Amica Silentia Lunae* for the *Egoist* and in July 1919 a more puzzled (and puzzling) review of *The Cutting of an Agate*, which appeared in the *Athenaeum* under the headline 'A Foreign Mind'. Although 'never weary' of Yeats's voice, in his attempts to grapple with *Per Amica*, Eliot finds its 'accents'

---

[14] *Knowledge and Experience in the Philosophy of F. H. Bradley* (London: Faber & Faber, 1964), 143, 165.

[15] Reviews of *Mens Creatia* by William Temple, *International Journal of Ethics* (July 1917), 542–43; *Religion and Philosophy* by R. G. Collingwood, *International Journal of Ethics* (July 1917), 543.

strange and 'cannot fathom his argument through all its mazes'.[16] One has a certain sympathy with this. Relating his own spiritualistic experiences to Neo-Platonism, particularly that of the seventeenth-century thinker Henry More, Yeats expounds his burgeoning ideas on mask and anti-mask, on the role of the daemon in individual human destiny and on the nature of the soul and its progress after death. Eliot thinks he can understand the first part of the book, but 'is quite lost' in the second part, 'Anima Mundi'.

Yeats, he confesses 'is lost to me, in some delicious soft mist as that in which Venus enwrapt her son', and yet 'as there is no one else living whom one would endure on the subject of gnomes, hobgoblins, and astral bodies, we infer some very potent personal charm of Mr. Yeats'.[17]

He does, however, manage to quote three passages from the book with approbation. The first is one in which Yeats asserts that modern culture 'with its doctrine of sincerity and self-realization' has 'made us gentle and passive', whereas the Middle Ages and Renaissance were right to found their culture on 'the imitation of Christ or some classical hero'. This chimed with Eliot's own contempt for the rationalizing theology and sociology of the day, exemplified in his 1916 review of Hastings Rashdall's *Consciousness and Christ* where he denounced liberal theological doctrines in which '[a]ll that is anarchic, or unsafe or disconcerting in what Jesus said and did is either denied or boiled away by "the principle of development"'. For Canon Rashdall, he goes on, 'the following of Christ is "*made easier*" by thinking of him "as the being in whom that union of God and man after which all ethical religion aspires is most fully accomplished"', and adds tartly that many 'saints found the following of Christ very hard, but modern methods have facilitated everything'.[18] In similar vein he was to condemn Sorel's *Reflections on Violence* as typical of the scepticism of the present, 'a torturing vacuity which has developed the craving for belief', and dismisses the book as 'representative of

[16] Review of *Per Amica Silentia Lunae* by W. B. Yeats, *Egoist* (June-July 1918), 87.
[17] *Ibid.*
[18] Review of *Consciousness and Christ: Six Lectures on Christian Ethics* by Hastings Rashdall, *International Journal of Ethics* (October 1916), 112.

the present generation, sick with its own knowledge of history, with
the dissolving outlines of liberal thought, with humanitarianism'.[19]

Eliot also commended Yeats's dictum that it 'is not permitted to
a man, who takes up pen or chisel, to seek originality, for passion is
his only business'. His increasing preoccupation with the question of
tradition and individual talent, found this challenge to originality for
originality's sake appealing. In an essay on Stendhal and Flaubert of
1919 he stressed that the two novelists 'were men of far more than the
common intensity of feeling, of passion', and that it was 'this intensity,
precisely, and consequent discontent with the inevitable inadequacy
of actual living to the passionate capacity, which drove them to art
and to analysis'.[20] In a review of Yeats's father's letters the previous
year he had applauded the old man's observation that poetry is 'truth
seen in passion', and was particularly struck by his comment that 'the
poet does not seek to be original, *but the truth*', a reflection, says Eliot,
that 'strikes through the tangle of literature direct to the subsoil of
the greatest... Ordinary writers of verse... deal in imagination or in
"ideas"; they escape from one to the other, but neither one nor the
other or both together is truth in the sense of poetic truth. Only old
ideas "part and parcel of the personality" are of use to the poet'. This,
he adds, 'is worth repeating to our American contemporaries who
study Freud'.[21] It would also have been worth repeating, apparently,
to Henry Adams, an uncontemporary American too old to have read
Freud, but whose life-long attempt at self-education failed according
to Eliot because 'he was unaware that education—the education
of an individual—is a by-product of being interested, passionately
absorbed'.[22]

Eliot also found Yeats's attack on Wordsworth and Wordsworth's
influence of value. In May 1918 he himself complained in the *Egoist*

---

[19] Review of *Reflections on Violence* by Georges Sorel, *Monist* (July 1917), 478–79.

[20] 'Beyle and Balzac', review of *A History of the French Novel to the Close of the
Nineteenth Century* by George Saintsbury, Vol. II: *Athenaeum* (30 May 1919),
392–93.

[21] 'The Letters of J. B. Yeats', review of *Passages from the letters of John Butler Yeats*,
selected by Ezra Pound, *Egoist* (July 1917), 89.

[22] 'A Sceptical Patrician', review of *The Education of Henry Adams: An Autobiography*,
Athenaeum (23 May 1919), 361–62.

of the inability of English commentators to criticize Wordsworth: although a poet 'of assured though modest merits', he was, Eliot reflected ruefully, one of those poets who 'punish us from their graves with the annual scourge of the Georgian Anthology'.[23]

In the two years between this article on *Per Amica* and Eliot's review of *The Cutting of an Agate*, something soured. Yeats's 'potent personal charm' seemed to have worn thin and his 'accent' (now identified unequivocally as Irish) sounded a good deal more grating. In 'A Foreign Mind' 'mutual illumination' is at its very dimmest. Eliot conveys his distaste for Yeats through a combination of knowingness, racial prejudice, and assumed urbanity. The book under review was a collection of essays and observations in which Yeats traced his literary development over the preceding fifteen years and discussed in particular the influence upon him of the Japanese Noh drama and the life and death of John Synge. In this sense it is palpably less 'esoteric' than *Per Amica* but nonetheless Eliot's tone has moved from benign bafflement to malign mystification: 'The difference between his world and ours is so complete as to seem almost a physiological variety, different nerves and senses'.[24] The argument of the review is centred on the attempt to fathom the alien nature of Yeats's mind and suggests that if 'we' could reach any conclusions about him that ought to 'illuminate our understanding of Irish Literature'. However, Yeats's mind is found to be 'independent of experience' and so 'different from ours' as to elude interpretation. So, it seems, are his dreams: the dreams of even Blake and Poe are 'continuous with normal mentality', but 'Mr. Yeats's dream is identical with Mr. Yeats's reality'. Eliot concludes that this remoteness is the product of a mind 'extreme in egoism' and thus 'a little crude', and that there 'is something of this crudity, and much of this egoism, about what is called Irish Literature'. It is, he claims, also a feature of the work of James Joyce, which is crude but has powerful feeling: 'the fault of Mr. Yeats's is that it is crude without being powerful'. This weakness of

---

[23] 'Observations', review of *Others, an Anthology of the New Verse*, ed. Alfred Kreymborg, *Egoist* (May 1918), 69–70.

[24] 'A Foreign Mind', review of *The Cutting of an Agate* by W. B. Yeats, *Athenaeum* (4 July 1919), 552–53.

Yeats's prose Eliot finds similar to that of his verse and puts it down to the fact that 'the objects upon which it is directed are not fixed'. Then, in a final sentence, he makes what in the context of the article is the astounding concession that it 'must always be granted that in verse at least Mr. Yeats's feeling is not simply crudeness and egoism, but that it has a positive, individual and permanent quality'.

This exaggerated insistence on the difference between Yeats's mind and the world as it exists is underscored by Eliot's repetition of second person plural pronouns. In most of his reviews of this period Eliot adopted a sparing editorial 'we', which usually articulated a position of neutral scepticism. In this article, however, the pronoun takes on a stable and normalising authority against which Yeats's aberrations are to be measured. Thus 'we are confirmed in the conviction' that Yeats 'is not "of this world"—*this* world, of course, being our visible planet with whatever our theology or myth may conceive as below or above it'. The editorial tone also adopts a complicit Englishness: 'When an Englishman explores the mysteries of the Cabala, one knows one's opinion of him, but Mr. Yeats on any subject is a cause of bewilderment and distress'.

This apparently authoritative and stable 'we' was a mask, and a mask which slips at significant junctures in the course of the article. The fact is that the article reveals less about Yeats than it does about Eliot, who was under intense emotional and physical stress at this time. At the end of June 1919 he confided to his mother that he had varicose veins and dental problems, and that for 'the first two days of this week I was too tired to be good for anything. Then I did another review, which took two days'.[25] It is tempting to imagine that that the recalcitrant review was the article on Yeats, but in any case, as his wife confided to a friend on 16 July, he was 'full of nerves' and 'really not well'.[26] His lack of worldly success was worrying him not only on his own account but also that of his family. In early January 1919 he had sent John Quinn a manuscript to place in America, explaining it was 'all I have to show for my claim—it would go toward making my

[25] TSE, *Letters* I, 367.
[26] *Ibid.*, 381.

parents contented with conditions—and towards satisfying them that I have not made a mess of my life, as they are inclined to believe'.[27] The very day after these words were written, on 7 January 1919, his father died thinking his son a failure.

This injected further anguish into his troubled state. Apart from his physical ailments, he was also at a point of decision and change. His lately widowed mother, as well as his former teachers, were pressing him yet again to return to America and, in weighing his inclination not to go back, he was obliged to analyse the consequences of remaining in England. Ironically, much of Eliot's anxiety was caused by his own alien status and thus the very title of his review of Yeats is tendentious. For who, we may ask, was the more foreign— the subject, Yeats, whose primary address had been London for forty-four of his fifty-four years, or the reviewer, Eliot, who had lived in England for just on five years. Eliot was, moreover, intensely aware of his position as an outsider. The letters he wrote in 1914 and 1915, shortly after his arrival in London and Oxford, are, understandably, full of observations on the otherness of England, but, despite (or perhaps because of) his marriage, these feelings became more rather than less acute. In March 1917 he told one of his Harvard professors that he intended to write a book on the English who 'are in fact very different from ourselves'.[28] On 2 July 1919, just two days before the publication of 'A Foreign Mind', he described to his brother what it was like to live in England in terms that verge upon paranoia: 'Don't think that I find it easy to live over here. It is damned hard work to live with a foreign nation and cope with them—one is always coming up against differences of feeling that makes one feel humiliated and lonely. One remains always a foreigner... It is like being on dress parade—one can never relax. It is a great strain.... People are more aware of you, more critical, and they have no pity for one's mistakes or stupidities... They are always intriguing and caballing; one must be very alert. They are sensitive, and easily become enemies'.[29]

27   *Ibid.*, 315.
28   *Ibid.*, 188.
29   *Ibid.*, 370.

But if Eliot was uncomfortable with the English—he told his Mother that trying to get recognized in English letters was like 'breaking open a safe'[30] (outsider now as outlaw)—he was even more uncomfortable with America and Fellow-Americans. America, he assured his brother, had no 'understanding or respect for the individual. The gregariousness of the life appals me'. Whereas in England, he found, one could be oneself. What struck him about the Americans he met was 'their *immaturity of feeling*, childishness',[31] and he told Quinn that England was an environment more favourable to the production of literature. If, then, both Yeats and Eliot are foreigners in London, there is this significant difference: Yeats had powerful ties to Ireland, where he was not only acknowledged as a national poet, but as a director of a successful theatre and a public figure whose pronouncements made news. Eliot, on the contrary, was trying to escape from America, which at this time he despised for its plebeian democracy and lack of cultural maturity.

But, as we have seen, for Eliot Yeats was a particular kind of foreigner: an Irish foreigner. And he had always had trouble with the Irish. As late as August 1921 he told Richard Aldington that Desmond MacCarthy was 'of course an Irishman, that is to say he belongs to a race which I cannot understand'.[32] In reviewing Pound's translations of Japanese Noh plays in 1915 he applauds his echoes of Anglo-Saxon and Provencal. These, he says, give 'added charm', while the Celtic echoes, which Pound also introduces, are condemned as 'offensive'. Quite why they are offensive rather than charming he does deign to reveal, but adds with faux magnanimity that he has 'no prejudice against the Irish drama, although I think that a large part of its popularity is due to tricks of idiom, just as I suspect that the reputation of Irish girls for beauty is due to their being called "Colleens"'.[33] A Bostonian Brahmin disdain for things Irish runs intermittently through Eliot's criticism and letters at this

---

[30] *Ibid.*, 476.
[31] *Ibid.*, 370.
[32] *Ibid.*, 574.
[33] 'The Noh and the Image', review of *Noh, or Accomplishment* by Ernest Fenollosa and Ezra Pound, *Egoist*, August 1917, 102–03.

time and we might remind ourselves that he even dubs the unlovely hero of a number of his early poems with the Hibernian patronymic 'Sweeney'.

Given all this, does Eliot think it ever possible to accommodate to a different culture? Of course, since he himself is seeking just such an accommodation, he does, and he suggests in another review that for Henry James the 'fact of being everywhere a foreigner was probably an assistance to his native wit'.[34] But it is not James who provides the supreme example of the successful literary expatriate, but Ivan Turgenev, whom Eliot describes in an article of December 1917 as 'in fact, a perfect example of the benefits of transplantation; there was nothing lost by it; he understood at once how to take Paris, how to make use of it'.[35] Turgenev 'knew how to maintain the role of foreigner with integrity', a position that was for him 'a source of authority, in addressing either Russian or European; authority but also isolation. He has a position which he literally made for himself.... It is not a position of popular appeal, as he neither aped French writing nor exploited the Russian backwater. He used Russian material naturally, with the simplicity of genius turning to what its feelings know best; he recognized, in practice at least, that a writer's art must be racial— which means, in plain words, that it must be based on the accumulated sensations of the first twenty-one years. But he combined in the same highest degree the insight into the universal sameness of men and women with appreciation of the importance of their superficial variations. He saw these variations—the Russian variations—as the artist and not the showman'. Eliot seems to be marking out a job-description for his own 'transplantation' here, but if anyone currently in London had achieved what Eliot says Turgenev achieved in Paris, it was surely Yeats. One questions the term 'backwater' in relation to either Russia or Ireland (although at this period Eliot would certainly have thought it a just description of the United States), but his account of what Turgenev did with his 'Russia material' chimes closely with what Yeats was doing with his Irish resources.

[34] In Memory of Henry James', *Egoist*, January 1918, 1–2.
[35] Review of Edward Garnett's *Turgenev*, *Egoist* (December 1917), 167.

Eliot would certainly have rejected such a comparison at this time, being convinced that Yeats had spent his childhood and youth in England so that Ireland was in the nature of an enchanting holiday destination for him. As such Yeats's experience perhaps offered itself (although he never quite says this) for a showman's rather than an artist's exploitation. Eliot is in the curiously paradoxical position of denying Yeats the entitlement to Irish 'race' since he believes he did not have 'the accumulated sensations of the first twenty-one years', and yet also wants to suggest that in him if anywhere we can come at an understanding of the 'Irish mind'.

Yet it is not just, or even mainly, Yeats's Irishness that distresses Eliot: it is his philosophical and theological heterodoxy. Significantly, he associates him with the 'Fantastics', a fifth-century heretical sect who, he reminds us, 'held that the visible Jesus, who grew to manhood and mixed with mankind, was a phantasm; at a certain moment the son of God assumed by the banks of Jordan full-grown the similitude of humanity. He was not really incarnate, but divinely deceived the world... Mr. Yeats might be such a fantastic avatar... [and]... controversy might rage... about the question whether Mr. Yeats really feels and thinks, or whether the deception, if it is the case, is derogatory to his divinity'. No matter how tongue-in-cheek, this analogy has resonance, not only because Yeats himself was to address such questions about the physicality of Jesus in his plays *Calvary* and particularly *Resurrection*, but also because the mystery and possibility of Incarnation was a recurrent theme in Eliot's poetry throughout his life. The allusion to the Fantastics comes from Book Five of *The Decline and Fall of the Roman Empire*, in which Gibbon discusses the various fifth-century heresies which centred on the actuality and meaning of the Incarnation. What particularly annoys Eliot—who had been for many years grappling with the philosophic grounds of reality and belief—is that Yeats seemed 'in his disembodied way, to happen on thoughts, thoughts of 'wisdom', and if we are not convinced, it is because we do not see by what right he comes by them'.[36] This suggestion that Yeats is cheating in his theological and

[36] 'A Foreign Mind', 553.

philosophic thinking by taking illicit short cuts is as hostile as Eliot ever became towards with him.

That said, he continued to snipe over the coming months. In the course of review in the *Athenaeum* on 3 October 1919, he consigned Yeats to the third of the four generations of poets currently writing in English. These were 'the middle-aged', a category which, he ambiguously remarked, included 'Mr. Yeats and a small number of honoured names'.[37] Does the conjunction 'and' register inclusion in or exclusion from the 'honoured names'? That it might be the latter is implied in Eliot's review of Ezra Pound's *Quia Pauper Amavi*, in the *Athenaeum* of 24 October 1919, where he remarked that what was 'not dependent upon the assimilation of medieval literature' in Pound's early work 'seemed to be slightly distorted by the influence of Mr. Yeats, although a more powerful intelligence than that of Mr. Yeats was visible. There was, of course, the much more beneficent influence of Browning'.[38]

Given these dismissive gestures, it is perplexing that Eliot in his elegiac lecture on Yeats should specify 1919 as the year in which his 'enthusiasm had been won by the poetry of the older Yeats', and opens up the possibility that his impertinencies of this year were an attempt to resist an enigmatic presence which loomed large and unignorable in London literary life. The attempt to disengage or at least belittle the sway Yeats exerted over his close and admired friend Ezra Pound (evident in his review of *Quia Pauper Amavi* above) may also be in part a displacement of the anxiety he felt more generally about the influence of Yeats. As early as the death of Swinburne in 1909 Yeats had declared himself now 'King of the Cats' and, although never a likely candidate for inclusion in *Old Possum's Book*, he was over the ensuing decade increasingly regarded thus by influential critics and the Establishment, with unanimous election to the Royal Literary Society's Academy of Letters, the award of a Civil List pension, and the offer of a knighthood.

---

[37] 'Murmuring of Innumerable Bees', review of *Coterie: An Illustrated Quarterly*, *Athenaeum* (3 October 1919), 972.

[38] 'The Method of Mr. Pound', review of *Quia Pauper Amavi* by Ezra Pound, *Athenaeum*, 24 October 1919, 1065–66.

What changed in 1919 was that Eliot came in out of the cold. He suddenly, to recall his own metaphor, cracked open the safe of London literary life. A couple of months after writing 'A Foreign Mind' he informed his mother that he had been asked to contribute to the *Times Literary Supplement*, which he extravagantly described (but he was writing to his Mom) as 'the highest honour possible in the critical world of literature',[39] and a little later he was asked to be the English representative of a promising new American periodical, the *Dial*, and to elicit contributions from, among others, Yeats. He was also, partly through his wife, an honoured guest at Lady Ottoline Morrell's Thursday evening receptions, and, he explained to his mother, 'there has been a great deal of jealousy and excitement aroused among all the people who were not invited'.[40] The publication of his influential book of essays, *The Sacred Wood*, in November 1920 further consolidated his literary presence and André Gide was to ask him to become London correspondent for the *Nouvelle Revue Francaise*.[41] Most important of all, and despite a nervous breakdown, he was working on a long poem, *The Waste Land*, which he knew to be good, and entering into negotiations with Lady Rothermere to become editor of the *Criterion*.

His attitude towards the Irish—or at least towards certain Irishmen—softened. He had already begun reading *Ulysses* in the *Little Review* with growing admiration and in August 1920 met Joyce in Paris, when at Pound's behest he embarrassedly presented him with a parcel containing a second-hand pair of boots. Neither Joyce nor his writings seemed any longer 'crude'. Shortly after the meeting he told Sydney Schiff that Joyce was 'a quiet but rather dogmatic man, and has… a sense of his own importance' (i.e. he had balked at being patronized with a pair of old shoes). 'He has a sort of gravity', Eliot went on with a tell-tale distinction, 'which seems more Protestant than Catholic. He is obviously the man who wrote his books—that is, he impresses you as an important enough personage

---

[39]   TSE, *Letters* I, 404.
[40]   *Ibid.*, 437.
[41]   *Ibid.*, 610–11.

for that'.[42] Eliot's admiration for Yeats grew partly as a consequence of his admiration for Joyce and particularly his admiration for the way Joyce was using myth.

Ellmann suggests that Yeats's pursuits were in Eliot's mind when he wrote in his poem 'A Cooking Egg': 'I shall not want Pipit in Heaven: | Madame Blavatsky will instruct me | In the Seven Sacred Trances', although Yeats's transient interest in Madame Blavatsky had long since run its course. We might at first reading detect a similarly satirical purpose in the portrayal of Madame Sosostris in *The Waste Land*, but the relationship here is more complex. Ellmann reminds us that Madame Sosostris is 'not made entirely a charlatan',[43] and it is significant that Jessie Weston, whose *From Ritual to Romance* provides a number of the most significant motifs in *The Waste Land*, introduced into the poem by Madame Sosostris, consulted Yeats in establishing the place of the Tarot cards in the mystical tradition. Eliot's realization that he and Yeats had more in common in their use of mythology than he had perhaps supposed is registered in his famous defence of *Ulysses*, a book which had a declared influence on *The Waste Land*. Here Eliot establishes an almost apostolic succession of influence in which Yeats is the precursor. In 'A Foreign Mind' he had included Joyce with Yeats in what was a general critique of Irish literature as egotistical and crude. His reading of *Ulysses* and his immediate recognition of its contemporary significance forced him to reassess his wilful impatience with both Yeats and Irish writing. Although well known, the passage in which he publicly acknowledges Yeats's importance bears re-quoting:

In using the myth, in manipulating a continuous parallel between contemporaneity and antiquity, Mr. Joyce is pursuing a method which others must pursue after him…. It is simply a way of controlling, of ordering, of giving a shape and a significance to the immense panorama of futility and anarchy which is contemporary history. It is a method already adumbrated by Mr. Yeats, and of the need for which I believe Mr. Yeats to have been the first contemporary to be conscious…. Psychology… ethnology, and *The Golden Bough* have concurred to make possible what was impossible even a

---

[42] *Ibid.*, 494.
[43] *Eminent Domain*, 91.

few years ago. Instead of narrative method, we may now use the mythical method. It is, I seriously believe, a step toward making the modern world possible for art.[44]

Eliot's jibes about gnomes and hobgoblins in Yeats's work were now a thing of the past, and indeed by the time he wrote the review of *Ulysses* he had re-established social and literary contact with him. His appointment as editor of the *Criterion* in 1922 led him to contrive a meeting which turned out to be of mutual benefit. Eliot's editorial policy, as he explained to a German correspondent, was to combine 'those of the older generation who have any vitality and enterprise, with the more serious of the younger generation, no matter how advanced'.[45] On 22 October 1922 he wrote to Ezra Pound that he would 'be delighted to have a few poems of Yeats, but so far I have had to go on the principle of asking people whom for one reason or another I felt pretty sure of getting, and as Yeats does not particularly like me, I believe, there appeared no reason why he should consent if I wrote to him direct. Could you do anything in the matter?' And he added 'I think it is particularly important to reserve the *verse* contributions to the really first-rate people. For that reason I should very much like to get Yeats.... I do not think that the *Criterion* can afford to print verse, for the present at least, except by people who really know their job. Hence my desire to get hold of Yeats'.[46] It is unlikely that Pound, who by now had moved to Paris, and who had in any case an ambiguous attitude to Eliot's new venture, took any action, and the intermediary was not to be him but the Eliots' new hostess Lady Ottoline Morrell, with whom Yeats stayed in November 1922. During that visit she evidently gave him a copy of *The Sacred Wood*, and also set up what turned out to be a very successful meeting between the two men in London on 3 December 1922, for which Eliot wrote to thank her:

I wired Yeats after hearing from you and consequently lunched with him.... I enjoyed seeing him immensely; I had not seen him for six or seven years and this was really the first time that I have ever talked to him for any

[44] 'Ulysses, Order, and Myth', *op. cit.*, 480-83.
[45] TSE, *Letters* I, 710.
[46] *Ibid.*, 766–67.

length of time alone. He is really one of a very small number of people with whom one can talk profitably about poetry, and I found him altogether stimulating.[47]

Yeats in his turn had written to his wife immediately after the meeting, telling her that 'Eliot has just lunched with me, & we have talked Joyce, poetry & the parallel dream for three hours' (Yeats's conversation still centring on psychical research apparently), and he went on: 'I am charmed with Eliot & find that I have a reasonable liking for his "Sacred Wood"' (*CL InteLex* 4229). The poetry they discussed evidently included Eliot's own, for soon after the meeting he defiantly informed his brother Henry Eliot that he considered his 'Sweeney poems as serious as anything I have ever written, in fact much more serious as well as more mature than the early poems but I do not know anybody who agrees with me on this point except Vivien and William Butler Yeats who have both said much the same thing about them'.[48] Eliot also presented Yeats with a copy of the opening number of the *Criterion*, which contained the first printing of *The Waste Land*, since a couple of weeks later Yeats told him that he found the poem 'very beautiful' but added cautiously (and forgivably) that 'here & there are passages I do not understand—four or five lines' (*CL InteLex* 4264). Eliot was touchingly and even humbly grateful for Yeats's kind words, replying on 21 January 1923 that is was 'a very great satisfaction to me to know that you like *The Waste Land*. When it is brought out in this country in a month or two as a book, with notes, I shall send you a copy and hope to have at some time, either in conversation or by letter, a detailed statement of your criticism. It is quite possible that the passages ought to be repaired'.[49] And he was just as delighted by Yeats's offer to send an article for the *Criterion*, promising that he would do his best to include it in the next number 'which in that case', he added expansively, 'will be the best number of the year'.[50] He did in fact inscribe a copy of the first English edition

---

[47] *Ibid.*, 806.

[48] TSE, *Letters* I, 803.

[49] *The Letters of T. S. Eliot, Vol. II: 1923–1925*, eds. Valerie Eliot and Hugh Haughton (London: Faber & Faber, 2009), 22. Hereafter TSE, *Letters* II.

[50] *Ibid.*

of *The Waste Land* on 26 April 1923 to Yeats 'in admiration of his work' (*YL* 90).[51]

The poem genuinely intrigued Yeats, and that for at least two reasons. In the first place, it seemed to suggest a return in contemporary literature to concerns and themes that had animated the earlier work of the Irish literary revival. In his preface to *The Cat and the Moon* of 1924 (Eliot published the play itself as one of the 'two good things' in the July *Criterion*[52]), he told Lady Gregory that in certain recent Irish plays, including his and hers but not those of the realists, he detected 'an odour, a breath, that suggests to me Indian or Japanese poems and legends.... something in Irish life so old that one can no longer say this is Europe, that is Asia'. This led him to speculate whether younger writers would 'take up our theme again, urged thereto by some change in the world's thought too subtle to be attributed to any book?', and finds evidence that they might in that 'the other day when I read that strange 'Waste Land' by Mr. T. C. [*sic*] Eliot I thought of your work and of Synge's; and he is American born, and Englishman bred, and writes but of his own mind' (*VPl* 1308).

Since Eliot was calling in *The Waste Land* upon the work of comparative mythologists well-known to Yeats, the similarities he detects grow out of the 'mythical method' as described by Eliot and are less mysterious than he wants to believe; nevertheless, he is correct in perceiving an affinity between himself and the apparently dissimilar Eliot. Nor was that affinity merely a shared interest in *The Golden Bough* and *From Ritual to Romance*: the detection of 'a breath' that suggested India, a breath that had stimulated both of them in their earlier years, was to bring the two closer together in Yeats's final decade, when Eliot would authorize the publication of a series of Indian texts sponsored and introduced by him.

---

[51] Eliot in fact slightly 'repaired' this version in ink, correcting 'A crowd flowed under London Bridge' to 'over London Bridge' (7); 'In which sad light a coloured dolphin' to 'a carvèn dolphin' (9); and in the notes altering the publisher of *From Ritual to Romance* from 'Macmillan' to 'Cambridge' (29). Since WBY already had the *Criterion* printing of the poem, he left most of the pages of this presentation copy uncut.

[52] TSE, *Letters* II, 383.

Yeats was also intrigued by *The Waste Land* because he was aware that Eliot was becoming influential among the young. His friend and patron, the Irish-American lawyer John Quinn, had written in July 1922 to inform him that in America 'Eliotism is the fashion. Amy Lowell and a dozen others here are now imitating Eliot, just as fifteen or twenty years ago they imitated your poetry' (*LJQ*, 287–8). This is the sort of news that a writer greets with mixed feelings, but in 1931 Yeats gained an insight into how younger Irish writers regarded Eliot when he read Thomas MacGreevy's *Thomas Stearns Eliot: A Study*. To a great extent the views that MacGreevy, a poet and art critic whom Yeats himself had introduced to Eliot, reinforced his own: that Eliot was 'a poet of undoubted genius', but that much of his early poetry ('Prufrock' and 'Rhapsody on a Windy Night' are counted as exceptions) is satirical and often too arch and knowing; that Eliot 'scarcely ever… finds something to write gratefully about'; and that what gaiety he has is a perverse 'scoring off of life'.[53] For MacGreevy *The Waste Land* was the apogee of Eliot's work, and he argued that *Ash Wednesday* and the subsequent poems showed a falling off.

In thanking MacGreevy for a presentation copy of the book, Yeats assured him that he was 'entirely delighted' with it, finding in its writing a 'momentum' the want of which in 'even the fine passages of Eliot always chills me, his words remain separate, each well-chosen and rightly placed but groups of words do not run together until they are a new single word…. A master of English, he insists upon speaking every word with the same care as if it were a foreign tongue'. Although he concedes that there are 'other things in Eliot', and that perhaps if he had *The Waste Land* beside him he 'might have nothing but praise of him', he feels that Eliot is trying, but failing, to write like Shakespeare 'and his very effort makes him unlike, he is dancing among eggs' (*CL InteLex* 5458). Yet he could not ignore the revolution that Eliot had wrought in poetry in English and the following year warned his friend Joseph Hone that in translating Mario Rossi's essay on Berkeley from the Italian

[53] Thomas MacGreevy [also McGreevy], *Thomas Stearns Eliot: A Study* (London: Chatto & Windus, 1931), 1, 24, 27.

'sea' should never become 'ocean' or 'main' or its 'blue' become 'azure' or a 'wave' a 'billow'. If you were a poet not a prose writer you would not use these words because you would feal very acutely that we are in a frenzy of reaction against all the old conventions. I should have warned you that Elliot, who is himself the most typical figure of that reaction, would refuse the essay on that account. Think of his bare poetry (*CL InteLex* 5606).

Not for nothing does Eliot in *Four Quartets* identify a shared concern when he has his compound ghost tell him that 'our concern was speech, and speech impelled us | To purify the dialect of the tribe'.[54]

    The concern with language is also an important aspect of Eliot's reappraisal of Yeats. He reread Yeats's canon in 1933 in preparation for a course on 'Contemporary English Literature' he was giving at Harvard. In his notes he asked 'Why deal with Yeats?' and answered his own question with the observation that from 'the late '90s to what I call the Anglo-American movement, everything can be dealt with in relation to Yeats. His variety of interest, his resourcefulness and development'. He divided Yeats's career into three phases: first the nineties, then the Irish Movement, and finally what he described as the 'Post-Pound Period'; the first two stages he found of little interest, and insisted that Yeats's influence began with the third—and to such an extent that, although Yeats had been born in 1865, Eliot regarded him 'as my contemporary'. He was particularly concerned with Yeats's theory of symbolism and with his image-making power; while speculating as to whether he was too deliberate in cultivating certain of his metaphors, he emphatically concluded that 'Yes the great progress is in clarity and simplicity, in finesses of metre'.[55] He also praised Yeats's labours in the Abbey Theatre, both as a dramatist and as an administrator: 'Fought for tolerance, civilisation, throughout', his notes read, 'Yeats kept the real spirit of the theatre alive. Whatever is going is in his debt. (Myself and Auden) Vital importance of theatre for the future'.[56] Eliot himself had already tried to assist Yeats's fight for 'tolerance' and 'civilization' in the *Criterion* of December 1928 by trenchantly supporting his opposition to the

---

[54] TSE, *Collected Poems and Plays*, 194.
[55] TSE notes, Harvard. I am very grateful to Ron Bush for drawing these to my attention.
[56] *Ibid.*

Irish Censorship Bill, backing given impetus both by his admiration for Yeats's campaign and by his fear of the threat of a more insidious censorship in Britain.[57] Eliot's interest in Yeats's contribution to the theatre was no doubt inspired by his own ambitions to become a dramatist, but may have been given a more immediate spur by a lecture on the Irish Theatre that Yeats delivered at Wellesley College on 8 December 1932, a narrative strand of which was the fight for 'tolerance, civilization' exemplified by the Abbey Theatre's refusal to surrender its artistic independence and integrity in the face of onslaughts from both government censorship and nationalist propaganda.[58] It is probable, but not certain, that Eliot, who was spending the year as Norton Professor at nearby Harvard, attended this lecture.[59] He himself had given a poetry reading at Wellesley on 17 October 1932 at the invitation of Elizabeth Manwaring, a Professor of English there and the author of a well-regarded book on the influence of Italian landscape on eighteenth-century English culture. She had been given an introduction to Eliot by his brother-in-law when she visited England the previous summer, and had struck up a friendship with him and, significantly, with his wife Vivien, at a time when the marriage was in a state of terminal disintegration.[60] It was the strength of that friendship (and the fact that she chose the poems he was to recite) which seems to have persuaded a very

---

[57] 'The Censorship and Ireland', *Criterion*, December 1928, 185–87.

[58] Yeats gave the lecture under the auspices of the Barnswallows Drama Association, which had mounted a production of *The Land of Heart's Desire* in Wellesley just over a month before. A somewhat garbled anonymous account of the talk in the *Wellesley College News* reports Yeats as saying that the early productions of the Irish dramatic movement 'were felt by the authorities to be a public menace', that *The Playboy of the Western World* 'had to be acted under police protection, but the Theatre finally won a victory over public opposition' and that since then 'many new writers have added to the repertoire of the Irish Players, but none of the plays touches on propaganda, and they are all founded on a passionate desire for service to country'.

[59] See frontispiece. It is not clear just where in the Boston region or at what function this photograph was taken.

[60] Elizabeth Wheeler Manwaring (1879–1949), had been educated at Wellesley College and returned to teach there, becoming Professor of English and Head of Department. Her acclaimed *Italian Landscape in Eighteen-Century England*, 'a study chiefly of the influence of Claude Lorrain and Salvator Rosa on English taste, 1700–1800', had appeared in 1925.

reluctant Eliot to read his own work at all, but once that ordeal, scheduled for the late afternoon, was over they enjoyed a pleasantly sociable evening with other members of the faculty. It is probable that over the course if the evening she mentioned Yeats's impending visit and invited Eliot to attend both it and the dinner which preceded it,[61] although the only evidence for this is an unattributed reference in Richard Ellmann's *Eminent Domain*, where it is the occasion of an (also unattributed) anecdote which has achieved some currency as an example of the continuing discordance between the two men. According to this story, Yeats was seated next to Eliot at the dinner 'but oblivious of him, conversed with the guest on the other side until late in the meal. He then turned and said, "My friend here and I have been discussing the defects of T. S. Eliot's poetry. What do you think of that poetry?" Eliot held up his place card to excuse himself from the jury'. John Haffenden shrewdly dismisses this story as 'surely apocryphal', on the grounds that (as Eliot himself attested) Yeats was unfailing gracious to younger writers. It is also barely conceivable that Elizabeth Manwaring would not have mentioned Eliot's presence to Yeats, or that Yeats, despite his poor eyesight, would not have recognized him at the pre-dinner reception. It is suspicious, too, that so scrupulous a scholar as Ellmann does not on this occasion give any source for his information, and one suspects that the temptation to open his chapter on Yeats and Eliot with the dinner anecdote (*Eminent Domain*, 89) must have been irresistible, supporting as it amusingly appears to do his thesis of their 'long, languid incompatibility'. In fact, not only is there no corroboration

---

[61] Elizabeth Manwaring was generally attentive in extending invitations to Eliot. She also arranged an outing with him to a recital by Jan Paderewski on 30 October 1932, and she invited him to dine with her in February 1933, 'a great pleasure' to which he looked forward 'with keen anticipation'. On 28 February 1933 Eliot presented her with an inscribed copy of *The Swiss Family Robinson*. On her visit to England in the summer of 1933 she pleased him by generously offering to visit the estranged and partly deranged Vivien, although she was recalled to the USA by the sudden illness of a colleague before this could done. She was one of the three American correspondents to whom Vivien wrote in early 1934, when she belatedly realised how terminal the separation from Eliot really was (see *The Letters of T. S. Eliot, Vol. 6: 1932–1933*, edited by Valerie Eliot and John Haffenden, 15, 466, 479, 544, 602, 633, 640 n.).

of the story, but no firm evidence that Eliot did in fact visit Wellesley at all on Thursday, 8 December 1932.[62]

If Eliot's admiration for Yeats's poetry and drama had been rising steadily since 1919, their philosophic views, though far from 'languid', were still incompatible, and after Eliot's conversion to Anglicanism in 1927 (he was, as it happens, received into the Church by William Force Stead, also a friend and frequent correspondent of Yeats) took on a theological inflection.[63] This is most clearly felt in a series of lectures he gave in Virginia in April 1933, five months after their supposed meeting at Wellesley and subsequently published as *After Strange Gods*, which represent a significant misreading of Yeats, even if it is almost the opposite of the misreading advanced in 'A Foreign Mind'. Now, so far from maintaining that 'a peculiar Irish genius', if it exists, 'ought to be discovered in him', Eliot suggests that Yeats's association with Ireland was, initially at least, adventitious, indeed little more than a romantic enthusiasm. Since, Eliot claims, Yeats was brought up in London, Ireland was for him 'rather a holiday country, to which its sentiment attached itself'. We might remind ourselves that Yeats did not merely holiday in Ireland, but was born there, spent a good deal of his childhood in Sligo and lived in Dublin for six years during his adolescence. His espousal of Irish themes and traditions, although a conscious decision, was thus not the casual sentimental choice that Eliot suggests.

As in 'A Foreign Mind', it is not Yeats's position as an Irishman that is the main preoccupation in *After Strange Gods*, but his position as a theologian. Eliot takes a crucial text, the passage in

---

[62] James F. Loucks in his article 'The Exile's Return' (*ANQ*, Spring 1996), giving the date of the encounter as '*November*' 1932, cites Ellmann as his source (17), and no mention of Eliot's attendance appears in the *Wellesley College News* or in Eliot's letters at this time. However, given the proximity of Wellesley, the availability of his sister, Ada Sheffield, and her husband in providing transport, his friendship with Elizabeth Manwaring, and his respect for Yeats, it is probable that he did make the journey from Harvard, although it would have meant a fairly tight schedule since he held a regular weekly At Home for his students and acquaintances on Wednesday afternoons, and he was due to deliver the fourth of his Norton Lectures, 'Wordsworth and Coleridge', on Friday, 9 December.

[63] See David Bradshaw, '"Oxford Poets": Yeats. T. S. Eliot and William Force Stead', *YA19* 77–102.

Autobiographies quoted above, in which Yeats laments the deprivation of 'the simple-minded religion of my childhood', and concludes that by the age of sixteen he was taking up the Arnoldian idea that Poetry can replace Religion, 'and also the tendency to fabricate an *individual* religion'.[64] This was inaccurate: in the 1890s Yeats constantly refuted Arnold's views on literature and religion with those of Blake, and so far from fabricating a private religion he was desperate to find traditional, if unorthodox, authority for his 'religious' sentiments. Eliot bolsters his argument by citing I. A. Richards' contention that Yeats had surrendered himself to trance, to dissociated phases of consciousness, and that the revelations vouchsafed by these states were 'insufficiently connected with normal experience'. He carries Richards' remarks further, arguing that Yeats's supernatural world was the 'wrong supernatural world': it was 'not a world of spiritual significance, of real Good and Evil... but a highly sophisticated lower mythology'.[65] This is a charge which, on these terms, could presumably be leveled at much of Eliot's own pre-Conversion poetry, and not least *The Waste Land*. It also overlooks the profound change in Yeats's thinking which caused him, as he himself put it, to get down 'off his stilts' in 1900. If his early writings are concerned with an attempt to elude evil in the quest for an Edenic unity, shortly after the turn of the twentieth century a poem like 'Adam's Curse' (as its title suggests), and aphorisms such as 'we begin to live when we conceive life as a tragedy' (*Au* 188; *CW3* 163) indicate a realization that the earthly paradise was unobtainable, that after such knowledge forgiveness does not come easily. Something of this Eliot concedes in his concluding sentences, where he adopts a more conciliatory, if inadequately concessionary, tone: 'he has arrived at greatness against the greatest odds; if he has not arrived at a central and universal philosophy he has at least discarded, for the most part, the trifling and eccentric, the provincial in time and place'.[66]

---

[64] *After Strange Gods: A Primer of Modern Heresy* (London: Faber & Faber, 1934), 44.
[65] *Ibid.*, 45–46.
[66] *Ibid.*, 47.

For various reasons Eliot never allowed *After Strange Gods* to be republished, and there is evidence that in the years following its appearance he amplified his view of Yeats's poetry, revised his ideas on Yeats's relationship with Ireland and tempered his views on Yeats's heterodoxy by accepting its correspondence with Indian philosophy. His new appreciation of Yeats's position in contemporary literary life seems to have been a product of his Harvard lectures on 'Contemporary English Literature', and were succinctly stated his commemoration of Yeats's seventieth birthday in the *Criterion* of July 1935. Here Eliot addresses the long perplexity of Yeats's Irish ethnicity and rethinks it in terms of his developing ideas of centre and periphery, a notion which he was to amplify in *Towards a Definition of Culture*, and which, in turn, has affinities with his theory of tradition and individual talent. Just as he regarded tradition as depending for its continuing vigour on the vitality of individual talent, which in its part is schooled by that tradition, so a vibrant culture depends on its centre being reinvigorated, but not overwhelmed, by its more diverse edges. Thus, even when he was devoting an overwhelming amount of his time and energy to the theatre in Ireland, 'Mr. Yeats in Dublin performed as great a service to English literature, and belonged as much to it, as Mr. Yeats in London', and this because, Eliot believed, 'the future vitality of English literature will depend very much upon the vitality of its parts, and their influence upon each other'. He went on to argue that this diversity was 'not a petty question of employing one's native Doric, which is merely a nuisance', nor was it 'a question of being sentimental about the old homestead and the landscapes of childhood', the very attributes he had hitherto detected in early Yeats and which caused him to deny Synge 'universality'. Now, however, he is able to accommodate and welcome Yeats's Irish identity because it is an enriching part of his English identity. What is essentially Irish about Yeats is, Eliot confesses, 'impossible fully to define', but it is 'most effectually expressed through rhythm', and is 'something which can best be expressed, and most successfully maintained, through poetry'. Crucially in Eliot's definition of culture, the centre must hold, and Yeats work has contributed effectively to that. In his '*literary* Nationalism therefore' (Eliot does not distinguish other forms of nationalism, nor ponder their possible relationship with literature), 'Mr. Yeats has performed a great service to the English language'. And, ironically, Eliot sees the chief element in this service as his chastening of language, a feature Yeats's had persistently, if not always approvingly, thought pre-eminent in Eliot's own poetry. In his 'latest and greatest period', Eliot insisted, Yeats 'has tended to divest itself of the more superfluous stage properties of Ireland, and is perhaps all the more Irish for being unaffectedly so. There is a rhythm, an intonation, a way of making the simplest statement in the fewest and barest words, which belong to Mr. Yeats and to no one else'. This has produced a paradoxical situation in which his 'influence upon English poetry has been great and beneficial; upon Irish poetry it seems to me to have been almost disastrous'. A paradox for Yeats and perhaps for literary historians, but not for Eliot: on the contrary, it is 'just what you should expect'. Those poets who can have a beneficial influence on contemporary English (or Irish) literature must either be 'considerably removed in time' or current writers 'from outside'. Given this, Irish poets 'must shift for themselves', since 'no nation owes its great poets a debt of gratitude for their influence upon their immediate successors', but England's gratitude to the outsider Yeats 'is without this reservation, for his influence, wherever apparent, has been wholly salutary'.[67] The 'Foreign Mind' has, it seems, been entirely naturalized.

Eliot's new sympathy with Yeats also extended to his philosophic interests and in his capacity as a publisher he gave him enabling assistance with three books on Indian thought. Both men had long been fascinated by Indian philosophy, although Eliot's approach had been more academically rigorous. The fascination was fuelled by the increasing importance of comparative mythology which found in Sanskrit (as in the Celtic languages) important insights to Indo-European languages and early European culture.

Yeats had in part been introduced to eastern thought by A. P. Sinnett's *Esoteric Buddhism*, which led him to help found the Hermetic Society in Dublin and to become associated with, but

---

[67] 'A Commentary', *Criterion* (July 1935), 611–13.

never actually join, the Dublin Theosophical Society. His interest in the East was focused when he met the young *chela* Mohini Chatterjee, who accompanied Madam Blavatsky to Europe in 1884, and was invited to Dublin by Yeats and his friends in 1885. As Yeats recalled, it was his 'first meeting with a philosophy that confirmed my vague speculations and seemed at once logical and boundless' (*Au*, 91–92). At the age of only twenty-seven Chatterjee, although a Brahmin, was hardly a seasoned Sanskrit scholar and, as P. S. Sri has argued, distorted the Vedanta though an interpretation coloured by Theosophy and Walter Pater (*YA11* 61–76). Nor was Yeats's allegiance to Theosophy as committed as that of his friends George Russell and Charles Johnston. Although he frequented Madame Blavatsky's London Lodge, he had fundamental doubts about her hidden Mahatmas, as about her manipulation of psychic phenomena, and he complained to John O'Leary that she and her followers were 'turning a good philosophy into a bad religeon' (*CL1*, 234). It was not until the early 1930s that he began to make a more concentrated study of the 'good philosophy' of the East.

Eliot's study had been systematic from the beginning. Harvard was at the forefront of the study of Indian philosophy and from 1911–13 he took classes with two internationally renowned scholars. With Charles Lanman he learned Sanskrit and Pali, and read *The Bhagavad Gita* and the sacred texts of Buddhism. James Woods, another leading Orientalist and a particular advocate of Eliot, taught him 'Philosophical Sanskrit', which included the study of Yoga System and Patanjali's Sutras (upon which Woods was currently writing a scholarly commentary). Yet, although his study was more academic, Eliot's purpose in pursuing Indic studies was close to that of Yeats, and his attitude towards Indian thought and religion more receptive and sympathetic than that of his professors, who never doubted the superiority of the Western over the Eastern tradition. Like Yeats, he was ready to see connections between Eastern and Western thought. The Fire Sermon section of *The Waste Land* draws upon both Buddhist and Christian sources, while the poem ends with a triple invocation in Sanskrit taken from the 'Fable of the Jungle' in the *Brihadaranyaka Upanishad*, 'Datta, Dayadhvam,

Damyata', and concludes with the repeated 'Shantih', 'a formal ending
to an Upanishad', compared to which, Eliot's notes assure us, "'The
Peace which passeth understanding" is a feeble translation'.[68] These
allusions at once discourage an overtly Christian interpretation of the
poem, invited by its quotations from St Augustine, and its settings in
Gethsemane and Emmaus, and also universalise its theme of quest.
Krishna's injunctions to Arjuna on the field of battle, cited in the
third part of *The Dry Salvages*, also serve to broaden the reach of a
more avowedly Christian poem, and Krishna's sentiments also inform
Eliot's 1943 poem 'To the Indians who died in Africa', dedicated to
men who fought on a real as opposed to mythological battlefield.

The Indian allusions in Eliot's work are a form of parallelism,
which extend his poems' philosophical implications beyond the
Western tradition, but they remain predicated upon that tradition.
For Yeats India held out more radical possibilities, nothing less than
the promise of achieving the revolution in Western consciousness
he had ardently sought in the 1890s. In his Introduction to *The Ten
Principal Upanishads* in 1937 he recalled that in his youth

we talked much of tradition, and those emotional young men, Francis
Thompson, Lionel Johnson, John Gray, found it in Christianity. But now
that *The Golden Bough* has made Christianity look modern and fragmentary
we study Confucius with Ezra Pound, or like T. S. Eliot find in Christianity
a convenient symbolism for some older or newer thought... Shree Purohit
Swami and I offer to some young man seeking... vast sentiments and
generalisations, the oldest philosophical compositions of the world'.[69]

Two years earlier, in his essay, 'The Mandookya Upanishad',
published by Eliot in the *Criterion*, he had likened the transformation
experienced by the Indian pilgrim to the acquisition of Unity of
Being: 'The initiate, all old Karma exhausted, is "the Human Form
Divine" of Blake, that Unity of Being Dante compared to a perfectly
proportioned human body' (*E&I* 483). As in his preface to *The Cat*

---

[68] *T. S. Eliot. The Waste Land: A Facsimile and Transcript of the Original Drafts*, ed.
      Valerie Eliot (London, Faber & Faber, 1971), 149.
[69] *The Ten Principal Upanishads*, put into English by Shree Purohit Swami and W.
      B. Yeats (London: Faber & Faber, 1937), 10.

and the Moon, he continued to count Eliot as part of this movement, arguing in his Introduction to *The Ten Principal Upanishads* that between 1922 and 1925 'English literature, wherever most intense, cast off its preoccupation with social problems and began to create myths like those of antiquity, and to ask the most profound questions. I recall poems by T. S. Eliot, *Those Barren Leaves* by Aldous Huxley, where there is a Buddhistic hatred of life, or a hatred Schopenhauer did not so much find in as deduce from a Latin translation of a Persian translation of the Upanishads'.[70]

The spur to Yeats's new interest in India was Sri Purohit Swami, who, after years as an itinerant monk, had arrived in London at the end of February 1931, eager to prepare his version of the *The Bhagadavad Gita* for publication. Thomas Sturge Moore, whom he met that April, helped him in this task and also introduced him to WBY, who urged him to write an autobiography. He immediately set to work, but Moore was now too busy to assist him, as, initially, was Yeats (who assured AE that, in any case, his preoccupations were 'Greek not Indian'[71]). This stance altered dramatically when he read the first few chapters in manuscript early in 1932; they so 'overwhelmed' him that he volunteered to write an Introduction and pressed the 'masterpiece' on his own publisher, Macmillan. *An Indian Monk* appeared in October 1932, whereupon the Swami and Yeats turned their attention to the account of a spiritual journey by his friend and 'Master' Bhagwān Sri Hamsa, a book which also significantly deepened Yeats's absorption with India and for which he also offered to write a preface. He explained to Olivia Shakespear in October 1933 that his 'essay on The Tibetan Travels of his Master with the Swami… has taken me two months at least', but had 'grown to have great importance in my scheme of things' (*CL InteLex* 5458). Unfortunately, *An Indian Monk* had not sold as well as hoped and, notwithstanding Yeats's forceful advocacy, Macmillan refused to commit themselves to another book by the same author. Finding a replacement publisher proved difficult until Yeats, making the most

---

[70] *Ibid.*, 9.
[71] WBY letter to George Russell (AE), 29 Oct 1931; *CL InteLex* 5533.

of his friendly relations with Eliot, lobbied him to take it, and on 20 January 1934, after what seem to have been drawn-out deliberations within the firm, he was able to inform Shri Purohit that he just received 'an answer & a most satisfactory answer from Faber & Faber' (*CL InteLex* 5996), who estimated that the book would 'not have a large sale but will continue to sell for a long time' (*CL InteLex* 5998). From now on Eliot became an important factor in the collaboration between Yeats and the Swami. There is evidence that he himself was not entirely convinced by the Swami's reliability or scholarship, but in the light of Yeats's enthusiasm and support, and his own interest in Indian thought, he was willing to disregard his scruples.

Indeed, he unwittingly did much to keep the collaboration going. It is evident that by the spring of 1934 Yeats, in ill-health and with major projects of his own in hand, was trying to disengage from the Swami. His Introduction to *The Holy Mountain* had taken far more time and effort than he had anticipated, as did the correction of the manuscript and of the proofs which he was currently reading. He refused to accept the Presidency of the London Institute of Indian Mysticism, set up by the Swami's British followers to promulgate his teachings, informing him on 21 May that 'as I have edited those two books, you have already what support my name can give you', and advising him 'to make somebody 'president' who can bring you new support, or serve you the better for the honour. I wish you all good luck' (*CL InteLex* 6046). But the Swami's good luck depended very largely on Yeats's continuing support and he was not so easily to be shaken off. He was now eager to publish his translation of *The Bhagadavad Gita*, and had begun work on the Upanishads. In early August, just as *The Holy Mountain* was reaching the bookshops, he had a long interview with Eliot, possibly set up by Yeats so that he no longer had to act as a go-between. He reported back that Eliot had 'said he was very much interested in my mission and promised to do his best', adding that Eliot 'immensely liked your essay in the "Criterion", and wished you could write more. I think he will write to you'.[72]

---

[72] Sri Purohit Swami to WBY, 1 Aug 1934 (NLI). The essay was 'Initiation on a Mountain', published in *Criterion* (July 1934).

Eliot did write, to ask Yeats to contribute an introduction to the Swami's version of the *Gita* but Yeats instantly passed the buck back to him: 'All I could do for the Swami book', he insisted,

is write a couple of pages taking some one point. I gave three months to my essay for 'The Holy-Mountain' but now I am writing against time to keep my sister's press going. His work wants one or other of two things, or both of them, to introduce it. One of those things is a schoolurly introduction by a learned orientalist.... The other thing (suplement or substitute) in a few words by some man of letters (not me; my bolt is shot). You have studied Indian philosophy a few words from you would vouch for him to a modern audience I cannot reach. It would be a mistake to send him forth again as my God-child. Perhaps somebody could show how his sacred texts are related to ours, his movement to our movements' (*CL InteLex* 6076).

Eliot declined the honour of introducing *The Geeta*, and, after failing to persuade the Swami to send the book to George Allen & Unwin, commissioned a preface from His Highness Sir Sayaji Gaekwar, the reformist Maharaja of Baroda, a powerful political and social figure, but for this assignment perhaps no substitute for a major poet.

Part of Yeats's reasons for refusing to write an Introduction was, as he says, the pressure of other work, but it was also because that text did not engage his imagination in the way that the Swami and Hamsa books had. The Upanishads, the ancient Sanskrit treatises, expounding and elaborating the scriptures of the Vedas in mystical terms, were more compelling, and a few days after the publication of *The Holy Mountain* and his long talk with Eliot, the Swami sent Yeats some typed translations of them. In thanking him on 29 August Yeats wished he 'had asked you to include in 'The Holy Mountain' a translation of *Mandukya Upanishad* as your master heard the supernatural voice singing it' (*CL InteLex* 6091), and the Swami took him up on this. In October Yeats called on Eliot and agreed to write a prefatory article for the Swami's version of the Upanishad to appear in the *Criterion*. Publication was delayed by two serious bouts of ill-health Yeats suffered in the late winter and mid spring of 1935 and did not appear until July. By that time, he and the Swami had made plans to collaborate on a translation of all the major Upanishads and, helped by Gwyneth Foden, with whom the Swami enjoyed, and later did not at all enjoy, an ambiguous relationship, arranged to avoid the rigours of a British winter by working on the project in warm and sunny Majorca.

They evidently hoped that Faber & Faber would publish the volume when completed, but Eliot, who had been eager for Yeats to introduce *The Geeta*, was more circumspect about the Upanishads, even with the association of his name, and Yeats had to use a good deal of ingenuity to keep him sympathetic. He astutely turned a less than warm review of *The Geeta* in the *Spectator* (which wondered 'why this translation was made, when there are so many other vivider and no less accurate versions'[73]), to his advantage by firing off a letter to Eliot, dismissing it as 'silly' and enclosing two letters—almost certainly solicited—from his friend Frank Sturm, 'a fine scholour in English & other tongues', as he assured Eliot, ecstatically praising the Swami as a translator (*CL InteLex* 6330). The gambit worked and two weeks later, in thanking Sturm for the letters, Yeats revealed that Eliot had 'said they were "a great encouragement"' (*CL InteLex* 6343).

Not, however, encouraging enough to coax Eliot off the fence and the Swami, Yeats and Mrs Foden set out for Majorca in late November 1935 still without a contract. Work on the translations was seriously delayed when Yeats suffered a life-threatening collapse caused by nephritis and a heart problem which triggered serious difficulties in his breathing. The success of the project was threatened in different way when the Swami and Mrs Foden had a blazing row. She flounced back to London and in the early summer he returned to India. When, after a long recuperation, Yeats was well enough to take a ship home he found that Mrs Foden was trying to sabotage the edition of Upanishads by blackening the Swami's reputation, particularly at Fabers. As he complained to Dorothy Wellesley in June 1936, her latest effort had been to call on Richard de la Mare, one of the publishers at Fabers who was responsible for seeing the Swami's books though the press, to

tell him that the Swami did not know Sanskrit but had translated the Upanishads from the vernacular & that he is not a Swami. Then she wrote

---

[73] 'The Geeta', *Spectator* (30 August 1935), 336.

to T. S. Elliot hinting that a homo-sexual scandal—or so my informant understood T. S. Elliot to say—might overwhelm the Swami at any moment. The object is to scare Faber & Faber so that they may reject our translation (*CL InteLex* 6594).

He found himself in the delicate position of refuting Mrs Foden's malicious allegations at the same time as trying to close a deal over publication with Eliot. In early July 1936 he sought out a pretext to give Eliot a gentle nudge:

> I dont know if you have come to any conclusion yet about the Upanishads, and I dont want to hurry you. I write to make the suggestion that if you accept you might care to have (say) one of the minor Upanishads, or some part of a[n] Upanishad, given by an appendix with the Sanscrit words and the ancient music which accompanies it (*CL InteLex* 6604).

Eliot took the hint and within days of receiving the letter formally accepted the book, later entitled *The Ten Principal Upanishads*. The translations were a collaborative effort and without Eliot's admiration for Yeats and his work it is unlikely that he would have contracted this, or perhaps any of the Swami's books. This was certainly true of the last book the Swami published with him, a translation of Patanjali's *Aphorisms of Yoga*. Since one of his favourite Harvard professors, James Wood, had written what was universally considered the definitive scholarly edition of Patanjali, Eliot was suspicious of the Swami's less rigorous treatment and accepted it, as Yeats revealed, only 'subject to my writing a preface' (*CL InteLex* 6915). Eliot also sounded him out as to whether he had had any hand in the translations, and he was obliged to confess that 'Yes I had something to do with the general character of his book & did some revision of text' (*CL InteLex* 6916). He exacted revenge for Eliot's doubts in his Introduction with a light tilt at the famous poet who had commissioned it, when, using information he must have got in conversation with Eliot himself, he insisted upon the superiority of imaginative translation over academic exactitude. 'Some years ago', he began,

> I bought The Yoga-System of Patanjali, translated and edited by James Horton Woods and published by the Harvard Press. It is the standard edition, final, impeccable in scholastic eyes, even in the eyes of a famous

poet and student of Samskrit [*sic*], who used it as a dictionary. But then the poet was at his university, but lately out of school, had not learned to hate all scholar's cant and class-room slang, nor was he an old man in a hurry.[74]

Yeats's old man's hurry was one of the things about him that most impressed Eliot. Another was his career as a dramatist and theatre administrator, and, as we have seen, he counted himself and Auden 'in his debt' for keeping 'the real spirit of the theatre alive'. In the autumn of 1934 Yeats and Eliot combined with Auden and others in a practical project to keep this real spirit alive by setting up the Group Theatre. Yeats, as he explained to the actress Margot Collis, was particularly pleased to have Eliot in the scheme 'because he represents a movement that has grown all over the world and is strong at the Universities. It seeks modernness in language and metaphor and helps us to get rid of what Rossetti called "soulless self reflections of man's skill" but it does throw out the baby with the bath-water' (*LMR27*). Among the organisational and artistic problems that prevented the initiative developing quite as planned was the production of Eliot's *Murder in the Cathedral*, which had been commissioned by Canterbury Cathedral and therefore could not be fitted into the London programme. Reading the script forced Yeats to reconsider his persistent accusation that Eliot's language was plain and monotonous: it was, he reported to his wife in April 1935, 'no play but magnificent speach', and few days later elaborated on this: 'Elliots play is about the murder of Becket, half play half religeous service as spoken poetry exceedingly impressive.... It will require magnificent speaking, its oratory is swift & powerful' (*CL InteLex* 6225). That September, and back in Dublin, he attended a lecture on the play at the Abbey Theatre, given by Martin Browne, with recitations by Robert Speaight, reporting to Eliot that it was all so moving that the audience called for more and that he would 'like to get up a performance here but do not know if it is possible. I will discuss it with the Abbey board' (*CL InteLex* 6330).

[74] *Aphorisms of Yoga* by Bhagwān Shree Patanjali; done into English from the original in Samskrit [*sic*] with a commentary by Shree Purohit Swami (1938), 2.

More frequent meetings to discuss Group Theatre policy led a warmer friendship. Although Yeats's cantankerousness sometimes made Eliot want to kick him down the stairs, he came away from a lunch with him in October 1934, as he told Ottoline Morrell, with an increased liking and admiration for the old poet.[75] These sentiments led him to contribute towards the present of a Rossetti drawing to mark Yeats's seventieth birthday, an occasion he also celebrated with a generous tribute in the *Criterion*, where he asserted unequivocally that Yeats 'has been and is the greatest poet of his time', and that he could 'think of no poet, not even among the very greatest, who has shown a longer period of development than Yeats…. Development to this extent is not merely genius, it is character; and it sets a standard which his juniors should seek to emulate, without hoping to equal'.[76]

Notwithstanding this, and his delight in *Murder in the Cathedral*, the question of why Eliot's poetry commanded such a following continued to puzzle Yeats, and arose again when, early in 1935, he began work on an anthology, *The Oxford Book of Modern Verse*, divulging to Olivia Shakespear that the problem he had set himself was '"how far do I like the Ezra, Elliot, Auden school & if I do not why not?" Then this further problem "why do the younger generation like it so much? What do they see or hope?"' (*CL InteLex* 6191). Although he took advice from Eliot on the selection of American material for the book, his assessment of his poetry disappointingly reverted to what it had always been. He ignored the 'magnificent language' of *Murder in the Cathedral*: while he mentions this play and *The Waste Land* in his introduction, he does not select passages from either of them in the book itself. Nor does he print anything from 'Prufrock', 'Gerontion', or 'Ash Wednesday'. Indeed, the majority of the poems he chooses are early works, wilfully selected to enforce his view of Eliot (re-enforced by his reading of MacGreevy, which they echo closely) that Eliot was a satirist, writing in scorn of the limitations of the modern world, and in this sense negative in style and approach. This had certainly been the more general view of Eliot

---

75 See Robert Medley, 'The Group Theatre 1932–9', *London Magazine* (January 1981), 47ff.
76 *Criterion* (June 1935), 612–13.

fifteen years before, a fact that Eliot himself bemoaned in a letter to his brother of 15 February 1920: 'even here I am considered by the ordinary Newspaper critic as a Wit or satirist'.[77] By 1935 this perception had significantly changed—but not it seems in the case of Yeats. The poems representing Eliot's later style and manner are represented only by 'The Journey of the Magi' (a theme that Yeats had also handled in both poetry and prose, and which register their preoccupation with, and different approaches to, Incarnation), and a very brief extract from 'The Rock'. By contrast, most of the poems Yeats printed from his own work were very recent—the earliest dated from 1914, but the large majority were taken from *The Winding Stair* which had only been published in 1933. In restating his view of Eliot as a satirist, Yeats, who had recently accused him of trying to write like Shakespeare, now compared him to Pope:

Eliot has produced his great effect upon his generation because he has described men and women that get out of bed or into it from mere habit; in describing this life that has lost heart his own art seems grey, cold, dry. He is an Alexander Pope, working without apparent imagination, producing his effects by a rejection of all rhythms and metaphors used by the more popular romantics rather than by the discovery of his own, this rejection giving his work an unexaggerated plainness that has the effect of novelty.

Even in *The Waste Land*, in which Yeats admits there is 'much that is moving in symbol and imagery', there is also 'much monotony of accent'. And in considering the influence of religion in enriching Eliot's emotional life and latest poetry, Yeats argues that 'his religion... lacks all strong emotion; a New England Protestant by descent, there is little self-surrender in his personal relation to God and the soul' (*OBMV* xxi-xxii; *CW5* 191–92). In spite of this robust, not to say partial, criticism, Yeats was eager to remain on good terms with Eliot and when on 1 November 1936 the Observer alleged that in his introduction to the Oxford Book he had preferred Cecil Day Lewis and Louis MacNeice to Eliot, he wrote at once to him that he had 'done nothing of the kind' (*CL InteLex* 6704).

---

[77] TSE, *Letters* I, 441.

The very reception of his Anthology, especially the attacks on it by the then Communist Stephen Spender over his omission of the War Poets, provided him to his satisfaction with the answer he was looking for as to Eliot's appeal, as he announced in 'Modern Poetry', a radio programme broadcasted by the BBC in October 1936. Here Eliot, 'the most revolutionary man in poetry during my lifetime', is seen as the first and most powerful voice to register the disillusion of the War and the years *entre les deux guerres*: 'No romantic word or sound, nothing reminiscent... could be permitted henceforth. Poetry must resemble prose, and both must accept the vocabulary of their time; nor must there be any special subject-matter.... The past had deceived us: let us accept the worthless present' (*E&I* 499; *CW5* 95).

Had he lived, Yeats might have been obliged to revise this view, but he died before Eliot published *Four Quartets*, his last major poem (although he did read *Burnt Norton*). *Four Quartets* is a poem that owes a good deal to Yeats, who had complained in *The Oxford Book of Modern Verse* that there was 'little self-surrender' in Eliot's 'personal relation to God and the soul'. This cannot be said of *Four Quartets*, which is perhaps the most directly personal of Eliot's poems, and one in which the necessity of selflessness and self-surrender is a recurrent theme, as is the articulation of a personal relationship with God and the soul. The courage to adopt this new manner for so fastidious and intentionally impersonal a poet as Eliot seems to have derived in great measure from Yeats, and it is quite possible that Yeats's criticism had spurred him to this mode. Moreover, the 'unattended moments' of the poem, those crucial 'hints followed by guesses' that may make possible some consciousness of the infinite, seem in concept and description to owe something to Yeats's account of the ascetic's experiences in 'Initiation on a Mountain', an essay which Eliot had published in the *Criterion* in July 1934:

Nor is supernormal sense confined to the moments of concentration; he will suddenly smell amid the ordinary occupations of life, perhaps in the middle of winter, an odour of spring flowers, or have an unimaginable sense of physical well-being that is described as a transformation of the sense of touch, or meet in empty places melodious sound, or a fine sight' (*E&I* 464).

In *The Dry Salvages* Eliot describes

> ...the unattended
> Moment, the moment in and out of time,
> The distraction fit, lost in a shaft of sunlight,
> The wild thyme unseen, or the winter lightning
> Or the waterfall, or music heard so deeply
> That it is not heard at all, but you are the music
> While the music lasts.[78]

But the posthumous presence of Yeats is more palpable than this, for he constitutes the chief component of the 'familiar compound ghost' whom, in Little Gidding, Eliot accosts during the London blitz. Even if we do not identify Yeats from the poem (and it is difficult not to), Eliot makes it clear in various drafts that it was Yeats he had in mind, although he took pains to avoid a too obvious identification. Originally he had thought of modelling the revenant on Ser Brunetto from Canto XV of Dante's *Inferno*, but as he wrote on he had to get rid of Brunetto since

the visionary figure has now become somewhat more definite and will no doubt be identified by some readers with Yeats.... However, I do not wish to take the responsibility of putting Yeats or anybody else into Hell and I do not want to impute to him the particular vice which took Bruno there'.[79]

This is a remarkable passage in Modernist literature: one great poet summons up another to question him about the value of a life not merely dedicated to poetry but the value of life itself. (Yeats had done something similar, but not identical, in interrogating Red Hanrahan, one of his own creations, in 'The Tower'.) The answers are uncompromising and uttered in a language and tone far from the 'unexaggerated plainness' of which Yeats had accused him

> 'Let me disclose the gifts reserved for age
>   To set a crown upon your lifetime's effort.
>   First, the cold friction of expiring sense

---

[78] TSE, *Collected Poems and Plays*, 190.
[79] Quoted in Helen Gardner, *The Composition of 'Four Quartets'* (London: Faber & Faber, 1978), 176.

> Without enchantment, offering no promise
>   But bitter tastelessness of shadow fruit
>   As body and soul begin to fall asunder.
> Second, the conscious impotence of rage
>   At human folly, and the laceration
>   Of laughter at what ceases to amuse.
> And last, the rending pain of re-enactment
>   Of all that you have done, and been; the shame
>   Of motives late revealed, and the awareness
> Of things ill done and done to others' harm
>   Which once you took for exercise of virtue.
>   Then fools' approval stings, and honour stains.
> From wrong to wrong the exasperated spirit
>   Proceeds, unless restored by that refining fire
>   Where you must move in measure, like a dancer'.[80]

Helen Gardner argues that Eliot found in Yeats a voice he echoed with a difference. He thought of Yeats as the poet of middle age and she lists the many references to middle age in *Four Quartets*, suggesting that the line in the poem about old men's 'fear of fear and frenzy' is an echo of 'Grant me an old man's frenzy' in 'An Acre of Grass'. But in this, as in other late poems, Yeats does not fear fear and embraces frenzy as an agency of imagination and self-knowledge. It was for this, more than his poems of middle age, that Eliot most praised him. In fact, at this period, which alas constituted the effective end of his own creative career, Eliot seems almost obsessed with Yeats's extraordinary capacity for self-renewal and change over a lifetime. In his Dublin Lecture of June 1940 he extolled him for 'exceptional honesty and courage to face… change', and picked out his poem 'The Spur' as a powerful example of this. He also discussed his play *Purgatory* and, although differing theologically from Yeats, was almost certainly thinking of this in giving *Little Gidding* its purgatorial ambiance. Typically, he asserts, older poets are reduced to mimicking their early work, or leaving their passion behind, or succumbing to the worst temptation of all: 'that of becoming dignified, of becoming public figures with only a public existence—

---

[80] TSE, *Collected Poems and Plays*, 194–45.

coat-racks hung with decorations and distinctions, doing, saying, and even thinking and feeling only what they believe the public expects of them. Yeats was not that kind of poet'.[81] It is a Yeatsian capacity for perpetual reappraisal that the familiar compound ghost *Little Gidding* insists is the key to human experience, reaffirming what Eliot by now already knows

> the pattern is new in every moment
> And every moment is a new and shocking
> Valuation of all we have been.[82]

In conclusion we may note that the strategically important appearance of Yeats in *Four Quartets*, the care which Eliot took there in appropriating Yeats's voice, which was not his own voice, together with the number of earlier examples of Yeats and Eliot defining their own poetic methods and ideas against those of the other, greatly complicates and modifies Ezra Pound's 'benevolent speculation... as to whether the two poets 'neglected to develop a mutual illumination'. There was 'insemination' at important points in their careers and Eliot, towards the end of his writing life, certainly found an 'illumination' in the example and practice of Yeats, an illumination which had its effect on *Four Quartets*.

But are we entitled to ask why that illumination did not do more for Eliot? Yeats is the great example for him of a poet who goes on, year after year, remaking himself and his art. Yet Eliot himself conspicuously failed to do this and for the last two decades of his life the poetry dried up, though not of course the prose writings on culture, religion, and society. It would be unfair to categorize this Eliot in his own terms as becoming merely 'dignified', one of those 'public figures with only a public existence—coat-racks hung with decorations and distinctions'. Eliot did not say merely what the public expected of him, but he did acquire a public gravitas—not for nothing was he dubbed 'the Pope of Russell Square'. Yeats—and perhaps we come back to his favourite punctuation, the question mark—never

[81] *On Poetry and Poets*, 257.
[82] TSE, *Collected Poems and Plays*, 179.

managed to acquire this sort of certainty, and it is his intellectual and emotional restlessness which animates and charges the poetry he continued to write even on his deathbed. In a note written late in January 1929, he recorded that he disliked the word 'belief', and went on: 'We, even more than Eliot, require tradition and though it may include much that is his, *it is not a belief or submission, but exposition of intellectual needs*… I feel as neither Eliot nor Ezra do *the need of old forms, old situations that, as when I re-create some early poem of my own, I may escape from scepticism*'.[83] For scepticism not belief is Yeats's default position, or, as he put it in *Per Amica*: 'We make out of the quarrel with others, rhetoric, but of the quarrel with ourselves, poetry'.[84]

[83] Quoted in Richard Ellmann's *The Identity of Yeats* (London: Faber & Faber, 1964), 240.
[84] *Myth* 331.

http://dx.doi.org/10.11647/OBP.0081.08

The Cantwell Collection[1]

Compiled by Crónán Ó Doibhlin

THE CANTWELL COLLECTION (with the agreement of Dr Eamonn Cantwell) is an open collection within the Boole Library, University College Cork, and the Library has added a small number of significant titles to the collection since the original gift in 2006. The Collection was first exhibited at the Boole Library, UCC, 24 June-30 July 2003, and it complements other Boole Library collections such as the Cuala Press Collection, and the Dolmen Press Collection of the Yeats scholar and distinguished publisher, Liam Miller.

The accompanying catalogue, *W. B. Yeats: A Collector's Gift* was compiled by Olivia Fitzpatrick and a team of assistants and was available at the exhibition, which opened with the inaugural lecture of the series: see above p. 3. Catalogue details not pertaining to provenance and to be found more generally in *Wade*, have not been repeated here. A few details of provenance for some items have been added to this list. The provenance of each title was not specifically recorded prior to 2006 unless noted in the UCC Library catalogue record. Errors in *A Collector's Gift* have been silently corrected.

---

[1] Further information may have been gathered since this article was prepared for publication. If you would like to find out if any further information has been discovered that may help your own research, why not write to the author at c.odoibhlin@ucc.ie? Quite apart from anything else, feedback is always welcomed.

PART 1: MATERIAL CATALOGUED SINCE 1996

These items are all part of the Cantwell Donation and have been checked against the listing in *W. B. Yeats A Collector's Gift* (2003).

Yeats, W. B. *The Wanderings of Oisin: and Other Poems.* London: Kegan Paul, Trench & Co., 1889. Cantwell 821.9 YEAT *Wade* 2, http://library. ucc.ie/record=b1335114

Yeats, W. B. *The Countess Kathleen and Various Legends and Lyrics.* Boston: Roberts Bros.; London: T. Fisher Unwin [c.1892?]. Cantwell 822.9 YEAT *Wade* 7, http://library.ucc.ie/record=b1334707

Yeats, W. B. *Poems.* London: T. Fisher Unwin; Boston: Copeland and Day, 1895. Cantwell 821.9 YEAT *Wade* 16, http://library.ucc.ie/record=b1335011

Yeats, W. B. *Poems.* London: T. Fisher Unwin, 1899. Cantwell 821.9 YEAT *Wade* 17, http://library.ucc.ie/record=b1334718

Yeats, W. B. *Poems.* London: T. Fisher Unwin, 1901. Cantwell 821.9 YEAT *Wade* 18, http://library.ucc.ie/record=b1107517

Yeats, W. B. *Poems.* London: T. Fisher Unwin, 1908. Cantwell 821.9 YEAT *Wade* 20, http://library.ucc.ie/record=b1334705

Yeats, W. B. *The Tables of the Law AND The Adoration of the Magi.* London: Elkin Mathews, 1904. Cantwell p 824.9 YEAT *Wade* 25, http://library.ucc. ie/record=b1335026

Yeats, W. B. *The Wind Among the Reeds.* London: Elkin Mathews, 1899. Cantwell 821.9 YEAT *Wade* 27, http://library.ucc.ie/record=b1334713

Yeats, W. B. *The Shadowy Waters.* London: Hodder and Stoughton, 1900. Cantwell 822.9 YEAT *Wade* 30, http://library.ucc.ie/record=b1334717. This copy is stamped on the flyleaf: *Cappagh, Co. Waterford*, the address of Percy Arland Ussher.

Yeats, W. B. *The Celtic Twilight.* London: A. H. Bullen, 1902. Cantwell 824.9 YEAT *Wade* 35, http://library.ucc.ie/record=b1335021

Yeats, W. B. *Where There is Nothing: being Volume One of Plays for an Irish theatre.* London: A. H. Bullen, 1903. Cantwell 822.9 YEAT *Wade* 44, http:// library.ucc.ie/record=b1335031

Yeats, W. B. *Poems, 1899–1905*. London: A. H. Bullen; Dublin: Maunsel & Co., Ltd., 1906. Cantwell 821.9 YEAT *Wade* 64, http://library.ucc.ie/record=b1335129. This copy is inscribed and annotated by Peter Allt.

Yeats, W. B. *The Collected Works in Verse and Prose of William Butler Yeats*. Stratford-on-Avon: Imprinted at the Shakespeare Head Press; London: Chapman & Hall limited, 1908. Cantwell 821.9 YEAT v.1–8 *Wade* 75–82, http://library.ucc.ie/record=b1334681. Inscribed: Dorothy Archibald.

Yeats, W. B. *William Butler Yeats Poems: Second Series*. London: A. H. Bullen, 1913. Cantwell 821.9 YEAT Reissue of *Wade* 83, http://library.ucc.ie/record=b1335100

Yeats, W. B. *Deirdre*. Stratford-upon-Avon: Shakespeare Head Press, 1911. Cantwell p 822.9 YEAT *Wade* 87, http://library.ucc.ie/record=b1335084. The error on the back cover has been corrected.

Yeats, W. B. *The Green Helmet: an Heroic Farce*. Stratford-upon-Avon: Shakespeare Head Press, 1911. Cantwell p 822.9 YEAT *Wade* 89, http://library.ucc.ie/record=b1334901

Yeats, W. B. *Plays for an Irish Theatre*. With Designs by Gordon Craig. London: A.H. Bullen, 1911. Cantwell 822.9 YEAT *Wade* 92, http://library.ucc.ie/record=b1004597. Inscribed by Peter Allt, and with his annotations and line numbering.

Yeats, W. B. *The Land of Heart's Desire*. London: T. Fisher Unwin, 1912. Cantwell p 822.9 YEAT *Wade* 94, http://library.ucc.ie/record=b1334904

The Poetical Works of William B. Yeats: In Two Volumes. New York: The Macmillan Company; London Macmillan & Co., Ltd., 1912. Cantwell 821.9 YEAT Vol. 2 only sub-titled *Dramatical Poems Wade* 98, http://library.ucc.ie/record=b1335136

Yeats, W. B. *Poems*. London: T. Fisher Unwin, 1912. Cantwell 821.9 YEAT *Wade* 99, http://library.ucc.ie/record=b1335109. Inside front cover: Ex libris Derek Marlowe. On facing page, Kathleen Greenwood 1912.

Yeats, W. B. *A Selection from the Poetry of W. B. Yeats*. Leipzig: Bernhard Tauchnitz, 1913. Cantwell 821.9 YEAT *Wade* 103, http://library.ucc.ie/record=b1335040

Yeats, W. B. *Reveries over Childhood and Youth.* London: Macmillan & Co., Ltd., 1916. Cantwell 824.9 YEAT *Wade* 113, http://library.ucc.ie/record=b1087963

Yeats, W. B. *Responsibilities and Other Poems.* New York: Macmillan & Co., Ltd., 1916. Cantwell 821.9 YEAT *Wade* 115, http://library.ucc.ie/record=b1335024. Inscribed: D. W. Ranken 1916.

Yeats, W. B. *Per Amica Silentia Lunae.* London: Macmillan & Co., Ltd., 1918. Cantwell 828.9 YEAT *Wade* 120, http://library.ucc.ie/record=b1334912

Yeats, W. B. *The Wild Swans at Coole.* London: Macmillan & Co., Ltd., 1919. Cantwell 821.9 YEAT *Wade* 124, http://library.ucc.ie/record=b1335099

Yeats, W. B. *The Cutting of an Agate.* London: Macmillan & Co., Ltd., 1919. Cantwell 824.9 YEAT *Wade* 126, http://library.ucc.ie/record=b1087911. Inscribed: E. T. Abell from A. K. D. i.iv.19.

Yeats, W. B. *Four Plays for Dancers.* London: Macmillan & Co., Ltd., 1921. Cantwell 822.9 YEAT *Wade* 129, http://library.ucc.ie/record=b1087999

Yeats, W. B. *The Trembling of the Veil.* London: Privately Printed for Subscribers only by T. Werner Laurie, Ltd., 1922. Cantwell 824.9 YEAT *Wade* 133, http://library.ucc.ie/record=b1335068

Yeats, W. B. *Later Poems.* London: Macmillan & Co., Ltd., 1922. Cantwell 821.9 YEAT *Wade* 134, http://library.ucc.ie/record=b1335283

Yeats, W. B. *Plays in Prose and Verse: written for an Irish Theatre, and Generally with the Help of a Friend.* London: Macmillan & Co., Ltd., 1922. Cantwell 822.9 YEAT *Wade* 136, http://library.ucc.ie/record=b1087916. Title page embossed with Presentation Copy stamp.

Yeats, W. B. *Plays and Controversies.* London: Macmillan & Co., 1923. Cantwell 822.9 YEAT *Wade* 139, http://library.ucc.ie/record=b1335278

Yeats, W. B. *Essays.* London: Macmillan & Co., Ltd., 1924. Cantwell 821.9 YEAT *Wade* 141, http://library.ucc.ie/record=b1087883. Inscribed: Ruth Jameson.

Yeats, W. B. *Early Poems and Stories.* London: Macmillan & Co., Ltd., 1925. Two copies. Cantwell 828.8 YEAT *Wade* 147, http://library.ucc.ie/record=b1087986. Two copies, only one of which was part of the original donation, and which is inscribed 'Mrs Jameson from W. B. Yeats January 24, 1926'.

Yeats, W. B. *A Vision: an Explanation of Life founded upon the Writings of Giraldus and upon Certain Doctrines attributed to Kusta ben Luka.* London: Privately printed for subscribers only by T. Werner Laurie, Ltd., 1925. Cantwell 824.9 YEAT *Wade* 149, http://library.ucc.ie/record=b1335033

Yeats, W. B. *Autobiographies: Reveries over Childhood and Youth and The Trembling of the Veil.* London: Macmillan, 1926. Cantwell 828.9 YEAT *Wade* 151, http://library.ucc.ie/record=b1087958. Inscribed: Ruth Jameson, 1926.

Yeats, W. B. *Poems.* London: T. Fisher Unwin (Ernest Benn, Ltd.), 1927. Cantwell 821.9 YEAT *Wade* 153, http://library.ucc.ie/record=b1335290. Inscribed: T. W. Marsh 1930.

The Augustan Books of English Poetry W. B. Yeats. [London]: Ernest Benn, Ltd., [1927] Cantwell p 821.9 YEAT *Wade* 155, http://library.ucc.ie/record=b1334724

Yeats, W. B. *Stories of Red Hanrahan and the Secret Rose.* Illustrated & decorated by Norah McGuinness. London: Macmillan & Co., Ltd., 1927. Cantwell 823.9 YEAT *Wade* 157, http://library.ucc.ie/record=b1087991

Yeats, W. B. *The Tower* London: Macmillan & Co. Ltd., 1928. Cantwell 821.9 YEAT *Wade* 158, http://library.ucc.ie/record=b1087946

Yeats, W. B. *Sophocles' King Oedipus: A Version for the Modern Stage.* London: Macmillan & Co., Ltd., 1928. Cantwell p 822 SOPH Two copies. *Wade* 160, http://library.ucc.ie/record=b1334896

Yeats, W. B. *The Winding Stair.* New York: The Fountain Press, 1929. Cantwell 821.9 YEAT Copy 383. Signed by the author. *Wade* 164, http://library.ucc.ie/record=b1335094

Yeats, W. B. *Selected Poems: Lyrical and Narrative.* London: Macmillan & Co., Ltd., 1929. Cantwell 821.9 YEAT *Wade* 165, http://library.ucc.ie/record=b1131345

Yeats, W. B. *Three Things.* London: Faber & Faber, Ltd., 1929 Cantwell p 821.9 YEAT *Wade* 166, http://library.ucc.ie/record=b1334720

Yeats, W. B. *Words for Music Perhaps and Other Poems* Dublin: Cuala Press, 1932. Cantwell 821.9 YEAT *Wade* 168, http://library.ucc.ie/record=b1198818

The Winding Stair and Other Poems. London: Macmillan & Co., Ltd., 1933. Cantwell 821.9 YEAT *Wade* 169, http://library.ucc.ie/record=b1334709

Yeats, W. B. *Letters to the New Island*. Edited with an introduction by Horace Reynolds. Cambridge, Mass.: Harvard University Press, 1934. Two copies. Cantwell 828.8 YEAT *Wade* 173, http://library.ucc.ie/record=b1087881. One copy Cantwell, the other previously UCC General Collections.

Yeats, W. B. *Wheels and Butterflies*. London: Macmillan & Co., 1934. Cantwell 822.9 YEAT *Wade* 175, http://library.ucc.ie/record=b1335281

Yeats, W. B. *The Collected Plays of W. B. Yeats*. London: Macmillan & Co., Ltd., 1934. Cantwell 822.9 YEAT *Wade* 177, http://library.ucc.ie/record=b1114721

Yeats, W. B. *A Full Moon in March*. London: Macmillan & Co. Ltd., 1935. Cantwell 821.9 YEAT *Wade* 182, http://library.ucc.ie/record=b1335086

Yeats, W. B. *The King's Threshold*. London: Macmillan & Co., Ltd., 1937. Cantwell p 822.9 YEAT *Wade* 189, http://library.ucc.ie/record=b1334900

Yeats, W. B. *A Vision*. London: The Macmillan Company, 1937. Cantwell 824.9 YEAT *Wade* 191, http://library.ucc.ie/record=b1335042

Yeats, W. B. *A Vision*. New York: The Macmillan Company, 1938. Cantwell 824.9 YEAT *Wade* 192, http://library.ucc.ie/record=b1335042

Yeats, W. B. *The Herne's Egg: a Stage Play*. London: Macmillan & Co., Ltd., 1938. Cantwell 822.9 YEAT *Wade* 195, http://library.ucc.ie/record=b1335066

Yeats, W. B. *New Poems*. Dublin: Cuala Press, 1938. Cantwell 821.9 YEAT *Wade* 197, http://library.ucc.ie/record=b1198652. This copy belonged to Sean McEntee.

Yeats, W. B. *Last Poems & Plays*. London: Macmillan & Co., Ltd., 1940. Cantwell 821.9 YEAT *Wade* 203, http://library.ucc.ie/record=b1129949

The Poems of W. B. Yeats. London: Macmillan & Co., Ltd., 1949. Cantwell 821.9 YEAT v.1–2 *Wade* 209 & 210, http://library.ucc.ie/record=b1334677. Copy n. 86 of this two-volume set.

Yeats, W. B. (ed. & select.) *Fairy and Folk Tales of the Irish Peasantry*. London: Walter Scott, Ltd., [1888]. Cantwell 398.2 YEAT *Wade* 212, http://library.ucc.ie/record=b1129952

Poems of William Blake. Edited by William Butler Yeats. New York: The Modern Library [192-]. Cantwell 821.7 BLAK *Wade* 222, http://library. ucc.ie/record=b1335001. N. 91 in the ML series, limp boards, bound in green fabricoid. The endpapers are designed by Lucien Bernhard which dates the volume to *c.*1925–29; see: http://www.modernlib.com/Identifiers/ endpapers/endpapers.html

The Oxford Book of Modern Verse, 1892–1935 chosen by W. B. Yeats. Oxford: Clarendon, 1936. Cantwell 821.9 OXFO *Wade* 250, http://library.ucc.ie/record=b1079733

W. B. Yeats Manuscripts and Printed Books Exhibited in the Library of Trinity College, Dublin, 1956. Dublin: Printed for the Friends of the Library of Trinity College by C. O. Lochlainn at the Sign of the Three Candles, [1956] Cantwell p 821.9 YEAT *Wade* 346, http://library.ucc.ie/record=b1335013

Yeats, W. B. *The Speckled Bird.* Edited by William H. O'Donnell. Dublin: Cuala Press, 1973–74. Cantwell 823.9 YEAT and Cantwell 823.9 YEAT v.1 [Edition in two volumes], http://library.ucc.ie/record=b1131345 (The online catalogue is erroneous here).

Yeats at the Municipal Gallery. Dublin: Charlemont House, 1959. Cantwell p 821.9 YEAT, http://library.ucc.ie/record=b1334898

PART II: ACQUIRED BY LATER DONATION FROM J. Kearney, Blackrock, Cork

W. B. Yeats, a Centenary Exhibition [Dublin]: National Gallery of Ireland / Gailearaí Náisiúnta. na hÉireann, 1965. Cantwell 759.2915 YEAT, http://library.ucc.ie/record=b1308240

PART III: ACQUIRED BY UCC BY PURCHASE SINCE 2005

Yeats, W. B. *John Sherman, and Dhoya* / Ganconagh [i.e. W. B. Yeats]. [2nd ed.]. London: T. Fisher Unwin, 1891. Cantwell 823.9 YEAT *Wade* 4, http://library.ucc.ie/record=b2027643

Yeats, W. B. *The Secret Rose.* With illustrations by J. B. Yeats. London: Lawrence & Bullen, 1897. Cantwell 823.9 YEAT *c.*101 *Wade* 21, http://library.ucc.ie/record=b2027697

Yeats, W. B. *Is the Order of R. R. & A. C. to remain a Magical Order?* Written in March, 1901, and given to the Adepti of the Order of R.R. & A.C. in April, 1901 D.E.D.I. [i.e., W. B. Yeats] London: 1901. Strongroom Cantwell 135.43 YEAT *Wade* 33, http://library.ucc.ie/record=b1682566. John Quinn's copy with his bookplate.

Yeats, W. B. *Stories of Red Hanrahan.* Dundrum: Dun Emer Press, MCMIV [1904]. Cantwell 823.9 YEAT *Wade* 59, http://library.ucc.ie/record=b2048779

Yeats, W. B. *The Bounty of Sweden: a Meditation, and a Lecture delivered before the Royal Swedish Academy and Certain Notes.* Dublin, Ireland: The Cuala Press, 1925. Cantwell 828.9 YEAT *Wade* 146, http://library.ucc.ie/record=b2048781

Twenty-one poems. S Dublin: Dun Emer Press, 1907. Cantwell 821.9 TYNA *Wade* 238, http://library.ucc.ie/record=b2048778

Wade, Allen. *A Bibliography of the Writings of W. B. Yeats.* London: Rupert Hart-Davis, 1951. Cantwell 016.8289 YEAT. W *Wade* 303, http://library.ucc.ie/record=b2028518

Symons, A. J. A., comp. *A Bibliography of the First Editions of Books by William Butler Yeats.* London: First Edition Club, 1924. Cantwell p 016.9289 YEAT.S, http://library.ucc.ie/record=b2028517

RESEARCH UPDATES
AND OBITUARIES

http://dx.doi.org/10.11647/OBP.0081.09

W. B. Yeats's *Mosada*[1]

Colin Smythe

AS IS WELL KNOWN to all collectors of the works of W. B. Yeats, *Mosada. A Dramatic Poem*, printed by Sealy, Bryers, & Walker of Dublin in 1886, is the most sought-after and most valuable of all his works, with copies selling for many tens of thousands of pounds.[2] Wade accords it the status of being Yeats's first 'book',[3] while yet firmly stating that it is an 'off-print from *The Dublin University Review*, June 1886' (*DUR*, 473–83).

---

[1] Further information may have been gathered since this article was prepared for publication. If you would like to find out if any further information has been discovered that may help your own research, why not write to the author at cpsmythe@aol.com? Quite apart from anything else, feedback is always welcomed.

[2] In *Yeats: The McC. Gatch Collection* Maggs Catalogue 1492 (London: Maggs Bros., 2015), item 162, *Mosada* is described as 'one of the black roses of modern literature' (46).

[3] See Allan Wade: *A Bibliography of the Writings of W. B. Yeats* (London: Rupert Hart-Davis, 1951), n. 1, an attribution followed in *Wade* (1968), 19; John Hayward: *English Poetry. A Catalogue of First & Early Editions of the English Poets from Chaucer to the Present Day* (Cambridge: Cambridge University Press, for the National Book League, 1947), n. 294. In this article I refer to Wade's bibliographies as Wade (1908), and the three editions published by Rupert Hart-Davis in 1951, 1958 and 1968 as Wade 1, Wade 2 and Wade 3.

Being a second use of the type, this separate publication was a reprint as far as the printers were concerned. Such is acknowledged on the front cover, which Wade uses as a facing illustration, where it is stated between rules '*Reprinted from THE DUBLIN UNIVERSITY REVIEW*', while below 'DUBLIN': are the words 'PRINTED [rather than PUBLISHED] BY SEALY, BRYERS, AND WALKER', followed by their street address (see Plate 4 above, p. 16). Yeats himself stated that it was thus, but his use of such terms as 'reprinted' and 'publication' was not necessarily bibliographically exact.[4] To Katharine Tynan, it was 'privately printed'.[5] It was probably available for distribution in late October or the first week of November 1886. The absence of a price on the cover could mean that it was undecided at the time of printing, but A. J. A. Symons states that it was sold for one shilling.[6]

The first the Dublin public knew of its appearance was a note in the November issue of the *DUR*:

We are glad to note the publication by MESSRS. SEALY BRYERS & WALKER of the powerful and pathetic poem, 'Mosada' contributed to a recent number of this REVIEW by Mr. W. B. Yeats. The reprint contains a pen-and-ink portrait of the author by Mr. J. B. Yeats—a very beautiful and characteristic piece of work admirably reproduced on zinc by a Dublin engraver, Mr. Lewis. (958)

This notice of 'publication' is more a mere advertisement than a review, of course, yet it mentions no price and does not seem to seek a wide sale. William M. Murphy claims that '[t]he volume had little sale. Papa and Willie gave copies away liberally'.[7] Writing in 1939, P. S. O'Hegarty, the Dublin book collector and bibliographer (among

---

[4]   See below, his 1923 inscription in item 13.
[5]   See her *Twenty-Five Years: Reminiscences* (London: Smith, Elder & Co., 1913). It is here that she declares *Mosada* 'privately printed... a far cry from that to a limited edition at six guineas. Possibly *Mosada* made me sure of what he was. It has beautiful passages' and at the time of writing Tynan still had it, 'somewhere' (256).
[6]   A. J. A. Symons, *A Bibliography of the First Editions of Books by William Butler Yeats* (London: The First Edition Club, 1924), 1.
[7]   See William M. Murphy, *Prodigal Father: The Life of John Butler Yeats (1839–1922)* (Ithaca and London: Cornell University Press, 1978), 146–47.

many other things),[8] stated that before he had seen A. J. A. Symons's statement that the edition had been of 100 copies, he had believed that the number was fifty, because 'if 100 copies had been printed I would expect rather more copies to turn up than actually have turned up, especially in Dublin'. He continued '[Since this [type] was set up, I have been informed by Miss E. C. Yeats that the edition was 100.]'[9]

This present working note provides a numbered census of known, identified, surviving copies as well as a record of copies which have passed through the sale rooms but of which the present whereabouts are unknown. It also mentions copies which have been known in the past and which may no longer exist. It further describes the varying paper types on the known items, and essays various bio-bibliographical connexions.

According to Joseph Hone's biography of Yeats, the booklet had been brought about by John Butler Yeats, the poet's father who, assisted by his friend Professor Edward Dowden, 'collected a few subscribers', the principal one being his brother, the Rev. John Dowden (1840–1910), soon to be elected Bishop of Edinburgh (a position he held till his death). '[O]n hearing some years later of Yeats's rising fame and of the rarity of his early work, [the Bishop]

---

[8] Apart from being a bibliophile, P. S. O'Hegarty (1879–1955) joined the Post Office in Cork in 1897, from which he resigned in 1918 following his refusal to take the Oath of Allegiance, was a member of the Supreme Council of the Irish Republican Brotherhood, and was editor of its publication, *Irish Freedom* (from 1910 until its suppression in 1914), and was Secretary to the Irish Department of Posts and Telegraphs from 1922 to 1945. He was elected to the Irish Academy of Letters in 1954. His son Seán Ó hÉigeartaigh founded the Irish language publisher Sáirséal agus Dill, and his daughter, Gráinne, married WBY's son, Michael. His book collection was acquired in 1955 by the Kenneth Spencer Research Library of Kansas University, Lawrence, KA. See also Wayne K. Chapman, 'P. S. O'Hegarty and the Yeats collection at the University of Kansas', *YA10* 221–38 and Plates 5–7.

[9] P. S. O'Hegarty, 'Notes on the Bibliography of W. B. Yeats, I. — Notes on, and supplemental to, the existing bibliographies by Mr. Allan Wade and Mr. A. J. A. Symons, 1886–1922', *The Dublin Magazine* 14:4 (October–December 1939), 61–65.

jingled his episcopal keys and sent his daughter up to the Palace library to search for his twelve copies. Not one could be found'.[10]

Writing to his friend Coventry Patmore on 7 November, 1886, Gerard Manley Hopkins, then a fellow at the Jesuit-run University College, Dublin (a constituent college of the Royal, now National University of Ireland), mentioned that he had called on the young Yeats's father, 'by desire lately';

he is a painter, and with some emphasis of manner he presented me with *Mosada, A Dramatic Poem*, by W. B. Yeats, with a portrait of the author by J. B. Yeats, himself; the young man having finely cut features, and his father being a fine draughtsman. For a young man's pamphlet this was something too much; but you will understand a father's feeling.[11]

Yeats himself was clearly embarrassed by the portrait: in March 1904 he was to inscribe a copy belonging to John Quinn[12] (recently sold to a private buyer from the collection of Milton McC. Gatch[13]),

There was to have been a picture of some incident in the play but my father was too much of a portrait painter not to do this instead. I was alarmed at the impudence of putting a portrait in my first work, but my father was full of ancient & modern instances. (See Plates 33 and 5 above, p. 17).

And in the Roth copy now in the Harry Ransom Humanities Research Center, Austin, Yeats reiterated that he had had little choice in the matter:

It was my father who insisted on the portrait for he refused to consider any body's diffidence where a portrait was concerned, it was also his insistence that kept me bearded.

---

[10] Joseph Hone, *W. B. Yeats, 1865–1939* (London: Macmillan, 1942), 49–50; (New York: Macmillan, 1943), 52–53.

[11] See Claude Colleer Abbott (ed.), *Further Letters of Gerard Manley Hopkins Including his Correspondence with Coventry Patmore* (London: Oxford University Press, 2nd ed., 1956), 373–74.

[12] Lot 11340, sold for $300 at Anderson Galleries' auction of John Quinn's book collection on 20 March 1924, the last day of the sale, which had started on 12 November the previous year. This would have been £50.0.0 at the conversion rates prevailing at the time.

[13] See also *Yeats: The McC. Gatch Collection* (London: Maggs Bros., Ltd., 2015), lot 162, 46–47.

Plate 33. Frontispiece portrait of W. B. Yeats by John Butler Yeats (1886) in John Quinn's copy of *Mosada: A Dramatic Poem* with W. B. Yeats's 1904 inscription. Courtesy of Maggs Bros., London.

As can be seen from the Gatch inscription however, his embarrassment did not prevent him sending copies out for review.

Yeats himself kept no copy, and it would seem that none were sent to the six British Copyright libraries. Thin and flimsy as they were, they were all too easily lost. At present I know of only two copies in Ireland, that in the collection which I sold to the Dublin City Library in 1965, and the one in the National Library of Ireland, which it acquired in 2010. A third is claiming temporary residence there. In Britain I know of three, two in the Bodleian Library, and the one from the Gatch Collection described above, but all the other copies I know of are, I believe, in the USA—though, given the present secrecy of auction houses regarding their buyers, it is impossible to tell.[14]

My numbered census below, however, ranges beyond the fifteen copies of which I now know the whereabouts, or have recently seen, all but four of which are in institutional libraries. I begin the census with the only known review copy, because it was no doubt dispatched as soon as copies were received from the printers. Measurements are in centimetres, and in each case, the paper as described is that of the wrapper. It goes without saying that the measurements and paper types of those copies that neither I nor my informants have seen cannot be given, being unknown.

1. **Milton McC. Gatch collection, ex-Quinn (sold by Maggs Bros. in 2015 to a private buyer)** 21.5 × 13.8, plain paper. Front cover inscribed 'For Review with the Author's compliments'—circular stain on bottom half of front cover, lower extremities frayed, inner hinges restored. Inscribed to John Quinn (see above), lot 11340 in the Quinn sale, where it fetched $300.00. This, later the W. Van R. Whitall copy, was sold to Morton McMichael by mid-1935, possibly the presentation copy sold at Hodgson's on 20/6/34, lot 62, bought by Maggs for £40.00.[15] It was eventually sold to McC. Gatch at Sotheby's New York, 17 December, 1992, lot 345, $60,000.

It seems logical to assume that other review copies could still be extant. As none of the currently 'known but unaccounted for' copies (see list below) has ever been described as a review copy, the following brief account of known reviews is listed below.

The *DUR* review copy. The notice above (p. 240) surely indicates that the *DUR* had itself received a copy.

---

[14] At the time I was collecting in the 1960s, it was normal for firms like Sotheby's to issue a list of auction prices with the buyers' names—though these of course would often have been pseudonyms.

[15] In an ALS to Morton McMichael of 27 June, 1935, Elizabeth Corbet Yeats asks him where he obtained the copy and how much he had paid for it: 'If you care to tell me, I will not repeat it to anyone else if you wish, but I am immensely curious to know—none of the family have a copy'. See item 471, in the Maggs catalogue 1492, *Yeats: The McC. Gatch Collection* (London: 2015), 117.

The *Freeman's Journal* **review copy.** Used to review *Mosada* on 27 November 1886, 5—'When "Mosada" was first published in the *Dublin University Review*, we freely expressed our sense of its many excellences, and our appreciation of the promise that it gave. With sincere pleasure, therefore, we welcome its republication, and our only regret is that the author should have limited the edition to a very small number of copies' (5).

The Graphic **review copy.** Used to review *Mosada* on 26 March 1887, 'A very striking, though brief, dramatic sketch is "Mosada: A Dramatic Poem"' (23).

The *Manchester Guardian* **review copy.** Although not reviewed at the time of publication, *Mosada* is referred to in 'Books of the Week' on 15 October 1888, when reviewing *Fairy and Folk Tales of the Irish Peasantry*, WBY's 'tendency to mysticism and Orientalism, well known to those who are familiar with his striking lyrics and his more ambitious "Mosada" are real helps towards the due appreciation of the unwritten poetry of the most mystical people in Western Europe' (7).

This copy was later in the possession of a Dublin *Daily Express* reviewer who, when writing on *The Poems of William Blake* and *The Celtic Twilight* on 2 January 1894, noted 'We still possess his first published work, a poem entitled "Mosada" sent to the Man[*chester Guardian*] for review' (6). Again, when writing on *Poems* in the same paper, evidently the same reviewer remarked:

Those acquainted with Mr. Yeats's work will learn with sorrow that among the poems eliminated is the dramatic sketch "Mosada", which, rightly or wrongly, we deem the high-water mark of his achievements in poetry. It is one of the few poems from his hand with a deep human interest, and in this, if not on the ground of superiority of workmanship, we regret its omission in this, his first collected volume. The first and only edition of "Mosada" sent in 1886 for review lies before us.[16]

---

[16] 8 November 1895, 6. Possibly the reviewer was Ramsay Colles (see *CL1* 128), whose *In Castle and Courthouse: Being Reminiscences of 30 Years in Ireland* (London: T. Werner Laurie, 1911) opens with a sketch of the 1886 literary 'set' during Sunday pilgrimages to old Andrew Tynan's farmhouse, Whitehall, Clondalkin, at the foot of the Dublin mountains. For Colles, 1886 marks the beginning of

The Irish Monthly **review copy.** Katharine Tynan reviewed *Mosada* in the *Monthly* as the first item in 'Three Young Poets', March, 1887 (166–68). It is not known whether she did this from a separate review copy, or from her own presentation copy, for which see next item. The review, however, states that the DUR text has been 'reproduced' in 'its less perishable form', 'in pamphlet form, with a stiff paper cover' (166; also *CH* 66–67).

2. **Katharine Tynan / Beinecke Library copy,** Yale University [Ip Y34 886m] 21.5 x 13.8, silurian paper, lined white. Mentioned in Tynan's *Twenty-Five Years: Reminiscences*[17] it is inscribed 'Miss K Tynan from her friend and fellow worker in Irish Poetry the author': it was sold at Sotheby's on 1 April 1914 (lot 853) to Maggs for £6–10s. It now forms part of the Garvan Collection of Books on Ireland, set up in 1931 with funds provided by Francis P. Garvan (1875–1937) Yale Class of 1897, in memory of his parents, but there is no record of when it was purchased. It was exhibited, I believe, as item n. 1 in the Yale University Library's 1939 exhibition of Yeats's works, and so must have been acquired in the 1930s. Tynan had reciprocated by giving WBY a copy of her 1887 *Shamrocks*, now in the Smythe collection in the Dublin City Library, inscribed 'To dear Willie Yeats, with the belief in him and the affectionate friendship of the writer, May 30th'.

3. **Frederick J. Gregg's copy.** 21.6 × 13.7, silurian paper, lined white. Gregg (1864–1927) had been a contemporary of WBY's at the Erasmus Smith High School and in late 1886 was living at 6 Eccles St., Dublin. He published poems in the *Irish Monthly* and two were later in *Poems and Ballads of Young Ireland* (1888). However, 'El Greggo' (as John Quinn later termed him, emigrated

the Irish Literary Movement, and writers of and for *The Irish Fireside*, the newly revived *Dublin University Magazine* (in which had appeared 'Mr. Yeats's... finest dramatic poem, *Mosada*', and *The Irish Monthly* would cycle or walk out four miles to gather around Katharine Tynan who held court for such figures as Yeats, Frederick Gregg (see item 3), Fr. Matthew Russell, Douglas Hyde, Richard Ashe-King, and George Russell (20–27). This was the group, clearly, in which *Mosada* initially circulated.

[17] See above, n. 4.

to the U.S. in 1891 where he became a journalist on the *New York Evening Sun*: see *CL1* 7–8 esp n. 1. This copy was purchased by Alfred Tennyson DeLury (1864–1951) from C. Gerhadt & Co. Rare Books, New York, in May 1916 for $25.00.[18] DeLury was Dean of Arts at the University of Toronto and was an avid collector of works by Irish Literary Renaissance writers, as well becoming as a friend of the Yeats family. On his death his collection was donated to the University, which created the Alfred Tennyson DeLury Collection in the Fisher Rare Book Library. It would appear that his family kept back *Mosada* when they donated his remarkable collection to the University. A century with one family—no wonder no one heard of it for so long! Its recent reappearance—it was recently exhibited for sale at the 2016 London Olympia Book Fair—offers the hope that further copies will turn up. Gregg's copy is inscribed in an early hand 'To F. Gregg from his friend the Author'. It is also the original of the facsimile edition (Plate 34).[19]

---

[18] The relative values of pounds and dollars have of course varied much over the years with the dollar almost constantly gaining ground. Before World War I the conversion rate was in the region of US$6 to £1 sterling. It dropped almost continuously until when I started collecting in the 1960s it was $2.80 to the pound, soon to drop to $2.40, and since then, in the mid-1980s, they almost achieved parity, before the pound picked up. A very useful site for historical currency conversions is https://futureboy.us/fsp/dollar.fsp?quantity=&currency=pounds&fromYear. In 1916 $25 would be worth $511 now, while £14 would be worth $1,221. Thus in that year $25 would have converted to about £5–17s. Such was the slump in sterling during the War, that same £14 in 1913 would have been worth $1758.75 now, so it had dropped by about a third against the dollar in three years.

[19] Wade is incorrect in stating that the inscription was under the portrait: it is on the inside front cover. It would appear to have become detached and during otherwise careful restoration of the book evidently in DeLury's lifetime, and has been pasted back so that it now faces the first page of text. Given that Alfred Tennyson DeLury lived in Toronto, it would seem reasonable to assume that he arranged for the facsimile edition, and the 'few facsimile copies' seen by Pádraig Ó Broin must have been in the owner's possession. He probably saw the original and was bound to silence on the point of ownership. This note appeared in Wade 1. The only copy I have seen was in the collection of James F. Gallagher of New York, and had been dated 15 December 1949. It was not included in the Sotheby's sale of his collection on 11 July 1986. It is now in the Kenneth Spencer Library, University of Kansas, Lawrence KS, call number Yeats Y67, http://catalog.lib.

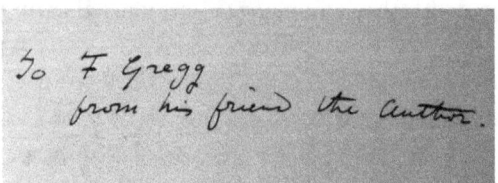

Plate 34. Yeats's inscription in his presentation copy to Frederick J. Gregg of
Mosada: A Dramatic Poem. © Colin Smythe and courtesy of private collection.
All rights reserved.

4. **Edward Dowden / Robert P. Esty & Frederic Dannay**[20] **copy.**
Present whereabouts unknown to me. Inscribed 'Prof. Dowden
with the author's compts'. 'Messrs. Hodgson in London yesterday
concluded the sale of the first and modern portion of the library
of the late Professor Dowden' (*Daily Express*, Dublin, 8/11/1913,
5), in which was doubtless included this copy of *Mosada*. Dowden
had died on 4 April 1913. It formed the last lot in the sale of the
collection of Robert Pegram Esty (1877–1958), of Philadelphia,
at the Parke-Bernet Galleries on 22 October 1963 (lot 411) with
an estimated price of $2,500–2,750, but selling for $3,750. It
was resold through Parke Bernet New York as part of Frederic
Dannay's collection on 16 December 1983 (lot 397), to 'Lyon'
for $30,000 (estimate $12,000–15,000). Given the number that
Bishop John Dowden received for his generous subscription (see
next item), it is almost certain that Edward Dowden must also
have had more than one copy.

5. **Bishop John Dowden's 12 copies,** as described above, also n.
9 above. Present whereabouts of all these is unknown, further

---

ku.edu/cgi-bin/Pwebrecon.cgi?bbid=3786311. The photostats were printed on
Vandyke paper on one side only, and stitched inside plain light brown kraft paper
covers, with page 12 cut out, leaving a half-inch stub. They were trimmed to
match the dimensions of the original.

[20] As well as an avid book collector, Frederic Dannay (1905–82) collaborated with
his cousin, Emanuel Benjamin Lepofsky (1905–71), who was professionally
known as Manfred Bennington Lee, in writing detective stories under the joint
pseudonym 'Ellery Queen'.

searches in Edinburgh this year were—not surprisingly—also fruitless. One hopes, nevertheless.

6. **Gerard Manley Hopkins copy.** Present whereabouts unknown. Presentation copy from John Butler Yeats mentioned in letter from GMH to Patmore, 7 November, 1886, probably no more than two days after their meeting in JBY's studio.[21] See also above, pp. 145-17 and 242 n. 10.

7. **'Miss Veasey' / Buhler.** Present whereabouts unknown. The copy in the C. Walter Buhler sale at Parke-Bernet Gallery (1/5/41 lot 130, $190) was inscribed 'Miss Veasey with good wishes for the New Year from her friend the author'. This was probably Ethel Mary Veasey (1863–1905) the elder sister of Harley [not Charles] Cyril Veasey (1865–1926), who protected the thirteen-year-old WBY from bullying at the Godolphin School (*Life 1*, 26). Their father Robert G. Veasey (1834–1912), was a clerk at the Bank of England. Ethel was a friend of Elizabeth Corbet Yeats, and is mentioned by name in a letter from ECY to Katharine Tynan, 29 Dec 1889 (Southern Illinois) quoted in *CL1* 203, n. 4. She had given a Christmas present in 1889 to ECY (a Spanish fan). Perhaps ECY encouraged her brother to reciprocate for the New Year with this copy of *Mosada*?

8. **T. W. Rolleston copy seen by Wade in 1908.** Its subsequent ownership history and present whereabouts unknown. T. W. Rolleston owned a copy which he lent to Allan Wade for

---

[21] According to William M. Murphy, Gerard Manley Hopkins already had a copy of *Mosada* when he was presented with this one: see Murphy, *op.cit.*, 146–47. All that is known, however, is that Hopkins had sent her three books by Robert Bridges instead of a single book, the implication being that KT had given a book to GMH. If so, it is more likely to have been her *Louise de la Vallière* (1885) than *Mosada*. Murphy also claims Hopkins went to call on JBY at KT's insistence. It seems likely that she was present in JBY's studio, but left before the end of the conversation, because she wonders how GMH 'and Mr Yeats finished the discussion on finish or non-finish': see KT to GMH [Sat.], 6 November in Abbott, *op. cit.*, 430, a letter which strongly suggests the meeting with JBY had taken place in the previous few days.

examination when he was compiling his 1908 bibliography. It is reasonable to assume that it would have been signed by WBY.

9. **Zena Powell / Dr F. S. Bourke.** Present whereabouts unknown. 3/12/1962, Sotheby's, to Wright, £580.00. Inscribed to 'Miss Zena Powell from her friend the Author'. In 1956 loaned by Dr F. S. Bourke to the Trinity College Dublin Library for the exhibition ('lower wrapper missing'). It was offered for sale by Mrs M. Whitley 'from the collection of the late Dr F. S. Bourke'. From the marked-up sale catalogue retained by Sotheby's there is a suggestion that the reserve was £700 and the copy was bought in. Nevertheless, the published listing of prices and buyers for the sale notes a figure of £580 sold to 'Wright'. It is likely that the copy in the 'private collection in Dublin' mentioned in the 1951 and 1958 editions of Wade (Wade 1 and Wade 2) was Dr Bourke's, and that obviously Brig. Gen. Alspach had not been aware of its subsequent history when editing Wade 3. The type of p. 18 of Wade 2 and Wade 3, which entirely relates to owners of *Mosada*, had no changes made to it between the editions. Sotheby's records give no idea as to its subsequent fate. The repeated catalogue description of the torn condition of the back cover makes it likely that this is the same copy sold at Hodgson's on 7 December 1933 (lot 426) to Lee for £27–10–0, and again by them on 17 July 1935 (lot 167) to Radcliff for £19–0–0, the drop in value perhaps indicating a further deterioration of the back cover, later lost in its entirety.

10. **John O'Leary / John Quinn / Berg Collection, New York Public Library, Astor, Lenox & Tilden Foundations.** 22.00 × 13.9, silurian 85% red, 15% blue, lined white. Lot 11339 in Quinn's sale catalogue, this too is an early presentation copy, inscribed 'Mr J O'Leary from his disciple and friend the Author W B Yeats'. (Plate 35). Sold for $260.00. At the time of the sale, and at the time of its acquisition by the Berg Collection, it was accompanied by a wrapper addressed to Quinn, postmarked 24 April 1903.

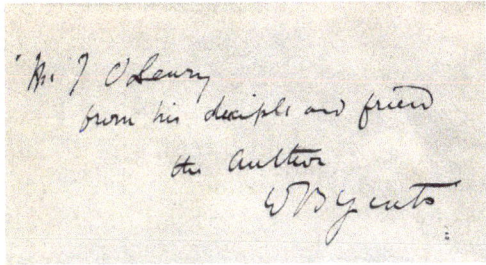

Plate 35. Yeats's inscription in his presentation copy to John O'Leary of *Mosada: A Dramatic Poem*. © the Henry W. and Albert A. Berg Collection, and the Astor, Lenox and Tilden Foundations, New York Public Library. All rights reserved.

11. Henrietta Alma Pollexfen / William Andrews Clark Memorial Library, University of California. 21.6 × 13.9 silurian, red threads, lined white (without checking the entire cover with a strong magnifier the non-existence of blue is not a certainty). It is inscribed 'H.A. Pollexfen from W. B. Yeats', which hardly indicates warmth (Plate 36). On the inside back cover there is the label of E[dward] W. Titus, who had bought this copy at Sotheby's on 19 December 1924 for £46. He published books at the Sign of the Black Manikin Press, 4 rue Delambre, Paris (14e), between 1927 and 1932.[22] Henrietta Alma Johnstone married WBY's uncle Frederick Henry Pollexfen (1852–1933) in 1881, they having eight, possibly nine, children before he filed for divorce in 1899, on the grounds of her adultery with Roland Edward Bennison. Following the divorce Frederick sued an unnamed borrower (Bennison?) for the loss of this copy which he had obviously kept, with some other books, an event mentioned in Clement Shorter's 'literary letter' in the 21 December 1901 issue of the *Sphere*. WBY, when writing a sympathetic valuation

---

[22] 'Editor's Gossip', *The Irish Book Lover* 15:4 (October 1925), reports the appearance of this sale in the current number of *Book Auction Records* as an 'interesting fact… an inscribed copy… published less than forty years fetched the handsome sum of £46' (54–55).

for the defendant, said he considered *Mosada* of no worth at this time, giving as his reason that there was no demand for it, but Frederick, the 'shabby relation' mentioned in WBY's letter to Lady Gregory of 22 December 1901, got Elkin Mathews to value it at £10. He was awarded £6–10s for the lot, with *Mosada* valued at £5 (*CL3* 139). This copy was later sold by the Parke-Bernet Gallery on 9 October 1951 (lot 707) for $390.

Plate 36. Henrietta Alma Pollexfen's copy of *Mosada: A Dramatic Poem.* © the William Andrews Clark Memorial Library, University of California, Los Angeles. All rights reserved.

12. **Thomas Edwin Butler Yeats / Grace Butler Yeats / National Library of Ireland.** 21.5 × 13.8, silurian paper, coloured fibres, lined white, lacking small piece at bottom of front cover, which has been repaired as has the damage to the back cover. Grace B. Yeats's copy, left to her by her father, and sold at Sotheby's, 13/7/2000, lot 78, £42,000; with a letter from her to her mother, October 1925, discussing the family and mentioning this copy of *Mosada*. It was later offered for sale by Bloomsbury New York, 21/4/2010, lot 105, $60,000, unsold at the auction, but bought

later. Grace Butler Yeats was WBY's second cousin once removed. A Canadian, she called to see him in Dublin, 13 October 1925: see John Kelly, *A W. B. Yeats Chronology* (Basingstoke: Palgrave Macmillan, 2003), 243. In a letter of 7 October [1925], WBY sets up the appointment for their meeting at 4.30 pm in 82 Merrion Square, remarking that 'I remember your father well & his father Matt Yeats—that old life is all very vivid to me' (*CL InteLex*, 4784). In her letter to her mother Grace writes: '...Tell Dad to hold on tight to his Mosada. The value is going up. Lolly has a lot of first copies of W.B'.s but not that. She says one of it was sold recently in London for £30. A friend of hers sold it for £6 and it was sold later for £30. So that 1/- was not a bad investment of Dad's...' (Plate 37).

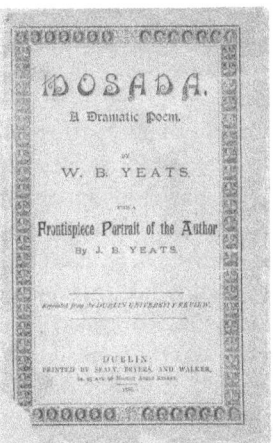

Plate 37. Grace Yeats's copy of *Mosada: A Dramatic Poem*. © the National Library of Ireland. All rights reserved.

13. **Harry Ransom Humanities Research Center, Austin** TX **[HRHRC] / William M. Roth copy,** 21.5 × 14.0 plain. Sold at New York's Anderson Galleries in 1926, offered by Scribner Booksellers, NYC, in their 1948 and 1949 catalogues for US$500, bought by William M. Roth, and sold (at cost) to The Harry Ransom Center, Austin TX, had been inscribed by Yeats when

in Dublin, 'The first copy that I have seen for many years. The play was published in the Dublin University Review & from that reprinted in the present form & had of course no success of any kind. It was my father who insisted on the portrait for he refused to consider any body's diffidence where a portrait was concerned, it was also his insistence that kept me bearded. WB Yeats Nov 10, 1923'. He added, on page 11, 'I read this through for the first time since it was first published. I wrote it when I was twenty one & think rather sadly that if a young man of that age sent in like work I [would] not be able to foresee his future or his talent. W B Yeats'.

William Roth had set up the exhibition of Yeats's works 'held in the Yale University Library beginning May 13, 1939' and written the catalogue / bibliography that accompanied it. He wrote to me in June 1982:

'In answer to your question—the bibliography came from a number of sources: the books shown at the Yale Library were their own plus mine—mostly the latter. I had put together a fairly complete collection plus letters, proof copies and manuscripts in days when buying both in shops in London and New York and at auction was fairly easy and inexpensive (corrected proofs of Countess Kathleen at $40). I also used a small collection at Mills College near San Francisco, the Harvard Library and the New York Public Library. The Quinn catalogue was, of course, helpful as was the excellent collection of James A. Healy in New York (I have no idea what ever became of his books).[23] Miss[24] Yeats was helpful, too.

After the war when I was working in the oil fields in Texas, it seemed to me the collection should be in safe keeping so I sold it to the University of Texas at cost—and regretted it ever since. Perhaps, however, it was just as well'.

---

[23] Healy gave them in 1948 to the Library of Colby College, Waterville, Maine, where they are located in the John and Catherine Healy Memorial Room [named after his parents] in Special Collections. He also created a collection of modern Irish history at the Hoover Institution in Stanford University, and added to the libraries of Boston College, Villanova, Cornell, Kansas University and the library of the American Historical Society, New York, as well as to the National Library of Ireland. For further details, see http://libguides.colby.edu/healy.

[24] The *Catalogue* states that this was Elizabeth Corbet Yeats.

14. **Bodleian Library, Oxford, 1** [Don. D. 85] 21.7 × 13.7 bound in thick, darker, pinker, paper, unlined, almost card. As a result cover is printed more solidly. Came via the Friends of the Bodleian from the family of the late Mr. J. G. Legge in 1940.

15. **Bodleian Library, Oxford, 2** [Arch. AA e 79] 21.7 × 13.8 silurian, 85% red, 15% blue, lined white (lighter colour than the text paper). Donated to the Library in 1957, but no information as to the donor.

16. **Dublin City Library's Colin Smythe collection.** 21.7 × 13.8, silurian red/blue. Bought at Sotheby's by Bernard Quaritch acting for Colin Smythe, 11 May 1964 £650. The front and back covers had separated and were stuck together with adhesive tape, which had degraded, before being repaired by its new owner. Some staining from the tape remains. It formed part of his collection sold to the Dublin City Library in 1965. Earlier provenance unknown (Plate 38).

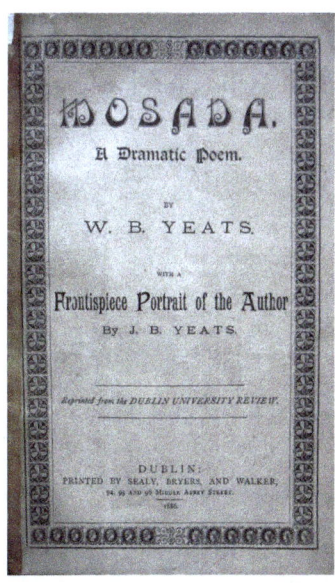

Plate 38. Dublin City Library copy of *Mosada: A Dramatic Poem*.

17. **Boston College, via Bradley Martin (d. 23/4/88) → Brian Leeming:** 21.5 × 13.7 silurian, lined. Original cover, minor fraying at extremities, vertical crease where formerly folded—bought by Bradley Martin in 1986[25]—Sotheby's New York, 1/5/90, lot 3340, $85,000.

18. **Houghton Library, Harvard University, Boston, MA.** 21.6 × 13.7 plain paper lined white. Provenance and date of acquisition unknown.

19. **University of N. Carolina, Chapel Hill, via George Mills Harper.** Yeats PR5904.M67 1886. 21.6 x 13.6, original wraps, some spotting, has a pale ochre/light brown thick paper cover, unlined, without the silurian flecks in the paper. Cyril I. Nelson (New York) → Anthony Hobson → Sotheby's, 28/6/96, lot 283, £42,000 ($64,680).

20. **Oliver Brett, 3rd Viscount Esher / Stuart Rose.** 21.5 × 13.7, plain paper. Esher sale 20 November 1946, bought by C.J. Sawyer on behalf of Lord Berwick for £54–0–0, exhibited National Book League, London, 1947. The title page of this copy was reproduced in the second edition of the NBL's catalogue of the exhibition, in which it appeared as n. 294. Lord Esher → Lord Berwick → James Gilvarry → Garden, Ltd [Haven O'More[26]/

---

[25] See Stephen Weissman's obituary of Henry Bradley Martin in the *Proceedings of the American Antiquarian Society*, 98:2 (October 1988), 216.

[26] There had been speculation as to whether this was his real name or whether it was a modification of 'Have No More'. In his *New York Times* review (20 August 1995) of Nicholas A. Basbanes' *A Gentle Madness. Bibliophiles, Bibliomanes, and the Eternal Passion for Books* (New York: Henry Holt, 1995), Philip Kopper summarises what is known about him: 'Another fabulous character is Haven O'More, who engaged in 'high-spot' collecting (buying the rarest, priciest books) while cloaking himself in mystery. It turns out that this high-living autodidact persuaded a rich young man [Michael Davis] to furnish $17 million for his lavish pastime. Mr. Basbanes proudly reports that his Freedom of Information Act request uncovered military records for a Haven Moore, who, he contends, is the same person. Haven Moore was a North Carolina farm boy who signed his name with an X during a World War II Army hitch—an extraordinary beginning for "this strange man who wanted so keenly to be proclaimed the world's greatest book collector"'.

Michael Davis] → James O. Edwards → Stuart Rose (by private treaty, April 2006). Phillips, Son & Neale 17/9/63 lot 289, £750 to House of Books, for a client, presumably James P. Gilvarry;[27] New York, Christie's New York, 7/2/86, lot 464, $33,000; Sotheby's New York, 10/11/89, lot 200, $80,000.

More inscribed copies may well turn up: who knows what may be sitting in some wealthy family's library? And, in addition to, or perhaps including those described or postulated above as 'present whereabouts unknown', I have yet to discover the present whereabouts of the following:

21. **Paul Lemperley Estate.** Sold at Parke Burnet Galleries, 5/1/40 (lot 1035) for $175.00.

22. **Arthur Barnette Spingarn's copy, with his bookplate.** Sold by Sotheby's London on 19/6/62, on behalf of 'a gentleman resident in New York', to The House of El Dieff [i.e., Lew D. Feldman] £820. In 1940 Spingarn (1878–1971) succeeded his brother Joel Elias Spingarn (1875–1939), a civil rights activist who was the second President (1930–39) of the National Association for the Advancement of Coloured People (NAACP) in the USA, holding the Presidency until 1965. In 1948 he sold his vast collection of material relating to the African-American experience to Howard University, and in 1966 he sold his art collections at the Parke-Bernet Galleries. The vendor of this copy also sold Maud Gonne's copy of *The Book of the Rhymer's Club* (lot 68) and Shaw's copy of the 1903 *Where There is Nothing* (lot 71).

23. **Thomas Rice Henn's copy seen by me *c*.1970.** This copy would have formed part of his Estate at the time of his death in December 1974, unless he had sold it after he showed it to me. In his Will he had stated that he had marked those books he wanted to go to St Catharine's College, University of Cambridge, and to the Sligo Museum, but neither have it. Following his death in December 1974, the residue of his books were sold on his widow's behalf by

Deighton Bell Booksellers, of Cambridge, who no longer exist, nor do its records for this period. Could this have been the copy (lot 573) sold at Sotheby's to El Dieff for £1,400 on 6 July 1971, and whose present owner is unknown? Mere guesswork, but the sale of a treasured possession might not be something one would talk about.

If we assume that every one of the 'unknowns' recorded is not one of the 'knowns', or the same one appearing a number of times, we are still left with approximately a fifth of those printed.[28] I have looked through all volumes of *Book Auction Records* from 1902 until they ceased publication in the 1990s, and have found about thirty copies offered for sale by auction (a couple of which failed to sell). Of these, eight lack any distinguishing marks, but the rest I have identified with absolute, or reasonable, certainty. One pricing oddity stands out: in 1989, when named copies were selling in New York for a minimum of $30,000, Mealy's of Dublin sold one unnamed copy for a mere £1,200 (22/3/89, lot 345).[29]

I have also very recently been studying the cover paper variants used on those extant copies of *Mosada* I have been able to see, not because they have any impact on value or give any indication of order of printing or any other reason, but purely out of curiosity, to provide additional information to what is known about the surviving copies and what little can be learned of the production process. I wish I had thought to do this when I accepted Oxford University Press's commission to complete the bibliography in 1980 as I could then have taken closer note of those copies that passed through the major British auction houses since then. Being unaware of the variants, the

---

[28] When I attempted to get descriptions of copies of *Eight Poems* (1916, *Wade* 114) for my article in *YA12*, I was able to track down only a similar percentage of each of the official Italian and Japan paper copies sold through the Poetry Bookshop, these being mostly in institutional collections.

[29] *BAR* does omit items—the Esher sale of *Mosada* in 1946 is missing, as are the two Quinn sale copies, and the 1927 Anderson Galleries copy eventually bought by Roth.

auctioneers never thought to be at all precise about the 'wraps', apart from noting their condition.

All the copies I have seen or know of can roughly be described as being bound in buff / light brown wrappers, and I saw seven copies in the latter half of 2013 alone. There are four cover-paper variants that I know of, listed below with their owners:

A. plain paper:
  Gatch [review copy/ex Quinn] (Plate 4, p. 16)
  HRHRC [ex Roth]
  Stuart Rose [Lord Esher copy]

B. plain paper thicker/heavier than that used for the text:
  Bodleian 1
  George Harper UNC Chapel Hill

C. plain paper, inner surface white, termed 'lined white':
  Houghton, Harvard

D. Silurian [granite] with c.85% red and 15% blue fibres, lined white:
  Bodleian 2
  Beinecke, Yale
  Berg, NYPL
  Boston College
  William Andrews Clark
  Dublin City Library [CPS]
  The Frederick Gregg copy
  National Library of Ireland [Grace Yeats: see Plate 37, p. 253]

The dimensions vary: the height 21.5 or 21.7 cm for the height of all the copies but one, and the widths between 13.6 and 14 cm. Wade gave it as 5¼"—13.4 cm—but all those I've seen are 13.6 cm or wider, hence my calling in the aid of the present owners. It is very likely that in using inches, Allan Wade approximated, choosing the

nearer quarter inch. I have not seen or had reported to me any copy
with the exact width given by him.

Dimensions: Height/width/paper type
[Wade's 8½" × 5¼" converts to cm 21.6 × 13.4]

21.5 cm

Stuart Rose	× 13.7	A
Gatch	× 13.8	A
HRHRC Roth	× 14.0	A
Beinecke Yale	× 13.8	D
Boston College	× 13.7	D
NLI	× 13.8	D

21.6 cm

Houghton	× 13.7	C
F. Gregg	× 13.7	D
UNC Harper	× 13.6	B
Clark/Pollexfen	× 13.9	D

21.7 cm

Bodleian 1	× 13.7	B
Bodleian 2	× 13.8	D
DCL Smythe	× 13.8	D

22.0 cm

| Berg | × 13.9 | D |

As to the paper covers, the printers must have used up whatever
paper they had to hand that was the right general buff colour, so
there would probably be a minimum of six to eight copies of each
variant, depending on sheet size, but, from the predominance of
silurian/granite paper copies, it is likely that these made up the
largest number.

The provenance of any book can be a fascinating insight into its history—or perhaps 'career'—since it was sold or was a gift from the author. Often, they are enhanced by bookplates, offering an insight into their owners, while the speed with which they are resold can reflect how said owners may look on them, occasionally, it would appear, as mere financial investments, soon to be disposed of at a hoped-for profit, not always realised. The study of the last century's sales has convinced me that missing copies will be found in the next decade or so: books for which one has paid tens of thousands of pounds/dollars do not get lost. Death tends to put a halt on a collector's intentions, but when a book, such as Frederick J. Gregg's copy, has been in the possession of one family for an entire century, for three generations, one has to recognise a very different—and rare—attitude towards it, and be amazed.

I am most grateful to Stuart Rose for describing his copy for me, and the following for their assistance in giving me descriptions of the copies of *Mosada* held in their libraries: Dr Isaac Gevirtz, Curator of the Henry W. and Albert A. Berg Collection of the New York Public Library; Richard W. Oram, Associate Director of the Harry Ransom Center, University of Texas at Austin; Nina M. Schneider, Head Cataloguer at the William Andrews Clark Memorial Library, Los Angeles; and Karen Spicher, Archivist at the Beinecke Rare Book and Manuscript Library, Yale University. I'm also very grateful to Dr Philip Errington of Sotheby's London for all his assistance, and to Gretchen Hause of Christies, New York, for finding catalogue entries of half a century ago.

http://dx.doi.org/10.11647/OBP.0081.10

Yeats and the Flying Dutchman[1]

Warwick Gould

THIS IS NOT a note on Yeats and Richard Wagner's opera *Der fliegende Holländer* (premiered in 1843). Instead, it concerns itself with the rôle played in the evolution of Yeats's thinking by the influential myth of the 'legendary ghost ship' that can never make port and is doomed to sail the oceans forever, captained by a species of the Wandering Jew figure. I trace thereby the source of his early play *Mosada* (1886), and the influence of the myth in the form in which Yeats originally encountered it, on a subsequent early poem and story, and gesture to the development of his interest in Purgatories.

Wagner's Dutch sea-captain is in search of a wife, Wagner having adopted from Heine the possibility of his Holländer's redemption by a woman's devoted love. His captain can come ashore every seven years in quest of such a wife, and Heine and Wagner transfer the action from the Cape of Good Hope to the North Sea (off Scotland in Heine, off Norway in Wagner). These are later variants upon a

---

[1] Further information may have been gathered since this article was prepared for publication. If you would like to find out if any further information has been discovered that may help your own research, why not write to the author at Warwick.Gould@sas.ac.uk? Quite apart from anything else, feedback is always welcomed.

mid-seventeenth century legend from the nautical folklore of colonial exploration and trade. The oldest extant version of *Der Vliegende Hollander* is said to date from the late eighteenth century.

Sightings in the 19th and 20th centuries reported the ship to be glowing with ghostly light. If hailed by another ship, the crew of the *Flying Dutchman* will try to send messages to land, or to people long dead. In ocean lore, the sight of this phantom ship is a portent of doom.[2]

Fanciful or visionary explanations of the glowing ship in the sky have slowly yielded to the meteorological explanation for such recurrent manifestations. The well-known refraction and 'bending' of light, that optical illusion or mirage, known as a *Fata Morgana* can, under certain extreme and frequently stormy differences of air temperature, whereby a ship more than hull down on the horizon can appear as a 'flying' (usually inverted) ship in the sky. In the past, however, reports of such bizarre sightings in travel writings fed legends, which grew by what they fed on. Moreover, in the legendary accounts, the site of the action is usually the Cape of Good Hope. As international trade expanded, what was repeatedly found in travel writings 'crossed over' in to imaginative literature and its derivatives (including Wagner's opera), particularly via early nineteenth century melodrama. Writers such as Scott, Tom Moore, Edgar Allen Poe—and possibly the Coleridge of *The Rime of the Ancient Mariner*—fed into a literary tradition carried forward via multiple vectors.[3]

One such vector was John Howison's story, 'Vanderdecken's Message Home; or, the Tenacity of Natural Affection' (1821). It offers a name for the captain of an Amsterdam ship, the Cape of Good Hope as location of his tribulation, and the recurring motifs whereby the ghost ship's crew offer letters to long-dead people (if

---

[2]   See https://en.wikipedia.org/wiki/Flying_Dutchman. It seems to have been a 'common story' by 1790: see John Macdonald, *Travels in Various Parts of Europe, Asia and Africa during a Series of Thirty Years and Upwards* (London: published by the author, printed by J. Forbes, 1790), 276.

[3]   See the brief, popular account in Jonathan Eyers, *Don't Shoot the Albatross!: Nautical Myths and Superstitions* (London: Adlard Coles Nautical, i.e., A. & C. Black, 2011), 68–71. Wikipedia offers something more substantial at https://en.wikipedia.org/wiki/Fata_Morgana_(mirage)#The_Flying_Dutchman.

accepted by passing vessels, such messages bring bad luck to those ship and their crew). Howison's Hendrick Vanderdecken captains a vessel which had left Amsterdam seventy years prior to the setting of his story. Frustrated by foul winds which prevent his rounding the Cape of Good Hope, the captain is asked if he will put into Table Bay and replies: 'May I be eternally d—d if I do, though I should beat about here till the day of judgment'.[4]

These strands of the legend are reworked by a far more influential English vector, Captain Frederick Marryat (1792–1848) in *The Phantom Ship*,[5] which Yeats seems to have read as a boy. The legend enjoyed an afterlife in such doggerel poems as 'The Flying Dutchman', by the Fenian convict, John Boyle O'Reilly (1844–90), to whom I return below.

Plate 39. Frontispiece to Captain Marryat's *The Phantom Ship* (1839; rpt. London: Richard Bentley, 1847) engraved by J. Crowse. Private collection, London.

---

[4]   *Blackwood's Edinburgh Magazine* 9:1 (May 1821), 125–31.

[5]   London: Henry Colburn; Philadelphia: E. L. Carey & A. Hart, 1839. The edition read by Yeats is unknown, and no edition remains in his library. The book was widely reprinted in the nineteenth century. The texts quoted below are taken from the London: Henry Colburn, 1839 edition and checked against later reprintings including the London: George Routledge & Sons, 1874 illustrated edition (possibly the edition used by the young Yeats); and Stroud: Nonesuch pb., 2006 editions, hereafter distinguished by date. *The Phantom Ship* is also available in a searchable Kindle edition. The London: Richard Bentley, 1847 edition has an engraved frontispiece by J. Crowse, and is perhaps a precursor to Gustave Doré's 42 magnificent illustrations for Coleridge's *The Rime of the Ancient Mariner* (London: Doré Gallery; Hamilton Adams & Co., 1876). For the Crowse image see Plate 39.

A SOURCE FOR *MOSADA*

Mosada's source has been long-sought.[6] In fact it has been equally long-forgotten and therefore unexplored. The editor of *The Irish Book Lover*, John Crone, in one of his 1925 'Editor's Gossip' columns noted that 'it has recently been brought to my attention that the opening scene [of *Mosada*]... bears a strong resemblance to a chapter in Captain Marryatt's [*sic*] "Phantom Ship"'.[7] Coming upon these words, I somehow *knew* that Crone's informant had been correct. Yeats himself had written a poem entitled 'The Phantom Ship'.[8] Accordingly I read the first novel by Marryat which I had attempted since *Mr Midshipman Easy* at the age at which little boys in the 1950s found adventure and romance in such books as Marryat's, R. M. Ballantyne's *The Coral Island* and Stevenson's *Treasure Island*.

Marryat's *The Phantom Ship* might well be subtitled *Son of the Flying Dutchman*. It is set in the mid-seventeenth century, opening in a cottage in the small town of Terneuse where the Dutchman's wife Catherine, prematurely wasted at forty years of age, is apparently possessed of some 'deep-seated, irremoveable, hopeless cause of anguish, never for one moment permitted to be absent from her memory: a chronic oppression, fixed and graven there, only to be removed by death'.[9] William Vanderdecken, a Catholic, has been gone seventeen years as Captain of the *Amsterdammer*, on his voyage to East India. After just six months, there had been a dreadful storm in Terneuse, the windows and shutters are blown in, and the Dutchman's apparition manifests itself on the storm, telling his wife that he 'hover[s] between this world and the world of Spirits'. For nine weeks Vanderdecken had attempted to round the Cape of Good Hope, had finally blasphemed, and now thinks he murdered his pilot. 'I struck at [the pilot, Schriften]; he reeled; and, with the sudden lurch of the vessel, he fell overboard, and sank'. The Dutchman then swears by a fragment of the true Cross (which

6   *NC* 453–54 lists what little sketchy work had otherwise been done on the subject.
7   *The Irish Book Lover* 15:4 (October 1925), 54–55.
8   *VP* 718–19, and first published in *The Providence Sunday Journal*, 27 May 1888 (3) as 'The Legend of the Phantom Ship', republished as 'The Phantom Ship' in *The Wanderings of Oisin and Other Poems* (1889) and then suppressed by Yeats— so well, one might think, that subsequent comment has been almost wholly discouraged ever since. The poem is quoted in full below, pp. 272-73.
9   *The Phantom Ship*, I:4–5 (1839); 2 (1874); 12 (2006).

he gives to his wife in a reliquary she thereafter wears around her neck and which, on her death, passes to her son, Philip), that he 'would gain [his] point in defiance of storm and seas, of lightning, of heaven, or of hell, even if I should beat about until the Day of Judgment'... an 'oath registered in thunder, and in streams of sulphurous fire'. His ship nearly founders, and 'in the centre of a deep o'erhanging cloud, which shrouded all in utter darkness, were written in letters of livid flame, these words—UNTIL THE DAY OF JUDGMENT'.[10] We will return to this irruption.

Philip has been encouraged to believe from infancy that his father is drowned, but at nineteen or twenty, is determined to go to sea against his mother's wishes. When pressed about his father, Catherine Vanderdecken has a stroke. Rallying before dying, she tells Philip the truth: far from drowning his father still exists, 'IN LIVING JUDGMENT... CURSED'.[11] He has left her a letter, now in a sealed room of the cottage, with his fortune. At this crucial moment in the story, the 'widow Vanderdecken was no more'.[12] Philip swears upon the relic that he will 'avert [his father's] doom, or perish'.[13] A sub-plot emerges in the growing love between Philip and Amine, daughter of one Mynheer Poots, the local doctor who has attended his dying mother. Amine is Muslim; her father had been captured by Moors, sold to a Hakim (physician), trained by him in all his 'knowledge of the art' and has converted to Islam to be freed from slavery. Poots then marries an Arab, acquires immense wealth, loses it and escapes with wife and daughter among the wild Bedouin—a narrative, one imagines, immensely gripping for the young Yeats who later would write 'Cycles Ago: in memory of your dream one July night' and the *Stories of Michael Robartes.*[14] Latterly Poots's only 'god is gold',[15] but Amine has learned some Arab medical secrets as well as Arab sorcery from her parents.

---

[10] *Ibid.*, I, 25–26 (1839); 8–9 1874; 19–20 (2006).
[11] *Ibid.*, I, 19–21 (1839); 11 (1874); 18 (2006).
[12] *Ibid.*, I, 27 (1839); 11 (1874); 20 (2006).
[13] *Ibid.*, I, 75 (1839); 30 (1874); 41 (2006).
[14] For 'Cycles Ago' (including full text), see Warwick Gould and Deirdre Toomey, "'Cycles Ago...", Maud Gonne and the Lyrics of 1891', *YA7* 184–93.
[15] The crispest summary is provided by Amine in the fifth chapter, *ibid.*, I, 100ff. at 115 (1839); 40ff. at 47 (1874); 56ff. (2006).

Philip goes to sea to learn his profession as a seaman, on a Dutch East Indiaman, the pilot of which is the mysterious and unearthly Schriften, who, despite being several times cast overboard, always seems to re-enter Philip's increasingly complex adventures in ship after ship, trying to steal his relic (Plate 40). Philip rises in the Company, until he is eventually a Master and part-owner of one of its ships. There are several inconclusive encounters with The Flying Dutchman's phantom ship on these voyages, and many pages of wreckages, adventures, and buried treasure in the Dutch East Indies and even Papua, doubtless thrilling to small boys. Amine's father dies of a poison he had intended to administer to Philip: Amine has, in giving the potion to her father, to all intents and purposes murdered him while discovering his murderous attempt on her husband. Eventually Amine and Philip sail together on a Dutch East Indiaman under his command. Wrecked and separated, she ends up in Goa where, with a small boy, Pedro, she invokes Arab sorcery and

gets a vision of Philip cast away on a desert island. Pedro is forced by the Inquisition to betray her by helping her to re-enact her sorcery in the presence of concealed Inquisitors (Plate 41).[16]

Plate 40. 'Philip Vanderdecken—that's the Flying Dutchman!' from *The Phantom Ship* (London: George Routledge & Sons, 1874). Private collection, London.

---

[16] Established as a branch of the Portuguese Inquisition (est. 1536) in 1560, suppressed 1774–78, abolished 1812: see https://en.wikipedia.org/wiki/Goa_ Inquisition, with broadly similar aims as those of the Spanish Inquisition: see below pp. 269–71and n. 21.

Plate 41. Then I was not mistaken',… cried Father Mathias, with looks of indignation; 'accursed sorceress! you are detected', from *The Phantom Ship* (London: George Routledge & Sons, 1874). Private collection, London.

Philip makes it to Goa in time to see her paraded and—refusing to renounce her Muslim faith in favour of a Christianity she has never espoused—burnt in an *auto-da-fe*. Pages and pages are devoted to the rituals, the meanings, and the elaborate trials and tortures of the (Portuguese) Goa Inquisition. Amine's death drives Philip into insanity, and when, years later, he recovers enough to travel back to Holland, he encounters the Dutchman's ship yet again. The crew press upon him mail to their loved ones, dead for many decades. By forgiving Schriften's sins he finds himself divinely empowered to confront the Dutchman with his relic of the true cross. The Phantom Ship, its crew, Schriften, and the whole 'insubstantial pageant' dissolves and leaves 'not a rack behind'.[17]

Of this tumultuous novel, Yeats takes for his *Mosada* its central element—a Moorish girl, inculcated into Arab sorcery, who refuses to recant, and who is set to die. Mosada sucks poison from a ring before recognizing her beloved Gomez (he is Vallance[18] in the

---

17 *The Tempest*, IV, i.
18 The name 'Vallance' (the spelling varies: see W. B. Yeats *The Early Poetry, Vol. I: Mosada* and *The Island of Statues*, ed. George Bornstein [Ithaca and London: Cornell University Press, 1987], 21–126ff.) acknowledges his origins in Valencia. Later in his reading, Yeats encountered in Balzac's *La Peau de Chagrin* (London: Dent, 1895; *YL* 111), 'Raphael *de* Valentin, if you please…. [the family has a coat of arms and] 'a fine motto: NON CECIDIT ANIMUS. We are no foundling child, but a descendant of the Emperor Valens, of the stock of the Valentinois, founders of the city of Valence in France, and Valencia in Spain, rightful heirs to the Empire of the East. If we suffer Mahmoud on the throne of Byzantium, it is out of pure condescension, and for lack of funds and soldiers' (48).

MSS) as the Inquisitor, Ebremar, just as he is too late to save her. Marryat's Amine is most certainly not in love with her Inquisitor and 'unrepenting faces her end' (cf., *VP* 273), embraced by her beloved husband.

Mosada's conclusion is admirably economical. At the beginning of the play we have been warned that Mosada and Gomez are what Shakespeare called 'star-cross'd lovers'. Azolar ('the star-taught Moor', whom we never meet) has told Mosada that 'it was decreed' that she and 'dark Gomez' (who believes that she and all her people are 'accurst | Of his sad God') will one day meet. The decree has come from

> ...those wan stars that sit in company
> Above the Alpujarras on their thrones:

And the meeting will take place

> ...when the stars of our nativity
> Draw star to star, as on that eve he passed
> Down the long valleys from my people's tents (*VP* 690–91).

Mosada expires in Ebremar's arms as monks and inquisitors enter.

First Inquisitor. My lord, you called?
Ebremar.　　　　　　　　Not I. This maid is dead.
First Monk. From poison; for you cannot trust these Moors.
　　　You're pale, my lord.
First Inquisitor (aside).　　　　　His lips are quivering;
　　　The flame that shone within his eyes but now
　　　Has flickered and gone out.
Ebremar.　　　　　　　I am not well.
　　　'Twill pass. I'll see the other prisoners now,
　　　And importune their souls to penitence,
　　　So they escape from hell. But, pardon me,
　　　Your hood is threadbare[19]—see that it be changed
　　　Before we take our seats above the crowd. (*VP* 704)

---

[19] The scene is full of Shakespearean parallels, most obviously in plot terms with the finale of *Romeo and Juliet*. It also echoes another love-death by poison, that of Cleopatra, in *Antony and Cleopatra* where Charmian's words in V: ii, 'Your crown's awry; I'll mend it, and then play' work similarly, if not, of course, as a command.

Ebremar's self-repression here is perhaps rather too savage for him plausibly to pass as a tragic lover, but Yeats may well have been working towards what he would later praise as Shakespearian tragic ecstasy.[20] His future as a lover being over, Ebremar clearly has a big future in the Church. The reader turns back to reflect on the Cardinal in the play's epigraph

'And my Lord Cardinal hath had strange days in his youth'—*Extract from a Memoir of the Fifteenth Century'.*

That date is a charmingly vague gesture. The Spanish *Tribunal del Santo Oficio de la Inquisición* was established in 1478 by Ferdinand, and was shaped to regulate those who had converted from Judaism and Islam, especially after 1492 and 1502 when Jews and Muslims were decreed to leave Spain or convert.[21] Yeats's quotation has never been traced and was, in all likelihood, invented for an imagined book. *"In dreams begin Responsibility". OLD PLAY'* comes to mind, as it too follows Walter Scott's practice with such devices.[22] For Marryat's Amine (in the fourteenth chapter of the novel), the prophetic dreams she has conjured after summoning the ghost of her dead mother with drugs and ritual dictate her subsequent course of action.

YEATS'S PHANTOM SHIP

In focusing on Marryat's Moorish girl who, with the prospect of punishment for heresy as a sorceress and seer by an Inquisition by means of the *auto-da-fe*, kills herself. Yeats takes over Marryat's Pedro, who, in his play, becomes the lame Cola, with maybe Amine's

---

[20] See, e.g., *E&I* 522–23; *CW5* 213.
[21] It was not abolished until 1834: see https://en.wikipedia.org/wiki/Spanish_Inquisition.
[22] See *The Phantom Ship*, II, 28ff. (1839); 131ff. (1874); 148ff. (2006); *VP* 269. On epigraphs see Warwick Gould, 'An Empty Theatre? Yeats as Minstrel in *Responsibilities*', in Jacqueline Genet (ed.), *Studies on W. B. Yeats* (Caen: Groupe de Recherches d'Etudes anglo-irlandaises de C.N.R.S., 1989), 79–118, at p. 82 and n. 20, where some of Scott's 'mottoes' from *The Monastery, The Abbot, Peveril of the Peak, Woodstock,* and *The Fair Maid of Perth* are cited.

Moorish doctor-father being hinted at in Yeats's Azolar.[23] *Mosada* otherwise offers no glimpse of Marryat's engagement with *The Flying Dutchman*, his crew, and Purgatory. In 1887 however, Yeats turns to this *topos* in his poem of the same name. The highlighted passages in the entire poem quoted below are those which focus on one aspect of the Flying Dutchman legend, i.e., that he, and his crew, are souls in Purgatory.

The Phantom Ship

Flames the shuttle of the lightning across the driving sleet,
Ay, and shakes in sea-green waverings along the fishers' street;
Gone the stars and gone the white moon, gone and puffed away and dead.
Never storm arose so swiftly; scarce the children were in bed,
Scarce the old and wizen houses had their doors and windows shut.
Ah! it dwelt within the twilight as the worm within the nut.
'Waken, waken, sleepy fishers; no hour is this for sleep',
Cries a voice at roaring midnight beside the moonless deep.
Hail dizzy with the lightning there runs a gathering band—
'Watcher, wherefore have ye called us?' Eyes go after his lean hand,
And the fisher men and women from the dripping harbour wall
See the darkness slow disgorging a vessel blind with squall.
'Bring the ropes now! Stand ye by now! See, she rounds the harbour clear.
God! they're mad to fly such canvas!' Ah! what bell-notes do they hear?
Say what ringer rings at midnight; for, in the belfry high,
Slow the chapel bell is tolling as though the dead passed by.
Round she comes in stays before them; cease the winds, and on their poles
Cease the sails their flapping uproar, and the hull no longer rolls.
Now a scream from all those fishers, for there on deck there be
All the drowned that ever were drowned from that village by the sea;

---

[23] There is a sense in which the Arab seer/sorceress theme persists through to the Solomon and Sheba poems, e.g., 'Solomon and the Witch' (*VP* 387–89) and to 'The Gift of Harun al-Rashid' (*VP* 460 ff.). Elizabeth Brewer Redwine groups the early 'enchantresses' Vivien (from *Time and the Witch Vivien* and its precursor, 'Vivien and Time'), Naschina (from *The Island of Statues*) and Mosada herself as projections from Yeats's early infatuation with Laura Armstrong, who, as he remarked to Katharine Tynan, 'woke me from the metallic sleep of science and set me writing my first play' (*CL1* 154–55). See Redwine's '"She Set me Writing My First Play": Laura Armstrong and Yeats's Early Drama', *Irish University Review* 35:2 (Autumn-Winter 2005), 245–58.

And the ghastly ghost-flames glimmer all along the taffrail rails
On the drowned men's hands and faces, on the spars and on the sails.
Hush'd the fishers, till a mother calls by name her drownèd son;
Then each wife and maid and mother calls by name some drowned one.
Stands each grey and silent phantom on the same regardless spot —
Joys and fears in their grey faces that the live earth knoweth not;
Down the vapours fall and hide them from the children of a day,
And the winds come down and blow them with the vapours far away.
Hang the mist-threads for a little while like cobwebs in the air;
Then the stars grow out of heaven with their countenances fair.

'Pray for the souls in purgatory', the pale priest trembling cries.

* * *

Prayed those forgotten fishers, till in the eastern skies
Came olive fires of morning and on the darkness fed,
By the slow heaving ocean—mumbling mother of the dead.
                                    (*VP* 718–19, emphases added)

In the *Providence Sunday Journal* of 27 May, 1888, Yeats's poem
had been titled 'A Legend of the Phantom Ship', and legend it is, or
was. It does not, in his rendition, achieve any Irish local habitation,
although one might read back into it some memories of life in the
fishing-port of Howth. This Phantom Ship has somehow netted
all of the drowned from one village—almost a foretaste of *Riders
to the Sea*.

   It is natural to wonder if this poem could have had an Irish
forebear and here one must turn again to John Boyle O'Reilly's 'The
Flying Dutchman'.[24] A sample from its conclusion follows:

Once more the lurid light gleamed out—the ship was still at rest,
The crew were standing at their posts; with arms across his breast

---

[24] The poem was first published in late 1867 in the hand-written newspaper, *The
   Wild Goose: A Collection of Ocean Waifs* aboard the *Hougoumont*, the last ship to
   transport convicts to Australia. A set of all seven issues, preserved by descendants
   of John Flood, another Fenian on the *Hougoumont*, was presented to the State
   Library of New South Wales, Sydney. O'Reilly, poet and journalist, escaped from
   Western Australia to America where he became editor of *The Boston Pilot* and a
   close associate of the leaders of Clan-na-Gael.

Still stood the captain on the poop, but bent and crouching now
He bowed beneath that fiat dread, and o'er his swarthy brow
Swept lines of anguish, as if he a thousand years of pain
Had lived and suffered. Then across the heaving, angry main
The tempest shrieked triumphant, and the angry waters hissed
Their vengeful hate against the toy they oftentimes had kissed.
And ever through the midnight storm that hapless crew must speed:
They try to round the stormy Cape,[25] but never can succeed.
And oft when gales are wildest, and the lightning's vivid sheen
Flashes back the ocean's anger, still the Phantom Ship is seen
Ever sailing to the southward in the fierce tornado's swoop,
With her ghostly crew and canvas, and her captain on the poop,
Unrelenting, unforgiven! and 'tis said that every word
Of his blasphemous defiance still upon the gale is heard!
But Heaven help the ship near which the dismal sailor steers,—
The doom of those is sealed to whom that Phantom Ship appears:
They'll never reach their destined port,—they'll see their homes no more,—
They who see the Flying Dutchman—never, never reach the shore![26]

The association of the tempestuous Vanderdecken with devilish
defiance, driving a ship around the Cape of Storms under a
supernaturally exorbitant press of canvas against impossible
weather—these are all aspects of the story familiar from such
vectors as Howison and Marryat. But it is only Marryat who offers
the defiant and repeated quests of the son of the Dutchman to
redeem him, together with his Moorish wife, her Arab sorcery, and
an *auto-da-fe*.

There is no evidence that Yeats knew O'Reilly's poem, though
he certainly knew of O'Reilly, because as editor of *The Boston
Pilot*, O'Reilly published Yeats's 'How Ferencz Renyi kept Silent'
on 6 August 1887, as well as his subsequent columns 'The Celt

---

[25] Bartolomeu Dias in 1488 gave the Portuguese name *Cabo das Tormentas* ('Cape of Storms') to what has since become more generally known as the Cape of Good Hope.

[26] See John Boyle O'Reilly, *Songs from the Southern Seas and other Poems* (Boston: Roberts Bros., 1873), 179–90 at pp. 188–90; *Songs, Legends, and Ballads* (Boston: The Pilot Publishing Company, 1878), 144–60 at pp. 159–60.

in London'.[27] Yeats, however, had found all he needed on the subject—and much more—in Marryat's novel. O'Reilly's poem is an intermediary by a man who, well-educated, had also presumably read Marryat before being transported, and the poem remains merely an Irish forebear, and analogue, and not, I think, a source. Yeats's abandoned or suppressed poems have perhaps understandably received very little critical comment.[28] 'The Phantom Ship' seemed a fairly unremarkable addition to the myth of the Flying Dutchman, and its identity of title with that of Marryat's novel merely confirmed Yeats's distinct *locus* of attention, a legend of Purgatory. Yeats's priest uses a Catholic catchphrase, words from the Prayer of St Gertrude, one of the most famous of the prayers for souls in Purgatory.

Eternal Father, I offer Thee the Most Precious Blood of Thy Divine Son, Jesus, in union with the masses said throughout the world today, for all the holy souls in purgatory, for sinners everywhere, for sinners in the universal church, those in my own home and within my family. Amen.[29]

Suppressing unsatisfactory poems even before—and certainly after— *The Wanderings of Oisin* meant rejecting those—including *Mosada* itself—which were foreign-based. Thus Yeats rejects e.g., 'Song of Spanish Insurgents',[30] or the Hungarian tale of 1848, 'How Ferencz Renyi kept Silent', even with its urgent political message for Ireland

---

[27] See *CL1* 20 and *passim*. Yeats's connection with O'Reilly was through John O'Leary. O'Reilly's paper then took Yeats's Irish Letters, 'The Celt in London': see *CW7 passim*. See also *CL2* 625. O'Reilly's poems are not represented in Sparling's *Irish Minstrelsy*, Yeats's *A Book of Irish Verse*, *The Cabinet of Irish Literature*, or *The Field Day Anthology of Irish Writing*.

[28] Deirdre Toomey and I seek to remedy that in working towards the next edition of Jeffares' *New Commentary*.

[29] It is 'a holy and wholesome thought to pray for the dead, that they may be loosed from sins' (2 Maccabees 12:46): see http://www.ourcatholicprayers.com/ prayers-for-souls-in-purgatory.html. According to tradition, God promised St Gertrude the Great, a thirteenth-century Benedictine nun and mystic, that 1000 souls would be released from Purgatory each time it is said devoutly (the Church having endorsed the doctrine of Purgatory from the Councils of Florence and Trent in the fifteenth and sixteenth centuries right up through Vatican II in the 1960s).

[30] See John Kelly, '"Song of Spanish Insurgents": A Newly Discovered Poem by Yeats' (*YA3* 179–81).

(the 'Hungary of the West', *VP* 709–15). But as his work grew more Irish, 'tribeless, nationless' poems set in 'No Man's Land' also had to go (*E&I* 205; *CW4* 151).

'THOSE WHO LIVE IN THE STORM'

The 'Irishizing' of the Purgatory *topos* was no easy matter for a poet from a Protestant background, but Yeats certainly tried it in the story suppressed after *The Secret Rose* (1897), entitled variously 'Those who live in the Storm' and 'The Rose of Shadow' (1894–97; *VSR* 227–31). Ostensibly a story arising out of 'the great storm of October, 1765' (*VSR* 231v.), 'The Rose of Shadow' concerns itself with the irruption during a violent storm of the ghost of one Michael Creed, the former lover of Oona Herne, into the cottage of her parents, Simon and Margaret Herne in Co. Sligo. Before gesturing to Yeats's further dependence on Marryat's novel, I will quote from it at some length because it is a rarely-accessed adjunct to the Hanrahan stories, suppressed by Yeats after its inclusion in *The Secret Rose* (1897).

Exactly a year before the events of the story, and during a storm, when the wind had blown 'along the mountain of Gulben [i.e., Ben Bulben] and out to sea'—an east wind in a region where the prevailing wind is westerly—Oona's brother, Peter, had killed Creed 'with a blow from a boat-hook'. Creed had been the 'master of a coasting smack, and

the terror of the little western ports because of his violence and brutality, and the hatred of all peaceful households because of his many conquests among women, whom he subdued through that love of strength which is deep in the hearts of even the subtlest of them. (*VSR* 228).

Since then, Oona has remained submissive. Yet, the night before the new storm 'as black and as bitter' as that which has raged exactly a year before, she had put a 'sod' from Creed's grave on the chair beside her bed.

'Come to me, alanna', it said; and I answered, "How can I come?" And it said, "Come with me when the wind blows along the Mountain of Gulben and out to sea". Then I was afraid, and I put it outside on the window-sill. (*VSR* 228).

She is curious about the fates of 'those who have done crimes' and 'those who have never confessed', and asks her mother 'are they put in a place apart, or do they wander near us?'

'Child', replied the old woman, 'my mother told me that some are spitted upon the points of the rocks, and some upon the tops of the trees, but that others wander with the season in the storms over the seas and about the strands and headlands of the world. But, daughter, I bid you think of them no more, for when we think of them they draw near'.[31]

After this wonderfully inclusive, evasive reply, Margaret Herne sprinkles her daughter with holy water. Her action confounds folk knowledge with Catholic gesture, a peasant reflex—of which I have heard in far more recent times—where ritual is reduced to superstition. But Margaret's action does presume a belief in a Purgatory, albeit imagined via Irish folklore rather than orthodox Catholic belief, and so a fair representation of Yeats's early attempts to grapple with local belief patterns.

Oona has begun to chant in a trance, a 'fitful, exultant air in a low voice', becoming more and more entranced as the storm rises and drowns her words before. It then becomes 'still, as though the beings that controlled it were listening also'. Her father interjects with a brutal blow to her mouth: her 'evil air' being one of Hanrahan the Red's who had sung 'it after he had listened to the singing of those who are about the faery Cleena of the Wave... it has lured, and will lure, many a girl from her hearth and from her peace'. Her mother adds that the song is

of a love too great for our perishing hearts... Hanrahan the Red is always seeking with wild tunes and bewildered words to answer their voices, and a madness is upon his days and a darkness before his feet. His songs are

---

[31]   *VSR* 228, folklore also found in 'The Curse of the Fires and of the Shadows' (*VSR* 45; *M2005* 120) and, for a note on Yeats's probable reading of T. Crofton Croker's *Researches in South of Ireland etc.* (1824) on this matter, see *M2005* 327 n. 12.

no longer dear to any but to the coasting sailors and to the people of the mountain, and to those that are ill-nurtured and foolish. Look, daughter, to the spinning-wheel... and be content (*ibid.*)

As 'wild words of love became audible' the temperature falls, and 'an icy feeling' begins to 'creep about the room and into their hearts, as though all the warmth of the world was in that low, exultant song'. When Peter Herne throws more turf on the fire, but it goes out: 'demons, whose coming kills the body of man, were in the storm listening to this evil song'. Oona brightens, and half rising from her chair sings 'in a loud and joyous voice:—

> O, what to me the little room,
> That was brimmed up with prayer and rest?
> He bade me out into the gloom,
> And my breast lies upon his breast.
>
> O, what to me my mother's care,
> The home where I was safe and warm?
> The shadowy blossom of my hair
> Will hide us from the bitter storm.
>
> O, hiding hair and dewy eyes,
> I am no more with life and death!
> My heart upon his warm heart lies;
> My breath is mixed into his breath.
>   (*VSR* 230–31; cf. *VP* 151–52)

While she had been singing,

an intense drowsiness had crept into the room, as though the gates of Death had moved upon their hinges. The old woman had leaned forward upon the table, for she had suddenly understood that her hour had come. The young man had fixed his eyes fiercely on the face of the girl, and the light died out of them. The old man had known nothing, except that he was very cold and sleepy, until the cold came to his heart.[32] At the end of the song the storm

---

[32] Yeats at the end of his life describes the 'the sudden enlargement of their vision, their ecstasy at the approach of death' of Shakespearean tragedy' in strikingly similar terms 'all must be cold... The supernatural is present, cold winds blow across our hands, upon our faces, the thermometer falls... "Tragedy must be a joy to the man who dies"' (*E&I 523; CW5* 213).

began again with redoubled tumult, and the roof shook. The lips of the girl were half-parted in expectation…

Suddenly the thatch at one end of the roof rolled up, and the rushing clouds and a single star flickered before her eyes for a moment, and then seemed to be lost in a formless mass of flame which roared but gave no heat, and had in the midst of it the shape of a man crouching on the storm.[33] His heavy and brutal face and his partly naked limbs were scarred with many wounds, and his eyes were full of white fire under his knitted brows' (*VSR* 231).

Plate 42. John Butler Yeats's illustration for 'The Rose of Shadow' in W. B. Yeats's *The Secret Rose* (1897). Private collection, London.

This irruption was illustrated by John Butler Yeats in the 1897 edition, on a slightly anticipatory facing plate (Plate 42). And there the story ends, except in *The Speaker* 21 July 1894 version, where it concludes

[33] See John Newton, *Olney Hymns, in Three Books: I: On select texts of scripture; II. On occasional subjects; III. On the progress and changes of the spiritual life* (London: Printed for J. Johnson, 1806), Bk II, Hymn 15, 'Light shining out of darkness' (William Cowper):
'God moves in a mysterious way
His wonders to perform;
He plants his footsteps in the sea,
And rides upon the storm' (255).

with dispensable sentences on the destruction of house and family by
the storm: 'The rest of the roof rolled up and then fell inward with
a crash, and the storm rushed through the house.... [they were all
buried in] the barony of Amharlish', under a 'tombstone to say they
were killed in the great storm of October, 1765'.[34]

Recovery of these abandoned words helps us to gesture back to the
story's source, in the opening chapter of Marryat's *The Phantom Ship*.
The *Amsterdammer* has been at sea for six months. Vanderdecken's
wife recalls a 'dreadful night' in Terneuse:

'...when the gale blows, a sailor's wife can seldom sleep. It was past
midnight, and the rain poured down. I felt unusual fear,—I knew not why, I
rose from my couch and dipped my finger in the blessed water, and I crossed
myself. A violent gust of wind roared round the house and alarmed me still
more. I had a painful, horrible foreboding; when, of a sudden, the windows
and window-shutters were all blown in, the light was extinguished, and I
was left in utter darkness. I screamed with fright—but at last I recovered
myself, and was proceeding towards the window that I might reclose it,
when, whom should I behold, slowly entering at the casement, but—your
father,—Philip—Yes, Philip,—it was your father!'... When he had entered
the room, the windows and shutters closed of themselves, and the candle
was relighted—then I thought it was his apparition and I fainted on the
floor.

When I recovered I found myself on the couch, and perceived that a cold
(O how cold) and dripping hand was clasped in mine. This reassured me,
and I forgot the supernatural signs which accompanied his appearance.... I
felt as if I had embraced ice.[35]

The captain then tells her that he has lost his ship and how, that
he 'is not dead, nor am I yet alive. I hover between this world and
the world of spirits' and of his blasphemy, his killing of the pilot,

---

[34] I.e., 'Ahamlish', which is in fact not a Barony but a Civil Parish of 50 townlands
in the Barony of Carbury to the north-west of Ben Bulben. Ahamlish Cemetery
(with Drumcliffe, one of the two principal cemeteries in North Sligo), lies between
Grange and Cliffoney and not far from Streedagh Beach, in the Townland of
Moneygold, i.e., Muine Dhualtach, or the field or good patch of Dualtach. I
thank Martin Enright, President of the Yeats Society, Sligo, for this information
and translation.

[35] *The Phantom Ship*, I, 23 (1839); 10 (1874); 19 (2006).

his oath on the fragment of the Holy Cross and the natural sign of its being supernaturally registered, the 'letters of livid flame' in the centre of a 'deep o'erhanging cloud' proclaiming 'UNTIL THE DAY OF JUDGEMENT'.[36] He leaves her a letter, the shutters and windows burst open again, and he 'sailed through the window... his form borne away like lightning on the wings of the wild gale, till it was lost as a speck of light, and then it disappeared'.[37] His wife, on telling this last detail, expires into the arms of her son.

Allowing for the difference between a cursed husband caught 'in living judgment' and a 'Demon Lover'[38]—which is another Celtic folk tradition to which Michael Creed has strong links—it is passages such as these which must have caught the imagination of the younger Yeats, and it is their attempt to capture such moments of irruption as moments when the 'supernatural is present' which fired his mind with visions of private purgatories.

YEATS'S PURGATORIES: A PRELIMINARY GESTURE

A growing interest in the Irish folklore record of Purgatory finds recurrent expression in Yeats's subsequent prose. A major trigger was provided by the visits of William Carleton and Caesar Otway to Station Island, Lough Derg, the ancient shrine of St Patrick said to provide access to a mouth of Purgatory; Otway being the helping hand in the editing of Carleton's 'The Lough Derg Pilgrim' for *Traits and Stories of the Irish Peasantry*.[39] In visionary experiments with Mary Battle, she saw the Gates of Purgatory (*Au* 267; *M2005* 28). The imagined spatial and geographical relation of Purgatory to Hell

---

36 *Ibid.*, I, 24–25 (1839); 12 (1874); 20 (2006). Vanderdecken's ghost uses modes of address which recall those of the ghost of old King Hamlet, repeating 'my time is short' and 'Mark me' as King Hamlet uses 'Brief let me be' and 'List, list, O, list!' (*Hamlet*, I, v.).

37 *Ibid.*, I, 26 (1839); 11 (1874); 20 (2006).

38 See Walter Scott, *Minstrelsy of the Scottish Borders* (Edinburgh: Adam and Charles Black, 1861), II, 195–98.

39 *YL* 347. For a modern reprint see Carleton's *Traits and Stories of the Irish Peasantry* with a Preface by Barbara Hayley (Gerrards Cross: Colin Smythe; Savage, Maryland: Barnes and Noble Books, 1990), I, 236–70.

and Paradise clearly preoccupied many of Yeats's peasant witnesses, with St Patrick's Purgatory recurring again and again in Yeats's and Gregory's early folklore harvests and studies.

Such 'broken bread' of the 'old Irish visions of the Three Worlds' (e.g., those of such medieval figures as St Adamnan in certain *c.* twelfth century writings which have been seen as influences on Dante's *Divina Commedia*)[40] supplied the Purgatory *topos*, found in a further story at one time considered for *The Secret Rose*, 'Michael Clancy, the Great Dhoul, and Death'.[41] 'The Prisoners of the Gods', 'The Broken Gates of Death', 'Away' touch on Irish beliefs about Purgatory,[42] as do the 'The Celtic Element in Literature' and the Blake essays in *Ideas of Good and Evil* and there are interesting scattered references either to Purgatory, or to St Patrick's Purgatory elsewhere in Yeats's occasional and abandoned prose. The revised and expanded version of *The Celtic Twilight* collects the very brief 'Concerning the Nearness together of Heaven, Earth, and Purgatory' (*M2005* 65). The orthodox doctrine of Purgatory was applied in such plays *The Unicorn from the Stars*, *The Cat and the Moon* and *The Hour Glass* (where the School Master has denied the existence of Heaven, Hell, and Purgatory).

> *Angel.*
> Though you may not undo what you have done,
> I have this power—if you but find one soul,
> Before the sands have fallen, that still believes,
> One fish to lie and spawn among the stones
> Till the great Fisher's net is full again,
> You may, the purgatorial fire being passed,
> Spring to your peace. (*VPl* 603–05)

As yet, none of Yeats's acquired Irish Purgatory-*lore* had been internalized. That process was initiated as he tried to bring into a unified field of consideration Irish folklore, modern 'spiritism' (as he

---

[40] For 'broken bread' see *Ex* 60; *CW5* 66. See 'Happy and Unhappy Theologians' (*M2005* 28–30 and, for the claimed influence on Dante, 240 n. 11).

[41] *UP1* 310–17; see also *VSR* xvii.

[42] *UP2* 74–87; 94–107; 267–83.

called what we might now name 'spiritualism'), and a reform of his own theatrical practices during WW1. In 'Swedenborg, Mediums, and the Desolate Places' (1914), in consideration of theatrical techniques appropriate to the 'pain of the ghost in a Buddhist purgatory', in his introduction to *Certain Noble Plays of Japan* (1916), Yeats moves towards what might be called 'belief self-assessment', which becomes unignorable in *If I were Four-and-Twenty* (1919).

But if I were four-and-twenty, and without rheumatism… I would go— though certainly I am no Catholic and never shall be one—upon both of our great pilgrimages, to Croagh Patrick and to Lough Derg… Europe has nothing older than our pilgrimages.[43] In many little lyrics I would claim that stony mountain or all Christian and pagan faith in Ireland, believing, in the exultation of my youth, that in three generations I should have made it as vivid in the memory of all imaginative men among us, as the sacred mountain of Japan is in that of the collectors of prints; and I would, being but four-and-twenty and a lover of lost causes, memorialize the bishops to open once again that Lough Derg cave of vision once beset by an evil spirit in the form of a long-legged bird with no feathers on its wings.[44]

A few years ago Bernard Shaw explained, what he called 'the vulgarity and the savagery' of his writing, by saying that he had sat once upon a time every Sunday morning in an Irish Protestant church. But mountain and lough have not grown raw and common; pillage and ravage could not abate their beauty; and the impulse that gathers these great companies in every year has outlasted armorial stone.

Then, too, I would associate that doctrine of purgatory, which Christianity has shared with Neo-Platonism, with the countryman's belief in the nearness of his dead 'working out their penance' in rath or at garden end: and I would find in the psychical research of our day detail to make the association convincing to intellect and emotion. I would try to create a type of man whose most moving religious experience, though it came to him in some distant country, and though his intellect were wholly personal, would bring with it imagery to connect it with an Irish multitude now and in past time (*CW5* 36–37; 310–11nn.; *Ex* 266–68).

---

[43] The abandoned epilogue (*c.* 1917) of *Per Amica Silentia Lunae* grows from Yeats's fascination with pilgrimages to St Patrick's Purgatory: see *CW5* 253–54.

[44] Later explored in the 'The Pilgrim', first published as *A Broadside* 10 (New Series) (October 1937): see *VP* 592–93.

Given that this was written after the period of intense re-engagement in the thought of Emmanuel Swedenborg,[45] in mediumistic practice and psychical research, it is clear that Purgatory was ripe for reinterpretation by this fundamentally Protestant mind. Yeats thought he had witnessed direct experience in spiritualistic practice of the accessibility, or 'nearness' of the dead.

THE RENDING PAIN OF RE-ENACTMENT

The way was thus clear for what then seemed Yeats's deepest thinking about Purgatory in the concept of the after-death 'Shiftings' in the first version of *A Vision*. See *CW13* 189–90). Further dramatic deployment followed *A Vision*, as in *The Words upon the Window-pane*.

Dr. Trench.

Sometimes a spirit re-lives not the pain of death but some passionate or tragic moment of life. Swedenborg describes this and gives the reason for it. There is an incident of the kind in the Odyssey, and many in Eastern literature; the murderer repeats his murder, the robber his robbery, the lover his serenade, the soldier hears the trumpet once again. If I were a Catholic I would say that such spirits were in Purgatory. In vain do we write *requiescat in pace* upon the tomb, for they must suffer, and we in our turn must suffer until God gives peace. Such spirits do not often come to séances unless those séances are held in houses where those spirits lived, or where the event took place. This spirit which speaks those incomprehensible words and does not answer when spoken to is of such a nature. The more patient we are, the more quickly will it pass out of its passion and its remorse. (*VPl* 944–45; *CW2* 470).

While Yeats was explicit in his denial that any 'character upon the stage spoke my thoughts. All were people I had met or might have met in just such a séance' including 'the old man who was half a Swedenborgian',[46] it is difficult not to remember that he himself attended scores of such séances, even if no longer of quite the

[45] See 'Swedenborg, Mediums, and the Desolate Places' (*Ex* 30–70; *CW5* 47–73).
[46] *Ex* 363–64; *CW2* 718.

Swedenborgian persuasion he had once been attracted to.[47] But the thinking was to go even deeper—and clearer in dramatic realization than it had been in *A Vision*. 'I never remember the dream so deep', wrote Yeats of the frenzy of excitement in which he wrote *Purgatory* (1938), his masterpiece in which Purgatory is a state of remorseless re-enactment rather than purgation. Nor was the play '"an allegory… My plot is my meaning"', he told the *Irish Times*[48] after the play had opened. At its first night—his last appearance at the Abbey—he told the audience that he had 'put into this play… my thoughts about this world and the next';[49] a crisp summation of a lifetime's brooding development via legend, folklore, and a constantly reconfigured set of beliefs in reincarnation and spiritism which make up this Protestant revision of Catholic orthodoxy in the social and political setting of the new Republic of Ireland.

T. S. Eliot remarked that in *Purgatory*, and only in that play, Yeats had 'solved his problem of speech in verse, and laid all his successors under obligation to him'.[50] When Eliot meets Yeats as the major spirit of his 'familiar compound ghost' in 'Little Gidding' and Yeats', as 'dead master' warns him of the third of the 'gifts reserved for age', the 'rending pain of re-enactment' | Of all that you have done, and been', I suggest that Eliot also understands Yeats's thinking on Purgatory.[51]

CONCLUSION

Though Yeats left Marryat behind, he could not rid himself of Purgatory. Reflecting on these matters at Schiphol Airport, hub of the Royal Dutch flag-carrier airline, I noticed the fuselage

---

[47] One recalls his statement to the Swedish press during his visit to collect his Nobel Prize, that he had even been inclined to be married in a New Swedenborgian church: see *Life 2*, 245–46 and n. 124, for this news percolating from the Swedish *Nya Kyrkans Tidning* (December 1923) and into the London Swedenborgian paper *New Church Life* (April 1926).

[48] *Irish Times* (13 August 1938). See also *Life 2*, 618–19; 627ff.

[49] *Irish Times* (10 August 1938).

[50] See T. S. Eliot, *Poetry and Drama* (London: Faber & Faber, 1951), 20.

[51] See Christopher Ricks and Jim McCue (eds.), *The Poems of T. S. Eliot* (London: Faber & Faber, 2015), I, 204–05.

motto—in English—'The Flying Dutchman'—under the company logo that KLM's intercontinental planes bear. I briefly wondered if I was suffering from ideas of reference, or whether the legend of the Dutchman is itself obsessional.[52] Airports being notorious, I soon recovered enough to see that Purgatory itself has received an upgrade—the motto gestures to ceaseless travel in the sky—even if the copy-writers had been oblivious to national legend. The Dutchman was only temporarily grounded at Schiphol.[53]

One of the privileges of editing this journal is that of re-visiting primary documents in the harmless drudgery of editing others' work. Reporting the appearance of *Mosada* in *Book Auction Records*, Colin Smythe's preceding article quotes some 'Editor's Gossip' from *The Irish Book Lover* in 1925.[54] Checking Smythe's quotation, I rediscovered as indicated above the source of *Mosada* in Marryat's novel. Perhaps advanced research is but the privilege of rereading primary documents and reviewing the new perspectives they open up.

---

[52] Perhaps Umberto Eco is right: 'Moral: there exist obsessive ideas, they are never personal; books talk among themselves, and any true detection should prove that we are the guilty party'. See his *Reflections on* The Name of the Rose (London: Secker and Warburg, 1985), 81.

[53] Other questionable attempts to update the legend include Albert Lewin's script and film, *Pandora and The Flying Dutchman* (1951). James Mason as the Dutchman is a John Singer Sargent figure, enraptured by the beautiful wife he has killed centuries ago. In 1930, his luxurious ocean-going yacht arrives in a Spanish Riviera resort after his latest seven-year bout at sea, and he works on a swagger portrait of her latest incarnation, Pandora (Ava Gardner). Alas, redemption through requital again eludes him.

[54] See above, See above, p. 251 n. 22, and p. 266. Bruce Stewart's 2004 edition of *The Irish Book Lover: An Irish Studies Reader Taken from Issues of* The Irish Book Lover *(1909–1957)* has also become an invaluable aid. See 'Publications Received' below, p. 460.

http://dx.doi.org/10.11647/OBP.0081.11

Yeats and Tukaram: 'An Asylum for my Affections'[1]

Geert Lernout

YEATS'S EPIGRAPH for *The Wanderings of Oisin* has had a shaky afterlife. Although the poet attributed it to 'Tulka', Yeats is sometimes credited with having written the phrase himself, and now, in any case, takes the credit for it, as Edna O'Brien demonstrates in a recent interview.[2] The romantic opposition between the world and the poet's inner nature seems to resonate not only with Irish novelists: the travel writer Leila Hadley used the first words as the title of a book, and uses Yeats's archaic wording in an epigraph, "*Give me the world if thou wilt, but grant me an asylum for my affections*" although she claims it as '*From the Icelandic* Tulka'.[3] And Yeats himself made use of the second part later when he complained to Pound that the American poet's work gave him 'no asylum for the affections'.[4]

---

[1] This paper was delivered as the second lecture in the series, on 3 June 2004. Further information may have been gathered since this article was prepared for publication. If you would like to find out if any further information has been discovered that may help your own research, why not write to the author at geert. lernout@uantwerpen.be? Quite apart from anything else, feedback is always welcomed.

[2] Sunday 6 February 2011, http://www.theguardian.com/books/2011/feb/06/edna-obrien-ireland-interview.

[3] Leila Hadley, *Give me the World* (London: Victor Gollancz, 1958), [p. vi].

[4] *The Letters of Ezra Pound: 1907–1941* (London: Faber & Faber, 1951), 121 (letter 84, To Kate Buss, May 1916).

287

Despite the resonance of the phrase, nobody seems to have known where it came from. In 1954, Richard Ellmann in *The Identity of Yeats* simply repeated that Yeats 'was quoting a sentence of Tulka' (320), without explaining who or what that was.[5] In *The Collected Works of W.B. Yeats*, Richard J. Finneran claimed the author as the Czech painter Josef Tulka, but he added: 'No source for the words ascribed to Tulka has yet been found, and it is possible that they were invented by Yeats'.[6] As recently as two years ago, the *Critical Companion to William Butler Yeats* mentioned the Czech painter and offered another vague possibility, 'the Swedenborgian writer Charles Augustus Tulk'.[7]

The real author of the momentous lines was the Mahārāshtra poet Sant [Saint] Tukaram (*c.*1598/1608–1649/50) who belonged to the Bhakti movement within Hinduism. Tukaram is the presumed author of a fluid collection of devotional poems that belong to the genre of the Abhanga: most of these poems end with one or two lines of ethical advice, ascribed to the poet who in that part of the poem calls himself Tuka.

We can't be sure where Yeats found the relevant lines, but a distinct possibility is the first volume of the 1871 book *Experiences of a Planter in the Jungles of Mysore* by Robert H. Elliot. The full flavour of the book is apparent in the opening sentence of the first chapter, under the title 'Myself':

In the year 1855 I sailed for India, with a trifling capital, and with that firm belief in my own capabilities which is common to youth, and which one looks back upon in after life with mingled feelings of wonder and amusement.[8]

Further indications of the book's general character are evident in the chapter titles that follow: 'My Native Neighbours' (II); 'Native Character—Private Relations of Life' (III); 'Native Character— Current and Written Opinions' (IV); 'Bribery' (V); 'Caste' (VI).

5   Richard Ellmann, *The Identity of Yeats* (London: Macmillan, 1954), 320.
6   *CW1*, 693.
7   David A. Ross, *A Critical Companion to William Butler Yeats: A Literary Reference to his Life and Work* (New York: Facts on File, 2009), 281.
8   Robert Henry Elliot, *The Experiences of a Planter in the Jungle of Mysore* (London: Chapman and Hall, 1871), I, 1. Hereinafter 'Elliot'.

The chapter that concerns us is the seventh, under the title 'Religion', which may have well been the only one that was relevant to Yeats. After a number of general remarks about the history of the Vedic faith and Brahmanism, and before discussing the influence of Christian missionaries, Elliot deplores the fact that in India 'Nothing, literally nothing' has managed to replace the ancient religion. Then he writes:

I am now, with an object which will be distinctly declared further on, going to give at considerable length an account of the life, and a number of quotations from the writings, of an old Maharatta poet, who lived about the end of the sixteenth and the commencement of the seventeenth century. The life and translations I take entirely from a most interesting article by Sir Alexander Grant, which appeared in the *Fortnightly Review* some years ago.[9]

Elliot points out that to the average English reader the sentiments in Tukaram's work seem so 'exalted and pure that it may be surprising to have emanated from any who had not read the Bible'.[10] In his brief biography he stresses the humble living conditions of the shopkeeper Tukaram, who after his death (and ascension in a heavenly chariot) was considered a saint by all who knew him.

Elliot then proceeds to 'give the whole of such portions of Tukaram as seem best to illustrate the tone of thought and feeling expressed by the Maharatta poet'.[11] All of the quoted poems express a mystic and quietist faith (which Elliot compares to 'Calvinism'), summed up in the final lines of each poem by a quotation from 'Tukâ', the moral of the story, expressed by the poet/saint. This is the full text of the tenth (of 22 poems or 'stanzas', as he calls them):

> Salvation is not difficult for us to obtain,
> It is clearly to be found in the bundle on our back.
> If we desire the pleasures of faith,
> Our longing for them shall be satisfied.
> You give, O God, each man his due and what is fit:
> Acknowledging it to be good, I accept it readily.

---

[9] Elliot, 296–97. Sir Alexander Grant's 'Tukaram, a Study of Hinduism' appeared in *The Fortnightly Review* 7 (January 1867), 27–40.

[10] Elliot, 297.

[11] *Ibid.*, 300.

> Tukâ says,—'If you like, give me this world,
> But give me an asylum for my affections'.[12]

Before quoting the next poem, Elliot provides an explanation of the rather puzzling final lines:

'The great object of horror', says Sir Alexander Grant, 'to the mind of a religious Hindoo, is the prospect of being born over and over again into this miserable world. Tukaram's resignation to the will of God is so great, that he professes himself ready to bear this curse of prolonged individuality, provided only that, as long as he is in this world, he may have God as the object of his affections'.[13]

After the last poem, Elliot moves on to the real reason for his discussion of the work by the saint. He believes that this particular indigenous tradition shows that the British attempts to convert India to Christianity are misguided and have been shown to fail. Since the missionaries will not succeed in converting the 'Hindoo lads' to the Christian faith, they might as well make sure to teach them 'the best possible form of the old Vedic faith', which would be monotheist and deistic, but not specifically Christian'.[14]

At the end of the chapter on religion, which also closes the first volume of the book, Elliot comes to a conclusion: missionaries should lead by example, not by trying to convert the natives while living the life of Europeans, but by living among the natives and the like, and by showing what a Christian life is really like.

Missionary work carried on after this fashion would, I feel well assured, be of incalculable benefit to the Indians, and would yield in good time an ample return. But, carried on as it is at present, I feel well assured, as I have repeatedly urged, that little good will ever be done to the cause of Christianity, and that the evils that have ensued from our misguided efforts have done, and are at this moment doing, an amount of harm to the cause of Christianity in Asia which is impossible to exaggerate.[15]

---

[12] *Ibid.*, 302.
[13] *Ibid.*, 302–03.
[14] *Ibid.*, 311.
[15] *Ibid.*, 318.

It is impossible to be certain that Yeats found the quotation of Tukaram in Elliot's book or in the *Fortnightly Review*. Both seem equally likely, but what they have in common is a certain distance from Christianity and a sympathy for the native religious traditions, which resulted in finding in Sant Tukaram's work a mystic deism that was thought not to be incompatible with the Christian tradition. Not all contemporary converts to Christianity seem to have agreed.[16]

The relevance of the motto to what Yeats was trying to do in *The Wanderings of Oisin* and in his esoteric philosophy in general, should be obvious. R. F. Foster in the first volume of his biography describes Yeats's involvement in the Dublin Hermetic Society in the mid-eighties as 'a local reflection of the fashion for Indian things which infused intellectual avant-garde circles in the 1880's. Later on in the same volume he points out that some of the poems in *The Wanderings of Oisin* look back to that period, 'using the language of Indian mysticism'.[17]

In the light of a retrospective view such as Foster's, it is worth stressing that the epigraph is not to be found in *The Wanderings of Oisin: and Other Poems* (1889), the collection which contains the first printing of Yeats's version of the Irish epic as well as a heterogeneous group of other poems, including a number on Indian themes. That book had functioned, like so many of Yeats's early editions, as a kind of *Collected Poems* to its date of issue, and when Yeats next published these poems, rewritten in many cases, in *Poems* (1895) he radically altered their overall *ordonnance* as well as their texts. *Poems* (1895) was heavily sectionalized and began with *The Wanderings of Usheen* [*sic*] as a section, adding the epigraph on the verso of the title and dedication, and making clear that the epigraph related only to the poem which followed. The other poems were regrouped as *The Rose* and as *Crossways*, the former privileged over the latter because 'the writer' 'in them has found, he believes, the only pathway whereon he can hope to see with his own eyes the Eternal Rose of Beauty and of Peace' while *Crossways* (which included the Indian poems) was

---

[16] For a contemporary reaction, see *A Letter to the Brahmos from a Converted Brahman of Benares* (Allahabad: Allahabad Mission Press, 1868).

[17] *Life 1*, 46 and 552 n. 80; 85.

consigned to the very back of the volume, by 'the writer', 'because in them he tried many pathways' (*Poems* [1895], v-vi: the third person expression is Yeats's).

An Indian epigraph to an Irish epic requires further explanation, but it gestures perhaps to a very personal and syncretic quest.

http://dx.doi.org/10.11647/OBP.0081.12

'I am sitting in a café with two French-Americans': W. B. Yeats, Max Dauthendey, James and Theodosia Durand. Durand's 'Communistic Manifesto'[1]

Günther Schmigalle

IN *THE TREMBLING OF THE VEIL*, Book IV, 'The Tragic Generation', W. B. Yeats recalls his visits to Paris, and in chapter XX, where he evokes 'many pictures [which] come before me without date or order' (*CW3* 264), we find the following reminiscences:

I am sitting in a café with two French-Americans, a German poet, Dauthendey, and a silent man whom I discover to be Strindberg, and who is looking for the Philosophers' Stone. One French-American reads out a manifesto he is about to issue to the Latin Quarter; it proposes to establish a communistic colony of artists in Virginia, and there is a footnote to explain why he selects Virginia: 'Art has never flourished twice in the same place. Art has never flourished in Virginia' (*CW3* 265).

An editors' note explains what the Philosophers' Stone is, refers to Strindberg's occult and Swedenborgian interests, and admits that 'the French Canadian with plans for a colony of artists in Virginia is untraced' (*CW3* 480–81, n. 102). In this note I shall try to trace him,

---

[1] The author can be contacted at the following email address: schmigalle2000@ yahoo.de

without forgetting that there were 'two French-Americans'. I also trace the 'manifesto'.

Max Dauthendey (1867–1918), 'a painter as well as a poet', as the editors specify in another note (*CW3* 516, n.15), writes in his autobiography[2] that when he established himself in London early in 1894, he made friends, in the pension where he stayed in 24 Upper Woburn Place, with a couple of young American artists. James, who wanted to be a sculptor, was from New York; his wife Theodosia, aspiring to be a painter, was a native of San Francisco. After meeting in Paris, they had married in London. They were members of a magical order and had come from Paris to London in order to deepen their knowledge of secret science, and, before the German poet's astonished eyes, they opened the doors of an unknown world. They read the works of Blake to him, they explained the chemistry of the stars and the life of the planets, and they put him in touch 'with the Irish poet Yeats who lived in London at that time and belonged to the same secret society as themselves. This man, too, longed for new ideals'.[3] Dauthendey recalls:

In the realms of the spirit, said Yeats, there are differences of force just like in the physical realms. He said he felt sure that the spirits of the old gods of his Irish home country, who had been driven away by the advance of Christianity, were still alive in the air above Ireland, and it was possible to call them and make them return'.[4]

'At that time', the German poet records,

a play by Yeats was performed in the Drury Lane Theatre in London. The poet invited both the American couple and myself to attend the first performance. I remember that the play attracted the whole literary world of London [...] But I didn't understand anything of the play and I thought it was the spring air which made me close my eyes in spite of the action

---

[2]   Max Dauthendey, *Gedankengut aus meinen Wanderjahren*, 2 Vols. (München: Albert Langen, 1913), hereafter *Gedankengut*. The translations of the quotations are mine.
[3]   *Gedankengut*, Vol. 2, 55.
[4]   *Ibid.*, 56.

happening on the stage. The only thing I remember is a lady sitting in a dark room, in front of a big fire burning in a fireplace, and behind her a window, blue with the light of the moon. But what the lady spoke to the ghosts or to human beings didn't enter my mind […] I felt a little ashamed when the Irish poet, tall, pale-faced, with black hair, asked us whether we had liked his play. I couldn't find anything to say. Later, at home, sitting near the fireplace in the simple room of the Americans, waiting for the tea water to boil, we started talking about the spirits again.[5]

Two years later, in February 1896, Dauthendey established himself in Paris. The American couple had returned to Paris, too, living now 'in an avenue near the Eiffel Tower, in a studio with kitchen and bedroom' (*Gedankengut*, vol. 2, p. 160). They gave him good advice when he decided to marry his Swedish girlfriend, lent him money for a trip to Germany, continued to talk about questions of occultism, and took him to visit,

at Neuilly, the last descendant of a Scottish king who lived in Paris and dedicated himself to Egyptology, staying with his wife in a beautiful house with garden, where on Sundays he received numerous ladies and gentlemen […] This same wise man, later, reestablished in Paris the ancient cult of Isis, and his wife became the priestess of Isis.[6]

It is not difficult to recognize MacGregor Mathers, his wife Moina and the house, 87 Rue Mozart in Auteuil (not Neuilly), which they occupied since the summer of 1895 and which also served as the Golden Dawn's Ahathoor Temple. The revived cult of Isis reached

---

[5]   *Gedankengut*, vol. 2, 56–55. Ithell Colquhoun's version is slightly different: 'On the way Dauthendey, who was short-sighted, dropped his glasses down a gutter-drain so could not see what was happening and slept peacefully through the historic occasion'. See her *Sword of Wisdom: MacGregor Mathers and 'Golden Dawn'* (London: Neville Spearman, 1975), 85. While Coloquhoun clearly embroidered some of her stories, she did know both Yeats and Mathers, and this detail has the ring of something told to her by Yeats possibly in his old age. They had met in 1937, see *CL InteLex* 6919.

[6]   *Gedankengut*, vol. 2, 161.

its culmination by a successful public performance in the Théâtre de la Bodinière in Paris, in March 1899.[7]

The four of them—Dauthendey, his wife Annie Johansson, James and Theodosia—then conceived a project to found an artists' colony, in order to escape from the capitalist and bourgeois society and find a way of living more in harmony with the rhythms of the cosmos. Artists' colonies were being founded in many places at that time, from Worpswede in Germany to the Eagle's Nest in Oregon. James elaborated a detailed project for the settlement, which corresponds to the manifesto mentioned by Yeats. The four friends considered a number of possible sites: Brittany, the Lake of Geneva, the French Riviera, Corsica, Spain, the South of the United States, California. The Dauthendeys tried Sicily, but they didn't like it. In the spring of 1897, James proposed 'New Carolina' [sic]—a slip of Dauthendey's pen, as James must have meant North Carolina, or perhaps—as according to Yeats—Virginia.[8] But Dauthendey didn't want to go to the United States, not even to North Carolina, so James changed the plan: the new destination was Mexico. In June, 1897, Dauthendey and his wife disembarked in Vera Cruz and travelled to the capital. But they didn't like Mexico any more than they had liked Sicily. When they met James and Theodosia, who had arrived in Mexico City by a different route, Dauthendey explained that he couldn't possibly stay. The Americans were disappointed and annoyed. The two couples separated forever. The Dauthendeys stayed in Mexico for five months before travelling back to Paris[9]

Let us return to Yeats's 'sitting in a café with two French-Americans'. This coffeehouse meeting took place most probably during his second stay in Paris in December 1896 or January 1897. He had known the two 'French-Americans' for almost two years. He had invited them when his one-act play *The Land of Heart's Desire* was

[7]   Ellic Howe, *The Magicians of the Golden Dawn: A Documentary History of a Magical Order, 1887–1923* (London: Routledge & Kegan Paul, 1972), 200. Hereafter '*Magicians*'.
[8]   *Gedankengut*, vol. 2, 220.
[9]   *Ibid.*, 225–43.

staged for the first time, as a curtain-raiser for John Todhunter's *A Comedy of Sighs*, in the Avenue Theatre (in Northumberland Avenue, not in Drury Lane), on 29 March 1894. Dauthendey, number four at the coffee table, describes their friendship with himself and with Yeats in his autobiography, but he mentions the 'Americans', as he calls them, only by their first names. Their full names appear in a letter he wrote to them from Paris to Atlanta on 3 May 1897: they were James and Theodosia Durand.[10] They were members, like Yeats himself, of the Hermetic Order of the Golden Dawn, and disciples of MacGregor Mathers. The Membership List of the Order of the Golden Dawn lists the Durands (191st and 192nd respectively in its address book) as initiated into the Isis-Urania Temple in London, James as 'Judah' and Theodosia as 'En Hakkore'.[11] It gives their address at their initiation on 28 February 1894 as 11 Rue Boissinade [*sic*, actually 'Boissonade'], Paris.[12] On that day, Yeats was in Paris, attending the first night of Villiers De Lisle Adam's *Axel* with Maud Gonne.[13] He had been in Paris since 7 February, staying with Matherses, seeing Verlaine (and failing to see Mallarmé, who was in England), and, on 24 February, had acted as Hegemon or Keeper of the Portal at a Golden Dawn ceremony at the Matherses' Ahathoor Temple. He returned to London on 29 February or shortly after (*ChronY* 32). Unless the Durands had been in London for some time

---

[10] Max Dauthendey, *Ein Herz im Lärm der Welt. Briefe an Freunde* (München: Albert Langen and Georg Müller, 1933), 144–46. From now on quoted as *Herz*.

[11] On the meanings of these mottoes, see below n. 9.

[12] This street runs between the Boulevard Montparnasse and the Rue Raspail, close to the Montparnasse cemetery. In the 1890s it was a quiet street, then still divided into two cul-de-sacs (separated by the park of a convent), where no vehicles were allowed to enter. It was therefore a favorite of both French and foreign artists and writers. The Durands, in 1894, lived at number 11; the Dauthendeys, recently married, in 1896, lived at number 6, almost opposite. They all, including Strindberg, Edvard Munch and many others, had their meals at Madame Charlotte's Crèmerie, Rue de la Grande Chaumière, a very short walk from there.

[13] See 'A Symbolical Drama in Paris', Yeats's review in *The Bookman*, April 1894 (*CW9* 234 and ff.). See also Warwick Gould, 'Yeats and Symbolism', in *The Oxford Handbook of Modern Irish Poetry*, ed. Fran Brearton and Alan Gillis (Oxford: Oxford University Press, 2012), 20–41.

before the date of their initiation (e.g., receiving instruction), it is possible that they had met Yeats for the first time at the Ahathoor Temple in Paris.

James Madison Durand was the 63rd member to achieve the 5=6 grade on 7 June 1895. His unchanged motto, 'Judah' was inscribed in Hebrew on the Second Order Membership Roll on this occasion. Mrs Theodosia M. Durand had achieved the same grade on the same day, but the scribe, who entered her name first, mistook the date as the 5th, and then clumsily overwrote 7th onto the Roll. Her motto stands unchanged as 'En Hakkore'.[14] The reason for demission of both members is given as 'away', but no date is given. It would seem that later they had attended the Ahathoor Temple.

Their membership in the Golden Dawn is confirmed by Ellic Howe, who explains that between June 1894 and November 1896, the Ahathoor Temple in Paris recruited eleven members, most of them expatriates from Britain and from the United States, and that it was also joined by two married couples who had already been initiated in England. One of these couples were James and Theodosia Durand.[15] He specifies that the Durands by then lived in 156 Avenue de Suffren, which corresponds to Dauthendey's 'in an avenue near the Eiffel Tower'.[16]

---

[14] In the Membership Roll of the Isis-Urania Outer Order the so-called 'Hebrew' motto for Durand is clearly 'Judah' in English (GBR 1991 GD 2/2/2). As initiated into the Inner Order the name is written on the vellum in Hebrew, in very uncertainly inked and corrected characters, as if done neither with a decent pen nor by a scribe familiar with Hebrew. Mrs Durand's motto is 'En Hakkore', which she takes from Judges 15:19, viz., 'Then God opened up the hollow place in Lehi, and water came out of it. When Samson drank, his strength returned and he revived. So the spring was called En Hakkore, and it is still there in Lehi'. Her motto translates as "fountain of the crier". There is a note in the G D address book which records simply 'away' for her. The original membership rolls of the Outer and Inner Orders of the Golden Dawn, GBR 1991 GD 2/2/2 and GBR 1991 GD 2/2/7a-b, held in the Freemasons' Hall Library, London WC2.

[15] *Magicians*, 295.

[16] Ibid., 156. See *The Golden Dawn Companion: A Guide to the History, Structure, and Workings of the Hermetic Order of the Golden Dawn*, compiled and introduced by R. A. Gilbert (Wellingborough: Aquarian Press, 1986), 152. Sebastiano Fusco claims that Max Dauthendey, too, was a member of the Golden Dawn and offers: 'Maxima Virtus—M. V.—James M. Durand. Mirum in Modum—M. I. M.—Max Dauthendey. Multa Cum Spe—M. C. S.—Mrs. Theodosia Durand'.

Their surname 'Durand' explains why Yeats should have remembered them as 'French-Americans', being of French origin: there is also a major concentration of the name in French Canada.[17] Yeats's French friend of 1896 and later, was his translator and reviewer, Henry-Durand Davray (see *CL2* 13 and n. 2, and *passim*), who had strong English connections throughout his life.

Theodosia's maiden name was Moore. She was a native of Santa Rosa, daughter of a judge, A. P. Moore, and of his wife Annie E. Moore, and sister of Virgil Moore, variously described as 'former San Francisco newspaper writer' and 'widely traveled Kansas City resident and former U. S. commissioner to Alaska'.[18]

If we wonder what became of these hopeful and ambitious young artists, the dictionary *Artists in California 1786–1940* by Edan Hughes provides the following entry:

DURAND, Theodosia (1863–1949). Painter. Born in California on November 25, 1863. Mrs. Durand was a resident of San Francisco in 1916–21, Santa Rosa in 1929–30, and San Diego in the 1920s and 1930s. She died at Modesto (CA) State Hospital on March 15, 1949. Exhibited: SFAA. 1916, 1918 (paintings on cement); SFAA, 1925 (Oils); Calif. Industries Expo, San Diego, 1926; GGIE, 1939.[19]

See his *Insegnamenti magici della Golden Dawn: rituali, documenti segreti, testi dottrinali* (Rome: Edizioni Mediterranee, 2007), 242. However, the source of Fusco's mottoes and of the information that Dauthendey was a member remains obscure and cannot be reconciled with the original records cited in n. 9, above.

[17] 'Most of the 1800–1900 given names in our family are French-Canadian in origin (Pierre, Nazaire, etc.) [...] The 'given' name of James, in the 1800's, suggests to me that James is one of the English Durands—a clan that is not connected to our Jean Durand lineage', explains Roger Durand in the name of the Durand Heritage Foundation (Message to the author by e-mail, 5 October 2015).

[18] 'Funeral Held for Widow of Jurist', *Oakland Tribune*, 4 January 1929; 'Brother and Sister United', *Macon-Chronicle Herald*, 22 June 1932. My thanks to Mike Durand for providing these articles from the database of the Durand Heritage Foundation.

[19] Edan Milton Hughes, *Artists in California, 1786–1940* (San Francisco: Hughes Publishing Company, 1986), 161. The online version of the dictionary offers some additional information: 'Mme. Durand graduated from the Government Fine Arts School in Paris. She taught art at the University of Washington prior to moving to California [...was] director of the CSFA [California School of Fine Arts] in 1918'. See http://www.askart.com/artist/Theodosia_Durand/10015490/Theodosia_Durand.aspx, page consulted 10 October 2015.

As for James Durand, Dauthendey provides some curious information about his family background: 'The American', he says, 'owned two little houses in New York, and by renting them he could more or less live without having to confront extreme misery. Now he wanted to sell them. His maternal grandfather, the founder of the Tiffany glass factory in New York, was a rich man, and James expected later to receive a considerable heritage from him'.[20] These details, too, find some confirmation in Ellic Howe's book, which quotes two letters on astrological problems written by James Durand to Frederick Leigh Gardner, another member of the Golden Dawn, on 30 September and on 28 October 1895. These letters had to do, among other things, with 'the problem of his grandfather's will and possible litigation [...] Durand had cast a horoscope for the exact moment when the question about his grandfather's will presented itself to him, but the answer was obscure' (*Magicians*, p. 156). On 28 October, James Durand wrote: 'V. H. Soror Vestigia [Mrs Mathers] did a Tarot for me and the result of the lawsuit showed a victory for me, but rather an empty one' (*ibid.*).

According to the official record, Charles Lewis Tiffany (1812–1902), the founder of the Tiffany Company, had four sons and two daughters from his marriage with Harriet Olivia Avery Young (1817–97), but none of his daughters married a Durand or had a grandson called James Durand.[21] Perhaps he had a daughter from an extra-marital union. If that was so, James may have been her son, and litigation may have become necessary when he wished to be recognized as such. In that case, what would an 'empty victory' be? Could it mean that James was finally recognized as Tiffany's grandson, but remained excluded from his grandfather's will?

James Durand's major claim to immortality seems to consist in the document which Yeats calls a 'manifesto' and which according to Dauthendey was published in New York and in London, while he

---

[20] *Gedankengut*, vol. 2, 199.
[21] https://en.wikipedia.org/wiki/Charles_Lewis_Tiffany#Personal_life, page consulted 10 October 2015.

himself translated it into German and sent it to a monthly review in Germany.[22] Following the lead of H. G. Wendt,[23] K. W. Obrath,[24] and Volker Zenk,[25] I have found two published versions of this text: 'Fondation d'une colonie d'artistes subvenant eux-mêmes à leurs besoins', published in *La Plume* on 1 January 1897, and 'The foundation of a colony of self-supporting artists. Appeal', published in *The Arena* (Boston) the same year. There are some slight differences between the English and the French versions (see Appendixes A and B), printed below on facing pages to facilitate close reading.[26] Both versions of the manifesto were published anonymously, though the 'Note by the editor of *The Arena*' quotes a fragment of a letter by J. M. Durand, sent on 14 November 1896 from Paris, 203 Boulevard Raspail[27] and explaining that the manuscript was composed by a 'body of artists' and that Durand had the honour of representing them.[28]

---

[22] *Gedankengut*, vol. 2, 222.

[23] Hermann Georg Wendt, *Max Dauthendey. Poet-Philosopher* (New York: Columbia University Press, 1936), 38–39, n. 22; from now on quoted as *Dauthendey*.

[24] Karl Wilhelm Obrath, *The Image of Mexico in Germanic Imaginative Literature* (Cincinnati: University of Cincinnati Press, 1975), 198, n. 15.

[25] Volker Zenk, *Innere Forschungsreisen. Literarischer Exotismus in Deutschland zu Beginn des 20. Jahrhunderts* (Oldenburg: Igel Verlag Wissenschaft, 2003), 348, n. 11.

[26] See pp. 312-33. The French version concludes with the following sentence: 'Un petit groupe international d'artistes est déjà formé et s'est efforcé de se procurer le terrain nécessaire au développement de la colonie' (A small international group of artists has already formed and has made an effort to obtain the necessary ground for the development of the colony), while in the English version, an endnote added by the editor of *The Arena* states that 'the Society is now organized, and [...] it includes one practical farmer among its members'.

[27] This was the address of the Grand Hôtel de la Haute Loire, where Yeats resided in January 1897 (*CL2* 70, n. 1), and Dauthendey in May of the same year (*Herz*, 144).

[28] The Dauthendey archive of the city of Würzburg, in a section called 'Gründung einer Colonie sich selbsterhaltender Künstler', keeps a total of nine pre-publication versions of the 'Manifesto': three manuscripts in German in the writing of Dauthendey, two manuscripts in English in the writing of James Durand, two manuscripts in Swedish in the writing of Dauthendey's wife Annie Johansson, and two typescripts in Swedish. One of the English manuscripts corresponds exactly to the printed version of *The Arena*; the other is a fragment of it. One of the German manuscripts is an exact translation of the printed French

If, as most likely, the coffee-house meeting of Yeats with the Durands took place in December 1896 or January 1897, and the French version of the manifesto was published in *La Plume* on 1 January 1897, the text Durand read out to Yeats was either to be published soon, or had just been published in Paris. And if, as Yeats writes, Durand wished to issue his manifesto to the Latin Quarter, publication in *La Plume* was the most efficient and also the most elegant way of doing it. During its existence in the years 1889–1914, this journal was the most important organ of the modernist generation of French poets, writers and artists. It was firmly anchored in the Latin Quarter, with its offices and exposition rooms in the Rue Bonaparte, its *soirées* every Saturday night in the smoky basement of the Café du Soleil d'Or (Boulevard Saint-Michel), and the more solemn banquets or dinners it offered on special occasions, in restaurants of a higher category, generally presided by a poet or writer of the older generation.

Yeats must have been impressed because Durand's manifesto was quite an elaborate document. Not many manifestos have footnotes, but this one does. The footnote he quotes from memory says: 'Art has never flourished twice in the same place. Art has never flourished in Virginia'. Fn. 2 in the English version of the 'appeal' says: 'As Art has rarely ever flourished in two countries in the same era, it is as if we must unite ourselves to the destiny of the place most worthy and favorable to Art'. This is a partial coincidence. In Yeats's memory, 'in the same place' is replaced by 'in the same era'; place is substituted for space. In fact the appeal contains no specific reference to a place which might be chosen for the artists' colony, neither in its English nor in its French version. It seems natural that Yeats's memory should have modified the text a little; but it is also possible, even probable, that Durand added the reference to Virginia when he read it out to him, or that Yeats chose, for his impressionistic 'pictures... without date or order', a sardonic touch of his own.

version of *La Plume*; another one, dated 'Paris September 96' records discussions about the selection of a site for the colony.

Why did Durand publish his manifesto unsigned? Perhaps out of modesty and humility, virtues which, as the text of the manifesto shows, ranked high in his scale of values. Or perhaps, after many discussions with Theodosia, Dauthendey, Annie Johansson, and probably others whom we have not been able to identify, he was really convinced that the text was a collective production of a group of artists. Or wished it to seem as such.

It is more difficult to determine how far the colony of artists Durand proposed to establish can be qualified as 'socialistic' (editor of *The Arena*[29]), or as 'communistic' (Yeats), or as plain 'communist' (Franz Blei[30]). There are some striking affinities between Durand's project and Brook Farm, the most celebrated utopian community of America, founded by George and Sophia Ripley, inspired by the ideals of Transcendentalism, and operating in the years 1841–47 at West Roxbury, situated about eight miles from Boston, Massachusetts. Henry James, who thought himself the first to write extendedly about Brook Farm, writes in his biography of Nathaniel Hawthorne: 'The thing was the experiment of a coterie—it was unusual, unfashionable, unsuccessful. It was, as would then have been said, an amusement of the Transcendentalists—a harmless effusion of Radicalism'.[31]

The founders of Brook Farm believed that by pooling labour they could sustain the community and still have time for literary and scientific pursuits. George Ripley's object was 'to insure a more natural union between intellectual and manual labor than now exists; to combine the thinker and the worker, as far as possible, in the same individual'.[32] The official name of Brook Farm was 'Institute of Agriculture and Education', and its associates were active as farmers,

---

[29] Benjamin Orange Flower was the founder of *The Arena* and its editor in 1889–96. In 1897, John Clark Ridpath assumed editorship.

[30] Franz Blei, *Zeitgenössische Bildnisse* (Amsterdam: Allert de Lange, 1940), 111. From now on quoted as *Bildnisse*.

[31] Henry James, *Hawthorne* (London: Macmillan, 1879), 77.

[32] Letter of George Ripley to Ralph Waldo Emerson, November 1840, quoted in Sterling F. Delano, *Brook Farm: The Dark Side of Utopia* (Cambridge, Mass.: The Belknap Press of Harvard University Press, 2004), 34, 61, 115. From now on quoted as *Brook Farm*.

but also as teachers in a boarding school which comprised all levels, from an infant programme to the preparation for college. Instruction in the area of 'Belles Lettres', for example, included Homer's *Iliad*, Virgil' *Aeneid*, Dante's *Divine Comedy*, Goethe's *Faust*, Schillers's *Song of the Bell*, and the plays of Racine and Molière, all of these studied in their original language; there was also an emphasis on music and dance.[33] Whatever education had been in Brook Farm; artistic practice was to be in Durand's projected colony. According to the manifesto, by 'giving part of our lives ... to raising our own sheep and cows, catching our own fish, and planting our own corn, even in a wilderness of modern civilization', the artists and poets settling in it would not only be able to sustain themselves and escape the laws of capitalist society, but also have enough space, time, energy, and independence to follow their artistic vocation. Physical labour was perceived, both in Brook Farm and in Durand's plan, as a condition of mental well-being and a stimulus for artistic creativity. By tilling the field in the morning and painting, sculpting or writing poetry in the afternoon, or vice versa, the artist in the projected colony seeks to abolish, in a way, the division of labor dominant in modern society, and hence, the alienation of man. This was the theory. In practice, however, a 'disproportionate amount of time ... had to be devoted to physical rather than intellectual labors'; the work-day was of ten hours in summer and eight hours in winter.[34] Nathaniel Hawthorne, after living and toiling at Brook Farm from April to November of 1841, has seriously questioned the possibility of a spiritualization of labour:

The clods of earth, which we so constantly belabored and turned over and over, were never etherealized into thought. Our thoughts, on the contrary, were fast becoming cloddish. Our labor symbolized nothing, and left us mentally sluggish in the dusk of the evening. Intellectual activity is incompatible with any large amount of bodily exercise. The yeoman and the

---

[33] Delano, *Brook Farm*, 35, 69–70.
[34] *Ibid.*, 53, 66–67.

scholar […] are two distinct individuals, and can never be melted or welded into one substance'.[35]

Brook Farm, the founder of which had been a Minister in the Boston Unitarian church, was variously described by its founders as 'city of God' or as 'A Glimpse of Christ's Idea of Society'; however, religious freedom was essential to its program. Likewise in Durand's manifesto, 'Every artist shall have perfect liberty for his own ideas of Art, his religious belief or opinions, and in his domestic life'. Brook Farm proposed and practised the emancipation of women, which is also an element in Durand's artist's colony:

There shall be a perfect equality between women and men, and women shall have a voice in all matters […]. A wife shall feel herself an independent self-supporting artist, choosing a manual occupation adapted to her physical strength, not depending on her husband; nor should he impose upon her the never-accounted-for small duties of the household.

Dauthendey was very much impressed by the way James Durand practised this principle in his everyday life with Theodosia.[36] George Ripley 'probably hoped that Brook Farm in its development would grow into a model community, and become the germ or nucleus of a new and better social organization'.[37] Likewise, Durand imagines that 'when the great nations shall have dashed themselves to pieces on the rocks they have formed around them, we will announce the new age of Spirituality and the Regeneration of the World'. Durand's manifesto, then, was communistic in the same sense that Transcendentalism was.

A few years after the closing down of Brook Farm, Nathaniel Hawthorne satirized it rather benevolently in his novel *The Blithedale*

---

[35] Nathaniel Hawthorne, *The Blithedale Romance*, ed. Seymour Gross and Rosalie Murphy (New York: W. W. Norton, 1978), 61.

[36] *Gedankengut*, vol. 2, 46–48.

[37] Orestes Brownson, Review of *The Blithedale Romance*, *Brownson's Quarterly Review* (October 1852), quoted in: Benjamin Franklin V. (ed.), *Nathaniel Hawthorne: A Documentary Volume* (New York: Thomson Gale, 2003), 193.

Romance. Durand's project was not even honoured by a satire; 'the founding of the colony', as Wendt says, 'came to naught' (*Dauthendey*, p. 39, n. 32). What was the cause of this failure? My view would be that the main cause for this failure was the selection of Mexico as the site of the settlement. Durand stipulates, as one of the conditions for the success of the artists' colony,

...union by fraternal sympathy with the people of a country already settled, having an Art future, where the soil shall favor the easy raising of food; with landscapes varied by hills, plateaus, woods, and watercourses; not too far inland.

These sensible political and geographical conditions were not met by Mexico. The solemn beauty of its deserts, forests, and mountains, and the real or potential fertility of its soil, did not convince the future colonists. If we read Dauthendey, the only one of the little group whose first impressions of the land of the Aztecs have been preserved, we find that cacti, mosquitoes, and vultures are the recurrent images of his travelogue, summing up the forbidding, infertile, and hostile nature of the country. Furthermore, heavily armed men at every corner, adventurers approaching the travelers to swindle them out of their money, create the impression of a country most imperfectly 'settled' ('policé', i.e. civilized, educated, in the French version). This impression was confirmed by the German consul, who, when the Dauthendeys finally consulted him, explained that

the interior of the country is very dangerous for foreigners. There are Spanish bandits who live in the Indian villages, and when they suppose someone has money, they may easily ambush and shoot him from behind. In this lawless country nobody troubles about a dead man. The murderer is never found. There are too many murders, and it would be too much work for the police to follow up all the murders which happen in far-away places. However, if we really wanted to cultivate some land and live peacefully in this country, we would have to be at least ten men and ten women, and even then it would be dangerous if we didn't speak the language and were no Catholics, for the Spaniards are very severe and fanatic in questions of religion.[38]

---

[38]   *Gedankengut*, vol. 2, 229–30.

The foundation of Brook Farm had been based on a joint stock company formed in 1841 by George Ripley and his wife along with ten other initial investors..[39] Durand, for his part, counted, to obtain the terrain for his projected community, on

finding [...] some one sympathetic to Art, who will provide land ready and cleared for cultivation, and small, simple dwellings, consisting of a room for sleeping, a room for eating, and a studio or study; also a few sheep, cows, and horses, and some farming implements,—enough to start with. In return for his faith and sympathy, poets, writers, and musicians will dedicate their poems and compositions, and sculptors and painters give their works in trust to him.

In other words, Durand's artists' colony needed a Maecenas. The necessity to find some benevolent rich man was always present in the deliberations of the four friends. In the beginning, Dauthendey says, he would have preferred settling in Germany; the Durands in the US; and he had to admit that in the US it would be easier to find some unoccupied land and some sympathetic millionaires.[40] In Paris, the four friends, after eliminating England, Scotland, Ireland, Germany, Switzerland, Italy, Greece, Spain, Russia, Turkey, Scandinavia, Holland, Belgium and France, as possible sites for the colony, arrive at the following conclusion:

So what remains is America. North America. Not the business world of New York and Chicago, but south of Washington there is a country with a climate as mild as France. Six hours by train from Washington. Mountains, forests, rivers and a marvellous climate. The air from the 'Blue Mountains' makes the summers cool, the land has been long cultivated, there are plenty of animals in the forests and in the rivers. Vanderbilt there has 80.000 acres of land. He will lend us land for the future Colony'.[41]

'Vanderbilt' is undoubtedly George W. Vanderbilt, youngest son of William H. Vanderbilt and grandson of 'Commodore' Cornelius Vanderbilt, who enjoyed visiting western North Carolina for its

---

[39] Delano, *Brook Farm*, 35, 69–70.
[40] *Gedankengut*, vol. 2, 222.
[41] 'Aufforderung zu einer Künstlerkolonie', manuscript n. 7, Würzburg, my translation (see above note 20).

mild climate and spectacular scenery. During a visit in the winter of 1888, he was inspired by a view from Asheville so spectacular that he purchased 125,000 acres of land to create his country home of Biltmore, with a double goal 'to house the monumental works of art he had been acquiring on his trips abroad' and 'to promote scientific forestry and farming'.[42] The landscape he chose for his new home corresponds to the one described in Durand's manuscript:

> The spot where his 5000 acre farm is situated is as beautiful as one may hope to see. On the broad plateau that extends from the Blue Ridge to the Alleghany Mountains, the general level of which is near to 2000 feet above the sea and surrounded by mountain peaks more lofty than any east of the Rockies, the place naturally is a sort of paradise. [...] From his library window Mr. Vanderbilt can see the Blue Ridge, the Alleghanies and their tributary mountain ranges rising and stretching away in the distance. He can see Mount Pisgah raising its pine clad head more than 6000 feet above the plateau. Black Dome, Clingman's Dome, Mitchell's Peak and a score or more of giants are near by. Between these, like silver threads, run the French Broad, the Hiawassee and near half a dozen other rivers. He may see if he wishes, the spots over in the Tennessee Mountains that have been made in a way famous by the charming stories of Charles Egbert Craddock.[43]

It is not known whether Durand and his friends talked or wrote to George W. Vanderbilt, though the phrase 'He will lend us land' sounds as if they had received some sort of promise from him. There were certainly many affinities between them. It is known that in his youth,

> he spent his time among his books, reading, studying philosophy, becoming fluent in eight foreign languages, and learning the histories of all the paintings in his father's gallery.[44]

---

[42] Arthur T. Vanderbilt II, *Fortune's Children: The Fall of the House of Vanderbilt* (New York: William Morrow, 2013), 274, 276.

[43] Foster Coates, 'Scholar of Plutocracy. George Washington Vanderbilt Woos Wisdom in Luxury. Croesus and Scaliger in one—Traits of the Wealthiest Suitor Who Ever Neglected Venus For Minerva', *The Galveston Daily News* (Houston, Texas), 27 August 1893.

[44] Vanderbilt, *Fortune's Children*, 271.

At Biltmore,

George led the life of a gentleman farmer, in his spare time studying the plants, birds, and animals of his principality, learning various dialects of American Indian tribes, and, for some obscure reason, translating contemporary literature into ancient Greek.[45]

Anyway, his immense fortune as well as his passion for art and for agroscience would have made him an ideal partner for Durand's project, at least during the years 1889–95 (construction of Biltmore) and 1896–1900 (prosperity of Biltmore). By 1900, he was running out of money, and by the time of his death in 1914 his fortune had been considerably diminished.

In Mexico, only the president could have assumed the role of Maecenas. In fact, the Durands arrived carrying a letter of recommendation for Porfirio Díaz.[46] When the Dauthendeys were received by him, he apparently offered to sell them cheaply all the land they wanted.[47] Although establishing colonies of immigrants was an essential part of Díaz's economic policy, the image of 'Art Befriender' sits uncomfortably upon the ageing caudillo, already three times reelected by 1897.

Dauthendey must have realized this. He was shocked when, during the celebrations on Independence Day (16 September 1897), a drunken man's clumsy attempt on the person of Porfirio Díaz was followed by a police assassination, causing one of the major political scandals in Mexican history. Claude Dumas has resumed the case:

Following the custom on that day, the official procession walked from the Government Palace to the Alameda where the ceremony in memory of the Independence was celebrated. When the President, accompanied by his ministers and his high officials, arrived at the Alameda place, an individual emerged from the crowd, crossed the barrier formed by the cadets of the Chapultepec Military School, and struck the President on the head with an unidentified object. The man, whose name was Arnulfo Aguero, was arrested

---

[45] *Ibid.*, p. 277.
[46] *Gedankengut*, vol. 2, pp. 230–31.
[47] Blei, *Bildnisse*, p. 112.

immediately and taken into custody. Porfirio Díaz, absolutely unscathed, then continued on his way and presided the planned ceremonies as usual. The emotions aroused by this event had hardly calmed down when it was known that the author of that strange attack had been stabbed to death by a group of unknown persons shouting 'Long live Porfirio Díaz!', when he was in a room of the central police station, immobilized by a straitjacket. The subsequent investigation proved rapidly that this assassination had been committed by the police itself, and ordered by its General Inspector, Eduardo Velázquez, with the help of various inspectors under his orders. Velázquez was imprisoned and a few days later found dead in prison with a pistol in his hand. In the subsequent trial, from 15 to 22 November, almost all the men responsible for the assassination of Arroyo were condemned to death; but when they appealed, the matter was put off, and after three years, the condemned men were acquitted, and even returned to occupy important official positions.[48]

The political crisis provoked by the so-called 'asunto Arroyo' threatened to disrupt the delicate balance of power in the country. Thirteen years later, Díaz's protracted dictatorship was swept away by a formidable revolution. Dauthendey used his own Mexican adventure and the elements of the so-called 'Arroyo scandal' for his successful novel *Raubmenschen* (*Men of Prey*).

Both the Brook Farm utopia, which enjoyed six years of reality, and Durand's artists' community, which remained a dream, were transformed into novels—the first one by Nathaniel Hawthorne, the second one by Max Dauthendey. As for James Durand, he still remains something of an enigma. Nothing is known today about his works of art and very little about his life; all that remains of him is the 'manifesto' he read out to Yeats one day, at a coffee-house table in Paris.

---

[48] Claude Dumas, *Justo Sierra y el México de su tiempo, 1848–1912* (México: UNAM, 1992), vol. 1, 391–92 (my translation). See also Jesús Rábago, *Historia del gran crimen* (México: Tip. de El Partido Liberal, 1897), and for a recent study, Claudio W. Lomnitz, 'Mexico's First Lynching: Crime, Moral Panic, Dependency', *Critical Historical Studies* 1:1 (2014), 85–123.

The Utopia that is envisaged in 'The Lake Isle of Innisfree' is a very different concept from that envisaged by Durand, not least because it envisages a solitary existence. And while Yeats had experienced F. J. Dicks's Theosophical commune in Ely Place, Dublin in 1891–92 (see *CW3* 193ff.), it had been a very urban—if earnest and idealistic—organisation. We may surmise from the handling of the anecdote that the Yeats who published *The Trembling of the Veil* in 1922, recalled the young poet in the Latin quarter with affectionate distance.

APPENDIX A

THE FOUNDATION OF A COLONY OF
SELF-SUPPORTING ARTISTS.
APPEAL.[49]

MEN AND WOMEN ARTISTS:

The time has come when we poets, painters, sculptors, and musicians must unite to free ourselves and Art from the overwhelming spirit of the age,—Commercialism and Sensuality.

The strong undercurrent of idealism impels us to become the prophets whose mission it is to herald the dawn of a new age of Heroism and Poetry which shall triumph over and check the further reign of a barbarous civilization.

We have suffered long enough in humility; we have begged our bread too often of editors, critics, and connoisseurs—Art speculators, who are the greatest hinderers of idealism, and have nothing to do with Art but to debase it; we will no longer sell our birthright. Those among us who have no means of sustenance need no longer be cut off from answering the voice of their soul. We must come together, as the strongest men and women of other nations when oppressed have done before, becoming intellectual pioneers of a new state.

To realize fully the hour, compare the spirit of Art, politics, and enlightenment of to-day with that of any other age. If we are artists we must despise our cities, our false civilization, and our cold, spiritless religions.

Let us, artists of all nations, withdraw ourselves from their midst, unmindful or our nationality and our present customs, in which we can have but little pride, estranged as we are from our own kind. As artists, we are brothers, and the difference in nationality cannot separate us. We will leave exhibitions, salons, and theatres (markets made for speculations) to journey men and hirelings who are willing to pamper the vulgar taste of the bourgeoisie. Art is ignored in this

---

[49] *The Arena* [Boston] 17 (1897), 642–51. The footnotes in this manifesto are James Durand's.

APPENDIX B

FONDATION D'UNE COLONIE D'ARTISTES SUBVENANT EUX-MÊMES A LEURS BESOINS[50]

Artistes, homes et femmes.

Poètes, peintres, sculpteurs et compositeurs de musique, le moment est venu de nous unir et de délivrer l'Art et nous-mêmes de l'esprit envahisseur de ce temps tout de Mercantilisme et de Sensualité.

Le mouvement latent d'idéalisme nous pousse à être ceux dont la mission est d'annoncer l'aube d'un âge nouveau tout à l'Héroïsme et à la Poésie qui doit triompher de la haine et mettre trêve brusquement au règne d'une civilisation barbare.

Voici assez longtemps que nous souffrons dans l'humiliation ; trop souvent, nous avons mendié notre pain auprès des éditeurs, des critiques, des amateurs et des différents intermédiaires,—les spéculateurs de l'Art ; nous ne voulons plus vendre le meilleur de nous-mêmes. Ceux qui, parmi nous, n'ont pas le moyen de vivre ne peuvent guère répondre aux voies de leur âme. Liguons-nous, comme firent les femmes et les hommes des autres nations lorsqu'ils furent opprimés, et devenons les pionniers intellectuels du nouvel âge.

Afin de mieux comprendre notre époque, comparez l'esprit de l'Art actuel avec celui de jadis, la société et l'éducation d'aujourd'hui avec celles du passé. Si nous sommes artistes, nous devons dédaigner nos cités, notre fausse civilisation et nos religions sans vie.

Artistes de toutes les nations, retirons-nous de ce milieu, sans nous arrêter trop à notre nationalité et aux mœurs actuelles, dont nous sommes peu fiers, éloignés comme nous le sommes de nos semblables. Comme artistes, nous sommes frères, et les différences de nationalités ne peuvent nous séparer. Nous laisserons les expositions, les salons et les théâtres (marchés créés pour les spéculations) aux manœuvres et aux salariés qui sont contents de flatter les goûts vulgaires de la bourgeoisie. L'Art est ignoré dans cet âge si peu initié

---

[50] *La Plume* [Paris], 1 January 1897, 10–15. The footnotes in this manifesto are James Durand's.

age, so uninitiated in divine things; and, being ahead of the age, we cannot look to it for support. To wait for destiny to help us is perhaps never to realize our hopes. There are those who have said they will *die* for Art; but we will *live* for it. Separated, we can do nothing against the reign of ignorance; scattered, our works will be destroyed, with the places unworthy of them, by the wars and revolutions which are already at hand.

Let us unite and return to the natural life of primitive men of the soil, which latter, as artists, we love; giving part of our lives (for Art's sake) to raising our own sheep and cows, catching our own fish, and planting our own corn, even in a wilderness of modern civilization; so keeping our intellects sacred to our Art and to the higher plane, and, like other laborers, dedicating our hands to the raising of our own food, that our bodies may become the stronger and more beautiful vehicles for our souls.

We are without experience, but we are intelligent women and men, not easily daunted, and are ready to study the most advanced methods and experiments, being prepared for failures at the first. If we are artists, we can dare. We will make our lives works of Art; like Hercules, we are ready to perform the labors of life. Though homeless, though countryless, though moneyless, though men naked cast on the earth, we are artists.

We will offer ourselves to the people whose country we shall inhabit, and will be ruled by their laws in force for aliens, living peacefully among them and speaking their language among ourselves. So may we make for ourselves an ark for Art; and when the great nations shall have dashed themselves to pieces on the rocks they have formed around them, we will announce the new age of Spirituality and the Regeneration of the World.

Practical.—As artists, to realize our ideals we must be practical women and men, and a natural mode of life is our first step.

Before the foundation of a colony which is to be the expression of Art and Ideal Life can be laid, a triple union must be established:

I. A union among young idealists, sympathetic by nature, having studied the Art of older nations and having tried to create works as

aux choses divines ; et de cet âge dont nous ne sommes déjà plus, nous ne pouvons attendre aucun secours. Attendre que le destin nous aide, c'est risquer de ne jamais réaliser nos désirs. Certains disent qu'ils veulent mourir pour l'Art ; nous, nous voulons vivre pour lui. Séparés, nous ne pouvons rien contre le règne de l'ignorance ; dispersés, nos œuvres, placées indignement, seront détruites par les guerres et les révolutions déjà à nos portes. Unissons-nous, et retournons à cette vie naturelle qui attirait les hommes vers le sol ; le sol que nous, artistes, nous aimons ; consacrons une part de notre vie, pour l'amour de l'Art, à l'élevage de nos moutons et de nos vaches, à la pêche de nos poissons, à la plantation de notre maïs, même dans la brousse de la civilisation moderne ; consacrons ainsi notre esprit à l'Art et au plan supérieur, et, comme les autres laboureurs, donnons nos mains à la production de notre nourriture et que nos corps deviennent de plus forts et de plus beaux véhicules de nos âmes.

Nous sommes sans expérience, mais nous sommes les hommes et les femmes intelligents, peu facilement détournés, prêts à étudier les méthodes et les expérimentations les plus avancées, préparés aux échecs de la première heure. Nous ne sommes pas artistes si nous ne savons oser. Nous ferons de nos vies des œuvres d'art ; comme Hercule, nous sommes prêts à accomplir les labeurs de la vie. Quoique sans foyer, sans pays, sans fortune, quoique jetés nus sur la terre, nous sommes artistes. Nous nous offrirons au peuple du pays où nous habiterons, et nous accepterons de vivre sous les lois qui concernent les étrangers, demeurant paisiblement parmi cette nation et usant de sa langue dans notre vie sociale. Ainsi construirons-nous une arche pour l'Art : et quand les grandes nations se seront brisées contre les rochers qu'elles ont formés autour d'elles, nous annoncerons au monde le nouvel âge de Spiritualité et de Régénérescence.

Partie pratique.—Pour réaliser notre idéal d'artistes, nous devons, nous aussi, devenir des femmes et des hommes pratiques, et commencer par vivre tout à fait près de la nature.

Avant la fondation d'une colonie qui soit l'expression de l'Art et de la vie idéale, il faut qu'une triple union soit établie.

1° L'union entre les jeunes idéalistes, attirés par une sympathie réciproque, ayant étudié l'art des nations du passé, et ayant essayé,

high in inspiration and as perfect in execution and external beauty, though new in poetic form, who know that the power to realize this is a gift from their own Divine source, whose expression, Art, should be as freely re-given to the world, and not sold any more than Love and Grace can be; those, namely, who are willing to live to execute and Art for Art's sake alone, knowing that Art can never be the product of one man; renouncing egoism, expecting no other reward than the joy of realizing the highest aspiration of their soul, and to this end giving up part of their hours to labor in the fields for their food, which labor has no corruption for the spirit.

II. A union with a mild but energetic climate, having a balance of sunshine, wind, and rain.[51]

III. A union by fraternal sympathy with the people of a country already settled, having an Art future, where the soil shall favor the easy raising of food; with landscapes varied by hills, plateaus, woods, and watercourses; not too far inland.[52]

A complete natural and universal scheme by which a man can live for his ideals, free from the struggle against hunger and want, must be a reflection of the idea intended by the Eternal Mind. Such a plan assumes that he shall have enough land at his disposal to meet his simple, natural requirements, as primitive man receives it, together with the sun and the rain, from Nature,—free. To obtain such land in a country having a near Art future, that is, where there is already some enlightenment, necessitates the finding of some one sympathetic to Art, who will provide land ready and cleared for cultivation, and small, simple dwellings, consisting of a room for sleeping, a room for eating, and a studio or study; also a few sheep, cows, and horses, and some farming implements,—enough to start with.

---

[51] A study of those countries which have produced an Eternal Art, such as Egypt, India, Greece, and Italy, will show that their climates were all the same—that is, warm but energy-giving.

[52] As Art has rarely ever flourished in two countries in the same era, it is as if we must unite ourselves to the destiny of the place most worthy and favorable to Art.

quoique nouveaux dans la conception poétique, de créer des œuvres d'aussi haute inspiration et d'exécution aussi complète ; les idéalistes qui savent que la puissance d'œuvrer est un don de leur propre *source divine*, dont son expression, l'Art, doit être aussi librement redonnée au monde que ce don a été donné, et n'être pas vendue plus que l'Amour ou la Grâce ; ces idéalistes qui sont décidés à vivre dans le but exclusif d'exécuter l'Art pour l'amour de l'Art sachant aussi que l'Art ne peut être le produit d'un seul homme, n'attendant d'autre récompense que la joie de réaliser les plus hautes aspirations de leur âme, consacrant, pour ce faire, une partie de leurs heures au travail des champs afin d'assurer leur vie matérielle, ce travail n'ayant aucune corruption pour l'esprit.

2° L'union avec un climat doux, mais vivifiant, où règnent harmonieusement le soleil, le vent et la pluie.[53]

3° L'union par la sympathie fraternelle avec le peuple d'un pays déjà policé, ayant un avenir artistique, où le sol favorise la production nécessaire à la vie où se trouvent des paysages variés par des collines, des plateaux, des bois et des eaux, ni trop près, ni trop loin de la mer.[54]

Un système complet, naturel et universel par lequel on peut vivre pour cet idéal, délivré de la lutte contre le besoin, doit être un reflet de l'esprit de l'Éternel. Un tel plan implique que l'homme aura à sa disposition aussi librement que le soleil et la pluie, un terrain qui suffise à sa vie simple et naturelle, ainsi qu'il en a toujours été pour les premiers occupants d'un pays. Pour obtenir ce terrain dans un pays ayant un prochain avenir artistique, c'est-à-dire où se trouve déjà une formation, il est nécessaire de trouver une personne dévouée à l'Art qui nous fournisse les terres prêtes pour la culture, de petites demeures composées de trois petites pièces simples, pour coucher, manger et œuvrer ; des moutons, des vaches, quelques chevaux, des outils de fermiers, bref, le nécessaire pour commencer.

---

[53] En examinant les pays qui ont produit un art éternel, l'Égypte, l'Inde, la Grèce, l'Italie méridionale, on se rend compte que leur climat était presque identique et celui-là était doux et vivifiant.

[54] Comme l'Art n'a jamais fleuri dans deux pays différents à la même époque, c'est comme si nous devions nous unir à la destinée de l'endroit actuel le plus favorable à l'Art et le plus digne.

In return for his faith and sympathy, poets, writers, and musicians will dedicate their poems and compositions, and sculptors and painters give their works in trust to him, to be placed in a temple on his land, made for them, to be open at times to his countrymen. Neither he nor his heirs—against whom he should secure us regarding the land—should have any power in our government, nor right to dispose of or remove the works we commit to his charge. We and our children shall have no claim on the land or other property; we shall both be bound by the sacred bonds of Art and honor.

Coöperative System.—For every colonist to have as much time daily as possible for the work of his soul, it is imperative to cooperate to produce food with the least labor possible, the labor being divided as equally through the four seasons as may be, the various kinds of work being distributed according to physique, natural preference, experience, and capability. All idea of producing that which can be obtained cheaper outside, or requiring the learning of a trade or the use of expensive machinery, should naturally be abandoned. Our crops and supplies should be limited to our exact needs to live frugally but well. A poet, concentrated on his work for four or five hours, may find more relaxation in the heavy labor of the fields, while a sculptor would perhaps be best suited to lighter work; both would do quickest and easiest that which is most opposite to their higher work.

There are days when the healthy brain-worker, incapacitated for his work, could do the labor for another who was profiting by an hour of inspiration, or while his own crops were ripening.

As one man's abstention from his higher work is worth another's, *time* shall become the tender for the colony. Our disdain for money will be sufficient to exclude it from circulation among us. The value of any product shall be reckoned by counting the time spent in its production, and a book shall be kept in which shall be recorded in a peculiar fashion the exact time spent each day over such product, and under each head the date of commencing. A yellow circle (O), symbolizing a day's cycle, from sunrise to sunrise, might represent twenty-four hours; an arc (⌒) one hour, and a point (.) five minutes.

Pour sa foi et sa sympathie, les poètes, compositeurs de musique, lui dédieraient leurs poèmes et leurs compositions, les sculpteurs et les peintres lui offriraient leurs œuvres en hommage ; ces œuvres seraient placées dans un temple construit pour elles, sur sa terre et ouvert gracieusement de temps à autre aux visiteurs. Ni lui, ni ses héritiers, contre les prétentions possibles desquels il doit assurer ces biens, n'aura aucun pouvoir sur notre gouvernement, ni le droit de disposer de nos œuvres commises à sa charge. Nous et nos enfants n'aurons aucun droit sus les terrains et autres biens mis à notre disposition. Nous serons liés par les liens sacrés de l'Art et de l'honneur.

Système de coopération.—Pour que chaque artiste dispose quotidiennement de la plus grande somme de temps possible afin d'œuvrer selon son âme, la nécessité s'impose pour lui de *coopérer* aux indispensables travaux matériels en un nombre d'heures infime, le labeur étant réparti aussi également que possible dans les quatre saisons, les différentes sortes de travaux étant distribués selon la force physique, les préférences naturelles, l'expérience et le talent. Toute idée de produire ce qui peut être obtenu à meilleur marché au dehors, ou ce qui demande l'apprentissage d'un métier, ou ce qui nécessite l'emploi de machines coûteuses, doit être naturellement abandonnée. Nos récoltes et nos provisions seront limitées selon nos besoins exacts de vie frugale, mais réconfortante. Un poète tout à son œuvre pendant trois ou quatre heures trouvera une diversion dans le dur labeur des champs, tandis qu'un sculpteur serait peut-être mieux approprié à un travail moins pénible ; le travail que tous les deux feront aisément, facilement, sera le plus opposé à leur travail artistique.

Les jours où un cérébral sain se trouverait incapable de travailler à son œuvre, il pourrait accomplir le travail d'un autre, inspiré à cette heure ou pendant que ses propres récoltes mûriraient.

Comme l'heure qu'un homme prélève sur son travail spirituel vaut l'heure d'un autre, le temps sera considéré comme valeur type pour la colonie. Notre dédain pour l'argent exclura ce métal de notre milieu. La valeur d'un produit quelconque sera établie d'après le temps dépensé pour sa production, et ce laps de temps sera noté sur un livre d'une manière particulière, la date du commencement d'un travail étant marquée sous l'indication de ce travail. Un cercle jaune symbolisant la durée d'une journée, du soleil levant à l'aube du lendemain, pourra représenter vingt-quatre heures ; un arc, une heure ; un point, cinq

Thus, the colonist producing flour shall plant a field of wheat sufficient for one season and sowing for the next, recording the actual time spent each day on the grain, from the time of breaking the soil to the grinding and putting into sacks. The total hours, divided by the amount of flour, will give the value of flour in hours for that season.

A second book might be used to record hours of provision given and received; thus, for three hours of corn, the colonist shall receive the same number of hours of another commodity, in this way carrying on a system of exchange and cancellation. Also, when one colonist assists another, his hours shall be credited to him.

Meat, Fowls, Milk, Butter, and Eggs.—Pasturing a small flock of sheep and keeping of pigs (which may be butchered outside by a butcher for a small share in the meat), raising of fowls and eggs, care of two cows, their milking and making of butter, would give employment to one or more families.

The Raising of Vegetables, Fruit, and Grain would give employment to a second colonist. The last-named could be ground by a small wind- or water-mill.

Fishing, the Making of Wine, Cider, or Beer, and Washing (by the aid of a small machine) to another; *Cooking, Baking of Bread, Preserving of Fruits, Preparing of Wood for Fuel,* to another; *Printing of Manuscripts, Making of Colors, Repairing of Tools, Carpentering,* etc., to another.

In order to avoid the repetition of cooking and dish-washing in each household, these may be done in a special place built for the purpose, with large oven, etc., situated within easy reach of every family. A large quantity and variety of vegetables, or other simple dishes, may be prepared there, and each colonist can send in his own meat when he requires it, the person in charge attending to the cooking. Dishes may be collected and washed all together by a quick process, and be returned to their owners in a small hand-wagon.[55]

---

[55] Such ideas will be, of course, open to discussion and experiment.

minutes. Ainsi l'artiste sociétaire chargé de produire la farine, après avoir planté un champ de blé suffisant pour une saison et semé pour la saison suivante, marquera le temps dépensé chaque jour à propos de toutes ses besognes, depuis le labourage du sol jusqu'à la réduction en farine du grain et à sa mise en sac. La somme totale des heures ainsi employées divisée par la quantité de farine produite, donnera en heures la valeur de la farine pour cette saison-là.

Un deuxième livre pourrait servir à marquer les heures de provisions données et reçues ; ainsi pour trois heures de maïs, un artiste sociétaire recevrait trois heures d'un autre produit ; de cette manière s'établirait un système d'échange et d'annulation. Ainsi quand un artiste sociétaire assisterait un de ses confrères, ses heures seraient créditées à celui-ci.

Viande, volailles, lait, beurre et œufs.—L'élevage des moutons et des porcs, les uns et les autres pouvant être tués par un boucher du dehors, lequel recevrait une parte de cette viande comme rétribution, l'élevage des poules, les soins à donner aux vaches, la fabrication du beurre, pourraient occuper une ou plusieurs familles.

La culture des légumes, des fruits, des grains pourrait occuper un deuxième groupe de sociétaires. Les grains seraient moulus par un petit moulin à eau ou à vent.

La pêche, la fabrication du vin, du cidre ou de la bière, le blanchissage, à l'aide d'une petite machine, seraient le lot d'autres familles. *La cuisine, la boulangerie, la conserve des fruits, la préparation du bois à brûler,* autant d'emplois pour divers sociétaires ; *l'imprimerie des manuscrits, la fabrication des couleurs, la réparation des outils, la charpente,* etc., autant de besognes à se partager.

Afin d'éviter à chaque ménage les longueurs inévitables de la cuisine journalière, l'alimentation générale pourrait être faite sur un grand four, dans un emplacement spécial choisi au mieux de la commodité de tous. Des légumes variés et d'autres plats simples pourraient y être préparés, et chaque sociétaire pourrait à son gré envoyer son plat de viande à la personne chargée des apprêts. La vaisselle et les couverts, nettoyés en masse par un procédé simple, seraient rendus ensuite à leurs propriétaires.[56]

---

[56] Les idées sont naturellement ouvertes à la discussion et à l'expérimentation.

Clothes.—A simple, natural, practical, and ornamental dress can be adopted by the colony; practical as to washing and durability. The cutting and sewing by machines of such costumes, as well as repairing, may be undertaken by one or more colonists, who would prefer such work to outdoor labor.

We shall be within easy communication with a doctor in case of need. With the simple, ready medicines and the experience of those among us, we shall be able to provide for any accident or emergency.

Résumé.—By returning to a simple, natural life; by wisely-disposed labor, equally distributed throughout the seasons, we can easily earn our simple, natural bread. Such sustained muscular activity as is necessary for the continued equilibrium of a great ideal worker to produce works of power and intellectual brawn (which is now the common need) will be enough to earn for him this bread and his liberty. Like the birds, not laying up food in barns, he would be free to follow the flights of his soul. The man and woman who go out to the fields, after hours of concentrated brain work, will be refreshed by the change of work, rather than fatigued. Such a regime means untiring activity, and Art.

Even those whom fortune has placed beyond the necessity of earning their bread, will know a nobler manhood for so doing, and will lessen the difficulties of the others by increasing the number of workers. Everyone who makes his own life a heroism strengthens his Art. Only a vigorous life and body can know and create a vigorous, lasting Art.

Our fields will be adjoining, our houses set within them; we shall have no walls nor streets, no barriers of civilization between us. Our gatherings will be on the sward in the shade of circling trees, to sing our poems and our praise. Here we shall recount the labors of the day; we shall become as the heroes of our works.

The painter and the sculptor will have a habitation for their works in a temple of their own conception; the musician and the poet will there give their own compositions and dramas. The poet will have his works translated and printed for his brothers and for the country of his adoption. The earth will be to us a more harmonious creating-

Vêtements.—Un costume simple, naturel, pratique et décoratif pour hommes, femmes et enfants, pourrait être adopté par la Colonie ; pratique, facile à nettoyer et de longue durée.

La coupe de ces costumes et leur couture à la machine, leurs réparations, pourraient être entreprises par les personnes préférant cet ouvrage au travail en plein air.[57]

Résumé.—En revenant à la vie simple et naturelle, avec un travail organisé judicieusement, distribué également entre les saisons, nous pouvons facilement produire notre subsistance. Une telle activité physique incessante, si nécessaire au grand travailleur idéaliste pour qu'il conserve son équilibre et produise des œuvres de haute puissance intellectuelle (un des grands besoins de ce temps), suffira pour lui assurer le pain et la liberté. Comme les oiseaux, il ne réservera pas de nourriture pour l'avenir, plus libre sera-t-il ainsi de suivre les envols de son âme. Celui, homme ou femme, qui s'en ira aux champs, après des heures de concentration, sera ranimé plutôt que fatigué par ce changement de travail. Un tel régime engendre une activité que rien ne lasse et fait renaître l'art dans toute sa pureté.

Même ceux que le destin a placés hors de la nécessité de gagner leur pain connaîtront des sentiments plus humains et plus généreux en travaillant ainsi, et diminueront les difficultés des autres en augmentant le nombre des travailleurs. Tout homme qui héroïse sa propre vie rend son art plus puissant. Car, seule, l'âme héroïque dans un corps vigoureux peut sentir et créer un art vigoureux et impérissable.

Nos champs se toucheront tous, s'étendant autour de nos demeures, sans murs, sans rues ni barrières de civilisations. Nous nous assemblerons sous les ombrages des clairières pour exécuter notre musique et chanter nos poèmes. Là, nous nous conterons nos travaux esthétiques du jour, nous deviendrons comme les héros de nos œuvres.

Le peintre et le sculpteur auront un vrai sanctuaire pour leurs œuvres dans un temple conçu par eux. Le musicien et le poète y entendront leurs compositions et leurs drames. Le poète aura ses

---

[57] La colonie possédera les médicaments nécessaires pour remédier aux accidents et aux maladies les moins graves ; pour les cas difficiles, elle se mettra en rapport avec un médecin.

place, where we may unite in one voice of praise to the Supreme Creator who has chosen us as his imitators.

Abiding by the laws of the country and governed among ourselves by Art, Fraternity, and Forbearance, ever crushing down selfhood within us, we should ride over many of the complications of life and bring nearer the realization of our ideals.

As the rays of the seven colors unite and form white, so, by the exchange of ideas and an amalgamation of the fittest of passing nations, we shall bring back an Art of eternal ideas born of Divine Inspiration and clothed in forms of pure intellectual beauty and of translucent imagination.

Subject to the laws of evolution bringing the downfall of commerce, the people of our adopted country will be raised to a union with Art, thus laying the foundation of a new faith and civilization, where wisdom reigns and erects monuments of beauty, and where the artist is priest.

"If I be lifted up I will draw all men unto me".

Government.—Every artist shall have perfect liberty for his own ideas of Art, his religious belief or opinions, and in his domestic life. But as a colonist he shall be governed by *Three Primordial Ideas*, by the recognition of which any artist can claim the right to *apply* for admission to the colony. These shall be the *unchanging* rulers of the colony, *without which it does not exist.*

I. To unite to create, individually and jointly, an Art for Art's sake, which is to express the highest aspiration of his soul, renouncing all egoism and distinction.

II. To devote part of the day to manual labor, so as to become self-supporting.

III. To crush down all selfishness, jealousy, envy, malice, and discord, and to live as far as possible the noble life of an artist.

Every artist should uphold the colony flag symbolic of these three ideas, which is to plant the symbol of Art in the land. A border

œuvres traduites et imprimées pour ses frères et pour le pays de son adoption. La terre sera pour nous, créateurs passagers, un champ d'action plus harmonieux où nous unirons nos voix, confondues en une seule louange au Créateur suprême qui nous a choisis comme ses imitateurs.

Soumis aux lois du pays et gouvernés entre nous par l'Art, la fraternité et la charité, faisant taire en nous l'amour de soi-même, nous nous élèverons au-dessus des difficultés de la vie et plus près de notre idéal.

De même que les rayons de sept couleurs produisent le blanc par leur union, de même, par l'échange des idées et l'amalgame des plus dignes d'entre les nations mourantes, nous ferons revivre l'Art des idées éternelles, né de l'inspiration divine, formé de beauté intellectuelle et de pure voyance.

Assujettis aux lois d'évolution, amenant la chute du mercantilisme, les peuples de notre pays adoptif seront élevés à l'Art, posant ainsi les fondations d'une foi et d'une civilisation nouvelles où régnerait la Sagesse, édificatrice de beautés, où l'artiste serait prêtre : « Lorsque je serai élevé, j'attirerai tout à moi. »

RÈGLEMENT

Chaque artiste conservera une entière liberté quant à ses idées propres en Art, sa croyance religieuse, ses opinions et sa vie intime. Mais en tant que sociétaire, il sera gouverné par *Trois Idées Fondamentales*, au nom desquelles tout artiste a le droit de solliciter son admission dans la Colonie. Ces idées sont les lois immuables, sans elles la Colonie ne saurait exister.

I.—Renonçant à tout égoïsme, à tout dédain, s'unir pour créer individuellement et collectivement un Art pour l'amour pur de l'Art, un Art devant exprimer la plus haute aspiration de l'âme.

II.—Consacrer une partie de la journée au travail manuel afin que chacun subvienne à son entretien personnel.

III.—Refouler l'amour de soi, la jalousie, l'envie, la malice et l'esprit de discorde, et vivre autant que possible la vie digne d'un artiste.

Chaque artiste se fera gloire de défendre ces trois idées, et le symbole qu'elles représentent, véritable blason à ses yeux, sera l'expression de l'Art sur cette terre. Un ornement, d'un dessin et

of appropriate design and color, or an emblem, may be worn as a decoration on some part of the dress adopted by him.

All questions and controversies shall be considered as belonging to one of two planes, to be decided accordingly. The first shall be the highest plane and of the soul. Matters of Art, Sentiment, Charity, Support of the Sick and Infirm, Education of Children, etc., shall be settled in this plane without debate, the colonist writing his pure and unselfish opinion, free from malice, and unsigned, as an address to the *highest and most sacred idea he knows*, depositing it to be read by the others and settled by silent vote. The Three Ideas shall rule this plane. All matters concerning manual labor, economy, exchange, etc., shall be settled by discussion and vote. The First Plane shall have the rule over this.

The musician, painter, poet, or sculptor, although free to carry out his own ideals of Art, has no right to give out any work or monument outside of his own house, that is, on colony commons, without the consent of the entire colony, the refusal of one person sufficing as a veto. That which is once given for the colony cannot be removed by him, neither can it be removed against his will, unless by the desire of all the rest. All should be united in the choosing of the position occupied by any work, or in the desire for the representation of any musical composition or drama. The quarrels and disputes of inartistic men do not apply to us. Although, as artists, our differences of opinion may be strong, the purity of our motives and our unselfish love of Art will reconcile them.

d'une couleur appropriés, ou un emblème, pourra être porté comme une décoration au costume adopté par chacun.

Toutes les questions et controverses seront considérées comme appartenant à deux plans, et discutées dans cet ordre. Le premier plan sera le plus élevé et celui de l'âme. Tout ce qui dépend le plus de l'Art, du Sentiment, de la Charité, de l'Assistance aux malades et aux infirmes, de l'Education des enfants, etc., sera réglé sans débats sur ce plan, le sociétaire écrira son opinion non signée sans tenir compte de ses intérêts personnels et sans intentions comminatoires, au nom de son idéal le plus élevé et le plus sacré, et il le soumettra à la lecture de ses frères et à leur vote silencieux. *Les Trois Idées* règleront ce plan. Toutes les choses relatives au travail manuel, répartition, échange, etc., seront réglées au moyen du vote après discussion. Ce plan-ci sera réglé par le premier.

Les musiciens, les peintres, les poètes ou les sculpteurs, quoique libres d'exécuter leur propre idéal en Art, ne peuvent pas placer une œuvre ou un monument en dehors de leur propre demeure, c'est-à-dire de la Colonie, sans le consentement de tous les sociétaires, le refus d'une seule personne suffit pour que l'interdiction soit prononcée. Ce qui est une fois donné pour la communauté ne peut être repris par le donateur, ni être enlevé contre la volonté dudit, mais seulement si la collectivité le désire. Tous devront se mettre d'accord lorsqu'il s'agira de choisir un emplacement pour une œuvre, ou d'accepter l'interprétation d'une composition musicale ou dramatique. Les querelles et disputes des hommes inesthétiques ne sauraient avoir lieu chez nous. Quoique nos divergences d'opinions artistiques soient intenses, la pureté de nos objectifs et notre pur amour de l'Art les concilieront toutes.

Admission des membres.[58]—Dans le but de préserver notre haut étendard de l'Art et de l'Idéalisme, l'admission des membres est considérée comme tout à fait sacrée, elle sera décidée sur le plan de plus Haut et réglée par les Trois Idées. Chaque sociétaire, encore une fois, devra se dépouiller de ses sentiments trop personnels et rester simple, sans faiblesse, prêt à défendre et à propager l'idéal le plus

---

[58] Editor's note: this paragraph is lacking in the Boston version. An eye-skip by the translator, perhaps?

Women. —There shall be a perfect equality between women and men, and women shall have a voice in all matters (as souls; the colonists have no sex). A wife shall feel herself an independent self-supporting artist, choosing a manual occupation adapted to her physical strength, not depending on her husband; nor should he impose upon her the never-accounted-for small duties of the household. If she have full care of the children, the support of the entire family would devolve upon the husband.

Children.—Children shall be at the expense and care of their parents until such time as they shall be old enough to be responsible and do real labor for their own food and clothing, and to record hoursin so doing. As young children they may go to the fields with their parents, to help them as much as they are capable of, the parents instructing them in practical farming. As soon as they show an inclination to study or follow the calling of any colonist, that colonist shall receive them fraternally at certain times as pupils, and impart to them his knowledge of they prove themselves worthy. And so shall our children help on Art and our labors. Such children, growing up naturally, with the idea of being self-supporting and free to follow their own aspirations, would become strong, simple, Art-loving souls. Every artist knows the mistakes and sufferings of his childhood, when forced to work and learn without an ideal in view, pampered and spoiled by reliance on parents who would make of him a small copy of themselves; raised to prudence and commercial nonentity, at last breaking away to follow the promptings of his own soul, which he wished to do from the first. The first principles of mathematics could be given to the child at the school of the district. The children could, if they chose, study subjects of their own fancy from books at hand, and form their own education by their own efforts and the

sacré de l'Art, il votera solennellement et silencieusement. Dûment proposé et soutenu par deux membres qui répondront de lui, il devra prendre connaissance, avant son introduction, des principes de la communauté. Aucune admission ne pourra être prononcée sans un vote unanime.

Femmes.—Une parfaite égalité régnera entre les femmes et les hommes, et elles auront voix dans toutes les délibérations (en tant qu'âmes, les colonistes n'ont pas de sexe). L'épouse doit se sentir une artiste indépendante et capable de subvenir à ses besoins, prenant une occupation manuelle adaptée à ses forces physiques, de telle sorte qu'elle ne dépendra pas de son mari ; les petits devoirs domestiques si accaparants et dont on tient si peu compte ne lui seront point imposés. Si le soin des enfants lui incombe, le mari doit supporter la charge de la famille entière.

Enfants.—Les enfants seront à la charge de leurs parents jusqu'à l'âge où ils seront conscients et en état de travailler pour leur entretien propre et de marquer les heures ainsi passées. Pendant leur enfance, ils peuvent accompagner leurs parents aux champs, les aider dans la mesure de leurs forces naissantes, et il appartient aux parents de les former pratiquement à la vie agricole. Aussitôt qu'un enfant montre des dispositions pour suivre la vocation de quelque sociétaire, celui-ci doit le recevoir fraternellement d'une façon périodique comme disciple, et lui faire partager ses connaissances, s'il le reconnaît apte à les recevoir. Ainsi nos enfants se développent naturellement, avec l'idée d'assurer l'indépendance de leur vie et, libres de suivre leurs aspirations, deviendront des âmes fortes, simples et aimant l'Art.[59] Les premiers principes de mathématiques peuvent être donnés aux enfants à l'école du district. Ils pourraient, à leur gré, étudier des matières de leur choix, avec l'aide de leurs éducateurs et faire leur éducation par leurs efforts personnels, libres de quitter la Colonie

[59] Chaque artiste se souvenant des erreurs et des douleurs de son enfance, lorsqu'il était forcé de travailler et d'apprendre sans idéal en vue, gâté et corrompu par la direction passive et molle imprimée par les parents, toujours désireux de faire une petite copie d'eux-mêmes ; élevé dans un sentiment de prudence exagéré et ridicule, et dans la crainte et le dédain de toute activité personnelle, et enfin obligé à recommencer sa vie pour suivre les impulsions premières de son âme.

aid of their masters, being free to go from the colony and seek other experiences if they choose. If they do not desire to become artists, as mere bread-laborers they shall have no right to occupy colony houses, but shall belong to the household of their parents until they are old enough to go elsewhere. They shall have no claim by right of birth to the house and land occupied by their parents, nor to their works of Art, except what may be their parents' private work, wealth, and possessions, which do not concern the colony in any way.

Servants. —Such colonists as have private means are free to hire servants for their household or to care for their children, but never to supplant them in their work in the fields; and no houses shall be built for such or other outsiders.

Models and workmen for sculptors and painters shall be at the latter's private expense.

Every colonist or family shall have a house alone, if he or they so desire; the Art Befriender would only be expected to supply a simple dwelling. All other accommodation, for servants, etc., as well as their keep, shall be at the private expense of the colonist. The idea is to maintain small farms which shall form altogether one large one, for those who have done with the luxury of civilization.

Fund. —It will perhaps be necessary for each to raise a trifle more than enough for actual consumption, against old age, sickness, losses, charities, repairs, and outside-colony expenses. All such surplus shall be deposited by each colonist; and if it be found that anyone has contributed more than his share it shall be returned to him in hours.

All surplus of perishable produce, such as eggs, vegetables, etc., may be taken to the nearest town and sold at the prevailing prices; and such necessaries as oil, sugar, medicines, tea, and coffee can be bought with the money and retailed to the others at cost in hours.

et de continuer ailleurs leurs expériences. Ceux qui ne désireraient pas devenir artistes n'auront pas le droit d'occuper les demeures de la Colonie, en tant que simples travailleurs, mais ils appartiendront à la maison de leurs parents jusqu'à ce qu'ils aient l'âge d'aller ailleurs. Ils n'auront aucun droit sur la demeure et la terre de leurs parents, ni sur les œuvres d'art de ceux-ci ; leurs droits seront restreints aux objets qui sont la propriété des parents, person-nellement, et qui ne concernent en rien la communauté.

Serviteurs.—Les sociétaires en état d'avoir des serviteurs sont libres de les conserver pour l'entretien de leurs demeures et les soins à donner aux enfants, ils ne pourront jamais se faire remplacer par eux dans les travaux matériels, et il ne sera pas fait d'habitation spéciale pour les serviteurs, ni pour aucune personne du dehors.

Les modèles et les ouvriers seront à la charge des sculpteurs et des peintres qui les emploieront.

Chaque sociétaire ou chaque famille pourra jouir d'une demeure particulière ; mais on n'attend pas du donateur ami de l'Art autre chose que de simples demeures. Tout ce qui concerne les serviteurs, entretien, etc., sera aux frais personnels du sociétaire qui les aura à son service. Le projet des fondateurs est de réunir des métairies pour composer une grande ferme et cette ferme attend ceux qui en ont fini avec le luxe des civilisations.

Fonds de réserve.—Il sera nécessaire de produire un peu plus que ne l'exigerait notre consommation actuelle, afin de soutenir la vieillesse, de soigner les malades, de remplir les devoirs de charité, de faire face aux dépenses exigées par les dommages, les réparations nécessaires et les achats inévitables au dehors de la Colonie.

Tout surcroît de production sera déposé par les sociétaires ; et s'il se trouve que quelqu'un ait produit au-delà de sa tâche ordinaire, on lui en tiendra compte au moyen d'un équivalent basé sur le système des heures expliqué plus haut. Tout surcroît de produits périssables, œufs, légumes, etc., peut être porté au marché le plus proche et vendu au prix courant ; l'argent de cette vente sera affecté à l'acquisition de ce que la Colonie ne pourrait produire, comme le pétrole, le thé, le café, les médicaments, etc., et ces matières seront livrées en détail aux sociétaires pour une somme d'heures équivalente à leur valeur.

Painters and sculptors requiring material other than that which can be produced in the colony, if they have no private means, will be obliged to raise extra produce to procure the same. An artist shall expect no pecuniary help from the colony in the execution of his works, unless it be the united wish of the colony.

Amendments.—Only a unanimous vote can make amendments to existing laws (excepting the Three Ideas) or make new ones.

NOTE BY THE EDITOR OF THE ARENA.

The foregoing "Appeal" was sent to us from Paris accompanied by a letter, from which the following is an extract:

PARIS, 14 November, 1896.

TO THE EDITOR OF THE ARENA:

DEAR SIR,—I have the honor to represent a body of artists sending you the manuscript composed by them, which they feel you will be pleased to publish for them in your review, believing the latter to be the most sympathetic to such an ideal movement, and that among your readers in America they will awaken the most interest.

J. M. Durand
203 *Boulevard Raspail, Paris.*

A more recent letter states that the Society is now organized, and that it includes one practical farmer among its members. Any person desiring to receive more particular information of this Artists' Colony, with the idea of cooperating with its members, will be put in communication with them or their correspondent for America on sending his letter to the care of the Editor of THE ARENA. The progress of this remarkable socialistic experiment will doubtless be watched with sympathetic interest by the whole civilized world.

S'il arrive que les peintres et les sculpteurs aient besoin d'un matériel que la Colonie ne puisse produire, ils se le procureront, à défaut de moyens personnels, par un surcroît de travail. Un artiste ne doit attendre aucune aide pécuniaire de la communauté pour l'exécution de ses œuvres, à oins que tous les sociétaires n'en manifestent le désir.

Amendements.—Il n'y a qu'un vote unanime qui puisse apporter des amendements à ce règlement (exception faite des Trois Idées reconnues immuables) ou des additions nouvelles.

Un petit groupe international d'artistes est déjà formé et s'est efforcé de se procurer le terrain nécessaire au développement de la colonie.

***

Tout artiste désireux de collaborer à ce projet devra écrire, pour supplément d'informations, au secrétaire de l'œuvre aux soins du Directeur de la Plume, 31, rue Bonaparte, Paris.

http://dx.doi.org/10.11647/OBP.0081.13

Three Letters from Yeats to the Anarchist, Augustin Hamon[1]

Deirdre Toomey

ON ABOUT 9 February 1899 Yeats wrote to Synge from his hotel in the Boulevard Raspail to admit that he had forgotten both the name and the address of the man at whose house he was to speak that night (*CL2* 358). This vagueness is not uncharacteristic.

By a Venn diagram of those who knew both Yeats and Synge in Paris, the editors of that volume fixed on Augustin Frederic Adolphe Hamon (1862–1945) a well-known Anarchist and editor of the anarchist journal *l'Humanité nouvelle: Revue internationale*, which he had founded in 1897. A translation of 'The Man Who Dreamed of Fairyland' had appeared there in September 1899 (the translation was probably by Hamon but no translator's name is given). Hamon later, with his wife Henriette, became Shaw's official translator, despite, according to Miron Grindea, being not at all confident of his English; however, Shaw overruled Hamon's protests saying, 'the dramatic liveliness of the reports you gave of some the Socialist Congresses

---

[1] Further information may have been gathered since this article was prepared for publication. If you would like to find out if any further information has been discovered that may help your own research, why not write to the author at yeatsresearch@sas.ac.uk? Quite apart from anything else, feedback is always welcomed.

[1897] had satisfied me... I saw in you the man to undertake the French version of my plays' ('G.B.S. and France' [*Adam International: London*, July 1956] p. 2). Further, the Flemish writer Robert de Smet insisted that Hamon could not even ask for directions in the street in English ('G.B.S and France', p. 3). Indeed, in the letters which follow it is evident that Hamon relied on Jerrold's help with Yeats's letters. Hamon, was a passionate defender of Shaw in the French press and Shaw had chosen Hamon and his wife Henriette partly because of their political position Hamon. Hamon had been part of the large exodus of French and Belgian anarchists who moved to England after 1894 when extremely hostile legislation against those who were believed to have Anarchist connections 'les lois scélérates' had been passed in France after the assassination of the President of France, by an Italian anarchist in 1894. Hamon's interest in Yeats is more of an enigma, although Anarchists and other radicals had been interested in Irish Nationalism, particularly in its physical force side for some time and Hamon would have been told by Synge of Yeats's part in the 1898 celebrations and of his membership of the IRB. In *John Millington Synge and the Irish* Theatre, Synge's friend Maurice Bourgeois recalled that Synge 'sometimes mentioned... M. Augustin Hamon' (London: Constable, 1913) p. 46. Whether Synge knew of Yeats's move to the pro-Dynamiting INA in 1895 is unknown, but this would have been of great interest to Anarchists. Synge probably met Hamon at a café, possibly the Café Harcourt, much frequented by expatriate Irish. Hamon also regularly attended Maud Gonne's Paris *salons*.

Yeats was very interested in the concept of 'spiritual anarchy', as exemplified in *Where there is Nothing*' (1902).[2] By contrast, Hamon

---

[2]   *VPl* 933. On that theme in Yeats's work from the three early stories intended as a concluding triptych for *The Secret Rose* ('Rosa Alchemica', The Tables of the Law, and 'The Adoration of the Magi') through such plays as 'Where there is Nothing' and 'The Unicorn from the Stars', see 'Yeats: A Noble Antinomianism', Chapter 9 of Warwick Gould and Marjorie Reeves, *Joachim of Fiore and the Myth of the*

was a very practical anarchist, concerned with workers' rights and Trade Unionism. He eventually became a socialist.

In 1899–1900, Hamon evidently sought some contribution to his journal from Yeats, and the following correspondence traces the background to Yeats's eventual appearances in *l'Humanité nouvelle.*

The Yeats/Hamon file emerged as a result of the diligence of Ron Heisler, a scholar and a renowned collector of Socialist pamphlets, in the archives of the International Institute of Social History, Amsterdam. The Institute holds 181 cases of Hamon's wide-ranging correspondence. Undated letters to Hamon were carefully dated by receipt, in accord with the well-known Anarchist slogan 'Anarchy is Order'. Thus, our editorial decision to propose Augustin Hamon's house as the forgotten venue for his speech in February 1899 for volume II (1997) of the *Collected Letters* has at last been justified by the discovery of these three letters in Hamon's archive. I have chosen to offer both sides of the correspondence, because of the involvement—on Hamon's side—of an unusual middleman, Laurence Jerrold (1873–1918) who was the Conservative *Daily Telegraph*'s Paris correspondent. He had also published a signed translation, 'Innisfree', in *Le magazine internationale*, 6, May 1896.[3] The issue is lost, and so the translation cannot be checked against 'l'Ile d'Innisfree', one of Yeats's 'Poèmes', in the December, 1899 number of to l'*Humanite Nouvelle* (the others were 'La Rose du Monde', 'Chanson' ('Impetuous Heart, be still') and 'Le Vent' ('The wind blows over the gates of the day' [*sic, cf., VPl* 210]). Jerrold also contributed a brief account of *Beltaine* as 'le Theatre littéraire' to *l'Humanite Nouvelle* in July 1899, and the journal also published 'l'homme qui connuit en songe le pays des fees' in its September,

---

Eternal Evangel in the Nineteenth and Twentieth Centuries (Oxford: Clarendon, 2001, revised and enlarged edition), 221–98 (pp. 273ff).

[3] I am grateful for the assistance of Yeats's bibliographer, Dr Colin Smythe, as to the particular issue, which had eluded Wade, cf. *Wade*, 433. Were it to surface for comparison with the 1899 version, and the versions to prove non-identical, it might merely be the case that Jerrold had chosen to revise the earlier version.

1899 number (*Wade*, p. 433). None of these translations was signed, but it is clear that Jerrold, if less prolific that (say) Henry-D. Davray among Yeats's early French enthusiasts, is likely to have translated the poems sent at Hamon's invitation as editor. What is certain, however, in the correspondence between Yeats and Hamon (who had difficulties in understanding either or both the English language and Yeats's hand), is that Jerrold plays a decisive rôle, as will be seen in the transcriptions below. Hamon kept up his Irish links and lectured to Irish Literary Society on 23rd November 1915, presumably on Shaw on whom he had written a monograph *George Bernard Shaw: The Moliere of the Twentieth Century* (London: George Allen and Unwin, 1915.)

Yeats's first letter was written from Woburn Buildings Euston Road is of March 1899 and is undated except by 'Saturday'. A recipient—Hamon or perhaps Laurence Jerrold—dates its receipt 5/3/99.

à rendre
[blue pencil, unknown hand, across top left corner]

18 Woburn Buildings
Euston Road.

Saturday ['5/3/99' added in blue pencil, unknown hand]

My dear Monsieur <deleted letter> Hamon:
I will send you copies of the poems you so kindly asked for in a few days. I have hitherto been unable to do so & am still unable, as my only copies are now with the printer who is printing a new edition.
Yours sinly
W B Yeats.

Yeats's text is in black ink on a bifolium, on the inner recto of which, in purple ink, appear a note from Jerrold to Hamon on the matter of the translations. Yeats's second letter follows this fragment, on letterhead paper.

21 mai 99
[Blue pencil, unknown hand]

à retourner | avec traduction | je ne peux pas lire

Nassau Hotel,
Dublin.
[printed rubric letterhead]

March

M y Dear Monsieur Hamon: I <enclose> send some poems at last. I have
procrastinated from day to day. At first I had no copy of my book & then
I <ha> was absorbed in the preparation for the performance of my play
'The Countess Cathleen'. The play is to be produced tonight & there is
likely to be a riot as the ultramontane organ has denounced me for heresy &
blasphemy.⁴ < illegible deletion, *c.*6 words >

Yr sinly
W B Yeats

Please turn over

[on verso]

I left this unposted amid the <illeg> bother of The Irish Literary Theatre!
My 'The Countess Cathleen' a play in verse has had a great triumph in
Dublin. I <enclose> send some papers which may interest you.⁵

---

⁴ Frank Hugh O'Donnell, a political enemy, had denounced the play in the *Freeman's
Journal* on 1 April 1899 and a further attack was rejected by the journal. Nothing
daunted, O'Donnell wrote a savage pamphlet attacking the play *Souls for Gold! A
Pseudo-Celtic Drama in Dublin*, widely distributed in Dublin. As a consequence, the
Daily Nation published an aggressive leader endorsing theological objections to the
play on 6 May. 'Ultramontane' in this context refers to those Catholics who defer to
the supreme authority of the Pope. It was commonly used in Ireland to refer to the
more rigid forms of Catholicism. See *CL2* 407ff. and Appendix, 669–80.
⁵ There were some disturbances during the performance mainly from students
from the Royal University (later University College, Dublin) this culminated in
a letter deploring the irreligious aspects of the play. James Joyce refused to sign
this letter. Yeats thought that this response indicated that the new Irish Literary
Theatre was a powerful force in Ireland. It is possible that he wrote this letter

A page follows, in which Jerrold has translated this letter into French, presumably for Hamon. Yeats's third letter succeeds it.

Woburn Buildings
Euston Road.

Yeats [pencil, unknown hand]
7 Juin 1900
[blue pencil, unknown hand]

Thursday.

My dear Monsieur Hamon: I have made a search & I find that I have not a single photograph of myself left. They are all rather bad & I am not sorry to have seen the last of them. There is a good portrait—not a photograph—at the beginning of the edition of my collected poems published by Fisher Unwin in 1899; & henceforth I am inclined to be known by that.[6]
I am very sorry not to be able to comply with your request.
I am yours very sincerely
WB Yeats

It is not known why Hamon had sought a photograph of Yeats: *l'Humanité Nouvelle* did not normally reproduce photographs. By 1899 Yeats had had few sittings for studio portrait photographs. The M. Glover portrait of 1889 or before, and the Frederick Hollyer photograph of 1893 or before, were well out of date.[7] O'Donnell dates the Elliot & Fry (Dublin) photograph to *c*.1899: it may be the one against which WBY had taken a decided view. Yeats's very favourable judgement of the 'highly emblematic portrait photograph taken by Chancellor of Dublin in November 1902 (see *YA3* plate 6) might be thought to reflect some relief at such a suitable replacement image—

shortly after 8 May 1898 and delayed posting for a while as he collected reviews from the Dublin papers as Hamon did not receive it till 21 May.
[6]   The frontispiece for *Poems* is by his father and is dated by John Butler Yeats 1899 (Plate 43).
[7]   The *American Monthly Review of Reviews* was to use the Hollyer image as late as December 1901. See William H. O'Donnell's revised checklist of studio portrait photographs, *YA8* 196ff., and also see *L*, facing p. 146.

he delightedly announced that it was "'the first good photograph" of him and was "really very good"'.[8] Although the Chancellor photograph gives prominence to WBY's emblematic floppy tie and his lock of hair, it is very clear that Yeats routinely preferred portrait drawings or paintings to photographs as his self-image (Plate 44).[9]

Plate 43. John Butler Yeats's frontispiece portrait of W. B. Yeats, in *Poems* (2nd ed., London: T. Fisher Unwin, 1899). Private collection, London.

Plate 44. The Elliott & Fry image of W. B. Yeats, said to be of 1899. Private collection, London.

8   O'Donnell, 'Portraits of W. B. Yeats: This Picture in the Mind's Eye', *YA3* 81–103 at p. 87.
9   See the *CL InteLex* correspondence over the selection of self-images for *CWVP* (1908), as well as O'Donnell, *ibid.*, 87.

http://dx.doi.org/10.11647/OBP.0081.14

Ghost-writing for Sara Allgood

John Kelly

GHOST-WRITING FOR SARA ALLGOOD[1] was a task which intrigued
and frustrated Yeats in almost equal measure (as, indeed, she herself

[1] Sarah (Sara) Ellen Allgood (1880-1950), the leading Abbey actress had,
appropriately, been born at 45 Mid-Abbey Street on 29 Nov 1880 (not 1883
as she later claimed). After attending Marlborough Street Training College,
Dublin, she worked as an upholsterer and French polisher, but began acting
with Maud Gonne's nationalist society, 'Daughters of Erin', and through them
became associated with the Fays. She joined of the Irish National Theatre Society
in 1903, appearing in Yeats's *The King's Threshold* in October of that year, and
acting regularly with the Company thereafter. After the resignation of Maire nic
Shiubhlaigh from the Society early in 1906, she assumed the place of leading lady
and stayed on until 1913, playing major female roles. From 1913 she began to
freelance on the English stage, appearing with the Liverpool Repertory Theatre,
and also at Annie Horniman's Gaiety Theatre in Manchester, although she
returned to the Abbey on short-term contracts until July 1915, when she landed
the title role in J. Hartley Manners' *Peg o' My Heart*, which was being toured by
the Alfred Butt Company. In 1916 she went with the play to Australia and New
Zealand, where she married her leading man, Gerald Henson. A daughter, born
in January 1918, survived only for an hour, and in November of that year her
husband died in Wellington, New Zealand, in the great influenza epidemic. She
returned to Europe in May 1920 and on 21 June arrived in Dublin, where she
appeared in several plays at the Abbey over that summer. In September 1920 she
opened in Lennox Robinson's *The Whiteheaded Boy* which enjoyed a long run at
the Ambassador's Theatre, London, and on tour, and in December 1921 began
a season with 'The Irish Players' at the Everyman Theatre, London. In August
1923 she returned to the Abbey, playing numerous parts, including on 2 March

often did). Maire nic Shiubhlaigh's resignation from the Abbey
Theatre Company in early January 1906 left the stage literally clear
for Allgood to assume the role of undisputed Irish diva, and she
enjoyed a commanding and growing reputation as an actress, not
only in Dublin but also more widely in Ireland and Britain, and
particularly in Belfast, London, Oxford, and Manchester. With her
increasing fame came requests for interviews, articles, and lectures.
Although a compelling presence when playing a role on the stage, she
was more diffident about writing and lecturing on her own account,
essentially because of insecurities about her education, which had
consisted of only a few years at a national school before the death
of her father obliged her to take up a job as upholsterer and French
polisher. Given this vulnerability, she turned to Yeats for help in
fulfilling journalistic or public-speaking assignments, with the result
that what appeared under her name sometimes owed a significant
amount to his composition. This is particularly evident in two cases:
'An Autobiographical Sketch' she contributed to the *Weekly Freeman*
on 20 March 1909, and, even more so, in a talk he wrote for her to
deliver to the Manchester Playgoers' Club in April 1910 (which is so
clearly his composition that it has bibliographical claims to be listed
as one of his works).

   Both commissions gave him more trouble than he had anticipated,
and the contribution to the newspaper also caused him intense
irritation, as he revealed to Lady Gregory in a letter written on the
day of its publication:

I had not told you that I wrote (this is private) Miss Allgood article in its
first form. That is to say I questioned her & got her to talk & made rather a

---

1924 what was to become her favourite role, Juno Boyle in O'Casey's *Juno and
the Paycock*. She had made a film while touring Australia in 1918, and in 1929
appeared as Mrs White, the heroine's mother, in Alfred Hitchcock's *Blackmail*,
the first British talkie. A year later Hitchcock cast her as Juno in the film version
of *Juno and the Paycock*. She moved to Hollywood in 1940, where she was cast
as Beth Morgan (this time the hero's mother) by John Ford in the 1941 Oscar-
winning *How Green Was My Valley*. She was subsequently offered a long-term
contract with 20th Century-Fox, which made her comfortably off but which
reduced her parts to a series of stereotyped Irish mothers and servants. Her final
screen appearance was as Mrs Monahan, a small role, in Fox's *Cheaper by the
Dozen* in 1950. She became an American citizen in 1945.

charming peace [*for* piece] of girlish self revelation. It needed some skill as she had to talk of herself without egotism. Well when I got it in 'the Weekly Freeman' at Limerick I found a most unwise long egotistical passage (it begins when she speaks of Synge) which was not only bad in itself but spoilt all my part by turning what had been boyant natural chatter into egotism by the light it threw on it. I find this was Henderson.[2] He has made her quote the 'Manchester Guardian' compliments about herself, quote Poels letter, quote & magnify out of all recognition a conversation (which was of course private) at Mrs Campbells supper in London & of which she had given me a rather different account. What was hardly more than vague compliment emerges as a definite offer of £100 a week from a Music Hall. I told him that it was like an interview with a second rate American actress. If it were in any paper more important than the Weekly Freeman it could do Miss Allgood a good deal of harm. He makes her tell how she did not want to act at the Playboy's last night because of the police. I am fealing thoroughly exasperated. This last thing about the police makes an earlier sentence of mine in which I made her sigh for a part that would enable her to look 'young & bea[u]tiful' look like an indirect attack on us. It is no use trying to explain things to Henderson. One might talk till midnight & he would not understand.[3]

Lady Gregory entirely sympathised with his vexation, replying on 21 March 1909 that she had

looked at Weekly Freeman & with real disgust—the change of style wd. have been evident even if you had not written. One looks across from a simple & charming sentence to the next column 'moved by the vehemence of my attack' etc—It is not Henderson I rage at, for we knew all along he was the froth & foam of the worst Dublin vulgarity… but that Miss Allgood should take him as an equal guide with you on a literary question, & fall so low, makes me despair of ever getting any understanding into those we are working with…. I wish above all that you had not to spend so much of yourself on them all.[4]

---

[2] William Alexander Henderson (1863-1927) had been secretary and business manager of the Abbey Theatre 1906-7, and was a staunch supporter of Sara Allgood. Despite the reservations of Lady Gregory (1852-1932) and Annie Horniman (1860–1937), respectively a director and the proprietor of the Abbey, he was reappointed secretary of the Theatre in February 1908, largely at Sara Allgood's urging.

[3] *CL InteLex* 1113.

[4] Berg.

W. A. Henderson, the unmarried Secretary of the Abbey, was clearly sweet on Allgood and his affection had not only begun to cost him the goodwill of the Directors, but in early 1911 was to cost him his job, when, contrary to strict instructions, he let her borrow a copy of her contract to strengthen her position in a dispute over pay and she refused to return it. In Part 1 below, I offer the piece from the *Weekly Freeman* on 20 March 1909.

1: THE WEEKLY FREEMAN

A GREAT IRISH ACTRESS OF TO-DAY.
THE NATIONAL THEATRE.
An Autobiographical Sketch
By Miss Sara Allgood

The editor of the Weekly Freeman[5] has asked me to contribute to his St Patrick's Day Number something about my associations with our National Theatre, and I do so with pleasure, trusting that my narrative will interest many in our work.

To commence at the beginning, there is a little hall in Camden street—for, I suppose, it is still there—it is at the back of a shop, and one goes into it by a door between two shops.[6] When I knew it, in the spring of 1903,

---

[5] The current editor of the *Weekly Freeman* was Matthew Michael O'Hara (1873–1927). As a former drama critic on the daily *Freeman's Journal* he retained his interest in the theatre. In January 1907 he had written an inflammatory anonymous review of *The Playboy of the Western World* which helped to stoke public outrage at the play.

[6] The then 'National Dramatic Society' had moved into the Camden Street Hall on 8 August 1902, and the following day the members appointed a committee with officers: Yeats as President, with AE (George Russell), Maud Gonne, and Douglas Hyde as Vice-Presidents. William Fay wrote to Yeats on 12 August 1902 (NLI): 'It is not large and would perhaps seat 200.... The hall is in Camden Street close to Harrington Street, and is no. 34. The trams pass the door, but it is so far from the street that there is no annoyance from tram bells. The stage is as deep as Clarendon Street [location of St Teresa's Temperance Hall, a former venue of the Fays' Company] but not so wide and we will have to resort to the simplest of scenery so as to have room to dress and store props during the shows'. The hall was rented for 12 months and the company moved in on 8 August, but only used it for one set of performances, from 4 to 6 December 1902, although it continued to serve for rehearsals and storage. The stage was less than six feet deep and, since there were no dressing-rooms, actors had to change costume

one had sometimes to push aside a tub of butter or a box of eggs before one could pass the threshold. It was here that I first met the group of players and playwrights whose work led to the foundation of the Abbey Theatre. I remember that the hall was very cold and very small; if full to the door, I doubt if it would have held more than forty people. The roof was leaky, for it was a wet night, and I had to move from the place where I was standing, because drops of rain fell upon me and made a puddle at my feet. When I joined the company,[7] the Hall was only used for purposes of rehearsal, but I hear from others that there were no dressing rooms, and that the company had to dress behind screens which were put on the stage for the purpose. The Hall had been a dream, and after one or two performances an impossible dream. I had known Mr. W. G. Fay when he and his brother played farces at the Coffee Palace,[8] though I had never played for him, and it was he who brought me to Camden street, and gave me a part in a revival of Lady Gregory's first play 'Twenty-five' and in the first performance of Mr. Yeats' 'King's Threshold'. A little before this I had seen the company setting out on their first London visit,[9] and felt

at the side of the stage. The auditorium, described by W. A. Henderson as 'a draughty ill-lighted hall and without fire', was approached down a long dark passage. From March 1903 until the opening of the Abbey Theatre in late 1904 the Company performed in the more satisfactory and commodious Molesworth Hall. For more detail and drawings, see Christopher Murray, 'Three Sketches by Jack B. Yeats of the Camden Street Theatre, 1902', *YA3* 125–32 and Plates 10, 11 a and b.

[7] Sara Allgood joined Maud Gonne's nationalist women's society Inghinidhe na hEirean (Daughters of Erin), and became a member of the dramatic class. Under its auspices she took the part of Lady Selina O'Brien in *The Harp That Once* by Alice Milligan, produced by William and Frank Fay on behalf of the Society at the Antient Concert Rooms on 26 August 1901. She gave a number of songs and recitations at coffee-houses and modest venues in Dublin through 1901 and 1902, and early in 1903, hearing that an 'Irish National Dramatic Society' had been formed, she approached Frank Fay about joining. With his encouragement, she began attending rehearsals in the Camden Street Hall, while he also gave her private tuition in acting and elocution. She made her first appearance for the Irish National Theatre Society, as it was now known, in March 1903.

[8] During the 1890s the Fays' amateur companies performed a variety of comedies, screaming farces, and melodramas in various venues throughout Dublin, but from January 1897 they began to stage their productions regularly but not exclusively in the Lecture Hall of the Coffee Palace Temperance Hotel in Townsend Street, sometimes as the 'Ormonde Drama Company' and sometimes as a 'Comedy Combination'.

[9] In Lady Gregory's *Twenty-Five*, first produced at the Molesworth Hall on 14 March 1903 and revived there from 14 to 16 January 1904, an emigrant returns to marry his sweetheart but, discovering that she is now the wife of an impoverished

Very Sorrowful at being Left Behind,

but when somebody at the end of 'Twenty-five' handed me a basket of flowers I felt that all my ambition had been satisfied. What more could one ask from life? My admirer was very kind, for the part was very small. After that I played one or two small parts in new plays—'Brigid' in Mr. Colum's 'Broken Soil', Kathleen in 'Riders to the Sea', and the mother, Mrs. Gillane, in 'Kathleen ni Houlihan'.[10]

It was in Lady Gregory's play, 'Spreading the News', that I achieved my first success. This play was first produced in December, 1904, at the opening of the Abbey Theatre. While the rehearsals were going on, the Mechanics' Institute was being turned into the Abbey Theatre, very timidly, for I thought that something would happen, but what, I did not know if I were found there, I went down day after day to see if the work went rapidly. I made excuses to get away from my place of business[11] for ten minutes or for half an hour. I pretended that I had some important message to deliver,

---

farmer, deliberately loses to him at cards to save his farm. Sara Allgood's first speaking part was as Princess Buan in Yeats's *The King's Threshold* on 8 October 1903. The Company's first visit to London took place on 2 May 1903 when they played well received matinee and evening programmes at the Queen's Gate Hall in South Kensington. Although disappointed to miss this, Sara Allgood was part of the no less successful second London engagement at the Royalty Theatre on 26 March 1904.

[10] Sara Allgood played Brighid MacConnell in Padraic Colum's *Broken Soil*, produced at the Molesworth Hall on 3 December 1903 and later rewritten as *The Fiddler's House*, and Cathleen, one of the daughters in J. M. Synge's *Riders to the Sea*, produced at Molesworth Hall on 25 February 1904. She took over the part of the mother, Bridget Gillane, in *Cathleen ni Houlihan*, when the play was revived as part of the opening programme of the new Abbey Theatre from 27 December 1904 to 3 January 1905.

[11] Sara Allgood was apprenticed as a French polisher and upholsterer to Messrs. P. J. Walsh & Sons, who sold high quality antique and modern furniture from their warerooms at 19 and 20 Bachelor's Walk, Dublin, and who also operated as cabinet-makers, upholsterers, valuers, house agents, and auctioneers. In her unpublished 'Memories' (Berg) she described the firm, which ceased trading in 1922, as 'a wonderful antique shop' which 'stood for everything that was of the best'. The architect and diarist Joseph Holloway (1861-1944) had sketched out a rough plan of the new Theatre by 15 April 1904 and work on converting the Mechanics Institute and adjoining premises began soon thereafter. Reconstruction continued through the summer and autumn, and the first rehearsals, which Sara Allgood attended, were held in the still far from finished building on 31 October 1904. The site of the Abbey was a few minutes' walk from Bachelor's Walk on the Dublin Quays.

but it was only to see if the Abbey stage was beginning to show itself in its new shape among the scaffolding and broken masonry.

At last the Theatre was ready, and we had our final rehearsals in it a few days before the opening of the Theatre. Till the performance and the applause I had no[12] idea that I had got anything, but a little part like those I had played before. I am afraid if I had dared I would have asked for the part of the deaf applewoman, because she is on the stage all the time. How finely W. G. Fay played that night. Frank Fay was not, I think, as fine in 'Baile's Strand' that night as he was a few months before in Mr. Yeats' 'King's Threshold'.[13] He was our elocution teacher and voice producer, and if my voice is expressive I attribute all to his teaching.[14] After that there

---

[12] The *Weekly Freeman* reads 'not'.

[13] As well as playing Bridget Gillane in *Cathleen ni Houlihan* in the opening programme of the Abbey Theatre, Sara Allgood also took the part Mary Fallon, the long-suffering wife of the lugubrious supposed murderer Bartley Fallon (played by William Fay), in the first production of Lady Gregory's one-act comedy *Spreading the News*. She made an immediate hit, the *United Irishman* of 31 Dec 1904 claiming (1) that that the 'chief credit of the success of the piece' was due to her, while John Masefield in the *Manchester Guardian* of 2 January 1905 (3) reported that 'her acting of an indignant countrywoman was excellent. She has a great fund of spontaneous humour, and when allied with so genuine a humourist as Mr. W. G. Fay she carries all before her'. Although Mrs Tarpey, who keeps an apple stall, is on stage throughout the play, and although her deafness is a source of the misunderstandings which constitute the plot, her part, being more choric and passive, does not offer the acting possibilities provided by Mrs Fallon. Most of the critics were respectful of Frank Fay's performance as Cuchulain in *On Baile's Strand*, and the only paper to share Sara Allgood's reservations was the *United Irishman* of 31 December 1904 which accused him (1) of 'a considerable amount of melodramatic acting', and alleged that 'neither in physique nor in his conception of Cuchullain's character did he show any relation to the heroic'. Frank Fay had taken the part of Seanchan, the hero and bard, in the first production of *The King's Threshold* on 8 October 1903, and was such a success that Yeats dedicated the play to the 'memory of Frank Fay and his beautiful speaking in the character of Seanchan'. His latest performances of the role had been at the Royalty Theatre, London, on 26 March 1904 and at a private staging in the Molesworth Hall on 26 April.

[14] In her 'Memories' Sara Allgood recalled that 'Frank Fay would be about twenty-five years old, when I first met him, I was almost fifteen. He was a short, ruddy-faced young man, very peppery and quick-tempered, but with a wonderful love and appreciation of the theatre. When he took notice of me and asked me to study elocution and learn everything connected with the stage, I was delighted. I used to go up to the Hall in Camden Street every Saturday—after I had finished my work in the shop, clutching my few shillings (wages) in my little hand—and with him I would work on my breathing; my Ah's and Oh's; my poetry reading; deportment; principles of voice production; the secret of articulation; how to

were disputes. What were they all about? They were very intricate, and a year ago I remember seeing at the Abbey a girl from the University of Chicago; she had a note book and pencil, and was asking questions of every one she met. She had chosen the Irish Dramatic movement as a Thesis for her University degree, and she was deeply interested in that split. When her Thesis is published we will all understand why we quarrelled.[15] Some were

pitch the voice. Then he would make me walk across and up stage, with books balanced on my head for poise; how to make an entrance; how to sit, and so on. He would get so intent on his teaching that time would be completely forgotten. I would work there all during the afternoon, for about five hours, without a stop. Then I would walk home, right across the city—about two and one-half to three miles—put on the kettle and drink countless cups of tea to get rid of my thirst as well as my tiredness'. She goes on to reveal that Fay later proposed to her, and, when she refused, 'wrote me back, saying he would wait, because he would rather have 'Hell with you that Heaven without you'. Elsewhere in 'Memories' she described 'him once keeping me on a poem for three months to get the right intonation on the word 'strange'... the same thing with a poem of W. B. Yeats. I had to say, 'It had become a glimmering girl', and I had to make my audience see a 'glimmering girl' by the tone of my voice'.

[15] The graduate student from the University of Chicago is unidentified and may be a device to deflect a fuller treatment of the theatrical quarrels of 1905–6. Certainly Sara Allgood is being faux naïve (or Yeats excessively diplomatic) in pretending to know little of them, since she was implicated, not least because of her rivalry with Maire nic Shiubhlaigh. To make possible the payment of certain members of the Company, the constitution of the Irish National Theatre Society was radically rewritten in the autumn of 1905, transforming it from a cooperative to a limited liability company. Lady Gregory, Synge, and Yeats held the majority of the shares in the new company, and thus now exercised a controlling interest in it. As a result over two-thirds of the members seceded from the Society, mainly because they objected to the more authoritarian and professionalized regime, but also for a variety of personal motives and jealousies, as in the case of Maire nic Shuibhlaigh, who took offence at being offered the same salary as Sara Allgood. Thus, when Padraic Colum appealed to Yeats [4 January 1906] to "bring the Society back together, he replied that 'a re-united society would be five wild-cats struggling in a bag'" (*CL4* 280; *CL InteLex*, 303). However, discovering that the seceders retained important legal rights under the terms of the patent, Yeats and the new National Theatre Society were obliged to buy them off, handing over costumes and a sum of £50. With this money they set up a rival group, formally instituted as 'The Theatre of Ireland' in late May 1906. Bad blood persisted between the two organizations for several years: Annie Horniman and Yeats accused the seceders of blackmail, while the Theatre of Ireland contended that Yeats had seized the hitherto democratic Irish National Theatre Society and bent it to his own self-interested purposes. In November 1908 Casimir Markiewicz (1874–1932) gave him a severe fright by threatening him with a libel action for allegedly claiming that the members who resigned from the old Irish National Theatre Society were a 'pack of thieves & blackmailers who stole £50 of his...

so angry that they seceded, and one of them in doing so left behind her for my legacy the part of

Kathleen Ni Houlihan.

I had wanted it for years. I got it; that is all I intend to remember about the dispute. There had been many Kathleens; every one had played it in their own way. Miss Maud Gonne's performance (the original Kathleen) I cannot clearly remember, as I was very young at the time. One of the other players who had taken the part before me had, I thought, been most struck with the supernatural element in the character. She gave us Kathleen as Ireland, immortal, spiritual, divine, if you will, but Ireland in sorrow, struggling without hope.[16]

Perhaps our sorrows are more spiritual than our joys. I had a different conception. I did not wish to make my audience feel that 'Kathleen' called that young man to a hopeless sacrifice. When I stand at the door re-chanting

> 'They shall be remembered for ever,
> They shall be alive for ever,
> They shall be speaking for ever,
> The people shall hear them for ever'. (*VPl* 229, 231)

I call into my thoughts all those who have died for Ireland. I say to myself their death was victory. Ireland, too, will be victorious. I fill myself with joy. 'Dervorgilla' that is the sorrow of Ireland, but 'Kathleen' looks in to the future.[17]

---

money', and later that month there was an acrimonious row over the inadvertent use of the Abbey name by the Theatre of Ireland, in consequence of which Annie Horniman banned them for ever from hiring the Abbey Theatre. Although Yeats had approved of her action at the time, by 1910 he was far more amiably disposed towards them and was evidently reluctant to revive contentious memories.

[16] The first Cathleen ni Houlihan was Maud Gonne, who played the part with electric effect at St Teresa's Hall from 2 to 5 April 1902 (when Sara Allgood was in fact twenty-one years of age). Thereafter the part was briefly taken by Helen Laird ('Honor Lavelle') and then by Maire nic Shuibhlaigh (who accentuated the 'supernatural element in the character') until her resignation from the Abbey Company in January 1906, at which point Sara Allgood made it hers and regularly received rave reviews.

[17] Lady Gregory's *Dervorgilla* is based on the romanticized but widely-held tradition that the elopement of Dervorgilla, wife of Tiernan O'Rourke, King of Breffny, with Diarmuid MacMurrough, King of Leinster, had led to the expulsion of Diarmuid and to his inviting Henry II and the Anglo-Normans into Ireland in 1170–1, and thus to the subsequent seven-hundred-year English occupation.

It is scarcely possible to omit from these memories, some reference to 'The Playboy', the most stirring and memorable event so far in my theatrical career. The widow Quin was

Scarcely a Part to my Liking,

but an actress cannot always choose and pick her part, but must loyally do her best with the character allotted[18] to her.[19] It must be said that Mr. Synge makes this comparatively easy, for all his characters are boldly and definitely outlined. In many plays the characterisation is vague and flabby, and out of a mass of dialogue, the moulding and vitalising is wholly left to the creative instincts of the players. Between these two kinds of dramatists, there is all the difference to the actors, between getting into a sack and into a close-fitting costume. All Mr. Synge's conceptions spring, like Minerva, fully developed from his head.[20] I had already played Molly Byrne in 'The Well of the Saints', and Maurya in 'Riders to the Sea', a part very precious

---

The play takes place outside Mellifont Abbey, where an anonymous and now aged Dervorgilla has been trying to expiate her guilt by dedicating her life to penance, prayer, and charitable deeds. In the course of the play her true identity is revealed, the lads and girls she has befriended turn against her, and she realizes that, despite all her efforts, she will never escape 'the swift, unflinching, terrible judgment of the young!'. In *Cathleen ni Houlihan* another old woman inspires young men to armed resistance against English domination and is transformed into a vigorous young woman with 'the walk of a queen'. *Dervorgilla*, had first been produced at the Abbey Theatre on 31 October 1907, but Lady Gregory rewrote it in the early summer of 1908 and the new versions was staged on 8 October of that year. Sara Allgood had made an immediate hit as Dervorgilla, and the play was often revived.

[18] The *Weekly Freeman* reads 'alloted'.

[19] Sara Allgood had played the Widow Quin (the *Weekly Freeman* reads 'Quinn') with great success from the first production of *The Playboy of the Western World* in January 1907. Her appearance, intonation, and comic timing made her particularly effective in the part of the feisty older woman who vies with Pegeen Mike for the attention of the Playboy, but in February 1911, tired of being cast in middle-aged or elderly roles, she refused to play it anymore and Eileen O'Doherty took it over.

[20] In Roman mythology Minerva, the goddess of wisdom, emerges fully armed from the head of Jupiter. Synge's conceptions may or may not have emerged 'fully developed', but their execution often took years to bring to fruition. As Sara Allgood goes on to remark, he 'laboured so long' over *The Playboy of the Western World*, which he began in September 1904 and was still revising up to its first performance at the beginning of 1907, and he was unable to complete *Deirdre of the Sorrows*, on which he had started serious work in October 1907, by the time of his death later this month.

to me, in which an eminent Manchester critic was kind enough to describe my impersonation as the finest old woman study on the English stage.[21] I will never forget, if I were to live as old as Maurya herself, that historic night when the curtain rose for the first production of 'The Playboy'. Naturally we were all in a state of trepidation. Mr. Synge's former works had been so bitterly assailed,[22] that we wondered how this play, his masterpiece, over which he had laboured so long, would be received. The play had been carefully rehearsed, and its production excited great expectations. The theatre was crowded that night, and many were turned away. Never did a band of Irish actors face a more cultured and representative Irish audience. Judges, barristers, solicitors, clergymen, artists, musicians, and literary men filled the stalls. Gaelic Leaguers, Sinn Feiners, University students—the

---

[21] Sara Allgood played Molly Byrne, 'a fine looking girl with fair hair', in the first production of *The Well of the Saints*, from 4 to 11 February 1905, although in later productions she was cast as the ancient blind crone Mary Doul. On 20 January 1906 she had switched roles in *Riders to the Sea*, from the daughter, Cathleen, to Maurya, the aged mother who in the course of the play loses the last of her eight sons. At Yeats's request, she was to recite Maurya's final speech at Synge's funeral later this month. Commenting on her performance as Isabella in the *Manchester Guardian* of 13 April 1908, 'C.E.M'. (i.e. C. E. Montague) wrote that, although 'the best we have seen', it was 'not, to our thinking, as perfect as her Maurya in 'Riders to the Sea', but then that is perhaps the finest piece of tragic acting that any English-speaking actress has done in our time, and her Isabel, though less fine, does not shame it'. Born in London of Irish parentage, the influential journalist Charles Edward Montague (1867–1928) was the theatre critic of the Liberal daily *Manchester Guardian*. He was a supporter of AEFH's Gaiety Theatre, and published selections of his drama criticism as *The Manchester Stage, 1880–1900* (1900) and *Dramatic Values* (1911). In a letter of 27 April 1908 Yeats told John Quinn (*CL InteLex*, 880) that he was 'after Archer and Walkley about the most influential' critic in England.

[22] Although *Riders to the Sea* was widely admired in Dublin, other plays by Synge had attracted opprobrium. *The Shadow of the Glen*, in which a husband feigns death to catch his wife in an adulterous relationship, had been attacked in the nationalist press on its first production in October 1903, when it occasioned the resignations of Maud Gonne and Douglas Hyde from the Irish National Theatre Society, as well as the departure of the then leading actors Dudley Digges and Maire Quinn, who subsequently emigrated to the USA. The controversy over its morality and authenticity flared up again in early January 1905, after its revival at the Abbey Theatre. His next play, *The Well of the Saints*, was roundly panned on its first production in early February and on 29 March of that year Lady Gregory explained to John Quinn (NYPL) that there was 'a strong undercurrent of feeling against Synge'. The received wisdom in Dublin was that his chronic ill-health had twisted his mind towards sensuality and morbidity, and rumours circulated in Dublin in the days before its premiere that there would be trouble during the run of *The Playboy*.

pick of the freshest intellect of the city crowded the balconies and the basements. The first act went splendidly amid laughter and applause, and curtain after curtain were taken. The second act followed, and was loudly applauded. Just in the middle of the third act, following a speech, which one of the actors had been instructed to cut out, the storm burst, and the house broke up in disorder. For a week the Theatre was

Turned into a Pandemonium.

It is not necessary here to recount the deplorable scenes that followed. The actors were the chief sufferers. For three or four nights the play was faithfully performed, but not a syllable was heard across the footlights. Rumours were prevalent that the stage would be rushed and the company maltreated. A force of sturdy policemen were placed in the precincts of the stage to guard against this, but nevertheless our nerves were shaken, and after the fearful strain of a week of turmoil, threatenings, and maledictions,[23] we were left in a state of total collapse. One incident occurs to me, which has not been recorded, in which I played an impromptu part. On Saturday—the evening of the last performance—just before the public were admitted, I found the theatre crowded with police. They were ranged all around the walls and up the centre of the pit benches. Acting on an impulse I rushed on the stage, and passionately informed them that unless they left the theatre I would not play that night. Moved by the vehemence of my attack they looked uneasily at each other, but of course they could only follow their instructions. I did not carry out the threat, for it would only have made matters worse, and I had no desire to make the position of the directors more painful and complicated than it was at the time.[24] The story of the

---

[23] The *Weekly Freeman* reads 'maledictions'.

[24] Trouble at the first production of *The Playboy of the Western World* erupted shortly before 11 p.m. on Saturday, 26 January 1907. In 'J. M. Synge and the Ireland of his Time' Yeats, who was in Scotland, recalls (*E&I*, 311) receiving a telegram informing him 'Audience broke up in disorder at the word shift'. When in the third act of the play the Widow Quin urges the Playboy, Christy, to make his escape from the village he retorts that 'It's Pegeen I'm seeking only, and what'd I care if you brought me a drift of chosen females, standing in their shifts itself maybe'. While the image was mildly erotic, 'shift' was an acceptable contemporary term for a female flannel undergarment but Holloway confirmed that it was 'this phrase that settled it!', adding that it 'was made more crudely brutal on the first night by W. G. Fay. '*Mayo girls*' was substituted for 'chosen females'. Following adverse publicity in the Dublin press, disturbances on Monday night were more sustained and violent and the management called in the police to keep order and arrest troublemakers. The services of the police were retained at each subsequent performance and so it is strange that Sara Allgood should have waited until the

Playboy went out to the end of the earth, and I have read accounts of it in newspapers from Korea, Australia, South Africa, Canada, United States, India, etc. It will go down the ages as one of the toughest fights in theatrical history, and posterity will not forget the little band of players, who, through eight performances, never deserted their posts, but unflinchingly faced the music, and played their parts through din and terrors of a great public upheaval. I may now say a few words on

My Two English Engagements.

To play Shakespeare is, perhaps, the highest ambition of every actor. To bound into a difficult and important role without long training and experience in minor parts very seldom happens in the profession. Yet this was my fortunate lot. Miss Horniman's Manchester Company had accepted an engagement to play 'Measure for Measure' during the great annual Stratford-on-Avon Festival, to which people come from all parts of the world. Mr. Iden Payne, who managed the Abbey Theatre for some months in 1907, was in difficulty to find some one to play the trying part of Isabella. He offered it to me, and, thanks to the kindness of the directors, I was enabled to accept it. Mr. William Poel, the great Shakespearean scholar, was the producer. We played it first in Manchester, and then went to Stratford-on-Avon.[25] In both places it was lavishly praised by the critics, and I was

very last show before making her remonstration. She may have been provoked by the fact that by Saturday the vehemence of the audience had greatly diminished, while the deployment of the police continued to be very unpopular in Dublin. Holloway, who attended both the matinée and the evening performances on that day, noted that by then the police, although 'as thick as blackberries in September' had 'no work to do & idly stood by'.

[25] Sara Allgood had played Isabella in William Poel's production of Shakespeare's *Measure for Measure* from 11 to 18 Apr 1908 to mark the official opening of AEFH's Gaiety Theatre in Manchester, before transferring to the Shakespeare Memorial Theatre, Stratford-upon-Avon, on 21 and 22 April. Although her contract, dated 25 March 1908 (Berg), was formally with Ben Iden Payne (1881–1976), the Gaiety's manager who had known her while working at the Abbey Theatre from January to June 1907, it was William Poel who had gone out of his way to engage her. As Robert Speaight notes in his *William Poel and the Elizabethan Revival* (1954), he had set his heart on Sara Allgood playing Isabella: 'although Sybil Thorndike was a member of the company, Poel would not accept her as Isabella. He had a great desire to see Sara Allgood in the part and persuaded Miss Horniman to engage her specially. Poel himself... played Angelo' (95). The production was widely reported in the local press on Monday, 13 Apr 1908, in reviews which gave glowing uniform praise to Sara Allgood's performance. William Poel (born William Pole; 1852–1934), actor, playwright, and Shakespearean scholar, had founded the Elizabethan Stage Society in 1895.

not overlooked, but the tribute I prize highest, was a letter I received from Mr. Poel on my return home, in which he said 'Your great success in the part was due to your personality and temperament being exactly suited for it. You are the best Isabella the stage has ever seen, because you came nearest in my opinion, to Shakespeare's conception and intention'. I should like to say something about Shakespeare's delightful birthplace, and all the charming places and buildings hallowed by associations dear to every player. I should like to express my joy at playing in the Shakespeare Memorial Theatre, to tell of the many notable actors I met, but space will not permit,[26] and I have still to relate my experience with Mrs. Patrick Campbell. Once again good fortune smiled, for I had the very great privilege of playing with and enjoying the friendship of the most brilliant and gifted actress on the English stage to-day. One step further—one experience more in my profession—from the romantic drama of Shakespeare to a classic play of Greece. Mrs. Patrick Campbell was kindness personified to me, and I shall never forget the help, the encouragement, the praise she found time to bestow on me during a very strenuous time when rehearsing 'Deirdre' and 'Electra' in London.[27] I

[26] Most of the actors Sara Allgood would have met in Stratford were members of the Benson Company. Francis Robert ('Frank') Benson (1858–1939), actor and theatre manager, had set up his own touring company in 1883, shortly after leaving Oxford. In 1886 he was asked to manage the spring Festival at Stratford-upon-Avon, which had been established in 1879, and he continued to direct it annually until 1916, by which time he had produced all but two of Shakespeare's plays there. Later in 1908 Benson asked Sara Allgood join his Company for February 1909 and also for three weeks at the Stratford Festival later that year, but Yeats and Lady Gregory refused to give her leave. Yeats, who had known Benson since early 1901 when they were planning his Company's Dublin production of *Diarmuid and Grania*, met him again in April 1908, during his visit to Stratford to see Sara Allgood play Isabella, a performance he described to Quinn on 27 April Quinn (*CL InteLex* 880) as 'wonderful.... She got a great reception from the audience'.

[27] Sara Allgood became a great friend of the celebrated English actress Beatrice Stella Campbell, née Tanner (1865–1940), who used the stage name Mrs Patrick Campbell, in November 1908, when Mrs Campbell, honouring a promise to Yeats, took the title role in a hugely successful production of his *Deirdre* at the Abbey. Sara Allgood acted with her as First Musician, and, as she later recalled in 'Memories', the Company 'were all thrilled and delighted, and a friendship began between Stella and myself that was only severed by death. Never will I forget her wonderful kindness, not only to me, but to the other members of the cast'. Mrs Campbell subsequently invited her to repeat the performance in London, and also play Chrysothemis, the sister of Electra, in Arthur Symons's translation of Hugo von Hofmannsthal's *Elektra*, staged in a double bill in a series of matinees at the New Theatre from 27 November to 11 December. 'What a lucky girl I was to be chosen by her for parts of such calibre', Sara Allgood enthused in her 'Memories',

might also tell how she perhaps wisely stood in the way of a very lucrative engagement. A man came into the Café Monico, where we were rehearsing 'Electra', and asked Mrs. Campbell if she knew of a lady who looked like Edna May, that Mr. Frohman wanted a girl who looked like her, to send out with some musical comedy.[28] He looked at me, and Mrs. Campbell promptly got up and stood between us. She said that

Frohman Would Give £100 a Week

if he could get a girl who would suit. She, however, advised me to stick to classical drama, and advice coming from one as experienced in everything pertaining to the profession is worth following.

The editor asks me to talk of all my parts, but they are very numerous, for we have a large repertoire now at the Abbey that I have played in. I think our audiences at the Abbey like me in 'Riders to the Sea', next after 'Kathleen ni Houlihan', but I will admit to you that I would like a long part with plenty of fine clothes, in which it would not be necessary to make up

'She paid me Ten Pounds a week, a huge salary to me at that time, and she also insisted that I be her guest all during rehearsals and the London season, so I had no hotel bill to pay. What a joy to me to be an honoured guest in her delightful little 'Queen Anne' house, 33 Kensington Square'. Yeats noticed the effects of this friendship, writing to Lady Gregory on 23 November 1908 (*CL InteLex* 994): 'I was greatly amused at the changed look of Miss Allgood. She has grown fashionable under Mrs Campbells instructions. It is like the transformation of people who go from the provinces to Paris in Balzac'. Mrs Campbell also offered to get her an engagement of £50 a week at the Coliseum to sing Folk Songs, and on 22 December 1908, shortly after her return from London, she informed Holloway that 'Mrs Campbell just fell in love with her—her kindness to her surpassed anything. She would not let her return until she was quite well. She would wish to keep her always'.

28 The Café Monico (named after its founders) had been established in 1877 in Shaftesbury Avenue and was enlarged in 1885–86 to the north of Piccadilly. Edna (the *Weekly Freeman* reads 'Enda') May was the stage name of Edna May Pettie (1878–1948), famous on both sides of the Atlantic as a star in Edwardian musical comedies, many mounted by the impresario Charles Frohman (1860-1915). Although an American, her break-through came in England, where she appeared as the heroine in *The Belle of New York*, a play which had disappointed in the USA but was a smash hit in London in 1898. She went on to enjoy a highly successful theatrical career, but had given up the stage in 1907, following her marriage to the millionaire Oscar Lewisohn. Sara Allgood was possessed of a much-admired singing voice and had the personality to carry off May-like roles, and at this time rumours were rife in Dublin that she was seeking engagements in a variety of English companies

a hundred years old.[29] Instead of talking about all these parts you will let me say, will you not, that it is pleasant playing at the Abbey, where we have nearly all known each other for years, and can take pleasure in one another's success.[30] We are confident that some day our movement will take its place in the intellectual history of Ireland, and through the slights and blights of its early stages it will yet emerge as an honoured possession and a glory of our native land. It will perhaps then be said of us, that we did a 'good deed in a naughty world';[31] although I fancy nowadays that there are many who think, that our deeds were very naughty in an exceptionally good world.

II: THE MANCHESTER PLAYGOERS' CLUB

If Yeats had ventriloquized Sara Allgood's voice in the *Weekly Freeman* article, he used her talk to the Manchester Playgoers' Club on 17 April 1910 to disseminate his own views on the place of the theatre. Although delivered by Allgood at the outset of an Abbey tour to the city, her address, uncontaminated by Henderson or any others, was almost entirely his work, and he complained to Lady Gregory that it had given him 'more trouble than I expected'. He had begun writing the speech in mid-March 1910, describing it as

---

[29] Yeats warned the newly appointed Abbey manager Norreys Connell on 8 April 1909 (*CL InteLex* 1135) that the actors would 'all insist on new clothes, for which they have a passion', and to remember that there was 'no crime they are not capable of to get them'.

[30] Since the Company was riven with feuds and jealousies, these remarks are far too cosy and naive. On 9 March 1909, even as Yeats was helping her write these words, Henderson spoke to Holloway (NLI) 'of the jealousies of the Company—especially of Arthur Sinclair who always posed as the leading man. He is a mass of conceit.... He is very hard to manage lately & kept the audience waiting for ten minutes last week just to annoy Miss Allgood'. Sara Allgood herself was to admit in her 'Memories' that her attempt 'to resume my duties as stage manager and producer', after her tour in *Measure for Measure*, was 'not for long': 'The company had become too difficult for me to manage, the biggest offenders were Arthur Sinclair, my sister Marie O'Neill, and Michael Dolan, so I asked the Directors to release me, and get someone for the position who would be obeyed'. Yeats later confided in L. A. G. Strong that peace in the Abbey company 'varied with the size of Sara Allgood's waist' (*Green Memories* (1961), 260).

[31] See *The Merchant of Venice* V i: 'How far that little candle throws his beams! | So shines a good deed in a naughty world'. Yeats, who was particularly fond of this scene, had used *The Merchant of Venice* as the text for a class in speaking poetry he ran for the Abbey Company in the spring of 1908.

a large piece of propagandist writing an anonimous attack on stage as convention, words that another mouth was ready to speak, a cockatrice's egg to be let fall into an innocent basket.[32]

Although he thought it 'now done' by 31 March, he was to continue working at it over the coming days. He had originally hoped to be present at the talk, but found it clashed with a speech he himself was to give at the annual Stage Society Dinner in London, and he havered between the two engagements. News that he might not be in Manchester after all greatly; she had already suffered a nightmare over the fear of his manuscript 'not reaching her in time', and, 'evidently in a state of terror', she dashed off a 'wild letter' to him.[33] The main trouble, as he saw it, was that there would be a discussion after her lecture, and she might be required to give an unscripted reply. After some reflection, he decided that he should nevertheless fulfil his obligation to the Stage Society, especially since it would be 'a good advertisement for the Abbey on the edge of our June tour',[34] but contacted the former Abbey manager Ben Iden Payne, asking him if he would reply to Sara Allgood's talk, a responsibility he himself was originally to have undertaken. As he explained, the speech was 'all right' but she had 'no experience in extempore speaking and would break down if she attempted it'.[35] Unfortunately the sympathetic Payne was unable to attend the lecture either, but evidently sent Yeats a letter of good advice, warning him, among other things, not to ask Edwin Heys, the business manager of the Manchester Gaiety, to reply as he was full of 'clumsiness and gaucherie'.[36] He may also

---

[32] Yeats to the writer, journalist, and student of the stage Huntly Carter (1875–1942), 31 March 1910 (*CL InteLex* 1321). In fable, a cockatrice was a legendary serpent, said to be able to kill by its glance alone, and which was supposedly hatched from a cock's egg.

[33] *CL InteLex* 1330, to Lady Gregory, 12 April 1910.

[34] *CL InteLex* 1333, to Ben Iden Payne, 13 April 1910. The Abbey Company were due to appear at the Court Theatre, London, from 30 May to 25 June.

[35] *Ibid.*

[36] Edwin Theodore Heys (1876-1937) was born in Stockport, the son of a leather merchant, and started business life in the cotton cloth trade. He served as business manager of the Gaiety Theatre, Manchester, from 1907 to October 1912, when he resigned to set up his own touring company, which, among other productions, managed the provincial tours of Stanley Houghton's immensely popular *Hindle*

have had a quiet word with the organisers of the event, and helped to ensure it received wide coverage in the Manchester press.

The meeting, held in the Midland Hotel, was in the safe hands of Councillor Walter Butterworth, a self-made glass manufacturer and a man of wide culture,[37] and Sara Allgood also brought her own team of supporters from the touring Abbey Company, comprising her sister, who acted as Maire O'Neill, Arthur Sinclair, Fred O'Donovan, J. M. Kerrigan,[38] and the ever-faithful Henderson. Despite her bad

Wakes. In 1920 he was on the board of the company that bought the Gaiety from Annie Horniman to convert into a cinema, and when this venture did not succeed he was associated with other cinemas in Bolton and Manchester. In 1909 he became deeply infatuated with Sara Allgood's sister, Maire O'Neill, but he had given Yeats and Lady Gregory considerable trouble by disputing their choice of plays on the Abbey's Manchester tours.

[37] Walter Butterworth (1862–1935) was at this time Chair of the Municipal Art Gallery Committee, in which capacity he helped build Manchester's impressive collection of Pre-Raphaelite pictures. He was also a member of the Manchester Playgoers' Club, the Literary Club and, as an accomplished linguist, of the Dante Society.

[38] These were leading members of the Abbey Company who were in Manchester from 18 to 23 April 1910, performing at Gaiety Theatre, as part of a tour which had included Belfast and Leeds. Mary (Molly) Agnes Allgood (1886–1952), the younger sister of Sara Allgood, took her stage-name, Maire O'Neill, from her maternal grandmother. She had been a member of the Daughters of Erin, and was, like her sister, a French polisher before taking her first Abbey part as Cathleen in *Riders to the Sea* on 20 Jan 1906. She went on to rival Sara Allgood as the Abbey's leading lady, and was currently engaged to Synge; she remained at the Abbey after his death in 1909, only leaving in 1911, when she married the journalist George H. Mair (1887–1926). Shortly after Mair's death she married Arthur Sinclair and toured with him, although the marriage was not a success. In later life she worked mainly on the London stage and in British film and radio. Francis Quinton ('Mac') McDonnell (1883–1951), who acted under the name Arthur Sinclair, had originally worked in a law office but joined the Irish National Theatre Society in late 1904, making his first appearance on 27 Dec 1904, the opening night of the Abbey Theatre. He subsequently became one of the leading actors in the Company, until his resignation in 1915. Sara Allgood had recently rebuffed his amorous overtures and, although supportive on this occasion, he was taking revenge by disrupting her work at the Abbey. Fred O'Donovan (1886–1952) was the stage name of the Dubliner Freddy Saunders. He joined the Abbey in February 1908 after answering an advertisement and made an immediate success in the part of James Walsh, the spoiled priest and anti-hero of W. F. Casey's *The Man Who Missed the Tide.* He consolidated his reputation over the following months and remained a leading member of the Company until late 1918, acting as Manager from 1917. Joseph Michael Kerrigan

dreams and panic attacks, the talk was very well received, winning not merely applause but cheers at its conclusion.

The following TS, dictated to a typist by Yeats and corrected in his hand in pencil and pen, is now in the National Library of Ireland, where it is tentatively attributed to Fay. It is evident from newspaper reports that Sara Allgood prefaced the typewritten talk (which begins 'It is pleasant coming to Manchester...') with some remarks on the history of the Irish Dramatic Movement, but even these, which, taken from the *Manchester Guardian* of 18 April 1910, are included here, have a rhythm and register more characteristic of Yeats than her, and were also probably written by him. Typing errors have been silently corrected in the following version, but deleted words, and misspellings in Yeats's own hand, are retained. In a very few cases words missing from the TS but necessary to the sense have been supplied from newspaper reports and appear in square brackets:

The Irish theatre movement started about 1897 or 1898. It is hard to fix a date, for, like all great artistic movements, it took its rise not from one individual but from many. When in 1898 Mr. Yeats and others made a practical attempt to stage their plays in Dublin they could only do so by importing actors from England. We began very humbly with one performance in the year in some obscure Dublin hall unsuited for dramatic performances. Later we performed twice or three times a year in the Molesworth Hall, and finally in 1904 we opened in the Abbey Theatre.[39] But the encouragement

(1885–1965) joined the Abbey Company in October 1906, after a short career in journalism, and made his first major appearance in Yeats's *Deirdre* on 24 Nov of that year. He gained rapid prominence as an Abbey actor, and appeared regularly until 1916, when he joined the Irish Film Company. In 1920 he emigrated to the USA, where he did stage and film work.

[39] Yeats, Lady Gregory, and Edward Martyn began planning a Dublin-based 'Celtic Theatre' in late June 1897 but the first productions of what had now become known as the Irish Literary Theatre did not take place until May 1899 (not 1898 as Sara Allgood states). The Irish Literary Theatre, financed by subscriptions and underwritten by Martyn, set itself a three-year programme and used English actors, including, in 1901, Frank Benson's Company. In the summer of 1901 Yeats discovered the Fays amateur Irish Company, the Ormonde Players, and allowed them to produce his *Cathleen ni Houlihan* in the cramped St Teresa's Hall in April 1902. The Fays quickly changed their Company's name to the Irish National Dramatic Society and subsequently registered it as the Irish National Theatre Society, taking an 'obscure Dublin hall' in Camden Street but mounting

we got from the public was still slight. How cheerfully we used to play to an audience of 30 or 40 people. How encouraging was the presence of two new people in the stalls. But those who came once came again, and the last night I played in Dublin, about two weeks ago, the theatre was packed.[40] Looking back on that modest beginning the result seems to me to be very wonderful.

It is pleasant coming to Manchester, there and in London and Oxford we have had our best welcome outside Ireland, and surely <it must mean> the approval of these three towns means that much of the best English intellect has thought well of us. We have done our work for the sake of our own people at home and their pleasure is of course our great aim, but we come to you to get a more impartial judgment, the very fact that our work touches on many things of importance to Ireland, & that it arouses passions that are deep in Irish hearts, prevents it being <cannot always be> quite impartially judged. In every time and in every land the artist has carried his work—sometimes beyond the borders of his own country—with the feeling

most of their productions at the more spacious Molesworth Hall in central Dublin. In 1904 Annie Horniman leased the Mechanics Institute, converted it into the Abbey Theatre, and successfully petitioned for the necessary Royal Patent. By eliding the Irish Literary Theatre with the Irish National Theatre Society Yeats is using Sara Allgood to make a polemical point, since arguments about the 'true' origin of the Irish National Theatre Society were by 1910 hotly disputed, and Yeats was being accused of having hijacked the drama movement for his own ends.

[40] Many reviewers and commentators remarked on the thinness of the audiences at the Abbey during its first two years. Some potential patrons were put off by its reputation for obscure artiness, others by the supposed unsavouriness of Synge's plays, but most were probably deterred by Annie Horniman's insistence that the price of the cheapest seats should be set at a shilling, twice that of other Dublin theatres. On 27 December 1910 the actor Ambrose Power told Holloway (NLI) that 'when anyone asks him if Yeats is a mystic poet? he invariably recalls one night he was on the stage before the curtain went up [on] *The King's Threshold*, & Yeats who was standing by him on hearing "a cheque" fall into the box exclaimed—"Another 'bob' in the Pit, Power".' A reduction of prices and the growing reputation of the Company had attracted larger audiences through 1908 and 1909, and Sara Allgood had just arrived in Manchester from a particularly profitable Easter Week. She had played Mrs Dempsy in a packed revival of William Boyle's *The Eloquent Dempsy* on 1 and 2 April 1910, the first production of this most popular play since Boyle had withdrawn it from the Abbey repertoire in February 1907 as a protest against the production of *The Playboy of the Western World*. It proved a huge success, and as the *Irish Times* reported on 2 April 1910 (8) 'provided one of the most amusing performances that a crowded house had ever listened to. It was simply impossible to resist the fun of the piece, and the audience were almost exhausted with laughter before the three acts had run their course'.

or at any rate the hope that he was being judged as posterity would judge. That I speak of posterity at all, perhaps you may say, shows that we take ourselves very seriously, you may not think it right for us to do that but we do take ourselves seriously. We believe our movement of great importance to Ireland. Ireland is a country where the wax is still hot, you can put a mark upon it that will last a long time.[41] The last Irish artistic movement was 60 years ago, the movement we call 'Young Ireland' and it is still shaping men's souls in a way that it must be hard for an Englishman to understand who lives in a country where the wax has hardened.[42] Perhaps every country must pass through a formative time and that England has long left that time behind her. But it is of my own art of acting that I wish to speak and not of these great general questions. I think what brought us into notice first was that we studied a new kind of life—a life that had found little or no representation on the stage—When travelling companies come to Dublin I notice that they bring little but the life of the drawing-room, that play after

[41] The metaphor of hot wax was a favourite of Yeats's. In 'Reveries over Childhood and Youth' he recalls (*Au* 101; *CW3* 104–05) foreseeing that Ireland's 'poetry when it comes will be distinguished and lonely', and beginning 'to plot and scheme how one might seal with the right image the soft wax before it began to harden'. Later in *Autobiographies* he explains that he thought the vision of an Irish literary revival, 'the sudden emotion that now came to me, the sudden certainty that Ireland was to be like soft wax for years to come, was a moment of supernatural insight' (*Au* 199; *CW3* 169).

[42] The Young Irelanders, a group of nationalist intellectuals and activists, led by the poet and journalist Thomas Osborne Davis (1814–45) and the journalists and politicians Charles Gavan Duffy (1816–1903) and John Blake Dillon (1814–66), used the weekly *Nation*, founded in 1842, to further a policy of cultural as well as political nationalism. In 1843 the editors brought out *The Spirit of the Nation*, an influential anthology of patriotic verse which went into numerous editions and exerted a shaping dominance over Irish poetry for the rest of the century and beyond. Yeats had been introduced to the work of the Young Irelanders by John O'Leary, an unwavering admirer of the group, but he soon became impatient of what he saw as the propagandist intent and careless technique of their writings, and began to deplore them publicly as a dangerous model. Despite this, the Young Ireland influence persisted, and informed the views of Arthur Griffith and others who had opposed his and Synge's attempts to introduce new voices into Irish literature. In *Synge and the Ireland of his Time*, which Yeats was to write over the coming summer, he complained that 'Young Ireland had taught a study of our history with the glory of Ireland for event; and this... wrecked the historical instinct... There was no literature, for literature is a child of experience always, of knowledge never; and the nation itself, instead of being a dumb struggling thought seeking a mouth to utter it or hand to show it, a teeming delight that would re-create the world, had become, at best, a subject of knowledge (*E&I*, 316–17; *CW4* 230).

play shows to us the life of rich people, the life of a very small class. Now, if I am to put into a sentence what we are trying to do, I must say that we are trying to do the opposite of all this; we study the characteristics—whether of speech or manner—in those classes which are most unlike that life of rich people, the life of that small class. It is the feeling of our country that <it tells> impells us to do this. The ordinary play-goer—certainly the play goers who pay most for their seats—wish to see their own life upon the stage or the life that they would like to live, whereas our audience wishes to see upon the stage whatever life that is most Irish and that is always a life of people who are far removed from that life of rich people which is much the same all over the world; above all it is the life of peasants. We made our first success—and still get most of our success—from our playing peasants; my own first parts that <succeeded> got me much applause[43] were in Lady Gregory's 'Spreading the news' and in Mr Yeats's 'Kathleen ni Houlihan'. During our time in Ireland there has been something like a cult of the peasant created very greatly by the Gaelic League, which goes for its teachers of Irish to the country people of Kerry, or of Galway or of Aran[,] who speak Irish amongst themselves.[44] Does not the peasant in every country preserve the memories and the legends of the race? Mr Yeats tells me that in the Norwegian intellectual movement, which climaxed in the work of Ibsen, they began with the study of the peasant and of the ancient Sagas of their country and made much use of this formula 'To understand the peasant by the Saga the Saga by the peasant'. That formula has been true of our movement in Ireland, also the peasant has been the key by which

---

[43] The replacement of 'succeeded' by 'got me much applause' is a pencil correction apparently in Sara Allgood's hand.

[44] The typescript has 'Arran'. Since the Gaelic League, which was founded in Dublin on 31 July 1893, had as its 'sole purpose... keeping the Irish language *spoken* in Ireland', it paid particular attention to those people, overwhelmingly peasants from impoverished rural areas, who were still native speakers. As the *Gaelic Journal* explained as early as November 1893 (227–28), the organizers of the League 'purpose at the earliest opportunity to change the venue of their work from Dublin to the Irish-speaking districts; to appeal to the Irish-speaking people... a race possessing splendid characteristics, preserved to them, no doubt, by the survival of their ancient speech and all that it has brought along with it down the stream of time'. The ensuing stereotyping of an idealized peasantry partly contributed to the animosity against Synge's and the Abbey's more robust portrayals, and Yeats was to later to observe (*Ex*, 401) that he and Lady Gregory had 'sought wisdom and the peasants' imagination' while 'Dr. Hyde and his League were different' in that they sought not the imagination but the peasant himself.

we would unlock the door of the past.[45] He remembers, just as the man of the commercial classes hopes, plans and looks into the future. I think that I can say we have put the Irish <peasant> country man for the first time upon the Stage, we have studied him, we know him in his own home and it is only by that knowledge that the peasant ever can be represented. International acting—acting which seeks to represent life without special national and local knowledge—the moment it passes beyond the cosmopolitan life of the drawing room and the dining room, is an imposture and an illusion.

How can you represent the life of a class which is extravagant, dramatic, emotional and therefore always intensely characteristic by a stage tradition? When the travelling Company comes to us in Dublin it acts the life it is accustomed to act with a skill born of great experience, but when it goes outside that, one is bored. Think of those Corsican peasants in 'The Corsican Brothers' are we not reminded of charades we have played wrapped up in table-cloths?[46] We feel that those lively players have certainly not studied in Corsica, we refuse to believe that they are peasants, the characterization does not go deeper than the table-cloth, nobody is to blame,

---

[45] This had been the gist of C. H. Herford's article, 'The Scandinavian Dramatists', which Yeats published in the first number of *Beltaine*, May 1899 (14–19), and Yeats was to cite the axiom on numerous occasions. In *Samhain* 1905 he wrote (4) that as was 'natural in a country where the Gaelic League has created a pre-occupation with the countryman, the greater number of our plays are founded on the comedy and tragedy of country life, and are written more or less in dialect. When the Norwegian National movement began, its writers chose for that maxim, 'To understand the saga by the peasant and the peasant by the saga'. Ireland in our day has re-discovered the old heroic literature of Ireland and she has re-discovered the imagination of the folk'. He was to repeat on 4 February 1912 that during 'the youth of Ibsen and Bjornson their phrase was 'To understand the peasant by the saga and the saga by the peasant' (*UP2*, 403; *CW10* 135), and he returned to this in 'If I were Four-and-Twenty' in 1919 (Ex, 278; *CW5* 44) and in 'A Defence of the Abbey Theatre' on 23 February 1926 (*UP2*, 467; *CW10* 203–07).

[46] *The Corsican Brothers* (*Les Frères corses*) was originally a novella by Alexandre Dumas, *père*, first published in 1844 and subsequently adapted many times for the stage and screen, notably by the Irish dramatist Dion Boucicault (1920–90), who first produced his stage version *The Corsican Brothers; or, The Fatal Duel* at the Princess's Theatre, London, in February 1852. The melodrama was frequently performed in Dublin through the last half of the nineteenth century and the latest productions there had been by Martin Harvey's English touring company at the Theatre Royal in October-November 1906 and again in November 1908. A play about Mediterranean islanders as represented by inauthentic metropolitan actors was a deft foil to the authenticity of Grasso's actors, authentic natives of another Mediterranean island.

you cannot get actors from Corsica every time the 'Corsican Brothers' is to be played and they would not know English if you did; but I imagine if you were to compare <them> the players I am speaking of with those Sicilian players—whom I am not so fortunate as to have seen—you would conclude that the International Theatre—however necessary—is an imposture.[47] No, the Theatre must be always National if it is to represent the full life of any country; it must gather up all local knowledge and treasure it; it must find some means of using an actor because of the characteristics that have come to him from living in the place he was born in, among the people he grew up with, from the people he has worked with, from the streets he has walked through, if he has an accent which belongs to his birthplace you must not make him feel that it is a difficulty in his way, it should be a power that he can use, if he can put it off at will so much the better, but his capacity for it is an artistic gift, a thing to cherish. You must not select your actors as if they were pebbles on the sea shore, chosen by some child for their roundness and smoothness. Surely the welcome we have found—and above all the welcome given all over Europe to those Sicilian players means that people are beginning to feel this? But of course you will require playwrights who love all that is strange, characteristic, unexpected in life, National and local, not cosmopolitan writers. There is no need to confine themselves to the peasant; every class below that small world wide class of well-to-do people <though> & in always increasing amount <when> as it approaches the peasant <departs> becomes local, capricious, characteristic. Our writers are gradually pushing their study here and there through Ireland into any class that contains any Irish characteristic <into other classes>, we are this moment rehearsing a play which is a study of the Workhouse Parlour in a little country town. It is the work of Mr Padraic Colum who grew up in that life, it is not the life of peasants but it keeps a memory as it were of the fields. The hero of the play is a Workhouse Master who all his life has done

---

[47] Yeats saw Giovanni Grasso's Sicilian Players at the Lyric Theatre in London in March and April 1910. In his London lecture, 'The Theatre', delivered on 7 March 1910, he contrasted the overflowing life of Grasso's actors and their plays with the moral realism of modern British drama as exemplified by John Galsworthy's *Justice*, observing that the latter was 'made for people who do not think about human life…. Mr. Galsworthy is writing for an age that is far more interested in commerce, business and all kinds of problems, far more interested in moral codes, revolutionary or otherwise, than in life'. In a lecture to the Boston Drama League on 28 Sept 1911, he identified Grasso's initiatives with those of the Abbey: 'In Sicily, where Grasso is creating a wonderful school of players, and in Ireland… [we] are putting upon the stage a real life where men talk picturesque and musical words, and where men have often strange and picturesque characters; that is to say, the life of far-away villages where an old leisurely habit of life still remains' (*Boston Evening Transcript*, 29 Sept 1911 [14]).

everything for his family but who now in his old age wishes to live on his pension by himself, he longs for freedom, but they have debts and cannot let the pension go. He is a dreamer, an idealist, but when he writes verses, writes pedantically about Venus and Aurora, of the ballads the country-men buy upon Market days, and in the clumsy uncertain rhythm of the ballads.[48]

[48] This was Padraic Colum's three-act tragedy *Thomas Muskerry*, first produced at the Abbey on 5 May 1910. On 27 February 1910 Colum told Holloway that the play was going 'into rehearsal tomorrow', but this was probably postponed until 18 March when Lennox Robinson took up his post as a producer at the Abbey. In the play events and his family conspire to bring about the degradation, ruin, and finally death of Thomas Muskerry, a conscientious and dignified old Workhouse Master, and the reviews in the Dublin daily papers, which appeared on 6 May 1910, ran the gamut from enthusiasm to repugnance. The rehearsals did not go smoothly: Sara Allgood, who played Mrs Crilly, Muskerry's selfish married daughter, complained to Holloway on 7 May 1910 that when she first read the script Robinson 'told her to put more emotion into it. Fancy telling her such a thing at first reading when she was merely feeling out the meaning of the part. She simply told him she couldn't & that he did not know what he was talking about'. Towards the end of the play a youthful poem of Muskerry's is discovered: 'In the pleasant month of May, | When the lambkins sport and play, | As I roved out for recreation, | I spied a comely maid, | Sequestered in the shade, | And on her beauty I gazed in admiration. || I said I greatly fear | That Mercury will draw near, | As once he appeared unto Venus, | Or as it might have been | To the Carthaginian Queen, | Or the Grecian Wight called Polyphemus'. It is little wonder that in form and language this is close to verse in the hedge schoolmaster tradition of the late eighteenth century, since (although Yeats was unaware of it) Colum had plagiarized it from a hitherto unpublished poem, recently collected by P. W. Joyce in his *Old Irish Folk Music and Songs* (1909), 201–02. Such effusions are imitation *aislings* (vision poems), in which the poet, out for a morning stroll, encounters a beautiful young woman whom he accosts in hyperbolic classical terms. It evidently reminded Yeats of another anonymous poem of 1790s, 'The Colleen Rue', which he probably first read in H. H. Sparling's *Irish Minstrelsy* (1888) and in which the poet asks: 'Are you Aurora, or the beauteous Flora, | Euterpasia, or Venus bright? | Or Helen fair, beyond compare, | That Paris stole from her Grecian's sight?' Padraic Colum (1881–1972) was himself the son of a Longford Workhouse Master who had been dismissed for alcoholism. The younger Colum became a clerk in the Irish Railway clearing house, and first met Yeats at the 1902 performances in St Teresa's Hall. Yeats encouraged him to write drama and his plays *Broken Soil* and *The Land* had been produced by the Irish National Theatre Society, the latter at the Abbey Theatre on 9 June 1905. He resigned from the Society early in 1906 but had accepted a commission from Yeats for *Thomas Muskerry*, his last significant work for the Irish Theatre. In 1912 he married the Sligo-born literary critic Mary Gunning Maguire (1884–1957), and emigrated with her to America in 1914. Apart from occasional visits to Ireland, they remained in the USA for the rest of their lives, although Colum spent more time in Dublin after his wife's death.

His speech too, is a mingling of peasant picturesqueness and the pedantry that comes of half education. It is a study in speech, the speech of a definite class and locality and indeed our writers have above all things studied speech, for they desire to get away in their writing as we do in our acting from that life that is the same all the world over that is why style is so important to them. Lady Gregory has made the most laborious study of the speech of the West of Ireland, I believe that she took down from the people very nearly two hundred thousand words of dialect before she had written a single play and J. M. Synge used to live for long periods in cottages on the Kerry mainland or in the Aran or Blasket Islands, writing down or getting by heart characteristics of speech. We too, in our acting give probably more study to speech as distinguished from pantomime than is usual with players, that is necessary where the style which is always among other things a form of music is elaborate <though> or unusual. Above all it is important in dialect, where the rhythm is as marked as it is in verse and perhaps more difficult because less definite, less subject to law. I am told that when Mr Tree played Synge's 'Tinker's Wedding' the other day, the substitution of the hard precise pronunciation, the continual emphasis of every word which is natural with people living a hurried, crowded life, in the place of the slow meditative, musical cadence of Irish country speech, with its rise and fall like a wave, took character out of the play and force out of it, robbed it of all its salt and sap and made it a dull impossible thing.[49] Sentences which are

[49] Five matinee performances of Synge's *The Tinker's Wedding* were given in November 1909 by The Afternoon Theatre Company at His Majesty's Theatre, the proprietor of which was the actor-manager Herbert Beerbohm Tree (1852-1917). Yeats, on whom Sara Allgood's account entirely depends, had seen the final performance on 25 November and wrote furiously to Lady Gregory the following day (*CL InteLex* 1229): 'I saw first act of Tinkers Wedding yesterday but could not stand any more—a most disgraceful performance—every poetical or literary quality sacrificed to continual emphasis & restlessness—a meretricious stage moonlight scene & Mona Limerick [who played the heroine]... with a cockney pronunciation, & a chocolate box make up.... One interesting thing I did notice—the continual emphasis & change of note made the speaches inaudible as they are in verse plays treated in the same way. This emphatic delivery & movement—which is the essence of the English idea of romantic acting—evidently fits nothing but plays written in short sentences without music or suggestion. I tried to analyse the general impression of vulgarity & found it came either from this emphasis, from the necessary seperation from life of players who had never seen the life they tried to copy or from a conventional standard of <beauty> handsomeness.... I have not had such a sensation of blind fury in a theatre for fifteen years'. The unnamed playgoer who coined the simile of running in a top coat presumably spoke not to Sara Allgood but to Yeats, who informed Lady Gregory that as he was leaving the theatre 'in a rage I met a member of our Abbey Audience & found him even angrier than I was. He had been denouncing it to the people round him'.

entirely right when rightly spoken, were long and overloaded. <because the emphasis> It was like a man running in a heavy top coat as one playgoer has said to me—'a heavy top coat that would have been very comfortable wear for a man walking quietly'—One must always remember that words are the principal expression of character and thought, otherwise we would carry on the business of life with pantomime. <Pantomime is of course of supreme importance upon the stage but in the noblest dramatic form it comes second and not first for it is only> I have seen it two or three times stated in quite intelligent criticism, that the perfect play would have no words at all, to say that indeed has become one of the unconventions of the conventional, which like other conventions are repeated <like> without thought. That is like saying that the perfect life would contain no speech, for after all the Theatre is Life—the life of the mind the life of the passions—an appeal to both eye and ear. The patriotic feeling of a large part of our audience has widened the subject matter of our art in other directions also. An English audience is but very faintly interested in let us say Alfred the Great[50] as compared with its interest in the life it lives or hopes to live or pretends to live, an Irish audience—or a section of it at any rate—is as much interested in real or legendary history as an Elizabethan audience. This has enabled our playwrights to make romantic drama and the drama in verse once more a reality; among the parts that I have been most applauded for are Lady Gregory's 'Dervorgilla'—a one act play about the woman who brought the Norman into Ireland and Mr Yeats's 'Deirdre' a tragedy in verse describing the life and death of an ancient Irish Queen, while J. M. Synge's 'Deirdre of the Sorrows' in which Miss O'Neill took the principal part has been <perhaps> one of the most <popular> successful plays of our season[51] and

---

[50] Alfred the Great (849–99), the only English monarch to be called 'the Great', is regarded as the creator of the English nation, in that he defended Wessex, the last remaining southern Anglo-Saxon kingdom, against waves of Danish invasions, and finally forced them to make peace. He also instituted a code of laws, reformed the coinage, founded the English navy, and supported the spread of education. Among the myths that grew up around him was that while sheltering from the Danes he allowed baking cakes he was meant to be minding to burn and was roundly scolded by the housewife, ignorant of his true identity. There was more English interest in Alfred the Great than Yeats and Sara Allgood supposed: he had been the subject of a number of plays and poems through the nineteenth century, and the recent millenary of his death had inspired many more between 1899 and 1902.

[51] For Dervorgilla see above, note 17. Sara Allgood took on the title-role of Yeats's *Deirdre* for the first time on 17 February 1909, and, although there were fears that she might lack the passion and intelligence for the part, or that she might imitate too closely Mrs Campbell's recent performance, still vivid in the public memory, she triumphed in the part, even winning over the initially pessimistic Yeats. The *Freeman's Journal* of 18 February proclaimed (9) that 'Miss Sara

this brings me back again to that formula quoted from the Scandinavians 'to understand the Saga by the peasant the peasant by the Saga'. Mr Synge once said to a friend 'By using dialect, by putting everything in the way it is imagined in folk-lore we may be able to re-create again historical drama'. This was just after Lady Gregory's 'White Cockade' which used the method

Allgood, in the title-role, achieved a triumph', that her performance 'throughout was marked with intense emotion', and 'stamped her once again as an actress of extraordinary powers'. The *Irish Times* of the same day (6) judged that her interpretation stood up to that of Mrs Campbell, and that in the scene with Conchubar 'she declaimed her lines with powerful effect, her dignity was queenly, and the emotional side of her acting was exceptionally praiseworthy'. Meeting Yeats after the matinee on 19 February 1909, Holloway told him (NLI MS 1807) 'it was a beautiful performance of *Deirdre* I had just seen—the best I had yet witnessed'; Yeats fully concurred, writing to Lady Gregory the following day that 'yesterdays performances of 'Deirdre' were the best performances of verse I have ever seen—it was all music—I mean taking it as a whole'. Holloway recorded that 'Miss Allgood was presented with a bouquet after *Deirdre*—this was the first bouquet presented to one of the Abbey players'. He also commented on the 'splendid house' that had gathered and was told by Henderson that the receipts of the matinee 'were the best they had had for a long time'.

Her sister was no less a success in Synge's posthumous *Deirdre of the Sorrows*, which opened on Thursday, 13 January 1910, when, as Holloway noted, 'all or nearly all literary Dublin was present'. Reviewers differed as to the quality of the play, but all agreed on the excellence of Maire O'Neill in the title role. The *Irish Times* of 14 January 1910 (10) hailed this latest *Deirdre* as 'the sweetest and most intimate of them all…. Miss Maire O'Neill has, in her Deirdre, far surpassed any previous work; it is one of the most beautiful characterisations we have seen on the stage'. The *Freeman's Journal* of 14 January (5) reported that 'Miss Maire O'Neill achieved a pronounced success…. Her depiction of the distraught wife whose murdered husband and brothers had been thrown into a yawning grave, beside which she stood, was intensely tragic'. H.S.D. [Henry Stuart Doig] wrote in the *Evening Mail* of 14 Jan that her acting was 'a remarkable triumph. She has the gift of poetical representation, of passion, or of pathos, and her dignified restraint adds a reserve of strength and conviction to her portrayal'. The *Daily Express* of the same day lauded the performance as 'a wonderful triumph… acted throughout with a weird pathos and rare beauty'. Yeats told Allan Wade on 3 February (*CL InteLex*, 1287) that 'Synge's "Deirdre" went finely and was even a financial success, it was much more successful than any of us expected'. He was using Sara Allgood to prepare Manchester audiences for the play: it was to receive its first production outside Dublin there three days after this talk, and her words may have helped encourage the enthusiasm of its reception. The *Manchester Courier* of 21 April 1910, announced (12) that "Deirdre's' first appearance in Manchester was hailed last night with immense satisfaction and delight by a gratifyingly large audience, while the *Manchester Guardian* of the same day maintained (6) that the 'acting of Miss Marie O'Neill in the second and third acts surpassed anything of hers that we can remember'.

first, then he went on 'Archaeology has killed historical drama, when we begin to write now we are so anxious to realize historical people in the terms of some past life, that we see them outside ourselves'.[52] I want to elaborate this point a little for the form in which Deirdre of the Sorrows was cast may puzzle you. Mr Synge, Lady Gregory and in a much lesser degree Mr Yeats, for he is limited by his vehicle of verse, write about history, ancient heroes and so on in a dialect which is not to them the speech of peasants alone, they think when they write of endless folk-stories in which kings and queens of legend and great historical characters are made to <speak in the cottages of the West> use it and <as> of a speech which though a living <tongue> speech in the cottages of the West resembles in its syntax and its use of metaphor the Irish language that <they> the heroes really did <speak> use or that their first creators <spoke> used. This language is to them a kind of witch's mirror in which the world reflects itself in a romantic shape without ceasing to live, but I am going outside my province and the subject I have set myself, I must get back to my own art. <Even if our work was not so closely associated with Miss Horniman and so much indebted to her it would still be impossible for me to finish without pointing out that her admirable theatre here in Manchester is also>

One other necessity as it seems to me of abundant drama[,] drama, I mean, full of life in its detailed and its total effect, whether in the acting or in the writing has been <given to y> made possible to you in Manchester, as to us in Dublin by the generosity of Miss Horniman, a great and rare generosity.[53] Wagner says somewhere or other 'That every remarkable play of antiquity was written for some one definite company, for some one group

---

[52] The plot of *The White Cockade*, a three-act tragi-comedy, first produced at the Abbey Theatre on 9 December 1905, centres on the farcically ignominious behaviour of King James II after his defeat at the Battle of the Boyne, including his hiding in a barrel to escape enemy soldiers. The 'friend' to whom Synge spoke was almost certainly Yeats, and in a note to the published version of the play Lady Gregory recalled that when 'my *White Cockade* was first produced I was pleased to hear that J. M. Synge had said my method had made the writing of historical drama again possible' (*Collected Plays* II (1970), 303).

[53] Annie Horniman had not only paid for Abbey Theatre in 1904, and subsidized it until 1910, but also established a repertory theatre company in Manchester. This had opened on 23 September 1907 at the Midland Hotel Theatre but (now named 'Miss Horniman's Company') moved to a permanent home at the Gaiety Theatre in March 1908 and was formally inaugurated 11 April (see note 25). The Abbey players appreciated Annie Horniman's generosity more ungrudgingly than Yeats and Lady Gregory, with whom she had quarrelled, and early in 1911 presented her with an engraved facsimile of the Ardagh Chalice and a signed vellum address expressing their thanks for her open-handedness.

of players, whose characteristics the dramatist could master and express himself through.[54] It is a great evil when a dramatist gets into the habit of building his work round about the personality of some <actor> one popular actor, but the reason of that is that it is only one, one actor who is more anxious to be himself than to act. The history of the Theatre has shown that whereas [in] a stock company each member of which plays many parts, something is created which is like a musical instrument and that author and stage-manager alike can play upon this instrument as they [never] can upon anything that is made out of the more or less accidental and casual association. Where a stage manager knows his players for a long time, he is not under the necessity of imposing upon them his own voice and ways. He can use all their ways, their tricks of speach, their habits of fealing. He can leave them freer and <know what they are going to do, and he can also help them more. They can express themselves> & so their work will give you the sensation of life instead of seeming, as acting so often does, a mere work of skill. And just as the Company itself becomes a kind of family, so does an audience which is grown fond of seeing the same people, night after night, bind itself to the player with a bond of sympathy, almost affection. Indeed this bond between player and public seems to me altogether essential, at least to the players and the playwright who are trying to make anything new. Both players and public require to be trained, trained for work of a new kind, and prolonged association makes them patient and ready to forgive each other much. We find in Dublin that every now and then we get an

---

[54] In his 1871 essay 'The Destiny of Opera' Richard Wagner points out that Shakespeare 'was a *play-actor* and *manager*, who wrote for himself and his troop.... *Lope de Vega*, scarcely less a wonder, wrote his pieces from one day to the next in immediate contact with his actors and the stage... there stands the actor *Molière*, in whom alone production was alive; and midst his tragedy sublime stood *Aeschylus*, the leader of its chorus.—Not to the Poet, but to the Dramatist must we look, for light upon the Drama's nature; and he stands no nearer to the poet proper than to the *mime* himself, from whose heart of hearts he must issue if as poet he means to 'hold the mirror up to Nature' (*Richard Wagner's Prose Works V*, trans. W. Ashton Ellis (1896), 142–43). Yeats probably knew of this passage from the paraphrase in Arthur Symon's review-essay, 'The Ideas of Richard Wagner', which had appeared in the *Quarterly Review* in July 1905 (73–108), and was reprinted in *Studies in the Seven Arts* in 1906. In the course of this extended survey of the prose works, Symons remarked (99) that 'Wagner points out the significant fact that from Aeschylus to Molière, through Lope de Vega and Shakespeare, the great dramatic poet has always been himself an actor, or has written for a given company of actors'. Yeats had read Symons's article eagerly in August 1905 and on 10 September told him that it 'touches my own theories at several points, and enlarges them at one or two' (*CL4*, 175; *CL InteLex* 214).

audience, much less sympathetic to our more daring attempts than is usual and when this happens someone will come into the green room and say: 'Did you notice that <there> they were all new people in the theatre. I hardly recognised a face'. Sometimes a holiday or a race meeting will bring us an audience of this kind.[55] <The people that make it up> The people that make up this new audience are just as intelligent as the old audience, but they have not learned how to see or to listen or what to look for, and what to wait for. The best audience of all, the quickest to take pleasure, the keenest in criticism is one in which there are many people, who have been many times to see the same play, who indeed know it so well that we hear at times a sort of gasp of distress in the pit, when a player forgets a sentence. I wonder if Miss Horniman's company has had a similar experience. Yes, the art of the theatre, like every other art depends upon friendly association between the artist and his public, <and more than any of them> upon the building up, as it were, of a kindly household of the arts, as little professional as may be, certainly not at all commercial, but above all things very human.

Although there was a discussion after the talk, Sara Allgood apparently played little part in it. According to Henderson, the contributions were 'good, bad & indifferent', although Heys lived down to Payne's low opinion of him, making 'some extraordinary statements' which he [Henderson] found himself, as he later informed the inveterate theatre-goer and assiduous diarist Joseph Holloway, compelled to arise & answer. Such as the Irish players could only act effectively Irish plays…. He also stated that Miss Horniman got the Abbey to play English as well as Irish plays there, only the *patent* prevented her & compelled her to play only pieces by Irish writers or on Irish subjects'.[56] This intervention did nothing to diminish the triumph of the evening and Sara Allgood, together with the Abbey actors who

---

[55] Such audiences were wont to appear during Horse Show Week performances in August and on national holidays. The latest example had been the Easter Week patrons, 28–30 March 1910, when the programme comprised *Deirdre*, *The Workhouse Ward*, and *Blanco Posnet*. Yeats wrote to Lady Gregory on 31 March (*CL InteLex* 1323) that the 'performance of 'Deirdre' last night was very good about the best there has been, but I thought the audience a little cold a less vigorous call for the actors at the end, I found on enquiry that it was strange audience probably drawn by the fame of 'Blanco' and by the holiday season. The night before it had taken Blanco like a popular melodrama, hissing the villain'.

[56] See Holloway NLI MS 1809.

had accompanied her, stayed on at the Midland Hotel for a convivial dinner hosted by the Playgoers' Club. She herself was confident that all had gone splendidly, assuring Holloway on 20 April that her 'address to the Manchester Playgoers, was very well received indeed, and that she was 'vain enough to think that it helped in a way, our success here this week'.[57]

[57] Sara Allgood to Holloway on 20 April 1910, NLI MS 1809.

http://dx.doi.org/10.11647/OBP.0081.15

JON STALLWORTHY (1935–2014)

Nicolas Barker

'I am a poet's poet', wrote Wilfred Owen on New Year's Day 1917. Jon Stallworthy, whose writing has brought Owen back to life, was the poet's poet of our time. A poet he became, first caught as other poets have been by nursery rhymes, and then by A. A. Milne and Kipling. Not much later he tried his own hand at it, and 'discovered that what I most wanted to do in the world was to write poems'. Twelve books of his poetry now tell how well he did that, but along with them went as many more books about other poets and their work: biography, criticism informed by practice, above all, line by line analysis that unravelled not just the meaning but the springs of inspiration.

He was born in London, his father come from New Zealand to further his career in medicine, eventually becoming professor of obstetrics and gynaecology at Oxford. Jon grew up in Oxford, better first at the sound than the meaning of words: asked 'What's your favourite college?' he said 'Gynaecollege'. The Dragon School opened his other senses, and his mind filled with other verse; from his father came forestry and rugby football, and from that Rugby School, where 'acres of vegetable prose' led to a master who 'saw a spark in the mind' and became his creative critic. His father took him back to his New Zealand roots, and national service to Nigeria in the

Royal West African Frontier Force. Back at Oxford and Magdalen College, he honed his rugby, and ambition turned to the Newdigate Prize for poetry. Third time lucky, he won it in 1958, and, more important, Jill Waldock, whom he married in 1960. Helen Gardner told him to study Yeats for a graduate degree, and Maurice Bowra introduced him to Mrs Yeats.

Over forty years, he found in poetry a vocation, but also a livelihood. All this he wrote down in *Singing School* (1998), an unsparing but joyous self-analysis of 'The Making of a Poet'. The Oxford University Press offered him a job as an editor and also published his first collection, *The Astronomy of Love* (1961). Publishing poetry proved as rewarding as writing it, and Jon and his colleague John Bell quickly built the best list of new poetry in the 1960s. An essay on 'Poet and Publisher' in the *Review of English Literature* in 1967 showed him master of his new trade. Posting to the Oxford University Press branch at Karachi made him new friends and opened his ears to a different kind of English, reflected in his next collection, *Out of Bounds* (1963).

Concurrently, his apprenticeship to Yeats continued. He passed the tests set by Mrs Yeats to those seeking access to the manuscripts. He learned first how to read the 'execrable' hand, then how to follow thought in its reiterated snatches, leaf by leaf, to the final text. Eighteen poems thus tracked to their sources produced a new portrait of the poet at work, published as *Between the Lines* (1963). It was also preparation for a cataclysm in his own life. The birth of his first-born son stirred new depths of emotion in a new long poem, often anthologized now, 'The Almond Tree':

> All the way to the hospital
> the lights were green as peppermints
>
> …
>
> I parked in an almond's
> shadow blossom, for the tree
> was waving, waving me
> upstairs…

> 　　　　　　　wave
> after wave beat
> on the bone coast, bringing
> ashore—whom?
>
> 　　　　　　New-
> minted, my bright farthing!
> …
> *your son is a mongol*
> the doctor said.
>
> How easily the word went in—
> clean as a bullet
> leaving no mark on the skin,
> stopping the heart within it
> …
>
> 　　　　　　　locked in
> your body you will remain.
> Well, I have been locked in mine.
> We will tunnel each other out…[1]

Root and Branch (1969) in the Phoenix Living Poets series introduced many to this new voice. *The Penguin Book of Love Poetry* (1973), unbuttoned and unhackneyed, shared a cover with the next collection, *Hand in Hand* (1974). Translation in partnership led to versions of Alexander Blok and Pasternak with Peter France, Polish poetry with Jerzy Peterkiewicz. Harder stuff was on the way. A bystander to the Oxford *Collected Letters of Wilfred Owen*, Jon was drawn in to write his biography during a sabbatical as Visiting Fellow of All Souls. *Wilfred Owen* came out in 1974 to universal praise; written without sentiment but with deeper understanding, it won the Duff Cooper Prize, the E.M. Forster Award and the W.H. Smith Literary Award, and has remained in print since.

Clouds were now drawing over the Oxford University Press, where Stallworthy had become deputy head of the Press's academic

---

[1] From 'The Almond Tree', in *The Almond Tree* (London: Turret Books, 1967), 7–12.

division, but in 1977 he was thankful to accept an invitation to Cornell as Professor of English Literature. Jill and he quickly acclimatized. The academic work was familiar; they found the perfect house, and explored the hills and lakes of upper New York State. Best of all were new friends, not only in the University but among other poets. Absence stimulated new exploration of old roots. *A Familiar Tree* (1978), illustrated by David Gentleman, followed generations of Stallworthys (from England to the Marquesas, to New Zealand and back to England again) over two centuries, in elliptical vignettes, terse yet vivid. *The Anzac Sonata* (1986) took its title from a longer meditation on nearer family history.

By now the Stallworthys were themselves returning to Oxford. Jon was next appointed first Reader then, in 1992, Professor of English Literature. He became a fellow of Wolfson College, and in 2006–08 acting President. Another biography, *Louis MacNeice* (London: Faber & Faber, 1995) won more plaudits, as did his editions of Henry Reed and Owen; *Rounding the Horn* (1998) collected all his poems to date. Increasingly war engaged his mind, in *Anthem for Doomed Youth* (2002), *Survivors' Songs from Maldon to the Somme* (2008), *Three Poets of the First World War* (2011), and in *The Oxford Book of War Poetry* (1984; new ed. 2014). His own last collection was titled *War Poet* (Manchester: Carcanet, 2014).

Instantly attractive, exceptionally handsome in youth, Jon Stallworthy was an electric presence in any gathering. Verbal wit came easily; so did lighter as well as serious verse. From deep wells of reading his own distinctive poetic voice comes through clearly. Like Henry Reed, he knew better than any poet of our time how paper-thin the barrier is between love and war. In his studies of other poets and of his own forbears in the past, and always in his own poetry, he explored with a tender precision, just as his father did anatomy, the wounds and joys that love and war engender.

Jon Stallworthy, poet and scholar of poetry, born London, 18 January 1935; married Gillian Meredith Waldock, 1960, two sons and one daughter; died Oxford, 19 November 2014.

http://dx.doi.org/10.11647/OBP.0081.16

KATHARINE WORTH (1922–2015)

Richard Allen Cave

It was fitting that at the funeral of Katharine Worth, who died on 28th January 2015 at the age of ninety-two, her daughter quietly read *The Wild Swans at Coole*. It had been the poem that Katharine had chosen to read and discuss with a poetry group in the home where she spent the final months of her life. The echoes and resonances at that moment were many and various: recall of the years Katharine taught at the Yeats International Summer School at Sligo; realisation of the extent to which Yeats like those swans was a constant in Katharine's life, absent for a while but always, dependably returning to consume her interest and commitment; awareness of the ripple-effect that her passionate endorsement of the need to stage Yeats's plays had on students and theatre professionals who came under the spell of her persuasiveness.

There were, too, memories of her stringent but kindly critical voice as lecturer, editor, author, theatre director and of her eagerness to accept the challenge of joining in debate with any dissenter to her view that Yeats's plays were theatrically dynamic, if the right conditions were met and the cultural context of his experiments with dramaturgy were understood. Beckett rather than Yeats might seem for many to be the figure who dominated the final years of her scholarship; and to some extent this is true, except it was precisely the study of Yeats's drama in its Irish and international contexts that gave Katharine insight into how best to approach Beckett's plays and their performative potentials at a time in the 1960s when (as her work on the panel creating and editing the Beckett sections of the *Cambridge Bibliography of English Literature* showed her) more attention was being paid to his fiction.

Katharine's first two book-length studies (the then required submissions for the M.A. as well as the Ph.D. degrees at the University of London in the 1950s, which she completed at Bedford College, working with Una Ellis-Fermor and Kathleen Tillotson) already showed the favoured direction her later publications would follow. On Shaw and Eugene O'Neill respectively, the theses did not discard traditional modes of literary criticism but extended them to embrace theatre history and nuanced appreciation of details of dramaturgy, particularly the visual dimensions of drama in performance.

This pioneering approach, strengthened over a number of ensuing monographs, prepared the way to engage readers imaginatively in the arts of performance; it became the hallmark of her quasi-improvisational lecturing style and informed at every level the construction of a syllabus for the Department of Drama and Theatre Studies that she in time established at Royal Holloway College in the University of London in 1978. It was to prove too to be the ideal approach to a study of Yeats's drama: not avoiding the felicities of the verse or the searching philosophy that underpins his invention, but exploring how greatly elements of performance continually enhance one's appreciation of them. Her quest was to establish the unity of Yeats's dramatic vision.

Katharine's first published monograph, *Revolutions in Modern English Drama* (London: G. Bell, 1972), would not appear at first glance to be advancing in a Yeatsian direction: it was a study of modern, chiefly English, playwriting but it elucidates challenging texts from the standpoint of their theatricality and (in terms of theatre history) from a wholly Yeatsian impulse, as encapsulated in her use in her chosen title of the word, 'Revolutions'. She carefully glossed her deployment of the term as embracing more than political or social upheaval; rather she preferred the creative implications of Yeats's pursuit of his philosophy of the gyres, in which change brought with it transformation, a return of the recognisably known that nonetheless encompassed a marked difference: the traditional reworked by a refreshingly individual vision. She examined in this light, for example, Pinter's staging of Joyce's *Exiles* (Mermaid Theatre, 1970) and John Barton's revival of *Murder in the Cathedral* (Aldwych, 1972), which consciously presented the play for an age far less uniformly Christian than originally envisaged by Eliot. Provocatively Katharine highlighted the technical, thematic and stylistic links between Noël Coward and Pinter, between Shaw and both Osborne and Stoppard, and between Wilde, Stoppard again and Orton.

The focus throughout all the chapters is on production and performance as (especially when considering revivals) a reaching back to the circumstances surrounding a work's initial staging, but also outwards to engage new, decidedly different audiences. New dramaturgy is continually examined in the context of the potential influences shaping its apparent originality. In many ways the book offers subtle (because not overly theorised) studies in the history of theatrical reception by not only audiences but also, and crucially, by playwrights in respect of their perception of and response to their predecessors' achievements. Forty years on, the monograph remains a potent and evocative history of post-war English theatre of the sixties and seventies.

If Yeats is to be detected as a shaping presence behind the methodology of *Revolutions*, there is no denying his absolute centrality in *The Irish Drama of Europe from Yeats to Beckett* (1978). From the founding of the Irish National Theatre Society it had always been part of Yeats's ambition to create a theatre culture in Ireland that would provide as welcoming a stage for international as for Irish drama. It may have proved a struggle to achieve this in practical terms because of strong opposition from Yeats's co-directors, but Katharine contended that on an inspirational level those same directors, Lady Gregory and Synge, were in fact open to international influences on their own creative work and usually on Yeats's recommendation. The strictures on acting style and methods of stage presentation embraced at the Abbey after 1904 were quite alien to English techniques at the time but wholly in line with innovations especially in contemporary French theatre.

Katharine was the first fully to explore the impact of Maeterlinck on Yeats's creativity as playwright and theatre director, mindful always of Yeats's uncanny ability to resist outright imitation, preferring invariably to adapt his influences to his own particular needs and ends. The same was true of his search for a hieratic dramaturgy where, though a marked stylisation prevail, a passionate intensity might nonetheless steadily be evolved. When he found Noh as his ideal model with Ezra Pound's help, again it was to work astonishing and highly original variations on the form. It was here that Katharine's approach came into its own: the visual dimensions of this new style (the use of masks, the bringing of dance to convey states of 'otherness', the use of music, not just to create atmosphere, but often to control the movement of actors within the playing space) were far from easy to gauge from the text. Katharine not only elucidated their significance and evoked their impact but showed how crucial they were to a perception of the dramaturgical design and to the intimations of the poetry that shaped the dialogue. Katharine made an irrefutable case for seeing Yeats as absolutely a man in and of the theatre.

But Yeats is only one privileged name in Katharine's title; Beckett is also present there; and one great strength of the volume is the confidence with which Katharine places Beckett firmly within the continuities of Irish dramatic culture. She draws nuanced affinities between Synge's plays and Beckett's and subtly defines how the particular grounds on which she has assessed the excellences of Yeats's richly varied dramas may be extended into as sensitive an appraisal of Beckett's. She was wonderfully attuned to the manner in which the facial features of some of Beckett's characters harden to become mask-like; to the near-choreographic patterning of stillness and movement in scripts that at times read almost like scores; to the musicality resonating on in voices that Beckett requires steadily to lose all vestiges of expression; to the poetry residing just beneath the surface of his prose; to the wit, stoicism and sheer inventiveness with which loss and approaching death are faced.

These qualities in Beckett's work were to receive even more searching treatment in two of Katharine's final publications: the highly personal monograph, *Samuel Beckett's Theatre: Life Journeys* (1999), which explores both her longstanding engagement with his work as reader, spectator and critic, and their personal friendship, as recorded in their correspondence; and the remarkable and deeply moving essay, 'Beckett's Divine Comedy' in Mary Luckhurst, *A Companion to Modern British and Irish Drama* (Oxford, 2006).

The wealth of scholarship in theatrical history and the critical acumen that are the hallmarks of Katharine's monographs were subsumed within her judicious editing for the Irish Dramatic Texts series of Yeats's *Where There is Nothing* and *The Unicorn from the Stars* (1987), in which she demonstrates in her Introduction the relative merits of each of the versions (the latter tighter intellectually, the former dynamic and provocative) and she edits to highlight those elements in each text. Her annotations not only draw attention to textual cruces but also to thematic and dramaturgical parallels with Synge's comedies and with earlier plays and poems by Yeats. Her account of Yeats's sources and influences while composing the dramas at two different periods in his career (Blake, Spenser, Nietzsche, Vedanta, Tolstoy) illuminate the ways in which Yeats could ably transform what are chiefly intellectual materials into stageable dramatic situations as well as (by way of extended revision and often with Lady Gregory's help) increasingly characterful dialogue.

Characteristically, Katharine finds grounds to redeem both plays as *plays* by revealing the theatrical vitality underlying their composition. The same is true of her monographs on two playwrights continually referenced throughout *The Irish Drama of Europe*. Oscar Wilde and Maurice Maeterlinck became themselves the subjects of intense and focused studies (published respectively in 1983 and 1985), partly as a consequence of researching and writing *The Irish Drama of Europe*, where Katharine had discovered how seminal their influences were. Wilde, generally at the time considered by critics and directors as markedly (almost exclusively) a verbal dramatist, she redeemed from such a limited view by demonstrating how complete a dramatist his texts show him to be, with his growing interest in effects of colour within the stage picture, in stage design and proxemics, in incorporating music and dance into the fabric of his dramas. To all appearances Maeterlinck is today a forgotten dramatist, but Katharine challenged that notion by approaching the range of his plays through the history of their performance, which she showed as being surprisingly steady and world-wide, varied in styles of presentation, richly open to imaginative interpretation, and demanding of actors, designers and directors many of the qualities she had earlier extolled as necessary for the adequate staging of Yeats's work. Yeats may not feature strongly in either volume, but there is no denying how powerfully Katharine's relish of the complex theatricality to be found in Yeats's dramaturgy guided her intellectual and imaginative scrutiny of his older contemporaries as purposefully as her engagement subsequently with Beckett. Always in her work there is that concern for revolutions, a joy in daring innovation accompanied by the excited recognition of continuities. Read in sequence, her monographs define an ever-expanding web of connections.

Yeats may have retreated to the background of Katharine's later published work, but she never lost her passion for his plays and poems, as generations of students and audiences to whom she lectured may attest; she continued to foster an enthusiasm in younger practitioners (Niema Ash, Sam and Joan McCready, and two of her colleagues, Poh-Sim Plowright and myself) where she recognised a developed practical ability that matched her commitment to see Yeats's plays regularly staged; and she advised for many years on the editorial board of *Yeats Annual*, guiding scholars addressing aspects of Yeats's dramaturgy with rigour and kindness, scruple and insight. Clarity of expression was the hallmark of her own style, though never at the expense of subtlety, nuance or wit. It falls to few critics to cultivate over time writing styles that are a close correlative of their actual speaking voices: Katharine Worth was so gifted. Her scholarship, framed in her distinctive 'voice' (the sense of her very presence in her style), is an enduring legacy.

'MASTERING WHAT IS MOST ABSTRACT':
A FORUM ON A VISION

http://dx.doi.org/10.11647/OBP.0081.17

A Vision: The Revised 1937 Edition, edited by Margaret Mills Harper and Catherine E. Paul, *The Collected Works of W. B. Yeats*, Vol. XIV (New York: Scribner, 2015), pp. li + 503. A Review Essay

Colin McDowell[1]

[R]eaders—and editors—must think for themselves
—Richard J. Finneran

I

Finally, with the publication of *The Collected Works of W. B. Yeats, Volume XIV: A Vision. The Revised 1937 Edition*, scholars have decent and readily available texts of the original 1925 edition of *A Vision* and Yeats's later version of 1937, both of them edited by Margaret Mills Harper and Catherine E. Paul. When I say 'readily available', I do not refer to the eBook versions also published by Scribner, which are available for purchase only in the United States. Whether this is testimony to the American view that only Americans matter, or whether it is simply due to demarcation disputes amongst publishers, I do not know: I can only say that it is an irritating restriction on scholarship. Nevertheless, the edition is a monument of scholarship and well worth placing alongside other major achievements in *The Collected Works of W. B. Yeats*, such as the editions of *Autobiographies* and *Later Essays*. Not only has the text been carefully collated, the edition includes generous quotations from the unpublished typescripts, a lengthy Editorial Introduction, tables of

[1]   colin.richard.mcdowell@gmail.com

'Proofs, Versions, Emendations, and Hyphenations', and 170 pages of notes. With this last in particular, it is as though the prior publication by George Mills Harper and Walter Kelly Hood of *A Critical Edition of Yeats's* A Vision *(1925)* had somewhat inhibited the textual apparatus of *The Collected Works of W. B. Yeats. Volume XIII: A Vision. The Original Version*, and only with this edition have the editors felt free to do as they would have wished as regards annotation. But this is mere speculation. It is also quite likely that the reviews of the earlier edition have guided the course of this one: Neil Mann's careful appraisal in *YA18* (265–96) in particular has surely had an effect for the better, as we shall see.[2]

In what follows, I am merely chipping away at the edges; it should not be seen as impugning the structural soundness of the achievement.

The reader new to *A Vision* who is looking for guidance as to what the book is about will not find it the Editorial Introduction to this edition. The reason may be that the editors did not wish to repeat material from their Editorial Introduction to the 1925 edition, which to some extent functions as an Introduction to both volumes; but a paragraph or two here may not have gone amiss.

This aside, the Editors' Introduction is typically dense, and may reflect Harper and Paul's over-familiarity with publication history and the ins-and-outs of manuscripts and typescripts. Reading of shorter previous studies may prepare the reader. One longs for the relative clarity of Richard Finneran's 1977 article 'On Editing Yeats: The Text of *A Vision* (1937)' (*Texas Studies in Literature and Language*, 19:1 [Spring 1977], 119–34), or Connie K. Hood's 'The Remaking of *A Vision*' (*YAACTS1* [1983], 33–67); but, admittedly, these are difficult matters, things have moved on since Finneran and Hood wrote, and you can only simplify so much without distortion.

Perhaps taking to heart Neil Mann's complaint that the editors' *A Vision. The Original Version* included only a single reference to contemporary reviews (*YA18* 265 n. 1), the editors have over-compensated here. While some of

---

[2]   The editors refer to 'Mann, "*A Vision* [1925]: A Review Essay"' several times (see *CW14* 381 n. 211; 382 n. 213; 448 n. 60). Since writing this paper, I have read Catherine Paul's review of the *Yeats Annual* in which Mann's critique appeared. There, she admits candidly that 'The second part of Mann's review has been extremely useful to us as we prepare our edition of that later version, as he enumerates errors, oversights, and misjudg[e]ments that we are grateful for the chance to consider and try to rectify', 'Yeats Annual Rebooted', *South Carolina Review* 46:1 (2013) 211, online version at http://www.clemson.edu/cedp/press/scr/articles/scr_46–1_paul.pdf.

these reviews may have contributed to how Yeats revised the work, most seem to have little relevance, and the editors don't manage to justify their inclusion, unless they are intended to provide light relief from the textual ins-and-outs of the rest of the Introduction: they certainly don't offer any help in coming to terms with the subject matter, but instead remind us what people say who feel they have to comment on what they do not understand. Nor do the editors mention that most of the reviews have been collected on Mann's website in any case, http://www.yeatsvision.com/Reviews.html, thus obviating the need for interested readers to track down musty journals. However, they do quote snippets from one review that Mann was unable to locate, and reference reviews of 'Stories of Michael Robartes and His Friends' that Mann did not include.

The editors also find space to indulge in some needless repetition, although perhaps it is just over-zealous signposting. For example, in two consecutive pages they inform us that 'We have charted a conservative course, keeping our emendations minimal, noting all in Appendix 1, Table 4', 'Although all our emendations are noted in Appendix 1, Table 4, we explain our principles here', and 'All emendations are noted in Appendix 1, Table 4' (*CW14* l-li).

As for errors and misprints not related to the difficulties of the system, the volume is surprisingly free for a book of this size and complexity: I have noticed only about a dozen. The most egregious error is the identification of Henry James as one of the philosophers Yeats was reading in 1926 (*CW14* xxvi), an error which necessitates an emendation to the Index as well, given that the James brothers are equally represented in this volume and the Index refers to only one of them. Nor did M. M. Rossi 'co-edit' Berkeley (*CW14* xxviii), certainly not for the book to which Yeats wrote an Introduction: he added a philosophical commentary to what is largely a biographical study. With misprints proper, Peter Liebregts' book is called *Centaurs in the Twilights* (*CW14* xvi: perhaps the phrase 'deer in the headlights' caused contamination); the philosopher R. G. Collingwood is given as 'R. C. Collingwood' (*CW14* 394 n. 52); 'Plunket' is printed as 'Plunkett', both in the text and the notes (*CW14* 185, 300 n. 24, 431 n. 46, 491), as per Yeats's misspelling (although it had been corrected, both in text and notes, by the same editors, in their edition of the 1925 version [*CW13* 361]); one of Yeats's poems is referred to as 'The Double Visions of Michael Robartes' (*CW14* 394 n. 55); the Index under 'Michael Robartes' directs the reader to the '"Michael Robartes Foretells" TS, 315n28' (*CW14* 492), whereas that reference is to a published passage in *CW13*; and the note on Gentile [*CW14* 350 n. 21] points the reader to 'n34 below', when the note is actually 35. But these are easily corrected minor matters. They do not detract from the solid achievement of the whole, and I mention them so that they may be corrected in any future printings.

The extreme shorthand of the notes gives a cramped impression and is occasionally confusing, it sometimes being unclear if the reference is to an internal page or an external source; see, for example, 'On Phidias's *Zeus Olympios*, see Pausanias, 5.11.1 (*Description of Greece*, Books 2–5, trans. W. H. S. Jones [Loeb, 1926], 436–37), and note 688 above' (*CW14* 453), where I have no idea what 'note 688 above' means. The following does not make for easy reading, but is no doubt useful: '*An Adventure* and its authors appear numerous times in the AS, and WBY mentions it in *AVA* (136, 286–87 n126) and elsewhere. See also *Plays* 722; *LE* 115, 270, 272, 354 n35b, 452 nn36 and 36a, and 360 n10. See *YVP* 1:307, 319, 3:290; *MYV* 1:179, 224–25' (*CW14* 408 n. 38; the quote from Moberly in the same note is of course from *LTWBY* 347–48, not *L* 347–48); but when the reader is faced with 'Robartes's death is alluded to in "The Adoration of the Magi" (*Myth1* 310, *Myth2* 202) and mentioned in notes to *Michael Robartes and the Dancer* (*VP* 821) and in Owen Aherne's "Introduction" to *AVA* (lviii–lix); see also 327 n. 1 and 339 n. 60' (*CW14* 341 n. 6), it is not immediately apparent to the uninitiated that the semi-colon signifies that the references which follow are to *CW14* itself.

To some extent, what one chooses to annotate is a subjective judgment, as is what one chooses to include in the annotation once chosen. Many of the annotations to the 1925 edition closely followed those of *CVA*, adding references to *Yeats's* Vision *Papers* where appropriate. The 1925 edition, being closer in time and subject matter to the system's genesis, called for more references to the automatic script and their publication in *Yeats's* Vision *Papers*, whereas this edition dictates more reference to the typescripts. However, the editors do not entirely eschew quotations from the automatic script, which is to be welcomed. Nor does interpretation loom large in the endnotes, as the editors' brief was to provide materials for interpretation and not the interpretation itself. Nevertheless, there are several passages that stray from this self-imposed limitation, and these also are to be welcomed, e.g. the note explaining that Yeats's 'right to left' in a particular passage should be 'left to right' (*CW14* 351 n. 29), or the note explaining why the astrological symbols have been reversed in the diagram of The Great Wheel from one edition to another (*CW14* 344–45 n. 1 #4). And given that there is a large overlap between the text of 'The Twenty-Eight Incarnations' and 'Dove or Swan' in the two editions, how do the editors handle those particular annotations? They appear to be largely the same; the changed passages are often helpful expansions or corrections pointed out by reviewers. For example, the long note on 'fabulous, formless darkness' (*CW14* 447–48 n. 60) credits Neil Mann's review of their 1925 edition for the proper attribution, while the note on the phrase 'the dog bays the Moon' (*CW14* 356 n. 50) has added a reference to the Tarot card 'The Moon', also via Mann. (I *do* have a quibble about the way the latter note has been handled. Reference to Kathleen Raine's *Yeats, the Tarot and the Golden Dawn* might have been more appropriate than reference to A. E. Waite's popularized account. Raine includes pictures of the card from the packs of both Yeatses, and quotes the meaning it had in the Golden Dawn, where there was no reference to Waite's misleading dog AND wolf.) In fact, most of the matters addressed in Mann's review have been remedied, as if they had been ticked off one by one. Paul's knowledge of Ezra Pound comes more into play in the Notes than it did in parallel passages in the earlier edition (e.g. on Dowson and Landor, not to mention Wordsworth (*CW14* 365 n. 102 compared with *CW13* 251 n. 131; *CW14* 354 n. 42 compared with *CW13* 238 n. 49; *CW14* 366 n. 108 compared with *CW13* 252 n. 137). Presumably Paul is responsible for the more obscure Ezra Pound references in the notes to 'A Packet for Ezra Pound' (see the reference to Massimo Bacigalupo's article in *Quaderni di Palazzo Serra*, *CW14* 310 n. 15), as well as later ones in 'The Completed Symbol' (e.g. *CW14* 433 n. 59); it is not however mentioned that Pound is probably the source for Yeats's initial interest in Grosseteste's theories of light, with Duhem only coming into play later (see *CW14* 140, 385–86 notes 11–12). Paul's expertise in Pound is also apparent in parts of the editorial introduction, where whole paragraphs are repeated from her 2011 article 'Compiling *A Packet for Ezra Pound*', including what I am reliably informed are faulty transcriptions of 'questions from Mary Devenport O'Neill' relating to *A Vision* (*CW14* xxix).[3] As an aside, Paul's article is listed in the Abbreviations as 'Paul', while Russell Murphy's essential study of the significance of Byzantium in the system, '"Old Rocky Face, look forth": W. B. Yeats, the Christ Pantokrator, and the Soul's History (The Photographic Record)', *YAACTS* 14 (1996), which is referenced more often, is not so listed, while the sole Index entry for Murphy is not to the first mention of him or his article, so that someone

---

[3] O'Neill was not a random correspondent as the O'Neills had known Yeats for some years and Mary Devenport O'Neill had often discussed *A Vision* with him. See Ann Saddlemyer, *Becoming George: The Life of Mrs W. B. Yeats* (Oxford: Oxford University Press, 2002), 177, 351 and *YGYL* 34 n. 1; also *MYV2* 412–14. Where *MYV2* has O'Neill asking if a daimon has 'any separate existence apart from human being to whom it belongs' (414), *CW14* xxix has 'Has a daimon any separate masters apart from human being to whom it belongs?' Although I have not seen the original, the former reading is obviously preferable from the point of view of the system.

looking for the full citation cannot find it easily. Nor is the Index complete with its references to Paul. Obviously, such problems do not occur with electronic editions of books.[4]

The annotations for 'The Great Year of the Ancients' in particular are very full, with copious quotations from Pierre Duhem's *Le Système du monde* and explanations of astronomical matters aimed at an audience which may find such topics confusing.

Some of the annotations illuminate in unexpected ways. The note to 'the Muses sometimes form in those low haunts their most lasting attachments' (*CW14* 19) compares it to Yeats's remark to Laura Riding that 'poets were good liars who never forgot that the Muses were women who liked the embrace of gay warty lads' (*CW14* 323 n. 65). However, checking Alexander Charles Sutherland's 1978 dissertation 'Yeats's Revisions of *A Vision*: A Study of the Text, with Appendices of Textual Variants and Annotations', Ph.D. diss., New York University, I find that he said it first. Sutherland's dissertation is referred to in the same note, but is not given as the source of this observation.[5] The fact that Sutherland was used perhaps explains why

---

[4] eBooks versions are essential for scholarly study, as the notes are more easily retrieved and the reader is not forced to rely on the vagaries of editorial indexing. Unfortunately, even major publishers do not seem to have thought things through with regard to scholarly eBooks, particularly when they publish older books that have had to be OCR'd: tables are printed as images because it is easier, words get run together, spaces occur where they shouldn't, and letters are misidentified. This publisher's sample for the eBook edition of *The Collected Works of W. B. Yeats Vol. VI: Prefaces and Introductions* has, in the first few paragraphs of the Editor's Preface, the following word-joins: 'specialinterest', 'Yeatsrevised', 'selectionof', 'willingnessto', 'revisionsmade', 'twosigned', 'never-publishedcollected', and 'thisto'. Needless to say, reading such a text can be wearisome. The ISBN for the eBook version of *A Vision: The Revised 1937 Edition* is given at the front of the hardback: ISBN 978-1-4767-9211-8. I have not seen the full version, for the reason given above. What I have seen is mercifully free of coding errors; I presume the text itself did not need to be OCR'd because of its newness.

[5] Sutherland 641. I do not wish to imply anything unethical here; things get lost in the course of editing long books, particularly when space is at a premium. To take an example of what is surely an unintentional omission, 'the Japanese interpreter of Botticelli' (*CW14* 150) is identified as 'Yukio Yashiro (1890–1975) [who] was an art historian and art critic who graduated from Tokyo University and studied in Europe from 1921 to 1925. In February 1926, just after the publication of *AVA*, GY gave WBY a copy of Yashiro's three-volume study *Sandro Botticelli* (London and Boston: The Medici Society, 1925)' (*CW14* 392 n. 42). As well as including information not in Sutherland, who tentatively identified the reference (Sutherland 872), Harper and Paul neglect to inform the reader of one of the essential sources used by them: the information about GY's gift is not from the standard biographies but comes from the inscription in *YL* 2304.

the reference is to Yeats's letter to Dorothy Wellesley in Wade's edition of the *Letters* and not to the original letter to Riding in *CL InteLex* 6563. I also find illuminating the note which juxtaposes a list of Indian schools of philosophy studied by Yeats with Dermott Mac Manus' claim that the Yeatses in later life gave up spiritualism in favour of 'the tradition of Indian thought' (*CW14* 384 n. 4). This is in spite of W. J. Mc Cormack's contemptuous dismissal of Mac Manus as 'the pseudo-Hindoo-guru' ('*We Irish' in Europe: Yeats, Berkeley and Joseph Hone* [University College Dublin Press, 2010], 63). (Alternatively, he is 'the swashbuckling fascist and Higher Hindu' in *Blood Kindred: W. B. Yeats, the Life, the Death, the Politics* [London: Pimlico, 2005, 13]; later, in the same book, the characterization 'the philosophical fascist and convert-Catholic, higher-Hindu' is used [285]. Mc Cormack is nothing if not tiresomely picturesque.) If only people and their aspirations could always be summed up so cavalierly.

II

Before getting on to the textual editing, I should clear a little ground. The editors dedicate their edition to Walter Kelly Hood and Connie K. Hood, who were the original designated editors of both volumes of *A Vision* for The *Collected Works of W. B. Yeats* (*CW14* xi). Walter K. Hood was of course one of the editors of *A Critical Edition of Yeats's* A Vision *(1925)*, contributing the bulk of the annotations, while George Mills Harper wrote the Editorial Introduction and added to the notes where reference to the Automatic Script was required. Walter K. Hood was to have contributed historical and explanatory notes for the projected 1937 edition, while Connie K. Hood was to have edited the text. Her unpublished 1983 dissertation 'A Search for Authority: Prolegomena to a Definitive Critical Edition of W. B. Yeats's 'A Vision' (1937)' Ph. D. diss., University of Tennessee, formed the basis for the intended textual emendations ('Search' vi, viii). It therefore has a direct bearing on Harper and Paul's project.

It is perhaps worth emphasizing that Hood's dissertation was completed before the main sources for the scholarly study of *A Vision* were published. *The Making of Yeats's 'A Vision': A Study of the Automatic Script* by George Mills Harper came out in 1987 (although Hood read the first four chapters before publication), while the first three volumes of *Yeats's* Vision *Papers* (under various editors) appeared in 1992. (The fourth and final volume was published in 2001.) It was written before O'Shea's *A Descriptive Catalog of W. B. Yeats's Library* (1985), the Compilation of the NLI *Collection List No. 60: Occult Papers of W. B. Yeats*, and the publication of the InteLex edition of Yeats's *Collected Letters*.[6] It was also completed just before the controversy erupted over the editing of Yeats's poems, when questions of delegation arose, and the idea was mooted and energetically defended by the late Richard Finneran, that a process was begun after Yeats's death 'of—not to put too fine a point on it—corrupting the texts which he had worked so hard to perfect'.[7] The enormity of the task undertaken by the Hoods, Connie K. Hood in particular, must be acknowledged, and Harper and Paul state that '[t]o observe that this edition would not have been possible without their extensive archival and contextual work is to understate drastically, and we are deeply in their debt' (*CW14* xi). This is by no means the sort of routine encomium you will find in books written by academics. Hood was nothing if not thorough; there is thus inevitably a large overlap between what she said in the historical narrative of her dissertation and what is covered by Harper and Paul in their Editorial Introduction. (They have of course updated and standardized the references.) Nevertheless, the resultant edition of the text differs from anything the Hoods would have produced, as I shall demonstrate.

Harper and Paul do not mention Finneran's charge directly, although they gesture towards his stance by using arch quotation marks around words such as 'corrected', 'authorial', 'intentions' and 'permission' (*CW14* xlviii-l). Finneran, of course, was one of the original general editors of *The Collected Works of W. B. Yeats*, a 'series invested in the authorial intentions of WBY' (*CW14* xlix). *A Vision*, however, is a special case, as it was originally based on the automatic writing of George Yeats, who by this fact can plausibly be called 'an author of equal standing' (*CW14* l) with her husband. Harper and Paul explain their problem as follows: 'First is the difficulty of ascertaining [Yeats's] intentions in the last version of the text published in his lifetime. Second is the question of what to do with emendations made to that

---

[6] Where I have given unsourced references to NLI numbers, I have taken them from *Collection List No. 60, Occult Papers of W. B. Yeats*, compiled by Peter Kenny (Leabharlann Náisiúnta na hÉireann, National Library of Ireland, [n.d.]), http://www.nli.ie/pdfs/mss lists/yeatsoccult.pdf. Kenny identifies most of the sources used by Hood.

[7] See Warwick Gould, 'W. B. Yeats and the Resurrection of the Author', *The Library* (1994) s6–16 (2): 101–34. The quotation is from Finneran's *Editing Yeats's Poems: A Reconsideration* (London: Macmillan, 1990), 39; it originally appeared in *Editing Yeats's Poems* (New York: St Martin's Press, 1983), 30. The epigraph at the head of this paper is from Finneran's essay 'Text and Interpretation in the Poems of W. B. Yeats', in George Bornstein (ed.), *Representing Modernist Texts: Editing as Interpretation* (Ann Arbor: University of Michigan Press, 1991), 31. I have taken it from Gould, 122.

text by trusted collaborators after his death' (*CW14* xlix). The difficulty of ascertaining Yeats's intentions is restricted by them to manuscripts, typescripts and galley proofs: more specifically, to the fact that there is not a complete record. I would stress, rather, the fact that Yeats himself was averse to proof-reading: he did, after all, have other calls on his time, was frequently ill during the relevant time-period, his eyesight was poor, and his spelling was notoriously bad.[8] Add to this the fact that *A Vision* is not a short piece of prose and its difficult subject matter makes for difficult proof-reading; it was also a book which Yeats could never finish to his own satisfaction.

Even if we had what Harper and Paul ask for, and lament the absence of, 'a complete extant setting copy' (*CW14* xxxix), I do not think this would resolve all questions of authorial intention: unless, of course, one takes an extremely restrictive view of what that entails. And, obviously, this is where questions arise of delegation to 'trusted collaborators'. Harper and Paul have decided to incorporate most of George Yeats's corrections as marked in various copies of *A Vision* (1937/38). The other trusted collaborator was Thomas Mark, to whom Yeats delegated copy-editing rights during his lifetime,[9] and who after Yeats's death mailed his corrected proofs to GY for

---

[8] It was not only his spelling that was notoriously bad; he sometimes could not even read his own handwriting; see William H. O'Donnell's 'Reading Yeats's Hand', in *YAACTS9* (1991), 87–94. Hood quotes a letter where AE admonishes Yeats: 'Your proof-reading is abominable. You are the worst culprit I know in this respect' ('Search' 165). Hood neglected to give the date of this letter, perhaps because it was from 1899; see *Letters from AE*. Sel. and ed. Alan Denson (London: Abelard-Schuman, 1961), 31. She suggests it got worse as he got older.

[9] See Gould, 'W. B. Yeats and the Resurrection of the Author', 114–17, for some of Yeats's comments on Mark. *CL InteLex* 5731 has Yeats's letter of 8 September 1932 to Harold Macmillan which reads, 'I would be very much obliged if you would give the enclosed letter to the admirable scholar who is assisting in the correction of the proofs of my new collected edition. It is partly a letter of thanks and partly an explanation of certain metrical tricks of mine which have puzzled him'. The 'enclosed letter' is not printed or noted here in the *CL InteLex*, but cross-reference should be made to *CL InteLex* 5733, which has 'Mention in letter from Mark, 16 September 1932. Discussing corrections and proofs of new edition of WBY's works', where the reference is to *LTWBY2* 543–44. The date of the *CL InteLex* letter should be changed from 'c. 15 September 1932' to 'on or before 8 September 1932', and its explanatory note emended to include specific quotations from the letter, as per that series' policy. Jon Stallworthy quoted sentences from it in his 1963 book *Between the Lines: Yeats's Poetry in the Making*, including the unambiguous statement 'I have never been able to punctuate properly. I do not think I have ever differed from a correction of yours in punctuation. I suggest that in the remaining volumes [of the projected Collected Edition] you do not

approval, apparently receiving it (*CW14* xlvi, 303 n. 78). Thus, it might be argued that they had been passed by 'an author of equal standing', meaning George Yeats, and should therefore be incorporated into an emended text. But this would involve too many assumptions about specifics. Harper and Paul have instead chosen to relegate Mark's corrections to the endnotes and an appendix, '[i]n keeping with established series policy' (*CW14* li).

However, even one of the original general editors of the *Collected Works of W. B. Yeats*, Richard Finneran himself, once thought that the 1962 London edition (copy-edited by Mark) was the best available (see Finneran's 'On Editing Yeats: The Text of *A Vision* [1937]', 124). This is despite the fact that it introduced errors into the text and did not make some corrections that had been made in the 1956/61 edition, which in itself had also introduced errors. The later Finneran would not have been so lenient: he had by that stage painted himself into a corner through being forced to defend his edition of the poems, and lost no opportunity to denigrate the work of Mark, and to a lesser extent, the work of GY. The editors of *A Vision* in *The Collected Works* overstate things to their own advantage when they write that 'We treat [in the section entitled EDITIONS AFTER 1937 (*CW14* xlvi-xlviii), a brief two and three-quarter pages] the editing process for those [1956/61 and 1962] editions, which rather than producing the definitive editions they advertised introduced further errors' (*CW14* xxv), as though those editions did not also introduce some readings that were preferable to those of the original edition.[10] The main point of the section appears to have been to demonstrate that the editing of the 1956/61 and 1962 editions meant that 'we are many textual stages away from the 1937 edition of A Vision' (*CW14* xlviii), and thus may safely be ignored. I remain unconvinced by this argument. All told, while it is hard not to agree with the editors

query your own corrections', from Gould, 115. The passage quoted by Gould from Charles Morgan's *The House of Macmillan (1843–1943)* should also be added, as presumably it is from the same source: 'For the first time there will be a satisfactory text of my work, thanks to your watchfulness and patience'. See also Note 10, below.

[10] In fact, the 1956/61 edition is the only one that claimed to be definitive: its title page included the subtitle 'A reissue with the author's final revisions', whereas the 1962 edition only claimed that it was 'Reissued with corrections'. It is to be regretted that Harper and Paul's edition does not include a textual collation such as that given in Hood's Chapter 6, where the reader can see at a glance the differences between the 1937, 1938, 1956/61 and 1962 editions ('Search' 239–48). Harper and Paul's Table 3 gives a collation with the 1962 text, but the reader is left to assemble a possible 1956/61 text from their Tables 1 and 2 (see *CW14* xlviii).

when they conclude that 'the ideal of a perfected text [is] impossible' (*CW14* l), I think the decision to restrict Mark's emendations to the endnotes and an appendix was not the best course of action.

Harper and Paul follow Connie K. Hood in espousing the editorial principle of least tampering with the received text. They write that their ideal is to present in its best possible light 'the 1937 edition of *A Vision*, the final version of the text over which W. B. Yeats had "authorial" control' (*CW14* xlviii), adding that

We have charted a conservative course, keeping our emendations minimal, noting all in Appendix 1, Table 4. In that same Appendix, Tables 1 and 2 compile changes marked by the Yeatses in their copies of *A Vision* (1937, YL 2434; and 1938, YL 2435), and these tables also note changes made in the copy of *A Vision* (1938) in the Alspach collection. Table 3 compiles corrections proposed for or made in posthumous editions of *A Vision*, comparing them with the 1937 text. These apparatuses allow readers both to reconstruct different published and imagined states of the text, and to consider our own editorial practice, and thereby to ruminate over the textual authority of Thomas Mark and GY while seeing what text WBY left behind (*CW14* l).

This is all admirably democratic, but perhaps it leaves too much to the reader. Hood also invokes a 'conservative course', writing that 'The editorial position of this [projected] edition is extremely conservative and at the same time broadly eclectic. Changes actually made in the text must be justified from manuscript sources prior to the 1937 edition (except for the three changes Yeats himself made on his wife's copy) except in a few cases where strong internal evidence suggests printers' or typists' corruptions (as "Phase 29" for "Phase 28" [cf. *CW14* 243, 269])' ('Search' 163). It is therefore of interest to see how the Hoods' projected edition would have compared with Harper and Paul's actual edition.

III

Finneran may not have accepted what he and George Bornstein called 'the weak argument of posthumous delegated authority' (*CW4* 324), but this of course does not absolve an editor from making his or her own editorial choices. At its simplest level, you would think that this would be a matter of reading the text as printed to see that the words make sense, that the sentences are grammatical, and that syntax is not tortured: in other words, routine proofreading and copyediting. This is what Thomas Mark did, and did well. Not to use his expertise to assist your own is to operate with one hand tied behind your back; simply listing his emendations in an Appendix is not the same thing as weighing his decisions against the text and against your own. Moreover, it is not just individual sentences that have to make sense. The reader needs to put the sentences into a coherent whole: passage has to be compared with like passage and consistencies (or their converse) drawn out. If there are inconsistencies, it would be ideal to ask the writer what was intended. When the author is not available, an editor should at least make some attempt to correct those minor inconsistencies where it is apparent that lack of attention was most likely involved. This of course should not be done silently; the reader must be given the arguments. If an editor chooses not to correct inconsistencies because his or her editorial principles dictate that this should not be done, then it would still be preferable if the reader could be confident that the editor was aware of them. There is a further consideration the reader may or may not choose to take seriously. Yeats believed the system was complete but that he did not always fully understand it. His text may therefore be regarded as an imperfect embodiment of the system, which the reader is invited to complete. I myself occasionally adopt this viewpoint as a heuristic device.

Harper and Paul's emendations, as set out in their Table 4, Emendations to the Copy Text (*CW14* 267–73), fall into three broad categories: spelling corrections, including titles of poems and proper names; GY's corrections to the Yeatses' copies of *A Vision* (1937) and *A Vision* (1938); and changes made to impose terminological consistency.

The first of these requirements, that of spelling, is I imagine one imposed by a combination of the publisher's house style and the requirements of the fourteen-volume *Collected Works of W. B. Yeats*. While it is sometimes difficult to distinguish between the two, publishers don't want to look as though they don't know their own business: their main concern is not to alienate readers by giving them the impression that they have been content with sloppy production.

I have no problems with the changing of poem titles from italics to roman type in quotation marks; after all, this is a process begun by Yeats and carried through by GY and Thomas Mark.[11] But the editors have also

---

[11] See Yeats's letter of 13 March 1935 to Harold Macmillan, where he writes, apropos of such things, 'I hesitate to lay such a burdensome task [as reading proofs of *A Vision*] upon Mr Mark for I suppose he would be the reader. I feel that my geometrical way of expressing myself may fill him with impatience or that he may find it impossible to revise efficiently without a greater study of my philosophical ideas than he should be expected to make. If however he could read the proofs for superficial errors, for lack of uniformity in the use of italics, capitals, etc., I should be greatly obliged to him' (*CL InteLex* 6199). As this letter also reveals, Yeats had the idea of trusting Frank Pearce Sturm with the task of

changed the spelling of proper names and have Anglicized Cyrillic names (*CW14* li). Thus, Yeats's 'Tolstoi' and 'Dostoieffsky', his 'Michael Angelo' and Leibnitz', have been modernized. You can see the point: no publisher wants to put off readers with unfamiliar spellings. It may be noted, though, that these spellings were perfectly acceptable when Yeats wrote. If you leave them as Yeats left them, they serve as a reminder to the reader of the time when the book was written; if you change them, you lose this flavour.[12] But other proper names have been corrected: Alcemon, Aeslepius, Philaus, Dionysius, Zazuki (although with the last, the editor's confusingly leave the misspelling of the InteLex *Collected Letters* without a 'sic' when they quote that source as saying that 'Yeats's "Zuzuki" is written mistakenly for "Susuki"', *CW14* 399 n. 72). This follows editorial procedure adopted in other volumes in *The Collected Works of W. B. Yeats*. However, for some unknown reason, Yeats's 'Grillion Club' has not been corrected to 'Grillion's Club', though the editors obviously know that the latter is correct, spelling it thus in the notes and index. Thomas Mark changed 'Leibnitz' to 'Leibniz' and 'Grillion Club' to 'Grillion's Club', but left the others. He emended 'Brama' in the quotation from Keats's 'Endymion' to 'Brahma' (cf. *The Poems of John Keats*, edited by Sidney Colvin [2 vols.; London: Chatto & Windus, 1920; *YL* 1055, 1:242), although this misspelling is left unremarked on by Harper and Paul (*CW14* 81, 243). Harper and Paul also change 'Crickmaa' to 'Cruchmaa' on the strength of GY's annotation (*CW14* 21, 228, 236, 326–27 n. 75), whereas a quick Google would seem to support Mark's 1962 spelling of 'Cruachmaa'. I leave it to Irish specialists to debate that one.

Some of these spelling corrections, as opposed to modernizations, may be seen as reflections of Yeats's intention, but it is a slippery slope. Hood, for example, suggests that 'Aeslepius' may be 'a printing error based on misreading of Yeats's poor handwriting' ('Search' 230), and one can imagine that at least some of the other misspellings have a similar origin. My preference would have been for the editors to refer to drafts and typescripts before altering the text; endnotes are the place for proper identification and spelling, as they would have been the place to note an emendation that had actually been made.

There is thus the large question of whether to emend the text on the basis of what George Yeats and Thomas Mark chose to do. Their corrections to

---

proof-reading for system errors, but this did not eventuate. See also the afterword to this essay by Warwick Gould.

[12] It may be worth mentioning that not even Finneran emended Yeats's 'Michael Angelo' in his edition of the *Poems*.

the text are available for inspection, as Warwick Gould once remarked.[13] We have seen above that Harper and Paul noted in an appendix GY's annotations in copies of *A Vision* (1937) and *A Vision* (1938), and many of them were incorporated by them into their text, presumably (although it is not stated outright) on the basis of GY's 'semi-authorial status' (*CW14* l). As test cases, let us examine two changes made on this basis by Harper and Paul where change might seem unnecessary.

The first is the word 'adaptation'. Harper and Paul change WBY's 'adaption' and 'self-adaption' to 'adaptation' and 'self-adaptation', basing their decision on 'GY in YL 2434'. Connie Hood explains, quite correctly ('Search' 223), that 'adaption' is a valid English word, and it appears in the *OED* with examples from Swift and Dickens. The original 1937 edition has examples of both 'adaption' and 'adaptation', with three of the former and one of the latter (see *CW14* 229, 249, 270 for the places where 'adaption' originally appeared; the unchanged 'adaptation' occurs on *CW14* 71). One might think that the word is GY's, since it is taken from the Automatic Script. However, WBY and GY use both spellings, if we are to trust the editors' transcriptions in the *Yeats's* Vision *Papers*. On October 24 1918, WBY asks, 'What do you mean by self-adaptation?' (*YVP2* 465), referring back to the session of January 3 (*YVP1* 192), which implies that the word first used is 'adaptation', and that it has been used by GY; while on February 1 1920, GY herself uses 'adaption' (*YVP2* 532). Personally, I prefer 'adaptation', but by crediting the amendment to GY's annotation alone, the editors gloss over the fact that the word had been the subject of debate between GY and Thomas Mark, and had been altered in both sets of Coole proofs (*CW14* 249).

The second word I wish to examine is 'cabbala' and its derivatives. The evidence of letters and early published texts suggests that Yeats originally spelt the word with a single 'b', although he varied between an initial 'k' and 'c'. In the 1937 edition of *A Vision*, Yeats used the forms 'Cabala', 'Cabalists' and 'Cabalistic', with the 1962 edition following this spelling consistently

---

[13] See Gould, 'W. B. Yeats and the Resurrection of the Author', 111: 'Whatever individual *textual* decisions George Yeats made, she appears to have acted in good faith. Some of them are open to challenge for the excellent reason that all can be inspected'. By 'inspected', Gould meant that scholars can study the roles of George Yeats (along with those of Yeats's publishers and publishers' readers) 'in vast archives of proofs and letters in at least ten separate locations in Britain, Ireland, and the United States'. Gould himself has been untiring in his excavation of these archives and in publishing his findings. My own inspection is limited to what Hood and various editors have chosen to print, but that in itself is sufficient for the limited purposes of this review.

and the 1956/61 edition fitfully.[14] Harper and Paul change all of these occurrences to a double 'b' on the authority of George Yeats; the source is given as 'GY in YL 2434' (*CW14* 267, 268, 273). In this case, however, we have definite proof that Yeats himself authorized Thomas Mark to make the change, at least insofar as the case of *Autobiographies* was concerned. Yeats had previously used 'cabalistic' (twice) and 'Christian Cabala' (once) in *The Trembling of the Veil* (1922) (although 'Cabbala' was also used once), while in the 1926/27 edition of *Autobiographies* the spelling varies, with the double 'b' having a preponderance due to addition of 'A Biographical Fragment' from *The Criterion*, with its seven usages (the inclusion of the new Section VI to 'Hodos Chameliontos' having added two occurrences of the single 'b'). Understandably, Mark queried the preferred spelling when he was correcting proofs for the *Edition de Luxe* in 1932. Warwick Gould and Deirdre Toomey explain: 'By underdotting "cabbalistic" in the text (*Au* 371) and scoring out Mark's alternatives, WBY had indicated his preference' (*Myth 2005* xcvi and note 26). GY and Mark were thus carrying out *Yeats's* decided spelling when they used the double 'b'. This example underscores that fact that it is unwise to assume that GY and Mark were simply imposing their own preferences; it also demonstrates the seriousness with which they undertook to carry out Yeats's expressed delegation.[15] The more one looks at this matter of delegation, the more arbitrary appears the decision to include George Yeats's annotations to copies of the 1937 and 1938 editions, but not to use the Coole proofs and the later London and

[14] Of course, when referring to von Rosenroth's *Kabbala Denudata* Yeats followed the spelling of the original title, as custom dictates (*CW14* 39). 'Cabala' appears to be the currently preferred spelling when discussing the Christian Cabala, 'Qabalah' the spelling used by occultists who wish to draw attention to themselves, and 'Kabbalah' that used when writing of Madonna or referring to Gershom Scholem and Moshe Idel (not to mention S. L. MacGregor Mathers and A. E. Waite) (see *CW14* 316 n. 30 for the editors' awareness of the different spellings). According to the website http://www.chabad.org/kabbalah/article_cdo/aid/380679/jewish/ KABBALAH-CABALA-QABALAH.htm, there are in fact 24 spelling variations, but we are concerned here with how Yeats spelt the word.

[15] Gould and Toomey note that George Yeats herself expressed dissatisfaction with several of Yeats's decisions. 'I do not like title [Mythologies]', she wrote, 'but even less do I like a change he [WBY] made from "discoveries" to "Explorations" which occurs in forthcoming "Essays"' (*Myth 2005* 493); however, as the reader must see, she did not impose her dislikes on the publisher. As an aside, Professor Gould advises me that the next printing of *Mythologies* will emend 'Rosa Alchemica' to 'The Tables of the Law' on p. xcvi, main text and n. 26. Here, I should like to thank Professor Gould for helpful comments on this review. Needless to say, any errors or omissions that remain are entirely my responsibility.

New York editions. The unexpressed assumption—if there is one—must be that there is a purely one-way traffic from the annotations to the Coole proofs; in point of fact, we simply do not know precisely when individual annotations have been made. Whatever the reasoning, the editors' decision is, at best, a half-hearted concession to those who argue that Yeats trusted others to carry out his wishes; but as the saying goes, those who try to please everyone end up pleasing no-one.

Some of Thomas Mark's emendations to *A Vision* have been made to correct syntax, to clarify what is being said, or simply to assist ease of reading. For example, he inserted a comma after 'to' in the phrase 'an appreciation of, or submission to some quality' (*CW14* 68, 242), but he did not change the earlier 'a sharing of or submission to divine personality' (*CW14* 65). He worried about Yeats's 'Certain London spiritualists for some years past have decked out a Christmas tree with presents that have each the names of some dead child upon it' (*CW14* 161), changing the 'it' to 'them' (*CW14* 256; although as Hood points out, 'A better solution would have been to rephrase as "presents each of which has the name of some dead child upon it"' ('Search' 232). He also tackled what Hood calls a 'confusingly phrased footnote' ('Search' 237) on *CW14* 195, which reads in part '"Mathematic Starlight" Babylonian astrology is, however, present in the friendships and antipathies of the Olympic gods'. (I think it is more of a headlong rush than a confusion.) Mark suggested rephrasing this to '"Mathematical Starlight", Babylonian astrology, is, however, present in the friendships and antipathies of the Olympic gods'. The change from 'mathematic' to 'Mathematical' is because Mark thought, quite reasonably, that Yeats was quoting the passage that the note was attached to (the first Coole proof has '"Mathematical Starlight", Babylonian astrology, is, [note: "al as in line 2?"]', *CW14* 261), where Yeats writes 'I can but see bird and woman [swan and Leda] blotting out some corner of the Babylonian mathematical starlight'. I myself would insert em dashes in the footnote, but Mark's solution is equally plausible. I also would not capitalize 'starlight'. Harper and Paul simply ignore the whole thing. Or take the following sentence: 'When *Passionate Body* and *Celestial Body* give way to *Mask* we dwell in aesthetic process, so much skill in bronze or paint, or on some symbol that rouses emotion for emotion's sake' (*CW14* 143). Mark would have us dwelling 'on' aesthetic process, not 'in' it (*CW14* 254). Harper and Paul do not change 'in' to 'on', and in fact give no sign that they have thought about the matter, although I think 'on' makes more sense.

Towards the end of 'The Great Year of the Ancients' there is a fairly well-known passage which contrasts an *antithetical* dispensation with a *primary*: 'A *primary* dispensation looking beyond itself towards a transcendent power is dogmatic, levelling, unifying, feminine, humane, peace its means and end; an *antithetical* dispensation obeys imminent power, is expressive, hierarchical, multiple, masculine, harsh, surgical'. It is the parallelism here that led Connie Hood to suggest that 'imminent' should be changed to 'immanent'. 'No manuscript source is available for this passage', she writes, 'but the sense of the sentence clearly requires "immanent" in contrast to "transcendent power" (263.5 [i.e. *CW14* 192]). Mark changed "imminent" at [the earlier passage at] 176.18 [i.e. *CW14* 131] but missed this instance' ('Search' 237). The earlier passage at *CW14* 131 reads: 'His work should neither be consciously aesthetic nor consciously speculative but imitative of a central Being—the *Mask* as his pursuer—consciously apprehended as something distinct, as something never imminent though eternally united to the soul'. Hood agrees with Mark here, and suggests replacing 'imminent' with 'immanent', but she bases her decision on 'VAMS', '[a] holograph manuscript of part of *A Vision* (1925)' (I presume this is the document called 'Version B' in *YVP4*, an early manuscript for 'The Great Wheel' and 'The Twenty-Eight Embodiments' [NLI MS 36,263/10/1–2]. I could be wrong, but all of the references match), as well as on what the sentence seems to say ('Search' 97, 229). Harper and Paul's edition of the 1925 version has a footnote relating to this sentence, but it does not take up the 'imminent/immanent' debate: 'VersB adds a final sentence to the paragraph at this point: "He is a moralist" (*YVP4*:232)' (*CW13* 89, 264 n. 226). The passage from *YVP4* 232 has 'as something never ~~imenent~~ imanent, though eternally | united to the soul. He is a moralist'. While Yeats's spelling is always suspect, the fact that he has changed the first 'e' implies that he had given some thought as to what letter should replace it. The table 'Comparison of *A Vision* with Proofs' in Harper and Paul (*CW14* 252) notes that both Coole corrections and the 1962 edition choose 'immanent' here, although the proofs as printed retained 'imminent'. Harper and Paul print 'imminent' both for this instance and the later one. They certainly do not mention the possibility that the word could be otherwise.

At one stage, Yeats refers to 'constellations [plural] of Goat' (*CW14* 184), which does not seem grammatical. Certainly one of the drafts has 'the Goat', as Hood explains:

252.21 constellation] The word is not in the corresponding place in MBY-VB 22 [MS 36,272/6/1–2; see NLI *Collection List No. 60*, 41 and *CW14* 430 n. 41]; thus the plural form is probably a printing error, produced by an attempt to read Yeats's handwriting on the galleys.

252.21 of the Goat] MBY-VB 22 contains 'the', but it was dropped in AV-B; Mark reinstated it in 62. ('Search' 236–7)

Harper and Paul quote the relevant passage from the typescript carbon in an endnote (*CW14* 430 n. 41) but do not make the correction. I suspect they quoted the passage simply because the sentence that follows is markedly different from the published version.[16]

There is one place where both Mark and Hood appear to have lapsed in their proofreading. On p. 151 of the 1937 edition, there is a missing letter at the end of line 3, an omission mirrored in the 1962 English reprint:

Is it an 's' or an 'n'? Harper and Paul think it is 'n' (*CW14* 112, 270), which makes a kind of sense only if you are allowed to start one sentence and end another. Hood, who is usually so thorough, does not mention the missing letter; the 1956/61 edition followed the wording of the same passage in the 1925 edition, and used the 's'. In their 1925 edition Harper and Paul themselves print 'is a fragment' (*CW13* 70).

A VISION   151

do I care if it is good or bad?" There is no "disillusion-
ment", for they have found that which they have
sought, but that which they have sought and found i
a fragment.

Mark also missed a badly punctuated passage describing the *Shiftings*. Yeats writes:

'For in a state of equilibrium there is neither emotion nor sensation'. In the limits of the good and evil of the previous life... the soul is brought to a contemplation of good and evil; 'neither its utmost good nor its utmost evil can force sensation or emotion'. (*CW14* 168–69)

The ellipsis here would seem to suggest that Yeats left something out of a passage he was quoting, which means that the middle statement must also be a direct quotation. Perhaps Mark was distracted by having to correct the '*Aeneids*' in the following sentence. Hood and Harper and Paul all quote the early version of this passage ('Search' 234, *CW14* 286), a passage

---

[16] The hasty reader may have trouble following Table 3 (*CW14* 259), where the '1st Coole correction' is 'of the Goat', 'As printed: 2nd Coole proofs' is 'of the Goat', whereas '2nd Coole correction' is given as 'of Goat'. Mark's notebook has the correction, as does the 1962 London edition. However, Harper and Paul explain that 'In most cases where the second-pull Coole proofs reverse a change made in the first pull, it is on the authority of the New York [1956/61] edition' (*CW14* 232). This is not the first time the second-pull Coole proofs reverted to a plainly inferior reading. Hood's suggestion ('Search' 231) that the earlier phrase 'precession of the Equinox' (*CW14* 149) is more usually written 'Precession of the Equinoxes' may be correct, but is not relevant to Yeats's passage, which is concentrating on the Vernal Equinox alone. Harper and Paul's endnotes on the precession are excellent (*CW14* 391 n. 38, 414–15 n. 1).

which makes it clear that there are two quotations and not three, as does the equivalent passage in *CW13* 190. Comparison with the original passage from the Automatic Script, helpfully noted by Harper and Paul (*CW13* 327 n. 35, *CW14* 411 n. 51), shows that the ellipsis occurs because the first part occurs after the second (*YVP1* 491). This source also has 'comprehension' instead of 'contemplation'.

Hood mentions several places where thorough proofreading alone might lead one to suspect the text needs emendation. For example, in 'A Packet for Ezra Pound', Yeats describes the occasion when his wife first began to talk in her sleep, 'and from that on almost all communications came in that way' (*CW14* 8). At first sight, it might be tempting to replace 'from that on' with 'from that time on' or 'from then on'. Hood prefers 'from that time on', referencing 'Yeats's Rapallo notebook, NL 13,577' ('Search' 96). However, it appears that 'from that on' is an Irish locution, as it was used frequently by Yeats in *Autobiographies*, as in the sentence 'From time to time from that on she gave me money' (*CW3* 304). Nevertheless, a note from Harper and Paul might have been welcome. Another questionable case occurs in the description of Phase 19: *CW14* 112, like *CW13* 69, has 'A certain actress is typical, for she surrounds herself with drawings by Burne-Jones in his latest period, and reveres them as they were holy pictures'. This would seem to require 'as if they were', which is the reading Hood chooses, basing herself on 'VAMS' ('Search' 97, 228; see *YVP4* 202 for 'as if they were'). Hood includes numerous passages in her chapter 'Textual Notes' along the lines of 'The sense of the sentence requires... but no textual authority exists for doing so' (e.g. 'Search' 221, 222, 224, 226, 228, 229). A typical example is the note on 'whirring' [*CW14* 172]: '"whirring" refers to sound and "whirling" to motion' ('Search' 235). (While we are on this topic, Yeats's idea that the sails of a windmill whirl in opposite directions or change their distance from each other [*CW14* 70, 147] is incorrect, a fact which no-one seems to have remarked on. This is the sort of error textual editing can do nothing about, beyond noting it). Harper and Paul themselves followed this procedure of emending by sense in *CW13* 359, where they changed Yeats's heading EXPANDING AND CONTRASTING GYRES (*CVA* 129; cf. *CW13* 104) on the grounds that 'section elsewhere speaks of contracting, but never of contrasting'. However, as we have seen, most of the examples I have given above of errors that should have been picked up by proofreading do not rate a mention with them.

I have few problems with the editors' standardization of the system's technical terms. In this, they are following in the footsteps of GY and Thomas Mark, who were simply carrying out WBY's wishes. It should be noted that there are differences in Italicization and Romanization between the editors' 1925 edition and their 1937 edition, so the standardization between the two is not always consistent. For example, the 1925 edition has 'When the *Will* predominates, and there is strong desire, the *Mask* or *Image* is sensuous' (*CW13* 16), whereas the 1937 edition has 'When the *Will* predominates the *Mask* or Image is "sensuous"' (*CW14* 64). The authority for the 'Image' part of this change, is 'GY in YL 2434' (*CW14* 269), and of course Yeats is here defining words, as per his instructors, hence the added quotation marks around 'sensuous'. The choice not to standardize 'Image' to all roman in 1925 (or to all italics in 1937) may or may not have been a conscious decision on the part of the editors; it seems as though Yeats changed his mind between the two editions ('Search' 111).

Harper and Paul note that there is one case where they have not imposed standardization:

> *Will*, one of the *Four Faculties* (*Body of Fate*, *Creative Mind*, *Mask*, and *Will*), is not regularized with the others. Since WBY also uses the word 'will' in its ordinary sense, and it is not always clear whether he refers to the common concept or the specialized term, we have yielded to the authority of the copy text for this word. (*CW14* li)

This is unexceptional, and they are not the first readers to have remarked on it. Another technical term, which is also in common usage, is '*Spirit*'; see *CW14* 171 where Yeats writes 'The *Spirits* before the *Marriage* are spoken of as the dead. After that they are spirits, using that word as it is used in common speech'. However, one must wonder why the copy-text's phrase '*Spirits* of the *Thirteenth Cone*' (*CW14* 166, 167 [twice]), with its de-italicized 'of the', has not been taken as the template for the similar phrase '*Spirit of the Thirteenth Cone*' (*CW14* 174 [three times], 175), which is entirely in italics. Although the former phrase occurs three times and the latter four, Hood admonishes: 'The added italics in "of the" probably resulted from a printing error. "Spirits" and "Thirteenth Cone" are separate terms' ('Search', 235).[17] I also wonder about the phrases '*Victimage for the Ghostly Self*' and

---

[17] Harper and Paul italicize the word 'spirits' in the following passage: '*Creative Mind* clings to *Body of Fate* until mind deprived of its obstacle can create no more and nothing is left but "the *spirits* at one", unrelated facts and aimless mind, the burning out that awaits all voluntary effort' (*CW14* 138). This is, I think, a special case: Yeats is quoting from the Automatic Script, where the phrase 'the spirits at one' frequently occurs (see the Indexes to *YVP*). Assuming that it is legitimate to change quotations, which is by no means a given, the question arises as to whether the word should be capitalized. In the Section of *CW13* entitled 'The Spirits at Fifteen and One', Yeats consistently capitalizes, although he does not italicize (*CW13* 198–99). The practice is inconsistent elsewhere (e.g. *CW13* 201 has lower case for 'spirits': 'the spirits at Phase 15').

'*Victimage for the Dead*' (*CW14* 174–75). The phrase '*Victimage* for a *Spirit of the Thirteenth Cone*' does not use italics for 'for a' (*CW14* 174). To emend the phrase to '*Victimage* for a *Spirit* of the *Thirteenth Cone*' would I suppose tend to emphasize that there are *three* technical terms involved here, and might overwhelm the reader, whereas if we treat '*Spirit of the Thirteenth Cone*' as a single technical term, the reader is less likely to take fright. Fright, I am afraid, is inevitable.

Of course, it is easier to impose consistency of terminology then to determine consistency of system. The former can be carried out mechanically; the latter needs engagement with what the text is trying to say. Mark is not always correct when he tries to engage with the system; he did not, after all, have access to the Automatic Script to assist him, although he did have access to George Yeats. In the 'Table of the Four Faculties' (*CW14* 71), the True *Mask* of Phase 4 is given as 'Intensity through emotions', whereas the description of Phase 18 informs us that its True *Mask* comes from Phase 4 and is 'Intensity through emotion' (*CW14* 108). Hood suggests 'emotion' for the former, giving 'VAMS' as her authority ('Search' 96; cf. *YVP4* 198, which has 'by emotion' instead of 'through emotion'), while *YVP2* 465 has 'intensity by emotion', as does *YVP3* 197, thus lending support to the singular. Again, Harper and Paul leave the text as it is, saying nothing in the endnotes, although their Table 3 shows us that Mark wanted to change the *later* mention to 'Intensity through emotions', a change that was carried out in the 1962 edition (*CW14* 248).

When it comes to more complicated system consistency, Mark is as lost as the next person. The following examples will give the reader some idea of the difficulties involved.

The reader may well wonder whether Yeats's phrase about Lunar South and Solar East should read 'Lunar South in Solar East' or 'Lunar South is Solar East'. It is the former on *CW14* 138; it is the latter in Yeats's note on *CW14* 146 and on *CW14* 183. Although Harper and Paul collate all of these references in an endnote (*CW14* 300 n. 31), they do not attempt to regularize the expression. That Yeats always puts the phrase in quotation marks suggests he is quoting from the Automatic Script, but I have been unable to find the phrase in *Yeats's* Vision *Papers*. The closest match occurs not in the AS itself but in the *Vision* Notebooks: 'Head, Heart, Loins & Fall do not refer to Wheel on which they are placed but mark the position of the Four Faculties at ♒ 30 on an interior wheel, when that wheel is taken to represent the Great Year. In this Wheel east on usual diagram is South... In dealing with life cone & after life cone we start at Lunar S & Solar East. Death is reached at Lunar East which is Solar N—we must therefore recognize that the Beatitude is at Solar W—CM Spirit at ♎ &

CB at 'ϒ' (*YVP3* 187–88). Here, the word used is 'is'. Also CF C5 has 'inner E is outer S' (*YVP3* 250). Connie Hood quite correctly suggests emending the first usage to be consistent with the other two ('Search' 97). The only reason that 'in' was even considered is confusion caused by the phrases 'Sun in Moon' and 'Moon in Sun' (*CW14* 60). There, the situation is different, with one tincture consuming the other; here, the one term is the equivalent of the other, although on a lower plane. Harper and Paul's endnote shows that they know the word should be 'is' (*CW14* 300 n. 31).

The careful reader of diagrams will also spot that there is a problem with the diagram of The Historical Cones which prefaces 'Dove or Swan'. As Neil Mann pointed out in his review of the Harper and Paul 1925 edition (*YA18* 293), the word 'WILL' was printed there as 'WELL' on the line cutting the cones 'a little below 250, 900, 1180 and 1927' (*CW13* 147). (Admittedly, it is hard to see, as a diagonal line of a cone bisects the 'E'.) Mann also noted that the colours had been transposed on the labels '12–13–14 (1380' and '15–16–17 (1550)'. Both of these errors of *CW13* have been amended by Harper and Paul in their 1937 edition, but a little above the same line they have substituted the incorrect '(120) 2–3–4' for the correct '120 (2–3–4)' (*CW14* 193). Of course, '120' is the year, while '2–3–4' are the phases. (Just to confuse matters further, the diagram in the automatic script on which this diagram is based used the parentheses for most of the years and left the phases naked [*YVP3* 61]). Jeffares in *A Vision and Related Writings* (London: Arena, 1989, 258) changes the correct '120 (2–3–4)' that occurs further down in the original diagram to the incorrect format, but is at least consistent. The 1956/61 and 1962 editions both retain the '(120)' error but have the correct 'Will', while the former drops '(19-' from '20–21) 1680' lower down on the right hand side. As explained by Hood, this error was introduced when the 1938 New York edition was produced by photolithography of the 1937 English edition: 'Following an agreement with Macmillan of New York, the 1937 London text was copied by photolithography by the Polygraphic Company of America and published on 23 February 1938. In spite of the ostensible accuracy of the photocopying process, one printing corruption was introduced into the 1938 text: on line 9 of the diagram on page 266, the 1937 version reads "(19–20–21)" but the 1938 text has "(20–21)". Since the 1956 text was photocopied from 1938, the corruption was perpetuated in 1956 and 1961' ('Search' 141). This means that there are *no* editions of *A Vision* with this diagram printed correctly, although it may be found drawn without error on Mann's website, at http://www.yeatsvision.com/History.html.

Mann in his review of the 1925 edition wrote:

On a minor note, it is clear from the diagram of the cones that 1050 is a key date, and the editors should have had the confidence to change 'The period from 1005 to

1180 is attributed in the diagram to the first two gyres of our millennium' ([*CW13*] 164), even though it is a mistake that persisted into all versions of *AVB*. (*YA18* 294)

Despite Mann's implied view that the editors were aware of the discrepancy here when they were preparing the 1925 edition, it is not evident to me that this was the case; however, they have emended the text in the 1937 edition, changing *CW14* 208.29 from '1005' to '1050'. The reason they give is that the latter is 'correct in The Historical Cones, p. 193' (*CW14* 272). I realize you can't put detailed explanation in a table, but this laconic entry glides over far too much: how do they *know* it is correct in The Historical Cones? I suspect the editors took Mann's word for it and then searched around for a reason; certainly they took his gentle admonition as a hint to lift their game. The date of '1050' is also used in *CW14* on pp. 192, 199, 207, not to mention the typescript on p. 292, and as the editors inform us, it is half of 2100, which is when the 'new Messiah' is due (*CW14* 444 n. 37); but the section heading, 'A.D. 1050 to the Present Day' (*CW14* 207), alone should have given sufficient warrant, never mind the previous section heading 'A.D. 1 to A.D. 1050' (*CW14* 199). The ultimate source for the date is of course the diagram of the Historical Cones drawn by 'Carmichael', as printed in *YVP3* 61.

The tendency to fudge with the sources of the editorial decisions is also apparent with the change from 'Domination through emotional constriction' to 'Domination through emotional construction' as the description of the True *Creative Mind* of Phase 20 (*CW14* 73). The 'Authority' given is that it is 'Correct on 91.24' (*CW14* 268), but surely when you are faced with only *two* usages of a phrase in a given text, you need an external authority to be able to make a decision as to which is correct, or else you need to engage in detailed contextual analysis which may or may not be conclusive. Once again, the reader will find that Neil Mann's review of the 1925 edition is the external source (*YA18* 291). Reference to the first three volumes of *YVP* is not entirely decisive.[18] In *YVP1* 257, we have

20 emotional domination
not quite
constriction in emotional—in intellectual domination

---

[18] I am assuming that the transcriptions in *YVP* are correct. Obviously, a definitive conclusion needs to be based on the manuscripts themselves, and even then inspection may not solve all difficulties. In this case, Hood admits that 'The word in VAMS can be read as either "construction" or "constriction"; the latter choice was perpetuated into AV-B' ('Search' 224).

whereas the table reproduced in illustration in *YVP3* 199 clearly has 'construction', with the endnote informing us that Yeats 'also changed "construction" in CG of P20 to "constriction" in *VA* 32' (*YVP3* 219 n. 57) (which does seem to beg the question). Hood ('Search' 96, 224) references 'VAMS' for the reading 'construction' (cf. *YVP4* 183, which has 'True Intellect Emotional construction in intellectual dominance').[19]

There are other places where the editors have left themselves some wriggle-room in their self-imposed strait-jacket. So far as I can see, both of the cases I discuss below are, at the very least, debatable. Normally, Harper and Paul relegate the corrections from the Coole proofs or Thomas Mark to Table 3, but there is one exception, and it looms large: they change 'the *thirteenth sphere*' from the 1937 edition (and the 1956/61 edition) to 'the *Thirteenth Cone*' in 'The End of the Cycle': 'The particulars are the work of the *Thirteenth Cone* or cycle which is in every man and called by every man his freedom' (*CW14* 219–20; cf. *CW14* 273, where the 'Authority' is given as 'Coole proofs'). This change is nowhere justified or debated; the editors simply mention it in passing as having been made by Mark in order to 'improve or correct the description of the system itself' (*CW14* xlvii). This was not a correction that Hood was going to make. It seems as though they just could not bear to forgo this change, given that it has been the subject of some debate (see, e.g., Finneran, 'On Editing Yeats: The Text of *A Vision* [1937]', 126–7).

There is an equally difficult emendation to consider. It stands out from the general uniformity of the 'Authority' column of Table 4, Emendations to the Copy Text, as the reason for the change is given as '"Version B" (*YVP4*:216)' (*CW14* 271). In the original 1937 edition, the text ran as follows: 'For the moment the desire for a form has ceased and an absolute realism becomes possible'; Harper and Paul change 'desire for a form' to 'desire for reform' (*CW14* 121), leaving the reader to find that it has been altered by consulting the table. However, if you check the source given,

---

[19] Certainly there are only two uses of the phrase 'Domination through emotional construction' in *A Vision* (1937), but there is a related phrase, 'constructive emotion', which occurs in the description of Phase 24, where the True *Creative Mind* (from Phase 6) is given as: 'Humanitarianism. through constructive emotion' (*CW14* 124). Harper and Paul note that Mark changed this to read 'Constructive emotion' in the 1962 edition (*CW14* 378 n. 188; cf. *CW14* 251), which makes it consistent with the True *Creative Mind* of Phase 6 in the 'Table of the Four Faculties' (*CW14* 71). (Remember that in the table, 'Each *Faculty* is placed after the number of the phase where it is formed, not after the phase which it affects' [*CW14* 70]). The first Coole proofs removed the errant full-stop from the original phrase. Harper and Paul leave it untouched.

'Version B', the text reads: 'The desire of reform has ceased, an absolute realism becomes possible': the word 'of' occurs instead of the word 'for' (*YVP4* 216). Thus, if they were going to change the text, the editors should have emended the text to 'desire of reform'. This wording is confirmed when we check the same passage in the 1925 edition (*CW13* 79): the attached endnote reads, 'The words "a form" are an error: see VersB, where the phrase reads "The desire of reform has ceased" (*YVP4*:216)' (*CW13* 261 n. 201). Yeats does seem to use 'desire of' when 'desire for' is meant, and it is unlikely that he would have been able to articulate the difference; see, for example, 'desire of expression' and 'desire of action and of command' (*CW14* 92) or 'Self-realisation attained will bring desire of power' (*CW14* 196). The emendation to 'desire for' surely owes its existence to Neil Mann's complaint about the same passage in the 1925 edition that 'leaving the mistake in the text seems the wrong way round for an edited text' (*YA18* 290).[20] Mann makes a slip in quoting the endnote, saying that 'it is noted that the draft in question gives "the desire for reform" ([*CW13*] 261)', so it appears that the editors, in making their change, worked from Mann's review rather than from their own sources. I can see why Mann endorsed the emendation to 'reform': after all, the preceding sentence of *CW14* concludes that, at Phase 22, 'there is neither change nor desire of change'. However, 'a form' also makes sense, given that the *Mask* is '[a] form created by passion to unite us to ourselves' (*CW14* 461), and Phase 22 is not a phase that values *Mask*: Phase 22 is the phase split between *antithetical* and *primary* in equal measures, eventually moving towards *primary*.[21] Here, of course, one faces the fact that detailed understanding is needed in order to establish what the correct text should be. I suspect that the Version B manuscript should be revisited

---

[20] In this case, for their 1937 edition, Harper and Paul have agreed with Mann's suggestion and have gone against the general series policy, which is precisely to leave the error in the text. They do not do this for the sentence 'Though the new *Husk* and *Mask* have been born, they do not *appear*, they are subordinate to the *Celestial Body*' (*CW14* 170). Instead they follow the procedure castigated by Mann for the 1925 edition. The endnote reads: 'An error: "*Mask*" should be "*Passionate Body*". As Neil Mann notes, "The Passionate Body gives rise to the Mask, and indeed Yeats shows how closely the two were fused in his thinking when he pairs 'the new Husk and Mask', a slip for Husk and Passionate Body", "The *Mask* of *A Vision*", *YA19* [2013], 186' (*CW14* 412 n. 56). One could argue, I suppose, that there was a manuscript basis to amend the text in the one case but not the other.

[21] If 'form' is intended, one must take into account its double meaning. Cf. *YVP2* 468: 'Is not the mask in subjective phases double—a form which we put on, a form which we desire, that which we become & that which we would possess', to which the answer was 'Yes'.

with this dilemma in mind: the words 'a form' and 'reform' as written by Yeats might well be indistinguishable. Failing a definitive answer from the manuscript, and given the complications involved, my own inclination is to trust the 1937 text here, set out the pros and cons in an endnote, and make no emendation.

Some of the emendations proposed by Hood but not taken up by Harper and Paul are based on those made by WBY or GY to their copies of *A Vision* (1925). (They have no problem using GY's emendations in copies of the 1937/38 edition, as detailed above.) These were first described in Finneran's 1977 article, printed in Edward O'Shea's *A Descriptive Catalog of Yeats's Library*, and more fully captured in Harper and Paul's edition of the 1925 version. The note in this last reads:

> The Yeatses kept four copies of *AVA* in their library: (1) number 83 of the six hundred copies printed (O'Shea 2433); (2) number 385 (O'Shea 2433b); (3) number 366 (O'Shea 2433a); and (4) number 498 (O'Shea 2433c). As Richard J. Finneran notes in his essay 'On Editing Yeats: The Text of *A Vision* (1937)' (*Texas Studies in Literature and Language* 19 [1977]: 121–22), the last three of these copies have postproduction corrections made by WBY and GY. The three tables that follow present the changes made to these three copies, with indications of the changes, who made them (when it is possible to distinguish whether the marking was made by WBY or GY, or in a few instances by Macmillan editor Thomas Mark), whether the change appears in one or more of the other copies, and if the correction was carried over into the 1937 edition. Page numbers are given for the original book (in parentheses) and this edition. (*CW13* 339)

More should have been made of these tables in the Introduction to the 1937 version, but the references are confined to the laconic sentence 'The Yeatses' marks in their four [*sic*] copies of *AVA-Laurie* suggest an early eye toward a corrected version' and its accompanying footnote (*CW14* xxviii and 300, n. 19), with sporadic mentions thereafter (*CW14* 302 n. 59, 356 n. 52, 357 n. 55). Perhaps the editors considered that decisions to carry the marginalia over into publication were made in an orderly fashion, so that anything that was not carried over was consciously rejected.[22] This of course

---

[22] There is one exception; this is the change from 'Temptation versus strength' to 'Temptation through strength' (*CW14* 73) in the Table of the Four Faculties. Harper and Paul take this change from an emendation in George Yeats's copy of *A Vision* (1925), YL 2433a. See *CW13* 341 and *CW14* 268, together with *CW14* 243, 355 n. 44 and 356 n. 52; this is one of the annotations that does not appear in O'Shea's YL. I confess I cannot make sense of the distinction the editors try to draw in the Introduction to the 1925 edition between 'those changes intended as corrections—as opposed to revisions' (*CW13* xlvi). This seems to me to be specious.

is mere assumption. Changes that Hood would have made on the basis of marginal notes written by Yeats himself in the 1925 copies, but which were not made in any edition, include 'return several times' instead of the more specific 'return up to four times' ('Search' 96, 164, 222; *CW13* 344) and 'The automatic script defines being as that which divides into *Four Faculties*' instead of 'By being is understood that which divides into *Four Faculties*' ('Search' 96, 222; *CW13* 345). Given that these changes were not made while Yeats was alive, and that other marginal notes in these copies have the air of Yeats or GY thinking aloud, perhaps Harper and Paul's caution is justified in these two cases; however, one does get the feeling that when they were editing the 1925 edition, they intended to make future use of 'Corrections to the Yeatses' Copies of *A Vision* (1925)'. Regrettably, any such intention got lost in the wash-up, so that an essential part of the writing of the 1937 edition is now relegated to Appendices in *CW13*.

One of the changes marked in one of the Yeatses' copies of the 1925 edition relates to the table 'Four Types of Wisdom'. This read, in 1925 (*CW13* 30),

At P. 4	Wisdom of Desire
At P. 12	Wisdom of Intellect
At P. 18	Wisdom of Heart
At P. 26	Wisdom of Knowledge

WBY's note is transcribed as 'the circled words "Intellect" and "Heart" in the grouping "Four Types of Wisdom" marked "transpose"' (*CW13* 346; not in *YL*). Hood writes, 'In AV-A #498 [=*YL* 2433c] Yeats marked the words "Intellect" and "Heart" for transposition; however, the printers misunderstood and transposed the two complete lines. See Yeats's note at 100.17–21' ('Search' 224). The passage in 1937 is emended as follows (*CW14* 74),

At P. 4	Wisdom of Desire
At P.18	Wisdom of Heart
At P. 12	Wisdom of Intellect
At P. 26	Wisdom of Knowledge,

and the note by WBY reads 'I give the Four Types of Wisdom as they were given. I have more than once transposed Heart and Intellect, suspecting a mistake; but have come to the conclusion that my instructors placed them correctly, the nature of the wisdom depending upon the position of the *Creative Mind*' (*CW14* 74n.). Had Hood's emendation been adopted, the table would have read:

At P. 4	Wisdom of Desire
At P.12	Wisdom of Heart
At P. 18	Wisdom of Intellect
At P. 26	Wisdom of Knowledge

I have not yet worked out what all of this means, although I imagine it has to do with the proposed table 'where the Four Faculties predominate' (*CW13* 340, 'Search' 125) and the passage that was retained, *CW14* 141, where the placement of the *Faculties* differs from those proposed. The 'wisdom of knowledge' and its connection with Phase 26 is mentioned on *CW14* 109, but there is little elsewhere on this subject. However, it is worthwhile following up Harper and Paul's endnote to 'The Four Types of Wisdom' in *CW13* 242 n. 73—there is no equivalent note in *CW14*—which reads 'See *YVP1*:183, 2:98, 3:207, for AS and notebook entries about the four types of wisdom'. *YVP1* 183 uses Phases 23 and 7 instead of 18 and 26: 'wisdom of heart at 23—wisdom of intellect at 12—wisdom of soul at 27—wisdom of desire or instinct at 4', whereas *YVP2* 98 corrects the phases to those used in the 1925 edition: '4. Can you devide Antithetical] & P[rimary] into 4. | 4. the wisdom of heart comes at 18 | wisdom of intellect 12 | wisdom of desire 4 | wisdom of knowledge 26', as does *YVP3* 207. *YVP1* 191 is also relevant but not specifically mentioned by Harper and Paul: '51. Can you explain with diagram why wisdom of heart & wisdom of intellect come so apparently out of place? | 51. no but I must go now—goodbye'. In other words, if we believe that Yeats is giving the Four Types of Wisdom as they were placed by his 'instructors', then Hood's suggested emendation is incorrect and Yeats did not wish to carry through on what was written in his personal copy. However, this still means that the phases should not have been listed out of order: Phase 12 should have been listed before Phase 18.

Although, as I have said, Harper and Paul are generous with the reprinting of rejected typescripts, there are several places where Hood suggests substantial additions to the copy text itself based on typescripts. At *CW14* 163 a footnote by Yeats ends: 'The Spirit is described as awakened from its sleep in the dead body'. I have always found this phrasing a trifle abrupt. Hood adds a lengthy continuation of the sentence from 'the carbon of the typescript which was sent to the printer as partial copy for *A Vision* (1937)' (NLI MS 36,272/6/1–2). The note appears to have been simply overlooked because it was typed on a separate page, and Hood's account of how it could easily have been missed is convincing ('Search' 97, 209, 233). Hood would also have included a diagram illustrating 'Lunar South is Solar East', placing it at the end of Section VI of 'The Great Year of the Ancients'. The source for this is a rejected typescript done after 1926 but before NLI MS 36,272/6/1–2. As Hood explains, two later unrejected typescripts, including NLI 36,272/6/1–2 itself, left a blank space for the diagram. The iteration before NLI 36,272/1–2 left a large space in which Yeats wrote 'Diagram' ('Search' 98, 236). Both of these items are of sufficient importance to have been brought to the reader's attention, either in the text or in the endnotes.

IV

I have mentioned numerous points of disagreement with Harper and Paul's editing of *A Vision* (1937). However, weighed against what has been accomplished, these are relatively minor, and are of interest primarily to specialists such as myself. I have a different idea of what textual editing means than the one they have (more or less successfully) adhered to; others may well agree with their idea rather than with mine. The reader with a pedant's eye for detail will still need to refer to Hood's dissertation for further sidelights; but, all things considered, my opening statement is something I would emphasize. The richness of the annotations and the publication of extended passages from the typescripts are in themselves enough to recommend this volume. Harper and Paul's edition of *A Vision: The Revised 1937 Edition* enlarges our understanding of Yeats's achievement; there is sufficient information here to keep scholars busy for years to come.

http://dx.doi.org/10.11647/OBP.0081.18

An Afterword: The Macmillan Archive and Editorial Policy[1]

Warwick Gould

It was to be expected that the Macmillan Archive would contain the historiography as well as the history of that firm: such is implicit in the nature of an archive as rich and comprehensive as this one. The notes for and drafts of Charles Morgan's *The House of Macmillan* (1843–1943), published in the centenary year show that Morgan utterly relied on Yeats's reader Thomas Mark (later a director of the firm), to do his devilling— the Archive, then being housed in the basement of the firm's premises in St Martin's Street.[2] With his unrivalled knowledge of the Archive, Mark very much preferred to be the self-effacing backroom scholar who could sift for Morgan a century of inner house history. What is surprising is that for large swathes of Morgan's book, the actual drafting is in the neat and unmistakeable hand of Mark himself.

These drafts are also found in typescript, and it is scarcely too much to say that Mark emerges as the ghost author. This gives an especial salience

---

[1] Further information may have been gathered since this article was prepared for publication. If you would like to find out if any further information has been discovered that may help your own research, why not write to the author at Warwick.Gould@sas.ac.uk? Quite apart from anything else, feedback is always welcomed.

[2] The existence of these still uncatalogued notes was first announced in Warwick Gould, 'W. B. Yeats and the Resurrection of the Author', in *The Library*, 16:2 (June 1994), 101-34 at pp. 115–16. They should be referred to as BL Uncat., 75 (d).

to Morgan's account of Yeats, which is concentrated in the chapter entitled 'Growing Younger'. Amid much else on Yeats, Morgan records that

...Yeats was delighted rather than annoyed by queries. He would sit down, pore over the doubtful line, seek and seek in his memory for a clue to the meaning that either his youthful ardour or some ancient misprint had clouded. But sometimes he himself was not available. His most esoteric work, *A Vision*, was full of conundrums which might or might not be intentional and were the harder to solve because Yeats was seriously ill in Majorca while the book was going through the press. "I don't expect many people to understand it", Yeats said. "In fact, I know only one man who *will* understand it all, and he is a doctor in Scotland".[3]

If one turns to Mark's pencilled draft of before 1943 one finds:

He was extremely pleased with the attention we gave to the production of his works, especially as regards the one-volume *Collected Poems* and Collected Plays. Nobody had looked after his proof for him before, and he was not at all good at correcting them himself. Spelling and punctuation had always, he admitted, been mysteries to him, and his handwriting often presented enigmas, so that there were many places where the text of his verse or prose as it stood was not, we felt sure, what he had originally intended. It might have been thought impudent to make such suggestions to the greatest living poet, but W.B.Y. was by no means offended—in fact he was delighted. When we went through the whole of his works for a projected complete edition (all seen and revised by Yeats, but held up by the war), he gave every such point the most careful attention, explaining his meaning where he thought it might have been missed, and writing to say, 'For the first time there will be a satisfactory text of my work, thanks to your watchfulness and patience'.[4]

His most esoteric work, *A Vision*, was packed with difficulties and conundrums, which were all the harder to solve because Yeats was seriously ill in Majorca while

---

[3]   Charles Morgan's *The House of Macmillan (1843–1943)* (London: Macmillan, 1943), 223.

[4]   Macmillan archive, Dep. 8910, The British Library., unpag. As Colin McDowell notes, this letter is missing from the Macmillan Archive and so from the *CL InteLex* edition. It was a private letter addressed to Thomas Mark, and was enclosed with a covering note sent by Yeats to Harold Macmillan from Riversdale on 8 September 1932: 'I would be very much obliged if you would give the enclosed letter to the admirable scholar who is assisting in the correction of the proofs of my new collected edition. It is partly a letter of thanks and partly an explanation of certain metrical tricks of mine which have puzzled him'. (*CL InteLex* 5731; TLS BL 55003 f 136) and marked by Macmillans 'To Mr Mark'. The letter was later shown to the late Jon Stallworthy in 1959 by Thomas Mark. See *VSR* xxii-xxiii and Gould, 'W. B. Yeats and the Resurrection of the Author', 115–16 and nn. It is to be presumed that the words Mark quotes here (also used, as above; see n. 2) and also by Morgan, are from that letter.

the book was going through the press *(and I have always imagined that in the end he sent the wrong set of proofs to the printers for press as final)*. I saw him at one stage, however, and said that I was not very comfortable because so much of the book was quite beyond me. He laughed and said, 'Oh, I don't expect many people to understand it at all. In fact I only know one man who *will* really understand it, and he is a doctor in Scotland'. (emphasis added)

After Mark was dead, and while I was still working on what became the 1981 first edition of *VSR*, this story of the wrong proofs for *A Vision* had been communicated to me by Mark's protégé Tim Farmiloe, though it was not until nearly ten years later that I unearthed Mark's written testimony as above. Mr Farmiloe, now long retired, had worked with Mrs Yeats from 1958, and filled Mark's shoes when *he* retired, and oversaw the inauguration of the *Collected Works*. Naturally I told other Yeats editors (including Professor Harper) about the existence of these papers when they came to the British Library to work on the Archive.

The consequences of this discovery were of course for the editors of *A Vision* to think through and, if possible, to reconcile with the emerging and, by the time of *CW14*, very definitely 'established series policy' (*CW14* li). The relegation of George Yeats's and Thomas Mark's corrections to the endnotes and an appendix (as Harper and Paul have done, and as McDowell notes above, *passim*, but see e.g., pp. 389, 396) is '[i]n keeping with established series policy' as indicated at *CW14*, li.

The formulation of that inconsistently applied policy is obscure. While it defies the evidence of the full Macmillan and Scribner Archives, it derives from Richard J. Finneran's calamitously untrue assertion of 1983 that '[Yeats] had not long been in his temporary resting place at Roquebrune before the process began of—not to put too fine a point on it—corrupting the texts which he had worked so hard to perfect',[5] an assertion which underlies *The Poems: A New Edition* (New York, 1983; London, 1984). Since that edition, the editorial value of archival evidence in the establishment of copy-texts had been vigorously contested. By 1994 a bibliography of the first ten years of a public controversy was available to the General Editors.[6]

Yet, it was certainly the case, as Colin McDowell hints, that some editors chafed under a 'series policy' which threw aside the surviving evidence of Mrs Yeats, Harold Macmillan, Thomas Mark and anyone else working

---

[5] Richard J. Finneran, *Editing Yeats's Poems* (London: Macmillan, 1983), 30; *Editing Yeats's Poems: A Reconsideration* (London: Macmillan, 1990), 39.

[6] See Warwick Gould, 'W. B. Yeats and the Resurrection of the Author', in *The Library*, 101–34 at pp. 133–34. The initial review referred in 'The Editor Takes Possession', *TLS*, 29 June 1984.

with Yeats in the 1930s and after as posthumous textual 'corrupti[on]'. In attempting to provide a rationale for the subsequent editorial practices of a *Collected Works* as a 'series invested in the authorial intentions of WBY' (*CW14* xlix), this 'series policy' (which broadly applies only to those of Yeats's works which would have appeared in the ill-fated *Edition de Luxe*, the *Coole Edition*, and the *Dublin Edition*), is handed down to editors. While there is the notably defiant exception of *CW3*, *Autobiographies* (1999) where William H. O'Donnell and Douglas Archibald were used the 1955 *Autobiographies* as copy-text, by 2002 the 'series policy' had hardened into a few unexplained (and certainly unjustifiable) *ex cathedra* pronouncements.[7]

A good example may be found in the editorial matter of *CW4, Early Essays*.

We have correlated our edition against the posthumous changes introduced into *Essays and Introductions* (1961) by George Yeats and Lovat Dickson, and earlier[8] Thomas Mark, but have not followed their readings as they lack Yeats's own authority and occasionally introduce new errors of their own. We have not accepted the weak argument of posthumous revision. (*CW4* 324).

This is not merely inexplicably unreferenced; it is also demonstrably incorrect. Yeats's own authority included numerous statements of delegation and his working practices show innumerable acts of delegated revision and emendation.[9] The implication that 'posthumous revision' by his widow and executrix and his trusted publisher's readers can somehow be evacuated of all authority is rendered all the more scandalous by Mark's memory that Yeats himself sent the wrong proofs of *A Vision* as passed for press. If that was the case, does it not compel a fundamentally different kind of consideration of all textual work on the 'editions after 1937' through to 1962? If so, it challenges the editorial horizon of the 'series policy'.

No one who has worked in the BL Macmillan Archive as a whole could but be impressed by the weight of the evidence which survives. Not all editors bothered—as I did—to interview Harold Macmillan, nor to seek

---

[7]   'The volume called "Mythologies" I need not see again. Your reader can complete the revision better than I could'. So wrote Yeats to Harold Macmillan on 5 July, 1932 (*CL InteLex* 5692, *M2005*, xxii). In the light of such statements by Yeats himself, the 'series policy' was so radically inappropriate to *Mythologies*, that my co-editor Deirdre Toomey and I had no option but to withdraw our edition after its submission in 2002, and to publish it outside the series in 2005.

[8]   In fact, Thomas Mark most certainly did work on *Essays and Introductions* (1961) and was later 'called out of retirement' to work on the 1962 *A Vision*. See Gould, 'W. B. Yeats and the Resurrection of the Author', 110 n. 40.

[9]   See, for example, above nn. 3 and 6.

out papers then in the Macmillan family's hands (and now in the British Library). Connie Hood certainly went to Basingstoke to review the Yeats papers gradually being assembled there by Mr Sydney Jacobs and Mr Derek Mirfin and others in the firm in the 1970s and 1980s. But under the 'series policy', the witness value of these papers has simply been elbowed out and editors given elbow room to re-determine texts themselves.

Once one concedes the *actuality* of contemporary and later in-house witnesses to an author's delegated textual processes (such as Thomas Mark and Tim Farmiloe), one is compelled to review all the work that Mark, Watt, Rache Lovat Dickson and George Yeats and others did towards the satisfactory presentation of Yeats's texts, and to admit it into the editorial horizon in which copy-texts are determined. If one consigns the evidence of the *Edition de Luxe*, *Coole* and *Dublin Edition* papers to the desert wastes of tabulated appendices, an editor can—even without intending to do so—puzzle or delude most of the readers most of the time. And yet the Archive remains, however, a silent and compelling rebuke to that dictated (but never justified) 'series policy', perversely and inconsistently applied as it is to some texts but not others, and, ultimately, based as it is upon editorial theory so obtusely inappropriate to Yeats and the publishing processes of his era that it is not even wrong.

http://dx.doi.org/10.11647/OBP.0081.19

God-appointed Berkeley and W. J. Mc Cormack's *'We Irish'
in Europe: Yeats, Berkeley and Joseph Hone* (Dublin: University
College Dublin Press, 2010), pp. x + 211.
A Review Essay

Colin McDowell[1]

'We Irish' in Europe is intended as 'part of a longer enquiry into the condition
of literary criticism in Ireland', to be followed by *Post-Murderism*, 'an account
of some Field Day manoeuvres', and a study of Joseph Mary Plunkett,
in this book entitled *Sweet Enemy* but recently published as *Enigmas of
Sacrifice: A Critique of Joseph M. Plunkett and the Dublin Insurrection of 1916*.[2]
Mc Cormack sees his overall strategy as an assault on the idea of system,
and the projected volumes as a whole have the vainglorious Balzacian title,
Critique of the Absolute (17, 131 n. 26). The unkind reader might equate an
attack on system with an inability to think straight or with an excuse for
inveterate maundering, and elect not to give assent to the assumption that
'systematic' equals 'totalitarian'; but important topics *are* involved here. Has
Mc Cormack chosen the most efficient way to raise them?

I came to this book to see what it could tell me about how Yeats
understood Berkeley and what Joseph Hone had to do with it, which is,
after all, what the subtitle promised. Readers may be interested in what Mc
Cormack has to say about Beckett and Berkeley; but while the excursions on
behalf of Synge and George Moore's *The Brook Kerith* may well be salutary

---

[1] colin.richard.mcdowell@gmail.com
[2] Now published (March 2016) by Michigan State University Press, March 2016,
ISBN 9781611861914.

423

one has to wade through a lot to get to them. The particularly heroic reader may also appreciate the pages on Adorno and those on Agamben, but even Mc Cormack realises he may be asking too much of his audience. 'Why', he asks, 'should any of this intrude on a study of W. B. Yeats and George Berkeley?' (87). Indeed, but the unrepentant author instead takes it as an opportunity to bemoan 'lapsed knowledge'—before embarking on a short digression about how no-one now reads Maria Edgeworth.

Unpacking the book's title may be helpful. Mc Cormack contends that Yeats's appropriation of Berkeley's phrase 'We Irish' is illegitimate, because Berkeley did not mean what Yeats wanted him to mean. The 'Irish' are European because Yeats and Hone (might have!) discussed Berkeley in Capri and Rapallo—Mc Cormack will later, on p. 160, paraphrase 'we Irish' as 'a short-term politico-philosophical Capri-based think-in of the 1920s'. But the Irish philosophy Yeats supposedly imagined—an idealism whereby the individual is subsumed into the State—apparently found its exemplification in Fascist Italy, the France of the Action Française, and Hitler's Germany.

This book has all of the faults of Mc Cormack's *Blood Kindred*.[3] Their strategy is to throw mud in the hope that some of it will stick. In *Blood Kindred*, assertion took precedence over well-researched fact; statements were made, withdrawn, then made again; accusations were whittled down, polished and repeated as mantras to foreclose thought. Irrelevant detail was piled on to disorient the reader. Innuendo was used to cover mere surmise; and if there were two interpretations one could place on behaviour, the less worthy was invariably chosen. Yeats was damned if he did something and damned if he didn't. Mc Cormack deployed the traps of the professional controversialist. *'We Irish' in Europe* is based on some initial research but Mc Cormack soon loses interest, filling out the book with whatever takes his passing fancy, all vaguely tied together by his assumption that he knows better than anyone else. Perhaps the digressions reveal that Mc Cormack doesn't have much that is new to say about Yeats and Berkeley, but he concedes little.[4]

---

[3]   *Blood Kindred: W. B. Yeats, The Life, the Death, the Politics* (London: Pimlico, 2005) was reviewed—generously—by David Dwan in *YA17* 403–07.

[4]   It takes little psychological insight to see that Mc Cormack's urge to rescue 'lesser' authors who have been hidden under the 'Yeatsian shadow' (16–17) is the obverse of the attack on Roy Foster which opens the first chapter. This is regardless of the validity of what is being said. If you want to point out that the Emperor has no clothes, you can do so; alternatively, you can draw attention to the way in which you do it. Authorial excesses do not always lead to the Palace of Wisdom, so a reader cannot be blamed who elects not to follow the winding paths by which Mc Cormack attempts to connect Yeats, 'resurgent sacrifice' (chapter 2.3ff.), and a lack of pity for those who lived their lives 'as though they had not been' (109).

For the parts of his book where the topic is actually addressed, Mc Cormack relies heavily on Donald T. Torchiana, *W. B. Yeats and Georgian Ireland*, Ch. 6, 'God-Appointed Berkeley' (222–65), as he must.[5] But he cannot refrain from the occasional aspersion, such as that Torchiana 'remains hostage to the terms of Yeats himself in "The Seven Sages"' (27). In his urge to distance himself from Torchiana, Mc Cormack omits some of the more salient points made in *W. B. Yeats and Georgian Ireland*. Coincidentally or not, the omitted passages are those which do not suit his thesis.

Torchiana (222–23) originally identified the soldier who said to Yeats that 'all the philosophy a man needed was in Berkeley' (*AVB* 19; *CW14* 15; elsewhere recorded as 'There is all the philosophy a man needs' (*UP2* 484, cf. *UP2* 489; *CW10* 218, 232). Mc Cormack initially accepts this: 'it seems likely that Yeats's informant was Colonel Jephson Byrne O'Connell (born 1886)' (3). A dozen pages on he writes: 'The onset of Yeats's enthusiasm has already been described in some detail wherein the honour of initiating the poet into the mysteries was divided between Lennox Robinson (1886–1958) and an unnamed revolutionary—*possibly* Jephson O'Connell'.[6] Whatever he means by 'described in some detail', or where, or even by whom, is unclear, as this is the book's first mention of Robinson, who bought Yeats the two volume 1784 edition of Berkeley's works after he had heard Yeats quoting the soldier's endorsement (*AVB* 19; *CW14* 15).

A dozen pages on, Mc Cormack returns to the topic, concentrating now on the word 'young' in one of Yeats's retellings: 'The revolutionary soldier has been identified as Jephson O'Connell by Donald Torchiana, apparently on the authority of Mrs Yeats; other candidates include Sean MacBride, Dermot MacManus, Patrick McCartan, Ernie O'Malley and Francis Stuart. If the revolutionary soldier's remark is taken to have been uttered *c.*1925, then McCartan and MacManus—and O'Connell?—can be eliminated on grounds of age and military inactivity.... While O'Malley certainly had the intellectual capacity, MacBride must be the most plausible candidate, being very young (b. 1904) and having the reputation as republican firebrand. In favour of O'Malley (b. 1898) is the fact that he and Robinson were on one occasion closeted awkwardly together... with every opportunity to discuss philosophy' (31n. 37). What to do with a statement like this last one is anyone's guess. Some pages later, apparently forgetting

---

Mc Cormack, of course, thinks it all the fault of the reader: 'We write, but nobody reads', he laments in the 'Epistle Dedicatory' (v).

[5] Evanston: Northwestern University Press; London: Oxford University Press, 1966, 222–65.

[6] Mc Cormack, 14, emphasis added. The reader of Mc Cormack must acclimatize to belittling rhetoric and the constant half-withdrawal of arguments proffered.

everything he had previously decided, Mc Cormack claims: '[t]he onset of Yeats's enthusiasm for Berkeley has already been described in some detail wherein the honour of initiating the poet into the mysteries [some phrases just *do* seem to write themselves] was divided between Lennox Robinson and an unnamed revolutionary—possibly Sean MacBride' (64). Further on, the word 'initiated' gets yet another working-out: 'At the end of 1925, Lennox Robinson (we are told) initiated Yeats into the reading of Berkeley' (90). It is hard to know what to deplore most about all the repetition and shilly-shally, but this is a published book, not an author mulling things over, so the blame must ultimately be laid at the feet of a hapless editor.[7]

---

[7] The book was originally twice its current size and that the early chapters were removed and others reshaped (v), so perhaps the phrase 'already been described in some detail' once had meaning. Mc Cormack is strangely determined to contest Torchiana's (and George Yeats's) identification, and to do so inconsistently. He had included a section in *Blood Kindred* entitled 'Jephson O'Connell and the National Army Mutiny' (226–31), but had not mentioned Torchiana in that context. He states, on the authority of MacManus, that 'O'Connell was an ordained Catholic priest of an English diocese, no longer exercising his vocation' (*Blood Kindred*, 227–28 and n. 451). If so, he may well be the Jephson Byrne O'Connell who can be found in the on-line archives of *The Tablet: The International Catholic News Weekly*, under the following 1916 entry for the diocese of Southwark: 'CLERICAL CHANGES.—The following clerical changes have taken place in the diocese:—The Rev. Jephson Byrne O'Connell, Ph.D., the Professor of Philosophy at the diocesan seminary, has gone to St Edmund's House, Cambridge, for further study', http://archive.thetablet.co.uk/issue/7th-october-1916/13/49246/news-from-the. If, like Mc Cormack, one is going to guess on the basis of 'intellectual capacity', then a professor of philosophy seems an eminently likely person to convince Yeats about Berkeley's merits. The O'Connell Yeats knew was a former pupil of G. E. Moore, although he was unable to explain Moore's philosophy to Yeats's satisfaction (*TSMC* 166–67; *CL InteLex* 5430). I leave to others to decide whether he qualifies as the Irish priest who told Yeats that 'Bertrand Russell is a prig and he is not the big man people think him, but there is a big man behind him—Moore of Cambridge. The pity is that Moore's mind is analytical and analytical alone' (*TSMC* 89–90; *CL InteLex* 4856). It is an open question as to what Yeats in 1925 might consider 'young'. One must wonder why Mc Cormack links the soldier and Robinson to advance O'Malley's claims. All Yeats says is that Robinson later bought him the volumes: he does not imply that Robinson and the soldier collaborated in the matter of Berkeley. John P. Frayne follows Torchiana's identification of the soldier (*UP2* 484, 489; *CW10* 218, 232). Roy Foster tentatively agrees with Torchiana, although he suggests that he 'could conceivably be Dermot MacManus' (*Life 2*, 730 n. 103). A. Norman Jeffares has consistently championed the claim of MacManus (1892–1975); see *NC* 273, *A Vision and Related Writings* (London: Arena, 1990), 384) and *W. B. Yeats: A New Biography* (London: Continuum, 2nd ed., 2001), 225. Fiorenzo Fantaccini follows Jeffares (*W. B. Yeats e la cultura italiana* [Florence: Firenze University Press, 2008], 77.

Of more moment than the question of who first brought Yeats to Berkeley is what Yeats made of him. Mc Cormack tells us he wants to sharpen the reader's sense of

> what Berkeley meant for Yeats in the 1920s or, rather, what Berkeley might be presented as—an exciting, paradoxical thinker in a decade of fudge and compromise, a local and yet intercontinental hero, a philosopher prince of the (reformed) church, a cultic presence unavailable to the latter-day mob, a trans-historic mind' (27)

Further informing us that '[t]he occasional, not to say opportunist, nature of Yeats's interest should not be underestimated' (37). Nor, I suggest, should it be exaggerated. Mc Cormack's correction of 'what Berkeley meant for Yeats' to 'what Berkeley might be presented as' is most probably intended as a conflation. For Mc Cormack, Yeats's interest in Berkeley, and one assumes in philosophy generally, 'was an intelligent but uncritical interest, fuelled by non-philosophical needs or desires—spiritualist, political, would-be absolute-ist' (175). For those interested in balancing the scales, it may be useful to quote Rossi's assessment of Yeats's attitude to philosophy:

> Nowhere have I met a more eager interest in metaphysics. Men usually follow only their own thoughts through philosophy. At the end they find themselves just as they were before. But Yeats asked *to know*. He was searching again and again for an explanation. You could not misunderstand his metaphysical interest for a pose. He sought occasions for thinking, for pitting his brain against metaphysics.[8]

Unlike Mc Cormack, Rossi actually *knew* Yeats; moreover, what he is saying tallies with my sense of what Yeats is doing when he discusses philosophic matters. That Yeats was sincere in wanting to know is demonstrated by the preface he wrote to *Essays 1931 to 1936*: 'I wrote always that when I laid down my pen I might be less ignorant than when I took it up' (*CW5* 84). This is not the statement of someone who wishes merely to convince someone else of his own intransigent ideas.

There are questions about Hone and Rossi's *Bishop Berkeley: His Life, Writings, and Philosophy* (London: Faber & Faber, 1931) that one might have expected Mc Cormack to address, if not resolve. He does say 'That Hone shared title page honours with the Italian philosopher is a bibliographical teaser to be resolved on another occasion' (63), and a chapter section will refer to 'the Enigma of "Hone and Rossi"' (56). The question of who wrote what—if that is what he means—is a legitimate line of enquiry, and (if drafts do not exist) I imagine one could look at what Hone published

---

[8] Rossi, quoted in Joseph Hone, *W. B. Yeats, 1865–1939* (London: Macmillan, 1942), 422.

about Berkeley before he wrote the book. Mc Cormack has compiled a useful listing of Hone's writings in Appendix IV, including some ephemera on Berkeley that do not appear in T. E. Jessop's *A Bibliography of George Berkeley by T. E. Jessop. With Inventory of Berkeley's Manuscript Remains by A. A. Luce.*[9] One could also read Rossi's other writings on Berkeley to see what is repeated in or from what Mc Cormack calls Hone and Rossi's 'avowedly collaborative book on Berkeley' (72). I presume that by 'avowedly' he is referring in a roundabout way to the fact that the book alternates, in a clumsy enough fashion, between biography with sketchy philosophical summaries and rather dense analysis, which in itself might be seen as a starting point for examination of the collaborative process. As for the question of why Hone got together with Rossi in the first place, some evidence does survive, although it is mostly ignored by Mc Cormack. In a postscript to his Introduction to *Bishop Berkeley*, Yeats says:

When I had finished these notes I read for the first time what Mario M. Rossi had added to the book. Had I read it earlier—it was not included in Joseph Hone's manuscript when first I saw it—diffidence might have kept me silent. And now I study with excitement this profound critic of philosophy, this scholar learned in all the schools who can make himself intelligible to the running man. He has given me my first full knowledge of Berkeley the philosopher; my knowledge of Berkeley the man I shall always owe to Joseph Hone's understanding of the Irish eighteenth century, his mastery of biographical detail.[10]

The Introduction itself is dated 'July, 1931'. Yeats refers to reading Hone's unpublished book in September 1930 (*Ex* 322). Then there is the letter in which Yeats tells Hone that:

Lady Gregory has just read your book & is delighted with it—I imagine she skipped the philosophy…. [Berkeley] is of the utmost importance to the Ireland that is coming into existence, as I hope to show in my introduction.[11]

We may I think still read this letter—I quote the rest below—as being written *before* Rossi expanded on Hone's philosophical portions, given that Yeats's Introduction is not yet completed. In fact, Hone himself credited Yeats with the whole idea of getting 'some professional philosopher to look

[9]　The Hague: Martinus Nijhoff, 1973 (2nd ed., rev. and enl.). I have been unable to consult these articles, but they do seem rather short.
[10]　*Bishop Berkeley: His Life, Writings, and Philosophy* (xxix), a passage that does not occur in *Essays 1931–1936*, nor in *E&I*. It is given as an Appendix in *CW5* 290.
[11]　*CL InteLex* 5409, 20 November 1930: *L* 779. Mc Cormack quotes it to sneer about Yeats's assessment of the future of Ireland (39).

over [my book]. In the end Rossi put in the philosophical commentary'
(*W. B. Yeats and Georgian Ireland*, 227). This surely implies that Yeats had a
stronger grasp of philosophic adequacy than Hone, and may be part of the
answer as to why Mc Cormack deferred his 'bibliographical teaser'. That
Hone himself used his knowledge of Italian culture to choose Rossi as the
'professional philosopher' is not under dispute.

The shilly-shally alluded to earlier about the Irish revolutionary soldier
probably occurred because it is of subsidiary interest to Mc Cormack's
principal thesis. Hone, he claims, 'introduced the poet to Berkeley's works,
even if he was not perhaps the first to recommend them' (3); alternatively,
'[t]he introduction was effected, or perhaps consummated, by Joseph Hone'
(28). 'It was Hone, indisputably', he avers, 'who nurtured the interest in
Berkeley during the latter half of the 1920s, not least by discreetly keeping
Yeats up to date with the bishop's reputation in fascist Italy' (3); moreover
'Yeats wished emphatically to endorse and indeed develop a philosophical
recommendation urged by Hone over many years' (10). The ambiguity of
'nurtured' and 'urged' is probably calculated: doubtless it simply means that
Hone published many articles on Berkeley in the 1920s, but the lazy reader
is intended to assume a more direct influence: for which, of course, Mc
Cormack offers little evidence (hence 'discreetly'). While he does admit
that it 'may be taken as non-contentious' that Hone 'was by no means the
only source of opinion available to Yeats' about Berkeley (63), the statement
appears to function merely as a legal disclaimer, as the whole tenor of his
book is that Berkeley was 'mediated' to Yeats by Hone (63). He will later say
that Hone influenced Yeats 'despite what one might call the impermeable
strength of Yeats's own intellect' (95); Yeats's mind, apparently, 'was of such
subtle power that it could not absorb new influences without converting
those novelties into something already compatible with its own essentially
irrational cast' (100).

Such remarks allow Mc Cormack to claim that Yeats learned all he
knew about Berkeley from Hone, but that at the same time he learned
nothing. Referring to Yeats's Introduction to Hone and Rossi's *Bishop
Berkeley*, he writes: 'Always happy to paraphrase other people's words to
suit his own purposes, Yeats particularly commended the *Commentaries* [sc.
the *Commonplace Book*]' (4). Elsewhere, he states that Yeats's knowledge of
current academic debates about Berkeley 'came through J. M. Hone, as he
made clear in his Introduction to *Bishop Berkeley* (1931)' (52 and n. 107).
The reference cited is *CW5* 103–12, i.e. the whole essay minus postscript.
Scholars generally do not give blanket references to support a quite specific
point: unless, that is, the reference does not support the point made. Earlier,
he had emphasized Hone's influence in alerting Yeats to Johnson's edition

of the *Commonplace Book*, giving the more restricted reference of *CW5* 103–04 (33 and n. 43). If you check those pages, nothing remotely like that occurs. Nevertheless, later Mc Cormack will write, as though a given, that Hone had 'success in persuading Yeats... to study the *Commonplace Book*' (151). As with so much of '*We Irish*' *in Europe*, this is assertion floating free; it is not scholarship.[12]

A similar slackness infects Mc Cormack's other main assertion about Yeats and Hone. 'For more than a decade', he writes, 'Hone was a constant mediator between Yeats and the Italian Idealist movement generally' (155). And, of course, by 'Italian Idealist movement' he means the philosophy of Italian fascism, and Gentile more than Croce. No evidence is offered for even the partial truth of this assertion, beyond the fact that Hone published several articles about Italy from the early 1920s onwards, coupled with fact

---

[12] The question of what Yeats learnt from Rossi (as opposed to Hone) about Berkeley's philosophy remains to be studied; I suspect it has much to do with an assessment of *Siris*. Rossi, of course, published a translation of the *Commonplace Book* in 1924 (*Gli Appunti (Commonplace Book), tradotti, commentati, ordinati, con introduzione, bibliografia e indici* [Bologna: Cappelli]). As the title suggests, Rossi arranged the notebooks thematically and did not follow the order of writing. The chances of this book influencing Yeats, even via Hone, are remote, although he *did* state in 1928 that it provided 'the only adequate commentary' (*CL InteLex* 5165). Torchiana quotes a letter of Rossi's in which he claims 'I am, just now, correcting the proofs of my last book on Berkeley, in which I maintain again the views Yeats accepted from me' (*W. B. Yeats and Georgian Ireland*, 227, n. 20). Torchiana quite rightly does not read Rossi as claiming that Yeats derived *all* of his interpretations from Rossi. Torchiana's 'Acknowledgments' is dated February 1965 (*W. B. Yeats and Georgian Ireland*, viii), so the book to which Rossi refers is probably *Introduzione a Berkeley* (Bari: Laterza 1970). *Introduzione a Berkeley* is not mentioned anywhere by Mc Cormack, although he sketches Rossi's later career and notes that the Hone family in Dublin have preserved 'two sets of marked-up proofs, one a translation of Berkeley's *Treatise on the Principles of Human Knowledge*, the other a study of the philosopher in Italian, both Rossi's work, both dating from 1955' (74). McCormack did not bother to see if the marked-up proofs had been published, although a quick check of *A Bibliography of George Berkeley* would have been sufficient: Jessop's book does appear in his own bibliography. The former marked-up proof sounds like *Trattato sui princìpi e Dialoghi*, trans. M. M. Rossi, 'Classici della filosofia moderna' (Bari: Laterza, 1955), while the latter is most probably *Saggio su Berkeley* (Bari: Laterza, 1955). Neither of these books is mentioned by Mc Cormack. *Saggio su Berkeley* is described by Jessop as 'Very controversial—"To save the poor bishop from his admirers"; he was a tyro in philos., and in scholarship a dabbler in second-hand information; his *De motu* and *Alciphron* are turningpoints [*sic*] towards a rationalist emphasis in *Siris*'. Rossi replied to two of the reviews but I have been unable to consult the reviews or responses (*Bibliography*, 126).

that Yeats knew Hone, so it *must* be true. But if this is correct—there was Pound, of course, as well as Yeats's independent reading, assisted by George Yeats's Italian when needed—why does Yeats write to Hone about things which Hone had supposedly educated him on, as though he is telling him something he didn't know?[13] Mc Cormack himself quotes the letter from Yeats to Hone of 20 November 1930, in which Yeats says:

> Gentile & other Italian philosophers found themselves on Berkeley & Rossi has the further advantage of being an authority on Berkeley's immediate predecessors & contemporaries. You & I are absorbed in Ireland but he sees Berkeleys [*sic*] European position' (39).

Yeats may well have been on occasion absent-minded, but Mc Cormack's thesis makes him look positively senile.

When Mc Cormack does address the question of what Yeats read and understood of Berkeley independently of Hone and Rossi, which surely should be a large part of a book such as this, he cannot resist a snide comment about 'Yeats's (so-to-speak) *independent* encounter with Berkeley'

---

[13] One should not underestimate the extent of independent reading. If a subject interested Yeats, he consulted standard reference works, as his annotations attest. Mc Cormack makes much of Yeats's reading of W. Tudor Jones' *Contemporary Thought of Germany* (*YL* 1027), but makes no mention of Angelo Crespi's *Contemporary Thought of Italy* in the same series (*YL* 436), despite it being a more than plausible source for Yeats's information about Italian Idealism. It also endorses a view of Italian Idealism consistent with that taken by Mc Cormack: Crespi calls contemporary Italian philosophy 'an extreme form of diseases from which we are all more or less suffering' (vii). Context of course is everything. You can choose to see these two books in the context of fascism; or can you see them as part of a series about contemporary philosophy, along with J. H. Muirhead's *Contemporary British Philosophy*, First and Second series (*YL* 1399 and 1400) or Bernard Bosanquet's *The Meeting of Extremes in Contemporary Philosophy* (*YL* 254). Yeats read Croce and Gentile for himself, and did not need to have them mediated. He apparently told Sturge Moore to read Gentile in late 1925 (*TSMC* 59; see also *CL InteLex* 4884, 23 June [1926]). Mc Cormack could have referred to Hone's *W. B. Yeats*, p. 368 for Yeats and the Italians, but chose not to, which is odd, given his ostensible topic. There, Hone informs us that Yeats attended Douglas Ainslie's lectures on Croce's aesthetics, but gives no date (there is no Index entry for 'Ainslie' in Mc Cormack). In Torchiana's 'Yeats and Croce', *YA4* 3–11, the date is given as 1923 via Virginia Moore (5). Hone also states that 'some phrase used by me about Gentile had caught his ear' (the context is educational reform). This doesn't sound like 'constant mediation'. Saddlemyer informs us that it was Pound who took the future George Yeats to Ainslie's lectures in 1914 (*Becoming George: The Life of Mrs W. B. Yeats* (Oxford: Oxford University Press, 2002), 39, 60).

(29). Unfortunately, the ground covered is less than that already surveyed by Torchiana who, writing long before O'Shea's *A Descriptive Catalog of W. B. Yeats's Library*, noted several books Yeats must have used (*Yeats and Georgian Ireland*, 225). As well as primary sources such as Johnston's edition of *Berkeley's Commonplace Book* (*YL* 159, 159a) and the edition that Lennox Robinson gave Yeats, the two volume *The Works of George Berkeley* (*YL* 160), there was the Everyman Berkeley, Mary Calkin's edition of Berkeley's selected works, and Collyns Simon's edition of *The Principles of Human Knowledge*. The last three are not in Yeats's library and are not mentioned by Mc Cormack. Although Torchiana does not say so, Yeats must also have read an edition of *The Commonplace Book* earlier than that of Johnston's 1930 edition, because he had read it by March 1926, when he said that '[m]y Berkeley is the Berkeley of the *Commonplace Book*' (*TSMC* 80; *CL InteLex* 4849).[14] As for books in Yeats's library which discuss Berkeley,

---

[14] Yeats stated in 1928, whilst attempting to persuade Macmillan to commission Hone to translate Rossi's *Gli Appunti*, that '[t]he only English edition [of the *Commonplace Book*] is in Frazers complete edition of Berkeley, and there the pages are in the wrong order. I have given some time to trying to understand the "Commonplace Book" and know therefore the great need for explanatory notes and introductions' (*CL InteLex* 5165). *The Commonplace Book*, now known as *Philosophical Commentaries* or simply as *Diaries*, was first published by Alexander Campbell Fraser in 1871, in *Life and letters of George Berkeley, D.D. formerly bishop of Cloyne; and an account of his philosophy. With many writings of Bishop Berkeley hitherto unpublished: metaphysical, descriptive, theological* (Oxford: Clarendon Press, 1871). Fraser republished it in 1901 in the first volume of his 4 volume edition of *The works of George Berkeley... including his posthumous works; with prefaces, annotations, appendices, and an account of his life* (Oxford: Clarendon Press, 1901). Yeats's quotations in the Introduction to *Bishop Berkeley* follow Johnston's wording rather than Fraser's. Torchiana (*Yeats and Georgian Ireland*, 225) adduces Yeats's reading of Calkins and Simon via T. L Dume's unpublished thesis, but could have referred to the Introduction to *Bishop Berkeley*, where Calkins is quoted, and *AV B* 190n., *CW14* 140n., where Simon is referenced. (In the original Introduction [xxiv] and the reprints in *Essays 1931–1936* [40] and the *E&I* version [406] Calkins is called 'Catkins'. This is corrected in *Later Essays* [*CW5*, 354, 518].) There are several printings of Collyns Simon. The original was *The Principles of Human Knowledge | Being Berkeley's Celebrated Treatise | On the Nature of the Material Substance | And Its Relation to the Absolute | With A Brief Introduction to the Doctrine and Full Explanations of the Text; | Followed by an Appendix with Remarks on Kant and Hume* (London: William Tegg & Co., 1878). There were also reprints in 1878, 1893, 1895, and 1899. The 'Everyman Berkeley', which Yeats carried in his pocket in 1931 (*Yeats and Georgian Ireland* references *Man and Poet*, 267), would have been *A New Theory of Vision and Other Select Philosophical Writings*, n. 483 of Everyman's Library, ed. Ernest Rhys, Introduction by A. D. Lindsay (London: J. M. Dent, 1910), or one of the reprints

Mc Cormack's research is desultory at best, after an initially promising start with Croce's *Logic as the Science of the Pure Concept* (*YL* 444), G. A. Johnston's *The Development of Berkeley's Philosophy* (*YL* 1025), and A. A. Luce's *Berkeley and Malebranche* (*YL* 1159)—although he says nothing that had not previously been said by Torchiana (225, 239, 252).[15]

O'Shea indexes only those works which have Berkeley as their principal subject, which are those mentioned by Mc Cormack, whereas a preliminary listing of works which treat Berkeley, or which prompted Yeats to add 'Berkeley' as an annotation, would include Bergson's *Matter and Memory*, Bosanquet's *The Meeting of Extremes in Contemporary Philosophy*, Charpentier's *Coleridge, the Sublime Somnambulist*, *The Encyclopaedia Britannica*, Erdmann's *A History of Philosophy*, where an annotation notes 'On Development of Berkeley's thought / Herman[n] Cohen' (*YL* 638), Gentile's *The Theory of Mind as Pure Act*, Hastings' *Encyclopaedia of Religion and Ethics*, Jones's *Contemporary Thought of Germany*, Russell's *An Outline of Philosophy*, Vasiliev's *Space Time Motion*, and Whitehead's *Science and the Modern World*. This last book has a lengthy endnote in part of which Yeats asks, 'Do we not get very close to Berkeley if as Whitehead advises we accept "naive experience"?' (*YL* 2258). Even Gentile's book is not examined in detail by Mc Cormack. It is reduced to a formula about merging of subject and object, but its explicit criticism of Berkeley is glossed over. After a brief aside on Bertrand Russell's views on Berkeley, Mc Cormack restricts himself to Tudor Jones so that he may segue into Germany—the Goethe Plakette gets its inevitable workout[16]—and from thence to Adorno and Husserl (see 1.3, *Yeats and German Thought in the 1930s*). Apparently a book on Yeats and Berkeley was best served by having Appendix IIA, 'A list of publications concerning twentieth-century German thought preserved in W. B. Yeats's library at the time of his death, with details of surviving manuscript annotation'. Despite the impeccably scholarly nature of this title, there are no details—Mc Cormack simply gives O'Shea numbers— and 'twentieth-century German thought' includes Eckartshausen (1752–

up to 1929 (1914, 1919, 1922, 1925, 1926, 1929). Like Mc Cormack, I have taken bibliographic details for Berkeley from Jessop's *Bibliography*, although I have also used the Internet Archive, where many of these books may be found.

15   Mc Cormack is mistaken in pointing out that the cutting from the *Irish Statesman* of 7 September 1929, Hone's 'The Dublin of Berkeley (1703–1710)', noted by Torchiana as an insert in Johnston, 'had disappeared by the time Parisious and O'Shea got to work' (30). It appears as *YL* 996. However, it is now listed as an insert in Croce's *Historical Materialism and the Economics of Karl Marx* (*YL* 443).

16   See K. P. S. Jochum's decisive 'Yeats and the *Goethe-Plakette*: an unpublished Letter' *YA15*, *Yeats's Collaborations*, 288–312.

1803), Fechner (1801–87), and McTaggart on Hegel (1770–1831), while
A History of Philosophy by Erdmann (1805–92) is not restricted to Germany
and obviously does not reach the twentieth century.

Strangely, the appendix omits what one would have thought an essential
article, 'Recent Philosophy: The School of Husserl',[17] baffling given Mc
Cormack's discussion at length of Husserl on Berkeley at length. He also
quotes Yeats's reference to Husserl from *On the Boiler* (45–45, 48–55), one
can only treat the omission as symptomatic of Mc Cormack's piece-meal
approach to scholarship.[18]

Having almost completed *A Vision*, Yeats came to Berkeley with his
own philosophy largely developed. He would have understood Berkeley in
the light of that philosophy and judged him accordingly, as Mc Cormack
concedes (30, 79, 128). He understood that Berkeley used the term 'spirit'
more or less interchangeably with a whole range of other terms, such as
'mind', 'soul', 'will', 'agent', 'self', and 'person'. He agreed with the Berkeley
of *The Commonplace Book* who said that 'Nothing properly but persons, i.e.
conscious things, do exist. All other things are not so much existences as
manners of ye existence of persons [i.e. they are ideas]' (*Commonplace Book*,
3–4). For Yeats, this is the thesis that 'we know nothing but spirits and
their relations' (*TSMC* 66, *CL InteLex* 4826), and that reality is 'a timeless
and spaceless community of spirits' (the phrase is from Yeats's 'Seven
Propositions', drafted in 1929. While Yeats further states that 'Each Spirit is
determined by and determines those it perceives, and each Spirit is unique',
he is nevertheless careful to stress that 'Though Spirits are determined
by each other they cannot completely lose their freedom. Every possible
statement or perception contains both terms—the self and that which it
perceives or states'.[19] One might suggest that, in his philosophical reading,

---

[17] *The Times Literary Supplement*, 18 April 1929 (Recent German Literature
     number). See *YL* 2146 for O'Shea's note: '[i]n an envelope inserted in [*YL*] 1052
     [*Kant's Critical Philosophy for English Readers*], labelled: Article on recent German
     philosophy from "Times Literary Supplement" ("German Supplement") April
     1929'.

[18] Mc Cormack wonders aloud whether the Husserl reference (*CW5* 435 n. 82)
     was originally part of *On the Boiler*, even suggesting that Hone may have foisted
     it on to George Yeats, because, of course, it had been Hone who 'very likely' has
     directed Yeats to Husserl in the first place (53 n. 108).

[19] I have taken my quotations of the 'Seven Propositions' from Neil Mann's website,
     http://www.yeatsvision.com/7Propositions.html, as at 22 December 2013). Mc
     Cormack chooses to see the idea of 'spirits and their relations' through the
     distorting glass of spiritualism (e.g. 37, 40), as though Yeats pictures the entirety
     of reality as Caspar the Friendly Ghost and all his cohorts floating around in the
     ether and getting up to japes. Spiritualism did not exist when Berkeley wrote,

Yeats looked at ways of asserting human values, whereas Mc Cormack would have it that he looked at ways of abolishing human values. Berkeley's philosophy allowed Yeats to maintain his belief in

the old humanity with its unique irreplaceable individuals' [while seventeenth century science and its modern offshoots—in the process of being turned upside-down by Relativity and Quantum Theory—has replaced human beings by] something that can be chopped and measured like a piece of cheese [thereby leading to] the stimulation and condonation of revolutionary massacre and the multiplication of murderous weapons (*Ex* 436).

It is to his credit that Mc Cormack quotes this passage, which one might think he would be tempted to agree with, but it is not to his credit that he immediately obfuscates with syntactical quizzicality designed to cast doubt on whether Yeats actually meant what he seems quite clearly to be saying; he then adds that it is atypical of Yeats anyway (51–2, 54). In *A Vision B*, Yeats places the word 'justice' in a prominent position (*AVB* 25; *CW14* 19). It is a concept which is also important to Mc Cormack (99), who does not acknowledge Yeats's similar concern. Neil Mann quotes an early draft of this passage:

The great tradition of philosophy, all the [illegible] speculation that descends from Plato &, Hegel sets before us the certainty or probability—for Kant only offers us probability—that he who has best imagined justice has best imagined reality' (NLI 30,757) (*YA19* 189; cf. *CW14* 325).

although it was very much in the air when McTaggart developed his philosophy. Yeats's mature view was that popular spiritualism 'is sentimental make-believe, a pantomime stage where disembodied spirits re-create their human loves and hates' (*Ex* 309), which is how Mc Cormack professes to understand Yeats's own viewpoint. When Mc Cormack writes that 'Yeats's motives in taking up the bishop in his exchanges with Sturge Moore include a desire to "prove" psychical phenomena' (36), it might be suggested that he has got it precisely around the wrong way: Yeats is using psychical phenomena, such as Ruskin's cat, to further a philosophic point about 'sense-data' (to use terminology he disagreed with). If you see a bent stick in the water, you see what you see, and all talk of refraction serves to obscure the fact. Likewise, if Ruskin saw his cat, he saw his cat. As Yeats explains to Sturge Moore, what is at stake is '*immediate* knowledge' (*TSMC* 66, *CL InteLex* 4826). It is what you make of what you see that is important, but it is no use denying what you have seen in the first place. He also explained 'However I try always to keep my philosophy within such classifications of thought as will keep it to such experience as seems a natural life. I prefer to include in my definition of water a little duck weed or a few fish. I have never met that poor naked creature H^2 O' (*TSMC* 69, *CL InteLex* 4830).

For Yeats, reality includes spirits with differing needs, while justice demands that the needs are accommodated in the manner which best allows each to fulfil his or her own potential. Mc Cormack writes as though Yeats thought in a moral vacuum.

For Berkeley, of course, God and spirits are the primary facts a philosopher must take into account. As Jessop explained, the themes of *The Principles of Human Knowledge* were '... to refute the scepticism that makes the existence of a corporeal world problematic, and to vindicate theism, and by these means to call knowledge back to the service of man, and man to the service of God'; while Berkeley himself wrote that his purpose was 'to demonstrate the existence and attributes of God, the immortality of the Soul, the reconciliation of God's foreknowledge with freedom of men, and by shewing the emptiness and falseness of several parts of the speculative sciences, to reduce men to the study of religion and things useful'.[20]

Because Berkeley begins from this stance, he was not ensnared in solipsism. Yeats also began, not from an empiricist base, but from the recognition that spirits existed. Gentile's actual idealism, on the contrary, embraced solipsism, at least according to his expositor Roger W. Holmes.[21] But, given Mc Cormack, it is necessary to stress that Yeats was not a solipsist. Harold Bloom has also written of Yeats's supposed 'ecstatic and reductive solipsism', and has suggested that '[t]he Higher Criticism of Yeats, when it is more fully developed, will have to engage the radical issue of his subjectivity'.[22] Bloom reads *A Vision* via *Per Amica Silentia Lunae*, where this characterisation may be valid, but as Margaret Mills Harper's book title has stressed, *A Vision* is 'wisdom of two'. There is no place for solipsism in a marriage. Gogarty's joke, which is repeated in Rossi's 1970 book, is perhaps too good to be true:

He [Yeats] went round to see George Russell and to try his newly found Berkeleyism on him.
'Russell, nothing exists but consciousness. The whole world depends on my being conscious of it'.
'Thank you, Willie', Russell answered, '...I wrote your poetry'.[23]

---

[20] A. A. Luce and T. E. Jessop (eds.), *The Works of George Berkeley Bishop of Cloyne* (London: Thomas Nelson & Sons, 1949), Vol. 2, 7.

[21] *The Idealism of Giovanni Gentile* (New York: Macmillan, 1937), Chapter 5, 'The Problem', 111–20.

[22] Harold Bloom, *Yeats* (New York: Oxford University Press, 1970), 372–73.

[23] Oliver St. John Gogarty, *William Butler Yeats: A Memoir*. With a preface by Myles Dillon (Dublin: Dolmen Press, 1963), 22. There is a less-polished version in *As I Was Going Down Sackville Street* (Penguin, 1954 edition, orig. published

Yeats's response to the charge of solipsism was the one he made to Sturge Moore: 'The belief that all is experience does not mean that there is no truth unknown to us for there are unknown minds, but it does mean that there is no truth where there is no mind to know it' (*TSMC* 86; *CL InteLex* 4855). One of these 'unknown minds' is God. Yeats explained his position to Sturge Moore in March 1926,

> I agree with what [G. E. Moore] says about the later Berkeley, who was a Platonist. My Berkeley is the Berkeley of the *Commonplace Book*, and it is this Berkeley who has influenced the Italians. The essential sentence is of course 'things only exist in being perceived', and I can only call that perception God's when I add Blake's 'God only acts or is in existing beings or men'. (*TSMC* 80; *CL InteLex* 4849)

The Blake quotation as used here obviously chimes with the sentiments expressed in the 'Seven Propositions' with its 'community of spirits', although Yeats early and late will refer to 'God' as a separate transcendent being. Mc Cormack will claim that 'if the Last Case perceiver, God, is elided from Berkeley's thesis, the result is a diagnosis of solipsism, even group solipsism, or a template for eternal surveillance' (109), but what Yeats is saying fits neither of these.[24] As for the contrast between early and late Berkeley, Yeats will later say, in the Introduction to *Bishop Berkeley*, that he thought Berkeley may have come to believe what he himself puts forward here as his own belief, but that he dared not say such a thing in public. The

---

1937, *YL* 754), 82: 'you are as good (or as bad) a Berkeleian as Yeats, who holds that all existence depends on the percipient, or rather he held it until Æ pointed out an objection with, "Very well, Willie, then I am responsible for both your existence and your poems"'. The clumsier phrasing suggests that there may have been some truth in the story, or it might simply mean that Gogarty had not worked up his joke sufficiently. Rossi was treated to Gogarty's more streamlined version: 'Oliver Gogarty mi raccontava che quando W.B. Yeats prese il primo contatto con Berkeley e Gogarty stesso gli spiegò quel che Berkeley diceva, Yeats se ne entusiasmò, alla prima, e corse dal famoso scrittore AE (George Russell) a dirgli: "Russell, la tua esistenza e tutto ciò che esiste deve la sua esistenza alla mia percezione…". Al che AE ribatté: "Grazie, Mino: vuol dire che sono stato io a scrivere anche le tue poesie"' (*Introduzione a Berkeley*, 227 n. 34).

24 By "Last Case perceiver' he means that if all other percipients are removed then only God remains to validate the existence of what is otherwise unperceived. Mc Cormack gratefully filches the phrase 'group solipsism' from John Russell Roberts' *A Metaphysics for the Mob: The Philosophy of George Berkeley* (Oxford: Oxford University Press, 2007, 4), but ignores the ways Roberts explains it is not applicable to Berkeley, perhaps because his arguments on this are equally applicable to Yeats.

following passage from that Introduction is essential for an understanding
of how Yeats interpreted Berkeley.

Berkeley wrote in his *Commonplace Book*—The Spirit—the active thing—that
which is soul and God—is the will alone'; and then remembering the mask that he
must never lay aside, added: 'The concrete of the will and understanding I must call
mind, not person, lest offence be given, there being but one volition acknowledged
to be God. Mem. Carefully to omit defining Person, or making much mention of
it'. Then remembering that some member of his secret society had asked if our
separate personalities were united in a single will, a question considered by Plotinus
in the Fourth Ennead but dangerous in the eighteenth century, he wrote, 'What
you ask is merely about a word, unite is no more'. Number had no existence being
like all abstract ideas a part of language. It is plain however from his later writings
that he thought of God as a pure indivisible act, personal because at once will and
understanding, which unlike the Pure Act of Italian philosophy creates passive
'ideas'—sensations—thrusts them as it were outside itself; and in this act all beings—
from the hierarchy of heaven to man and woman and doubtless all that lives—share
in the measure of their worth: not the God of Protestant theology but a God that
leaves room for human pride. (*Bishop Berkeley*, xxv-xxvi; *CW5* 110.)

There are some interesting questions raised here which might give Mc
Cormack pause, but which, given his totalitarian all-or-nothing stance, do
not. Yeats's charge that 'the Pure Act of Italian philosophy'—read 'Gentile'
for 'Italian philosophy'—does not leave 'room for human pride' should be
noted. It is precisely this charge that is brought against Gentile in Angelo
Crespi's *Contemporary Thought of Italy* (*YL* 436). As Yeats has noted, Gentile
is also denying that there is a part of spirit that is not act, i.e. that spirit can
sometimes be passive. This is a problem that all interpreters of Berkeley
must face. If spirit is simple, how can it be both active and passive? For
Berkeley, it is the fact that we have ideas which we do not create, i.e. that we
are passive in perception, that demonstrates the existence of another spirit
who has created them.

We have seen that Mc Cormack characterised Yeats's interest in
philosophy as 'would-be absolute-ist' (175). Yeats came to dislike about
Gentile is precisely the absolutism whereby the human mind becomes the
be-all and end-all and would have agreed with Berkeley that there was only
one spirit whose mind could be described as '*pure* act', with no admixture
of passivity, and that is God ('the Pure Act or Eternal Instant, source of
simultaneity and succession alike' [*Bishop Berkeley*, xxi n.; *CW5* 352n. 25a]).
Yeats confessed that 'I am always, in all I do, driven to a moment which is
the realisation of myself as unique and free, or to a moment which is the
surrender to God of all that I am' (*Ex* 305), whereas Gentile avoided this

situation by eliminating God from the equation, declaring that his mind as pure act was capable of accomplishing all that had traditionally been the provenance of God.

From Gentile's God's eye view, history itself became meaningless, and human beings become mere pawns in the unfolding of a totalitarian spirit. Yeats did not agree.

Hegel's historical dialectic is, I am persuaded, false [Yeats writes] 'and its falsehood has led to the rancid ill-temper of the typical communist and his incitements or condonations of murder. When the spring vegetables are over they have not been refuted, nor have they suffered in honour or reputation'.[25]

Yeats had early learned the distinction between a contrary and a negation, and this distinction lies behind the above sentence, as he explains in *A Vision B*:

"Contraries are positive", wrote Blake, "a negation is not a contrary".... I had never put the conflict in logical form, never thought with Hegel that the two ends of the see-saw are one another's negation, nor that the spring vegetables were refuted when over.

Yeats appends a note to 'logical form' in which he says that 'Croce in his study of Hegel identifies error with negation' (*AVB* 72 and note; *CW14* 53). In *What Is Living and What Is Dead of the Philosophy of Hegel* (*YL* 448), Croce uses the terms *distincts* and *opposites* instead of *contraries* and *negations*. Yeats, one should note, called Gentile 'the Italian Hegelian philosopher'.[26] Crespi's book on *Contemporary Thought of Italy* (*YL* 436) showed quite clearly, in 1926, how Gentile's philosophy leads to the negation of the individual in the interests of the State 'or, under this name, of any faction or mob which by fair means or foul succeeds temporarily in seizing the helm' (*Contemporary Thought of Italy*, 198). There is a difficult annotation made by Yeats on p.

---

[25] *Ex* 429–30n.; *CW5* 432 n. 65. Mc Cormack quotes a passage from W. Tudor Jones's *Contemporary Thought of Germany* which states that 'Hegel introduces alien elements from the natural world and conceives of these as pure thought' (44). Observing that Yeats has marked this passage, he comments: 'There is no way of judging from the single bar line in the margin whether Yeats regarded this with approval, curiosity, incomprehension, or hostility'. Obviously, though, you could look at what else Yeats had to say about Hegel. Mc Cormack has clearly examined the volume (O'Shea does not identify the marked passages).

[26] *Aphorisms of Yôga by Bhagwan Shree Patanjali, Done into English from the original in Sanskrit with a commentary by Shree Purohit Swami and an Introduction by W. B. Yeats* (London: Faber & Faber, 1938), 19; *CW5* 179.

160 of Crespi which is relevant to this topic: 'I (let us say) negate Swinburne, as part of an historical movement. But as transcendental ego I recreate his world. The transcendental ego may not be dialectical, but only empirical'. While the concept of negation occurs on this page, the annotation appears to be related to the wider context of Crespi's argument. I suggest that Yeats read further on in Crespi's chapter and returned to this page in order to make his comment, which seems to incorporate Crespi's later collapsing of Gentile's 'Transcendental Ego' into a merely empirical one (*Contemporary Thought of Italy*, p. 175: 'in such a synthesis the Empirical... does not cease to be empirical.... [or else] the Transcendental [is] a mere abstraction'). I thus take the annotation to mean that Yeats does not follow Gentile and accordingly would reject the transcendental ego *if* it is not dialectical, if it tries to treat contraries as opposites and thus have the opposites cancel each other out. This may be compared with the passage in the Introduction to *Aphorisms of Yôga* (p. 19; *CW5* 179), where Yeats characterises the idea that 'ultimate reality is the Pure Act', as that wherein 'the actor and the thing acted upon, the puncher and the punching-ball, [are] consumed away'. This is not a consummation that he wishes.[27]

Mc Cormack steers clear of contemporary debates about the status of Berkeley's immaterialism. Is he a subjective idealist or a realist? An early phenomenalist? A pragmatist before his time? An empiricist?[28] Nor does he

---

[27] In this assessment of what Yeats is saying in *Aphorisms of Yôga*, I disagree with Gerald Doherty, who says of this passage that 'Yeats applauds Gentile'. See Doherty, "The World That Shines and Sounds: W. B. Yeats and Daisetz Suzuki", *Irish Renaissance Annual* 4 (1983), 68. In his 1937 book on *The Idealism of Giovanni Gentile*, Roger W. Holmes notes that, for Gentile, 'even the four-fold division of Croce's must go. Any multiplicity, be it that of the mind and something outside of the mind or even a division of the activity of the mind, is arbitrary' (*The Idealism of Giovanni Gentile*, 7–8). As Yeats's annotations to Croce demonstrate (*YL* 444, *YL* 446), he would have been reluctant to dispense with Croce's idea. In *A Vision*, he writes, 'The *Four Faculties* somewhat resemble the four moments to which Croce has dedicated four books', although he thought that Croce did not go far enough because he made 'little use of antithesis and antinomy' (*AVB* 82 n.; *CW14* 61 n.). For Yeats and Croce, one should consult Torchiana's 'Yeats and Croce', already mentioned. This is the same as the Torchiana article listed in Mc Cormack's bibliography as 'Yeats and Italian Idealism'. Mc Cormack points out that Yeats lost interest in Gentile by 1934 (70), implying that mere fickleness was to blame.

[28] Mc Cormack's characterization of Berkeley as 'the advocate of tar-water' (63) is symptomatic of an unacknowledged contempt, although he probably thinks he is merely being entertaining. When he actually expounds Berkeley's philosophy,

examine how Yeats draws distinctions between different forms of idealism, both in the Introduction to *Bishop Berkeley*, where he says that he thinks Kant more an idealist than Berkeley, who was 'idealist and realist alike'—an opinion with which most Berkeley scholars would now agree—and Hegel and his successors more than Kant (*Bishop Berkeley*, xxiii; *CW5*), and in the letters to Sturge Moore, where he discusses realism and idealism at length (e.g. *TSMC* 77–78, 89,99; *CL InteLex* 4840, 4856). While Mc Cormack notes that Bradley had his own version of idealism (138), he does not quote Yeats's scathing assessment of the man, and one presumes, of his philosophy, in *A Vision*:

Professor Bradley believed also that he could stand by the death-bed or wife or mistress and not long for an immortality of body and soul. He found it difficult to reconcile personal immortality with his form of Absolute idealism, and besides he hated the common heart; an arrogant, sapless man' (*AVB* 219n., *CW14* 159n.).

Nor does he discuss McTaggart, who is Yeats's preferred idealist. The perennial problem of the One and the Many is early, and correctly, identified by Mc Cormack as a key to Yeats (17), but at no stage does he quote Yeats's confession about 'the realisation of myself as unique and free', or of 'surrender to God' (*Ex* 305, above p. 439). Mc Cormack also admits that Eastern thought might have similar concerns. One of his main concessions (in a fn.) is worth quoting in full. Raising the spectre of Yeats's concordance with the 'Einsteinian concept of space-time', which 'revived issues discussed by the ancient Greeks', he dismisses it by claiming that it is inconsistent with Yeats's supposed view that all questions must be drawn to 'a mind-totality in which even the dead and the living enjoyed no distinction one class from the other'. Ignoring the fact that Yeats, like everyone else, drew just such

he does so via Ronald Knox's limerick about the tree in the quad (78–79; the phrase merits a separate Index entry under 'Berkeley': there are references on pp. 55 and 156 that are not indexed). It is possible that this is a trap for the unwary, although it might signify laziness and a distaste for philosophy unless it has first been mediated—and vetted—by Adorno. However, Mc Cormack does note, via Roberts, that Berkeley never said 'Esse est percipi' as it is usually quoted— the reader of Roberts could hardly miss his discussion, as his first chapter is provocatively titled 'The Berkelian Basics: Why *Esse* Is Not *Percipi*'—but he prefers to discuss grammatical fine points rather than follow up on what Roberts has to say about the topic (151, 168). While his Bibliography does include several modern works on Berkeley, Mc Cormack only discusses those which have a predominantly literary focus. He appears to have learnt little about Berkeley's philosophy from David Berman, whom he thanks in the Acknowledgements.

a distinction (where has he ever said that he does not?), he proceeds with some casual Orientalism:

It can be argued that Yeats is not at odds with Eastern Philosophy on this point; the problems arise when he wishes to hold a non- or anti-individuating theory of mind and, at the same time, to act as an individual agent of power in relation to others considered likewise as individuals; to be at once eastern and western, passive (or contemplative) and active. Few occasions or contexts for resolution of these opposites arise without concomitant issues whether defined in moral terms or otherwise (e.g. through mysticism, 46 n. 90).

This passage is noteworthy in several respects. First, it is one of the few occasions where Mc Cormack concedes what most of his book seeks to deny, that Yeats at any time wanted to act 'as an individual agent of power in relation to others considered likewise as individuals'. Secondly, it is an admission that there are contexts in which the One can be invoked which do not involve fascistic thought. Thirdly, it acknowledges that attempts to resolve these opposites carry with them other issues. Yeats would have agreed with the last point. The unwarranted assumption is that Yeats *wanted* to resolve the issue of the One and the many. For him, on the contrary, 'human reason' cannot reconcile the claims of the One and the many: 'Could those two impulses [towards the One or towards the many], one as much a part of the truth as the other, be reconciled, or if one or the other could prevail, all life would cease' (*Ex* 305). Doubtless Mc Cormack would see this as an embrace of irrationalism rather than as an acknowledgment of inevitable paradox.

Mc Cormack's book is long on rhetoric and short on analysis. He does not give even a minimal account of what was promised at his book's outset, how the 'idealism' of 'Berkeley is reconceived, misbegotten and generally deformed in the "mind" of Italian idealism as swaddled by fascism' (8–9). It is simply stated as fact. When Mc Cormack writes that 'the Berkeley available to Yeats in 1927 was not the model of 1733 (or earlier); it was the complex of Berkeleyan text-in-interpretation advanced by Croce, Gentile, Papini, Rossi and Hone from a place avowedly totalitarian' (100), that is virtually the extent of the argument. Later, he will say 'Enough has been said about the transmission, and inevitable misprision, of Berkeley's thought from the eighteenth century through to the present, especially its Italian phase' (155), whereas little has in fact been said on this topic. Alternatively, the distinction between the 'real' Berkeley and Berkeley as interpreted is ignored and the two idealisms are simply conflated: he will write, for example, of how '[t]he idealist of the Berkeleyan-Yeatsian stripe' sees no difference between perpetrator and victim because '[t]he notion of individual minds is an inadequate realisation of mentality for, in Yeats's words, there is One Mind only', and besides, a physical beating is all in the mind (83–84). However, his juxtaposition here and elsewhere (e.g., 40, 100, 104) of Berkeley's thesis with death camps and beatings by fascist goons no more touches Berkeley or Yeats than did the pain in Dr Johnson's foot when he refuted Berkeley by kicking a stone; the criticism is at the same level of comprehension, and will win applause only from those who are likewise searching for easy victories.[29] But putting aside the placing of blame with Berkeley and Yeats, is Mc Cormack correct to believe that some forms of idealism are complicit with murder or, perhaps more accurately, do not give one a platform from which to denounce such things? Is he also correct to warn about the dangers of a cult of sacrifice for the greater good? Surprisingly enough, it is here, just when you think Mc Cormack is at his most cantankerous and unbalanced, his most *unforgiving*, that his book may perform a valuable service: his exaggerations and distortions are in fact provoking, and they may prod his readers into clarifying what they think—if they have not been driven to dismiss him completely, which, given his antagonistic stance and writing style, is a very real risk.

Much of *'We Irish'*, like its predecessor *Blood Kindred*, is an extended complaint that people in the 1920s and '30s did not see what fascism would become. In other words, it judges people of that era according to post-Holocaust standards, and of course, they are found wanting. Is this unfair? Obviously so, but it is not a futile exercise. Abstractions and ideology predominate in current political debate. Slogans like 'national security' and 'war on terror' help to condone abrogation of human rights and the massacre of innocents. Mc Cormack is right to excoriate the complicity of the 'wee Irish' (vi) and their analogues world-wide in support of 'greater' ideologies. When he writes of the situation where 'even value itself [is] susceptible to conversion into its opposite' (129), it is a necessary warning. The competing demands of reality and justice are our continuing burden, as Yeats well knew. Mc Cormack chooses to entomb the poet in a cocoon of innuendo and assertion, thereby missing anything of value to be found in his writings.

---

[29] What Jessop said about Dr Johnson may be applied to what Mc Cormack says about victim and perpetrator: Johnson may have kicked the stone, but he missed the point (quoted by Luce, *Berkeley's Immaterialism*, 80).

The final lines of 'The Man and the Echo' can serve as sufficient rebuttal
of Mc Cormack:

> O Rocky Voice,
> Shall we in the great night rejoice?
> What do we know but that we face
> One another in this place?
> But hush, for I have lost the theme,
> Its joy or night seem but a dream;
> Up there some hawk or owl has struck,
> Dropping out of sky or rock,
> A stricken rabbit is crying out,
> And its cry distracts my thought. (*VP* 633)

http://dx.doi.org/10.11647/OBP.0081.20

Winifred Dawson, *The Porter's Daughter: The Life of Amy Audrey Locke* (Published by the author: Winchester, printed by Sarsen Press, 2014), pp. xiv + 138

Jad Adams

Amy Audrey Locke is best known as the muse for William T. Horton, Yeats's illustrator and his companion in the esoteric. Now for the first time, she has her own biography, written by a woman who herself was a poetic muse—five of Philip Larkin's poems were written to Winifred Dawson. She does not mention it here, but her friendship with Larkin, who she met when both were working at the library of Queen's University, Belfast in the 1950s, may have been part of her inspiration for writing this book. Another point of connection is that both she and Amy Locke always worked in archives and libraries. Dawson stumbled across Locke while working as a specialist librarian in Winchester.

Locke was born in Winchester in 1881, the daughter of a butler at Winchester College who became the College's porter. The bookish Amy won a scholarship to Somerville and started on a lifelong career as a writer of local and aristocratic family histories. She often worked in the British Museum reading room, in the 'ladies section' until 1907 when segregation ended. Here, she met Arundell Esdaile, who at this time was the Assistant Keeper (Second Class) of Printed Books. They fell in love—a problem, as he was already married to Kitty, a relative of the famed Benson family. Esdaile and Kitty both make an appearance in Arthur Benson's diaries. Esdaile wrote Locke a slim volume of, it must be said, indifferent verse. Kitty, who bore him three children, wrote a rather better volume of her own, in heart-breaking distress at her husband's unfaithfulness. Kitty Esdaile was to become the leading authority on post-mediaeval sculpture in England.

Esdaile and Locke's relationship stopped short of sex, as he was to record, though

> several times we were mortally near it. But I might have got her with child, and not only made my own home impossible, but broken the hearts of her poor parents. Her thought for them was her main motive for withholding the last favour; she practically said as much.

That 'practically' suggests a woman of considerable reticence.

Esdaile brooded over Amy Locke's labours at the British Museum, surveying with contempt some of the characters he saw reading there. He respected Yeats, but with reservation,

> Great poet that he was, Yeats was utterly uncritical, and anybody, however intellectually or morally empty, could impose on him by claiming to be a mystic ... The Room at one time abounded in such riff-raff, who had no legitimate occasion to be there at all.

Esdaile's harsh tone is doubtless because one such, William Thomas Horton, was to supplant him in Amy Locke's affections. Horton had experienced a lonely childhood and solitary youth and as a man was seeking a Vision of the Spirit, which Locke provided, becoming his 'human Messenger' who inspired the 'legend in line and verse' that became *The Way of the Soul*, published in 1910. A more prosaic way of expressing it is that he fell in love with her. She responded in true bibliophile fashion with a review of this book in the *Occult Review* for December 1910.

Locke and Horton both lived in the Vale of Health, Hampstead, not far from each other, then moved in together early in 1915, to 63 Cartwright Gardens, just south of the Euston Road, and of course very close to Yeats's own rooms in Woburn Buildings. Yeats visited for occult conversations, responding to invitations such as Horton's 'if you could manage it, stay for supper which would be of fruit as our friend [Locke] & I are practically fruitarians' (p. 81).[1]

Locke and Horton worked together on a children's story called *Tiny Tim's Flyship* with 22 typed sheets by Locke and 18 black and white illustrations by Horton. Unpublished except for the sections reproduced here, it is now in the Horton papers in Reading University Library.

---

[1]   See also *LTWBY* 268–69, and George Mills Harper, *W. B. Yeats and W. T. Horton: the Record of an Occult Friendship* (London: Macmillan, 1980). The letter is of 20 July, 1914.

It was Yeats's belief that they 'lived together Platonically', but he provided little by way of evidence for this view. The summoning of the ghost of Horton in 'On All Souls' Night' is of course very familiar.

> Horton's the first I call. He loved strange thought
> And knew that sweet extremity of pride
> That's called platonic love,
> And that to such a pitch of passion wrought
> Nothing could bring him, when his lady died,
> Anodyne for his love.
> Words were but wasted breath;
> One dear hope had he:
> The inclemency
> Of that or the next winter would be death.
>
> Two thoughts were so mixed up I could not tell
> Whether of her or God he thought the most,
> But think that his mind's eye,
> When upward turned, on one sole image fell;
> And that a slight companionable ghost,
> Wild with divinity,
> Had so lit up the whole
> Immense miraculous house
> The Bible promised us,
> It seemed a gold-fish swimming in a bowl. (*VP* 471)

Yeats supplemented this with a very touching picture of Horton in the 'Dedication' to Moina Mathers ('Vestigia') of the 1925 version of *A Vision*. There Horton, though unnamed, is fully described as the third of his fellow-students with whom early conversations provide occasion for 'commendation' or 'expostulation' in his more mature writings, even when those fellow-students are 'estranged or dead'.

A third lived through that strange adventure, perhaps the strangest of all adventures—Platonic love. When he was a child his nurse said to him—"An Angel bent over your bed last night", and in his seventeenth year he awoke to see the phantom of a beautiful woman at his bedside. Presently he gave himself up to all kinds of amorous adventures, until at last, in I think his fiftieth year but when he had still all his physical vigour, he thought "I do not need women but God". Then he and a very good, charming, young fellow-student fell in love with one another and though he could only keep down his passion with the most bitter struggle, they lived together platonically, and this they did, not from prejudice, for I think they had none, but from a clear sense of something to be attained by what seemed a most needless trampling of the grapes of life. She died, and he survived her but a little time during which he saw her in apparition and attained through her certain of the traditional experiences of the saint. He was my close friend, and had he lived I would have asked him to accept the dedication of a book I could not expect him to approve, for in his later life he cared for little but what seemed to him a very simple piety (*CW13* liii).

Winifred Dawson does not explicitly state that Locke was adored by men but died *virgo intacta*, but that is the implication of her quotes on the intimate side of Locke's romantic life. Virginity may well have had some esoteric meaning in Horton's cosmology, but Dawson does not explore it. However, she does provide a great service in recovering a letter from Locke to Horton in response to a request from Yeats (via Horton) of 18 January, 1915. That letter from Locke (of 1 February 1915) is absent from George Mills Harper's *W. B. Yeats and W. T. Horton: the Record of an Occult Friendship*,[2] but Dawson prints it in full. It offers the fruits of her research for Yeats on the usurer Joseph Damer (1630–1720), including a transcription of Swift's epitaph and his (and Stella's) longer 'An Elegy on the death of Demer [*sic*] the Usurer; who died the 6th of July 1720', a family tree, and extracts from two letters of Horace Walpole's on Damer's heir. Yeats had been preoccupied by the story of Damer, a subject of the scorn of William Dall Heffernan (the Blind, *c.*1700–60), if fitfully, then certainly since late 1888 (see *CL1*, 115–16). Now Locke had undertaken some research for him on Damer in the British Museum, and at a time when he was preoccupied by Spiritualism. On 3rd February Yeats thanked her through Horton from Coleman's Hatch, inviting Locke and Horton to one of his Monday evenings and acknowledging her 'invaluable letter about Daimer [*sic*]. He was just the sort of person to be still walking'.[3] He was shortly to write to Lady Gregory about the representation of ghosts on stage and to urge the revival of her *Damer's Gold*.[4] There can be little doubt, too, that Yeats was attracted to Audrey Locke's physical type, for on 15th October 1915 he invited Horton and Locke to meet her 'double', 'Seraphita', i.e.,

---

[2]   See above n. 1. See Harper's item 43, p. 124, where this letter can now be inserted. Copyright reasons prevented Harper, who prints Horton's extant letters, from doing more than summarizing the Yeats side of the correspondence, which is now fully available in *CL InteLex*.

[3]   *CL InteLex* 2584, 2597, 3 February [1915].

[4]   *CL InteLex* 2638, to Lady Gregory, 27 April 1915. The play can be found in Ann Saddlemyer (ed.), *The Comedies of Lady Gregory, being the First Volume of her Collected Plays* (Gerrards Cross: Colin Smythe, 1971), 133ff. The letter can also be found in App. 1 of the third volume, pp. 413ff.

his current mistress, Alexandra ('Aleck' sometimes 'Alick') Schepeler with whom he was discussing visions as he prepared to write to his own 'double', 'Leo Africanus'.[5] It becomes clear from subsequent letters to Schepeler that neither she nor Yeats was in doubt as to Horton's instability of mind:

> Here is the usual Horton prophesy or rather evangelization. He left it next day. So I am not the only dark man in your tortuous existence. He leaves similar anouncements for me from time to time but much more denunciatory. I wonder when I am to see you.[6]

Early in 1916, Yeats issued an invitation to Horton and Locke to visit him, only to receive a reply that Locke was in a private nursing home. She was suffering from acute mastoiditis, a serious bacterial infection of her inner ear, which was to kill her on 19 June 1916 at the age of 35. Horton believed he continued to be 'in communication' with her, until his own death three years later. Esdaile, who eventually became Secretary of the British Museum, continued to pine for Locke, until he died in 1956.

Dawson died in 2014. She was not a natural writer of narrative, and the movement from fact to fact is rather jerky, rather than a fully digested flow that a natural biographer would provide. Locke never really comes to life as she would in the hands of a writer with more imagination; the images of her in this book by Horton are the most vital evidence of the spirit she possessed. Still, it is valuable that Locke has a book bringing together all the information which can reliably be known about her, and Dawson's labours must be applauded. Yeats scholars will value this book for what it fills out for them.

This biography falls into that category of book on more obscure subjects which now have to be self-published because small publishers have virtually ceased to exist. Nonetheless, it is of an extremely high standard, on acid-free paper, with a good level of copy editing and well produced illustrations, with many in colour. There are no notes but an adequate bibliography and index.

---

[5] See *CL InteLex*, 2781–82, 2788, 15 October, 1915, to Horton and 16, 25 October to Schepeler.

[6] See *CL InteLex* 2788, to Alick Schepeler, 25 October [1915] which encloses Horton's mad letter of 22 October, which is not in Harper, *op. cit.* See also *CL InteLex* 2838, also to Schepeler [26 December 1915].

http://dx.doi.org/10.11647/OBP.0081.21

Brian Arkins, *The Thought of W. B. Yeats* (Bern: Peter Lang, 2010), ISBN 978-3-03911939-4, pp. xi + 192; J. P. Mahaffy, *Rambles & Studies in Greece*, with an Introduction and Commentary by Brian Arkins (Ulster Editions and Monographs 17; Gerrards Cross: Colin Smythe, 2012), ISBN 978-0-86140-430-8, pp. 29 + 241

Michael Edwards

I begin with a statement of disinterest. I have known Brian Arkins for over a decade, primarily in my former role as 'Extern' (as they are known in Ireland) to the Classics Department at NUI Galway. I have also enjoyed his company over more than the odd tipple, Arkins being not only a great *raconteur*, but an expert in literature both classical (he was the Honorary President of the Classical Association of Ireland in 2005) and Irish of all kinds (critical studies of Desmond Egan and James Liddy, as well as various studies of the influence of classical literature on Irish writers such as Joyce and Yeats). I come to Yeats as a complete amateur—Mahaffy I am more familiar with as a professional classicist. I should add that I have no axe to grind with Mahaffy, the one-time opponent of Sir Richard Jebb, to whose *Selections from the Attic Orators* I myself contributed part of a new introduction in 2005.

I read *The Thought of W.B. Yeats* with a deep desire to learn more about the great man, and I was not disappointed. The book essentially falls into two parts. In the first, by means of a series of penetrating essays through which (as even the most inexperienced reader of Yeats such as myself would expect) runs the theme of antinomies. Arkins explores Yeats's thought on a variety of topics, beginning with opposites themselves ('All Things Doubled: The Theme of Opposites in Yeats') and moving on to 'Yeats and Religion', 'Yeats and Sex' and 'Yeats and Politics'. For me, the chapter on sex was perhaps the most interesting and informative, not (I aver) through prurience, but because this is an area of study in which Arkins excels, having published extensively on Latin love poetry, including Propertius and Catullus (see, for example, his 1982 book *Sexuality in Catullus*). In the second part, Arkins takes *A Vision* as his starting-point for an assessment of Yeats's views on history and human character ('Apocalypse: Yeats's *A Vision*'), surveys Yeats's use of classical literature. 'Further Greek Themes in Yeats' builds on Arkins' 1990 *Builders of My Soul: Greek and Roman Themes in Yeats*: this new chapter does not in fact confine itself to Greek, but covers Latin as well. It analyses in detail four important features of Yeats's style, the use of embedded sentences, questions and 'the' and 'that', and the combination of two nouns. Again as a classicist, I found the analyses of Yeats's renderings of Sophocles and his attitude to Latin literature (his use of Lucretius, Catullus, Virgil and Propertius, balanced by his rejection of Latin in *On the Boiler*) of particular interest, while as a student of grammar and rhetoric I was absorbed by the chapter on Yeats's style, 'Passionate Syntax: Style in the Poetry of Yeats'.

My criticisms of *The Thought of W.B. Yeats* are not so much directed at the content. I would not presume to challenge Arkins on Yeats, but perhaps an explanation of the terms 'primary' and 'secondary' epic on p. 104 would help to strengthen his point there. As Arkins knows, the genuineness of the ending of *King Oedipus* is debated, the clue being in '[t]he seven lines of rather clumsy Greek', p. (120).

But the proof-reading! Or rather the lack of it. I found myself correcting far too many typographical errors—a distraction serious enough to give pause for thought when one reads, e.g.

'Yeats's religious *Weltanschauung* involved belief in a transcendent reality, the immorality of the soul and reincarnation' (p. 9).

Further, the book would certainly have benefited from closer editing. I note, for example, that Dryden's name does not appear in the Index; had it been, an attentive editor might have realised that the lines of his translation of Lucretius quoted on p. 135 have already been quoted on p. 52—and, worse still—so have Yeats's quoted words to John Sparrow. Mind you, the prize must go to the opening four lines of 'Politics', which appear on pp. 8, 67 and 161 without cross-reference.

Those niggles aside, *The Thought of W.B. Yeats*, while by no means easy reading, will offer something of interest to a range of audiences, including professional Yeats scholars.

Mahaffy's *Rambles* have served a similar function since the first edition of 1876. Of course, many sites are now very different from what he saw, and 138 years of scholarship have given rise to challenges to many of his confident assertions (born of Mahaffy's tremendous scholarship, I hasten to add)—is the site of the Battle of Marathon 'absolutely fixed by the great mound', the *Soros* that is the burial place of the Athenian fallen (p. 80)? And a great deal of money and Elgin-inspired national pride has gone into the construction and layout of the still new Acropolis Museum, whereas for a doleful Mahaffy '[n]othing is more melancholy and more disappointing than the first view of the Athenian museums' (p. 28).

Only the scholarly pedant or the completely unromantic, however, could fail to be enraptured by Mahaffy's tales of life, ancient and (for him) modern. Arkins's edition again draws on his long experience and deep knowledge of matters both classical and Irish. With an excellent introduction to 'Mahaffy: Classicist and Philhellene' that sets the work in its context, and copious notes in 51 pages of learned and perceptive commentary (at random, p. 215: 'Mahaffy at his most colonial'…; 'the beehive tombs of Orchomenus that were discovered by Schliemann—Mahaffy's 'treasure-houses'—are unlikely to have any connection with the prehistoric Minyans'), this volume is both a welcome new edition of a classic work of scholarship, and a significant contribution to the study of ancient Greece and its reception in the nineteenth century.

http://dx.doi.org/10.11647/OBP.0081.22

Olivia Shakespear, *Beauty's Hour*, edited by Anne Margaret Daniel (Richmond, VA: Valancourt Books, 2016), pp. 89. Foreword, Introduction, and Notes by the Editor. ISBN 978-1-943910-40-3

Deirdre Toomey

'Who ever had a like profile?—a profile from a Sicilian coin' is Yeats's celebrated tribute to his first lover Olivia Shakespear, after looking at her image in the 1895 *Literary Yearbook*. That image is reproduced as the cover of this attractive volume from the enterprising Valancourt Press. Yeats was probably thinking of the 'Arethusa coin', one of the most beautiful of all Greek coins, from the period of rule of Dionysius I (397 BC-343 BC), which represents the profile of the naiad Arethusa, patron of Syracuse, with a horse and palm on the verso. The resemblance to the classical profile so admired by Yeats is striking, as are the elaborate masses of waving hair in a Greek knot.

'Beauty's Hour', scrupulously edited here by Anne Margaret Daniel, was written by 1894 and published in *The Savoy* in August and September 1896. It was Olivia Shakespear's sole contribution to this journal which also published many of the poems which Yeats wrote to her during their affair of 1896. 'Beauty's Hour' is, as Anne Margaret Daniel points out in her introduction, a strange work to come from the pen of a very beautiful woman. The story turns on the plain face of the highly intelligent heroine Mary Gower which inhibits her hopeless for love for Gerald Harman. By a personal act of will she becomes briefly beautiful and experiences Gerald's love in her new identity. The editor points to various models, for a plain heroine; both Jane Eyre and Marian Halcome in Wilkie Collins's *The Woman in White* are plain. Indeed, Marian's quasi-masculine ugliness causes a crisis of sexual response in the hero. As Walter realises, despite her perfect body,

'The Lady is ugly!' He feels 'a sensation close to that helpless discomfort familiar to all of us in sleep, when we recognise yet cannot reconcile the anomalies and contradictions of a dream'. Marian's half-sister Laura is a conventional helpless fair beauty, but it is Marian who dominates the novel. To her indignation, the arch villain Baron Fosco falls deeply in love with her, and Walter Hartwright lives in a strange *ménage-à-trois* with Marian and her now mentally enfeebled half-sister, in which triangle Marian and he are, as it were, the parental couple, protecting Laura from Baron Fosco.

Charlotte Bronte was defiant in making her heroine 'little and marked', which she did in a direct challenge to her sisters, whom she saw as 'morally wrong' in making their heroines beautiful as a matter of course, as was the norm in nineteenth-century fiction. Even Dorothea Brooke, although a bluestocking with scholarly aspirations, is given beauty far removed from that of her homely creator. In *Villette*, Bronte's heroine is also plain and in *Middlemarch*, Eliot gives us an ordinary looking secondary heroine in Mary Garth. However, Elizabeth Gaskell in *Wives and Daughters* contrasts the conventionally beautiful Cynthia with Molly, whose darker beauty will last, when her blonde stepsister's red and white complexion will coarsen.

'Beauty's Hour' is a novella and it is unlikely that any writer no matter how skilled or sophisticated would have been able to extend such a narrative, given the challenge of a plain heroine. Wilkie Collins was writing a plot-driven sensation novel, so Marian's 'ugliness' in *The Woman in White* is not as important as her intelligence and strength of character. Anne Margaret Daniel rightly compares Shakespear's novella to *The Picture of Dorian Gray* which also has a supernatural element, which thus allows for an extended narrative which can chart the corruption of Dorian and the sinister preservation of his youth and beauty and in which art (the portrait of Dorian) finally triumphs.

So we are left with a puzzle, why did Olivia Shakespear choose a plain heroine? In 'Beauty's Hour' she refers to the Beauty of the second class, whose claims to beauty might be disputed. Shakespear may have thought herself to be in this category, as hers was a dark beauty in a period in which fair beauty was idealised. We know that Yeats began his eccentric courtship of Olivia Shakespear by telling her of his love for Maud Gonne, an approach he had already used with Eva Gore-Booth. We do not know whether at any stage in his courtship, he had shown her a photograph of Maud Gonne. However, according to John Masefield, Yeats had 'a large photograph of a woman'—undoubtedly of Maud Gonne—on the wall of his rooms in Woburn Walk. This would have been a reminder to Olivia of her rival, who was exceptionally tall (Olivia was quite short) and who had red gold hair and a pale apple blossom skin rather than a skin 'a little darker than a Greek's'. Olivia Shakespear would have had leisure to examine this when she attended one of Yeats's Mondays in Autumn 1896, when she also met Henry-D. Davray who had called 'Beauty's Hour', 'une... jolie fantasie' in the *Mercure de France* in October 1896.

In allowing us to reflect on this enigma, Valancourt Books and Anne Margaret Daniel have done us a service by republishing 'Beauty's Hour'. Like many of thst press's rediscoveries it has a supernatural motif.

I noticed one minor slip in the otherwise careful editing of this text. In her introduction Daniel quotes a telling passage from Lady Gregory's Diary in which she describes her first visit in Winter 1897 to Woburn Buildings',very small and draughty... I wish poor W cd be better waited on—his room had not been done up'. Lady Gregory is referring not to interior decor, as the editor reads it, but to his bed not having been made nor his bedroom cleaned by Mrs Old, his housekeeper, who had to travel from Islington and possibly did the housework later in the day. Mrs Old was evidently not expecting an afternoon call from Lady Gregory, ready to measure for curtains. Yeats later referred to Mrs Old as 'no Angel'.

Valancourt Books has also republished Henry Mercer's *November Night Tales* an impressive quasi-supernatural series, positioned somewhere between Poe and M. R. James, which includes a fatal book story ('The Wolf Book') set in the Balkans, as well as *Manfroné; or, The One-Handed Monk* (1809), a novel which turns up as circulating library fare in Thackeray's 'A Shabby-Genteel Story' and Sheridan le Fanu's first novel, *The Cock and Anchor* with its hilarious account of two low-lives dressing for an evening at Dublin Castle. 'Beauty's Hour' is an impressive addition to this list, and one hopes that Valancourt will also consider republishing Olivia Shakespear's *Rupert Armstrong* (1898), the novel which is closest to the *milieu* of W. B. Yeats.

Publications Received

In addition to the books reviewed above, copies of the following have been received by April, 2016, and will be considered for review in *Yeats Annual No. 21*.

Wayne Chapman	*Yeats's Poetry in the Making: Sing Whatever Is Well Made* (Basingstoke and New York: Palgrave Macmillan, 2010), pp. xx + 358.
Wayne Chapman (ed.)	*The South Carolina Review*, 48: 2 (Spring 2016), ISSN: 0038-3163. Contains Neil Mann's essay review, 'The Fascination of What's Accurate' on Chapman's *Yeats's Poetry in the Making: Sing Whatever is Well Made*, pp. 211–19. ISBN 978-0-230-27191-3
Denis Donoghue	*Metaphor* (Cambridge, Mass.; London: Harvard University Press, 2014), pp. 232. ISBN 9780674430662
Declan J. Foley (ed.)	*Yeats 150: William Butler Yeats 1865–1939* (Dublin: Lilliput Press, 2016), pp. xii + 588. ISBN 978 1 84351 645 3. Following the editor's introduction, and Helen Vendler's 'Seamus Justin Heaney', there are 313 pp. of 'Academic Essays', some of them reprintings of published pieces. In order of placement, these essays are by Maneck H. Daruwala, Deirdre Toomey, Warwick Gould, José Lanters, Patrick J. Keane, Denis Donoghue, Peter Kuch, Colin Smythe, Neil Mann, Tomoko Iwatsubo, Lucy McDiarmuid, Anne Margaret Daniel, Bruce Stewart, Carolyn Masel and John Purser. Three essays on 'The Plays' follow, by Richard Londraville, Sam McCready and Melinda Szüts, 'The Yeats Family', essays by Ann Saddlemyer, Hilary Pyle, James L. Pethica, Elisabeth Ansel, Martin Mansergh. 'Tír Na Nóg' with essays by Glen Cavaliero, T. R. Henn (1901–74), Vincent Buckley (1925–88), and Alec King (1904–70).

'Scholars' includes pieces by Doug Saum, Craig Kirk, Katy Plowright and Kristóf Kiss; while 'W. B. Yeats Poetry Prizes' off a list of the iYeats Poetry Competition, and the Poetry Ireland Secondary Schools Competition, plus W. B. Yeats Poetry Prizes in Australia and New York. A final section on 'Sligeach: Sligo—"The Place of Shells" and Slí Dhá Átha—"The way of the Two Fords"' includes six pieces. 'Notes on Contributors' follow, with a list of Subscribers, Bibliography and Index.

Wayne E. Hall — *Dialogues in the Margin: A Study of* The Dublin University Magazine (Washington: Catholic University of America Press, 1999; Gerrards Cross: Colin Smythe, Ltd., 2000), pp. x + 252. ISBN 9780861404339.

Francesca Knox and David Lonsdale (eds.) — *Poetry and the Religious Imagination. The Power of the Word I* (Farnham: Ashgate, 2015), pp. 240. ISBN 9781472426246.

Francesca Knox and John Took (eds.) — *Poetry and Prayer. The Power of the Word II* (Farnham: Ashgate, 2015), pp. 262. ISBN 978-1472426215

Lucy McDiarmid — *Poets and the Peacock Dinner: The Literary History of a Meal* (Oxford: Oxford University Press, 2014), pp. xviii + 212. ISBN 9780198722786

Barry Shiels — *W. B. Yeats and World Literature: The Subject of Poetry* (Farnham: Ashgate, 2015), pp. x + 200. ISBN 9781472425539.

Bruce Stewart (ed.) — *The Irish Book Lover: An Irish Studies Reader Taken from issues of* The Irish Book Lover *(1909–1957)*, with an Integrated Index by Bruce Stewart, and an Introductory Lecture by Nicholas Allen (Gerrards Cross: Colin Smythe, Ltd., 2004. ISBN 0861404556. Princess Grace Irish Library: 14).

Sonja Tiernan — *Eva Gore-Booth: An Image of Such Politics* (Manchester: Manchester University Press, 2012), p. xviii + 277. ISBN 978-0-7190-8232-0

Helen Vendler — *The Ocean, the Bird and the Scholar: Essays on Poets and Poetry* (Cambridge, Mass.; London: Harvard University Press, 2015), pp. x + 444. ISBN 9780674736566. Contains with 26 other essays, 'Fin-de-Siècle Lyric: W. B. Yeats and Jorie Graham', 27–42.

Nathan Wallace — *Hellenism and Reconciliation from Yeats to Field Day* (Cork: Cork University Press, 2015), pp. x + 194. ISBN 9781782050681.

SESQUICENTENARY FICTION AND OTHER BOOKS ON ASPECTS OF YEATS'S LIFE AND CAREER

Patricia Hughes	There are now two further books in Patricia Hughes's 'William Butler Yeats and Honor Bright Series', viz., *An Analysis of Selected Poetry by William Butler Yeats between 1918 and 1928* (2014) and *Who Killed Honor Bright? How William Butler and George Yeats Caused the Fall of the Irish Free State* (2015). The series is published by Hues Books. The first volume was reviewed in 'Mummy Truths?' by Deirdre Toomey, *YA17* 483–85.
P. R. Jennings	*W. B. Yeats and the Secret Masters of the World* ([n.p.]: Peter Fludde and Partners, 2013), pp. 257..
Marguerite Mulligan McGlinn	*Murder in the Yeats Castle* [Kindle Edition] (Bryn Mawr: Thomas W. McGlinn, 2014).
Anthony J. Quinn	*The Blood-Dimmed Tide* (Harpenden: Oldcastle Books (No-exit Press, 2014), pp. 256. ISBN 9781843444657.
Orna Ross	*Secret Rose: Her Secret Rose* (2015) by Orna Ross and *The Secret Rose* (1897) by William Butler Yeats (London: Font Publications, 2015), pp. xvi + 543. ISBN Ebook: 9781909888180; ISBN Pbook Pod: 9781909888173; ISBN Hardback: 9781909888258.

This book need not end here...

At Open Book Publishers, we are changing the nature of the traditional academic book. The title you have just read will not be left on a library shelf, but will be accessed online by hundreds of readers each month across the globe. OBP publishes only the best academic work: each title passes through a rigorous peer-review process. We make all our books free to read online so that students, researchers and members of the public who can't afford a printed edition will have access to the same ideas.

This book and additional content is available at:
http://www.openbookpublishers.com/product/380

Customize

Personalize your copy of this book or design new books using OBP and third-party material. Take chapters or whole books from our published list and make a special edition, a new anthology or an illuminating coursepack. Each customized edition will be produced as a paperback and a downloadable PDF. Find out more at:

http://www.openbookpublishers.com/section/59/1

Donate

If you enjoyed this book, and feel that research like this should be available to all readers, regardless of their income, please think about donating to us. We do not operate for profit and all donations, as with all other revenue we generate, will be used to finance new Open Access publications.

http://www.openbookpublishers.com/section/13/1/support-us

Like Open Book Publishers

Follow @OpenBookPublish

Read more at the Open Book Publishers BLOG

You may also be interested in...

Yeats's Mask—Yeats Annual No. 19
Edited by Margaret Mills Harper and Warwick Gould

http://dx.doi.org/10.11647/OBP.0038
http://www.openbookpublishers.com/product/233

The Living Stream—Yeats Annual No. 18
Edited by Warwick Gould

http://dx.doi.org/10.11647/OBP.0028
http://www.openbookpublishers.com/product/194